Textile Fabrics
and
Their Selection

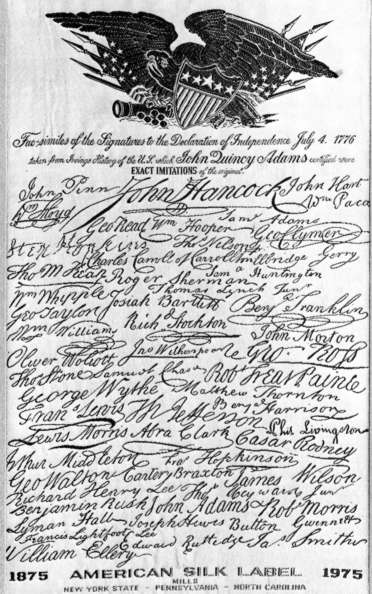

A woven label reproducing the signatures of the Declaration of Independence. It was first woven in 1876 for a Centennial exhibition. An original hangs in the Smithsonian Institution as an example of outstanding workmanship. The pattern for the facsimiles of the signatures of the Declaration uses 2,600 Jacquard cards. Courtesy of the American Silk Label Company.

SEVENTH EDITION

Textile Fabrics
and
Their Selection

ISABEL B. WINGATE

A.B., M.S. in Retailing, Ph.D.
Professor Emeritus of Retail Management
Institute of Retail Management
New York University

PRENTICE-HALL, INC., Englewood Cliffs, New Jersey

Library of Congress Cataloging in Publication Data

Wingate, Isabel Barnum.
    Textile fabrics and their selection.

    Bibliography: p.
    Includes index.
    1. Textile industry. 2. Textile fabrics.
I. Title.
TS1449.W5 1976   677   75-34352
ISBN 0-13-912840-9

© 1976, 1970, 1964, 1955, 1949, 1942, 1935
by Prentice-Hall, Inc., Englewood Cliffs, New Jersey

Printed in the United States of America

10 9 8 7 6 5

Prentice-Hall International, Inc., *London*
Prentice-Hall of Australia, Pty. Ltd., *Sydney*
Prentice-Hall of Canada, Ltd., *Toronto*
Prentice-Hall of India Private Limited, *New Delhi*
Prentice-Hall of Japan, Inc., *Tokyo*
Prentice-Hall of Southeast Asia Pte. Ltd., *Singapore*

Contents

v

APPENDICES

Foreword

At a time in life when most people feel they have made their contributions to society, and justifiably so, Dr. Wingate has not only kept current with the rapidly changing technology of textiles and consumer demands but has made this information available in the form of a new textbook revision. Since Dr. Wingate has written probably the most comprehensive textile consumer orientated college textbook published, many of us regretted that the 6th edition of *Textile Fabrics and Their Selection* was becoming inadequate in view of the rapidly changing technology and consumer demands. Upon reviewing her 7th edition, I am delighted to find all of the excellent qualities in textbook writing still retained. Good organization with appropriate Titles, Summary, Review Questions, Projects, and a Glossary of Terms at the end of each chapter helps the student to study in an organized manner. It aids in applying the knowledge to current consumer needs and in easily defining unfamiliar terms.

In addition to the above mentioned format, for which Dr. Wingate is so well known, she has up-dated the material taking careful note of both major and minor changes in the textile field. Of special interest to the professor and the student will be such information as: addition of the new generic fibers, new dyes and dyeing methods, new methods of computer-aided control of fabric construction, and the new Federal Trade Commission Laws on Care Labeling and the Flammable Fabrics Act. In addition she includes current information in Part II, Selection of Appropriate Fabrics. The Appendix has also been made more useable for students by grouping charts and listings together where they can be quickly located.

I am eagerly anticipating the use of this new revision in my course in Consumer Textiles.

G. Katherine Watson
Associate Professor
Home Economics Department
Bradley University

Preface

The textile industry continues to be a rapidly changing one, creating new fibers and yarns and manufacturing them into useful and decorative products for clothing and home furnishings, as well as for industrial purposes.

In 1776, except for imports from abroad, virtually all clothing and home furnishings were made in the home. The farmer raised the raw material and his wife spun the yarn, wove the cloth, colored it, and made it into garments and household textiles.

But the Industrial Revolution with its factory production brought a dramatic change. In 1791, Samuel Slater brought to America the secret English methods of carding and combing of yarns; and in 1814, Francis Cabot established the first completely power-operated textile plant where all steps in the manufacture of cloth were performed. For over 100 years, although there were great improvements in mechanical methods, the raw materials used were the natural fibers, particularly cotton, wool, linen, and silk. Late in the Nineteenth Century, chemists created the first man-made fiber, rayon, which commercial importance early in the Twentieth Century. But it has been only recently that the genius of the chemical industry has led to a wide variety of man-made fibers that, in the United States, at least, surpasses the natural fibers in importance. The spectacular changes in production have been supported by changes in customer demand, growing out of a rapid increase in population and in per capita income, changes in life-styles, and in the demand for new end uses to which textile products might be put.

These ever-increasing consumer demands have resulted in new creations in fibers, yarns, and finishes of textile fabrics. To illustrate one of the recent creative style developments in textiles is the old familiar staple twill denim with its blue warp and white filling, originally used for jeans. It has now become a fashion fabric. It may now be striped, checked, plaid, embroidered, or printed, have a brushed surface, or a faded look. It will even stretch.

The consumer's right to know has led to new and revised government regulations. Accordingly, the text discusses federal laws and F.T.C. rulings intended to inform the consumer of the fiber content of each article: the Flammable Fabrics Act to protect the consumer from dangerously flammable fabrics, and the Permanent Care Labeling Act to provide instructions for proper care permanently attached to articles of clothing.

There have been many new developments since the sixth edition of 1970. Accordingly, the following topics are now added: the Permanent Care Labeling Act; the new generic man-made fibers; innovations in textured and stretch yarns; computer-aided control in Jacquard weaving, knitting, and shade-matching; new fabric printing processes; improvements in man-made fibers; and many more.

Probably the greatest single contribution to this seventh edition is the complete revision of the chapters on man-made fibers. There are now three chapters instead of two. The first of these chapters, "Rayon and Acetate and the Consumer," was revised and up-dated by Celanese Fibers Marketing Company. The second chapter, now called "General Purpose Non-Cellulosic Fibers and the Consumer," and the third chapter, "Special-Purpose Non-Cellulosic Fibers and the Consumer," were revised by a committee organized expressly for this purpose by the Educational Director of the Man-Made Fiber Producers Association. Readers of the manuscript included major executives in the companies holding membership in the association. Each spent generously of his time and expertise in working on this manuscript.

An entirely new section on home sewing has been developed for a part of the chapter on "Women's and Girls' Wear." Included are guides to buying fabrics for use for various occasions; the making of a garment in light of requirements for garment serviceability; special guides for sewing textured woven fabrics and sewing knitted fabrics; points to consider in selecting women's and girls' ready-made dresses, sweaters, shirts, and other garments.

There has been an up-dating of all chapters, particularly "Care of Textile Fabrics," "Linen and the Consumer," "Period Styles in Home Furnishings and in Rugs," and "Draperies, Curtains, and Upholstery." Approximately a third to half of the illustrations are new.

Merchandise knowledge can be acquired by the consumer from experience in buying, using, and caring for textile articles. It can be learned from reading informative advertising and labels on merchandise, from well-informed salespeople, from knowledgeable friends and associates, and from formal classroom study.

Many years of experience in teaching textiles have proved that, of all methods, formal instruction can most quickly and accurately organize and present product information. This product information, coupled with an emphasis on the selling points of textile fabrics, will aid the retail salesman in helping the consumer make a wise selection.

But a mere presentation of facts is insufficient. The reader must assimilate the facts and apply them through study and experimentation. To assist in learning these facts, the first edition of this book was written in 1935. Subsequent revisions have attempted to keep its content up to date.

The Laboratory Swatchbook for Textile Fabrics, published by W.C. Brown, Dubuque, Iowa, soon to be in its seventh edition, endeavors to give the reader an opportunity to apply the facts to actual cloths. The organization of the experiments follows exactly the Table of Contents in this book.

Textile Fabrics and Their Selection is divided into two parts. Part I covers the intrinsic characteristics of fabrics. This information is basic to judging the grade of a fabric, to estimating its probable performance, and to determining the care required in order to get maximum performance. Part II emphasizes the importance of the selection of appropriate fabrics for specific uses in apparel and home furnishings, and discusses the factors to be considered in examining the construction of garments and household textiles. The plan for use of this text is flexible. It can provide for a year's course in textiles, with Part I covering the subject matter for the first semester and Part II for the second semester. The text can also be used for two separate courses in fashion fabrics: "Fashion Fabrics in Apparel" and "Fabrics in Home Furnishings." For the apparel class, subject matter may include Chapters 1-8 and 16-18; for the home furnishings class, Chapters 1-2, 8, 10-16, and 19-21. It will be noted that Chapters 1 and 2 are repeated. Since one course should not be prerequisite for the other, students in both courses must familiarize themselves with the terminology from the beginning. For adult education, ten two-hour lectures the first term and eight the second term have proved effective. It should also be noted that in the *Swatchbook*, yarns, weaves, and finishes are emphasized for collecting and evaluating data on household textiles.

I am indebted to my students for information that they have brought to classes; to manufacturers who have arranged market trips for students for the purpose of acquainting them with the features of their lines and their methods of promotion; and to many buyers and salesmen in retail stores for their help in discussing new merchandise, styles, assortments, and prices. I am particularly obliged to the following experts who have revised and up-dated portions of the manuscript for this seventh edition. These have been arranged according to the topics in the book to which they made contributions.

Topic	Contributor	Title at the Time of Assistance	Subject Matter
Textile Education	Rudolph C. Geering	Chemical Engineer and AATT member	Curricula in textiles
Teaching Textiles to Consumers	Geraldine Sparks	Consumer Information, Celanese Corporation	Consumer information provided by manufacturer
Teaching Textiles to Salespeople	Winifred Cole	Training Director, Ohrbach's, N.Y.	Merchandise information provided by department store
Teaching Textiles to High School and College Students	Bernice Mattis Rassoules	Teacher, Roosevelt High School; Lecturer, Fashion Institute of Technology	Up-dating the 1968-69 curricula
Basic Weaves	David H. Lipkin	Vice President, Home furnishing Division, American Silk Mills	Up-dating the entire chapter
Knitting and Other Constructions	Charles Reichman	Editor, *Knitting Times*	Up-dating the chapter
Silk and the Consumer	Grace Beller	Executive Vice-President, International Silk Assoc. U.S.A., Inc.	Up-dating the chapter
Linen and the Consumer	Frances Hanson	Director for the U.S. of the Belgian Linen Association	Up-dating the chapter

(continued)

Topic	Contributor	Title at the Time of Assistance	Subject Matter
Cotton and the Consumer	William Nunn	Cotton Council International, Memphis, Tenn.	Up-dating the chapter
Wool and the Consumer	B.J. Trumpbour	Manager, Public Relations, Wool Bureau, Inc.	Up-dating the chapter
Dyeing and Printing	Robert Tellis	Research and Development Division, Ciba-Geigy Corp.	Up-dating section on dyestuffs
Rayon and Acetate and the Consumer	Sherry Kelner	Supervisor, Public Relations, Celanese Corporation	Up-dating the chapter
Man-Made Fibers and the Consumer	Fisher Rhymes and eight-member committee	Education Director Man-Made Fiber Producers Association	Up-dated two chapters
Household Textiles	June Mohler	Formerly Sales Promotion Manager, Fieldcrest Mills	Up-dated chapter
Period Styles in Home Furnishings	Phyllis Edelman	Project Coordinator, Board of Cooperative Educational Services, Nassau County, N.Y.	Up-dated section on period styles in home furnishings
Rugs and Carpets	Pat Eells	Public Relations, Mohasco Industries	Up-dated section on rugs and carpets
Draperies and Curtains	Arthur H. Wingate	Market Representative, Draperies and Curtains, DuPont	Up-dated the chapter
Drycleaning	Albert E. Johnson	Director, Seal and Trade Relations, International Fabricare Institute	Prepared a section on drycleaning
Care of Textiles	Mildred Gallik	Soap and Detergent Association	Provided information on care of textiles

The author is especially grateful also to the following manufacturers, trade associations, magazines, and others for their assistance in providing illustrations, and answering many questions about their products.

Allied Chemical Corporation
American Association of Textile Chemists and Colorists
American Cyanamid Company
American Enka Corporation
American Fabrics Magazine
American Institute of Laundering
American Iwer Corporation
American Silk Label Company
American Textile Manufacturers Institute, Inc.
American Textile Reporter/Bulletin
American Textiles, A Clark Publication
The American Yarn Spinners Association, Inc.
Antiques Magazine
The Asian Society
Belgian Linen Association
Bigelow Sanford Carpet Co., Inc.

Dick Blick (identification of parts of the loom)
Mrs. J. Orton Buck (drawings)
Carbide and Carbon Chemical Company
Carborundum® Company
Carleton Voice, Carleton College (Minn.)
The Carpet and Rug Institute, Inc.
E.C. Carter & Son, Inc.
Celanese Fibers Marketing Company
Chatham Research and Development Corporation
The Chemstrand Corporation
Cheyney Brothers Inc.
Ciba-Geigy Corporation
Cone Mills, Inc.
Consumers' Research, Inc.
Consumers' Union of the U.S., Inc.
Cotton Incorporated
Cranston Print Works Company
Crompton-Richmond Company
Deering Milliken Research Corporation
E.I. DuPont de Nemours & Co., Inc.
Eastman Chemical Products, Inc.
Firestone Tire and Rubber Company
FMC Corporation
Forstmann Woolen Company
Franklin Process Company, a division of Indian Head Yarn Company
Good Housekeeping Consumers' Guaranty Administration
Hercules, Inc.
Jonas Grushkin (photos)
Industrial By-Products and Research Corporation
International Fabricare Institute
International Silk Association
Irish Linen Guild
Kent-Kostikyan, Inc.
Kleinert's, Inc.

Knitted Outerwear Times
Man-Made Fiber Producers Association, Inc.
Max Mandel Laces, Inc.
Men's Fashion Association of America
Monsanto Company
National Cotton Council
National Plastic Products Company
Owens-Corning Fiberglas Corporation
J.C. Penney Company
Jack Pitkin (photos)
Quaker Lace Company
The Sanforized Company, a division of Cluett Peabody & Co., Inc.
Scalamandré Silks, Inc.
Soap and Detergent Association
Southern Research Laboratory of the U.S. Department of Agriculture
Spring Cotton Mills
Textile World
TIME-LIFE Books
Uniroyal, Inc.
United States Testing Company, Inc.
Warwick Dyeing Corporation
Wellington Sears Co., Inc.
Wool Bureau, Inc.

Textile Fabrics
and
Their Selection

Fabric Construction and Buying Motives

PART ONE

Why Study Textiles

1

While drinking coffee one morning, Mrs. Dale happened to read a newspaper advertisement for men's permanent press corduroy slacks. The price seemed reasonably low. She decided to go to the store to see what they were like, so she read the ad further. "Permanent press takes the classic bag out of the knees. The slacks resist wrinkles, need no ironing after machine washing and drying. Made of 50 percent polyester and 50 percent cotton blend. They come in solids, prints, and in a broad range of colors with excellent fastness qualities. Sizes 34 to 44 waist." Yes, her husband could use a new pair of slacks in corduroy. But how can permanent press take the bag out of the knees? Wouldn't she really have to do a bit of touch-up ironing? And what is a polyester/cotton blend?

Fortunately for Mrs. Dale, a salesperson at the store had the necessary knowledge to answer her questions. She told Mrs. Dale that permanent press is a *durable press*, a term used to describe a garment that will retain its shape for its wear-life. Therefore, knees would not bag, creases in the slacks should remain sharp, seams flat and nonpuckering, and the surface texture smooth. No ironing is needed. As for the polyester/cotton blend, the clerk explained that in a blend two different types of fibers (raw materials) are mixed together, in this case in equal proportions of polyester and cotton. Polyester is the family name of a man-made raw material, or fiber, whereas cotton is a natural fiber obtained from a hollyhock-like plant. Polyesters are characterized by crease resistance, shape retention, ease of care, and nonabsorptiveness. Cotton has a natural luster, is not very strong or abrasion-resistant, but has good absorptive quality. By blending polyester and cotton, the fabric is strengthened, is more lustrous and more abrasion- and crease-resistant, and sheds water, which makes it dry faster than all-cotton. The cotton content makes the fabric more comfortable because it is soft and absorbs perspiration in warm weather. A permanent, or durable press, finish is applied to the fabric and set through the use of heat. (See *durable press*, Chapter 7).

Mrs. Dale was convinced that these slacks were well worth the price, so she purchased two pairs.

A complexity of materials and manufacturing processes is involved in making textile products. Consumers have a right to know what they are buying, what they can expect in service for the prices they have to pay, and the right to fair adjustments of complaints. Not only the salesperson

FIGURE 1.1. Consumer Rights and Responsibilities. (Courtesy of Celanese Fibers Marketing Co.)

but also the copywriter should be able to give the customer informative facts about the merchandise in terms that the customer can understand. (See Fig. 1.1, Consumers' Rights and Responsibilities.)

Since approximately 75 percent of total department store sales volume is from sales of merchandise wholly or partly textile (woven, nonwoven, knitted, felted, and laminated cloths), instructions for salespeople in information about textiles is essential.

TEXTILE EDUCATION

TEACHING SALESPEOPLE

In the small dry-goods store, salespeople still acquire much textile information through experience. This method of learning is often a slow and discouraging process. A shortcut to learning is the classroom instruction in textiles that training departments in retail stores may give their salespeople, supplemented by regular meetings conducted by the buyer of the department.

In the larger department stores and chains, the prime source of textile

4

information comes from pamphlets, films, fact cards, and texts provided by the manufacturers, vendors, and textile associations. The essential information is usually provided by the buyer or department manager at morning meetings. Emphasis is naturally given to new items added to the assortment. In chain stores, the pertinent information is compiled at headquarters and distributed to the department managers in the various units. The store's training department may teach the subject matter, and it is often responsible for writing informative booklets and providing the buyers with teaching materials for the main store and branches and for chain-store units. Sometimes the training department gives "reinforcement" instruction. When a new product appears in stock, the manufacturer's representative may present pertinent facts about it to salespeople. Part-timers are given the same textile information as the regular salespeople, and by the same executives.

The main difficulty lies in training part-time salespeople and contingents who come in only for the busy season, when all the store's efforts must be concentrated on sales volume and when formal training can at best be for only one or two hours. Probably the best solution to the problem of training contingents and part-timers is a well-organized sponsor system in each department. A sponsor is a person named by the management to assist in training a new salesperson when he or she comes into the department. The sponsor may receive the sales of the new person for the first few days, or remuneration for each person trained, or both.

To improve salesmanship, one store put on a "show-tell skit" for its salespeople. The purpose of this skit was to emphasize dramatically the value not only of showing the customer the merchandise but of telling her at the same time the pertinent facts about it in an accurate way. After the salespeople had seen this skit, shoppers checked on the merchandise information given customers by these salespeople.

Another store has developed the "role-playing" method. Briefly, the staff trainer selects from her group of trainees a person to represent the salesperson and another to represent the customer. The trainer tells them about the merchandise in the department (even though no physical goods may be there). Her description of merchandise location, color, and price is so vivid that the role-players can see it in their mind's eye. The person to play salesperson then is asked to leave while the trainer gives the person playing customer instructions on the type of customer he is to be. He may be told he may purchase an item only if he is really "sold." He may buy the highest priced item only if the salesperson has convinced him of its superiority. Then the demonstration sale takes place. Both salesperson and customer are left to their own devices, the customer trying to be true to the role. This method most nearly simulates an actual sales situation.

Many progressive stores encourage their sponsors and junior executives to take textile courses in high schools, colleges, museums, and other outside institutions. Stores may pay part of their employees' tuition if they pass the course. Sometimes textile experts from outside organizations give courses in the store.

EDUCATION IN THE HIGH SCHOOL AND COLLEGE

Most commercial high schools that offer a course in retail selling include the subject of textiles as an important part of that course. In cooperative high schools and in schools whose students spend part of their time in store service, a knowledge of textiles is invaluable, for much time is spent by students in stock rooms and in the selling of textile merchandise. Even if a store offers a course in textiles as a part of initial training, part-time employees very often miss such instruction. Frequently classes are held in the morning, and high school students cannot get to the store before noon. This fact is also true of the high school boy or girl who sells in a store on Saturdays only. Yet the store expects a high school salesperson to be at least as good as the regulars in the department. Accordingly, the courses in the school should help measurably.

Often high school students find that their store service consists of wrapping, packing, marking, and other routine work. Although this type of work is a necessary part of anyone's store training, a knowledge of textiles is a step to selling. In the average department store up to 80 percent of the departments are devoted to the sale of all-textile or partly textile merchandise.

Commercial high schools, both day and evening, and community colleges offer textile courses, which are frequently required for graduation from a program in retailing. Others offer retailing courses under the department of business education or under the commercial or home economics department. The courses vary in length from one to three years. A great many courses in retailing are now given in high schools and department stores by teachers provided through government appropriations under the Vocational Education Act of 1963.

The four-year college student who majors in home economics or retailing will find textiles and clothing a part of the course. Many women's colleges have broadened the scope of their home economics courses to include the study of textiles. Frequently, textiles is taught as part of a college general marketing or business program in appropriate specializations.

PLACE OF INDUSTRIAL RESEARCH AND GOVERNMENT DIRECTION IN TEXTILE EDUCATION

This era of man-made fibers and the competition among them, plus the advent of blends (mixtures of various fibers), has caused those in the textile industry to realize the need for more and better consumer research and for improvement in textile training for the industry.

The industry is constantly trying to determine what fiber, mixture, or blend is best suited for an intended use, how the fabric can be dyed so it will serve most satisfactorily, and how the consumer should care for it. When, through research, the textile manufacturer can say, for example, "We have proved that a blend of 55 percent wool and 45 percent Dacron polyester is the most satisfactory blend for a man's business suit," and can give consumers logical reasons why, the consumer will have one of his most confusing problems in clothing selections solved. Only through a vast amount of research would this decision be possible. Any research necessitates trained men and women. For textile training, the industry supports education and research in numerous institutions.[1]

The federal government has also played an active role in the development of industrial standards and public education. In 1962 a

---

[1] See Appendix B for a list of schools and research organizations active in the field.

National Consumer Advisory Council was appointed by President John F. Kennedy to concern itself with consumer welfare, protection, education, and labeling. with Dr. Helen Connoyer as chairwoman. Subsequently, in President Lyndon Johnson's administration, this post was held by Esther Peterson and later by Betty Furness. She was succeeded by Virginia H. Knauer as President Richard Nixon's Consumer Aide. Knauer continued under President Gerald Ford as Special Assistant to the President of Consumer Affairs. These people have arranged conferences of executives in the textile industry, scientists, and consumer representatives to help eliminate consumer complaints involving factual content or lack of it on labels and the loss of care labels in washing. The mandatory labeling regulations discussed later in this chapter are the result of joint efforts of the federal government and the textile industry.

VALUE OF TEXTILE TRAINING IN ACHIEVING A CAREER

IN RETAILING

Although most high school courses do not attempt to turn out expert salespeople in specialized lines, they do equip the student with merchandise facts in which the customer is most interested so that, in a retailing capacity, the salesperson can advise the customer intelligently.

He is taught the inherent characteristics of the raw materials and how they may affect performance and care of the finished cloth. He is taught how to judge the probable durability (wearing quality) of a fabric and how to advise the customer on the care of a fabric. He is also taught to interpret informative labels and tags.

The college graduate with a textile background will probably feel more secure in such positions as assistant buyer, fashion assistant, or copywriter. His training should be a help in moving up to the next higher position.

IN INDUSTRY

If the person trained in textiles wishes to enter the textile industry rather than retailing, he or she should consider the two major divisions—production and sales. For production, the plant needs textile engineers, research workers, specialists in fabric development (such as cloth designers), head chemist and assistants, head physicist and assistants, department directors, quality-control specialists, and analytical testers (technicians). In science and engineering, there are openings for mechanical, electrical, and industrial engineers in areas of optimum plant scheduling; time study; fiber and fabric testing, grading, and analysis; and quality control. In data processing, the field is growing and includes programming, analysis, sale and profit forecasting, estimating, sales and administrative records, and inventory control. There are also career opportunities in the manufacturing of textiles and textile products and in the administrative and secretarial supporting services.[2]

After the fabric is constructed it is called "grey goods" and must go through special processes called *finishing*, *dyeing*, and *printing*. These

[2] *Your Career In Textiles: An Industry, A Science, An Art* (American Textile Manufacturers Institute).

three processes are done by converters, commission dyers, printers, finishers, or the finishing divisions of vertically organized textile firms. The designer who creates a printed fabric design may be employed in a converter's studio, work for an independent studio, or free-lance. The colorist paints the designer's sketches and the repeat artist plans the method of engraving the design. Frequently, the converter or fabric manufacturer employs a stylist who supervises the whole design process from the forecasting and planning through the execution in the finishing plant. Actually a stylist (sometimes called designer-stylist or fashion coordinator) works with the production end of the business when she works with creative designers, and she coordinates this work with the sales division when she works with the dress designer in selling the idea of how the particular fabric design would work into the dress designer's creation.

In the sales division of the textile industry there are merchandising and promotion jobs as publicist or public relations manager (arranges programs and speaks to women's clubs and schools to promote goodwill of the firm), assistant publicist (reports on how the firm's goods are selling in the garment trade and does some writing of press releases), company representative (travels to instruct consumer groups on the product, arranges promotions for stores on the itinerary, and finds out what consumers want), copywriter, merchandiser (decides when market conditions are right to sell the product), and salesperson in the sales office or on the road. There are increasing numbers of jobs for women as fabric designers, publicists, company representatives, copywriters, and fashion coordinators.

OTHER CAREERS

In addition to jobs in retail stores and textile plants, there are other opportunities for young people who have acquired a thorough knowledge of textiles. They may become designers of women's, children's, and men's apparel, fashion editors for trade and consumer publications, home economists, technicians in textile laboratories, and teachers in high school and college.

> Graduates with a B.S. degree from a four-year college, such as New York State College of Home Economics at Cornell University, have taken positions as textile technician, designer of children's clothing, assistant buyer of apparel, fashion editor of a large women's magazine, fashion editor for a home economics publication, and home economics teacher in junior and senior high schools. Instruction on the graduate level emphasizes professional development. Research, especially in investigating textile end uses, is pertinent. Graduates with an M.S. degree from the aforementioned college hold positions as college teacher or university professor, apparel designer, statistician in the quality-control program of a fiber producer, statistician for a textile economics publication, museum curator, textile and clothing specialist with the Cooperative Extension Service, textile research worker in a university or commercial laboratory, textile technician, head of the consumer products laboratory in the research and development division of a fiber producer, supervisor of home economics in public schools, and home economist with a state welfare agency.[3]

---

[3] Vivian White, "Textile Education in Home Economics: A New Approach." Proceedings American Association of Textile Chemists and Colorists (AATCC).

Big business has brought the consumer many lines of improved goods and new goods. The complex processes used in their production have disguised the old products completely, and many new goods are so utterly novel that the consumer does not know whether they can be washed without shrinkage and without changing color, whether the color is sunfast, of what fiber the material is made, and how to care for the finished article so that it will give its money's worth.

The American Home Economics Association has been an important instrument in consumer education and protection. In cooperation with technical societies, it assists in the setting of standards and is a major instrument in educating the consumer to make an intelligent choice.

For the typical consumer without ready access to the more technical and professional sources of information, the label now attached to most textile products is the major supplement to the personal inspection of the product. Other guides now also often made available are seals of approval, ratings and guarantees, advertisements, and the presence of an informed and intelligent sales force.

INFORMATIVE LABELS

Mandatory Content and Performance Labels. A tag or label attached to the merchandise usually gives the consumer information about qualities inherent in the merchandise. Under federal law, the Textile Fiber Products Identification Act (TFPIA),[4] a tag or label must give the name of the raw material (fiber content) of which the fabric is made. Such a label must remain affixed to the merchandise until it is sold to the ultimate

[4] "Textile Fiber Products" as defined by the TFPIA means "... any fiber finished or unfinished incorporated in a household textile article and includes any yarn or fabric used in a household textile article. Such articles mean wearing apparel, costumes and accessories, draperies, floor coverings, furnishings and beddings, and other textile goods of a type customarily used in a household regardless of where used in fact."

FIGURE 1.2. Label showing fiber identification, performance features, and care. (Courtesy of Celanese Fibers Marketing Co.)

9

consumer. This law, which was passed by the Congress of the United States in August, 1958, and became effective March 3, 1960, required that the label include not only fiber content but also percentage by weight, in order of importance of each fiber used in an article. The manufacturer's (sponsor's) name and address or registered identification number also must be given on the label, and the country of origin must be given for imported fabrics. A list of generic or family names of fibers and their definitions compiled by the Federal Trade Commission is included in the act. Unfortunately, however, because of the technical nature of the definitions, some generic terms like "polyester" and "acrylic" cannot be readily comprehended by the consumer. These requirements are a step in the right direction to guide consumer purchases. But fiber content is not the sole criterion for judging how a fabric will perform. Of equal significance affecting use and performance are the following factors: (1) type and quality of the yarn, (2) type of fabric construction, (3) quality of the finishes including the coloring of the fabric, and (4) features of the construction of the garment or home furnishing.

The label may be made up by the manufacturer or by the retailer. The retailer's label must subscribe to the TFPIA, and the retailer must keep a record of the data that appeared on the label together with the vendor's name. In fact, department stores, retail chain organizations, wholesalers, manufacturers, and the federal government have contributed informative labels. But it is difficult to standardize data that appear on a label. The TFPIA, in requiring fiber content and the sponsor's name, has taken a valuable step in that direction. In so doing, the government has imposed a mandatory standard. The Wool Products Labeling Act is also mandatory, since federal law requires that all products containing wool fibers, with the exception of rugs and upholstery, must be labeled. Type of wool (new wool, reprocessed wool, and reused wool) must be disclosed on these labels.

Since fur fibers may be used in textile blends, the Fur Products Labeling Act of 1951, amended in 1961, should be included here. The act requires that in advertising a fur, the name of the animal from which the fur comes must be used. The use of the name of any other animal is not permissible. The name of the animal and the country of origin must appear on the label. An original pelt cannot be altered without naming the pelt that was used in the alteration. A simile to describe a fur quality, or a deceptive use of the adjectives "domestic" or "imported," is not permissible.

The Flammable Fabrics Act, passed in 1953 and amended in 1954, is also mandatory. The objective in this case is to prohibit the sale of fabrics or clothing that would be so flammable as to be dangerous when worn.

In 1967 Congress passed the Consumer Product Safety Act, setting up a Consumer Product Safety Commission. The responsibilities for implementing the Flammable Fabrics Act as well as other hazardous substance and safety acts were assigned to the new commission, which requires that many textile products carry labels indicating that they meet the flammability standards set. (See Chapter 7.)

The Wool Products Labeling Act, the Flammable Fabrics Act, and the Textile Fiber Products Identification Act were intended to protect the consumer against deception in labeling and, with the exception of the Wool Act, against the misrepresentation of merchandise in advertising.

These laws are also intended to protect the manufacturer against unfair methods of competition. The Federal Trade Commission administers these laws. A retailer who fails to follow the regulations receives complaints, cease-and-desist orders from the commission, and unpleasant publicity. The Wheeler-Lea Act of 1938 made violation of a cease-and-desist order punishable by a fine up to $5,000. Appeals for review of the case may be made to a circuit court of appeals.

Mandatory Care Labels. The rules discussed above do not require that information on how to care for textile products be included. While many manufacturers did provide such information, the tags were easily removable and were frequently not available for future guidance. Accordingly, in 1972 the Federal Trade Commission put into effect a new regulation requiring that most apparel and home furnishings carry permanently attached labels, good for the life of the article, giving care and maintenance information. These may be woven or printed labels, sewn, glued, or fused to the products themselves. In the case of yard goods, except remnants, the care instructions are to be printed on labels that carry a code that corresponds to the label at the end of each bolt.

FIGURE 1.3. Certified washable and dry cleanable seal. (Courtesy International Fabricare Institute.)

These labels are given to the customers at the time of purchase and may be sewn to the finished garments. Products that are exempt from the above requirements include those that do not require routine cleaning, such as hats and gloves, and articles sold for $3 or less that are completely washable, such as undershorts containing no wool. The standard terminology appearing on labels is discussed in Chapter 16.

Informative Labels Voluntarily Applied. Grade standards and labels of the ABC variety, often used on canned foods, are not applied to textile products. To the consumer, a combination of various features, including style, is more important than a narrow definition of quality. However, many voluntary labels and advertisements do provide information that denotes quality. For example, the phrase *pima cotton, 2 x 2 mercerized broadcloth, sanforized* can mean a great deal to the trained consumer. *Pima* means that the cotton fibers are extra long, except for Sea Island the best quality. The term *2 x 2* means the yarns are made of two single stranded yarns twisted together; they are more durable than single yarns of the same diameter. *Mercerized* means that the cloth has been treated with chemicals to give added strength and luster. *Sanforized* means that there is not more than 1 percent residual shrinkage (¼ inch to a yard). Thus, with good quality cotton fiber, strong yarns, luster, and minimum shrinkage, this broadcloth should prove serviceable for a tailored blouse or shirt.[5]

Voluntary Industry Standards and Labels. There are standards voluntarily developed by industry that are used as a basis for labeling consumers' goods. Such standards may be set up by a manufacturer for a product he makes. The purpose is to make products which are uniform and quality controlled. Most of these voluntary standards in the textile industry are the result of the general consensus of the parties involved. For example, the USA Standard L22 was the result of a voluntary agreement of almost thirty trade associations representing various segments of the textile industry, technical societies, and consumer groups. Minimum requirements based on features deemed essential to the satisfactory performance of various types of textile merchandise in their respective end uses were specified in L22.

An example is the proposed standard for girls' blouse or dress woven fabrics. It includes breaking and tearing strength; dimensional change in laundering and dry cleaning; absence of odor; colorfastness to light, perspiration, crocking, atmospheric gases, laundering, and dry cleaning; yarn shifting or slippage; retention of hand (feeling of fabrics); character and appearance; seam strength; and features of the garment other than the fabric.

Textile merchandise that meets these voluntary standards could bear a tag with the L22 designation signifying the kind of performance that was guaranteed for this item. These standards formed a basis for care labeling discussed earlier in this chapter.

Standards and methods of testing have been established by various technical societies and trade associations, particularly the United States American Standards Institute (USASI) (formerly the American Standards Association), the Association for Textile Technology (AATT), the American Society for Testing and Materials (ASTM), the American Association of Textile Chemists and Colorists (AATCC), and the International Fabricare Institute (IFI).

SEALS OF APPROVAL BASED ON STANDARDS
AND GUARANTEES

The National Bureau of Standards of the U.S. Department of Commerce has worked out commercial standards for (1) testing a fabric's colorfastness to sunlight, perspiration, laundering, and crocking (rubbing off of color); (2) control of shrinkage; and (3) crease resistance. (See Chapter 8 for a discussion of standardized methods of testing and reporting.) Although manufacturers are encouraged by the National Bureau of

---

[5] Brief mention should be made of the British "Tel Tag" system designed to provide useful, accurate, and readily comprehensible information for products at the point of sale. Performance or wear information is provided, but not care. The information furnished on the tags must be substantiated by official tests. Some major appliance manufacturers in this country and a leading department store chain have adopted the plan. The tags prove of value to salespeople in presenting the merchandise, but generally accepted standards for many of the specifications given have not been developed.

Standards to use self-identifying quality-guaranteeing labels or tags to indicate that a set of specifications has been met or exceeded, these guarantees are not enforced.

Conformity to Quality. Standards set by the USASI in cooperation with technical societies and with groups of manufacturers, retailers, dry cleaners, and consumers permit the manufacturer to label goods as meeting the Institute's standards. These standards cover many phases of quality.

Laboratories may give goods that pass their tests certified seals of approval or of quality for use in labeling and advertising. One of the best known consumer education and protection programs is that of Good Housekeeping Magazine. Since 1885, the magazine has maintained high levels of good taste and exercised strict editorial judgments in the consideration of products it will accept for advertising and for use of its seal. These judgments, based on investigations by the technical staff of the Institute, comprise the basis of the Good Housekeeping Consumers' Refund or Replacement Policy.

Under this policy, if any product or service advertised in any issue of the magazine is defective, Good Housekeeping will, upon verification of the complaint, replace such product or service, or refund to the consumer the price paid for it. The details of this Consumers' Policy are stated on page 6 of each issue of the magazine.

Should certain advertisers wish to use the seal beyond the pages of Good Housekeeping Magazine, such as on labels or in advertisements in other media, they may do so. (See Fig. 1.4.) The use of the seal is contingent upon the advertiser's signing an agreement governing its use. Again, endorsement of a product and the claims made for it are based on investigations made by the Good Housekeeping Institute.

FIGURE 1.4. Good Housekeeping Consumers' Seal. (Reproduced courtesy of Good Housekeeping.)

There are also some well-known textile manufacturers' guarantee programs. A guarantee, in strictly legal terms, means that if an article has not lived up to its promise of performance, the guarantor (company) will replace the item or return its original price to the consumer within a stated period of time. The Everfast color guarantee was the first program of this type. In 1921 Everfast Fabrics, Inc., guaranteed money back on the purchase price of the fabric plus the construction cost of the garment. In 1962 Monsanto introduced its Wear-Dated program, which guaranteed the replacement of a garment or refund of money if it failed to give normal wear for a year. The Dow Badische Company guarantees two acrylics—Zefkrome and Zefran II—money back or replacement guarantees on apparel that does not give one year's normal wear. The Allied Chemical Corporation's program has a three-year guarantee for commercial or contract carpets. J. P. Stevens & Co., Inc., offers a ten-year guarantee for its fiber glass screening. The Collins and Aikman Corporation has a Certifab program for a garment's face fabric bonded or laminated to a Certifab tricot made of Celanese acetate. The guarantee is for one year against fabric separation in normal use when dry cleaned or laundered as specified by the garment manufacturer.[6]

The Celanese Licensed Trademark program attempts to develop the confidence of the trade and the consumer in Celanese's good fabric performance. It strives to make known that a Celanese hangtag means exactly what it says. To qualify for a licensed fiber trademark, a company's fabric must pass specific Celanese tests for specific end uses. Since the Celanese Corporation is a fiber manufacturer, it must make sure that the quality of its fiber in the tested fabric has been maintained. Only a few fiber companies have this type of program, and only a few of their brand names are included in their programs. In guiding the fiber into the appropriate end uses, the fiber company must work with the mill, converter, finisher, dyer, printer, manufacturer, and retailer. Celanese must assure the members of the textile industry and the quality-conscious consumer that the nature and quality of the product are controlled through testing for the promised performance. The company feels that this assurance is worth the price because it protects the industry's profitability and insures the consumer against false claims.

The Consumer Service Bureau of *Parents' Magazine* also indicates by a seal its approval of merchandise that has passed its standard laboratory tests.

RATINGS

Textile research laboratories are generally of two kinds: (1) public laboratories that test fabrics for anyone on a fee basis (the United States Testing Company organized in 1880 represents this type); and (2) private laboratories that test fabrics for manufacturers and retailers (in some cases the laboratory may serve as a quality control agent for certain manufacturers). Better Fabrics Testing Bureau is an example of a private organization.

In addition, large chain stores may have their own laboratories for research and quality control. Large department stores may also maintain testing bureaus for analyzing customers' complaints and for maintaining standards of quality.

When informative labeling is lacking, the consumer often consults *Consumer Reports* or the *Consumers' Research* magazine for guidance about the purchase of textiles and other products. *Consumer Reports* is a monthly publication of Consumers Union of United States, Inc., a nonprofit organization established in 1936 in Mount Vernon, New York. *Consumers' Research* magazine is published monthly by Consumers' Research, Inc., a nonprofit organization established in 1929 in Washington, New Jersey. These organizations are testing agencies established for

---

[6] The face fabric is guaranteed not to separate from the tricot fabric.

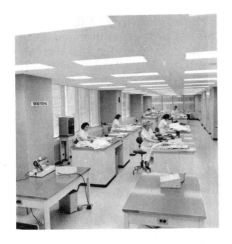

FIGURE 1.5. Interior view of Textile Testing Preparation Area. (Courtesy of J.C. Penney Co.)

the purpose of making science more effectively serve the interest of the consumer. They provide the buyer with the same type of advisory service that the technical staff provides for its own industrial establishment. The subscriber to Consumers Union will find in its *Consumer Reports* ratings of items that have been tested. For example, when Consumers Union judges the test samples to be of high overall quality and appreciably superior to non-check-rated items tested for the same report, they are rated by a check mark (√), meaning acceptable. A rating of one item sold under a brand name is not to be considered a rating of other items sold under the same brand name, unless so noted. "Best buy" ratings are given to products that rate high in overall quality but are also priced relatively low; they should provide more quality per dollar than acceptable items in that set of ratings.

Retailers feel that the consumer is entitled to know what she is buying

FIGURE 1.6. Seal of quality of the Nationwide Consumer Testing Institute Inc., a wholly owned subsidiary of the United States Testing Co., Inc. (Courtesy of the United States Testing Company, Inc.)

and how an article will perform in use. The knowledge of what a product will do should be carried from the mills on through garment manufacturing plants to the retailer and right on to the consumer. To this end, the National Retail Merchants Association and the USASI developed the washing and dry cleaning instructions previously described.

ADVERTISEMENTS

One of the most powerful tools for consumer education is advertising. Informative advertising goes hand in hand with informative labeling.

The TFPIA specifies that the required information for labels be shown in the advertisement of textile fiber products *in those instances* where the advertisement uses terms which are descriptive of a method of manufacture or construction, which is customarily used to indicate a textile fiber or fibers or by the use of terms which constitute or connote the name or presence of fiber or fibers. In contrast to the labeling requirements, advertising does not have to specify percentages of fiber present but simply list fibers in order of predominance by weight. Fiber or fibers amounting to 5 percent or less shall be listed as "other fiber" or "other fibers." This regulation applies to display signs used as advertising media but it does not apply to signs merely directing customers to the location of the merchandise.

A fiber trademark may be used in an advertisement of a textile fiber product but the use of such trademark requires a statement of fiber content (including percent by weight) in at least one instance in the advertisement. When a trademark is used, it must appear in immediate proximity and in conjunction with the generic name of the fiber. The generic name of the fiber shall appear in plain, legible type or lettering of the same size or conspicuousness as the trademark. Also, when a fiber trademark or generic name is used together with nonrequired information, it must in no way be false, deceptive, or misleading, as to fiber content. Nonrequired information is permissible in conjunction with an advertisement of a textile fiber product if it is truthful, nondeceptive, not misleading, or not detracting from the required information.

Swatches and samples used in display or to promote textile fiber products are not subject to labeling requirements provided:

1. Samples and swatches are less than two inches in area and the data otherwise required on the label appears in the accompanying promotional piece.
2. Samples and swatches are related to a catalogue to which reference must be made to make a sale and such catalogue nondeceptively gives information required for labels.
3. Samples and swatches are not used to make sales to the ultimate consumer and are not in the form intended for sale or delivery to the ultimate consumer.

Labeling or advertising of textile fiber products may *not* employ any names, directly or indirectly, of fur animals. Names symbolizing a furbearing animal through custom or usage may not be employed, i.e., "mink," "mutation," "broadtail." However, references may be made to furs which are not in commercial use, such as "Kitten soft" or "Bear Brand."

Should a textile fiber product contain the hair or fiber of a fur-bearing animal in amount exceeding 5 percent of the total weight, the name of the animal producing the fur is permissible provided the name is used in conjunction with the words "fiber," "hair," or "blend," as, for example: "80% Rabbit hair/20% Nylon."

The term "fur fiber" may be used to describe the hair or fur fiber or any mixtures of any animals other than sheep, lamb, Angora goat, Cashmere goat, camel, alpaca, llama, or vicuña where such hair or fur fiber or mixture exceeds 5 percent of the total fiber weight of the textile fiber product, and no direct or indirect reference is made to the animals involved; for example, "60% Cotton/40% Fur fiber" or "50% Nylon/30% Mink hair/20% Fur fiber."

But mere facts used without emotional appeal are not usually so successful as a combination of the two. Newspaper advertising that is truthful and at the same time informative builds customer confidence in the store. Mail-order houses have tried to improve their catalogues through better informative descriptions of their merchandise.

The radio put consumer education on the air in the form of consumer quizzes, lectures by educational speakers, and talks by executives in merchandise and fashion divisions of stores. Television demonstrates merchandise in use. Fashion shows, informative interviews on how to select a given item of merchandise, and a daily television woman's magazine are a few ways television brings consumer education into the home.

Women's and men's fashion and decorating magazines and special articles and fashion columns in newspapers are read by an increasing number of consumers.

In the past, advertisers have been held responsible for the accuracy of their claims and for the safety of their products. But the advertising media have not. As a result, many unsafe products, such as flammable clothing and home furnishings, have been advertised. Since federal agencies, such as the Consumer Product Safety Commission, are unable to enforce but a small portion of the quantity of goods placed on the market, it is now being suggested that the advertising media share this responsibility. While few can be expected to set up testing bureaus, all could refrain from publishing and broadcasting ads until their sponsors show evidence that their products present no health and safety problems.

AN INTELLIGENT SALES FORCE

Even when an adequate label is appended to the merchandise, the salesperson is the chief disseminator of merchandise information, since many customers never read the label. Suppose a customer wants a pair of boys' jeans for her seven-year-old. Before the advent of nylon or polyester blends, the customer had only a choice of all-cotton in navy blue. Nowadays, she has a choice of loden green, light blue, wheat, and other fashionable colors. They come in regular, slim, and husky cuts. Over half of them are durable press. Weights range from 10 to 14 ounces per square yard. There is a choice of all-cotton or cotton plus an appropriate percentage of polyester or nylon.

The salesperson who serves this customer had had instruction from her buyer and therefore could be of real assistance. She gave some practical information on all-cotton jeans: the heavier the better for tear and bursting resistance. But a lighter weight material, say an 11-ounce blend of cotton with 20 percent nylon or 50 percent polyester, will be about as durable as a 14-ounce all-cotton denim. As for color, yes, dark colors may darken the wash water. Durable-press blends are usually more resistant to abrasion, owing to a high percentage of man-made fiber. The salesperson can also point out strength features, such as reinforced bar tacks at each end of the hip pockets; the stitching of the side pockets for maximum security; the reinforcement of the fly at the bottom by rivets and bar tacks; the self-locking pull tab and double-stitched zipper tape; the waistband joined to the body by multiple rows of stitching; and double or triple seams wherever there is stress and strain.

Terminology on labels that requires interpretation resolves into a training problem for the retailer. The buyer is the logical interpreter of such information because he is in a position, if he does not know all the terms himself, to get the correct meaning from (1) the manufacturer who sold him the goods, (2) the store's testing laboratory, or (3) a textile consultant outside the store. In some stores a textile expert in the training department assists the buyer in training his salespeople and helps him in other ways when necessary.

Recognition of Consumers' Buying Motives. For some consumers, a brand name of merchandise may be a motivating factor in selection. For other consumers, factual information is demanded for satisfaction.

If the consumer can judge the wearing quality of a fabric, she is more likely to get her money's worth. To determine wearing quality, one must recognize the inherent characteristics of a fabric, such as the kind of raw material (fibers) used, the strength and evenness of the yarns, the construction or weave, and the permanency of the dye or the finish. Textile education attempts to teach the consumer (1) to recognize and interpret the inherent characteristics of a fabric in light of its intended use and (2) to judge the wearing quality in relation to the price.

A customer who comes to purchase a textile fabric may not ask a single question; yet the salesperson who can determine the customer's likes and dislikes through conversation and sales talk will usually make a sale. The salesperson can also determine whether the customer is trying to satisfy her physical and social needs. The customer's image of herself, or what she would like to be, is a consideration. Perhaps she considers herself a leader. Hence she must have something new, different, high style. Perhaps she doesn't want to be out of place in her social group and therefore conforms to what they will recognize as acceptable.

The discriminating consumer has at least some of the following questions in mind when she buys a fabric:

1. Is this suitable to my needs and wants? (suitability)
2. Can it be worn for a number of different occasions or purposes? (versatility)
3. Will it conserve time and effort? (convenience)
4. Will it wear well? (durability)
5. Will it be warm in winter? Is the texture suitable? (comfort)
6. Will this material be easy to dry clean, launder, protect from moths, mildew, and so forth? (care)
7. Is the article safe to use, either flame resistant or nonirritating to the skin? (safe)

8. Is the fabric good-looking? Will it look good on me? Will it go well with other garments or with the surroundings in which it will appear? (becomingness)
9. Is it in fashion? (appearance)
10. Does the price come within my means? Is it a "good buy?" (price)
11. Do I want to buy this merchandise because of associations it calls to mind? Because someone else has something like it and because I don't want to be out of style? (sentiment)
12. Will ownership of this merchandise give me a sense of possessing something unique and of great rarity? (pride of ownership)
13. Will people be impressed with my selection? Is it in line with what my group recognizes as acceptable? (recognition)
14. Does this merchandise satisfy a creative urge, particularly in yard goods? (creativity)

In question 8 the customer is considering the "ensemble idea"—the harmonious relationship of fabrics, color, and fashion-rightness, not only among various units of apparel worn together, but also among home furnishings. She may also ask herself: Is my selection in line with my self-image?

In answer to question 9, if the fabric is in accord with prevailing tendencies and modes of expression, if it has beauty, becomingness, and fashion-rightness, it looks good in use.

In question 10, the customer is also asking, "Am I getting my money's worth?" If the customer is limited in the amount of money she can spend for an article, the price is of great importance as a buying motive.

Many people buy old tapestries, laces, and rugs, not necessarily because of durability, but for the satisfaction of acquiring collections of fabrics that few people own. Other purchasers want materials that call to mind

FIGURE 1.7. A Sunday Merchandise Fair, Huancayo, Peru. (Courtesy of Professor Henry A. Rutherford, North Carolina State University, and *Textile Chemist and Colorist,* February 1973, published by the American Association of Textile Chemists and Colorists.)

pleasant associations. For example, to a man whose childhood was spent in Asia Minor, where beautiful rugs are woven, rugs would recall boyhood. Such a person's buying motive is based on sentiment.

Rivalry is an instinct, and the striving to equal or excel forms an appeal to the customer who buys to "keep up with the Joneses." This customer thrives on recognition.

Few consumers need to consider all these factors before making a purchase. To one customer price is paramount; to another, style; to another, becomingness; to another, possibly comfort. Knowing the factors inherent in the merchandise, the salesperson can relate the factors to the buying motive. For the man who wants comfort, durability, and ease of care in a shirt, the salesperson can recommend Dacron polyester and cotton blend, emphasizing the strength (durability) and convenience of polyester (no starching or ironing required; quick drying) and the absorptive value of cotton (absorbs perspiration without feeling clammy).

SUMMARY

The well-informed consumer is the one who can recognize and interpret the inherent characteristics of a textile fabric in the light of its intended use. With knowledge of facts about the goods, she can judge its probable wearing quality and can determine whether she is getting her money's worth. Consumer education in textiles may be obtained through courses in merchandise information given by high schools or colleges. The consumer is being protected and informed as a result of federal legislation. The government has also realized the value of courses in retailing which are now given in high schools and department stores with federal support under the Vocational Education Act of 1963.

Furthermore, progressive retailers have established the policy of informative newspaper, radio, and television advertising. Likewise, mail-order houses have rewritten their catalogues so that the consumer may have better informative descriptions of their merchandise.

Retailers have also realized that the consumer depends upon the salesperson for merchandise information, and therefore they have developed training programs toward that end. It is the salesperson who must determine the consumers' buying motives and, knowing the factors inherent in the merchandise, relate those factors to the buying motives.

Discriminating consumers are those who plan to get their money's worth. A person who gets value for the price paid is the one who knows the characteristics inherent in a fabric that affect the qualities of *suitability, versatility, durability, convenience, comfort, care, safety, becomingness, appearance, price, sentiment, pride of ownership, recognition, and creativity.*

**REVIEW
AND
DISCUSSION
QUESTIONS**

1. With what aims are courses in textiles given to salespeople in department stores?
2. By what means may the new salesperson acquire a knowledge of the textiles that he or she is selling?
3. What practical value has a textile course to a high school student?
4. Why are individual research and education important for the textile industry?
5. (*a*) Why is a knowledge of textile fabrics important to the consumer?
   (*b*) How can he or she acquire such merchandise information?
6. (*a*) Of what value is an informative label to the consumer?
   (*b*) What limitations do informative labels have?
7. (*a*) Name the federal laws pertaining to textiles

(b) What are the objectives of each law?

(c) How are these laws enforced?

(d) Are the provisions of the TFPIA sufficient to give the consumer adequate information about the inherent qualities of a fabric to enable him or her to decide how it will perform in a given use? Why?

8. What is the responsibility of the buyer in training salespeople in the selling points of certain merchandise?

9. (a) What is the chief objective of the Flammable Fabrics Act?

(b) To what textile products does this Act apply?

(c) What are the functions of the Consumer Product Safety Commission?

10. (a) Describe the application of mandatory care labels.

(b) How do these labels aid the home sewer?

11. In what ways is the government attempting to control textile standards?

12. What is the educational value of advertising to the consumer?

13. What is meant by the phrase "getting your money's worth"?

14. (a) List the questions a customer may have in mind when she comes to purchase a textile fabric.

(b) Which question or questions are the most important to you when you plan to buy (1) underwear, (2) hosiery, (3) a dress, (4) a suit, (5) a coat, (6) handkerchiefs, (7) curtains?

15. Explain which is meant by *sentiment* as a buying motive; by *recognition* as a buying motive.

16. Give an example, preferably from your own experience, in which the salesperson related the inherent factors in the merchandise to the buying motive.

PROJECT

1. (a) Clip an advertisement for a particular item of clothing, such as a dress, suit, hosiery, underwear, or hat.

(b) Underline all terms descriptive of the merchandise.

(c) List any terms that you believe a consumer would have difficulty in understanding.

(d) What are the chief merits of the advertisement?

2. Visit the yard-goods department of a department store in your community. Observe one salesperson in the department. Notice whether she seems to give intelligent answers to the customers' inquiries about the merchandise. Notice how she displays the goods and the way in which she cuts it from the bolt. Observe the measuregraph (the device fastened to the farther side of the counter) and the way it is used by the salesperson to measure the goods and to compute the sale.

(a) When you leave the department, recall your observations and rate the salesperson as excellent, good, fair, or poor. Give 60 points if the salesperson gave the customer intelligent information about the merchandise; 10 points if the salesperson displayed the goods attractively; 20 points if she cut the goods straight and with no apparent difficulty; 10 points if she computed the sale quickly by reading the figures on the measuregraph.

(b) Judging from the rating you have given the salesperson, what type of training would help her to improve her selling job?

3. (a) Visit a large department store and check at least five articles of apparel and five of home furnishings made of textiles. Determine whether the federally required care labels are attached and note whether the piece goods regulations are followed. Review this chapter to determine what articles are exempt.

(b) Talk to five typical consumers to determine their attitude toward the use of care labels. Do they feel that the value they gain exceeds some increased prices to cover the cost of the research involved and the cost of preparing the labels?

(c) If the entire class will make an extensive survey of consumer attitude toward care labels, it is suggested that the results be sent to the U.S. Consumer Product Safety Commission in Washington, which re-evaluates its regulations from time to time.

GLOSSARY Broadcloth—A tightly constructed cotton fabric in plain weave with a fine crosswise rib.

Buying motives—Reasons why consumers select a certain product for an intended use.

Buying points—Facts that the consumer considers important in selecting an article for a particular use.

Cloth—See *Fabric*.

Consumer—The purchaser of merchandise for certain uses—that is, wearing apparel, household textiles, food, and hard lines.

Consumer education—The process of helping the consumer to become a more intelligent buyer of goods and services and a wiser user of what he has, a more prudent manager of his finances, and a better-informed consumer-citizen.

Cooperative program (in school or college)—A program in which the student spends part-time in store service.

Delamination—The separation of the layers of fabric in bonded goods.

Fabric (textile)—A material formed of fibers or yarns, either by the interlacing method of weaving, by the interlooping of knitting, by braiding, felting, bonding, or laminating.

Fiber—The basic unit used in the fabrication of textile yarns and fabrics.

Grey goods—Textile merchandise as it comes from the loom (after it has been constructed) before it is finished.

Informative label—A tag that gives a description of qualities inherent in the merchandise in order to aid the consumer in appropriate selection for her needs and to give instructions for proper care of her purchase.

Merchandise—Any finished goods ready for consumer purchase.

Merchandise information—Facts about goods that will aid the consumer in selecting a suitable article for her needs.

Nylon—A man-made textile fiber largely derived from petroleum, chemically combined with air and water.

"Role-playing" method—A method of instructing trainees in selling situations in retail stores.

Selling points—Facts about a product that are stressed by the salesman in selling and that help the consumer make a selection suitable to her needs.

"Show-tell" skit—Method by which the salesperson demonstrates *and* explains pertinent facts about the merchandise.

Textile fabric—See *Fabric*.

Textiles—All materials that can be or have been formed into yarns or fabricated into cloth. See *Fabric*.

Fiber Content
of
Textile Fabrics

2

A customer was fingering a forest of hangtags attached to a dress she was trying on. The salesperson offered assistance, and the customer remarked, "I've found it. The dress is made of 50 percent polyester and 50 percent cotton. Is this fabric going to stand machine laundering?" "Oh yes," replied the salesperson without looking at the attached care label now required by federal law. Fortunately, the salesperson gave the right answer. She knew that cotton launders easily, is absorptive and comfortable; that polyester is a family name of man-made fiber characterized by strength, resilience, crease and abrasion resistance, shape retention, and ease in care. When the salesperson found the care label, it read "Machine washable." She was right but she had made an educated guess based on the *fiber content* (raw materials) in the dress fabric.

FIBERS, YARNS, AND CONSTRUCTION

A fiber is a hairlike unit of raw material of which cloths are made—for example, cotton, linen, rayon, silk, wool, nylon, and polyester.[1] The fiber is the basic unit of which a fabric is made. To see what a fiber looks like, unravel a thread, called a *yarn*, from a sample of sheer cotton cloth. Untwist the thread. Each of the tiny hairs that make up the yarn is a fiber. To make a yarn, several fibers are grouped (often twisted) into a strand. Cloth can be constructed from fibers or yarn in eight different ways:

1. *Weaving* is the interlacing of two sets of yarns at right angles.
   a. *Warp* (end) is yarn that runs lengthwise in a woven fabric.
   b. *Filling* (woof, weft, pick, shot) is yarn that runs crosswise in a woven fabric. These fillings are carried over and under the warp yarns.
   c. *Selvage* is the outer finished edge on both sides of the fabric. The selvage is formed by the filling yarn, which loops around the outside warp yarn to form an edge that does not ravel. Warp yarns always run parallel to the selvages. (See Fig. 2.3).
2. *Knitting* is the construction of an elastic, porous fabric by means of needles. One or more yarns form a series of connecting loops that support one another like a chain.

[1] The TFPIA defines a "fiber" or "textile fiber" as "a unit of matter which is capable of being spun into yarn or made into fabric by bonding or by interlacing in a variety of methods including knitting, weaving, braiding, felting, twisting, or webbing, and which is the basic structural element of textile products."

23

FIGURE 2.1. Fibers are shown at the loose end of a yarn that has been pulled away from the piece of cloth shown at the bottom of the picture. (Photo by Jack Pitkin.)

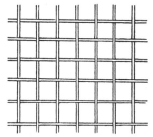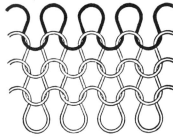

FIGURE 2.2. Left: Construction of a plain woven fabric. Right: Construction of a plain knitted fabric.

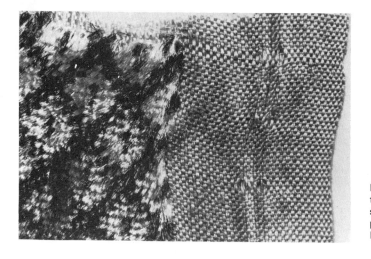

FIGURE 2.3 The selvage is the plain strip of fabric shown in the right half of the picture. (Photo by Jack Pitkin.)

FIGURE 2.4. Types of fabrics. (a) felted; (b) non-woven; (c) bonded; (d) crocheted; (e) braid—three strips of knitted jersey; (f) unbonded; (g) knotted; (h) laminated.

25

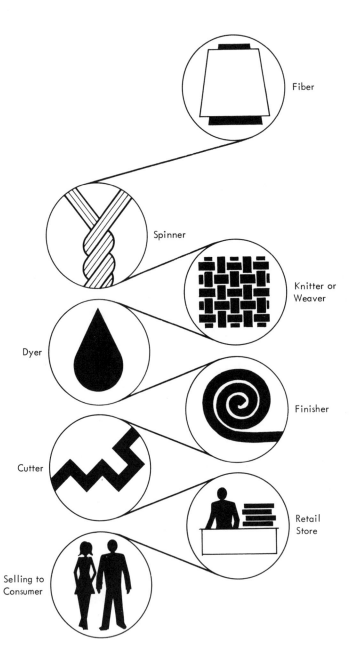

Fiber

Spinner

Knitter or Weaver

Dyer

Finisher

Cutter

Retail Store

Selling to Consumer

FIGURE 2.5. How fabric is made—from source to consumer.

3. *Crocheting* is a construction made with just one hook or needle. A chain of loops is formed from a single yarn.
4. *Felting* is the process of matting fibers together by heat, steam, and pressure to form a fabric.
5. *Knotting (or netting)* is a process of forming an openwork fabric or net by tying yarns together where they cross one another. *Tatting* is a form of knotted lace that is made with a shuttle filled with yarn.
6. *Braiding (or plaiting)* is an interlacing of three or more yarns or strips of cloth over and under one another to form a narrow flat tubular fabric.
7. *Bonding* is a process of joining two or more layers of cloth together with a layer of adhesive, or pressing fibers into thin webs or mats that are held together by adhesive, plastic, or self-bonding agents. Bonded webs are referred to as "nonwoven fabrics." For methods of producing nonwoven fabrics, see Chapter 6.
8. *Laminating* is a process of uniting a piece of fabric to a sheet of urethane foam (a plastic frothy mass)—especially the joining of a surface fabric to a foam plastic back.

Cloths or "fabrics" are known as "textile fabrics" when they are made from fibers by one of the aforementioned methods.[2] Leather is not a textile fabric because it is not made of fibers and is not constructed into a fabric by any of the eight methods listed here. (Sometimes, however, leather is cut into narrow strips and woven into the uppers of sport shoes. In such cases it has been made into a textile fabric). Paper used for stationery is not a textile fabric for the previously mentioned reason. A man's panama hat, however, is a textile fabric because it is woven from straw. A disposable pillowcase is made of bonded web—a nonwoven goods (textile).

Textiles are fabrics or fibers from which fabrics are made. The word textile is derived from the Latin verb *texere*, meaning "to weave." Although the term originally applied only to woven fabrics, the present definition includes fabrics made by other methods of construction, such as knitting, felting, crocheting, knotting, braiding, bonding, and laminating.

Textile merchandise is woven, knitted, crocheted, felted, knotted, braided, bonded, and laminated. All other merchandise is called "nontextile merchandise." China, glassware, leather shoes and riding boots,

FIGURE 2.6. A label showing correct use of generic terms defined in the Textile Fiber Products Identification Act. (Reproduced courtesy of Cone Mills, Inc.)

[2] According to the TFPIA, "Fabric means any material woven, knitted, felted or otherwise produced from, or in combination with, any natural or manufactured fiber, yarn, or substitute therefor."

stationery, wooden and steel furniture, jewelry, and silverware are some nontextile items.

Classification of textile fibers. Two main classes of textile fibers are used in consumer goods: (1) natural fibers and (2) man-made fibers.

**NATURAL
TEXTILE
FIBERS**

These fibers that grow in nature can be divided into three groups: (1) animal, (2) vegetable, and (3) mineral. (See fiber classification, p. 36.)

ANIMAL FIBERS

Wool and Silk. The animal fibers that are most used in consumers' goods are wool, which is the protective covering of the sheep, and silk, cultivated or wild, which is the product of the silkworm and is obtained from its cocoon. Silk and wool will be discussed in Chapters 11 and 12 respectively.

Less important fibers include hair fibers from camels, rabbits, goats, cats, horses, and cattle. They differ microscopically from wool and, as a rule, are stiffer and more wiry than wool and do not felt well. Cashmere, a goat fiber, and camel's hair, however, are quite soft.

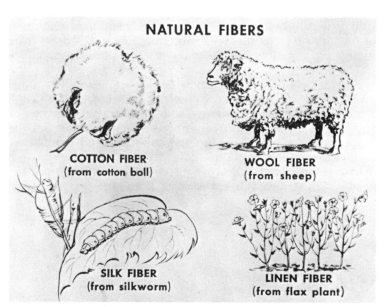

NATURAL FIBERS

COTTON FIBER
(from cotton boll)

WOOL FIBER
(from sheep)

SILK FIBER
(from silkworm)

LINEN FIBER
(from flax plant)

FIGURE 2.7. Before the advent of man-made fibers, clothing and other textile goods could be made only from fibers which nature provided, mainly, cotton, wool, silk, and linen. (Courtesy of Man-Made Fiber Producers Association, Inc.)

Cat hair and cow hair can be used as textile fibers, but they are used mostly for fur felts. Cow hair, although harsh and coarse, can be made into blankets and carpets, but it should be mixed with other fibers. The sources and properties of hair fibers will be discussed in Chapter 12.

VEGETABLE FIBERS

Cotton and Linen. Cotton and linen are the most common vegetable fibers used in consumers' goods. Cotton comes from the cotton plant, a small bush related to the hollyhock. Linen, called "flax fiber," is obtained from outside the woody core of the flax plant. Both of these fibers are vegetable because they contain a large amount of cellulose, of which the cells of plants are constructed.

Modified Cellulose Fibers. Cotton fibers can be treated with a bath of caustic soda either after they are made into yarn or after the cloth is constructed. The purpose of this treatment, called "mercerization," is (1) to give strength to the fibers, (2) to increase luster, and (3) to improve their affinity for dye. Linen is rarely mercerized because it is naturally stronger than cotton and possesses good natural luster.

The physical properties of the cotton fiber can be modified by cross-linking of molecules. This technique improves a fabric's wrinkle recovery and is thus important for wash-and-wear. (See Glossary for a definition of cross-linking.)

Minor Vegetable Fibers. These include: *Ramie or rhea, hemp,* and *sisal* a fiber from the nettle-like East Indian shrub. It is also produced in China, Egypt, Kenya, and the United States. *Jute* comes from fibers within a wooded stalk of a plant about twelve feet tall grown primarily in India.

Hemp. This fiber is grown in the Philippine Islands, Yucatan, Mexico, Central America, the West Indies, and India. Italy, Poland, France, Japan, and the United States (Kentucky) also raise hemp. Ramie, jute, and hemp will be discussed more fully in Chapter 10.

Sisal. Often called *sisal hemp*, this is a hard fiber larger and stiffer than the bast fibers, flax, hemp, jute, and ramie. Sisal grows on large plantations in Java, Haiti, Kenya in East Africa, West Africa, and Central America. We import most of our sisal from the first three countries. Approximately 4,000 to 6,000 plants can be grown to an acre, and an interval of three years is required from the time of planting until harvesting.[3] White fibers are obtained from the leaves of the Agave plant (*Agave sisalana*) by the process of decortication (the removal of the outer woody portion to obtain the fiber). The fibers are dried and bleached in the sun and are sold in bales. Principal uses are for cordage, ropes, and binder twine. Sisal is weakened by salt water but not so easily by fresh water. It is adapted for use in women's straw hats.

The uses for sisal.[4] The main use for sisal fiber is in the manufacture of strings, twines, and ropes. Before World War II, the trade found it difficult to interest shipowners and navies in using sisal ropes, because sailors generally criticized the harshness of the ropes and also maintained that they did not "give" in the same way as Manila ropes. However, during the war, when Manila supplies were cut off, sisal ropes had to be used, and the trade has kept a considerable amount of business in peacetime. Low-grade fiber is used for sacks, but these are not very popular because of their coarseness.

In agriculture, baler and binder twines use a considerable amount of sisal fiber. A growing use of low-grade fiber is in the mat and carpet

[3] J.M. Matthews, *Textile Fibers*, 6th ed., ed. H.R. Mauersberger (New York: John Wiley & Sons, Inc., 1954), p. 377. *Dictionary of Textiles* ed. Isabel B. Wingate (New York: Fairchild Publications, Inc., 1967).

[4] Result of research written especially for *Textile Fabrics* by Tongoni Plantations, Ltd. Christo Galanos, Director, Nairobi, Kenya.

industries. Pile carpets are being manufactured successfully in Holland. And on the continent of Europe and in England sisal for matting is beginning to supersede the better-known coir matting.

Coir. This is a hard, reddish-brown fiber obtained from the outer shell of the coconut. These fibers have to be removed from the fruit, then softened in water and pounded to remove the wooded husk. Coir is prepared by hand or by machines with fluted iron rollers that crush the husks. Then a revolving drum studded with sharp teeth tears out the woody husks. Broken fibers that fall from this drum are dried in the sun, then cleaned and used for mattresses. The finer grades of mattress fiber can be made into rope and cocoa matting. After washing, cleaning, and hackling (combing), the stronger, coarser fibers are made into hanks and sold for brushes, primarily to the European market. From strips of leaves of the coconut palm, a thread can be made that is elastic, lightweight, and waterproof. It is used in mats, bags, hats, and slippers.

Paper. Made mainly from linen, cotton, and hemp rags, and from straw, bamboo, jute, and wood, in sheet form paper is a nontextile. But fine strips of paper made of wood pulp can be twisted into yarn and properly treated so that they are usable in floor coverings and porch furniture. Ordinarily, paper used in the manufacture of so-called fiber rugs is weak when wet, and if thoroughly drenched will become mush.

Paper is closely allied to rayon. In one process especially, purified cellulose is rolled out into sheets of cardboard before it is treated with chemicals to form the viscous solution. (See Chapter 13).

Although paper may be so treated as to present a good appearance as a textile fabric, it is not durable, comfortable, or serviceable as a textile yarn. Consumers should consider carefully before they purchase fabrics containing paper.

Disposable items come under the classification of *throwaway fabrics* and are really nonwoven goods made of webs of cotton, nylon, or polyester that are fused or bonded with a cementing medium such as starch, glue, casein, rubber latex, one of the cellulose derivatives, or synthetic resins.[5]

Kapok. A vegetable fiber that comes from a plant or tree grown chiefly in Java, the West Indies, Central America, India, Africa, South Asia, and Brazil, kapok is a silky fiber, finer than cotton, but it is not adaptable to spinning; hence, it is not used in woven cloth. Mattresses and pillows are filled with kapok. It is cheaper than hair but not so durable or resilient. Kapok dries quickly and so is servicable for bedding used at the seashore. Life preservers made of kapok are buoyant and light in weight, but after a season's use can become heavy and nonbuoyant.

Grass, Rush, and Straw. Cured prairie grass from Minnesota and Wisconsin is bound together into a rope for weaving into grass rugs for sun rooms, porches, and summer homes. Rush, generally made of reeds that grow in sluggish waters of Europe and the Far East, is similarly used in rugs.

---

[5] Disposable items include hospital sheets, pillowcases, diapers, curtains, and wiping cloths.

Straw fibers are obtained from stems, stalks, leaves, and bark of natural plants. Following are names of straws, many of which are woven into hats: baku (fibers of bari palm of Ceylon and the Malabar Coast), balibuntal (from unopened palm leaf stems), leghorn (from a kind of wheat grown in Tuscany), milan (from Milan, Italy), panama (from Toquilla straw of Ecuador), toquilla (from Jippi-Jappa leaves), tuscan (from bleached wheat stalks grown in Tuscany).

MINERAL FIBERS

Asbestos is a mineral obtained from rocks primarily in Quebec, Southern Rhodesia, South Africa, and Russia. Asbestos from Canada and U.S.S.R. can be spun and woven into cloth because its fibers are more than one-quarter inch long. White, soft, and silky, they resist all liquids except strong acids. Woven products of asbestos include fireproof suits, protective clothing, gloves, and safety curtains in theaters. Asbestos cloth with a metallic layer of aluminum bonded to it reflects heat.

Thin sheets of gold, silver, or aluminum foil can be cut in strips and used as yarn for luxury fabrics.

The natural fibers that we have been discussing continue in top place from the standpoint of world production, even though they have dropped from 68 percent of total production in 1966 to 58 percent in 1974, with man-made fibers increasing from 32 percent to 42 percent. In the United States natural fibers are relatively much less important, with only 31 percent of total production; man-made fibers account for the rest.

Cotton is by far the major natural fiber, accounting for over 89 percent of the world's natural fiber production. Its production is still on the increase; wool production has been declining slowly; and silk is about holding its own in actual poundage but not in percentage of the total.[6]

MANUFAC-TURED OR MAN-MADE FIBERS

According to the TFPIA, the term *man-made fiber* "...means any fiber derived by a process of manufacture from a substance which, at any point in the manufacturing process, is not a fiber." This act lists the generic or family names and definitions for manufactured fibers established by the FTC for use in labeling and advertising. No other names may be substituted for these generic names unless and until established by the FTC.

Rule 7 of this act lists 20 generic names of manufactured fibers, along with their respective definitions. (See Chapters 13, 14, and 15 for technical definitions.) It will be noted that the definitions of these generic names by the FTC are couched in technical, chemical terminology that a salesperson or consumer would not be likely to understand. Yet these terms must be used by labelers and advertisers just as the generic names of the natural fibers—cotton, linen, silk, wool—are used. Familiarizing consumers with these terms requires considerable training of salespeople

---

[6] Data on world production from the *Textile Organon* for June 1975. Percentage of natural fiber production in the United States based on poundage of mill consumption reported in the *Man-made Fiber Fact Book* (for 1974) of the Man-Made Fiber Producers Association, Inc.

TABLE 2-1. Classification of Man-Made Fibers

Fibers Derived from Pure Cellulose	Chemically Derived Fibers	Fibers Derived from Non-Fibrous Natural Substances
Rayon (purified cellulose)	Nylon (polyamide)—largely derived from petroleum, chemically combined with air and water.	Rubber (natural or synthetic rubber)
Acetate (cellulose acetate)	Acrylic (resin)—coal, air, water, petroleum, limestone	Glass (molten glass)
Triacetate (modified acetate—higher ratio of acetate to cellulose)	Modacrylic (modified acrylic)—acrylonitrile, and other materials	Metallic (metal, plastic coated metal, metal coated plastic, or core covered completely by metal)
	Polyester (resin)—coal, air, water, petroleum	
	Saran (vinylidene chloride)	Azlon (protein—casein, peanuts, corn)
	Vinyon (vinyl chloride)	
	Olefin (propylene gas and ethylene gas)	
	Vinal (polyvinyl alcohol)	
	Nytril (vinylidene dinitrile)	
	Spandex (polyurethane)	
	Anidex (elastomeric acrylate)	
	Aramid (elastomeric aromatic polyamide)	
	Novoloid (phenolic)	

so that they can explain adequately. Simplification of these definitions should be most helpful in this training.

In order to comprehend the meanings of the generic terms, a general description of broad bases for classification of manufactured fibers should be helpful.

FIBERS DERIVED FROM A CELLULOSIC BASE

Some fibers, such as rayon and acetate, have a base of natural plant cellulose, the same as cotton. Other fibers are based on protein found in milk, soybeans, or corn meal. Others are based on natural rubber from the rubber tree. Still others are derived from sand (silicon) made into glass marbles.

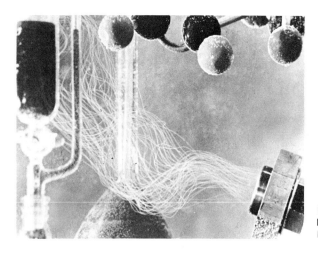

FIGURE 2.8. Chemically developed fibers being extruded through spinnerets. (Courtesy of Man-Made Fiber Producers Association, Inc.)

Rayon. Made both from wood pulp (obtained from western hemlock and southern pine) and from cotton linters (fibers adhering to cotton seeds), the raw materials used in making rayon contain a large amount of cellulose. Rayon, like other manufactured textile fibers, is made by converting the base raw material into a solution that can be extruded through small holes in a nozzle or jet and then hardened into fiber.

Rayon Fibers Made from Modified Cellulose. By treating the cellulose chemically, rayon fibers are changed (modified) in such a way as to create properties different from the usual rayon. These properties may include improved strength dry and wet, wrinkle recovery, crimping to give a kinky, wool like appearance, dimensional stability (retention of size and shape), and new styling possibilities. (See Chapter 13 for a full discussion of rayon and acetate.)

Acetate. Made from wood and sometimes from cotton linters (waste), acetate fibers are derived from chemical compounds of cellulose (cellulose and acetyl).

Until the FTC revised its ruling on rayon, which took effect February 9, 1952, acetate was called "rayon." But, because acetate fibers are not pure cellulose, as are rayons, but are cellulose plus acetyl, the fibers require different care by consumers than do the pure cellulose fibers. Rayon is a vegetable fiber, and acetate is a vegetable and chemical fiber. Common trade names for acetate are Acele, Estron, and Celanese. (Chapter 13 has a further discussion of acetates.)

Modified acetate fibers. Acetate fibers may be modified by stretching the acetate yarns generally in steam, and then treating them with an alkaline bath. Such a yarn has high tenacity. Dye can be added to the spinning solution called solution spun, or dope-dyed fibers. Fabrics made from these fibers are fast to sunlight.

Triacetate. This thermoplastic material contains three acetate components. Arnel is a trademark of the Celanese Corporation of America for triacetate fibers and yarns. These fibers are more resistant to heat than are regular acetate fibers. (See Chapter 13.)

FIBERS DERIVED FROM A NONCELLULOSIC BASE

Nylon, Acrylic, Modacrylic. The fibers in this classification are all "produced in a test tube." This means that the fiber-forming substances are not natural bases but complex chemical compounds. These same compounds used for extruding textile fibers may be used for plastics (nontextiles) and for finishes and coatings of textiles. There are many resins (plastics) used for textile fibers, such as polyamide resin used for making nylon fibers and acrylic resin (at least 85 percent acrylonitrile units) used for making acrylics like Orlon and Acrilan. When acrylic fibers are modified by using 35 to 85 percent acrylonitrile units, then resultant fibers are classified as modacrylics (modified acrylics). Trademarked fibers Elura and Verel are modacrylics. (See Chapter 14 for a discussion of these fibers.)

Polyester. A fiber-forming substance made from a chemical composition of ethylene glycol and terephthalic acid is generically classified as polyester. Trademarked fibers in this category include Dacron, Kodel, Fortrel, and Vycron. (See Chapter 14.)

Spandex. Polyurethane plastic resin is used for spandex, of which a well-known trademarked fiber is Lycra. (See Chapter 15.)

Vinyon, saran, nytril, vinal. Vinyl derivatives or various types are used for making manufacturered fibers. For example, a vinylite resin is used for the fiber vinyon, vinylidene chloride is used for saran, vinylidene dinitrile for nytril, and vinyl alcohol and acetal units for the vinal class of fibers that have achieved considerable commercial success abroad but have not appeared as yet on the American scene.

Olefin. The paraffin-based fibers, polyethylene and polypropylene, are classified generically as olefin. Trademarked fibers of this class include Herculon and Marvess. (See Chapter 15.)

NATURAL AND SYNTHETIC RUBBER-BASED FIBERS

A manufactured rubber fiber is used for an elastic yarn, uncovered or covered with various textile threads. These yarns are used for knitted and woven goods. Trademarked fibers of this class are Lastex (natural rubber) and Contro (synthetic rubber). (See Chapter 15.)

Metallic-based fibers. Manufactured fibers composed of metal, metal-coated plastic, or a core completely covered by metal come under this classification of manufactured fibers. A familiar trademark of metallic yarn is Lurex.

Glass. Glass fibers are made from melted glass marbles. The molten glass is extruded through a nozzle with tiny holes similar to the one used in forming nylon fibers. Glass fibers are fireproof. A well-known trademarked name is Fiberglas.

Anidex. This is a manufactured elastomeric fiber that stretches and recovers; an elastomer of an acrylic closely allied to acrylic fibers and acrylic plastics. (See Chapter 15.)

Azlon. A manufactured fiber produced from proteins found in casein, peanuts, soya beans, and corn kernels. Azlon is not produced in the United States.

Aramid. This is the name given by the F.T.C. in 1974 to a class of aramatic polyamide fibers that differ in properties from the more conventional nylons. Produced by Du Pont under the trademarks Nomex and Kevlar. These fibers are fire-retardant. (See Chapter 15.)

Novoloid. A generic name for a noncellulosic man-made fiber made from a cross-linked polymer derived from carbon, hydrogen, and oxygen. Its production by U. S. Carborundum Co. began in 1972.

The genius of researchers in the field of chemistry, especially in the United States and England, accounts for two great modern industries— man-made textiles and plastics. The two fields are closely related with the chemical composition from which nylon and polyester are extruded into textile fiber being the same as that molded, cast, or laminated into plastic materials of many sorts.

In the United States, man-made fibers account for about 70 percent of all textile fibers consumed, leaving only about 30 percent for the natural fibers. The older cellulosic fibers (rayon and acetate) account for only some 17 percent of the man-made fiber production, with the rest represented by the noncellulosic fibers.

Table 2-2 throws light on a major reason for the inroads into natural and cellulosic fibers by polyester, the leading noncellulosic fiber. Cotton, rayon, and wool increased in price until recently while polyester declined. Rayon prices have continued to move upward but cotton and wool have recently been declining. Polyester staple (cut into short lengths for spinning) has now moved up in price to about the level of cotton, making blends of the two practicable. With wool prices now lower, the supply of wool goods is likely to increase.

TABLE 2-2. Market Price of Selected Textile Fibers[a]
$/LB.
Annual Averages

	1965	1971	1973	1974	Est. 1975
Polyester Staple(1)	$ .84	$ .38	$ .38	$ .44	$ .48
Rayon Staple(2)	.27	.27	.33	.51	.53
Cotton(3)	.31	.33	.61	.55	.45
Wool(4)	1.25	.67	2.47	1.62	1.55
Wool(5)	1.19	.66	1.58	1.13	.88
Polyester Filament(6)	1.55	1.15	.88	.88	.80

(1) 1.5 denier $1\frac{1}{2}''$ staple
(2) 1.5 and 3.0 denier regular rayon staple
(3) Strict low middling, $1\frac{1}{16}''$ Memphis territory
(4) Graded territory, 64's—Good French combing
(5) Graded fleece, $\frac{3}{8}$ blood, 56's—58's
(6) 150 denier on tubes

[a]Prepared by the market analyst of a major fiber manufacturer.

In Appendix B, the table entitled "Generic Groups of Man-Made Fibers" presents the generic names of the manufactured fibers, their chief characteristics, uses, trademarks, features, and producers. In general, the companies listed in the table make both fibers and yarns. The majority do not make fabrics.

Table 2-3 summarizes the broad, general classification of fibers.

A classification according to the basic raw material from which each class of fiber is derived appeared in Table 2-1. With this guidance, the

TABLE 2-3

Natural Fibers	Manufactured or Man-Made Fibers
I. Animal	I. Fibers Derived from a Cellulosic Base
silk	rayon and modified fibers
wool	acetate and modified fibers
hair	triacetate
II. Vegetable	II. Fibers Derived from a Noncellulosic Base
cotton	nylon
linen	acrylic
ramie	modacrylic
jute	polyester
hemp	spandex
paper	anidex
kapok	azlon (protein-based fibers)
sisal	vinyon, saran, nytril, vinal
coir	olefin
grass	natural & synthetic rubber-based fibers
straw	metallic-based fibers
rush	glass
III. Mineral	aramid
asbestos	novoloid

generic classification of manufactured fibers established by the FTC under the TFPIA should be more meaningful. (Chapters 13, 14, and 15 contain full discussions of man-made fibers.)

THE CONSUMER'S INTEREST IN FIBERS

The consumer is not usually interested in identifying fibers per se. The TFPIA requires that all fibers used in a fabric be listed on a label in percentages by weight. This tag or label is to remain affixed to the article until it reaches the consumer. The consumer is interested in how certain fibers will perform in use in a finished cloth. She wants to know how the use of certain fibers in a cloth will affect its durability, suitability, comfort, ease in care, and attractiveness. These factors are the consumers' buying criteria. The Permanent Care Labeling Act of 1972 requires that finished articles of wearing apparel must have a permanently attached label.

The use of more than one fiber in a fabric might (1) give the fabric more uses than if it had one fiber, (2) give it a different feeling or "hand," (3) overcome a definite drawback of the other fiber or fibers, (4) lower the cost, or (5) give it a different appearance or style value.

There is an increasing amount of mixing of fibers. A fabric is a *mixture* if each individual yarn is composed of a particular fiber. For instance, the warp, or up-and-down yarn, might be made of acetate, and the filling, or crosswise yarn, might be of rayon. The acetate is more dimensionally stable than the rayon. The rayon filling provides the texture with surface interest of the fabric.

A fabric is a *blend* if each yarn is composed of two or more different fibers. To make a blend, different fibers are mixed together before the yarn is spun. There is an increasing amount of blending being done today, particularly where the newer man-made fibers are concerned. The technical problem lies in the percentage of man-made fibers that must be added to make the fabric best suited to the particular use for which it is intended. Nylon blended with wool adds strength to the wool. One technologist states that each 1 percent of nylon increases the strength of a woolen yarn 3 percent. But the consumer might want to know about a specific use: "Is the presence of nylon in a wool blend advantageous for use in upholstery, for example?" The answer would be affirmative, because nylon adds strength and abrasion resistance—two important factors in this end use.

The consumer may want to know why wool yarns are used in the warp, and cotton in the filling, of a flannel shirt. The mixed fabric is less expensive than 100 percent wool and is easier to launder (less apt to shrink). This example illustrates that more than one fiber in a fabric may make the garment less expensive to care for because it can be washed at home. Since wool-and-cotton flannel is not as warm as all-wool flannel, it is more comfortable in overheated apartments. The label reveals that the fabric contains both wool and cotton, and the consumer can sense the presence of cotton by touch.

SENSE OF TOUCH

While the sense of touch is not very reliable in helping the consumer identify textile fabrics (because of the man-made fibers and blends), she can still learn much from the hand, or feeling, of a cloth. Such factors as warmth, coolness, pliability, texture, bumpiness, smoothness, or strength of a fabric can be discerned by the sense of touch.

To develop a sense of touch, grasp the edge of a cloth between the thumb and index finger, with the thumb on top. Rub the thumb and forefinger across the cloth, then lengthwise, then in a circle. Each time a fabric is felt, words that best describe the feel should be brought to mind: pliability, elasticity or "give," warmth, softness, smoothness, and so on.

When is a cloth pliable and when is it elastic or resilient? By pliability is meant the degree of flexibility or give a fabric possesses. If a fabric is gripped by the thumb and forefinger of each hand and pulled crosswise and then lengthwise, it will give; and a fabric that has give is said to be pliable. A fabric that returns to its original shape and form after stretching is said to be elastic or resilient. An all-wool jersey, to be considered satisfactory, should be resilient. A jersey dress that bulges at the elbows because it lacks resilience is unsatisfactory.

By smoothness is meant the ease with which the fabric slips if pulled between the fingers.

For the comparison of texture, the following fabrics are suitable: acetate satin and nylon satin, both of which have smooth, slippery surfaces; cotton flannel and wool flannel, which have soft surfaces. Compare nylon shantung and polyester shantung. Both fabrics have bumpy textures. A terry toweling and a crash toweling, however, should not be compared, for their surfaces are entirely different and consequently would not give fair comparisons.

Fibers alone will not determine the hand or feel of a fabric. The type of yarn used, construction, and finish will contribute to the hand of a cloth. In general, all that can be said is that fabrics made of vegetable fibers are usually cooler than animal fibers of the same weight. A 100 percent cotton fabric is lifeless to the touch unless it is treated in the finish to give it a hand. A 100 percent linen fabric is cool and pliable (leathery) to the touch. A fabric of 100 percent silk is smooth, fairly slippery, and soft. A 100 percent wool is warm and comparatively resilient, and 100 percent polyester feels crisp and resilient.

SENSE OF SIGHT

Luster (or sheen), fuzziness, fineness, and coarseness of a fabric may be observed. A Qiana nylon satin has a rich luster; a cotton flannel has a fuzzy surface; a linen table damask has a flat, smooth surface; a silk chiffon is fine and sheer; an acetate shantung looks bumpy. Texture of a fabric is easily observed.

On the basis of fiber content, sight, and touch, a consumer can decide whether the fabric has the suitability, attractiveness, ease in care, durability, and style-rightness that she requires in a given use. The informed salesperson should be able to help her make a decision.

Sometimes a manufacturer's brand name on a label may help the consumer come to a decision. The name "Harris Tweed" representing a wool coating fabric is quite satisfactory for this use. Seals of approval of organizations mentioned in Chapter 1 may also help the consumer to come to a decision to purchase.

INTEREST OF THE MANUFACTURER IN FIBER IDENTIFICATION

To the manufacturers of cloth garments and household textiles the TFPIA has made fiber identification a *must*. It is they who are responsible for seeing that fiber content is specified on labels or tags. Who knows better what fibers went into a fabric than the manufacturer of the grey goods?

INTEREST OF THE RETAIL BUYER IN FIBER IDENTIFICATION

The retailer is legally responsible for subscribing to the TFPIA. He relies on his vendor to supply him merchandise that is labeled to conform to the act. Should the labels become detached from the merchandise or should imported merchandise be unlabeled, it becomes the retail buyer's responsibility to have labels made and affixed to the goods.

If the buyer is unable to identify fiber content himself, and most buyers do not have either the time or the equipment, then the merchandise must be sent to a testing bureau. With the advent of two or three different fibers in a blend and the variety of man-made fibers that can be blended with each other or with natural fibers, fiber identification is not easy.

LABORA-
TORY
METHODS
OF FIBER
IDENTI-
FICATION

While no attempt will be made here to give data on scientific testing procedure, an attempt will be made to show the complexity of fiber identification under the TFPIA.

Thirteen different classes of fibers (acetate, acrylic, modacrylic, nylon, olefin, polyester, rayon, saran, spandex, cotton, flax, silk, and wool) can be identified with certain modifications by seven tests.[7] The tests and a summary of the procedures follow.

1. *Resistance to heat and flame.* A preliminary inspection is made to obtain information on the fabric's distinct characteristics. As a part of this preliminary inspection, the heat and flame test should be applied to note the effects of heat, the burning characteristics, and the burning odor of the sample. The results of this test can be used in determining what subsequent tests are to be made.

Test Procedure: Slowly move a specimen of the fiber to be tested toward a small flame and observe the reaction of the fiber to heat. Then push one end of the specimen directly into the flame to determine the burning characteristics of the fiber. After removal from the flame, observe the fiber's burning characteristics again and note the burning odor. (Burning odor can be compared with that of known fibers.) Then allow the specimen to cool and check the characteristics of the ash.

You can use groups of fibers, short lengths of yarn, or small pieces of fabric as test specimens, unless the product to be tested contains a combination of yarns or a blend of fibers. In such cases, select individual fibers as test specimens from the textile material with the aid of a magnifying glass.

(The behavior of fibers in the flame test appears in Table 2-4. No changes have taken place since this table was prepared.)

2. *Microscopic examination.* (See Appendix A for longitudinal and cross-sectional photomicrographs of various fibers.) It is advisable to make the first microscopic examination with low magnification (50 to 60 X). The results of this test should verify or modify the conclusions reached in the preliminary inspection. If more microscopy is needed, groups of fibers (A.S.T.M. Test D 276-60T) from the specimen should be mounted and examined at a higher magnification (250-500 X). The longitudinal appearance of the fibers should be compared with photomicrographs of known fibers. If further examination is needed, the cross-sectional appearance of the fibers should be studied.

3. *Solubility tests.* After completing the microscopic test, fibers are divided into groups for identification by solubility. If one already knows the identity of one or more fibers, he can verify this by testing a specimen to determine whether fibers dissolve or disintegrate in selected liquids (organic solvents as well as acids and alkalis).

4. *Stain tests.* Various manufacturers of dyes make special stains for fiber identification. The manufacturer provides test procedure and cards showing typical colors resulting from staining the principal fibers. The procedure is simple, but identification may be difficult because in an intimate blend all fibers may be stained about the same color. In this case,

[7] See *Textile World*, III (December 1961), 47-59. Procedure for all fiber identification given in this section.

TABLE 2-4. Behavior of Major Fibers[a]

Fibers	Approaching Flame	In Flame	Removed from Flame	Ash Characteristics
Acetate	Fuses away from flame	Burns with melting	Continues to burn with melting	Leaves brittle, black, irregular-shaped bead
Acrylic	Fuses away from flame	Burns with melting	Continues to burn with melting	Leaves hard, brittle, black, irregular-shaped bead
Modacrylic	Fuses away from flame	Burns very slowly with melting	Self-extinguishing	Leaves hard, black, irregular-shaped bead
Nylon	Fuses and shrinks away from flame	Burns slowly with melting	Usually self-extinguishing	Leaves hard, tough, gray, round bead
Olefin	Fuses, shrinks, and curls away from flame	Burns with melting	Continues to burn with melting	Leaves hard, tough, tan, round bead
Polyester	Fuses and shrinks away from flame	Burns slowly with melting	Usually self-extinguishing	Leaves hard, tough, black, round bead
Rayon	Does not fuse or shrink away from flame	Burns without melting	Continues to burn without melting	Does not leave a knob or bead
Saran	Fuses and shrinks away from flame	Burns very slowly with melting	Self-extinguishing	Leaves hard, black, irregular-shaped bead
Spandex	Fuses but does not shrink away from flame	Burns with melting	Continues to burn with melting	Leaves soft, fluffy, black ash
Cotton	Does not fuse or shrink away from flame	Burns without melting	Continues to burn without melting	Does not leave a knob or bead
Flax	Does not fuse or shrink away from flame	Burns without melting	Continues to burn without melting	Does not leave a knob or bead
Silk	Fuses and curls away from flame	Burns slowly with some melting	Burns very slowly; sometimes self-extinguishing	Leaves soft, fluffy, black ash
Wool	Fuses and curls away from flame	Burns slowly with some melting	Burns very slowly; sometimes self-extinguishing	Leaves soft, fluffy, black ash

[a]Prepared for *Textile World*, December 1961. Copyright 1961 by McGraw-Hill Book Company

a stain from another manufacturer may prove more suitable, or examination under a microscope may prove helpful.

5. *Melting-point test.* A single fiber is placed between 19-millimeter microcover glasses on a calibrated Fisher-Johns melting-point apparatus. The fiber temperature is raised to the melting point.

6. *Moisture-regain test.* In this test, the specimens are all made of one kind of fiber or of two fibers that can be easily separated from each other. A specimen of fiber is first dried, weighed, and conditioned in air at 70° F., 65 percent relative humidity. To determine the moisture regain, record the percentage increase in weight of the fiber specimen during conditioning.

7. *Specific gravity test.* A fiber specimen is placed in a liquid of known specific gravity and is observed to determine whether it sinks or floats. This is a method of differentiating among fibers.

Other tests for identification include a refractive index test and an infrared spectrum test (an infrared spectrophotometer is used to scan the spectrum of a solvent cast or melt-pressed film or potassium bromide disk made from a specimen of the fiber). These spectra can also be used to identify fibers within a generic classification. Another test is heat discoloration. A fiber specimen is exposed for a specified time in air at 350° F. The discoloration of this specimen is to be used as a standard for comparison with discoloration of an unknown specimen. Since mechanical properties of fibers vary with different classes (such as breaking strength and breaking elongation), these properties can sometimes be used as means of fiber identification.

SUMMARY Although consumers are not particularly interested in the fibers themselves, they are interested in what effect the different fibers will have on the use and care of a fabric. A knowledge, then, of the classification of textile fibers is the first step in the study of textile fabrics. A knowledge of their classification will help in recognizing them in use.

Blends of various fibers will probably increase in importance because the blending of proper amounts of certain fibers will give the consumer a fabric that should serve her purpose better than one fiber alone. The noncellulosic manufactured fibers, particularly, can do much for giving "plus" qualities to blends; the public is learning that these man-made fibers can give increased wearing quality, crease and wrinkle resistance, and ease in the care of fabrics in which they are used. The consumer should realize that these manufactured fibers are no "miracle fibers." Each fiber has certain advantages and drawbacks, and the selection of one fiber or fibers over others for an intended use is the problem of the technologist. There is no one all-purpose fiber. In later chapters the reader will discover what each fiber can do in use.

REVIEW QUESTIONS
1. (*a*) What is a natural fiber?
   (*b*) What is a man-made fiber?
2. (*a*) Name the most widely used natural fibers.
   (*b*) List the man-made fibers derived from cellulose.

(c) How do acetate fibers differ from rayon?

3. (a) What is Orlon, Dacron, Verel?

(b) What is nylon? How does it differ from polyester?

(c) What is Aramid? Anidex?

(d) Give an important selling point for each fiber.

4. Explain the making of metallic yarn.

5. (a) How are glass fibers made?

(b) What are the uses of spun-glass fabrics?

6. Explain the difference between a mixture and a blend.

(a) What are the advantages of the use of more than one kind of fiber in a fabric?

(b) What do you think the future of blends will be?

7. (a) What is the importance of a knowledge of textile fibers to the consumer?

(b) To the textile manufacturer?

(c) To the retail buyer?

8. How may a good sense of touch be developed?

9. What adjectives best describe the feel of (a) pure silk, (b) rayon, (c) linen, (d) cotton, (e) wool?

10. In what way can a knowledge of manufacturers' brand names aid the consumer in identifying textile fabrics?

PROJECT

1. For one month check the advertisements in a daily newspaper to determine the end uses for each of the classes of generic fibers. Also check the trademark of each generic fiber. Compile the data to show for what articles the manufactured fibers are being used. Analyze the data and come to some conclusions as to where the fiber and yarn companies have markets for their various products.

GLOSSARY

Acetate—A manufactured vegetable and chemical fiber derived from cellulose.

Acrylic—A generic name of fibers made from arcylic resin (at least 85 percent acrylonitrile units).

Anidex—A manufactured fiber in which the fiber-forming substance is any long chain synthetic polymer composed of at least 50 percent by weight of one or more esters of amonohydric alcohol and acrylic acid.

Aramid—A generic name of a class of aramatic polyamide fibers that differ from conventional nylons.

Azlon—A generic name for manufactured fibers with a protein base.

Bicomponent fiber—A continuous-filament man-made fiber composed of two related components, each having a different degree of shrinkage. Stretch results from crimping of the filament.

Blend—A mixture of different fibers in the same yarn.

Bonded-face fabric—The side of a bonded fabric used as the face (right side) of the cloth in a garment or other end use.

Bonding—A process of joining two or more layers of cloth with a layer of adhesive, or pressing fibers into thin webs or mats that are held together by adhesive, plastic, or self-bonding.

Braiding (Plaiting)—Forming a narrow band by intertwining several strands of cotton, wool, or other materials.

Crimp—A term referring to the wavy appearance of a fiber or yarn.

Cross-linked cellulose—A term referring to the way cellulose molecules are linked to produce changes in the fiber's physical properties.

Cuprammonium process—One of the processes used in making rayon.

Dimensional stability—Ability of a fabric to keep its shape and size.

End use—Intended use by the consumer.

Felting—A method of producing fabric or interlocked fibers by an appropriate combination of mechanical work, chemical action, moisture, and heat. Processes of spinning, weaving, or knitting are not employed.

Fiber content—Amount of basic unit (raw material), such as cotton, polyester, wool, nylon, and so on, used in the fabrication of a textile fabric.

Filament—A variety of fiber characterized by extreme length (continuous). Examples are rayon, nylon, acrylic, polyester, and other man-made fibers.

Filling—Yarns that lie crosswise in a fabric from selvage to selvage, sometimes called weft or woof (in rugs).

Finish—Treatment of a cloth after the grey goods come from the loom or knitting machines.

Glass—A generic name for fibers made of glass.

Hand—A general term referring to the feeling of a fabric or yarn obtained by touching or handling; that is, soft, smooth, pliable, springy, stiff, cool, warm, rough, hard, and limp.

Knitting—The construction of an elastic porous fabric by means of needles. One or more yarns form a series of connecting loops, which support one another like a chain.

Knotting—A process of forming an openwork fabric or net by tying yarns together where they cross one another.

Laminating—Bonding a foam or sheet of plastic to a cloth.

Latex—Natural rubber (raw material) for fibers.

Metallic—A generic name of manufactured fibers composed of metal, metal-coated plastic, or a core completely covered by metal.

Mineral fibers—Textile raw material obtained from minerals in the earth, such as asbestos, silver, gold, copper, and the like.

Mixture—A fabric composed of two or more kinds of yarns, each yarn made of one kind of fiber.

Modacrylic—A generic name for modified acrylic fibers derived from 35 to 85 percent of acrylonitrile units.

Modified cellulose fibers—Cotton fibers treated with caustic soda to give strength, increased luster, and improved affinity for dye. Modification of a fiber changes its physical and chemical properties within the limits of a generic family.

Natural fibers—Textile raw material that grows in nature: cotton, linen, hemp, jute, ramie, kapok, silk, wool, and hair fibers.

Nontextiles—Merchandise that is not constructed by weaving, knitting, felting, knotting, or braiding. Nontextiles include such items as china, glassware, leather, cosmetics, jewelry, wooden and steel furniture, silverware, electrical goods.

Novoloid—A generic name for a man-made noncellulosic fiber made from a cross-linked polymer derived from carbon, hydrogen, and oxygen.

Nylon—A generic name for manufactured fibers derived from polyamide resin.

Nytril—A generic name for manufactured fibers derived from vinylidene dinitrile.

Olefin—A generic name for manufactured fibers derived from polypropylene and polyethylene.

Polyamide—A resin made by condensation (a chemical rearrangement of atoms to form a molecule of greater weight).

Polyester—A generic name for manufactured fibers made from a chemical composition of ethylene glycol and terephthalic acid.

Polymer—Large molecule produced by linking together many molecules of a monomeric substance.

Polymerization—The way in which small molecules unite to form large molecules.

Rayon—A man-made textile fiber derived from cellulose. Two processes are used in this country to produce rayon: viscose process and cuprammonium process.

Rubber—A generic name of a manufactured fiber in which the fiber-forming substance is comprised of natural or synthetic rubber.

Saran—A generic term for manufactured fibers derived from vinylidene chloride.

Selvage—The outer finished edge on both sides of a fabric.

Spandex—The generic name of a manufactured fiber derived from polyurethane plastic (resin).

Staple—A term descriptive of the average length of any fiber.

Synthetic fibers—Man-made textile fibers derived from natural bases or chemical bases.

Texture—The appearance of the surface of the fabric.

Thermoplastic—A resin that, with the application of heat and pressure, can be molded and remolded.

Tow—A continuous loose rope of man-made filaments drawn together without twist.

Vinal—The generic name of a manufactured fiber derived from alcohol and acetal units.

Vinyon—The generic name of a manufactured fiber derived from vinylite resin.

Viscose—A process of making rayon.

Warp—The yarns running lengthwise in a woven fabric parallel with the selvage.

Weaving—The interlacing of two sets of yarns at right angles to form a fabric.

Yarn—A generic term for a group of fibers or filaments, either natural or synthetic, twisted or laid together to form a continuous strand suitable for use in weaving, knitting, or some other method of intertwining to form textile fabrics.

Textile Yarns: Their Manufacture and Uses

3

In Chapter 1 our consumer learned that fibers of which textile fabrics are made are very important for judging how a fabric will perform in a given use. But kind of fibers used is not the sole criterion. Yarns, construction, and finish must also be considered. In this chapter, yarns will be discussed, and in subsequent chapters, construction and finishes will be considered.

A yarn is a strand of fibers or filaments, either natural or man-made, which have been grouped together or twisted for use in weaving, knitting, or other methods of constructing textile fabrics. The type of yarn to be manufactured will depend on the fibers selected, the texture, or hand, of the fabric to be made, and qualities such as warmth, resiliency, softness, and durability required in the fabric's end uses. In addition, the weave and the finish used will depend on kinds of fibers and yarns, end use of the fabric, and price.

The final fabric can be thought of as a linked chain, each link representing a process in the manufacturing of the chain. One link is fibers, another yarn, another construction, another finish. The final fabric can be of no better quality than the links of which it is composed. If, however, the fibers, construction, and finish of the fabric were not of the same excellence as the yarn, then the fabric could not be excellent in quality.

CLASSIFI-CATION OF YARNS ACCORDING TO USE

Yarns may be divided into two classifications according to their use: weaving yarns and knitting yarns. Thread, a special purpose yarn, will be discussed later in this chapter.

WEAVING YARNS

Yarns to be used for warp, the lengthwise direction of a cloth, are generally stronger, tighter twist, smoother, and more even than filling yarns (crosswise yarns in a cloth).

KNITTING YARNS

These may be divided into yarns for hand knitting and yarns for machine knitting. Knitting yarns are more slackly twisted than yarns for weaving. Hand-knitting yarns are generally ply, whereas those for machine knitting can be either single or ply. The following are some of the yarns that are used for hand knitting:

1. *Baby yarns.* Yarns of 100 percent wool or wool and rayon in light or medium weight for infants' garments.
2. *Dress yarns.* Plain or novelty yarns in all-wool, blends, or mixtures with cottons and rayons.
3. *Fingering yarns.* Two- or three-ply, light and medium weight, smooth, even diameter for children's and other apparel.
4. *Germantown.* Soft wool, medium weight for women's and children's sweaters and blankets.
5. *Shetland floss.* Soft, lightweight, fluffy yarn for infants' and children's sweaters.
6. *Sock yarns.* Especially spun wool or nylon yarn for knitting socks.
7. *Worsted* (knitting). Soft, well-twisted, heavy wool yarn for sweaters; very strong and durable.
8. *Zephyr yarns.* Very fine, soft, 100 percent wool yarns for lightweight garments.

Special yarns are also sold for hand embroidery. Embroidery floss is a slack or medium-twisted ply or cord-type yarn. For darning, softly spun yarn is wound on spools, balls, or cards.

YARN MAKING

PHYSICAL STRUCTURE

Yarn making is generally the second step in the manufacture of textile fabrics. Methods of manufacturing yarn depend on the type of fibers used and the type of yarn required. However, certain terminology is common to all yarns. For instance, a single yarn is one strand of fibers or filaments grouped or twisted together. When two or more single yarns are twisted together the final yarn is called *ply.* Two-ply yarn is composed of two singles, three-ply of three singles, and so on. A cord is the result of twisting together ply yarns in a third operation. The types of yarn just described are regular yarns. Then there are novelty yarns that may be either single or ply. When plied, there is often a core or center yarn with other yarns twisted about it to give textural effect. Frequently these yarns are bound to the core by other strands to hold all yarns together. Furthermore, there are *textured* yarns—continuous-filament man-made fibered yarns that have been geometrically modified or otherwise altered to change their basic characteristics.

METHODS OF YARN MANUFACTURE

Raw fibers arrive at the yarn manufacturers in different forms. For example, cotton is in bales; wool in fleeces; cultivated raw silk in strands, waste and wild silk in bales; flax in bundles; rayon, acetate, nylon, and the other manufactured fibers on tubes, cones, cops, spools, or skeins.

The natural fibers are restricted in length. For example, cotton staple ranges from ¾ to 1½ inches long; linen averages 18 to 20 inches long in best grades. Man-made fibers are continuous or are cut up into predetermined lengths called *staple fibers.* If a fabric is to resemble cotton, the tow (groups of continuous filaments) is cut up into staple. Obviously, the basic processes for making yarn will vary. However, certain fibers are prepared for yarn by similar processes.

In general, fibers are blended or mixed before yarn manufacture actually begins. Cotton, wool, spun or waste silk, spun rayon, spun acetate, spun nylon, and many of the noncellulosics are made into yarn by carding and combing. Although the machinery and the details of these processes vary with the fibers and from mill to mill, the terms and purpose of the operations are comparable.

Carding separates the fibers and puts them in a filmy sheet called a *sliver*. In cotton, this operation removes dirt and short fibers. Wool fabrics are made of woolen yarn, which is carded only; or of worsted yarn, which is both carded and combed. For woolen yarn, three carding operations put the fibers into a thin sheet or sliver suitable for yarn.[1] Staple man-made fibers are made into yarn in the same manner as cotton or wool, depending on the intended use of the fabric.

Not all wool yarn is combed. Yarns that are carded only are called woolen yarns. These yarns are used for such fabrics as blankets, tweed coating and suiting, wool flannel, and wool broadcloth. Worsted yarns are both carded and combed, and longer fibers are selected for worsteds than for woolens. One long combing machine, operating slowly to avoid breaking the long fibers, makes the sliver. In combing worsteds, the short fibers are removed and the fibers laid parallel. The sliver is drawn out to its desired width and thickness. Worsted yarns are used in fabrics such as tropical worsted, gabardine, whipcord, worsted flannel, and wool sharkskin.

Combing of cotton is necessary when fine, uniform yarns are needed to give sheerness, luster, smoothness, and possibly durability. All cotton yarns are carded, but not all cotton yarns are combed. Only about 8 percent of cotton yarns are combed. For combing, longer staple cottons are selected. Combing makes the fibers parallel in the sliver and removes the shorter fibers. The sliver is drawn out narrower and narrower, depending on the fineness of the yarn to be made. Spun silk fibers are also combed to lay fibers parallel and to remove the short ones. Man-made staple fibers intended to resemble combed cotton or worsted yarns would be combed.

HACKLED AND WELL-HACKLED YARNS

Hackling is the process by which flax is prepared for linen yarn. The purpose of hackling is to disentangle the flax fibers and to lay them in a sliver. For fine, even yarns, the fibers must be long and parallel, hence more hackling is necessary. When yarns are well hackled, those in the trade may say the yarns are combed. At any rate, the purpose of the operation and the results are similar to combing.

REELING AND THROWING

Raw silk is the long-fibered silk that is reeled from the cocoon and twisted into yarn. Several yarns are combined and twisted onto bobbins. If ply

---

[1] See *carding of cotton*, Chapter 9; *carding of wool*, Chapter 12; *combing of cotton*, Chapter 9; *combing of worsted*, Chapter 12.

yarns are required, the strands are combined and twisted together. The combining and twisting is called *throwing*. The machine that performs this operation is a *throwster*. (See Glossary, Chapter 3.)

Rayon, acetate, nylon, polyester, glass, and other man-made filament ply yarns, hard-twist voile, and crepe yarns are thrown. The term "thrown," then, applies to reeled-silk ply yarn and to man-made filament ply yarns in high twist. Regular filament yarns result from grouping fibers together so they lie parallel.

SPINNING

The spinning operation draws out the roving (very slackly twisted sliver) and puts in the required amount of twist. The purpose of twist is to bind the fibers together and to hold in the ends of fiber. Generally speaking, the tighter the twist, the stronger the yarn. This is true to a certain point; then the yarn weakens and may finally break. Long fibers like linen and long-fibered raw silk do not require so much twist to give strength as do cotton and short rayon staple fibers. A low or slack twist makes a more lustrous, softer yarn than a tight twist. Slack-twisted yarn is needed when the fabric is finished with a nap (fuzzy surface). When a yarn is twisted to the point of knotting, a crepe yarn results. Warp yarns are usually twisted

FIGURE 3.1. The old-time art of spinning with a wheel is not dead. This college girl is housed with a group of students who are interested in arts and crafts and natural history. (Courtesy of *Carleton Voice,* Carleton College, summer 1974.)

FIGURE 3.2. Chiffon, showing crepe yarns.
(Photo by Jack Pitkin.)

tighter than filling yarns because warp yarns have to stand tension in the loom in weaving. One way to identify warp and filling yarns is to compare amounts of twist in each yarn. Warp is frequently tighter. There are exceptions, however. Warps are generally stronger and therefore harder to break. A ply yarn is stronger than the combined strength of the single yarns composing it. Similarly, a cord is stronger than a ply yarn of the same size.

Twist may be put into yarn in spinning or in subsequent plying operations. The direction of twist (right or left) and number of twists (turns) to the inch may be determined by a testing device called a twist counter. The number of turns to the inch can also be determined by very nontechnical means—a real rule-of-thumb method. Although the result may not be very accurate, the test will serve to compare amount of twist of other yarns tested by the same method. Unravel from a fabric about a two-inch length of yarn. Grasp the yarn between the thumb and index finger of each hand. Leave about one inch of yarn in tension between the hands. A right-handed person should keep his left hand stationary. With the right hand, turn the yarn slightly until the direction in which the yarn untwists is evident. Then, still holding the yarn taut, roll the end between the thumb and index finger of the right hand. Each time the yarn rolls over constitutes a twist. A single yarn will pull apart when it is untwisted. When a ply yarn is untwisted, stop counting the twists when the single yarns lie parallel. The fibers will not pull apart in a ply yarn.

Single yarns are made in two directions of twist, right and left. The right twist is effected by twisting the sliver clockwise, and the left twist results from a counterclockwise motion. Right-twisted yarns are identified as Z twist, and left-twisted yarns as S twist. If a paper clip is attached to the end of a single yarn, and the end is allowed to hang free, the end will rotate. If the end rotates in a clockwise direction, the inherent twist is S; if in a counterclockwise direction, the yarn is Z twist. To make a ply yarn, the singles are usually twisted in one direction and the final ply twist in the opposite direction; for example, Z/S (Z is the direction of the twist for the singles and S is the ply twist). But a ply yarn may be S/S or Z/Z. A cable cord is S/Z/S or Z/S/Z; a hawser cord is S/S/Z or Z/Z/S. Cords, in addition to being made by twist, may be braided, woven, or knitted.

FIGURE 3.3. "S" and "Z" twists.

A practical illustration of how alternate direction in twist is used is in the filling yarns of rough and flat crepes. These crepes are often identified in the trade by their filling yarns as "2 x 2," which means 2S alternating with 2Z twists in the fillings of these fabrics. Two-by-two broadcloth, however, means two-ply yarn in warp and filling—not alternate direction in twist.

The word "spun" refers to a yarn that has been twisted by spinning. It also applies to a yarn made of staple fibers (man-made) that have been twisted into yarn. Hence, nylon yarn made of staple fibers is called spun nylon. "Spun dyed" has another connotation. This term is synonymous with "solution dyed," which means that the dyestuffs are put into the viscous solution before extrusion, and then the dyestuff is locked in the fiber when the fiber hardens. In the same manner, man-made fibers which have a high luster may have dulling agents added to the fiber-forming substance before spinning.

SIZE OF YARNS

To distinguish differences in weight and fineness, yarns are given size numbers called counts, lea, or denier. The term "count" applies to the size of cotton, wool, and spun yarns. The term "lea" applies to linen yarn, and "denier" to reeled-silk and filament man-made yarns.

For cotton and spun yarns, the standard used is 840 yards of yarn to the pound. If 840 yards of cotton yarn weigh one pound, the count is #1. If it takes 8,400 yards to weigh a pound, the count is #10, and so on. The higher the numerical count, the finer the yarn.

There are two methods of computing sizes of woolen yarns: one method, the American run count, will be discussed here. If 1,600 yards weigh one pound, the count or size is #1, a very coarse yarn. The higher the number, the finer the yarn. The size of worsted yarns is determined by the number of hanks of 560 yards weighing one pound. If one 560-yard hank weighs one pound, the count or size is #1. If 5,600 yards weigh one pound, the count is #10, and so on. Yarns numbered 30s to 40s ("s" means single yarn) are very coarse. (See Chapter 12.) The higher the number, the finer the yarn.

Linen yarns use a lea of 300 yards as a base for figuring size. To find the size of the yarn, divide the number of yards weighing a pound by 300 yards. For example, if 3,000 yards weigh one pound, the count of the yarn is 3,000 ÷ 300, or 10. The higher the number, the finer the yarn.

The size of filament man-made yarns and reeled-silk yarns is designated in terms of denier. Denier (pronounced den'yer) is equal to the weight in grams of 9,000 meters of yarn. In yarns, 9,000 meters = 9,842.4 yards. If

50

9,842.4 yards of yarn weigh 150 grams, the yarn is 150 denier. If 9,842.4 yards weigh 75 grams, the denier is 75. Since the length of the yardage weighed is always the same, the yarns that weigh more must be larger in size. The lower the denier number, the finer the yarn. The number of filaments in a given filament yarn is indicated with the denier number; that is, 100—74 means 100 denier yarn composed of 74 filaments (See Chapter 11 for the computation of International Denier in reeled silk.) A proposed universal yarn numbering system called "Tex" expresses the weight in grams of one kilometer length of yarn. Such a system was suggested in 1873 at an international conference in Vienna. But it was not until 1956 that action was taken when ten nations attending an International Conference for Textiles unanimously voted to adopt the system. Tex can be applied to all fibers. It is intended to replace the many diverse yarn numbering systems. As the metric system is more widely adopted here, the use of tex measurements should increase accordingly.

COLORING OF YARN

When a yarn is dyed before it is woven, it is said to be *yarn dyed.* Plaid ginghams are good examples of this method of dyeing.

Yarns can also be printed before weaving. It is common practice to print warp yarns before they are woven into cloth. By use of a white or

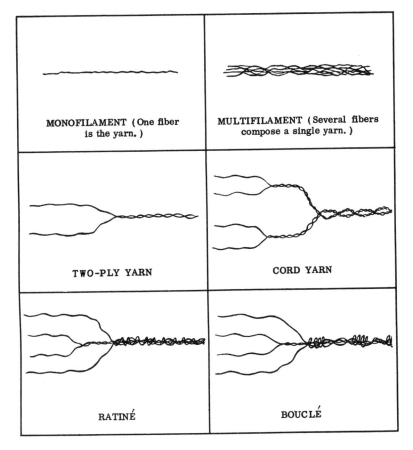

MONOFILAMENT (One fiber is the yarn.)

MULTIFILAMENT (Several fibers compose a single yarn.)

TWO-PLY YARN

CORD YARN

RATINÉ

BOUCLÉ

FIGURE 3.4. Yarn construction.

solid-color filling with the printed warp yarns, a hazy grayed effect is produced in the design. A cloth with the warp printed before weaving is called a warp-printed fabric.

Space-dyed fabric is made of yarns that have color applied by dipping or spotting various places along the yarn. This is done to warp and/or filling yarns.

HOW TO IDENTIFY ORDINARY OR CONVENTIONAL YARNS

Yarns used in clothing and home furnishings may be classified in two general types: (1) ordinary or conventional, and (2) novelty.

CARDED AND COMBED YARNS

It is important to know the fiber content of a yarn first in order to tell what has been its processing. If the fibers are cotton or wool or a blend of these fibers, carding and combing will be the processing required in manufacture. If man-made staple fibers are spun into yarn to resemble cotton or wool, these yarns will be spun on the cotton or wool systems and therefore will be carded and combed, too.

To identify a carded cotton yarn, untwist the yarn to the point where it pulls apart. Discard one piece of the yarn that has pulled apart. From the broken end of yarn, pluck out several fibers. Note whether the fibers are very short—less than one inch. Also note whether the fibers seem to branch out in all directions—are not parallel. If this is the case, the cotton yarn is probably carded only. If the yarn pulls apart and does not separate into two or three distinct yarns, then the yarn is a single. If the cotton yarn has long fibers (approximately one inch or over), all about the same length and lying parallel, the yarn is probably combed.

After identifying the yarns, the whole cloth should be studied. Notice whether the diameters of the yarns are quite even and smooth. If so, the yarns are probably combed. A very fine, even yarn, like one found in organdy, is combed.

LINE AND TOW LINEN YARNS

Everyone is familiar with dish towels that are 100 percent linen but are bumpy in texture. These towels are made of tow linen, which is poorly hackled yarn made of short fibers that are removed from the sliver in the hackling process. When a yarn is untwisted, short fibers of varied lengths branching out from the yarn will identify tow.

Handkerchief linen is a good example of line yarn made of long fibers that lie parallel in the sliver to make a smooth, even-diameter, fine yarn. Such yarns have been well hackled.

WOOLEN AND WORSTED YARNS

To identify a woolen yarn used for clothing and home furnishings, excluding rugs, proceed as for cotton by untwisting it. Note whether the fibers average less than two inches, and branch out from the yarn in all directions. If so, the yarn is carded only and is a woolen.

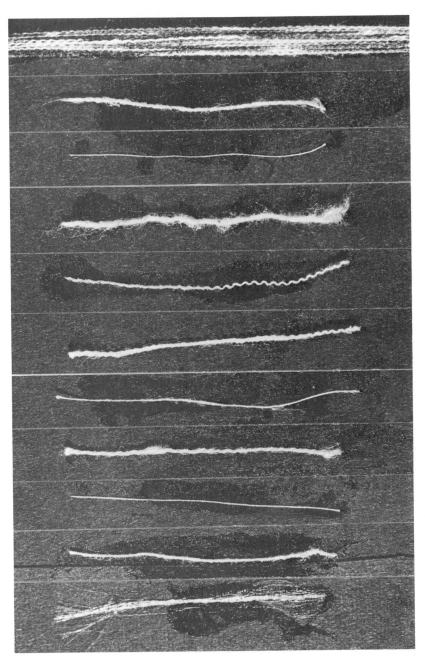

FIGURE 3.5. Types of yarns. Top to bottom: a. space-dyed yarn; b. carded cotton; c. combed cotton; d. carded woolen; e. combed worsted; f. tow linen; g. line linen; h. spun silk; i. reeled silk; j. spun rayon; and k. filament rayon. (Photo by Jack Pitkin.)

To identify a worsted yarn, proceed as before by untwisting the yarn. Note whether the fibers average more than two inches, are all about the same length, and lie parallel. If so, the yarn is combed and is a worsted.

Reeled Silk Yarns. The term "reeled" applies to long-fibered silk. Again, the fiber content is important to know first. If silk is reeled, the yarn is often lustrous, and there is usually less twist than for spun silk. The fibers will fan out or shred apart when the yarn is untwisted.

Filament Yarns. Filament yarns of man-made fibers have similar features. The fibers are continuous, and they lie parallel and fan out when the yarn is untwisted. These yarns may be dull or lustrous depending on their end use. When various types of monofilament yarns are combined and twisted together, a "combination" filament yarn is formed.

Generally speaking, the greater the number of filaments in a yarn, the stronger and more pliable and supple the yarn. Some yarns may consist of one filament, as in nylon hosiery or saran fabric for beach chairs. Such yarns are called monofilament, as opposed to the multifilament yarns.

Spun Yarn. Short lengths of silk fibers may be twisted (spun) into yarn called "spun silk." The yarns of spun silk are generally dull and cottony and usually have considerable twist to hold in the short ends (spun silk is made of shorter fibers than reeled silk). When the yarn is untwisted, fibers do not lie parallel and are of varied short lengths. Similarly, short man-made fibers of cut or broken filaments of desired lengths may be spun into yarn to resemble cotton, wool, or worsted. Spun yarns are more irregular, more fuzzy and bulky than filament yarns of the same weight. Therefore these yarns are suitable for warm, porous fabrics and nonsmooth textured cloths.

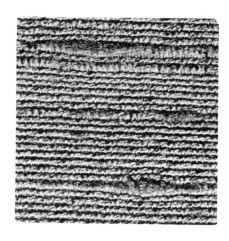

FIGURE 3.6. Shantung, showing slub fillings. (Photo by Jack Pitkin.)

Spun yarns of man-made fibers have fibers of the same lengths, because the tow (a strand of continuous filaments) is cut all one length: the length of cotton, if the yarn is to resemble cotton, wool to resemble wool, and so on. The texture of the cloth and evenness of the yarn should help in determining what processes have been used to manufacture the yarn.

A type of spun yarn called a "blend" is a combination of two or more staple fiber types (either man-made or natural) that are blended together before the fibers are spun into yarn. Fabrics made of such blended spun yarns are called "blends."

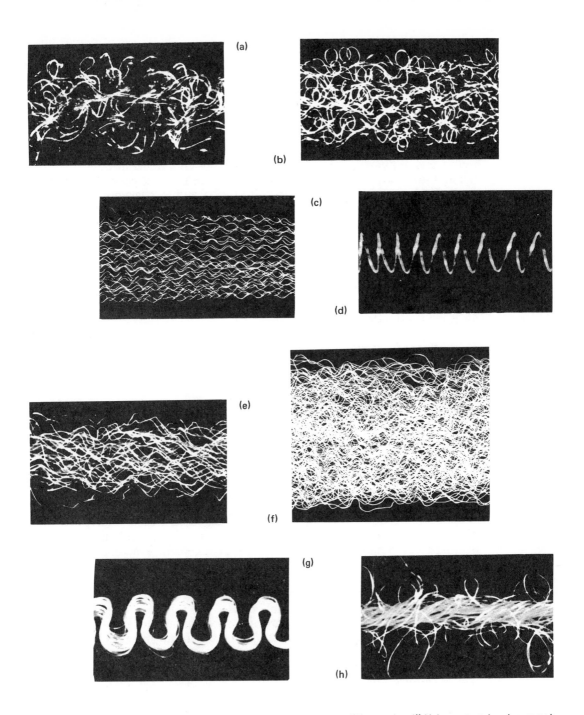

FIGURE 3.7. Basic methods of texturing yarn. a. "Conventional" Helanca stretch nylon yarn; b. A typical "False-twist" type stretch nylon yarn; c. Miralon gear crimped nylon yarn; d. Agilon (crimped type) nylon monofil yarn; e. Spunize textured yarn nylon; f. Producer textured "Blue C" nylon yarn; g. Knit-de-knit textured nylon yarn; h. Taslan textured nylon yarn. (Courtesy of Monsanto Company.)

55

56
*Fabric
Construction
and
Buying
Motives*

TEXTURED YARNS

Texturing is a process that gives the normally smooth, continuous filament yarns, of the noncellulosic fibers, crimps, loops, coils, and crinkles. Thus, the rugged performance of these fibers is augmented with luxurious bulk and/or stretch. These fibers are made more closely to resemble the natural fibers they simulate for clothing purposes. They are made suitable for a wide range of apparel for which smooth, continuous filament yarns are not appropriate. The yarns most often texturized are nylon and polyester. In fact, about half the nylon yarns now used for apparel are textured and of the fibers used in knitting yarns, polyester is in the lead, especially, for double-knit fabrics, and to a lesser extent tricot.

There are a great many highly ingenious techniques for texturing the noncellulosic yarns. These may be considered under two headings: Mechanical methods and Chemical methods.

Mechanical Methods.

a. Classical or three-staged method. This is the oldest technique; it was developed by the Heberlein Company in Switzerland. There are three stages in production:

1. Twisting of the yarn
2. Heat-setting the yarn in its twisted form
3. Untwisting the yarn

Such yarns are bulky. They have loft and a small amount of stretch (10 to 15 percent). Familiar brands of yarn made by this method are the original Helanca and Cheveux D'Ange (Billion & Cie, France).

b. False twist. This process is essentially the same as the classical process but is a refinement, since it is a continuous operation, not three separate ones. (See Figure 3.8). Notice the false-twist spindle. This is the most used process in the world. The same basic false-twist process produces both a heat set and a stretch yarn. Actually, the stretch yarn is simpler to produce because it is made in three stages: twist, set, and untwist. The set yarn is made in four stages: twist, set, untwist, and heating to stabilize or destroy the twist in the yarn. Trademarked names of stretch yarn of the false-twist type are Fluflon, Superloft, and some Helanca. A similar duo-twist process, which uses no spindle, makes a yarn with a lower twist. Two yarns are then twisted together, heat-set, separated, and wound on individual cones.

c. Draw-textured. This is a process wherein a partially oriented, or undrawn, yarn is drawn and textured in the same manufacturing step, usually on a false-twist texturizing machine. It is primarily used to make polyester and nylon apparel yarns.

d. Crimped yarns. In one method, yarns are made by a stuffer-box technique. Straight filaments are "stuffed" tightly into a heated box. When removed, the yarn resembles a "v" or sawtooth. The Ban-Lon fabrics are produced by a trademarked Textralizing ® process, which is licensed by Joseph Bancroft & Sons Co. The Textured Yarn Co. of Philadelphia produces its Tycora by this method. This is a bulky, lofted yarn—not a stretch yarn. Uses of the yarns include women's dress fabrics, sweaters, and men's knitted sport shirts. "Spunized" yarns by the Allied

Chemical Corporation Fibers Division are crimped by the teeth of two heated gears which mesh, so that the configuration of the yarn is like the gear teeth. Instead of texturing a single end of yarn, J. P. Stevens & Co., Inc., textures a multiple number of ends in warp formation. The crimping process therefore makes the crimps uniform throughout the length of these warp yarns. Crimps per inch can be varied according to the end use. Blouse, pajama, dress, and tricot lingerie fabrics may be made with these yarns.

e. Knit de-knit. Any hand knitter has had the experience of unraveling her work. The raveled yarn resembles a rounded sawtooth. The steps in the process include three stages in one continuous operation:

1. Knitting of a tubular fabric
2. Heat-setting the fabric
3. De-knitting (unraveling) the fabric

This method does not make a stretch yarn. A crepe or bouclé textured fabric results from this technique. Brand names are Bucaroni and Antron Crinkle.

f. Curled or edge-crimped yarns. The filament passes over a heated blade that causes alternate surfaces of the yarn to be flattened, much as one curls a ribbon by running it over the blade of a scissors. Curled yarns, which have moderate stretch, are produced chiefly under a license from Deering Milliken Research Corporation, with the trademark Agilon. They are used primarily for women's nylon hosiery.

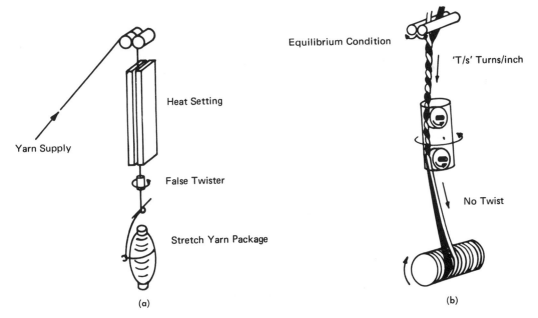

FIGURE 3.8. a. This figure shows schematically how a false twister is used to produce stretch yarn. b. Yarn is twisted above the false twister, it is heat set and relaxed while in the twisted condition, and then completely untwisted as it leaves the false twister. A continuous, delicate balance is maintained wherein downstream twist exactly cancels upstream twist. (Courtesy of *Textile World.*)

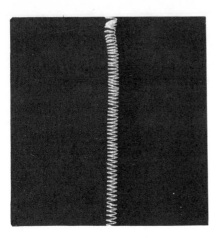

FIGURE 3.9. Monofilament Agilon yarn. (Photograph courtesy of Deering Milliken Research Corp.)

g. Air-bulked (air-jet) or looped yarns. A filament yarn is subjected to an air jet that blows a number of loops per inch into the individual filaments, both on the surface and in the *yarn bundle.* Textures of smooth, silky, or worsted-like textures, as well as woolen and heavy chenille types, can be achieved. Core and effect yarns are obtainable under the registered trademark Taslan by Du Pont. The yarn so formed does not have stretch properties, but it has increased bulk and texture not unlike spun yarn. Another brand name for air-jet yarns is Skyloft, by American Enka.

h. Thick and thin yarns. Yarns of varying diameters are produced by varying the diameters of man-made fibers. (See Chapter 12.)

Chemical Methods. In the mechanical processes described, texturizing depended on twisting and the application of heat, the exception being the thick and thin yarns. In some instances, texturizing is chemical. Generally two polymers with different ratios of shrinkage are used. Upon the application of heat, one polymer shrinks more than the other, in the solution forced through the spinneret, thus crimping the whole yarn. Since texturizing is done at the source, it is said to be "producer-textured." A yarn of this type is Cantrece, made by Du Pont.

A bright future seems indicated for textured yarns. There are new markets in men's knitted suits, children's wear, outer wear, and textured tricot and full-fashioned knits. Textured polyesters, so important today in clothing, may be in short supply during any energy crisis because about 1 percent of the nation's petroleum is used by the man-made fibers industry, which supplies 70 percent of all fibers used by American textile mills.[2]

Merits, Problems, and Uses of Textured Yarns. Bulked-yarn fabrics are more comfortable than fabrics made from filament yarn. Bulked-nylon fabrics, for example, tend to approach the general physical characteristics of cotton and wool staple knit fabrics with respect to thickness, weight, opacity, density, packing factor, surface characteristics, and thermal conductivity. Some men may remember the coldness and clamminess of the first filament nylon shirts. Synthetic yarns now used in woven shirts are often textured.

[2] *Man-Made Fiber Fact Book,* Man-Made Fiber Producers Assn., 1974, p. 11.

Furthermore, in addition to improved comfort, textured yarns have a better appearance; better resistance to pilling (unless filaments break); greater durability and evenness; and improved covering power because of their bulk. Problems of fuzzing from abrasion, matting, or breaking of the filaments, which may result in pilling, have confronted the technician.

The quality of textured yarn has improved owing to the increase in production speed and the continuous and automatic processing from start

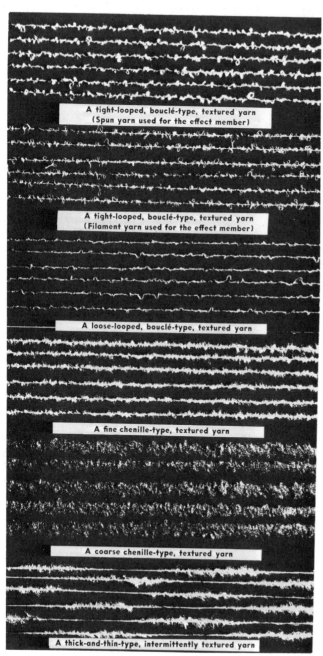

A tight-looped, bouclé-type, textured yarn
(Spun yarn used for the effect member)

A tight-looped, bouclé-type, textured yarn
(Filament yarn used for the effect member)

A loose-looped, bouclé-type, textured yarn

A fine chenille-type, textured yarn

A coarse chenille-type, textured yarn

A thick-and-thin-type, intermittently textured yarn

FIGURE 3.10. Examples of Taslan textured specialty yarns produced from continuous filament yarns (note exception at top) by multi-end texturing. (Photograph courtesy of E.I. DuPont de Nemours & Company, Inc.)

to finish. These improvements are noted in the texturing equipment of the United States, France, the United Kingdom, Germany, Italy, and Japan. While utility model texturing machines are available for under $65,000, a better quality draw-texturing model would cost about $210,000.

The "converter" of man-made fibers has reached a new and higher status. He is the throwster who used to be a twister of silk. Now he twists continuous-filament man-made fibers. Originally he performed only a commission service, but now he is responsible for custom designing of yarns for specific markets. His goal is variety and flexibility of the products.

KINDS OF NOVELTY YARNS

Fabric designers are constantly bringing out fabrics with novelty yarns to stimulate sales through a wider, more diversified variety of fabrics. Textural effects obtained by use of novelty yarns would be impossible with any ordinary yarn.

Novelty yarns are made on a novelty yarn-twisting machine by combining different types of yarns in various ways. The weight of novelty yarns may vary from a few hundred yards per pound to as fine as 20,000 yards per pound or more.[3]

Novelty yarns are used in knitted sweaters and dresses, contemporary drapery and upholstery fabrics, and the decoration of men's and women's suiting fabrics. Such yarns are often made with blends of natural and man-made fibers. In any case, they are designed for a specific end use, and they can be varied by numerous possible combinations of fibers, twist, ply, and color.

These novelty yarns are popular:

1. *Bouclé* is one of the most used novelty yarns. It is characterized by tight loops that project from the body of the yarn at fairly regular intervals. It is often made of a combination of rayon and cotton or wool. Bouclé is used in knitted sweaters, both knitted and woven dresses, and upholstery fabrics. Ratiné is similar in construction to bouclé, but the loops are twisted continuously and are not spaced.

2. *Chenille* is a term derived from the French for "caterpillar." It refers to a special soft, lofty yarn with pile protruding on all sides. Wool (worsted) is generally blended with other fibers. This type of chenille yarn is used for knitted outerwear. In coarser yarns, chenille is used to obtain prominent surface effects in coats and suits. A more common type of chenille yarn, often called *chenille fur*, is used for chenille rugs. (See Chapter 20.)

3. *Metallic yarn* is metal foil or steel, aluminum, gold, or silver, coated on both sides with plain or plastic colored film, and then cut into narrow strips. Metallic yarns coated with plastic do not tarnish. Recent metallic yarns have been produced by bonding aluminum foil between two clear layers of plastic film. This is called the *foil* type of yarn. A second kind, called the *metallized* type, uses a layer of polyester film (Mylar) treated with vaporized metal that is subsequently bonded between two clear

[3] *Novelty yarns* (a pamphlet), by Philadelphia Penn Worsted Company.

layers of film. Polypropylene, acetate, and cellophane films may also be used. For colors other than silver, color pigment can be added to the bonding adhesive. The quality of these two types of metallic yarn depends on the type of clear film used, plus the resistance it and the adhesives have to stretching and wet processing. To provide strength and to prevent stretching, these yarns are often wrapped with nylon or high-tenacity rayon.[4]

4. *Nub yarn* is made by twisting one end around another many times within a short space, causing enlarged places (nubs) on the surface of the yarn. Sometimes a binder is used to hold the nub in place. Nubs are generally spaced at varied intervals. Nub yarns are sometimes called knap yarns.

5. *Paper yarns*[5] are made by slitting and wet-twisting paper to form individual strands of yarn, and then are knitted or woven like other yarns. Since these yarns have strength, they are suitable for bagging, fiber rugs, automobile seat covers, hats, and handbags.

6. *Plastic yarns* are coated yarns made of natural or synthetic fibers that have been dipped into a protective coating of plastic.

7. *Splash yarn* is really an elongated nub that has been tightly twisted about a base yarn. A *seed yarn* is a very small nub, often made of man-made yarns applied to a dyed or natural base yarn.

8. *Slub* is a soft, elongated nub. The yarn forming the slub may be continuous or may be made of tufts of roving inserted at intervals between binder yarns.[6]

WHAT IS THREAD?

The chief difference between yarn and thread lies in the method of twisting strands together. If a six-cord cotton thread is to be made, six strands of yarn are twisted together. Each strand is balanced in twist and the finished thread approximates a perfect circle in cross section. Like yarn, thread is inspected and reeled into hanks.

In hank form, thread can be mercerized, bleached, or dyed. It is then wound on spools, inspected, and boxed.

A good thread must be (1) even in diameter, to move under tension easily and quickly through the eye of the needle; (2) smooth, to resist friction caused by sewing; (3) strong enough to hold seams firmly in laundering and in use; and (4) elastic enough to make stitches that will not break or pucker.

Sewing threads are made of cotton, linen, silk, rayon, nylon, and polyester. The size of cotton and linen thread is indicated on the end of the spool. As we have already mentioned, the higher the number, the finer the thread. For special uses such as luggage, shoes, carpets, bookbinding, gloves, umbrellas, upholstery, and awnings, special sewing threads are made. Special thread called *buttonhole twist* is made for buttonholes. Just a few yards of thread are wound on a spool for this purpose. Special thread in gold is made for crocheting and tatting.

Research has revealed that apparel made from water-repellent fabrics

---

[4] These yarns should not be confused with nonwoven cloth. See *Bonding*, Chapter 2, p. 27.

[5] See Fiber rugs, Chapter 20.

[6] Roving, see Glossary at end of chapter.

gives the wearer better protection when the seams are sewed with a thread that has been made water repellent.

Nylon thread is recommended for nylon fabrics, but other threads may be used. A nylon thread is difficult to break and should be cut with scissors. A cut thread is easier to put through the eye of a needle and will avoid pulled seams. It should be remembered that fewer stitches to the inch can be made when sewing nylon. On tightly woven fabrics as few as seven stitches to the inch may be used. Nylon's strength makes a long stitch possible.

IMPARTING STRETCH TO CLOTHING FABRICS

As we have seen in connection with texturing, stretch may be imparted to yarns by certain of the texturing methods in use. But there are other ways to provide the quality of stretch in clothing and other finished goods. The whole question may be logically considered at this point since the yarn used is an important consideration.

Stretch garments have the ability to extend and recover rather than remain rigid. Stretch garments are akin to skin. Just as our skin moves freely as we bend or twist, so do stretch garments move with the body. Nonstretch garments may be so rigid as to be uncomfortable because they constrict bodily movements.

Fabrics, then, are made to stretch for three reasons: comfort, control, and fashion. Freedom of movement is desirable in active sportswear, in suit jackets, and in straight skirts. For foundation garments, ski pants, and swimsuits, body control or support is needed. For a trim, slim, sleek look in ski pants, jumpsuits, and slacks, fashion plays an important role.

Stretch woven fabrics, which originated in Europe in the early 1950s, were used principally for ski pants. Originally they were made of Helanca yarn with stretch nylon warp and acrylic filling. In 1960 Pucci, the Italian designer, introduced sportswear made of a fabric with stretch nylon warp and silk Dupioni filling. The stretch concept grew in importance. But with the advent of durable press, stretch was eclipsed for a time. However, durable press has helped to bring back stretch. Pants manufacturers added stretch to their durable press offerings. A men's shirt manufacturer employed stretch as a durable press principle in his use of stretch batistes for shirts. Another manufacturer added all-rayon stretch dresses to his line. With the increased use of textured yarns, many of which are of the stretch type, an upward trend in stretch fabrics has been evidenced.

Stretch may be imparted to the end product in the fiber stage, the yarn stage, the fabric construction, or the finishing stage.

IN THE FIBER STAGE

Of the natural fibers, wool has the most stretch. Its natural crimp can be increased by the application of certain chemicals and by the twist, set, and untwist method (already explained in connection with texturizing), when done in the wet state at a temperature of 212° F or higher. This treatment has been found to increase the stretch of two-ply worsted yarn to about 100 percent. A resin application on the yarn prior to untwisting has been found in a laboratory test to increase the amount of stretch significantly.

Elastometric fibers, particularly rubber and spandex, stretch much more than wool. Natural rubber was one of the first materials used to give stretch to clothing. The familiar trade name Lastex is still in use. Another trade name is Contro. Rubber deteriorates from exposure to oxygen in the air, continuous flexing, chlorine, salt water, sunlight, contact with bodily oil, perspiration, cosmetics, and repeated laundering. Rubber's usage includes surgical supports, tops of men's socks, support hosiery, bindings, foundation garments, swimsuits, trimmings, and sewing thread.

Spandex, a man-made polyurethane fiber, has supplanted rubber for many uses. Its stretchability is comparable to rubber. It is one-third lighter in weight than rubber, and twice as strong. Hence it can be made much finer—a reason why fabrics of spandex are lighter and more sheer with the same control features and stretch properties as fabrics made with rubber. Furthermore, Spandex is unaffected by sunlight, water, most oils and oil-based cosmetics, salt water, and dry cleaning agents. However, white spandex may yellow in usage, and chlorine bleach may degrade and yellow the fiber quickly and severely. Trade names of spandex fibers include Blue "C," Lycra, Numa, and Vyrene.

Spandex and rubber, covered or uncovered, may be woven or knitted into fabrics. Uncovered yarns give good elasticity but an undesirable rubbery feel to the fabric. When spandex is used as the core of a yarn, with other fibers wrapped spirally around it, the yarn has considerable stretch, a bulkier hand, and a more pleasant feel than uncovered yarns. Core spun yarn, as these covered yarns are called, are used in such fabrics as batiste, flannel, gabardine, lace, poplin, seersucker, taffeta, and twills. Yarns stretch about 25 to 40 percent on the average in these fabrics.

The T.F.P.I.A. has been amended to allow "the disclosure of any fiber present in a textile product which has clearly established definite functional significance." Prior to the amendment, the act required that all fibers constituting over 5 percent of a fabric be listed on the label or hangtag according to the generic name. Frequently a small percentage of spandex in a yarn was unidentified. Since as little as 1 percent spandex in a yarn gives stretch, it is highly desirable to have the generic name specified.

IN THE YARN STAGE

It has been noted that some of the three-stage textured yarns may stretch; that the false-twist method is the dominant stretch-yarn process in use today; and that the curled or edge-crimped technique develops a certain degree of stretch in the yarn. Uses for heat-set stretch yarn include infants' wear, ski wear, lingerie, sportswear, and swimsuits.

The stretch yarns used in a woven fabric may be either in the warp, in the filling, or in both, depending upon whether stretch is desired in the length of the fabric, the width, or in both dimensions.

IN THE FABRIC FINISHING STAGE

Knitting as contrasted with weaving imparts a great deal of stretch to the finished garment and will be discussed in Chapter 6. In woven fabrics, the simplest and least expensive method of imparting stretch is called "slack mercerization." Mercerization was described in Chapter 2 as a treatment of cotton yarns or fabrics under tension in a bath of caustic soda. When only warp yarns are held in tension, the loosely held filling yarns shrink. This shrinkage is permanently set by a chemical treatment that provides stretch and recovery properties ranging from 13 to 22 percent beyond its

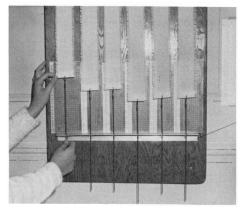

FIGURE 3.11. Test for woven stretch fabrics. After working stretch level is determined, fabrics are tensioned at proper level for two hours on the Extension Tester. (Courtesy of American Institute of Laundering.)

finished width. To be sure, this range is lower than stretch from elastomeric fibers and heat-set yarns. Also, recovery is said to diminish with wear and repeated laundering. Stretch levels for different end uses will be discussed in Chapter 17. The care of stretch fabrics will be considered in Chapter 16.

SUMMARY The type of yarns used has an effect on the fabric's texture, hand, warmth, weight, resiliency, durability, and luster.

Specifications for a particular yarn are determined by the fabric's end use. Ply yarns, for instance, are desirable in men's broadcloth shirts, in tropical worsted suitings, and in women's cotton voile dresses. In the first two uses, ply yarns give strength to the fabrics; in the third use, ply yarns in tight voile twist give the characteristic thready feel of voile and also give strength.

Yarns differ in weight and fineness, and in sheerness, smoothness, fuzziness, nubbiness, and elasticity—all varied to create qualities required in the final fabric.

Yarns may be classified according to structure (single or ply, direction of twist, size, or count), or use (as warp, filling, or other purposes). The present text has considered three classifications: (1) ordinary yarns; (2) textured and/or stretch yarns; (3) novelty yarns.

There have been innumerable pluses built into stretch fabrics. Therefore stretch should be a plus factor and not a sole selling point. Stretch fabrics

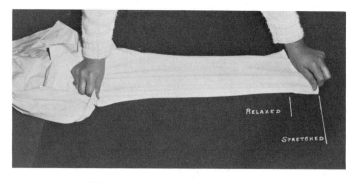

FIGURE 3.12. Sleeve of shirt manufactured of stretch fabric containing Polyester, cotton, and spandex. (Courtesy of American Institute of Laundering.)

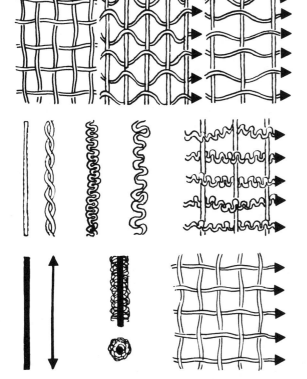

FIGURE 3.13. Mechanical or chemical stretch processing "buckles" the yarns; stretch occurs when the yarns are extended to their unshrunk length. Degree of stretch is usually low; recovery properties are slow.

FIGURE 3.14. Twist texturing induces a coil or crimp in filament yarns. Yarns then provide stretch characteristics to the woven or knit fabric. Degree of stretch is both high and long-lasting.

Figure 3.15. Core-spun yarns incorporate the stretch of a core of Lycra spandex inside a bundle of staple fibers. Performance and esthetics are those of the covering yarn; the stretch is high, recovery properties are strong and permanent. (Photographs courtesy of E. I. DuPont de Nemours & Company, Inc.)

should be used only where their properties are genuinely useful and beneficial to the consumer. The degree of stretch must be adequate to the function.

REVIEW QUESTIONS

1. (a) Define: core yarn, textured yarn, solution-dyed yarn, Germantown yarn, bouclé yarn.
   (b) Describe the methods of making textured yarn. Give a trade name of each type.
2. (a) What yarns are carded?
   (b) What yarns are combed?
   (c) Give the advantages of combed cotton yarns.
   (d) What are the differences between woolen and worsted yarns?
3. (a) To what types of yarn is the word "spun" applicable?
   (b) For what purposes are spun nylon yarns used?
   (c) What are some advantages and drawbacks of stretch yarns in woven fabrics?
4. (a) In what ways does twist affect the yarn?
   (b) Of what value is it to know the number of turns to the inch?
   (c) What is meant by a S twist? a Z twist?
   (d) Of what value is it to know direction of twist?
5. Explain the terms:
   (a) Count of yarn
   (b) Denier
   (c) Monofilament yarn
   (d) Multifilament yarn
6. Which is finer yarn, 30 denier or 15 denier? Explain your answer.

7. Which is finer, 100s cotton yarn or 150s cotton yarn? Why?
8. (*a*) What are novelty yarns?
   (*b*) What effect have they on the finished cloth?
9. (*a*) How are metallic yarns made?
   (*b*) What is the purpose of metallic yarn?
10. (*a*) How are yarns used?
    (*b*) What are the differences between thread and yarn?

**EXPERI-
MENT**

1. Using the technique for identification of yarns given in this chapter, take yarns from the following fabrics:
   (*a*) Dress satin (*f*) Stretch corduroy or stretch denim
   (*b*) Brocade (*g*) Silk organza
   (*c*) Shantung (*h*) Fiberglas marquisette
   (*d*) Donegal tweed (*i*) Sailcloth
   (*e*) Tropical worsted (*j*) Linen crash

   Answer the following for each yarn:
   (*a*) Regular or novelty yarn?
   (*b*) If regular, indicate:
      1. Single or ply
      2. Carded or combed, hackled
      3. Spun or filament, reeled
   (*c*) If novelty, indicate:
      1. Name of yarn
      2. How made

GLOSSARY

Air-bulked yarn—A textured yarn that is made by subjecting the filaments to air jets, which blow loops both on the surface of the yarn and in the *yarn bundle.*

Blended yarn—A strand of fibers produced from two or more constituent fibers that have been thoroughly mixed (blended) before spinning.

Bouclé yarn—A novelty yarn characterized by tight loops projecting from the body of the yarn at fairly regular intervals.

Bulky yarn—A yarn that has been textured to give it bulk without increasing weight.

Cable cord—The result of twisting singles together in various directions of twist, such as S/Z/S or Z/S/Z. See S *twist* and Z *twist.*

Carding—An operation in yarn making that separates the fibers and puts them in a filmy sheet called a sliver.

Chenille yarn—A soft, lofty yarn, somewhat rough in texture. See *Chenille fur,* Chapter 19.

Combination yarn—A ply yarn composed of two or more single yarns of the same or different fibers or twists.

Combing—An operation in yarn making that makes the fibers parallel in the sliver and removes the shorter fibers.

Construction—The way a cloth is fabricated. Construction includes weaving, knitting, felting, knotting, bonding, braiding, laminating, and so on.

Continuous filament—See *Filament yarns.*

Cord—The result of twisting together ply yarns in a third twisting operation.

Count of yarn—Size of yarn as distinguished by its weight and fineness. This term is applied to cotton, wool, and spun yarns.

Crimped yarn—A textured yarn made from man-made fibers that have been crimped to resemble wool.

Curled yarn—A textured yarn made by a heated blade that "curls" the filaments.

Denier—Size of silk and filament man-made yarns. See *Count.*

Double and twist yarn—A two-ply made from single yarns of different colors. A mottled effect is produced.

Durable press—A measure of garment performance. Features include (1) shape retention; (2) durable pleats and pressed creases; (3) durably smooth seams; (4) machine washability and dryability; (5) wrinkle resistance; (6) fresh appearance without ironing.

Filament yarns—Made of long continuous man-made fibers.

Fingering yarns—Light, medium weight, two- or three-ply yarns for hand knitting.

Frill or spiral yarns—A corkscrew effect produced by twisting together a fine and a coarse yarn.

Hackling—The process by which flax is prepared for yarn.

Hand—The feel of a fabric. See *Texture.*

Hawser cord—The result of twisting together singles with various directions of twists.

Lea—Size of linen yarn. See *Count of yarn* and *Denier.*

Line yarn—Well-hackled, even linen yarn made of long fibers.

Loop yarn—The slack-twisted strand is twisted to form loops or curls. This strand is held in place by one or two binder yarns.

Metallic yarn—Metal foil either wrapped around natural or synthetic yarn or coated on both sides with plain or plastic-covered film cut into strips.

Monofilament yarn—A yarn made of one filament (as in nylon hosiery).

Multifilament yarn—A yarn consisting of a number of filaments.

Paper yarn—A strand made of paper that is slit and twisted in web form.

Permanent press—See *Durable press.*

Plastic-coated yarns—Made of natural or synthetic fibers that have been dipped into a coating of plastic.

Ply yarn—Composed of two or more single yarns twisted together.

Raw Silk—Reeled silk wound directly from several cocoons with only a slight twist.

Reeling—Winding of silk filaments directly from cocoons.

Roving—Intermediate stage in yarn manufacture between sliver and yarn. A single strand of fibers having very little twist.

S twist—A left-hand twisted yarn.

Seed yarn—A very small nub often made of dyed man-made fibers applied to a dyed or natural-base yarn.

Sheath-core yarn—A very bulky yarn of synthetic fibers consisting of a core of fine denier fibers with considerable shrinkage and a cover or wrapping of coarse denier relaxed fibers.

Single yarn—One strand of fibers or filaments grouped or twisted together.

Sliver—A filmy sheet of fibers resulting from carding. See *Carding.*

Slub—An elongated nub. Slub yarn is identified by its elongated nubs.

Solution dye—Dyestuffs are put into the viscous solution before fibers are hardened.

Space-dyed yarns—Those yarns that have been dipped in dye or spotted in various places along the yarn.

Spinning—The process of drawing and twisting fibers together into yarns or thread.

Spiral—See *Frill yarns.*

Splash yarn—An elongated nub yarn that has been tightly twisted about a base yarn.

Spun yarn—A yarn twisted by spinning; also yarn composed of man-made staple fibers.

Stretch yarn—A textured yarn that has good stretch and recovery. It may also refer to yarns made of fibers that have elastic properties or to those yarns whose elastic properties are obtained by alterations of the basic fiber.

Texture—The surface effect of a fabric; that is, stiffness, roughness, smoothness, softness, fineness, dullness, and luster. See *Hand.*

Textured yarn—Any filament yarn that has been geometrically modified or otherwise altered to change its basic characteristics.

Thick and thin yarn—Produced by varying the diameters of man-made fibers.

Thread—A special type of tightly twisted ply yarn used for sewing.

Throwing—The combining and twisting of strands of reeled silk into tightly twisted yarn.

Tow—Poorly hackled, uneven linen yarn made of short fibers. It may also refer to strands of continuous filaments to be cut in lengths for spun yarn.

Turns—See *Twist.*

Twist—The number of times (turns) one inch of yarn is twisted.

Woolen yarn—A carded yarn made of relatively short fibers of varying lengths.

Worsted yarn—A combed yarn made of long-staple wool fibers.

Yarn dyed—Yarn that is colored (dyed) before it is woven into cloth.

Z twist—A right-hand twisted yarn.

Zephyr yarn—Very fine, soft, 100 percent wool hand-knitting yarns.

Basic Weaves:
Plain,
Twill, and Satin

4

When a customer sends a garment with a hole burned in it to be rewoven, she is often astounded by the price she must pay. She does not realize that the reweaver must match the yarns exactly and must make an entirely new cloth in the same woven-in pattern as the original. The reweaver must do a very high-quality darning job. First, he puts in the up-and-down yarns (warps or ends) spaced the same distance apart as the fabric's warps, then he works in the crosswise yarn (filling) over and under the exact number of warp yarns required to match the pattern.

Like the reweaving of a small hole, whole cloth (fabric by the yard) is woven with two sets of yarns (warps and fillings) interlacing at right angles. *Weaving*, then, is the process of interlacing two sets of yarns at right angles. This operation is done either on a hand or a power loom. If one set of yarns forms loops—one loop caught into another and one row of loops hanging on the one below—the cloth is made by *knitting*.

Weaving and knitting are two processes of making cloth. Weaving is the most common method, although knitting has become more important because new and improved knitting machines make cloth more quickly, more satisfactorily, and with more attractive patterns.

DEVELOP-MENT OF WEAVING The principles of weaving were known to primitive man. He knew how to make baskets and mats by interlacing twigs, reeds, and grasses. But these fibers were long and required no spinning into yarn. Man learned later how to twist together short fibers, such as wool and cotton, to form yarn; and woven cloths for clothing and home use were made on a *loom*.

The first hand loom was crude. It is chronicled that *warp* yarns—the lengthwise yarns in a fabric—were suspended from a limb of a tree and held in tension by stone weights at the ends near the ground. The loom of the American Navajo Indian shows warp yarns tied between two sticks. In less primitive looms a wooden frame was made to hold the warps; when strung parallel in this frame, they resembled the slats of a bed.

In early looms the crosswise yarns, or *fillings*, were carried over and under each of the warp yarns (as is done in darning). A sharpened stick was used for this purpose. Greater speed in weaving was attained when the *harness* (composed of *heddles*) was developed. It was found that the filling yarn could be interlaced with the warps much more quickly if each warp

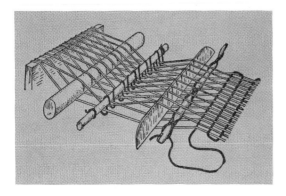

FIGURE 4.1. Primitive weaving device. A sword separates alternate warp yarns to form the shed. The needle carrying the filling yarn is being passed through the shed. (Courtesy CIBA-GEIGY Corporation.)

FIGURE 4.2. Four-harness hand loom. (Photograph courtesy of Dick Blick.)

yarn could be raised and lowered automatically so that the fillings could be shot through. This separation is done by the harness, and the operation is called *shedding*.

The hand loom in Figure 4.2, equipped with four harnesses, is designed to weave a variety of articles, such as neckties, collars, cuffs, belts, scarfs, table mats, and shopping bags. It has an extremely simple mechanism and can be operated by an amateur.

This loom is constructed like an inverted letter "T." The *bottom frame* corresponds to the crossing of the "T." The *main upright frame* is placed at the middle of the bottom frame and perpendicular to it. There are four harnesses (four frames suspended from the main upright frame). These frames hold a series of wires called heddles, each of which has an eye like that of a needle.

The cylindrical spool, called a *warp beam*, at the back of the loom holds warp yarns. To prepare the loom for weaving, the warp yarns are passed (1) up over the *breast beam* (the bar just above the spool of warp);

(1) through the eyes of the heddles; (3) through the *reed* or swinging frame in front of the heddles; (4) over a breast beam in front of the loom; and (5) around a cylinder, called a *cloth beam* or *merchandise beam*, to which they are attached. When a portion of material has been woven, it is wound on the cloth beam. If a cloth is several yards long, the entire yardage of warp yarns cannot be in tension on the loom at once;

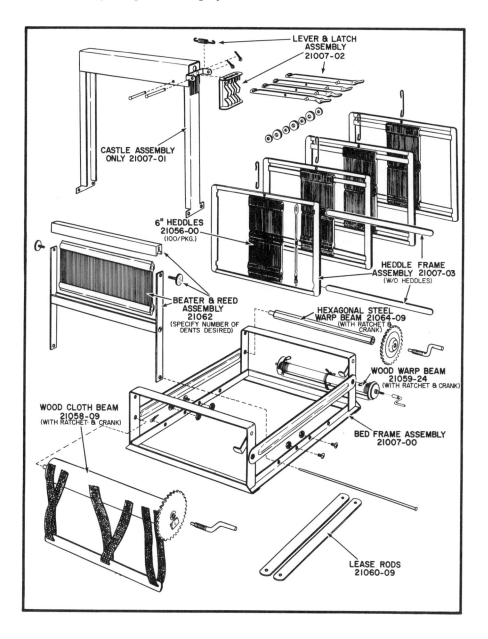

FIGURE 4.3. Parts of the hand loom. (Courtesy of Dick Blick.)

accordingly the rest of the warp is wound on the warp beam, which unwinds at the speed the cloth is woven.

Just below the nameplate in Figure 4.3 are four hooks, each suspended from an arm of a lever at the upper right of the main upright frame. Each hook is attached to the upper bar of one of the heddle frames or harnesses. Each heddle, or flattened wire, suspended between the upper and lower bars of the harness, controls the warp yarn that is threaded through its eye. The purpose of the harness is to raise groups of warps to form a shed so that the shuttle can be passed through the separate warps. Figure 4.3 also shows the *shed*.

To make the plain weave, a two-harness loom is sufficient. The weaving method, if a two-harness loom is used, is as follows: warps 1, 3, 5, 7, 9, and so on are threaded through the heddles of one harness, and warps 2, 4, 6, 8, 10, and so on are threaded through the heddles of the other harness.

The reed frame located directly in front of the harnesses swings forward to beat the last filling inserted against the previous fillings in order to make a compact construction.

A two-harness loom can make only a plain weave or its variations. Looms with more heddle frames are necessary for more elaborate weaves in which more than two combinations of warp yarns must be raised. A simple twill weave may be made with a four-harness loom. Some looms have 19 to 25 harnesses.

All woven cloth is made on some kind of loom. Power looms have supplanted the hand looms and have taken weaving from the home into the factory. Intricate designs, once considered masterpieces of the hand loom, can now be duplicated quickly and inexpensively by machinery.

THE SHUTTLELESS LOOM

A more recent development is the shuttleless loom, which carries the filling yarns through the shed by the use of rapiers, grippers, air jets, or water jets. The rapier and the gripper shuttle systems were established some time ago; they are broad looms that carry filling yarn from outside the loom, as opposed to the conventional shuttle looms that contain their own supply of filling within themselves. Some would argue that a loom with a carrier or projecting part extending through the warp shed is not a shuttleless loom. The present text will include these two systems as well as the newer jet looms. One machine, manufactured in Spain by Maquinaria Textil del Norte de España, South America, is available in the United States from the American Iwer Corporation. This machine weaves with any kind of yarn. It produces upholstery, worsted and curtain fabrics, burlap, blankets, shirtings and linings, dress goods, automotive materials, decorative fabrics, and domestics (common cotton cloth, such as sheeting). It can weave up to eight different yarns and colors. No separate bobbin winding machinery is required. French shuttleless looms (MAV weaving machines—Société Alsacienne de Constructions Mécaniques) combines some of the best technology of two continents in specialty weaving.[1]

[1] *Textile World,* June 1968, p. 51.

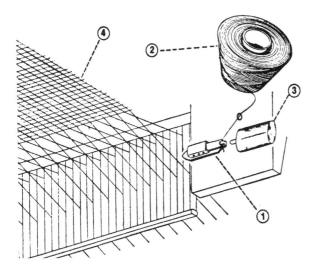

FIGURE 4.4. The shuttleless loom. Projectile (1) takes yarn from cone (2) and is shot by means of a pressure chamber (3) into the fabric in the loom (4).

American Silk Mills in Plains, Pennsylvania, has 40 MAV looms. They are said to be far less noisy than the conventional loom and speedier (220 picks per minute compared with 160 p.p.m. on conventional shuttle looms). Each loom equiped with two Jacquards produces weave patterns twice as long as one conventional Jacquard, without repeats. The card pattern for the machine is smaller, and it is easier to cut and store than the conventional Jacquard. These looms, 54 and 71 inches wide, are used for dress goods; men's dinner jackets, cummerbunds, and neckties; and ultramodern draperies. However, at the terrific speed that the filling streaks through the tension devices, heat and friction occur. A replacement of the rapier-like needle ends that hold the end of the filling is required at times. Other looms make six widths: 40, 44, 50, 64, 82, and 90 inches.

FIGURE 4.5. A Model 1800 Iwer shuttleless loom utilizing a Jacquard head to weave a blanket material in eight colors. (Photograph courtesy of American Iwer Corporation.)

73

In addition to Spain and France, the following countries have shuttleless looms in operation: West Germany, Switzerland, Japan, Czechoslovakia, Italy, England, Belgium, Ireland, Sweden, Canada, and the United States.

In 1967 the Draper Corporation had some 6,000 shuttleless looms in mills in the United States.

The textile industry's progress in the newer shuttleless looms will come gradually as new looms are installed and improvements in loom motions and parts are made. An important advantage of these looms is their speed, which increases production and hence profits. Greater profits, in turn, mean higher wages. Also, weavers prefer to work in the quieter weave rooms.

FOUR OPERATIONS IN CONVENTIONAL WEAVING

The steps in weaving may be summarized as follows:

1. After the warp threads (called *ends*) have been strung into the frame of the loom, the warp yarns are separated. This is the first operation; it is called *shedding*.
2. The filling is carried through the shed. This operation is called *picking*. The term probably originated before the invention of the shuttle and the heddles, when every other warp had to be picked up, as in darning, so that the filling could be passed over and under the warps. Each time the filling is carried across the cloth, one pick is made. A *pick* is synonymous with a *filling*; an *end* is synonymous with a *warp*.
3. Each filling or pick is pushed up against the previous filling by the reed frame. This process is called *battening*.
4. The warp is released from the *warp beam*, and the finished cloth is taken up on the *merchandise beam*. This operation is called *letting off and taking up*.

These operations are repeated over and over again until the cloth is the desired length.

THE SELVAGES

In yard goods the outer edges are constructed so they will not ravel. These finished edges are called the selvages (self-edges) and are often made with heavier and more closely spaced warp yarns than are used in the rest of the fabric. Tape selvages are firmer and wider than plain selvages. For towels, sheets, and drapery and curtain fabrics, tape selvages give added strength to the edges. Selvages vary in width from one-quarter to three-eighths inch. The warp yarns always run parallel to the selvages.

COUNT OF CLOTH

The yarns used for warp and those used for filling are frequently not of the same diameter; and those used for one dimension may be closer together than those used for the other. Usually there are more warp yarns than filling yarns to the inch, because the strain on a fabric that is being used comes primarily on the warp. Some cloths, like ginghams, are closely woven; others, like voile, are loosely woven. If the cloth is held to the light, the porosity of the fabric or the closeness of the weave can be discerned. Ordinarily, a closely woven fabric keeps its shape better, shrinks less, slips less at seams, and wears longer than a loosely woven cloth of similar texture and weight.

The closeness or looseness of the weave is measured by the count of the cloth. This is determined by the number of picks and ends (warps and fillings) to the square inch. A small pocket magnifying glass, called a *pick glass* or *linen tester*, is used for this purpose. Several warp yarns and several fillings are removed from the cloth. If the fabric is light in color, a piece of black material is put under it, or vice versa. The linen tester is then set against the raveled edge. Since the usual opening in the tester is 1/4-inch square, the yarns are counted in this space (first the number of warps, then of fillings). Then the number of the yarns that run each way is multiplied by four to give the count per inch. A pin sometimes helps in separating yarns for counting.

The textile weaving mill does its count of cloth at the loom. An electric-impulse mechanism counts the picks for each of ten looms on each of three shifts of personnel, plus the total picks per loom. Counters (actual counting mechanisms) remote from the loom are now set in a panel with a glass door. These count data are easy to read, encourage competition between shifts, and keep production high. In older mills, each loom has its own pick clock or counter.

If the count of the cloth is 80 warps and 80 fillings to the inch, the count is expressed as 80 × 80, or 80 square. If there are 60 warps and 50 fillings to the inch, the count is expressed as 60 × 50. This count is found in a plain gingham of medium quality. The count of surgical gauze is approximately 28 × 24. In comparison of the two counts, a 96 × 88 cloth is considered the higher-count cloth because it has more picks and ends (warps and fillings) to the square inch than has surgical gauze. There are, then, high-count and low-count cloths.

Since the yarns are closer together in high-count cloths than they are in low-count cloths, there is less danger of the yarns slipping out of place and causing a shreddy effect. Low-count cloths may be woven with only a few yarns to the inch, either to make the fabric lightweight and porous or to cheapen it.

The consumer can test the strength of a weave by gripping two edges of the cloth and, with thumbs close together, pressing the thumbs downward on the cloth as hard as possible, and turning the cloth over as pressure continues. If the fabric gives way when hard pressure is exerted, the cloth will not be durable. Any slipping of yarns will also show weakness in the construction of the fabric, and will make an unsightly, weak seam.

BALANCE OF CLOTH

The proportion of warp yarns to filling yarns is called the *balance* of a cloth. If the number of warps and the number of fillings to the inch are nearly the same (not more than ten yarns difference), a cloth is said to have good balance. The gingham whose count is 60 × 50 would be considered a fair-balanced cloth. Gauze with a count of 28 × 24 also has a good balance. A sheeting with 61 warp ends and 40 picks (61 × 40) has poor balance because there are too many warps and two few picks. Even though the sheeting is woven in the plain weave, ordinarily a strong construction, there are so few fillings that the warps will slip over them very easily, causing a shredded effect. If this cloth were held to the light, the yarns would seem to run all one way—lengthwise. The cloth count is substandard for a sheeting and is not durable.

Good balance is very important in cloths that have to stand hard wear and many washings. Sheets, pillow slips, and towels for glasses and dishes, for instance, should have good balance. A cloth is not always durable, however, just because it has a balanced count. The count of a cloth may be 58 × 50, which looks like a splendid balance, but the cloth may not prove durable if the warps are only half as coarse and half as strong as the fillings. On the other hand, a cotton broadcloth may have an off-balance count, say 144 × 76 (about twice as many warps as fillings). In this fabric, the fillings are larger than the warps to give a crosswise ridged effect; hence there are fewer fillings than warps to the inch. Better grades of broadcloth have ply warps and single fillings (2 × 1) to make up in tensile strength for the fine warp yarns used. Best grades have both warps and fillings plied (2 × 2). A buyer, then, must consider both the comparative sizes and the tensile strengths of warp and filling yarns. The warp should be the stronger and usually the more tightly twisted.

The count of cloth and the count of yarn should not be confused. The former denotes the number of picks and ends to the square inch; the latter indicates the weight and diameter of the yarn.

CLASSIFICATION OF WEAVES

The ways in which the filling yarns are interlaced with the warps change the appearance of the fabric and produce many intricate designs that are woven into the cloth. Weaves are named according to the system or design followed in interlacing warp and filling yarns.

The different weaves are named as follows (each weave will be discussed in this and the following chapter in the order given):

1. plain	6. dobby
2. twill	7. leno or gauze
3. satin	8. swivel
4. pile	9. lappet ⎫ *ornamental*
5. Jacquard	10. clipped spot ⎬ *embroidered*
	11. schiffli embroidery ⎭ *effects*

PLAIN WEAVE

In this, the simplest weave, the filling is passed over one warp yarn and under the next, alternating in this manner once across the cloth. The second time across, the filling passes over the warp yarns it went under, and under the warps it went over on the previous row. The third time across is a repetition of the first; the fourth repeats the second; and so on. (See Figure 4.6.)

POINT-PAPER DESIGN

Each weave can be presented in a squared paper design. For intricate woven-in patterns, designers use the point-paper pattern. Those who do not know how to use it often find their designs impractical from the weaver's standpoint. Figure 4.6 illustrates the pattern for plain weave.

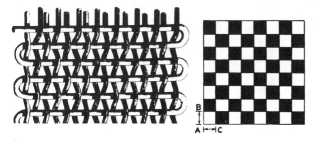

FIGURE 4.6. Left: Plain weave, showing interlacement of warp and filling yarns. Right: Point paper design for the same construction.

White squares are filling on the face—warp on the back. The warp runs lengthwise of the paper, and the fillings run crosswise. The diameter of filling yarns are the same size. The diameter of the filling yarn is represented by AB. AC represents the diameter of a warp yarn.

CLOTHS MADE IN THE PLAIN WEAVE

The plain weave is sometimes called cotton, taffeta, or tabby weave. Some of the most durable fabrics are made in this construction. The weaving process is comparatively inexpensive because the design is so simple. Plain-weave cloths can be cleaned easily, and when firm and closely woven, they wear well.

A partial list of plain-weave fabrics follows:

1. *Cottons.* Gingham, percale, voile, plissé crepe, batiste, calico, chambray, cheesecloth, chintz, crash, cretonne, muslin sheeting, cambric, lawn, organdy, shantung, unbleached muslin, scrim, crinoline, bunting, buckram, canvas, flannelette
2. *Linens.* Handkerchief linen, art linen, crash toweling, cambric, dress linen
3. *Nylons and other man-made fibered fabrics.* Organdy, lingerie crepe, shantung, taffeta, shirting (many of these constructions are also made in blends with natural yarns and with other man-made fibered yarns)
4. *Rayons and/or acetates.* Taffeta, georgette, flat crepe, seersucker, ninon, organdy, voile, rough crepe, chiffon, challis
5. *Silks.* Taffeta, organza, voile, Canton crepe, crepe de Chine, flat crepe, chiffon, pongee, shantung, silk shirting, broadcloth, habutai, China silk
6. *Wools.* Homespun, challis, crepe, batiste, some tweeds, voile
7. *Blends and mixtures of the various fibers*

FIGURE 4.7. Plain weave. (Photo by Jack Pitkin.)

FIGURE 4.8. Point paper design for striped dimity.

VARIATIONS IN PLAIN WEAVE THAT PRODUCE DIFFERENT EFFECTS

Rib Variation. The plain weave without any variation, as is found in sheeting and unbleached muslin, does not make a particularly interesting fabric. Several methods can be used to make a plain-weave fabric more attractive. The first is to produce a ribbed or corded effect by using fillings much heavier than warps, as in poplin, or by using warps much heavier than fillings, as in dimity. The former method is the most common. Bengaline and faille have regular fillingwise ribs; cotton broadcloth has a fine, irregular, broken fillingwise rib.

A striped effect is produced by alternation of fine and heavy warps at regular intervals, as in striped dimity or corded madras shirting. In addition, fine and heavy fillings may be alternated to produce a crossbar effect. Examples of this are crossbar dimity and tissue gingham.

The durability of fabrics in the rib variation of the plain weave may be questionable if the rib yarns are so heavy that they slip over or cut adjacent finer yarns. Such might be the case in striped dimity. The rib must be completely covered by many finer yarns, and the difference in weight between the rib yarn and other yarns should not be too great if wearing quality is to be assured. In heavily corded fabrics, like ottoman and bengaline, good coverage of the ribs is vital because abrasive wear occurs first on top of the ribs.

FIGURE 4.9. Rib weave
striped dimity.

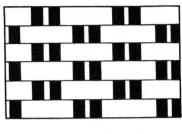

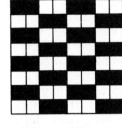

FIGURE 4.10. 2 X 1 basket weave.

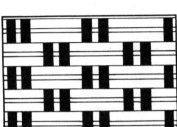

FIGURE 4.11. 2 X 2 basket weave.

Basket variation. The basket variation of the plain weave is interesting from the design point of view, but it is not so durable as the average rib variation. One or more filling yarns are passed alternately over and under two or more warp yarns. If one filling yarn passes alternately over and under two warp yarns, the weave is called 2 X 1 basket. This weave is common in oxford shirting. The fabric is sometimes made in 3 X 2 (two fillings pass over and under three warps). A 3 X 2 oxford makes an interesting woman's blouse when made of colored warp yarns and white fillings.

In Figure 4.10 the 2 X 1 basket weave shows one large filling yarn used for every two warp yarns. If a filling is exactly twice the size of a warp, the interlacing of one filling and two warps forms a design of a perfect square; if either set of yarns is not in this proportion, the interlacing of one filling and two warps makes a design in the form of an oblong.

In Figure 4.11 two fillings pass alternately over two warps. Warps and filling yarns are the same size. A 4 X 4 or 8 X 8 basket weave is found in monk's cloth.

The basket weave is a decorative weave, but it is loose; therefore it permits slippage of yarns and stretches, and it may shrink easily in washing. Monk's cloth frays badly unless it is bound on the cut edges.

VISUAL DESIGN OR EFFECT

In both the rib and basket variations of the plain weave, there are structural changes in the point-paper designs. (See Figures 4.8 through 4.11.) But the following ways of varying the plain weave may be employed, without structural changes, to give a visual effect (design) that is quite different from the usual appearance of the plain weave. Textural and new color effects can be produced by—

1. *Varying the size of yarns.* When uneven yarns are used at irregular intervals (hit or miss), a roughened, bumpy texture is the result. Crash, shantung, and pongee illustrate this use of different sizes of yarns at irregular intervals. Modern drapery fabrics employ such visual effects. (See Chapter 21.)

Another rough texture can be produced with different sizes of ply yarn, as in ratiné and bouclé. Each ply yarn may be made up of different sizes of single yarns with varying amounts of twist.

2. *Varying the number of warp and filling yarns.* The count of cloth is dependent on the number of warps and fillings to the inch; the more yarns to the inch, the closer the weave and the higher the count, and vice versa. The fewer the warp and filling yarns to the inch, the more porous and open the cloth, providing the yarns are fine. Cheesecloth, gauze, voile, and theatrical gauze are low-count cloths. Batiste, lawn, organdy, and cotton broadcloth are considered high-count cloths.

3. *Variations made by use of different degrees of twist in yarns.* If the warp or the filling is twisted so hard that it crepes or crinkles, the appearance of the cloth is textured. Crinkled bedspreads of seersucker are made from yarns with different degrees of twist and tension in the loom. Creping, such as is found in flat crepe, Canton crepe, rough crepe, and crepe de Chine, is made with tightly twisted fillings, alternating right-hand and left-hand twisted yarns (S and Z twists). (See Chapter 3.)

Another variation is made with one set of yarns twisted tightly, but not enough to crepe or crinkle, and fillings twisted so loosely that a nap can be raised in the finishing process. Flannelette is an example.

4. *Combinations of different textile raw materials.* Some cloths are made more attractive by the use of yarns of different textiles or blends of different raw materials. A novel visual effect is produced by the use of a black cotton warp and orange jute filling. A metallic yarn put in here and there in a wool crepe is very attractive because the metallic yarn is so much more lustrous than wool that it shows up to advantage. Alpaca and romain crepes are made of acetate and viscose yarns plied together to form an abraded yarn. The shiny viscose ply and the dull acetate ply give varied luster and sparkle. Metallic yarns may be introduced in any weave for effect. (See Chapter 3.) Matelassé, a fabric with acetate face and rayon back, is a good example of high shrink rayon and low shrink acetate yarns.

5. *Variations made by use of fibers or yarns dyed in different colors.* A cloth with a colored warp and a white filling gives a grayed effect. Cotton chambray has this appearance. End-to-end madras, a men's shirting, is quite similar to chambray, the greatest difference being that in the former dyed and white yarns alternate in the warp. This cloth has less depth of color than chambray because there are more white yarns in it. Yarn-dyed stripes are common in madras shirting.

Plaid gingham is made with a series of colored yarns and a series of white yarns used alternately in both warp and filling. This alternation makes the plaid effect. Linen crash may be made with the insertion of large, irregular fillings dyed a different color from the rest of the yarns. Wool tweeds and homespuns use yarns of different colors. Fibers dyed different colors when in raw stock produce cloth with a mottled effect. Gray flannel with a mottled appearance is made in this way.

6. *Variations in dyeing and finishing.* Printing, piece dyeing, and various finishes will vary the appearance not only of plain-weave fabrics but also of all other weaves. Variations due to different fiber combinations, kinds of yarn, and methods of dyeing, printing, and finishing vary the appearance of the cloth but do *not* affect the *structural* design (the weave).

TWILL WEAVE

Twill is the most durable of all weaves. In this weave the filling yarns are interlaced with the warps in such a way as to form diagonal ridges across the fabric. These diagonals, called *wales*, may run from upper left to lower right [Figure 4.12(a)], from upper right to lower left [Figure 4.12(b)], or both ways in the same cloth [Figure 4.13]. If the wales run from upper right to lower left, the weave is called a *right-hand* twill; if the wales run from upper left to lower right, the weave is called a *left-hand twill*; if the wales run both ways, the weave is a *herringbone*.

The twill weave may also be called the serge or diagonal weave. In a piece of coarse serge the filling yarn passes over two and under two warp yarns, alternating across the cloth. This is the first pick. For the second pick, or second time across, the filling passes over two and under two warps, but it laps back on the ground on the previous row, thus forming a stair pattern. In serge the twill runs in the same direction as the twist in the yarns. Point-paper designs for two types of twills appear in Figures 4.12(b) and (c).

In the even twill [Figure 4.12(b)], the filling passes over the same number or warps as it passes under. The wale on the right side of the cloth is represented by the black squares. In this weave the wales and the valleys between them are the same width. On the wrong side of the cloth the wales run from upper left to lower right.

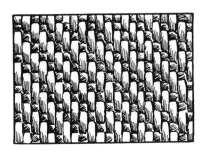

(a)

FIGURE 4.12. a. Interlacement of yarns in uneven twill weave. Wales run from upper left to lower right in this illustration. b. Even twill weave. Wales run from upper right to lower left in this illustration. c. Uneven twill weave. Wales run in the same direction as in (a).

1 2 3 4 5 6 7 8 9 10 11

(b)

1 2 3 4 5 6 7 8 9 10 11

(c)

FIGURE 4.13. Herringbone weave. Left: Point paper design. Right: Cloth. (Photo by Jack Pitkin.)

The uneven twill [Figure 4.12(c)] shows diagonals in black squares on the right side of the cloth. The filling passes under more yarns than it passes over (under 2 and over 1). A twill pattern might also require the filling to pass over 1 and under 3, 4, 5, 6, or over 2 and under 1, 3, 4. To recognize even and uneven twills, compare the width of a wale with the width of a valley between two wales. If the wales and the valley are the same widths, the twill is even; if they are of unequal widths, the twill is uneven. If the valleys are narrower than the wales, the wales stand out predominantly.

Below is an outline of the shedding that forms the even twill in Figure 4.12(b). Beginning at the right, the warps are lifted in the following combinations to allow the shuttle to pass under:

First row (top)	warps 1, 4, 5, 8, 9, etc.
Second row	warps 11, 8, 7, 4, 3, etc.
Third row	warps 2, 3, 6, 7, 10, 11, etc.
Fourth row	warps 10, 9, 6, 5, 2, 1, etc.
Fifth row	repeat first row

In Figure 4.12(b) it takes 4 picks (rows) to complete a design; 4 series of warps must be lifted and 4 harnesses must be used. This twill construction is called a *4-shaft* twill. A quick method to determine the number of shafts required is to add together the number of warp yarns the filling goes over and under. In this case, over 2 under 2. Therefore, 2 + 2 = 4 shafts. It is known as 2/2 twill or 2 × 2 twill.

The outline of shedding for the construction in Figure 4.12(c) is as follows (the method is the same as already mentioned):

First row (top)	warps 1, 2, 4, 5, 7, 8, 10, 11, etc.
Second row	warps 11, 9, 8, 6, 5, 3, 2, etc.
Third row	warps 1, 3, 4, 6, 7, 9, 10, etc.
Fourth row	repeat first row

Another 4-shaft twill is the 3/1 twill or 1/3 twill. Since it takes 3 picks or rows to complete a design and 3 series of warps must be lifted, this weave is called a *3-shaft* twill. Using the quick method: the filling goes under 2 and over 1 (2 + 1 = 3 shafts required) for 2/1 twill. This system automatically tells the number of shafts by simple addition.

VARIATIONS OF THE TWILL WEAVE

The most common variation of the twill weave is the *herringbone.* In this weave the diagonal runs in one direction for a few rows and then reverses and runs in the opposite direction. The effect resembles the backbone of a herring, as the name, implies. Figure 4.13 shows a point-paper design of a herringbone weave. Either the even or the uneven twills can make a herringbone, but, in either case, there must be a variation in the weave at the apex of the ∧ in order to reverse the wales.

Other variations of the twill may be made to form diamond patterns, as demonstrated by some worsted cheviots. Passing the filling over a large number of warps at a time produces a heavy, corded wale, common in whipcord. The wales may be broken at intervals or may curve or wave for a more unusual effect. If the twist of the yarns runs opposite to the pattern, a rough twill is made.

Variations in the use of fiber blends and yarns of different sizes, qualities, colors, and finishes make possible many visual effects in the twill weave, as in the case of plain weaves.

ADVANTAGES AND DISADVANTAGES OF TWILL WEAVES

Twill weaves usually make fabrics closer in texture, heavier, and stronger than do plain weaves. This is why twills are so suitable for men's clothing fabrics. Also, it is possible to produce more fancy designs in twills than in plain weaves. As has been seen in the illustrations, more elaborate shedding is needed for the twill than for the plain weave. Therefore twill cloths may cost more. Twills do not show dirt so quickly as plain weaves, but once they are dirty, they are harder to clean.

CLOTHS IN TWILL WEAVE

Cloths made in twill weave may be classified as follows (it will be noticed that the twill is frequently used for cottons and wools):

1. *Cottons.* Jean, ticking, drill, Canton flannel, denim, gabardine, covert cloth, khaki, serge
2. *Linens.* Ticking and table and towel drills
3. *Silks.* Twill foulard, serge, surah
4. *Wools.* Serge, worsted cheviot, gabardine, covert, flannel (twill or plain), tweed (twill or plain), unfinished worsted, broadcloth, sharkskin
5. *Rayons, acetates, and blends.* Gabardine, surah, foulard, flannel

SATIN AND SATEEN WEAVES

Why do satins have sheen? In what way are they different from the dull-finished silks?

Any consumer may have asked these questions. The answer to both questions is that the type of cloth construction called the *satin weave* gives great sheen to a fabric and reflects the light better than dull-finished fabrics in plain or twill weave do.

The consumer should notice that whenever she feels a silk or rayon dress satin, the hand slips more easily lengthwise than crosswise of the fabric (the right or shiny side should be felt). The reason is that more warps than fillings are exposed on the right side. If the fabric is turned over, more fillings than warps are visible. The sheen of the fabric runs warpwise on the right side. Dressmakers must be sure that dresses are cut so that the sheen runs lengthwise of the dress.

When there are more warps than fillings on the right side of the fabric, the weave is called *satin.* If more fillings than warp show on the right side, the weave is called *sateen* or *satine.*

Cotton, if highly mercerized, may be woven in the satin weave, as in cotton satin for linings; but ordinarily the fuzz on cotton yarns makes long floating warps undesirable.

Both satin and sateen weaves use the principle of the twill. In fact, some authorities call these weaves *rearranged* or *skipping* twills. In this discussion, however, the twill and the satin are considered separately. In satin and sateen weaves there is a semblance of a broken diagonal, but the interlacings of the warp and filling are placed as far apart as possible to avoid the forming of a wale. In the satin construction the warp may not interlace with the filling for 4 to 12 yarns. Thus, varying lengths of warp are left exposed on the surface of the cloth. When a warp skips seven fillings before it interlaces, the weave is called an 8-shaft satin; if the warp skips five yarns, the weave is a 6-shaft satin, and so on. If the filling skips four yarns before interlacing with a warp, the weave is a 5-shaft sateen weave, and so on. Point-paper designs of the satin and sateen weaves appear in Figures 4.14 and 4.15.

Figure 4.14 illustrates a long-float satin weave. The warp floats over 11 filling yarns. The blackened portion represents warp yarns brought to the face of the fabric. A predominance of blackened squares denotes a predominance of floating warps. Figure 4.15 illustrates a short-float sateen weave.

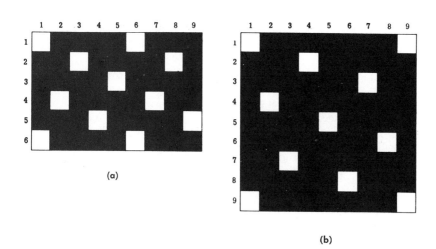

FIGURE 4.14. a. Four-float satin weave; b. Seven-float satin weave.

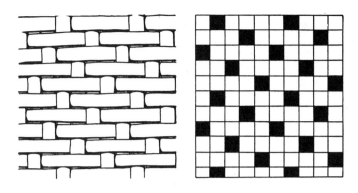

FIGURE 4.15. Short-float sateen weave.

ADVANTAGES AND DISADVANTAGES OF SATIN AND SATEEN WEAVES

These constructions produce smooth, lustrous, rich-looking fabrics that give reasonably good service if they are not subjected to excessive hard wear. Short-float fabrics are more durable than long-float fabrics, for the former have less exposed yarn to catch on rough objects; long-floats, although they increase the sheen of a fabric, snag and pull if there are any protrusions or splinters on furniture.

When style calls for luxurious fabrics for formal wear, satin is often chosen. It is an especially suitable fabric for coat linings because its smooth surface allows coats to be slipped on and off very easily. In general, it sheds dirt well, but a bright rayon in a long-float satin weave will often have a metallic sheen that may appear greasy after continuous wear.

The satin weave usually requires more shafts in the weaving than do the plain or twill weaves, thereby increasing the cost of production. For instance, in the design in Figure 4.14, the filling passes over 1 and under 4 warps, so 5 shafts are required (4 + 1 = 5). When the filling passes over four or more warp yarns, the weave is *sateen*.

VARIATIONS IN THE SATIN AND SATEEN WEAVES

Warp yarns may be twisted loosely, and long floats may be used to produce a high sheen. When a softer, lower luster is desired, warp yarns may be twisted more tightly and the floats may be shortened.

By the use of creped yarns of reeled or spun silk for filling and very loosely twisted reeled silk for floating warps, a warp satin face with a creped back can be made; the lustrous, smooth reeled-silk warps are thrown to the face of the fabric in warp floats, while the tightly twisted, dull, creped filling yarns are kept on the back. The fabric is reversible and is called satin crepe. Likewise, cotton or spun-silk yarns may be used for the filling. Since the warp made of lustrous reeled silk covers the face of the fabric, the cotton or spun silk can be carefully concealed. Since rayons, acetates, and nylons are woven in the same satin construction as are silks, their appearance can be changed in a similar manner.

The finishing processes and the amount of twist in the yarn affect the feel of the fabric. For example, a cloth may feel soft after the weaving;

85

but, if stiffened in finishing, the fabric will feel more crisp, less soft, and less elastic.

The sateen as well as the satin weave may be varied. If highly mercerized cotton yarns are used, the sheen of sateen will be increased. The sateen weave can be used in combination with the satin weave in making elaborate figured designs. (See Chapter 5.)

CLOTHS MADE IN SATIN AND SATEEN WEAVES

The materials that are made with the satin weave are antique satin (millions of yards per year), bridal satin, cotton satin, dress satin, satin bengaline, satin crepe, satin faille, slipper satin, and Venetian satin. Sateen is made in the sateen weave.

IDENTIFICATION OF WARP AND FILLING

The plain, twill, and satin weaves are the three fundamental weaves. Before studying more complicated ones, the reader should learn how to distinguish warp from filling in these weaves and how to choose between them for various uses.

In a large piece of yard goods it is easy to tell warp from filling, for the selvages, or finished edges, run parallel to the warp. But if there are no selvages and the consumer has only a sample of cloth of mail-order size, other methods to distinguish warp or filling must be used.

IN PLAIN WEAVE

The count in plain-weave cloths is usually the determining factor. There are generally more warps than fillings to the inch. In a square count cloth, 80 X 80, the way to identify warp is first to break a yarn in each direction to compare breaking strengths. The greater breaking strength is usually the warp because the warps are generally twisted more tightly—with the exception of the creped cloths like flat crepe and satin crepe, in which the filling is the more tightly twisted yarn. In rib variations of the plain weave, the ribs of cotton broadcloth, cotton poplin, bengaline, grosgrain, and faille run fillingwise, but the rib in Bedford cord runs warpwise. In 2 X 2 and 4 X 4 basket weaves the warps can be recognized by their twist or by their greater strength. In 2 X 1 basket weave there is usually one large filling to two close, parallel warps. The uneven bumpy yarns in pongee and shantung run fillingwise.

RIGHT AND WRONG SIDES OF A FABRIC

To tell the right side from the wrong side of a plain weave cloth is often difficult unless it is on a bolt, in which case the cloth may be folded with the right side inside to keep it clean. If one side of a fabric is more lustrous than the other side, the shinier side is the right side. A printed fabric design usually shows more clearly on the right side. In ribbed fabrics, the rib is often more distinct on the right side. Slub-yarn fabrics often show the slub more predominantly on the right side. Napped cloths are softer and fuzzier on the right side.

IN TWILL WEAVE

The side on which the wale shows up more clearly is the right side—unless the fabric is napped, in which case the side with more napping is the right side.

With the right side to the observer, the fabrics should be turned until the wales run from the upper right corner to the lower left corner, or vice versa. When the sample is held in this position, the warp should run up and down, and the filling crosswise. Warps are usually stronger and more tightly twisted than fillings. Sometimes warp yarns can be distinguished from filling yarns by the amount of wave or kink in them. Fillings are likely to be more wavy, because they are not held in tension in the loom as they go over and under the warps.

IN SATIN OR SATEEN WEAVE

If the fabric is extremely lustrous and smooth, the consumer may suspect it is a satin construction. First the finger should be run over the cloth to determine in which way the floats lie. The way the finger slips more easily is the way the floats run. If the fabric is silk, rayon, acetate, or a synthetic mixture, or a blend of these fibers, the warp floats, and the weave is satin. Silk and cotton mixtures, rayon and cotton, and acetate and cotton also have warp floats. If the fabric is all-cotton, the float is usually fillingwise. But the cotton satin that is used for coat linings—called farmer's satin—has a warp float.

GUIDES TO CON-SUMERS IN CHOOSING WEAVES

The consumer should know first the factors that enable one to choose suitable fabrics from the standpoint of type of fibers and yarn and should consider second the fabrics from the standpoint of construction or weave. In this chapter the three basic weaves—plain, twill, and satin—have been discussed.

If suitability is a factor of major consideration, the consumer should carefully consider the purpose for which the fabric is to be used. The plain weave is probably the most serviceable of all weaves. It is easy to dry-clean and to launder, wears well, is becoming to the majority of people, is comfortable, is usually in style in one cloth or another, and is comparatively inexpensive. However, loose weaves (the basket in particular) are more likely to shrink than are close weaves. The more the yarns slip or give, the more danger there is of their shrinking. A twill in wool keeps its press and shape well when used for suitings. For daily business wear, a plain-weave wool or silk crepe requires little pressing and is always becoming. For infants' wear, plain or twill cloths are best. Twill weaves do not show dirt so quickly as plain weaves, but more effort is required to clean them. For boys' wear, the twilled worsted is a durable suiting. For girls, a plain weave or a twill are both good. Many mothers prefer plain weaves for fabrics requiring frequent laundering and twills for wool goods.

Satins are impractical for active sports and for hard daily wear. There is the danger not only that they will snag, but also that in time they will look greasy. If style calls for a lustrous sheen for evening, the consumer should choose satin—provided she is not too stout—for satins tend to make a large woman look larger. Style and becomingness go hand in hand. If wearing quality is a factor in selecting satin, a short float should be chosen. Beauty, appearance, and style usually govern the choice of satin.

Since the satin weave requires more complicated machinery than do the plain or twill weaves, it is more expensive.

SUMMARY   Plain, twill, and satin weaves with their variations are considered the three basic weaves in the construction of textile fabrics. The weaves are arranged according to the simplicity of their manufacture (with the plain weave as the simplest) and according to the frequency of use.

The plain weave is made from all types of textile yarns, but it is most common in cottons. Twill, the strongest weave, is used mainly when durability is the prime requisite. The satin and sateen weaves are beautiful but may not be durable. The satin weave is most common in silks, rayons, acetates, and synthetics, where beauty depends upon richness of sheen. The sateen weave is found in a few mercerized cotton fabrics, and it appears in combination with the satin weave in elaborate woven-in patterns. Fancy weaves are discussed in the next chapter.

REVIEW
QUESTIONS

1. (*a*) What is weaving?
   (*b*) What is a loom?
   (*c*) How is the loom prepared for weaving?
   (*d*) Describe the action of the loom.
   (*e*) Can weaving be done without a shuttle? How?
2. (*a*) How is the plain weave made?
   (*b*) Draw a point-paper design to illustrate the plain weave.
3. In what ways may the plain weave be varied—
   (*a*) In actual construction?
   (*b*) In visual design or effect?
4. (*a*) What are the advantages of the plain weave?
   (*b*) What are its disadvantages?
5. Draw a point-paper design to illustrate (*a*) a rib weave; (*b*) a 2 X 2 basket weave; (*c*) a 2 X 1 basket weave.
6. (*a*) What is meant by the count of cloth?
   (*b*) How does count of cloth differ from count of yarn?
   (*c*) Why is the count of cloth important to a buyer of cottons or linens?
7. (*a*) Explain the construction of a twill weave.
   (*b*) Draw a point-paper design to illustrate a 4-shaft twill, a 3-shaft twill.
8. (*a*) What are the advantages of a cloth made in twill weave?
   (*b*) What are its disadvantages?
9. (*a*) In what respect does the satin weave differ from the twill weave?
   (*b*) Explain the construction of the sateen weave.
   (*c*) Draw a point-paper design illustrating a 5-shaft warp satin weave.
   (*d*) Draw a point-paper design illustrating a 5-shaft filling sateen weave.
10. Which of the three standard weaves is—
    (*a*) The most durable? Why?
    (*b*) The most beautiful? Why?
    (*c*) The most serviceable? Why?
11. List ten fabrics made in (*a*) plain weave, (*b*) twill weave, (*c*) satin or sateen weaves.
12. Define: float, 4-shaft twill, point-paper design, warp, heddle, pick, shuttle, end, selvage, filling, balance of a cloth, letting out and taking up, breast beam, merchandise beam, wale, herringbone, shedding, high-count cloth, crepe, pick glass.

EXPERI-MENTS

1. *Identification of warp and filling.* Examine a number of swatches. Be sure you have the right side, the more lustrous side, toward you. Note whether or not there is a selvage to indicate which dimension is the warp. If there is no selvage, unravel a yarn either way. Which yarn is stronger? Which yarn has the tighter twist? Which yarn was in tension on the loom? Which yarn has the more kink in it? Which yarn, then, is the warp?

2. *Identification of weave.* Mount each sample on a sheet of paper with the warp running lengthwise of the paper. With the aid of a pin or a pick glass, look at the filling and count the number of warps it goes over and under. Write down the system of shedding used for each row. When does the design repeat? Are there wales in the fabric? Are there floats? Are there ribs? Is the design like the plaiting of a splint basket? What is the name of the weave? Draw a point-paper design to illustrate the weave.

3. *Count of cloth.* Unravel a number of yarns both ways to make wide, frayed edges. If the fabric is of a light color, put it against something black, and vice versa. With the aid of a magnifying glass, or better, a pick glass, count the number of yarns to the 1/4-inch, first one way of the cloth and then the other way. Express the count of the cloth by giving the number of picks and ends to the inch. Does the cloth have good balance? Why? Will the cloth wear well? Why?

4. *Test for durability of the weave.* Grip opposite edges of the cloth tightly. Put your thumbs together and press down hard on the fabric. Does the cloth tear? Does the weave become badly distorted? Is the weave durable?

PROJECTS

1. Construct a cigar-box loom, using the illustration on page 70 as a guide. Use knitting yarns or pieces of string and construct one or more of the three basic weaves.

2. Use strips of paper about one-quarter inch wide. Two colors are preferable—one for warp and one for filling. Interlace these strips of paper to form a paper mat of plain weave. Then make the twill and satin weaves. These mats should be kept in the textile notebook or manual.

GLOSSARY

Balance of cloth—Proportion of warp yarns to filling yarns.

Balance of count—Number of warps and fillings to the inch are nearly the same.

Basket weave—Variation of the plain weave in which two or more filling yarns are passed alternately over and under two or more warp yarns.

Battening—Pushing each filling (or pick) against the previous filling. See *Reed.*

Cloth beam—See *Merchandise beam.*

Count of cloth—Number of picks and ends to the square inch.

Drill—A strong cotton fabric in an uneven twill weave.

Even twill—Filling passes over the same number of warps it passes under.

Filling—Crosswise yarn in woven cloth.

Float—In a satin weave, the number of fillings a warp skips over before interlacement. In a sateen weave, the number of warps a filling skips over before interlacement.

Frame—See *Harness.*

Harness—The frame holding warp yarns, which are threaded through the eyes of its heddles. See *Heddles.*

Heddles—Series of wires held by the frame or harness. Each wire has an eye like that of a needle through which a warp yarn is threaded. Heddles are raised to form the *shed.* See *Shedding.*

Herringbone weave—Variation of the twill in which the wale runs in one direction for a few rows and then reverses.

Letting off—Releasing warp yarns from the warp beam as the weaving operation proceeds.

Linen tester—See *Pick glass.*

Loom—A machine for weaving cloth. It is operated either by hand or by machine.

Merchandise beam—Cylinder in the loom on which finished cloth is wound (taken up). It is synonymous with *cloth beam.*

Pick—See *Filling.*

Pick glass—A magnifying glass for counting cloth, also called a *linen tester* or *pick counter.*

Picking—Carrying the filling through the shed.

Plain weave—Each filling yarn passes successively over and under each warp yarn, alternating each row. A synonym is *tabby weave.*

Point-paper design—Squared paper pattern to represent a certain weave.

Reed—This frame, located directly in front of the harnesses, swings forward to batten the last filling inserted against previous fillings. See *Battening.*

Rib weave—A variation of the plain weave made by using fillings heavier than the warps or vice versa.

Sateen weave—Characterized by floats running fillingwise. See *Float.*

Satin weave—Characterized by a smooth surface caused by floats running warpwise.

Selvage—See Glossary, Chaper 2.

Shedding—The raising and lowering of the warp ends by means of the harness and heddles to form the shed (passage) for the filling yarn to pass through from one side of the loom to the other.

Shuttleless loom—A machine that carries the filling yarns through the shed by the use of air or water jets and grippers.

Structural design—A woven-in design, as opposed to one printed on a fabric.

Tabby weave—See *Plain weave.*

Taking up—Winding up finished cloth on the merchandise beam as weaving proceeds.

Twill weave—Filling yarns are interlaced with the warps in such a way that diagonal ridges are formed in the fabric.

Uneven twill weave.—The filling passes under more yarns than it passes over.

Wales—Diagonal ridges characteristic of the twill weave.

Warp beam—Cylindrical spool at the back of the loom on which warp yarns are wound.

Weaving—A process of making cloth by interlacing two sets of yarns at right angles.

Weft—See *Filling.*

Fancy Weaves:
Pile, Jacquard, Dobby,
and Leno

5

Luxurious velvets with downlike textures, elaborate brocades with intricate woven-in designs, small geometrical patterns, and cobwebby lace effects are quite impossible to make on the plain harness loom described in Chapter 4. These fancy effects call for either special looms or attachments for the regular harness loom; the actual weaving is usually slower than standard weaving; and the price of these elaborate effects is higher than that of the plain weaves. Nevertheless, these fabrics are in demand; they are attractive and often high style.

PILE WEAVE

Cloths with soft, downy textures are velvets, velours, and plushes. All three of these fabrics are made in pile weave. The right side of these cloths consists of soft, clipped yarns, called *pile*. The wrong side of the fabric is smooth, with no pile and with the weave showing distinctly.

Pile weave is not an entirely new construction, for it uses the plain or twill weave as its base. The back of the fabric indicates the basic weave. But the soft pile made from extra yarns is the novelty. There are five methods of making pile. These are discussed in the following pages.

THE WIRE METHOD

Good-quality velvets, plushes, and Wilton and Axminster rugs are made with extra warp to form the pile. One set of warps interlaces with the filling to form the plain- or twill-weave ground of the fabric; the other set of warps forms the pile. When a row of pile is made, the warp yarns to form the pile are first raised by the harness to form the shed. Then a wire is inserted through the shed, much as filling yarn is shot through. The size of this wire is determined by the size of the pile to be made. When the set of warps to form the pile is lowered, it loops over the wire and is held in place by the next filling. The wire is then withdrawn. As this is done, a small, sharp knife attached to the end of the wire cuts the pile warp loops. The ground is then woven for a certain number of picks; then the wire is again inserted to form the pile. If the pile has not been cut evenly by the wires, the fabric is sheared again with a device like a lawn mower.

Sometimes the pile is left uncut: a wire with no knife is used, or a number of filling threads are substituted for the wire and are then withdrawn. Frieze used for upholstery is usually made with uncut loops.

FIGURE 5.1.   A carpet in a pile weave by the wire method (uncut pile).

THE TERRY-WEAVE METHOD

A less expensive method of pile weaving omits the wire. Groups of warps are held in tension for the groundwork of the fabric. The warps that form the pile have their tension released at intervals and are thus shoved forward. The tension is restored, and the battening up of the filling causes these warps to appear in loops. The easiest way to make this construction is to use four harnesses, two for the slack pile warps and two for the tight ground warps. On the first shed, pile warps are raised; two fillings are shot through this shed, but are not battened by the reed. The pile warps are lowered, and a third filling is shot through to interlace with the ground warps. Then all three fillings are battened back. Because the tension on the pile warps is loose when the fillings are battened, the pile warps appear in loops. This is known as a three-pick terry cloth because two picks go under the looped pile and one pick goes between two rows of pile. Figure 5.2 shows the ground of terry with pile removed. The ground weave of the fabric is a variation of either plain or twill. The pile is usually on both sides of the fabric (pile yarns alternate in forming loops on the face and the back of the cloth). However, the pile may be made to form stripes or designs. Turkish towels are woven in this manner. Instead of "pile weave," use the name "*terry* weave" when referring to turkish toweling. Terry cloth used for bathrobes is made in this construction. Loops are uncut in terry cloth and in turkish toweling. The loops make the surface absorbent. Terry facecloths, beach robes, and bath mats are also made in this manner.

FIGURE 5.2. The three thread system in a Martex terry towel. (Photograph courtesy of Wellington Sears Co., Inc.)

THE FILLING PILE METHOD

In both the wire and terry methods of making pile, extra warp yarns form the pile. To make corduroy, velveteen, and some plushes, extra fillings are floated over four or five warps. (See Figure 5.3.) The floats are cut after weaving, and then the cut ends are brushed up to form the pile. These floats require precision cutting in the center of the float by a special device equipped with knives. In corduroy, characterized by a pile stripe or wale alternating with a plain wale (no pile), a separate cutting knife is necessary for cutting the floats of each wale. If there are 5 wales to the inch in a wide-wale corduroy 40 inches wide, then 20 cutting knives would be required. A wide-wale cloth can have all the wales cut in one operation. Very narrow wale, called *pinwale*, would have 16 to 23 wales to the inch. Pinwales are fed through the cutting machine twice. Velveteen and filling plush have an all-over pile construction. The grounds of all these fabrics are either plain or twill weaves—the twill is the stronger. Hence a twill-back velveteen is more durable than a plain back. Another point in

FIGURE 5.3. Left: Grey goods with wire inserted. Right: Finished corduroy. (Courtesy of Crampton-Richmond Company. Photos by Jack Pitkin.)

93

durability is the way the pile is held to the ground. If a pile loop is pulled from the fabric, its shape will be a *V* or a *W*. A *V* reveals that the pile filling has interlaced with only one warp yarn, whereas a *W* reveals an interlacement with three warps. *W* is more durable because it is held to the ground by three warps instead of one.

THE DOUBLE-WEAVE AND BACKED-CLOTH METHOD

Many average grade millinery and transparent velvets are woven double; that is, two cloths are woven at the same time, face to face. Two sets of warps and two sets of fillings are used, and an extra set of warps binds the two cloths together. Either the plain, rib, twill, or satin weave may be used as the ground. The effect is not unlike a sandwich, with the extra set of binding warps corresponding to the jam inside. When the cloth is woven, a knife in the loom cuts the binding yarns, making two separate fabrics with sheared pile surfaces. (See Figure 5.4.)

Reversible coating may be woven double but is not cut apart like velvet. This double weave makes a thicker, warmer cloth that can be worn with either side out. Matelassé crepe for women's dresses is also woven double. The tight plain-weave back keeps the heavy blistered crepe on the right side from stretching out of shape.

Similar to the double cloth is the backed cloth. Whereas a true double cloth has two sets of fillings, a backed cloth has two sets of fillings and one set of warps or two sets of warps and one set of fillings. A cotton

FIGURE 5.4. Double cloth. Fabric held open to show fifth yarn joining upper and lower cloths together.

FIGURE 5.5. Backed cloth. Upper cloth is black, lower cloth is white. Since there are only four yarns used, one cloth is part of the other cloth so they cannot be completely separated. Upper left shows amount cloth can be separated. (Photo by Jonas Grushkin.)

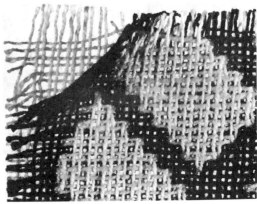

bathrobing in double-weave construction and some blankets use two sets of fillings and one set of warps, and heavy satin reversible ribbons in two colors often use two sets of warps and one set of fillings. Backed cloths cannot be cut apart.

THE RUG METHOD

Hooking, tufting, tying, chenille, and buried pile are ways of making pile for rugs and carpets. These methods will be discussed in Chapter 20.

PILE FABRICS OF FUR FIBERS AND MAN-MADE FIBERS

Real fur, fur blended with rayon or cotton, nylon, acrylic, or modacrylic imitation fur may be used as pile. The back may be the same fiber content as the pile or a different fiber content. According to the TFPIA, the fiber content of pile fabrics, excluding rugs, must be labeled in percentages of fibers as they appear in the product by weight. Or, if desired, pile may be stated separately, and the ratio between the pile and the back or base must be stated. (See Chapter 1 for the identification of fur fibers under the TFPIA.) Some pile fabrics are woven as double cloth and are cut apart like velvet; others are made by the filling pile or terry methods, and still others are knitted. (See Chapter 20 for the labeling of pile rugs and carpets.) In the finishing process the pile can be printed to resemble leopard, for instance; or it can be processed to look like broadtail or ermine; or it can be sheared to resemble other furs. Sometimes the pile is curled to resemble Persian lamb. But the TFPIA has specified that textile fiber products may not employ any name directly or indirectly of fur-bearing animals, such as mink, mutation, and broadtail. (See Chapter 1 for other points on labeling of fabrics made of fur fibers.)

IDENTIFICATION OF WARP AND FILLING

In the pile construction, extra sets of warps or fillings make the pile. Velvets made of silk or synthetic fibers have extra warps forming the pile. To identify warp and filling, fold the fabrics first one way and then the other. The direction that shows distinct rows of pile is the filling direction. To check for accuracy, a yarn can be unraveled in each direction. One yarn looks like a caterpillar because the pile is clinging to it. Since extra warps make the pile in the fabrics mentioned, the *filling* yarn holds the pile and resembles the caterpillar. The pile does not adhere to the warp yarns. In cotton velvet, velveteen, and in some plushes, extra fillings make the pile. When yarns are unraveled both ways, one yarn holds the pile; this caterpillar-like yarn is the *warp*. The filling yarn will be smooth. Folding the fabrics shows distinct rows of pile lengthwise because extra fillings form the pile. No folding is required to identify the warp of corduroy. The wales run warpwise.

In terry weave with uncut pile, the best way to identify the warp is to pull a loop. Notice the direction from which it pulls. Since extra warps form the loop pile, the direction from which the loop pulls is the warp. A selvage always eliminates any complicated methods of identifying warp and filling.

96
*Fabric
Construction
and
Buying
Motives*

GUIDES TO THE BUYER OF PILE FABRICS

If pile construction is used for silk, man-made fibers, or fur, these textiles are presented to the consumer in their richest, most luxurious textures. Pile fabrics feel soft and downy. Silk pile takes a rich, deep color, especially when one looks directly into the pile. If the pile is pressed down, the fabric takes on a silvery, satin cast.

Pile fabrics are warm and hence are best used for fall and winter wear. Transparent velvet with a long rayon pile and a loosely woven rayon back is not so warm as a fabric with a short pile and a tightly woven back. An all-silk velvet is warmer than a silk with a cotton back or rayon pile.

Pile fabrics are becoming to young and old. A downy pile texture softens the face. Some women think they cannot wear velvets because the pile makes them look stout, but if a fabric is made correctly so that the pile creates shadows of depth, the silhouette becomes indistinct, and the illusion of slenderness is achieved. Very short pile makes a woman look more slender than does long pile. Seams in the garment are made inconspicuous by the pile covering.

For velvet dresses, dressmakers usually cut the fabric so that the pile runs up. The wearer then can appreciate the richness of the fabric by looking into the pile. Another reason for having the pile run up is that the pile is less likely to mat from friction. Velvet is suitable for afternoon and evening wear. It drapes well, especially when it is all silk, and looks effective in both tailored and feminine lines. Cotton velvet is stiffer and seems more bulky when made into dresses. Velvets and corduroys can be made spot-resistant and of durable press. Corduroys are frequently made water-repellent for raincoats. And there are some washable velvets.

In upholstery, pile fabrics look soft, cushiony, and inviting. Pile upholstery is warm-looking in summer, and so may be covered with lighter fabric covers.

THE CARE OF PILE FABRICS

Upholstery pile fabrics should be brushed frequently. If the pile is made of wool or mohair, a brushing first against the pile and then with the pile will usually remove matted spots.

It is best to steam velvets and velveteens to remove creases and matted spots. A good way is to hang the fabric near the shower bath. Very hot water, hot enough to make steam, should be run from the shower for about ten minutes, but at no time should the fabric be allowed to get wet. When it is removed from the steam, it should be shaken gently and hung over a line (with the pile out) or on a hanger to dry. A garment should not be worn until the pile is thoroughly dry. Water spots can usually be removed by steaming, but other stains can best be removed by a reliable dry cleaner. Transparent velvet has rayon pile, and although it can be steamed in the same way as silk velvet, care should be taken not to shake it while it is wet. Two kinds of finishes are used on cotton and rayon velvets, namely, spot- and stain-resistant, and crush-resistant. No problems are evidenced on the former type of finish; the latter may reflect light differently when pile is distorted. A steam brushing may cause the pile to resume its original erect position.

Velvets and velveteens may be steamed by still another method. Stand a hot iron upright on the ironing stand; place a damp cotton cloth over the iron to generate steam; pass the velvet slowly over the damp cloth, with the pile away from the cloth. Velvets should never be ironed flat.

The terry weave generally appears in towels, bath mats, and bathrobes. The fibers are usually cotton. Since the pile is uncut cotton yarn, the fabric washes well and should be fluffed not ironed. The more loops on the surface of the fabric, the more absorbent the cloth. Bath mats may have rayon pile and cotton groundwork. While these fabrics are most attractive, their laundering quality and durability are questionable.

Friezé, a upholstery and drapery fabric, may be made in wool, in mohair, and in cotton. It is a very durable, uncut-pile fabric that dry-cleans satisfactorily, but, since the dirt settles between rows of pile, frequent brushings are essential.

FACTORS DETERMINING THE WEARING QUALITY OF PILE FABRICS

The lashing of the pile to the back of velvets, fabrics of fur fibers, and plushes is an important factor in determining wearing quality. As has been stated, some pile yarns are passed around only one background yarn before showing a cut end again on the surface. One interlacing of the pile is not secure; the V-shaped pile pulls out easily. If the pile yarns are woven over and under three yarns before they reappear on the surface, the resulting W-shaped pile will not pull out so easily. When pile pulls out, bare spots appear on the fabric. No one wants a bald velvet. If the fabric is a tight weave and the pile is close, the cloth is likely to wear better than a loosely constructed one.

Several factors must be considered in judging the wearing quality of a terry cloth: (1) Are the loops firmly held so that they will not pull out in laundering? (2) Will the ground warp yarns stand the strain of hard wear? (3) Will the selvage pull out? The first factor depends on the number of fillings used to interlace with the warp for every horizontal row of loops. If only one filling yarn interlaces with the warp for every horizontal row of looped pile, the cloth is termed *1-pick*. The construction is not durable, because one filling or pick is not enough to keep the pile warps from pulling out. A 3-pick cloth is an average quality. Better grades may be 4-, 5-, or 6-pick.

The weakness in ground warp is overcome if ply yarns or more ground warps and fewer pile warps are used. Although the resultant fabrics may have decreased absorptive qualities, their durability is increased.

Selvages often fray because the fillings or binding threads are loosely twisted and weak, or because only a few of the fillings come all the way to the edge and bind the outer warps. In some inexpensive towels fake selvages may be found; two towels are woven together (side by side on a loom) and then cut apart. The cut edge, which is not bound, frays at the first use.

CLOTHS MADE IN PILE WEAVES

Fabrics that can be made in pile weave are shown in Table 5-1. "Man-made fibers and blends with natural and man-made fibers."

TABLE 5-1.

Cotton	Rayon	Silk	Wool	Man-made fibers and blends with natural and man-made fibers
velveteen	transparent	plush	velour	plush
velour	velvet	velvet	frieze	velvet
terry cloth	chenille	velour	corduroy	chenille
frieze	Lyons-type	chenille	plush	velour
corduroy	velvet		tuffed rugs	rugs
chenille	crush-resistant		Wilton rugs	frieze
plush	pile face		Axminster rugs	
rugs			oriental rugs	

JACQUARD WEAVE

Up to this point no explanation has been made of how beautiful floral designs or elaborate figures are woven into a cloth. How are shamrocks woven into linen tablecloths? What makes the basket of flowers in the upholstery damask? How is the wide border with the sailboat made in the turkish towel? There are two methods of making all-over figured weaves: the *Jacquard* and the *dobby*.

The most elaborate designs are woven on an intricately constructed loom called the Jacquard loom, and the weave of these fabrics is called the Jacquard weave. (See Figure 5.6.) The loom was invented by a Frenchman, Joseph Marie Jacquard, in 1801. Elaborate designs could not be made on the regular harness loom that makes the plain, satin, and twill weaves, because intricate designs require many variations in shedding. So it was necessary to find a means of controlling not a series of warps but individual warps. The Jacquard loom supplied the need.

This loom is very expensive and requires a room with a fairly high ceiling to house it. Several weeks to three months are needed to prepare the loom for making a new complicated pattern, and the weaving operation is comparatively slow. Many, however, consider Jacquard-woven cloths the most beautiful and most interesting of all. The price is correspondingly high. Since the Jacquard loom is extremely complicated, and a detailed explanation would be too lengthy, only an outline of its workings will be given.

The design for the cloth is worked out in point-paper pattern first. Instead of harnesses, a series of oblong punched cards not unlike a large punched I.B.M. card controls the raising of the warps. As many cards are made as there are picks in the design. In other words, if there are 4,000 picks or fillings to be shot across before the same design is repeated, 4,000 cards must be made, which involves much labor and expense.[1] The cards are laced together in proper order and are rotated over an oblong cylinder on the upper part of the loom. From a frame hang long cords that hold fine steel wires, each with an eye through which a warp yarn is threaded. If the cloth is to have 4,500 warps, there will be 4,500 of these wires, one to control or lift each warp. It is quite evident that a great deal of effort and work are required to thread 4,500 warps through the eyes.

[1] Compare with Jacquard-weave patterns for shuttleless looms, Chapter 4.

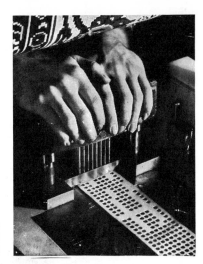

FIGURE 5.6. a. Punching the cards for a Jacquard pattern. b. A Jacquard loom. (Photographs courtesy of Bigelow-Sanford Carpet Co., Inc.)

At the top of the loom each of these many cords is attached to a horizontal wire called a needle. These needles press forward against a card. The needles that go through the punched holes in the card pull on the cords that raise the warps to form the shed. The shuttle shoots through. The card just used is automatically passed on by a partial turn of the needles. Again and again the principle of shedding is carried out until all the cards have been used once. The pattern is then repeated.

100
*Fabric
Construction
and
Buying
Motives*

In view of the skill required to make the cards, the labor and time required to set up the loom, and the slow action of the loom, it is small wonder that Jacquard weaves are expensive. Even though the use of the same cards again and again helps to decrease the price, the weaving is accomplished very slowly. To save expense, when one cloth is completed, new warps are tied to the old ones and pulled through the loom, and another cloth is begun. Jacquard attachments are used on many types of looms and knitting machines.

The Jacquard weave is really a combination weave; two or more of the basic weaves are combined in the same cloth. For example, in table damask the design may be a sateen weave with filling floats, and the background may be a satin weave with warp floats. (For the difference between single and double damask, see Chapter 19.) The sheen in the design runs in the opposite direction from that in the background, with

FIGURE 5.7. Pattern for a Jacquard weave.

FIGURE 5.8. A traditional damask in Jacquard weave with 100 percent Enka nylon warp. (Photograph courtesy of American Enka Corporation.)

the result that the design stands out clearly. Different colored yarns for warps and fillings make an even sharper contrast.

In a brocade the background may be a warp satin and the design may be a fine twill or plain rib. Rayon and cotton damask draperies are made with mercerized cotton in the design and rayon in the background. In borders of turkish towels the design may be in pile weave and the background in plain or basket weave.

COMPUTER-AIDED CONTROL IN JACQUARD WEAVING
The speed of controlling Jacquard woven designs can be aided by the computer. Since it takes a long time to produce a point-paper design (some 200 hours for one design), the computer can scan the pattern very rapidly and, by means of an electronic unit, convert the warp and filling paths (the overs and unders) into a binary number form that can be "read" by the computer. A point-paper design is thrown on a television screen. At this point, the designer can change the pattern by drawing on the screen with a light sonic pen. Hence, the pattern is a row-by-row representation of the design. This information is used to control the mechanism in textile patterning machinery.

While direct control of the machinery by computer may prove too expensive, automation shortens the lead time between the design concept and the production of a sample. Fast sampling may be economical because styling approval can be given quickly. More than one version of a design can be made so there is more opportunity for experimentation in the designing process. Manual card cutting will be eliminated, for sampling as well as for large-scale production, because the computer can employ punched paper tape that is standard for computer usage. Consequently, no special personnel need be trained and paid competitive wages for Jacquard card cutting. The magnetic tape required for making the final design can be stored in the computer for future use. Hence, in the computer-aided system, the information remains in the computer and can be used to control the design directly. (For *computer control in knitting,* see Chapter 6, p. 119.)

IDENTIFICATION OF WARP AND FILLING IN JACQUARD WEAVE

If a combination of satin and sateen weaves is used, the warp usually floats in the background and the filling floats in the design when observed from the right side of the cloth. In fact, the warp is most easily distinguished if the background is observed first. If the background is plain or twill weave, the principles of identifying warp and filling in these constructions should be applied. (See Chapter 4.)

FACTORS GOVERNING THE DESIRABILITY OF JACQUARD WEAVE

As the satin construction appears frequently in either the background or the design of a Jacquard weave, the length of the float affects the wearing quality of the fabric. This principle is especially true in table damasks, which have to stand much friction and laundering. If long floats are used the fabric shows a higher sheen, but durability is decreased. Cotton used

102
*Fabric
Construction
and
Buying
Motives*

in long floats is apt to lint as a result of friction. A loose weave in Jacquard construction is a great deal weaker than a tight, close weave. In selecting a cloth with a Jacquard weave, the purpose for which the fabric is intended and the kind of wear expected should be carefully considered.

CLOTHS MADE IN JACQUARD WEAVE

Jacquard cloths listed in Table 5-2 may be made in natural and/or man-made fibers.

TABLE 5-2.

Cotton	Linen	Rayon	Silk	Wool
damask terry cloth (with Jacquard designs or borders) tapestry	damask borders of huck towels	damask brocade lamé	damask brocade tapestry lamé	damask tapestry

DOBBY WEAVE

Small designs can be made inexpensively by the *dobby* attachment that is put on the plain harness loom. The dobby is an English invention. A chain of narrow strips of wood with pegs inserted in each indicates the pattern. These strips take the place of the cards of the Jacquard loom. Each strip of wood represents a pick in the design. The pegs raise the harness to form a shed. A second chain controls the shuttle. The dobby attachment may control as many as 32 harnesses, whereas the plain harness loom can control 19 to 25 harnesses.

An American invention called the *head-motion attachment*, which is also connected to the plain harness loom, performs an operation similar to that performed by the dobby.

Simple, small geometrical figures in which the repeat in design appears often (every 16 rows, possibly) can be satisfactorily made by these two devices. Since a woven-in design of this character was originally made only by the dobby attachment, the construction of these designs is still called dobby weave, even when the head-motion attachment rather than the dobby is used. Figure 5.9 shows a point-paper design for the dobby weave.

FIGURE 5.9. Point paper pattern for a dobby weave.

BIRD'S-EYE

Used for diapers, this is made in dobby weave, and is characterized by small diamond-shaped figures with dots in the center. Small figures in the stripe of men's woven madras shirting are usually of dobby weave, as are also small, woven-in patterns in men's ties. Nail-head or bird's-eye sharkskin men's suiting is made in dobby weave.

HUCKABACK, OR HUCK TOWELING

This is made of slack-twisted cotton or linen yarns (dobby weave) in small geometrical designs. (See Figure 5.10.) It is absorbent, slightly rough cloth used mostly for face towels, although bird's-eye piqué and waffle cloth are made in a similar manner. The durability of huckaback depends on the balance of the count and the tensile strength of warp and filling; the closer the weave, the more durable the fabric. The dobby-weave design, when used for huckaback toweling, is sometimes called the honeycomb weave.

LENO WEAVE

Lacelike effects, such as are found in marquisette curtains, dishcloths, and some thermal blankets, are made by a *leno* attachment; consequently, the weave is called the *leno weave.* Leno weave comes in both curtain-weight and dress-weight fabrics, many of which are lace-like and diaphanous. In weaving, adjacent warp yarns are twisted around each other, usually in pairs. Both warps may be twisted like a figure eight, or one may be held in tension and the other twisted about it. The filling passes through the twisted warps. If one warp is in tension, and one warp twists, the weave may be called gauze. Surgical gauze is plain weave, however.

Sometimes the leno weave is combined with the plain or basket weaves to produce a lacy mesh called lace cloth. Again, a fabric of plain weave may have stripes of leno weave.

Mosquito netting uses the leno construction. The fabric is made of loosely twisted yarns, and the weave is coarse compared with marquisette. After the fabric is woven, it is heavily starched to prevent dirt from sticking to it. Heavy warps and heavy fillings may be inserted at intervals to add strength.

Considering their open construction, cloths of leno weave are durable. The figure-eight twist of the warp not only adds strength to that set of

FIGURE 5.10. Huck toweling, a fabric in dobby weave.
(Photo by Jack Pitkin.)

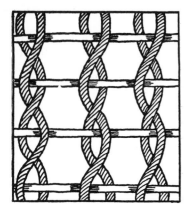

FIGURE 5.11. Leno weave.

FIGURE 5.12. Figured marquisette, a fabric in leno weave.

yarns, but also prevents the filling from slipping. This weave is found in cotton or in rayon and cotton mixtures in which cotton is used for the warp and rayon for the filling. Leno is also used in nylon, acrylic, polyester, or glass-fibered curtain marquisette. This weave is not an expensive one. Lenos are extensively used in coarse yarn drapery casement fabric, most recently with fire-retardant yarns or finishes.

ORNA-MENTAL EMBROID-ERED EFFECTS Patterns similar to embroiderv can be woven into cloth at the time the groundwork is woven. The difference between these patterns and Jacquard or dobby patterns is that embroidered effects can be pulled out by hand without injury to the rest of the cloth. Dobby or Jacquard patterns are such an integral part of the whole fabric that they cannot be removed. There are four types of these embroidery-like patterns.

CLIPPED-SPOT DESIGN

This is an ornamental woven effect most commonly used on cotton fabrics. An extra filling yarn generally of different size or color from the regular fillings is shot through at regular intervals in the weaving of the cloth. This extra filling is floated at points between the designs. After the cloth is woven, the floated yarns are raised so that the shearing knives may

104

be run over these floats to cut them. The cutting is similar to that in corduroy. A single design consists of several parallel filling yarns. Swivel and clipped spot give the same effect. (See Figure 5.13.)

SWIVEL DESIGN

Extra bobbins called "swivels" carry extra filling yarns several times around a group of warp yarns to give an effect of being tied. The yarn is clipped at the end of a figure. The design, therefore, consists of one thread only. Imported dotted swiss made in Switzerland may be made in this manner. (See Figure 5.13.) Most swivel patterns are woven into cotton fabrics. In this country the clipped-spot and flock-dotted designs have almost replaced swivel.[2] Rayon yarns can be used for swivel designs, but rayon is too slippery to stay in well. To ascertain the wearing quality of a swivel design, pull out a cut end. If the yarn pulls out very easily, the design is not likely to be durable.

LAPPET DESIGN

Still another pattern resembling embroidery is made by the lappet attachment. Needles threaded with yarns for the design are set upright in front of the reed, but the design yarns threaded through them do not pass through the reed. By moving the needles sideways, simple designs are woven over the regular filling yarns. A true lappet design thread is often carried in a zigzag line and is woven without being clipped. (See Figure 5.13.)

The essential difference between a lappet design and a swivel is that in the swivel the design is done with extra *filling* yarns, which are cut off short at the end of each design. The lappet pattern appears only on the right side of the fabric, since the floats forming the pattern are fastened to the ground fabric only at their extremities. Lappet designs are made of one continuous yarn and are not clipped.

[2] See the Glossary.

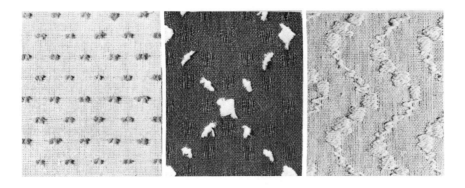

FIGURE 5.13. Left: Clip spot (wrong side). Center: Swivel (wrong side). Right: Lappet (right side). (Courtesy of Stoffel & Co. Photos by Jack Pitkin.)

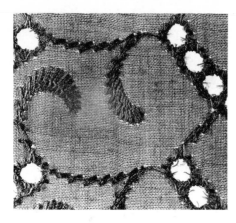

FIGURE 5.14. Eyelet embroidery done by the Schiffli machine. (Photo by Jonas Grushkin.)

Lappet, swivel, and clipped spot are all woven fabrics; none is embroidered, although the effect is that of machine embroidery.

SCHIFFLI EMBROIDERY

Intricate machine embroidery on fabrics such as batiste, lawn, organdy, and piqué is generally done by the Swiss-patented Schiffli machine. The embroidery yarn may run in any direction, not just fillingwise as in clipped spot or zigzag as in lappet. Eyelets may be embroidered by the Schiffli machine. (See Chapter 17.)

GUIDES TO PROPER SELECTION OF WEAVES

A consumer should have a few general principes in mind when selecting a woven fabric. The purpose for which the fabric is to be used is very important. Some weaves are made for strength and durability; others are made for beauty, richness of texture, and design. In the former category are the plain and twill weaves; in the latter, satin, Jacquard, dobby, pile, and leno. To be sure, there are gradations of strength and durability in each classification. For example, a poorly balanced count in plain weave will not wear so well as a good balance. A rib weave may have ribs that are so large as to be out of proportion to other yarns in the fabric and consequently may cut the finer yarns. In pile weave, if the pile is lashed under only one background yarn, it will pull out more easily than pile woven over and under three background yarns. If a fabric is suited to the purpose for which it is intended, it will give good service.

The consumer should determine the durability of the weave. Several factors influencing durability must be considered. First, the warp and filling yarns should be spaced evenly. Second, the weave should be straight, to insure both strength and good appearance. Third, there should be no broken yarns or other defects in the weave. Fourth, the weave should be close, both to produce strength and to minimize shrinkage. Fifth and last, the selvages should be strong.

Do the style, novelty, beauty, and appearance of the fabric govern the price? Does the intricacy or elaborateness of the construction of the cloth govern the price? Are age and hand workmanship the chief factors? Do the raw materials and the weaving justify the price asked? The consumer should answer these questions for herself and then come to a decision.

SUMMARY Elaborate weaves, such as pile, Jacquard, dobby, and leno, should be purchased not so much for their wearing quality as for their beauty and appearance. The pile weave in velvets and in fabrics made to resemble fur has a richness of texture and a depth of coloring not found in other constructions. Terry weaves in turkish towels have soft, absorbent surfaces and may have beautiful Jacquard borders. Leno weaves are purchased for their lacy, porous effects. In dress fabrics this weave is sheer and dainty. Jacquards are characterized by elaborate and intricate designs of remarkable beauty. Their price is correspondingly high. Dobby weaving makes simple geometric figures inexpensively. Embroidered effects produced by the lappet, clipped spot, and schiffli methods add to cloths interesting designs that are not integral parts of their construction.

REVIEW QUESTIONS

1. (*a*) Outline four methods of making pile weave.
   (*b*) Name a cloth that is woven by each method.
2. How is the durability of pile weave determined (*a*) in fur-like fabrics? (*b*) in terry cloth?
3. (*a*) How matted pile in a velvet dress be restored to its original condition?
   (*b*) What instructions should the salesperson give a customer for cleaning and caring for pile fabrics used as upholstery?
4. (*a*) By what methods can fabrics be made to resemble fur?
   (*b*) Explain briefly the law for labeling and advertising such fabrics.
5. (*a*) Explain the action of the Jacquard loom.
   (*b*) How may the Jacquard loom be controlled by a computer?
   (*c*) Give the advantages of computer control.
6. How can the consumer tell whether the fabric is made on a Jacquard or a dobby loom?
7. What advantages has dobby weaving over Jacquard weaving? Explain fully.
8. What factors determine the wearing quality of a Jacquard weave?
9. (*a*) Explain the construction of the weave found in marquisette.
   (*b*) What are the purposes of this weave?
   (*c*) Is this weave usually durable? Why?
   (*d*) For what fabrics is this construction used?
10. (*a*) Describe a method of weaving the dots in dotted swiss.
    (*b*) How can the durability of these dots be determined?
11. (*a*) What is the difference between swivel and clipped-spot designs?
    (*b*) Which weave is the more economical in the use of embroidery yarn?
    (*c*) How can one tell the difference between swivel, lappet, schiffli, Jacquard, and dobby patterns?
12. What factors determine the durability of any weave?
13. Define 3-pick terry weave, ground warp, fake selvage, double-cloth weave, pile, velveteen, Jacquard cards, long float, huckaback, pile warp.

EXPERIMENTS

1. *Identifying fancy weaves.* Feel each fabric and look at it closely. Does the fabric have pile? Does it have a woven-in design? If so, is it small, or large and intricate? Is the design an integral part of the cloth or can it be pulled out without injury to the fabric? Is the construction open and lacelike?
   (*a*) What is the name of each weave?
   (*b*) Which yarns are warp?
2. *Determining the wearing quality of fancy weaves.*
   Tearing test. Tear a sample of material. If the fabric tears easily, the cloth will not wear well.

108

*Fabric
Construction
and
Buying
Motives*

Seam test. Make a seam by pinning two edges of material together. Grip the fabric on either side of the seam. Pull the fabric. Does it show elasticity or does it split immediately? If the fabric splits easily, it will not wear well.

Pulling test. Grip the fabric at opposite edges; then pull slowly and evenly. Note how much strength it takes to split the fabric. Then pull the cloth with quick jerks. The fabric that will best stand quick, jerky pulling is the strongest.

GLOSSARY

Backed cloth—A variety of double cloth that has two sets of fillings and one set of warps or two sets of warps and one set of fillings. See *Double weave.*

Clipped-spot design—Ornamental woven effect in which extra filling yarn is shot through at regular intervals in weaving of a cloth. The extra filling yarns are floated and later cut between designs. One design consists of several clipped parallel filling yarns.

Corduroy—A pile fabric identified by warpwise pile wales alternating with plain wales. See *Filling pile method.*

Dobby weave—A type of construction in which small geometrical figures are woven into the cloth.

Double weave—Two cloths are woven at the same time, face to face. Two sets of warps and two sets of fillings are used. One set of warps binds the two cloths together. The two cloths may or may not be cut apart. See *Backed cloth.*

Filling pile method—Extra fillings are floated over four or five warps. The floats are cut after weaving and then the cut ends are brushed up to form the pile. See *Corduroy.*

Flock-dotted—Designs of short fibrous materials printed in or onto the fabric with the aid of an adhesive. Electrostatic and lacquered applications of designs are two methods used. The former is durable in washing and drycleaning; the latter may be nondurable.

Fur-fiber fabrics—Cloths woven of hair or fur fiber intended to resemble fur. In order for a manufacturer to use this term, the T.F.P.I.A. states that the fiber content of a fabric must be hair, fur fibers, or any mixtures of animals (other than wool-producing animals) in excess of 5 percent of the total fiber weight of the textile fiber product. No direct or indirect reference to the animals' names is permitted.

Jacquard cards—Oblong punched cards used to control the raising of warp yarns in a Jacquard loom.

Jacquard weave—A construction characterized by very intricate woven-in designs. A special Jacquard loom makes these designs by controlling each warp yarn.

Lappet—An ornamental embroidery effect woven into a cloth by a series of needles. The design, often in zigzag effect, is not clipped.

Leno weave—A lacelike construction made by twisting adjacent warps around each other like a figure eight. The fillipasses through the twisted warps.

Pile—The cut or uncut loops composing the surface of a pile fabric.

Pile weave—A construction characterized by soft, looped yarns called *pile.* Pile may be on one or both sides and may be cut or uncut.

Pinwale—Pertaining to a cotton corduroy with very narrow wales (16 to 23 wales to the inch). See *Wale.*

Schiffli—Machine embroidery. The embroidery yarn is carried by a boat-shaped shuttle that can move in all directions to make intricate designs.

Swivel—Ornamental design woven in by extra filling yarns. Each design consists of one thread only, covering only the distance of one figure.

Terry cloth—Absorbent fabric made with uncut pile loops. See *terry-weave method* in the text.

Three-pick terry cloth—Two picks (fillings) go under the looped pile and one pick goes between two rows of pile.

Velvet—Pile fabrics made of silk or man-made fibers in which extra warps usually form the pile by the wire method. The double-weave method may be used for average-grade transparent velvet.

Velveteen—A cotton pile fabric usually made by the filling pile method and characterized by a plain weave or twill back.

Velour—A cut pile fabric. Term is applied to cloths with a fine raised finish; to a cotton cut pile fabric with thicker pile than cotton velvet; to a woolen; and to knitted goods with the feeling of woven velour.

Knitting
and
Other Constructions

6

"That which is or may be woven" is a definition of the noun "textile" in one standard dictionary. This definition is correct as far as it goes, but who would say that the fabrics used in the making of a knitted sweater, a nylon hairnet, a felt hat, or a braided rug are not textile products? Yet none of these articles is woven; instead, they are all made into cloth by other methods, which include knitting, lace-making, felting, and braiding. Bonding and laminating should also be included.

Although weaving is the most usual way to construct cloth, knitting is the second most common method.

**INTRO-
DUCTION
TO
KNITTING**

How are knitted cloths made? For knitted fabrics a continuous yarn or set of yarns is used to form loops. For woven fabrics two sets of yarns are necessary. The knitted cloth is composed of rows of loops, each row caught into the previous row and depending for its support on both the row below and the row above.

Knitted fabrics have invaded the woven market owing to the increase in bonding and laminating processes, the need for a diversity of constructions, and the variety of fibers and finishes available. But knitted goods have grown primarily because of the distinctive properties of knitted materials—their resistance to creasing and mussing; their easy launderability; and their ease in production as compared to woven cloth. Knitted manufacture requires less lead time than woven construction; it can be switched readily from one fabric construction to another; it provides a comparatively speedier way in which design can be incorporated as compared with woven fabrics; and it is more economical as compared to the production of woven cloth.

**HISTORY
OF
KNITTING**

The knitting operation was supposedly invented in Scotland in the fifteenth century. The first stocking firms appeared in Nottinghamshire, England, in 1589. In 1758 the ribbing apparatus was invented by Jedediah Strutt. But it was not until the middle of the nineteenth century that circular machinery produced tubular fabrics. Now the improved circular knitting machines are most common. Some types of hosiery, underwear, and jersey are made in tubular form.

KINDS OF YARNS AND FIBERS

Since an object of knitting is to construct an elastic, porous fabric, the yarns are more loosely twisted than they are for weaving; and since some knitted fabrics must have napped surfaces, slackly twisted yarn is preferable. Yarn types include filament, spun, blended, and textured for man-made fibers.

The knitting industry's consumption of fibers and yarns has changed considerably over the years. Today, the principal raw material of the knitting industry is textured polyester yarn, and it is used primarily in circular-knit (largely double-knot) fabrics and to a somewhat more modest extent in warp-knit (principally tricot) fabrics. For sweaters, the prime raw material is acrylic fiber, followed by wool. In knit sport shirts, the major fibers are cotton and polyester/cotton, with the latter gradually displacing the former because it shrinks less, is stronger, and resists abrasion. Acrylic fibers are also used in this product area, in 100 percent form as well as in blends. In the manufacture of tricot fabrics, the major raw materials are acetate, nylon, rayon, and polyester. Polyester is a newer yarn in that field and is used primarily in textured form in the manufacture of 24-gauge outerwear fabrics for transfer printing.[1] In the construction fabrics (on the Raschel machine to be explained later in the chapter), knitters employ a wide range of raw materials, both spun and filament, with the latter both flat and textured.[2] The cloth manufactured on this machine is called a *Raschel fabric*. A good deal of novelty yarn is converted into cloth on Raschel machines. The chief raw material in the manufacture of fine-gauge women's hosiery is stretch nylon. Spandex is also used, particularly in the manufacture of support stockings and pantyhose, and in the newer, more popular contour top pantyhose. In half-hose and other similar types of casual hosiery, virtually all of the previously mentioned fibers are used, with man-made fibers significantly more important than either cotton or wool.

HAND KNITTING

Hand knitting is a craft in which the knitter may show little or much creative ability. If she follows instructions carefully, she will doubtless turn out an article of a given size, shape, and texture. Should she elect to vary the instructions for choice of yarn, colors, or stitches, she will create a unique and/or artistic item.

Before a novice can make any article for personal or home use, the basic stitches in knitting must be learned.

PLAIN STITCH

Hand knitters call this stitch *plain knitting*. Rows of stitches, or components of the loops, run crosswise of the fabric on both sides. The first row of loops is connected on the right side of the fabric; the second row is connected on the back; the third row is connected on the right side; and so on. These horizontal ridges are called courses. So, in the plain stitch, courses appear on both sides of the fabric. This stitch stretches more lengthwise than crosswise. Consequently it is not suitable for garments such as sweaters, hosiery, and underwear, in which the greater

---

[1] See Chapter 8.
[2] Textured yarn; see Chapter 3.

111

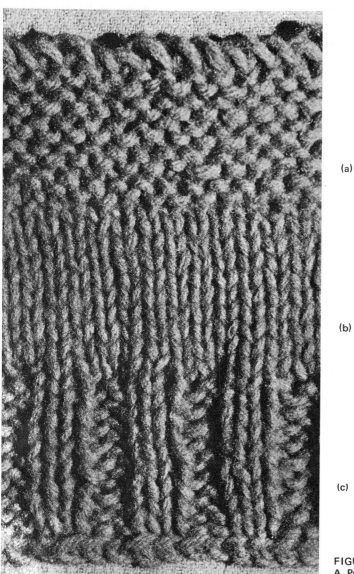

(a)

(b)

(c)

FIGURE 6.1. Hand knitting (right side).
A. Purl stitch or plain knitting; b. Flat
knit or stockinette stitch; c. Rib stitch.

stretch must be crosswise. High fashion sweaters, baby carriage covers, stoles, potholders, and dishcloths can be made with this stitch. (See Figures 6.1 and 6.2.)

STOCKINETTE OR JERSEY STITCH

In hand knitting utilizing the stockinette stitch, instructions call for plain knitting on one row and purling on the next, the steps alternating in this order until the fabric is finished. The stockinette stitch is identified by vertical ridges on the face and horizontal courses on the back. (See Figures 6.1 and 6.2.) Since the stockinette stitch stretches more in width than in

112

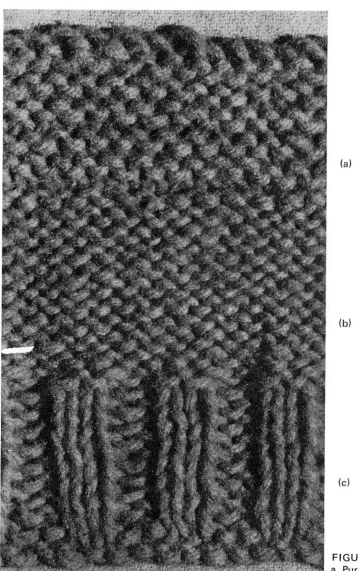

(a)

(b)

(c)

FIGURE 6.2.   Hand knitting (wrong side).
a. Purl stitch or plain knitting; b. Flat
knit or stockinette stitch; c. rib stitch.

length, it is particularly suitable for hosiery, dress fabrics, underwear, sweaters, bathing suits, coats, gloves, caps, and mittens. The stockinette stitch is generally found in tubular goods, but it may be used in flat materials. Where a flat-surfaced fabric with a crosswise stretch is needed, the stockinette stitch is most common. Jersey is a fabric made in this stitch.

RIB STITCH

This is a stitch used often for boys' hosiery, for the ribbed cuffs on sleeves and legs of knitted union suits, and for garter belts on socks. Lengthwise

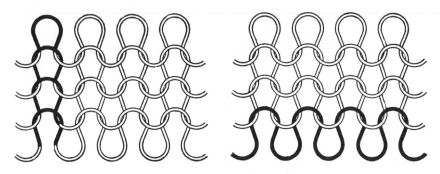

FIGURE 6.3.   Left: A wale in a plain circular knit fabric. Right: A course in a plain circular knit fabric.

FIGURE 6.4.   2 X 2 Rib knit (weft).

wales appear on the right and wrong sides of the fabric. (See Figure 6.3.) The hand-knit stitch is made by knitting two and purling two across the first row and then purling two above the two plain-knitted stitches and knitting above the two purled stitches on the second row. The result is called 2 X 2 rib. Each is two stitches wide, and each valley is two stitches wide.

Although this stitch is slower to make by machinery and requires more yarn than the plain stitch, it has an advantage in that it stretches in the width and generally returns to normal width after stretching.

We have discussed the three basic stitches in hand knitting: plain knitting stitch, stockinette or jersey, and rib stitch. There are many interesting effects possible by varying the basic stitches to produce openwork, tucks, cables, popcorn, and Jacquard patterns (argyle, for example).

MACHINE KNITTING   There are two basic types of machine-knitted cloth, namely weft knitted and warp knitted. The weft-type method forms loops running crosswise on the fabric and links each loop into the one on the preceding row. Hand knitting is done in this way. (The technical name for this type of knitting is weft knitting.) Weft denotes crosswise loopings in knitting.

The second type is called warp knitted. It cannot be done by hand. The machine for this operation is called a warp-knitting machine that produces mostly open width fabrics, but some warp-knitting machines can make tubular cloths. For warp knitting, parallel yarns must first be arranged in two tiers on the machine, with a needle for each warp yarn. Each needle makes a separate chain stitch, and the chains are tied together by the

114

zigzag of the yarns from one needle to the other. The resultant fabric, which has a cobwebby mesh, will not drop stitches, or "ladder," because loops interlock with one another both ways in the fabric.

The difference between these two methods of construction rests not only in the way they are knitted but also in their inherent properties. In general, weft-knit fabrics are heavier than warp-knit fabrics; they are also somewhat more resilient than warp knits. Furthermore, warp-knit fabrics tend to be more stretchy in the length, while weft-knit fabrics tend to have more stretch in the width.

CUT AND GAUGE

Cut denotes the closeness of weft knitting as determined by the number of needles per inch in a weft (circular)-knitting machine. It also refers to the number of needles per inch used in the construction of a weft-knitted (single and double knit) cloth. Compactness or stitch density of a single- or double-knit fabric is described as 18-, 20-, 22-, or 24- cut. The higher the cut number the finer the knitted fabric and vice versa.[3]

Gauge refers to the number of needles per inch or two inches of the needle bed in a warp-knitting machine or the number of needles involved on a one- or two-inch basis in the construction, respectively, of a tricot and a Raschel warp-knit cloth.[4]

Owing to the popularity of warp-knitted fabrics, mills design new constructions to increase the versatility of their products. Warp-knitted fabrics appear in dresswear, outerwear, men's shirts, and women's blouses.

[3] See Count of cloth, Chapter 4.
[4] See Glossary.

FIGURE 6.5. Warp knit. Left: Tricot (often identified as jersey). Right: Raschel (one of several types).

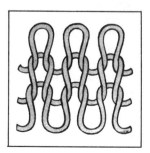
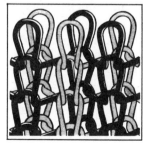

FIGURE 6.6. Weft knit. Left: Single knit (loops on one side of the fabric). Right: Double knit (loops on both sides of the fabric).

116
*Fabric
Construction
and
Buying
Motives*

WEFT-KNIT FABRICS: SINGLE AND DOUBLE KNITS

There are two major categories of weft-knit fabrics: single knits and double knits. Fabrics made on a rotary machine with one set of needles around the cylinder are called *single knits.* Fabrics that are knitted on circular machines with two sets of cylindrically disposed needles, each set placed and operating at the right angle to the other, are designated as *double knits.*

Weft-knitted fabrics are produced in tubular form only when they come off a circular machine, but if they come off a flatbed machine (horizontal bed or V bed) they emerge in open width. Similarly, it is possible on a two-needle bar Raschel machine to produce a circular (tubular), as against an open width, fabric. For example, mesh stockings of several years ago were produced in tubular form on flatbed (double-needle or 2-bar) Raschel machines.

Single knits. A few words of explanation of single-knit jersey apparel fabrics is in order. In the jersey stitch, vertical components of the loops appear on the right side and horizontal components (courses) are seen on the wrong side. See Figures 6.5 and 6.6. The face side of jersey usually has a softer hand than the reverse side. Jersey Jacquard or patterned fabrics can be knitted in two or more colors as can the striped fabrics. Patterns and stripes can vary widely; for example, horizontal and vertical stripes, tartans, checks, Jacquard, eyelet, and printed patterns (design printed *after* knitting). Jersey fleece, velour, and terry fabrics all originate in loops protruding from the surface of the cloth. These loops are subsequently cut and brushed or sheared, with the exception of terry which is left uncut. High-pile knitting is done by (1) sliver knit made by knitting of strands of individual fiber staple, or (2) loop-type made by cutting and whipping up the protruding cut ends to produce pile less deep than the former type. Plating is done by placing one yarn on the face and the other on the reverse side of a cloth. Laying-in is a technique done by placing a heavy or ornamental yarn between the loops of a fabric to make a lay-in cloth. Both plating and laying-in can be done in either a single-knit or double-knit construction.[5]

Double knits. Double-knit apparel fabrics also need explanation. An interlock fabric consists of two narrow ribs interknitted. It is usually plain solid color. Stripes or small designs such as checks can vary this simple structure. Ribs range from narrow (skinny) to broad widths. Non-Jacquard double jersey fabrics appear less rib-like than most double-knit fabrics, and resemble single-knit jersey fabrics. But since non-Jacquard double jersey fabric has the same appearance on both sides, it resembles interlock. Variations of the non-Jacquard double jersey are found in piqué, ottoman rib, Milano rib, and Ponte di Roma. Intermediate Jacquard and rib-Jacquard double jersey fabrics basically resemble in their composition non-Jacquard double jersey fabrics, except they have an

[5] "Facts About Knits: A Cutter's Guide to Basic Fabric Types," National Knitted Outerwear Association.

artistic design in two or more colors rather than a variation in the arrangement of fabric loops to create a stitch effect in self-color. Wide variation in width and depth of the knitted-in design is possible.

In knitting, different types of Jacquard constructions are not distinguished in the same way as in woven Jacquards. Knitters generally differentiate between full Jacquard and intermediate or mini-Jacquard. The former are patterns that are produced via a mechanical or electronic selecting mechanism for more than one complete revolution of the machine. The latter are patterns that are producible to the limit of one machine revolution and through the agency of a manually adjusted selecting means that cannot be changed unless a new pattern is required.

TABLE 6-1

Single Knit	Double Knit
Plain or patterned (Jacquard or striped) will curl at edges unless mechanically or chemically treated. Generally lighter in weight but weight can be reversed. Single-knit fabric categories: Plain or stitch varied fabrics, striped fabrics, jersey, Jacquard or patterned fabrics, raised surface fabrics, plated fabrics, lay-in fabrics, fleece, velour (cut pile loops), terry (uncut loops), high pile, openwork or eyelet.	Plain, patterned, self-colored, or as many as four colors. Will not curl at edges. Generally heavier in weight but weight can be reversed. Double-knit fabric categories: interlock, narrow and broad ribs, non-Jacquard, double jersey, intermediate Jacquard and rib Jacquard double jersey (to be explained).

WARP-KNIT FABRICS
Tricot, Raschel, Simplex, and Milanese

Of major interest in apparel are the four classes of warp knits: Tricot, Raschel, Simplex, and Milanese.

Tricot. The name comes from the French word *tricoter*, meaning to knit. The fabric has many surfaces: brushed, ridged, smooth, patterned, printed. Tricot fabrics are usually designated by the number of sets of warps or lengthwise yarns that are used in their construction. The most common kind of tricot is 2-bar tricot.[6] Two-bar tricot fabrics include tricot jersey, a fabric most widely used in lingerie, intimate apparel, printed outerwear, and the backing of bonded knits. It is also used in satin, sharkskin, tulle, and angel lace. Striped and patterned fabrics are included in this construction. Also produced are 3- and 4-bar tricots. The greater the number of bars used in making the tricot fabric, the more intricate the design.

[6] Bars guide the pattern in its production.

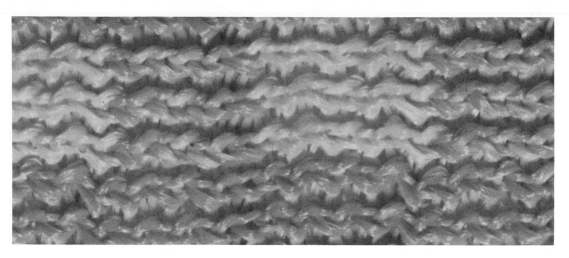

FIGURE 6.7. Three-bar tricot of Arnel/nylon.

Raschel Fabrics. These fabrics derive their name from the Raschel knit machine that produces them. This machine has a single or double alignment, horizontally, of needles of the latch type. The varieties of Raschel fabrics are greater than tricot. They range from wispy netting, lace and curtain fabrics to heavy plush and pile coating, and carpet fabrics. Openwork and crocheted effects come in this class of fabrics. Raschel can be single or double knitted, flat or tubular. A special device called a "chopper bar" can lay in heavier yarns to achieve a decorative surface effect. For men's suiting and trousers, it is possible to knit Raschel fabrics with similar patterns and stability of woven fabrics. Other types of Raschel fabrics include powernet for foundation garments and swimsuits; thermal cloth specially constructed for underwear; lace of weight and complexity of pattern similar to that made on Levers lace machines; netting that ranges in structure from flimsy hairnets to deep sea fishing or camouflage nettings. Lacey patterned net stockings and patterned one piece pantyhose in sheer and mid-sheer weights are possible. In short, Raschel is a most versatile fabric.

Simplex Fabrics. Simplex is a basic type of warp knit not used as extensively as tricot and Raschel in apparel. Actually a simplex fabric is nothing more than a double-knit tricot fabric. Tricot cloth is knitted with one set of spring beard needles on a tricot-type machine with two sets of needles. It looks and feels like weft-knit double jersey and is used for dress fabrics.

Milanese Fabrics. Another type of warp knit that is not too frequently used is Milanese, a name derived from the machine that makes the fabric. Its distinguishing characteristic is its diagonal, argyle-type pattern. Milanese is used as a lightweight dress fabric.

This discussion of weft and warp knits has not been exhaustive by any means. It is sufficient for the consumer and salesperson to have an appreciation of knitted cloths and their structures.

Jacquard knitting machines are now controlled by computers that translate designs into a form that the computer can read or scan, and it can speedily control desired variations in design and colors.

At least seventeen companies have developed ingenious computerized Jacquard pattern preparation systems that translate designs into instructions for the machines and make it possible to produce quick modifications in patterns and instructions, including preparation for a wide variety of color combinations.

While the systems on the market vary in details, they do make it possible to express a design electronically in terms of the sequence of stitches. The design to be put into computer readable form may be an original drawn by a designer, a print, a piece of knitted or woven cloth, or a piece of wallpaper. In many of the systems, a scanning unit scans the design very rapidly and, by means of a sonic pattern digitizer,[7] a point pattern of the stitch information is thrown onto a color television screen. There it can be modified in any way the designer wishes by drawing on the screen with a light sonic pen. In fact, a new design can be drawn directly on the screen and translated into a point pattern. When the pattern is judged satisfactory, a paper or magnetic tape or a disc pack is automatically prepared.

The data may be fed directly into the computer or stored on tapes or discs for future use. When ready for knitting, the master control in the computer processes the data into courses and relays. The output unit then presents the data to the knitting machine in a form that controls its operation. The number of stitches that the computer can handle varies

---

[7] An electronic unit that converts each tiny segment of a design into binary number form that can be "read" by the computer. The sequence of the electronic impulses produced controls the operation of the knitting machine and produces visual displays of the patterns.

FIGURE 6.8. Rockwell International Corp.'s Electroknit 48 electronically controlled double-knit machine. It has pattern control by magnetic tape or by all solid-state electonic pattern processor (EPP) featuring non-repeat pattern size of a magnetic tape version in full fabric widths by ten feet long. (Courtesy of *America's Textiles*, A Clark Publication.)

120
*Fabric
Construction
and
Buying
Motives*

from about 60,000 to as many as 500,000 in a large installation. Many existing knitting machines can be adapted for computer control.

However, mechanically controlled knitting machines still dominate production, although mechanical preparation for knitting is a long, arduous and costly process with steel tapes, drums, or wheels controlling the pattern. Electronics, on the other hand, can provide the fabric maker with a sample in a few minutes and can greatly reduce time and costs involved in setting up, making changeovers, and correcting errors before the pattern is run on the machine. The electronic equipment, however, is very costly, a factor that retards quick introduction. At present, there is no evidence that electronic machines will be replacing mechanically controlled knitting machines. The electronically controlled knitting machines are confined to making double-knit yard goods.

TRADE STANDARDS FOR KNIT GOODS

There are no tradewide standards of quality for knitted fabrics under consideration at present. Knitted fabric technologists, under the direction of the National Knitted Outerwear Association, have been developing specifications to describe the level of quality of knitted fabrics. They are attempting to group fabric performance factors into different classes, defining each class by different ratings. The group is also attempting to set up a uniform system to rate goods objectively for defects.

CARE OF KNITTED GARMENTS

Every woman knows how provoking it is to notice a dropped stitch or a run in one of her stockings. As each loop in knitting depends on other loops for its strength, a break in one loop affects all the loops below. Runs develop only in weft knitting. Hosiery can be made by regular warp knitting, but it is usually too heavy for the average consumer. If a consumer must have runproof underwear, she should buy a mesh. These fabrics have runs limited to only one direction, Runless, seamless nylon hosiery is a lock-stitch mesh.

To avoid runs in weft-knitted dress goods and underwear, it is advisable not to use pins, for they break the loops and start runs. When girdles or garter belts are worn, fasten garters in the garter welt at the top of the stocking. This welt is of stronger construction than the boot or body of the stocking, and if a run should develop in the garter welt, it will not run below the run stop. All runs should be mended as soon as they are discovered to prevent them from running farther. Often the application of run-stop fluid, nail polish, or even water to the ends of the run may stop it temporarily.

The consumer should know a few points about the hand laundering of knitted goods. Because of their great elasticity and open construction, they may shrink or lose shape when they are washed. Care labels will specify hand laundering if required.

1. To remove dirt, use a neutral soap and the same cupping motion of the hands as is used for delicate fabrics. (See Chapter 16.)

2. After rinsing, wrap cloth in a towel and squeeze out as much water as possible.

3. If possible, knitted fabrics should be dried flat, for the weight of water may pull a fabric out of shape and may break a loop and so cause a hole or a run. If knitted fabrics must be hung, however, it is better to throw them over a line than to attach them with clothespins. When using clothespins, attach them only to the reinforcement of the toe or garter welt in hosiery. Sweaters and blouses containing wool should be washed with an all-temperature detergent in cold water, rinsed, and either drip dried or machine dried with a "cold" or "warm" setting. Garments of an all-polyester or blends should be washed in warm or cold water, drip dried or machine dried at "warm" or "cold" setting. Laminated fabrics should be dry-cleaned only. In any case, follow and save the care label.

OTHER METHODS OF CONSTRUCTION

NET AND LACE-MAKING

Net is a geometrically shaped figured mesh fabric made of silk, cotton, nylon, polyester, rayon, or other man-made fiber. It comes in different sizes of mesh and in various weights. On the one hand, machine-made net is closely related to warp knitting because it is constructed on either a tricot or a Raschel warp-knitting machine; on the other hand, net is related to lace because many of the machine-made laces have geometrically shaped nets as their grounds. Bobbinet, made in a hexagonal-shaped mesh of rayon, nylon, silk, or cotton, is a popular fabric for evening dresses, veils, curtains, and trimmings. Like most nets and laces, bobbinet was originally made by hand on a pillow of the same width as the lace to be made. Small pegs or pins were stuck into the design. Thread was thrown around the pegs marking the design. When the lace was completed, the pillow was removed. (See *bobbin lace*, Chapter 19.) A closely constructed, very fine silk or nylon net is called *tulle*. The first nets to be made by machine were the warp-knitted tricots that appeared about the middle of the eighteenth century. At the beginning of the nineteenth century, a bobbinet machine that could handle yarns in three directions was invented and patented by John Heathcote. Shortly after that, a patterned lace loom was devised.

Another type of net is the knotted-square mesh type with knots in four corners to form the mesh. Originally made by hand and used by

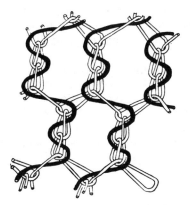

FIGURE 6.9. The structure of tulle fabric, the characteristics of which is the hexagonal shaped holes. Two guide bars are required, both fully threaded; the front guide bar knitting and the back guide bar laying-in. This net forms the basis of many patterned Raschel lace fabrics. (Reprinted, courtesy of *Knitted Outerwear Times*, official publication, National Knitted Outerwear Association.)

122
*Fabric
Construction
and
Buying
Motives*

fishermen, it is now made by machine. These modern fishnets of linen, cotton, or man-made fibers are used for glass curtaining in contemporary living rooms, sun porches and dens. (See Chapter 21)

A lace is an openwork fabric made of threads usually formed into designs. (See the description of various laces, Chapter 19.) By hand, lace can be made with needles, bobbins, shuttle, or hooks. Handmade lace is called real lace. When needles are used, the lace is called *needlepoint;* when bobbins are used the lace is called *bobbin* or *pillow;* when knotted with a shuttle, the lace is *tatting;* when made with a hook, it is called *crocheted.* Laces can also be made by hand with knitting or crochet needles.

Real lace was the only lace known until the invention of the lace machine in the early 1800s. This machine was later modified by several inventors, among them John Levers, whose name has come down to us via the Levers machine we use today.[8] Patterns of real laces can be reproduced on the modern lace looms, so we can now have their designs in quantity at a fraction of the cost of the handmade. Sometimes designs from various real laces will be combined in a single lace, which can be designated as *novelty lace.*

BRAIDING (OR PLAITING)

This is a method of interlacing (plaiting) three or more yarns or bias-cut strips of cloth over and under one another to form a flat or tubular fabric. These braided textile bands, which are relatively narrow, can be used as belts, pull-cords for lights, trimming for uniforms and dresses, tapes for pajamas, and some shoelaces. Several widths of plastic or straw braiding can be sewn together to make hat shapes. Similarly, braids of fabrics or yarns may be sewn together to make braided rugs.

FELTING

It is said that early peoples discovered what we know to be the felting process. By wearing the fur side of animal skins next to the body, these people discovered that the fur matted from the body's heat and perspiration and the pressure of the skin against the body. In our modern felting process, wool or fur fibers tend to mat or interlock when they are subjected to heat, moisture, and pressure. Hair of cows as well as hair of rabbits is used for woven felts and hair felts. Coarse hair of domestic cattle is used for inexpensive felted goods like insoles and underlays for rugs.[9] Fur felt hats are made from Australian, French, English, and Belgian rabbit fur.

Wool is probably most ideal for felting because the fibers swell in moisture, interlock, and remain in that condition when pressed and shrunk. When the fibers have been selected and, if necessary, blended with cotton or man-made fibers, they are carded into a flat sheet or bat. Bats are placed first one way and then the other in layers until the desired thickness is reached. Allowance has to be made for shrinkage, because steam and the pressure of heavy presses in the process of felting may

[8] "Lace," *Fairchild's Dictionary of Textiles* (1967), p. 325.

[9] "What Is Felt?" *Ciba Review,* XI, 29 (November 1958), 2-3.

increase the bats as much as 20 percent in thickness. To make the felt fabric stronger and more compact, the fabric is placed in warm soapy water, where it is pounded and twisted. For heavy felt, a weak acid is used instead of warm soapy water. (See *felting,* Chapter 12.) The cloth is then ready for finishing processes consisting of scouring, dyeing, possibly pressing or shearing, and treatment with special functional finishes to make it water-repellent, mothproof, and shrink-, crease-, and fire-resistant. Felt is made for men's and women's hats, women's skirts, vests, and slippers; also for table covers, padding, and linings. Woven felts have their place primarily in the industrial field.

LAMINATING

In Chapter 2 laminating was described as a process of joining a fabric to plastic foam. There are two ways to laminate foam to fabric:

1. *Wet adhesive.* A water-based acrylic compound is applied to the fabric, followed by curing by heat, which creates a permanent bond without affecting the draping qualities of the face fabric or the softness of hand.
2. *Foam flame.* The foam is made sticky with a gas flame. A small fraction of the foam's thickness is burned off. The foam in this case takes the place of an adhesive or binding agent.

BONDING

Bonding involves the making of a layered fabric by stitching layers of fabric together. This method is called the "fabric-to-fabric" method. Two layers of fabric are joined together by use of an adhesive, a binding agent, or heat. An example of layered fabric is a pair of girls' denim jeans that have been lined at the cuffs with plain flannelette. The flannelette has actually been stuck to the wrong side of the denim so that when the pants are rolled up the plaid shows.

Many homemakers have occasion to use this same principle to mend or reinforce clothing, sheets, or tablecloths with tape or patches by ironing the tape or patch with the binder side against the cloth. If the proper amount of heat and pressure is applied, the patch will adhere satisfactorily. Familiar brand names are Bondex and Irontex.

NONWOVEN CLOTH

In this process, the fibers are pressed into thin sheets or webs that are held together by a plastic adhesive. Rayon, cotton, or polyester are frequently selected for making this kind of cloth. Long fibers are preferable to give strength to the web. The fibers are first carded to lay them in a web (called a card lap). Methods of bonding are as follows:

1. A web is made by blending fibers that melt or fuse (nylon, acetate, vinyon) with fibers (cotton and rayon) that do not melt when heated. As heat is applied to the web, the nylon, acetate, or vinyon fuse just enough to hold the cotton or rayon permanently together.
2. Instead of heat, a solvent may be used to soften the acetate or plastic fibers.

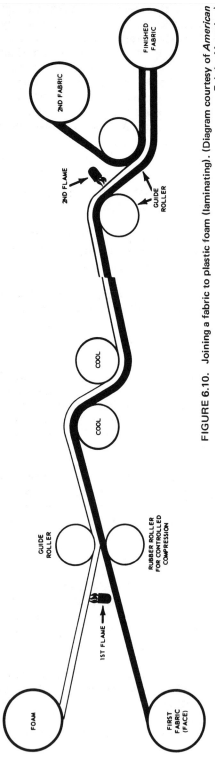

FIGURE 6.10. Joining a fabric to plastic foam (laminating). (Diagram courtesy of *American Fabrics Magazine*.)

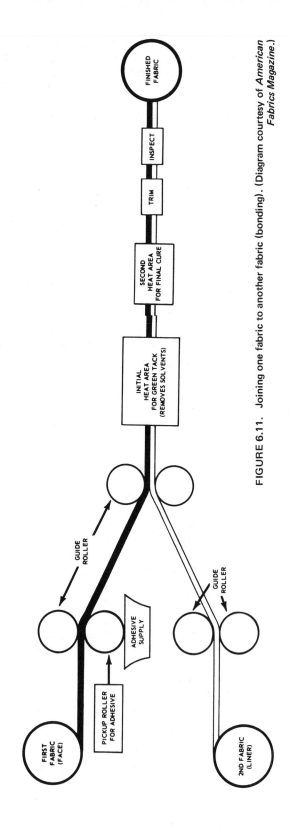

FIGURE 6.11. Joining one fabric to another fabric (bonding). (Diagram courtesy of *American Fabrics Magazine*.)

3. The web is sprayed or treated with a plastic binder to make the fibers adhere. Color can be added to the binder.

4. Bond. A bonded fabric is produced directly from the spinneret by electrically charging the extruded fibers and rubbing them over a suitable guide, releasing the tension, and moving filaments forward by air jet to a receiving surface. The electrical charge causes filaments to separate, loop, and crimp. The fiber web is bonded. In a dry-spun method, a solvent under pressure is kept above its normal boiling point. The frothing of the solution causes filaments to join at random points.

5. Spot-welding. In the spot-welding technique, a sheet of polyethylene or polypropylene is stretched lengthwise to orient the fibers' molecular chains. The disintegration into fibrous form results in a network of fine fibers that are relatively parallel to each other. Two or three layers of fibers can be spot-welded together.

Nonwoven fabrics have become increasingly useful. With crease-resistant and fire-resistant finishes, embossing, soft or crisp hand, increased flexibility, porosity, and printed designs, varied uses are made possible. A few important ones include draperies, towels, tablecloths, coat interlinings,[10] interfacings,[11] window shades, noncracking wallpaper, disposable tissues, diapers, bibs, and shoulder pads. Since bonded fabrics are inexpensive to produce, they are cheaper than woven or knitted constructions.

NEEDLE-WOVEN PROCESS OF CLOTH MAKING

This process is a variation of the nonwoven techniques. The method involves a so-called needle loom—a device that punches through a thick web of fibers, forcing the fibers from layer to layer until they gradually become entangled. An example of the use of this process is the Lantor blanket of lofty Acrilan acrylic web. A synonymous term is "needle punch," which is used in the carpet industry.

Needling as done by the Arachne machine feeds a web (cross-laid) into the back of a warp-knitting machine. Uses of the finished cloth include upholstery, windbreakers, and coats. The fabric is too stiff for dresses.

STITCH-THROUGH BONDED PROCESS

This is another variety of nonwoven goods. There are several ways of making stitch-bonded fabrics. A nonwoven batt of fibers is passed into a stitching or knitting device that makes a series of loops or a chain from a filament yarn in the batt. As the loops are formed under tension, a bonding or locking occurs, for the loops are in and on the nonwoven batt. The resulting structure is stable. The fabric can be piece-dyed, printed, resin-finished, or some other method. Uses include draperies, bedspreads, table covers, and blankets.

---

[10] Pellon is a popular brand name of a fiber fleece made from 60 percent wool and 10 percent camel's hair and other fibers. Pellon interfacing is predominantly nylon with some acetate and cotton. Fibers are bonded chemothermically.

[11] Keybak is a trademarked name of a nonwoven interfacing made of rayon and Du Pont virgin nylon. It is suitable for collars, cuffs, sleeves, waistbands, bodice fronts, jacket fronts and hemlines, and coat and skirt hemlines.

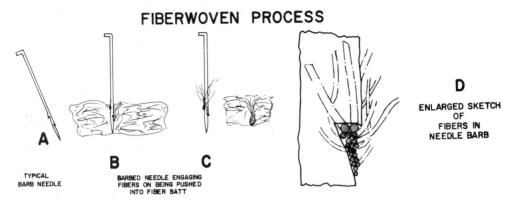

FIBERWOVEN PROCESS

A
TYPICAL
BARB NEEDLE

B   **C**
BARBED NEEDLE ENGAGING
FIBERS ON BEING PUSHED
INTO FIBER BATT

D
ENLARGED SKETCH
OF
FIBERS IN
NEEDLE BARB

FIGURE 6.12. The malimo structure is 3-dimensional. The background of this fabric is a polyester net made by a 2-yarn system. The crosswise yarn, or third yarn is needle-punched into the net background. In some fabrics the crosswise or lengthwise yarn is held to the background with a monofilament nylon or polyester yarn in a tricot knit or chainstitch construction. Fabrics may vary from very sheer to medium to heavyweight. The Malimo construction is used for draperies and curtains. (Courtesy Chatham Research & Development Corporation.) Fiberwoven is a registered trademark of the Fiberwoven Corporation.

THE SEWING-KNITTING PROCESS

While most simulated-fur pile fabrics are made by weaving or knitting the pile and the base cloth together in one operation, an inexpensive method is to use a Malipol[12] machine that punches tiny tufts of pile yarn through a base cloth, commonly of cotton in plain-woven or knitted construction. The tufts on the face side appear as rows of chain stitching on the back. When laminated, the foam sticks to the stitching, not to the base fabric, so that in heavy use or dry cleaning there may be some loss of pile. Long-pile fabrics so constructed are used for coatings, floor coverings, and blankets.

Short-pile fabrics are also made on the Malipol machine with the pile tufts punched through scrim or sheeting and held in place with an adhesive. The front side is calendered to lay the pile in one direction so that the fabric looks like crushed velvet. This has a variety of uses in clothing.

PROBLEMS OF SERVICEABILITY OF BONDED
AND LAMINATED FABRICS

Layered fabrics sometimes come apart (are delaminated) by abrasion, because the adhesive cracks and the face fabric separates from the backing. In dry cleaning, the fabric layers pull apart if the solvent solubilizes the adhesive. Designs formed by spot-welding discolor or disappear—a common occurrence in simulated quilted fabrics. Mechanical action in dry cleaning might cause separation of the fabric and obliteration of the design. However, there has been a decided improvement in resistance to delamination. Urethane backing could attract loose

---

[12] Other machines that use a similar technique are called the Malimo and the Maliwatt. The Maliwatt uses a fiber bat or web and interlaces stitching yarn to form a fabric. With the Malimo, warp yarns are laid on top of filling yarns and these are connected by a third yarn system of sewing thread.

soil or dye particles during dry cleaning or use. This often occurred with foam-backed place mats. The foam turned yellow or darkened owing to exposure to heat and atmospheric conditions. The outer layer of a garment changed color. Ripples and puckers might be caused by a shrinkage of one of the layers of the cloth. The spun-bonded fabrics might have finishes that are not colorfast to light, washing, and perspiration.

SUMMARY

Knitted goods are especially suitable for garments requiring a snug fit and elasticity. They are warm without feeling heavy, have good absorptive quality, and are hygienic. There are two methods of constructing knitted goods: weft and warp knitting. Although weft knitting has good elasticity, stitches may be dropped. On the other hand, stitches are not dropped in warp knitting. Also, in warp knitting the stretch is greater in the vertical direction.

Net-making is closely allied to knitting because machine-made net can be made on a warp-knitting machine. Many laces have net grounds and all have patterns.

To braid, three or more yarns are interlaced over and under to form a fabric. Braids are narrow goods, and several widths must be sewn together for shaped articles such as hats or rugs.

Felting is a nonwoven construction, although there is a woven felt. In felting, heat pressure and moisture cause the fibers to adhere. For bonding, a web of fibers is made and the fibers are held together by a binding agent. Felting is a much older process than bonding, but the two processes are closely allied.

Laminating is a process of sticking a fabric to a plastic foam material by a method similar to the construction of plywood in the nontextile field. Foam may be laminated to a knitted or woven fabric.

REVIEW QUESTIONS

1. In what respects does the knitted construction differ from the woven? Consider th yarns and the knitting operation.
2. (c) What are the three principal stitches in weft knitting?
    (b) For what purposes is each used?
3. What advantages has the plain stitch over the ribbed stitch?
4. In hand knitting contrast single and double knits.
5. (a) Describe warp knitting.
    (b) What advantages has warp knitting over weft knitting?
    (c) What fabrics are made by warp knitting?
6. (a) How do fabrics knitted in open width differ from circular- or tubular-knitted goods?
    (b) What are the advantages and the disadvantages of goods knitted by each method?
7. What instructions should salespeople give to customers on the care and laundering of knitted fabrics?
8. Explain the following constructions:
    (a) Bobbinet
    (b) Tatting
    (c) Fishnet
9. What braided articles are used in apparel? In home furnishings?
10. (a) Explain needle-woven or needle-punch construction.
    (b) Explain the stitch-through bonded technique.

128
Fabric
Construction
and
Buying
Motives

11. (*a*) Differentiate between bonding and laminating.
    (*b*) For what purposes are nonwoven fabrics used?
    (*c*) For what purposes are laminated fabrics used?
    (*d*) By what methods are fabrics laminated to foam?
    (*e*) Explain the merits and drawbacks of each method.

PROJECT   Visit the yard goods and lace departments of your local store. List in separate columns all fabrics that are (*a*) woven, (*b*) knitted, (*c*) net or lace, (*d*) felted, (*e*) bonded, (*f*) braided, (*g*) laminated, (*h*) other construction. What percentage of the fabrics listed comes in each category? What conclusions can you draw?

**EXPERI-
MENTS**

1. *Determining the stitch used in knitting.* Unravel a yarn from a sample. Does it unravel back and forth from the fabric? In which direction does it stretch more? Is it weft or warp knitting? Look at the right and wrong sides of the fabric and answer the following questions:
   (*a*) Are there courses on both sides?
   (*b*) Are there wales on one side and courses on the other?
   (*c*) Are there wales on both sides?
   (*d*) Does the fabric have an openwork or mesh design?
   (*e*) Is the surface roughened or puckered in the knitting operation?
   (*f*) Has a pattern been knitted into the fabric?
   (*g*) What stitch or combination of stitches is used in this fabric?
2. *Determining the durability of the fabric.* Hold the fabric to the light. Answer the following questions:
   (*a*) Do you see thick and thin places in the yarn?
   (*b*) Is the knitting regular?
   (*c*) Is it a close construction?
   (*d*) Does the fabric spring back to its original shape after stretching?
   (*e*) Will the fabric be durable? Why?
   (*f*) Will a garment made from this cloth keep its shape? Why?

GLOSSARY   Bobbinet—See *Net.*
Bonding—See Glossary, Chapter 2.
Braiding—See Glossary, Chapter 2.
Circular knit—Knitting in tubular form. Shaping is done by tightening or stretching stitches.
Cloqué—A raised effect Jacquard usually knitted from two colors.
Courses—Horizontal ridges (components of the loops) in weft knitting.
Curing—The application of heat to a fabric or garment to impart properties such as dimensional stability, crease resistance, water repellency, and durable press.
Cut—Number of needles per inch on the circular bed of a weft-knitting machine.
Double knit—Fabric knitted on circular machines with two sets of cylindrically disposed needles, each set placed and operating at a right angle to the other. See *Single knit.*
Drop-stitch knit—Open design made by removing certain needles at intervals.
Fashioning—A shaping process in making flat-knitted fabrics by adding stitches or by knitting two or more stitches as one to narrow the fabric.
Felting—See Glossary, Chapter 2.

Foam laminate—A construction made by laminating a synthetic foam to a woven or knitted fabric.

Full-fashioned—A term applied to sweaters and hosiery shaped by fashioning. See *Fashioning.*

Gauge—A term to describe the number of needles per inch in a warp-knitting machine (tricot and Raschel).

Interlock knitting—A process of making a compound fabric composed of two separate 1 × 1 rib fabrics interknitted to form one cloth—made on an interlock machine.

Jacquard patterns—Fancy patterns knitted in articles made by a special attachment of the knitting machine.

Jersey—A knitted fabric of cotton, wool, nylon, acetate, polyester, rayon, or blends with man-made fibers. It is usually made in stockinette jersey stitch or 2-bar tricot.

Knitted pile fabrics—Extra yarn introduced and drawn out in loops to form the pile that may or may not be cut.

Knitting—The process of constructing a cloth by interlocking a series of loops of one or more yarns. It may be done by hand or by machine.

Lace—An openwork fabric made of threads usually formed into designs. It is made by hand or by machine.

Laminating—The sticking of a fabric to a plastic foam.

Lisle yarn—Made of long-staple cotton of defined length in two or more ply and with a minimum twist for a given count specified by the F.T.C. rules for hosiery.

Mesh—A knitted or woven fabric with an open texture. It can be made of any fiber, mixture, or blend.

Milanese—A kind of warp knitting with several sets of yarns. Characteristic is its diagonal argyle-type pattern.

Net—A geometrically shaped, figured mesh fabric made in nylon, rayon, silk, or cotton. It has no pattern and is usually made on a warp-knitting machine.

Nonwoven fabrics—Webs of fibers held or bonded together with plastic, heat, pressure, or solvent.

Open width—Fabrics that come off a flatbed machine (horizontal or V bed).

Openwork stitch—A construction of open spaces purposely made at regular intervals across the knitted cloth. It is a variation of a basic stitch.

Plain stitch—A term used in hand knitting to identify a knitted construction with courses on both sides of the fabric.

Plated goods—Knitted fabrics that have one kind of yarn on the right side of the fabric and another kind on the back.

Purl stitch—Generically it is a weft-knit cloth and belongs in a separate class from single and double knits, which are also weft knits. Characteristics are similar to the reverse side of jersey, mostly for sweaters, in stripes and patterns.

Real lace—Handmade lace. See *Lace.*

Rib stitch—A weft knit identified by vertical ribs on both sides of the fabric—a very resilient stitch. When combined with the tuck stitch, it is called rib-and-tuck stitch.

Runless—A type of seamless nylon hosiery in a lock-stitch mesh.

Run-resistant—Knitted fabric constructed to make runs difficult. See *Interlock knitting.*

Single knit—Fabric made on a rotary machine with one set of needles around the cylinder. See *Double knit.*

Stockinette stitch—In hand weft knitting characterized by vertical wales on the face and horizontal courses on the back of the fabric. See *Plain stitch.*

Tricot—From the French *tricoter*, meaning to knit—a fabric made by a warp-knitting (tricot) machine. See *Two-bar tricot.*

Tubular knit—See *Circular knit.*

Tuck stitch—A variation of a basic stitch in weft knitting to make a knobby, bumpy, knitted texture. Unknitted loops are slipped from one needle to another. On the following row, the unknitted loops are knitted as regular stitches.

130

*Fabric
Construction
and
Buying
Motives*

Two-bar (double-bar) tricot—A warp knit in which two sets of yarns are required, one knitted in one direction and the other in the opposite direction. A ribbed surface results. It is synonymous with double-warp tricot knit.

Warp knitting—A process that makes a more dimensionally stable fabric than weft knitting. It is frequently run-resistant. Examples are tricot and Raschel.

Weft knitting—A process in which the thread runs back and forth crosswise in a fabric. See *Warp knitting.*

Finishes

7

A customer asks the salesperson, "If I buy these polyester/cotton slacks, and the label says they are machine-washable, will I have to press them?" "No," replies the well-informed salesclerk. "They are durable press, which means they stay smooth after washing and drying."

A *finish* is a treatment applied to the fabric after construction. The stiffness of organdy, the smooth, silky feeling of batiste, the colored print on cretonne, the watered or moiré effect on acetate, and the whiteness of table damask are all the results of finishing treatments to which the fabrics are subjected after they are made. A whole industry, called the *converting* industry, devotes itself to this finishing of cloth. The converter takes the fabrics from the mills and either treats them himself or has them treated to make them more attractive, more serviceable, and hence more salable. Before goods are finished they are said to be *in the grey* (or *greige*)—which does not necessarily mean gray in color.

There are the regular or basic finishes, such as napping, brushing, shearing, calendering, and the like, without which a fabric would not be suitable to sell. Basic finishes in some form have been applied to textile fabrics for centuries. Then there are the functional or special finishes that contribute a special feature to the merchandise. Permanent starchless, crease-resistant, and water-repellent are a few of the functional finishes. Finishing processes can be considered *mechanical* if they are done by copper plates, roller brushes, perforated cylinders, tenter frames, or any type of mechanical equipment. If fabrics are treated with alkalies, acids, bleaches, starch, resins, and the like, they are considered to have been subjected to *chemical* finishing processes. It is in the field of chemical finishes that the greatest developments have been made.

PERMA-NENT AND NONPER-MANENT FINISHES

PERMANENT FINISHES—An Overview

Some fabrics must be so finished that friction will not harm the surface; others must be crease-resistant; and some must be unaffected by light, perspiration, washing, or water spotting. Fortunately for the manufacturer, fabrics do not have to be finished to withstand every hazard equally well; if they did, the finish would, of course, be considered permanent. But permanency of finish is not usually determined in this

132
*Fabric
Construction
and
Buying
Motives*

way. If a cloth has a finish that will withstand whatever affects it in its particular use, the finish is considered permanent. For example, an evening dress does not have to be fast to light or to friction. A man's wool suit must be particularly fast to light and should be fast to friction, but it need not be fast to washing.

It is not wise to say that all types of any finish are permanent. For example, bleached silks may turn yellow sooner than bleached linens. One mercerized cotton broadcloth may lose its sheen in laundering sooner than another broadcloth. The mercerizing of the first piece may have treated only the surface of the fiber, whereas the mercerizing in the second piece may have penetrated to the core of the fiber. Permanency of finish is, of course, only a relative term.

Wash-and-wear finishes for cotton, first used in the late 1950s, have been improved considerably since then. Consumers found that early wash-and-wear cottons did not all perform as the term indicated. Most of them required ironing to make them look fresh and smooth. The resin in the finishing caused the cottons to have a heavy, somewhat stiff hand. Many of the first wash-and-wear cottons turned yellow if a chlorine bleach was used on them.

Now most of these finishes do not turn yellow. In fact, standards of quality have been set to insure good performance of wash-and-wear finishes. Quality manufacturers asked the Sanforized Division of Cluett, Peabody & Company, Inc., to establish a standard, whereupon they invented an electronic instrument (the Electronic Smoothness Evaluator), which has an electric eye that sees—and counts—every crease and wrinkle. A fabric after washing must dry without too many wrinkles to measure up to this standard. It must resist wrinkling, not shrink out of fit, have good tensile strength, and have good tear strength. Wash-and-wear cottons that come up to all five of the Sanforized Division's specifications bear the

FIGURE 7.1. Durable press label, front and back. (Courtesy Cone Mills Marketing Co.)

label "Sanforized-Plus."[1] Merchandise so labeled gives the consumer insurance of satisfactory wash-and-wear performance. Such a finish would be considered permanent.

The term "permanent press" indicates a long life in durability. Hence the term *durable press* is being used in this text. "A permanent or durable press garment, or any other end use textile product such as sheets or drapery, does not require ironing for the use life of the product under normal usage conditions."[2] Manufacturers' quality-control standards call for a certain level of performance in use.[3]

Some processes producing finishes that can be made to withstand a reasonable amount of wear without injury, and that are therefore called permanent finishes, include:

TABLE 7.1.

Cotton	Linen	Rayon	Silk	Wool
Bleaching	Bleaching	Printing	Bleaching	Printing
Glazing	Beetling	Dyeing	Dyeing	Dyeing
Dyeing	Dyeing	Moireing (if	Printing	Napping
Printing	Printing	resin-treated		Moth-repellent
Mercerizing	Shrinkage	and heat-set)		Shrinkage
Shrinkage	control	Shrinkage		control
control	Starchless	control		Wash-and-wear
Starchless	Crease-	Starchless		Durable press
Crease-resistant	resistant	Crease-resistant		
Wash-and-wear		Water-repellent		
Durable press		Durable press		
Cotton/polyester		(modified		
blends		rayons)		

Nylon	Polyester	Acrylics	Glass Fibers
Stiffening (resin)	Wrinkle-resistant	Crease-resistant	Crimp setting
Nonslip	Shape-retention	Permanent pleating	Wrinkle-resistant
Embossing	Heat-set	Water-repellent	
(heat-set)	Moireing	Heat set	
Moireing	Durable press	Moireing	
Durable press	(100% polyester	Durable press	
(cotton/nylon	and blends)		
blends)			
Durable press			
(100% nylon)			

Piece-dyed and printed fabrics may be fast to light, friction, and washing if their fibers have an affinity for the dyestuffs.

Beetling produces a comparatively permanent finish because the process flattens out the fibers themselves. Pressing tends to keep the fibers flat.

Nap wears off with friction but, if well made, does not wash off and is not affected by light. It is therefore generally considered a permanent finish.

[1] Sanforized-Plus is a trademark owned by Cluett, Peabody & Co., Inc., denoting a checked standard of wash-and-wear performance.

[2] Definition given at the Sixth Annual Conference of the American Association of Textile Technology (AATT), 1966.

[3] Fabrics that have passed the test for performance standards of the Sanforized Division of Cluett, Peabody & Co., Inc. are labeled Sanforized-Plus for wash-and-wear and Sanforized-Plus-2 for permanent press.

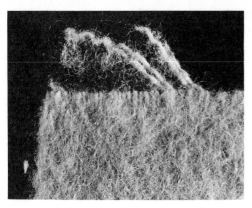

FIGURE 7.2. Fuzz on the yarns shows how napping raises short fibers in the yarns. (Photo by Jonas Grushkin.)

Many fabrics are now treated with plastic resin. The resin is fixed in the fiber so that it becomes a part of it and cannot be felt or seen even under a microscope. The resin doesn't change the surface of the fabric, but it adds resilience and hence muss resistance and reduces shrinkage in sponging and pressing. Flannels, light worsteds, and blankets so treated have better resistance to shrinkage. Oil-modified resins protect glass fibers. Cottons are often heat-set by applying resin first and then embossing. Wrinkle resistance and ease of care properties are given to cotton dress goods by using thermosetting resins, by using a catalyst, by curing at a high temperature, and preferably by washing afterward.

Glazed chintz and tarlatan may be treated with starch, glue, paraffin, or shellac and run through hot friction rollers to give the fabrics a high polish. These finishing materials are not permanent. However, plastic resins can be baked into the fabric to produce a permanent, washable finish. Everglaze is a trade name of such a finish.

Permanent or durable press is obtained through chemical treatment applied to either a fabric or a garment for the purpose of creating permanent shape, permanent pleats, permanent pressed creases, durable smooth seams, wrinkle resistance, machine washability and dryability, and a fresh-pressed look without ironing. If care instructions are followed, durable press finishes eliminate the need for ironing after laundering. To be effective, many fabrics should be tumble-dried. Trade names include Koratron, Dan Press, Super Crease, Coneprest, and many more. Durable press can also be added to stretch fabrics. The technology of durable press will be discussed later in this chapter.

FIGURE 7.3. Heavily sized costume cambric. Gathering of fabric at left shows stiffness of fabric. (Photo by Jonas Grushkin.)

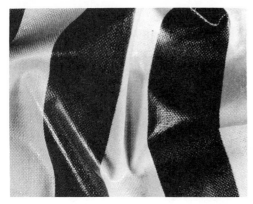

FIGURE 7.4. Chintz. Resin finished glaxing is permanent. (Photo by Jonas Grushkin.)

NONPERMANENT FINISHES

Surfaces that rub off when a cloth is brushed briskly are not permanent. Also, if the fabric loses its surface attractiveness or a good deal of its weight from cleaning or laundering, the finish is not permanent.

Sizing is a dressing that generally rubs off and washes out. With one or two exceptions, sizing is not permanent. Cotton organdy, when heavily sized, is not permanent, but when given a starchless resin finish, will come back to its original stiffness when the fabric is ironed. Glazed chintz, which is sized first and then calendered, is not permanent, but can be so treated that the cloth may be wiped with a damp rag in the same way as oilcloth.

Weighting is applied to both silk and wool and is not a permanent finish. If the finish washes out, the fabric becomes flimsy and shows its defects. Weighted silks water-spot easily. As the chief constituents of loading in wool are a chemical and moisture, this finish is also easily removed. Flocking, which can be removed by brushing, is not a permanent finish. A table damask may be recognized as cotton if fuzz or lint appears after the cloth is washed. Cotton towels that are carefully singed to imitate linen also become fuzzy after washing. Cottons singed preparatory to mercerization do not develop lint so quickly.

FIGURE 7.5. a. Pure silk (no weighting). Reeled silk yarns in warp and filling. Note the bead-like residue where the silk taffeta was burned. b. Weighted silk. Note the screen-like burned edge. (Photos by Jonas Grushkin.)

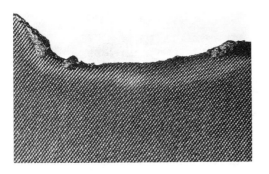

135

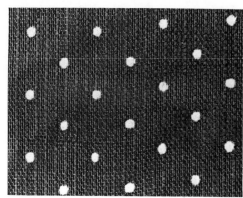

FIGURE 7.6. Flocking done by applying paste dots. Friction can remove paste dots. (Photo by Jonas Grushkin.)

Creping put in as a finishing process is not considered permanent unless heat-set. The roller type of creping comes out with the first washing, but the type put in by the caustic soda method is likely to be more permanent.

Embossing done by steam and rollers washes out and is not permanent. Heat-set treatment is permanent when done properly.

Moiréing can be made a permanent finish. The finishing of acetate cloth to produce moiréed effects that will withstand washings has been important for the moiré industry.

Tentering is a process of stretching a fabric to make it even. (See p. 138. If a cloth is stretched excessively to make it even in width, the fabric will return to its original size after laundering (it shrinks). Therefore a preshrunk fabric evenly tentered is important to the cutter of the garment. Later, when the consumer launders the garment, it is not likely to shrink to a narrower width.

Calendering is only pressing and is removed by washing and wear. This finish can be replaced by the consumer.

FIGURE 7.7. The tenter frame. After dyeing, the linen is dried to a uniform width. This picture shows the linen passing over hot air vents. (Photograph courtesy of the Irish Linen Guild.)

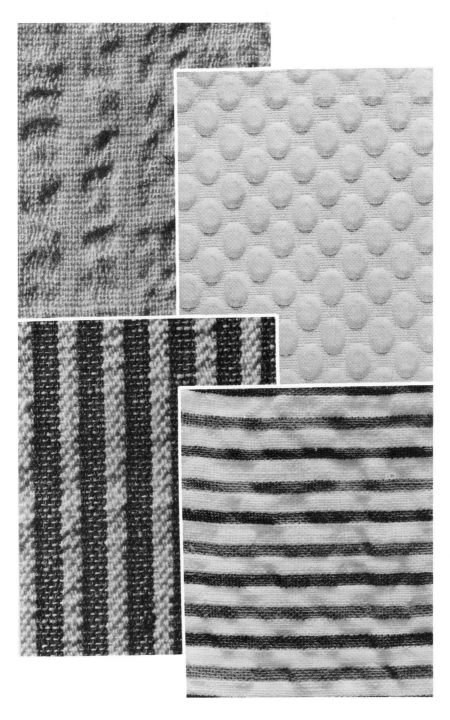

FIGURE 7.8. Top left: Crepes made by embossing. Top right: Crepes made by steam rolling. Bottom left: Crepes made by tension. Bottom right: Crepes made by caustic soda printing. (Photos by Jack Pitkin.)

138
*Fabric
Construction
and
Buying
Motives*

Some of the finishing processes that have been discussed in detail are mechanical in nature, including those that employ rollers, steam, and pressure. The rest of the finishing processes are chemical in nature and include weighting, mothproofing, and fireproofing; crease-resistant, ease of care, and water-repellent finishes; and bleaching, dyeing, and printing. (Dyeing and printing will be discussed in Chapter 8.)

The great improvements in finishing equipment and continuous finishing and dyeing operations have been primarily responsible for the wide variety of finished goods.

The consumer should be advised to consider, before a purchase is made, the purpose for which a fabric is to be used. Some finishes withstand laundering, sunlight, perspiration, and friction; others do not. The experiments at the close of this chapter should aid the consumer in making a decision.

PREPARA-TORY TREAT-MENTS

Before the basic or functional finishes can be applied, cloths usually are given some preparatory processing. For example, if a linen fabric not already bleached in the yarn is to be white or is to be dyed or printed, it is pretreated by being bleached. Hence, the following are not finishes because these treatments are done preparatory to finishing.

BLEACHING[4]

The object, of course, is to whiten the cloth, which comes from the loom grayish brown in color. Inexpensive cottons are often merely washed and pressed after coming from the looms and are sold as unbleached goods. The natural tan color of flax makes bleaching one of the most important processes in finishing linen. Wild silks are usually bleached before they are dyed. If a silk cloth is to be a light color or pure white, it must be bleached. Wool is frequently bleached in the yarn, but may be bleached after weaving or scouring.

[4] *Bleaching of cotton*, Chapter 9; *bleaching of linen*, Chapter 10; *silk*, Chapter 11; *wool*, Chapter 12; *rayon and acetate*, Chapter 13.

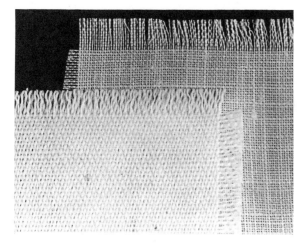

FIGURE 7.9.   a. Grey or greige goods; b. bleached fabric. (Photo by Jonas Grushkin.)

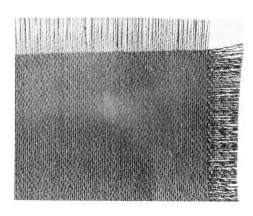

FIGURE 7.10. Mercerized cotton. (Photo by Jonas Grushkin.)

SCOURING

When scouring is done as a finish, it is called *piece scouring*. The purpose of the process is to remove any sizing, dirt, oils, or other substances that may have adhered to the fibers in the processing of the yarns or in the construction of the cloth. To avoid the formation of an insoluble soap film on the fabric, soft water is used for scouring.

DEGUMMING

Before a silk fabric can be dyed or other finishes applied, it must be degummed, unless the yarns were degummed before weaving. Boiling silk fabrics in a mild soap solution followed by rinsing and drying will accomplish this purpose. As a result, the fabric will have a beautiful sheen and will have a soft hand.

IMMUNIZING OF COTTON FABRICS—
A Chemical Modification of the Fibers[5]

Cellulose fibers, like viscose and cuprammonium rayons, take regular cotton dyestuffs; acetate fibers do not. (See Chapter 13.) Therefore, if cotton is treated with an agent such as acetic anhydride to change it from pure cellulose to an ester of cellulose (having the same chemical composition as acetate fiber) the cotton will be made immune to regular cotton dyestuffs and will take the same dyes as the acetates. The result is a paler stain on the cotton than on the acetate, but a wider range of colors is possible. Cross-dyed effects may be obtained by weaving immunized cotton with regular cotton. (See *cross dyeing*, Chapter 8.)

MERCERIZATION OF COTTON

Although this process can be done in the skein of yarn, frequently mercerization is done after weaving. Any type of cotton can be mercerized, but best results are obtained on long-staple cottons. (Newer rayon and cotton blends are now also being mercerized.) The process consists of holding the fabric in tension while treating it with a strong solution of sodium hydroxide at a uniform temperature of 70° to 80° F. Mercerization can be done before or after bleaching and occasionally after dyeing. In the last two instances, mercerization may be considered a basic finish. The purposes of mercerization are threefold: (1) to increase the

[5] *Fairchild's Dictionary of Textiles* (1967), p. 292.

fabric's luster; (2) to improve its strength; (3) to give it greater affinity for dye. (Further treatment of this subject is given in Chapter 9.)

BASIC FINISHES

Finishes that enhance the beauty and attractiveness of a cloth and cover defects appeal to the eye. Finishes that add weight, body, or warmth to a cloth appeal to the sense of touch.

FINISHES THAT APPEAL TO THE EYE

An unbleached cotton muslin is not considered a beautiful fabric, yet when the same fabric is bleached, brushed, singed, starched, printed, and calendered, it is attractive.

Unbleached muslin is commonly sold for household purposes, whereas a finished muslin print can be used for children's dresses, sportswear, and housedresses. Finishes that add attractiveness to a cloth will be described.

Shearing. After a nap has been raised on a cloth, it is sheared to make the surface smooth and uniform. Shearing is also done to even the pile. To make carved effects, designs and ground can be cut in different lengths. In the case of hard-surfaced fabrics such as gabardine, shearing removes all surface fibers. The process also serves to cut off knots, ends, or other defects. The shearing device has revolving blades similar to a lawn mower. Shearing can be applied to any of the textile fibers or blends.

Singeing. Smooth-surfaced cloths are passed over either heated plates or gas flames to remove projecting fibers. The fabric must be passed rapidly over the gas flame so only these fibers are burned.

Brushing.[6] For smooth-surfaced fabrics, such as cotton dress percale, brushing with rollers covered with bristles removes short ends of fibers. In the case of wool fabrics, brushing frequently follows shearing, because in the shearing process cut fibers fall into the nap and must be removed. Two-brush cylinders lay the nap in one direction and steam sets it. Brushing may be applied to any fabric.

Beetling. Linen damask has a glossy, hard, leathery feeling. To give this feeling, linen fabrics and cotton fabrics made to resemble linen are pounded (beetled) with little hammers. (See Chapter 10.)

Mercerization.[7] When mercerization is applied after bleaching or after dyeing, the process may be considered a basic finish.

Decating. Decating is a mechanical finish involving heat and pressure. It is applied to silk, rayon, and blends to set the luster and in wool especially to develop a permanent luster. It softens the hand, reduces shine, helps even the set and grain of the cloth, and delays the appearance of breaks and cracks. (See Chapter 12 on dry and wet decating of wool.)[8]

Tentering. To even fabrics in the width and to dry them, a tenter frame is employed. Pins or clips grip the fabric automatically by both selvages as the cloth is fed to the tenter frame. The distances between the

---

[6] See "Brushed Fabrics," *Fairchild's Dictionary of Textiles*, p. 84.
[7] See mercerizing, Chapter 9.
[8] For finishes for wools, see *fulling, gigging, napping,* and *steaming,* Chapter 12.

two sides of the frame can be adjusted to the appropriate width of the fabric. Creases and wrinkles are pulled out and the weave is made straight as the fabric is moved along the frame. The drying is done by machines, which either radiate heat from steam pipes or blow hot air through the fabric.

Calendering. After all chemical and mechanical finishes have been applied, the cloth is pressed, or calendered, by passing it between hollow heated rollers. If the fabric is to receive a high polish, the cloth is usually stiffened with sizing before it is calendered. The more heat and pressure applied, the greater the luster produced. Calendering, then, not only smooths out wrinkles but also adds sheen to the fabric. All cloths having a smooth, flat surface have been calendered.

When the consumer irons a fabric, she is really calendering it. In the making of velveteen, where flatness of surface is not desirable, the cloth is merely steamed while in tension; but it is not pressed. Calendering is an important finish for most cottons. It is used also for linen, silk, filament and spun rayons, and other man-made fibers when a smooth, flat surface is needed.

Variations of calendering operations include those producing moiréed, embossed, and glazed finishes.

Moiréing. One of the most interesting surfaces is the moiré finish. A cloth with a fillingwise rib weave is run between rollers engraved with many lines, and is thus given a watered effect. On acetate cloths, this finish will remain in good condition after the fabrics are laundered. Rayons may be given resin treatment to set the design.

Pressing. Pressing accomplishes the same result for wool as calendering does for other fibers. Calendering is really a pressing process, but the term is not applied to wool.

To press wool, the fabric is placed between heavy, electrically heated metal plates that steam and press the fabric. Sometimes the cloth is wound around a cylindrical unit that dampens the fabric and then presses it. This method can be used not only for woolens and worsteds, but also for rayons and silks.

Embossing. So that a design may be made to stand out from the background, the fabric is passed between steaming rollers that imprint or emboss the design on the fabric. This design is less expensive than a woven-in design. Rayon pillows are embossed in this manner.

Cotton piqué may be made to look like dobby weave by an *embossing* process. This finish is not a satisfactory one because it will not stay in after laundering unless it is heat-set.

Creping. As a finishing process, creping may be accomplished by passing the cloth between hot rollers in the presence of steam. These rollers are filled with indentations, the counterparts of the waved and puckered areas to be produced. This method is inexpensive, but the crepe will iron out and wash out unless a heat-setting treatment is used.

A more permanent creping is done by the caustic soda method. Caustic soda paste is rolled onto the cloth in stripes or figures. The fabric is washed, and the parts to which the paste was applied shrink. The rest of the cloth does not shrink but appears puckered or creped. Sometimes a paste that resists the effect of caustic soda is put on the cloth in spots

142
*Fabric
Construction
and
Buying
Motives*

where the fabric is not to shrink. The whole cloth is then immersed in caustic soda; the untreated spots shrink and the rest puckers or crepes. Crinkled bedspreads may be made in this manner. This method results in a more permanent crepe than does the first method.

Glazing. After fabrics are bleached, dyed, or printed, they may be given a stiff, polished, or glazed surface. Starch, glue, mucilage, shellac, or resin may be used to stiffen the fabric. Then smooth, hot rollers that generate friction are used. Chintz for upholstery and curtains is generally glazed.

Since the advent of resins in the finishing field, permanent-finish glaze can be applied to chintz and other muslins. The melamine formaldehyde or urea formaldehyde resins are used to give a smooth surface that resists oil. They produce a permanent finish.

Polishing. Polished cotton may be mercerized first and then friction calendered. These fabrics, which look shiny and shed dirt very well, are softer than glazed chintz. Cottons that are commonly polished are nainsook and sateen.

FINISHES THAT APPEAL TO TOUCH

Some finishes improve the softness of a fabric. For example, softeners and hand builders must be used on nearly all durable press fabrics. Since 1964 polyethylene emulsions have been found to improve abrasion resistance, sewability, and fabric hand. These emulsions have increased in use as softeners since the advent of durable press.

Other finishes give weight and body; others give crispness; others make the cloth warmer.

Napping. The warmth and softness of a wool flannel or a brushed wool sweater is partly due to the fuzzy soft surface called *nap*. Napping, then, is a process of raising short fibers of a cloth to the surface by means of revolving cylinders with metallic points. Cottons and synthetic fabrics of spun yarns may be napped to resemble wool in texture. (For the processes of napping woolens, see Chapter 12.)

Weighting. Weighting in silk is intended to replace boiled-off gum. If weighting is excessive, it can be employed to add body to an otherwise flimsy structure. The poor wearing quality of heavily weighted silks has been discovered by most consumers. Weighting is also accomplished in the finishing process when the weighting substance is put in the dye. (The practice of weighting fabrics will be discussed more fully in Chapter 11.)

To make a firmer, more compact wool cloth, manufacturers steam fibers (obtained by shearing a cloth or reused wool) into the back of a fabric. This is *flocking*. Its presence can be detected by brushing the back of the cloth with a stiff brush to see whether short fibers come out.

Sizing or dressing. To increase weight, body crispness, and luster, cottons are often stiffened. Substances such as glue, wax, casein, or clay are used. Sizing is not a permanent finish. (See Chapter 9 for a more thorough discussion of sizing of cotton.) Very soft, limp rayons and linens are often improved by some dressing. Permanent finishes to give stiffness, called *permanent starchless finish*, will be discussed under "functional finishes."

Starching. (See *sizing*.)

Inspection and repair. After the fabric is finished, visual examination to detect imperfection is a must. The process might consist of throwing the fabric over a horizontal bar[9] for examination under a powerful lamp. Visual examination is a final step for the finisher. The cloth must then have nubs, burrs, hair, slubs, and straw removed. Any knots must be opened and loose ends pushed through to the wrong side. If there are any exceptionally irregular yarns, they are pulled out and replaced. If any yarns are missing, they must be run in by hand.

SHRINKAGE Nothing can prove more distressing to a customer than to find the garment that fitted her perfectly before laundering shrunk to a size smaller afterward. The worst fabric offenders are cotton, linen, wool, and filament rayon. Acetate, silk, nylon, and the other synthetics are not subject to shrinkage, although the type of yarn used, the count of the cloth, and the type of finish are factors affecting this property of a fabric. For example, creped yarns and loosely constructed fabrics frequently shrink. Also, wool knitted fabrics, unless laundered properly, are likely to shrink.

PRESHRINKING (FTC RULINGS ON SHRINKAGE)

Prior to June 30, 1938, when the FTC issued its shrinkage rules, which are applicable to all woven cotton goods whether finished or not, the word "preshrunk" was misleading to the consumer. Many consumers were led to believe that if a fabric was labeled preshrunk, it would shrink no more. When the consumer washed the fabric, she often found it did shrink. In short, this fabric, after preshrinkage, had a capacity to shrink more. This capacity to shrink further is termed *residual shrinkage*.

According to the FTC ruling,[10] if the words "preshrunk" or "shrunk" are used on a cotton-goods label, the manufacturer must guarantee the maximum shrinkage. For example, "These goods have been shrunk (or preshrunk) to the extent that residual shrinkage will not exceed —— percent when tested in accordance with the recognized and approved standards or tests." A test devised by the American Standards Association has been recognized as a standard test by the FTC. Another suggested form of label may read: "Preshrunk—residual shrinkage 1 percent, or 2 percent." Terms such as "full shrunk," "shrinkproof," "nonshrinkable" are banned by this ruling if the goods so labeled have any further capacity to shrink.

In brief, if a manufacturer labels his goods as "preshrunk" or "shrunk" he must adhere to the FTC rules, but if he does not label his goods as "shrunk" or "preshrunk," then he need not indicate the percentage of residual shrinkage.

[9] See *perching, burling,* and *mending,* Chapter 12.
[10] The ruling applies legally to goods sold in interstate commerce.

Shrinkage can change a size dress 16 to a size 14 in bust, waist, and hip and to a size 12 in length. Even a 3 percent fabric shrinkage is undesirable. Should the collar of a man's shirt shrink 3 percent, a size 15 collar is reduced to 14½, and the sleeve shrinks ½ inch.

Cotton fabric shrinks because its yarns have been stretched during weaving and finishing. When the fabric is being laundered, the yarns relax and return to their normal position, thus causing shrinkage. Not all cottons shrink alike. They vary according to type and construction. Percales may shrink 3 to 8 percent. Flannelettes may shrink 10 percent or more.

SHRINKAGE CONTROLS

Almost everyone is familiar with the Sanforized label. Sanforized, as mentioned earlier, is a trademark owned by Cluett, Peabody & Company, Inc., which permits its use only on fabrics that meet this company's rigid shrinkage requirements. Fabrics bearing the trademark Sanforized will not shrink more than 1 percent by the government's standard wash test. Sanforized is not the name of a shrinkage process; it does not denote a method of shrinking; it *does* denote a checked standard of shrinkage performance.[11] Hence, when this Sanforized trademark is seen on a white broadcloth shirt the consumer knows that the fabric shrinkage will not exceed 1 percent despite repeated laundering. When she sees the trademark Sanforized-Plus by the same company, she knows the fabric has passed standard tests for proper performance in use of a wash-and-wear

[11] "How to Use the 'Sanforized' Trademark," a leaflet by the Sanforized Division, Cluett, Peabody & Co., Inc.

FIGURE 7.11. Trademarks of the Sanforized Co., Division of Cluett, Peabody & Co., Inc. Fabric shrinkage of labeled merchandise will not exceed 1 percent by government's standard test. **Sanforized®:** The familiar trademark found on piece goods, clothing, home furnishings, and domestics means the article will not shrink out of fit. **Sanforized plus®:** A trademark appearing on minimum-care merchandise. The item will not shrink out of fit. **Sanforized plus 2®:** A garment trademark found on durable press garments. The article will not shrink out of fit regardless of how it is laundered. **Sanfor Knit®:** A trademark for knit garments. It ensures lasting comfort and fit of garments after repeated home washing and machine drying. Can only be used by a licensed garment manufacturer. **Sanfor Set®:** A new tumble-dry shrinkage standard. No-iron without shrink loss in cotton denims. Ensures soft "hand," smooth appearance, reduces edge abrasion.

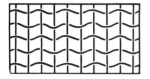
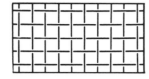
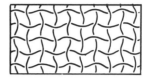

Fabric From Loom
Vertical Yarns Stretched

Finishing Processes
Stretch Yarns

Complete Shrinkage
Yarns Fully Relaxed

FIGURE 7.12. When fabrics are woven on a power loom, the warp (lengthwise) yarns are under constant tension (a). During commercial bleaching, dyeing, mercerizing, and other finishing processes, both warp and filling yarns are again subjected to stretching (b). When fabrics (not under tension) are dampened, all yarns become wavy and shorten—therefore, shrinkage occurs (c). The compressive shrinkage process is the most dependable and accurate method of shrinking fabrics. (Courtesy of The Sanforized Co.)

fabric. Similarly, Sanforized-Plus-2 refers to a fabric that has passed performance tests for durable press.

When a compressive shrinkage process is used on a fabric to eliminate customers' complaints of shrinkage, fabrics so treated gain in durability, because shrinkage increases the number of warp and filling yarns to the square inch (raises the count of cloth). The finish of the cloth is also improved, because the yarns are crinkled and drawn closer, and the fabric is dried against a polished cylinder. These processes give smoothness, soft luster, and improved draping possibilities. The compressive shrinkage process adds a few cents a yard to the price the customer must pay, but this increase is not exorbitant, since untreated cloth may shrink as much as 10 percent. Practically every cotton can be so treated—even mixed fabrics made of cotton, silk, and wool.

For rayon. Rayon fabrics and blends of these fibers may be stablized (so they will not shrink or stretch more than 2 percent) by resin impregnation. This treatment forms resin within the fiber rather than on the surface. Even though this treatment may change the hand, the advantage of shrinking control outweighs the disadvantages. Rayon shrinkage can also be prevented by chemical reaction (cross-linking) with acetals. Special additives are required to prevent excessive weakening of the fabric and to retain a pleasing hand and appearance. Another method utilizes a combination of dialdehyde, glyoxal, and urea formaldehyde resin. Fabrics so treated are said to be resistant to any temperature wash water and repeated launderings.

For the newer man-made fibers. The man-made thermoplastic fibers such as the polyesters and the nylons are heat-sensitive. They are usually heat-set during finishing to make them stable.

For wool. The four commonest methods of controlling the shrinkage of wool are (1) the chlorinating process; (2) the resin treatment; (3) treatment with enzymes that attack the fiber scales; and (4) microscopic coating of a polymer. (See Chapter 12.) In 1971 an improved ozone treatment under a British patent was announced.[12] Briefly, the process consists of premixing 14 volumes of air with one volume of chlorine gas before passing it through an electric discharge zone.

FUNC-TIONAL OR SPECIAL FINISHES

Finishes that are applied to fabrics to make them better suited for specific uses come in this category. In general, these finishes are newer than the basic finishes, many of them having been perfected during World War II.

ABRASION RESISTANCE

Abrasion resistance is a matter of the degree to which a fabric can withstand the friction of rubbing or chafing. The newer man-made fibers, such as nylon, acrylics, and polyesters, have good abrasion resistance, but the natural fibers do not have this property. To overcome this problem, fibers with high-potential abrasion resistance can be blended with fibers of low abrasion resistance (not a finish). The application of certain thermoplastic resins (particularly acrylic) may be used. The chief

[12] *Textile World*, April 1971.

FIGURE 7-13. Photomicrograph of fabric showing how the compressive shrinkage process alters its construction. The process does not impair a fabric in any way. On the contrary, the fabric is improved since, after shrinking, there are more threads per inch in both the warp and filling. As a result, the shrunk fabrics have greater wearing qualities and improved hand. (Courtesy of The Sanforized Co.)

objection to the use of resins lies in the fact that these finishes may increase wet-soiling of the fabrics.

In durable press cottons, abrasion resistance is reduced to a third or less of untreated fiber. In the original concept of durable press cotton, either the molecules were loaded with resin or the fiber structure was immobilized with cross-links. This reaction made the fiber brittle as well as resilient. No amount of softeners would overcome this fault while retaining the resilient property. Considerable research has been done along these lines. By 1967 the Southern Regional Research Laboratory (New Orleans, Louisiana) reported that cotton fabrics and garments made of blends of cotton fibers—part of which have been impregnated with certain thermosetting and/or thermoplastic resins and untreated cottons—show excellent ability to resist damage by abrasion during laundering.[13] A number of treatments have aimed to keep the cotton fiber slightly swollen while it is being cross-linked. Then there are possible improvements made in cross-linking agents. Finally, polyester blended with cotton compensates for loss of abrasion resistance and strength.

ABSORBENT FINISHES

For such articles as towels, bed linens, diapers, and underwear, the absorption of moisture is important. A treatment with ammonium compounds causes cottons, linens, and rayons to absorb water more readily.

A chemical finish has been found that corrects the hardness and lack of water absorbency of nylon. The use of this finish has improved the appearance, comfort, and salability of finished nylon hosiery and piece goods.[14]

AIR CONDITIONING

Short, fuzzy fibers are chemically sealed into the yarn. The fabric is thereby made more porous to permit circulation of air. Ventilation of the skin helps to make the fabric comfortable.

ANTIBACTERIAL FINISHES

In a study of perspiration made by the Chief Bacteriologist of the U.S. Testing Company, it was found that sterile perspiration, which is odorless, has no effect on fabrics and fabric finishes. The finish, if soluble, may be dissolved by perspiration just as by any other liquid, but sterile perspiration does not alter the chemical composition of the finish. Neither are the fibers weakened in tensile strength.

However, perspiration does not remain sterile. When perspiration is produced, it is immediately contaminated with various types of bacteria on the skin. Bacterial decomposition begins. It is this bacterial action that causes the odor of perspiration and has a deteriorating effect on the fabric.

Antiperspirants, applied under the arms, are commonly used to check perspiration, but they sometimes irritate the skin. To prevent the odor of perspiration, bacterial decomposition must be prevented. Germicides can be applied on the skin or on the fabrics. If the latter is the case, the

[13] *American Dyestuff Reporter* (February 1967), p. 23.
[14] Nylonex by W. F. Fancourt Company, Greensboro, N.C.

148
*Fabric
Construction
and
Buying
Motives*

germicide has to be carefully chosen. It must be colorless, in order not to stain the fabric, and odorless; it should not affect the dyes or finishes of the fabric, should not irritate the skin, and should not be removed by the first few washings. A few compounds have been found to possess these qualities. Fabrics treated with these germicides-fungicides have been found to be semipermanent (do not wash out in as many as forty washings) and to pass the sterility test of the U.S. Pharmacopeia. Fabrics treated with these compounds also sufficiently protect the wearer against the fungi that cause athlete's foot. This fabric treatment will prove effective for as many as twenty-five launderings.

Antibacterial finishes prevent bacteria-caused odors in textiles and/or the reduction of the changes of bacterial infections resulting from contact with contaminated textiles. Sanitized is a trademarked finish that protects fabrics from deterioration and odor-causing effects of bacteria, mildew, and mold.

ANTISLIP FINISHES

Seam fraying and yarns shifting (slipping) in the fabrics are common annoyances to the consumer. Finishing agents such as resins—hard, waxy substances remaining after distillation of volatile turpentine—have been used but are not generally durable to washing. Other chemical treatments reduce surface slickness but are not durable. Urea and melamine formaldehyde resins are the most durable of the finishing agents used to reduce yarn slippage.

ANTISTATIC FINISH

A chemical treatment applied to noncellulosic man-made fibers in order to eliminate static electricity is a boon to the consumer. An annoyance to the wearer is a nylon slip that clings to the body or to an outer garment; or a crackling sound as a coat is taken off; or acrylic slacks that cling to the legs on a cold, windy day. Static charge or static electricity is controlled in natural fibers and in rayon by the introduction of humidity in the air and by employing some weaving lubricants in the processing of the fibers. The newer man-made fibers, such as nylon, polyesters, and acrylics, are more difficult to process. Humidity is not the sole answer. Some type of coating must be used to carry away electrostatic charges built up on the fiber. For knit goods, Dow Badische has developed an antistatic process that will last for the life of the garment.[15] The homemaker can partially control static by the use of softeners such as Sta Puf, Downy, and Negastat in the wash water. Permanent antistatic agents have been developed by the finishing industry.

CREASE-RESISTANT FINISHES (CRF)

A crease is a fold or deformation of a fabric intentionally formed by pressing, while a wrinkle is unintentionally formed by washing and wearing. A wrinkle can usually be removed by pressing, but a crease is usually not removable. A durable press article should not have wrinkles.

[15] *America's Textiles Reporter/Bulletin*, April 1974.

Synthetic resins (melamine, epoxy, urea formaldehyde or vinyl) can be used to give resiliency. In one process, cloth is immersed in a resin solution that has a molecule small enough to permeate the cotton fibers. The fabric is then pressed between rollers to squeeze out the excess fluid. The impregnated cloth is heated until the molecules swell inside the fibers so that the resin cannot be removed by normal use, dry cleaning, or washing. A resin may be applied during the dyeing process or immediately after the dyeing when dyes have dried. Cottons so treated resist crushing, wrinkling, and creasing.

The Southern Regional Research Laboratory, Agricultural Research Service, U.S. Department of Agriculture, New Orleans, Louisiana, has developed several types of wrinkle-resistant finishes that cost only a few cents per square yard and can be easily applied in the usual equipment for resin finishing.[16]

Other strides have been made in crease-resistance experimentation. Modified starches called *oxidized starches* give crease-resistant finishes. Chemists also have discovered a compound that produces crease resistance as well as resistance to damage from chlorine after repeated washings.[17] The Electronic Smoothness Evaluator by Cluett, Peabody & Company, Inc., has already been described as the standard device for appraising the ability of a crease-resistant, wash-and-wear fabric to dry with a minimum of wrinkles after laundering. "Crease-resistant" does not mean that cotton so treated will not crease, crush, or wrinkle; it means that if and when wrinkles do appear they can be shaken out and hung out in the air.

The crease-resistant finish has been a great boon to velvets and to linens, in which crushing and wrinkling are highly undesirable.

Wash-and-wear finish insures minimum care of fabrics treated. (See *wash-and-wear*, p. 132.) The wash-and-wear concept was built on the idea that such a finish would prevent both the removal of permanent press

---

[16]Crease-resistant finishes developed at the Southern Regional Research Laboratory include formic acid colloid of methylolmelamine resin and formaldehyde finish. A no-wrinkle process, employing liquid ammonia, is being used on denim by Erwin Mills, a division of Burlington Industries Inc.

[17]This is an almost unpronounceable compound: 1, 3 Dimethyl—4, 5 dihydroxy—2—imidazolidinone. *American Dyestuff Reporter* (July 24, 1961), pp. 27-30.

FIGURE 7.14. a. Linen with crease resistant finish; b. Linen without crease resistant finish. Both fabrics were crushed in the hands. (Photos by Jonas Grushkin.)

150
*Fabric
Construction
and
Buying
Motives*

creases and the formation of wrinkles during wearing and washing. But durable press does more. It locks in the shape and locks out wrinkles for the life of a garment. Seams stay flat; no ironing. (See *durable press*, p. 158.)

Wrinkle recovery of fabrics can be tested by the American Association of Textile Chemists and Colorists Method 128—1974. The object of the test is to determine the appearance of textile fabrics after induced wrinkling. Three test specimens are used, 6″ x 11″ with the long dimension running in the warp direction of a woven fabric or the wale direction in a knit. A test specimen is wrinkled under standard atmospheric conditions in a standard wrinkling device under a predetermined load for a prescribed period of time. The specimen is then reconditioned in standard atmosphere for testing and evaluated for appearance with 3-dimensional reference standards.

Each of the three specimens is tested in turn. Then the observer, standing directly in front of the specimen four feet away from the board, assigns the number of the replica which most nearly matches the appearance of the test specimen. Number 1 rating is equivalent to WR1, the poorest appearance, while Number 5 represents the smoothest appearance and best retention of original appearance.

FLAMMABILITY FINISHES

The problem of flammability in textile fabrics came to the fore when some toddlers dressed in cowboy suits were fatally burned when they came too near a campfire. In another case, a woman wearing a sequin-trimmed gown accidentally came in contact with a lighted cigarette of a passerby. Suddenly her gown became a flaming torch. Disasters like the Cocoanut Grove and the Ringling Brothers Circus fires have shown the dangers of using flammable fabrics.

California was the first state to make rules and regulations relating to the sale of flammable merchandise. The fire marshall was designated as the person to decide on the flammability of an article. For aid in this extremely difficult task he consulted with textile experts in laboratory testing. The problem of fire hazards in wearing apparel was nationwide; it was present in every community. There was also the hazard of flammable wearing apparel that is shipped in interstate commerce. A problem of such import required federal legislation.

Accordingly, the 1953 Congress passed the Flammable Fabrics Act, which was amended in 1954. The purpose of this Act was to eliminate from the marketplace easily ignitable (dangerous) fabrics. In 1967 a new act was passed. Its purpose was to remove from the marketplace a wider range of articles of wearing apparel and interior furnishings that are so highly flammable as to be dangerous when worn by consumers or used in the home. For a few years the Secretary of Commerce, the Secretary of Health, Education and Welfare, and the FTC divided the responsibilities for enforcing this Act.

In 1972 the Consumer Product Safety Act was passed. This federal Act created the U. S. Consumer Product Safety Commission, which has broad jurisdiction over product safety. The Act also transferred responsibilities under the Flammable Fabrics Act to this Commission.

Regulations of Flammability. Following are federal regulations which implement the Flammable Fabrics Act.[18]

1. General Wearing Apparel (CS 191-53)—exclusive of interlining fabrics, certain hats, gloves, and footwear. Tests required to meet the standards: a piece of fabric in a holder at a 45° angle be exposed to a flame for one second. Flame must not spread up the sample for 3.5 seconds for smooth fabrics and 4.0 seconds for napped fabrics.

2. Large Carpets and Rugs. Carpets with areas over 24 sq. ft. (DOC FF1-70). Excludes linoleum vinyl tile and asphalt tile (nontextiles). Tests required: 9″ X 9″ samples which are exposed to a burning tablet on the center of each sample must not have a char length of more than 3″ in any direction. Test to simulate burning match dropped on carpet. Label carpet with "T" if flame-retardant has been applied. Fibers inherently flame-retardant not required to be labeled.

3. Small Carpets and Rugs (DOC FF2-72). Carpets with less than 24 sq. ft. surface area. Nontextile hard floor coverings excluded. Same tablet test as used for large carpets and rugs. Small carpets and rugs that do not pass this test must be labeled:

Flammable (Fails U.S. Dept of Commerce Standard FF2-70); Should not be used near sources of ignition.

Same requirement for labeling with letter "T" as prescribed for large rugs and carpets.

4. Mattresses and Mattress Pads (FF 4-72)

Includes ticking filled with a resilient material intended or promoted for sleeping upon, including mattress pads; but excludes pillows, boxsprings, and upholstered furniture.

Requires that the smooth, tape, and quilted or tufted mattress surfaces be exposed to a total of 9 burning cigarettes on the bare mattress and that the char length on the mattress surface be not more than 2″ in any direction from any cigarette. Two-sheeted tests are also conducted with 9 burning cigarettes placed between the sheets on surfaces as described above.

A sampling plan provides for premarket testing to detect noncomplying mattresses.

Mattresses which meet the standard are not required to have a label, although many manufacturers may attach a voluntary label stating that the mattress meets the standard.

Mattress pads must also pass the test. Those which have had a flame-retardant treatment must be labeled with the letter "T," and care labeling is required on the treated mattress pads to inform the consumer how to protect the pad against loss of flame retardance.

5. Children's Sleepwear, Sizes 0-6X (DOC FF 3-71)

Includes any garment (sizes 0-6X) worn primarily for sleeping (such as nightgowns,

---

[18] *Fact Sheet* (on flammability regulations), U.S. Consumer Product Safety Commission, Washington, D. C. 20207.

152

Fabric
Construction
and
Buying
Motives

pajamas, robes, and sleepers) but excludes diapers and underwear. Fabrics intended for use in children's sleepwear must also meet the standard.

Each of 5 samples is hung in a cabinet and exposed to a gas flame along its bottom edge for 3 seconds. The samples cannot have an average char length of more than 7″; no single sample can have a char length of 10″; and no single sample can have flaming material on the bottom of the cabinet 10 seconds after the ignition source is removed. This is required for both the new fabric or garment and after the fabric or garment has been laundered 50 times.

A sampling provides for premarket testing of fabrics and garments.

Sleepwear manufactured after July 29, 1973, must meet the standard. The manufacturer is not required to label the garment, but most manufacturers are voluntarily labeling, as follows:

Flame Retardant Fabric
This garment meets flammability requirements of Federal Children's Sleepwear Standard DOC-FF3-71 for sizes 0-6X.

Care labels must be attached if any agent or treatment could adversely affect the flame retardant qualities of the fabric.

6. Children's Sleepwear, Size 7-14 (FF 5-64)

Includes any garment (sizes 7-14) worn primarily for sleeping (such as nightgowns, pajamas, robes, and sleepers), but excludes underwear. Fabrics intended for use in children's sleepwear must also meet the standard.

Requirements are similar to but slightly less stringent than those for sleepwear sizes 0-6X.

A sampling plan will be used to test fabrics and garments.

Labeling: All sleepwear will have to bear permanent precautionary labels providing instructions for proper care.

State Laws and Standards. In addition to the federal law on flammability, there are some state laws and standards. For instance:

California: Law regulating the flammability of children's clothing (Senate Bill #1011)

Requires children's sleepwear, sizes 0-14, which is manufactured for sale, to meet federal flammability standards for children's sleepwear, sizes 0-6X.

Requires the state fire marshal to announce flammability regulations covering other articles of new children's clothing through size 14, effective July 1, 1975.

FLAMEPROOF AND FIREPROOF, FLAME-RESISTANT OR FLAME-RETARDANT FINISHES

It is estimated that 150,000 persons in this country are burned each year in accidents in which clothing is set on fire. Thousands are burned from bedding and home furnishings fires.

There is a slight technical difference between flameproofing and fireproofing. One authority defines a "flameproof" material as one "showing no afterflame or afterglow." "Fireproof" as applied to a material denotes ability to "withstand exposure to flame or high temperature and still perform the function for which originally intended."

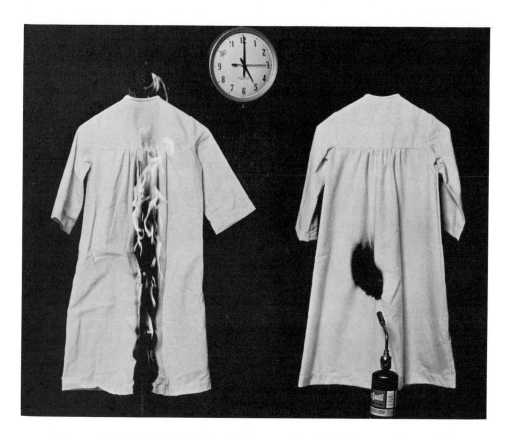

FIGURE 7.15. Self-extinguishing cotton flannel nightgown at right, treated with PROVATEX CP, a flame retardant compound developed by CIBA Chemical & Dye Company, chars but puts itself out when exposed to flame from a Bunsen burner. However, the untreated flannel gown at the left, which was exposed to a lighted match at the same time, became engulfed in flame in 15 seconds. (Courtesy of CIBA Chemical & Dye Company.)

There are several processes of rendering fabrics flameproof. One of the early processes involved an oil-in-water technique. Another process involves coating nylon or polyester fabrics with a new plastisol plus an adhesive bonding agent that will not drop off in molten drops when flame is applied to them. Three coats are given to each side of the fabric. The result is that there is no dripping under a gas flame and that burning stops when the flame is removed.

There is also a flameproof finish for acetate, nylon, and acrylic fibers, but the process cannot be used on cotton or rayon. This flameproofer is an emulsified clear liquid applied by specific methods in the dyebath.[19] Kiesling-Hess Finishing Co., Inc., has two types of flameproofing formulas: (1) Two Texpruf formulas, one which will withstand dry cleaning without losing its flameproof character, and a second Texpruf formula that will remain effective up to initial dry cleaning regardless of lapse of time, but will require reflameproofing after cleaning; (2) Pyroset

[19] This product is made by the Apex Chemical Company, Inc.

154
*Fabric
Construction
and
Buying
Motives*

and F I Retard NBX that withstands up to 20 dry cleanings and Flametrol "69" that provides permanent flameproofing.

Certificates or affidavits of flameproofing are required in most areas where local laws require such documents be issued by the processor who supplies them with each order.

The chief difficulty in flameproofing seems to be that, if, in overcoming combustibility, a large amount of material has to be applied to the cloth, it gives the fabric a different feeling.

One principle of fireproofing is to create a finish that smothers a flame as fire extinguishers do. Carbon tetrachloride or carbon dioxide has this effect. They cut off the supply of oxygen necessary to make a fire burn and fill the air about the flame with gases that do not induce burning.

Another principle is to treat the fabric with chemicals that, when heat comes in contact with the fabric, melt and cover the fabric with nonflammable film. Simultaneously, these chemicals give off a steam that, along with the film, gives the fireproof effect. Treatment with various carbonates and ammonium salts results in the creation of noncombustible vapors.

Flame-retardant fabric exhibits appreciable resistance to afterflaming (the continuation of flaming after the source of ignition has been removed). It is an untreated fabric that shows high resistance to afterflaming or a treated fabric that, after treatment, shows greater resistance to afterflaming than the untreated material.

A "Firegard" finish suitable for styled fabrics is produced by M. Lowenstein & Sons, Inc., who claim that it is nontoxic; that it does not support combustion once it is away from flame; that it lasts through fifty washings; and that it does not affect the natural softness of cotton flannel.

How can flame-retardant finishes insure protection? For a slightly extra cost (minimal in the case of small items) a treated flame-retardant fabric can save life or prevent severe burns.[20]

What fibers are comparatively flame-resistant? Wool will ignite but will burn very slowly and go out by itself. Man-made textile fibers (modacrylic) are inherently flame-retardant. They do not support combustion when exposed to flame or heat. A high-temperature-resistant fiber called Nomex by Du Pont does not support combustion. The FTC has given this fiber a generic classification called aramid. Nomex is used in space suits, military fabrics, and protective clothing. (See Chapter 16.) Another generic fiber is novoloid, sold under the trademark Kynol, of the Carborundum Co., Inc. Kynol chars without melting in high-temperature flames. (See Chapter 16.) Glass fibers are flame-retardant for their entire wear-life.

Cotton and rayon burn rather quickly but can, with the exception of very sheer garments, be treated with chemicals to make them flame-retardant. Rayon/acetate draperies of antique satin can be made to retard flame.

Chemicals that can impart flame resistance to polyester fibers are available. An agent used is tris (2-, 3-dibromopropyl) phosphate. It is not suitable for cotton.

[20] A fire-resistant finish called "Cease Fire" by Pickwick Draperies, Division of M. Lowenstein & Sons, Inc.

METALLIZED TREATMENTS

Woven fabrics may be coated with synthetic resin containing a good percentage of finely ground aluminum bronze. Such fabrics have increased insulation and are therefore claimed to be warm. Another method is to vaporize a variety of metals onto fabrics in a high vacuum to produce a metal coating less than 1/1000 millimeter thick. Still another method impregnates the textile material or fabric with aluminum. This finish, which may be added to one or both sides of the fabric, makes the fabric heat-resistant to 2500° F. It is claimed by the United States Testing Company that the aluminum coating preserves 96 percent of the heat from penetrating the material. The coating has many consumer and industrial uses, among them barbecue mitts and curtains for industrial furnaces.

Draperies with metallized linings reflect sunlight, hence keep out heat. When the room is being heated, the finish holds the heat in. Satins and taffetas respond well to metallized treatments. Trademarked names for these treatments include Milium, Temp-Resisto, and Therm-O-Ray.

MILDEW AND ROT-REPELLENT FINISHES

Mildew is a parasitic fungus that grows rapidly in warm humid weather. Fabrics of cotton, linen, rayon, and wool are particularly vulnerable to this fungus. Microorganisms present in the air and soil can grow on wet fibers. Consequently if clothing is not completely dry before it is put away, it can mildew. If clothing is improperly rinsed, soap or oils adhere to the fibers and provide a field for the growth of mildew.

Prevention of mildew is possible by treating the fabrics with nontoxic, odorless germicides. Certain metallic salts have this effect. For cotton, one method is to modify the cotton fiber so its surface is cellulose acetate, which is resistant to mildew. A resin impregnation of the cotton fiber, which prevents contact of the microorganism with the fiber, can be used.

Permanent rotproofing of cotton is possible through a treatment with a condensation resin. A new technique overcomes the drawback of loss of strength of the cotton fiber that resulted from conventional methods of applying condensation resins. If a suitable organic mercury compound is added to the rotproofing finish, then it is possible to protect cotton against surface mildew growth.[21]

The burying of treated and untreated specimens in soil rich in rot-producing fungi for a definite time is the test procedure for resistance of textiles to mildew and rot. When the specimens are removed from the earth, they are tested for breaking strength against controls.[22]

MOTH-REPELLENT TREATMENTS

To mothproof a fabric in the finishing process, colorless chemicals similar to dyestuffs are added to the dye bath. This treatment makes the fabric permanently moth repellent. Although this method is effective, the high cost of the chemicals required may make its use prohibitive. Another way

[21] Process by Ciba-Geigy, Basel, Switzerland.
[22] American Association of Textile Chemists and Colorists (A.A.T.C.C.) Standard Test Method 34-1952.

is to atomize the finished fabric with the mothproofing chemical, which is colorless, odorless, and harmless to humans. Fabrics so mothproofed are delivered to the garment manufacturer. The compound used in processing the fabric either poisons the moth or kills it upon contact.

Consumers and dry cleaners often make a fabric moth repellent by spraying it thoroughly with a mothproofing chemical. This treatment is not a finishing process (see p. 569 for methods of mothproofing upholstery). Paradichlorobenzene crystals or naphthalene mothballs are recommended for the closet where wool garments are stored. A clean fabric does not attract moths as quickly as a soiled fabric. Frequent exposure to sunlight is effective if the color is fast.

Wool or silk fabrics may be made moth repellent. Cotton, linen, and the man-made fibers do not attract moths.

To test for insect resistance, a specified number of insects (black carpet beetles, furniture carpet beetles, webbing clothes moths, or other species of insect pests) are allowed to feed on a fabric for fourteen days under controlled conditions of temperature and humidity. Below a set tolerance limit, textiles are considered satisfactorily insect-resistant, and above this limit they are considered to be inadequately protected (AATCC Standard Test Method 24-1952).

OPTICAL FINISHES

Luster. Mercerization has been described as a finish that increases a fabric's luster. Glazing and calendering also produce luster. The way in which a light is reflected from a fiber's surface owing to its transparency or shape produces luster. Silk has a natural sheen, and some man-made fibers may have considerable luster.

Delustering Treatments. In finishing, fabrics can be delustered by special heat treatments that change light reflection by softening the yarn and the surface of the cloth. Coating the surface of the fabric has a delustering effect.

Optical brighteners.[23] Consumers may find that many fabrics lose their whiteness, brightness, and clearness during the wear-life. To prevent this, optical brighteners have been employed. They are used as finishes and may be added to many home laundering agents. These brighteners become affixed to the fabric so that they appear to create brightness the way they reflect light. Some optical brighteners are built into the product to insure continued whiteness. The fluorescent material of the agent changes ultraviolet light wavelengths into visual wavelengths and remits them as such to give a fluorescent effect. Loss of energy of this fluorescent material through usage fails gradually to transform these light waves. Today, almost all soaps and detergents contain optical brightness additives that can be renewed with each laundering.

The effectiveness of optical brighteners, in a large measure, is based on the ultraviolet source of light, such as (1) natural sunlight, (2) fluorescent lighting, (3) ultraviolet or "black" lamps. Regular household light bulbs

---

[23] Optical brighteners are also called ultra violet brighteners (UV brighteners, fluorescent brighteners, and white dyes).

have no ultraviolet, so optical brighteners[24] are of no value under this type of lighting.

SLACK MERCERIZATION

The purpose of this finish is not so much to achieve luster, as it is to give for fabric elasticity. (See *mercerization*, p. 140, for a description of regular mercerization.) In slack mercerization, the 100 percent cotton or cotton blend fabric is immersed in a caustic soda bath without any tension so that yarns in the fabric shrink or buckle. Stretch is evident when the fabric is pulled to its unshrunken dimension. In this method, the amount of stretch and its durability are questionable. But this technique is inexpensive.

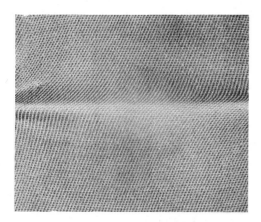

FIGURE 7.16. Slack mercerization. (Photo by Jonas Grushkin.)

STARCHLESS FINISH

To obviate the use of starch for a crisp finish that can be durable for repeated washings, cottons are treated with a resin (plastic). This starchless finish is permanent and does not dissolve in laundering. The fabric can be washed, and when ironed presents its original crisp appearance.

The permanent starchless finish is used on organdy, lawn, voile, and other sheer cottons. Fibers are sealed down by the starchless finish, so that cotton fabrics stay clean longer. Heberlein is the original Swiss process for permanent crisp-finish organdy. In this process chemicals fuse the cotton fibers, making the fabric smooth and lintless.

Permanent starchless finish can also be used on curtains, draperies, bedspreads, and sheer cottons for apparel. Embossed or frosty-etched white patterns, formerly put in cloth by weaving, can now be applied in the finishing process at moderate cost. When applied to plissé crepe, greater permanency of crinkle is obtained.

Starchless finish can be used on cotton, linen, silk, and rayon fabrics to insure permanent crispness without starch.

[24] J. J. Pizzuto, *Fabric Science*, rev. by A. Price and A. Cohen, (N.Y.: Fairchild Publications, 1974), p. 247.

158
*Fabric
Construction
and
Buying
Motives*

DURABLE OR PERMANENT PRESS

At the time of the fifth edition of this book (1964), durable press was a technical curiosity. In 1968 durable press became part of our household language, while today it is taken for granted.

Durable press or permanent press is not a specific finish per se. The term is used to describe ready-made garments and domestics (such as table linens and bed sheets) that continue to maintain a smooth appearance after many launderings and wearings, and require no ironing. Furthermore, durable press describes "ready-made textile articles that retain or resist the removal of creases or pleats intentionally put into these articles."

History of Durable Press. Prior to the development of durable press, certain cross-linking chemicals had been applied to cotton and rayon yards goods in the dyeing and finishing processes for the purpose of improving wrinkle resistance and reducing shrinkage. Garments made of these chemically treated and cured (baked) fabrics were known as wash-and-wear. However, these garments often required touch-up ironing, and few garments retained their creases or pleats after repeated wearings and launderings.

In short, these wash-and-wear fabrics were precured at the mill before the garment was constructed.

By adding two to three times as much resin as before to 100 percent cotton slacks and by precuring, excellent wrinkle resistance, crease retention, and dimensional stability were made possible. But reduced tensile strength and reduced edge abrasion became very noticeable. So the 100 percent cotton content of slacks was replaced by polyester/cotton and polyester/nylon blends. The cotton content gave required wrinkle resistance and the man-made fibers provided improved edge and flat abrasion resistance. However, the precuring as a flat fabric presented a problem in some garments because when the garment was constructed the fabric had a "memory" for its flat state and tended to return to that condition. Particularly was this a problem in retension of sharp creases in slacks, pleats in dresses, and nonpuckering seams. Where the shape of a garment and its pleats and creases were factors, methods had to be found to give "memory" to the shape of the completed garment. The answer was to postcure the garment (after garment construction).

Methods of Producing Durable or Permanent Press.

(a) Postcured or deferred cured. Polyester/cotton fabric is chemically treated at the mill or finishing plant, but it is not cured. The chemical component (a thermosetting resin) reacts with the cellulose fiber and is cured only when subjected to certain degrees of heat (325° F) for from 5 to 15 minutes. This is called post-, or deferred, curing because heat is applied *after* the garment has been constructed and pressed. Postcuring sets the pleats and the garment's shape permanently. The cotton content in the blend may lose strength and abrasion resistance in curing, but the polyester compensates for the cotton's loss in strength. This method was first marketed in 1964.

(b) Precured. A polyester/cotton blend is impregnated with resin and cured at the mill or finishing plant. Hence the method is called precured.

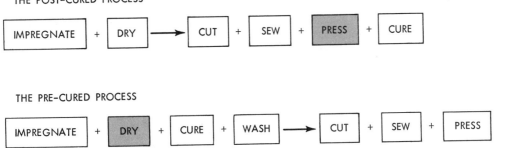

FIGURE 7.17. Flow diagrams of the post-cured process and the precured process. (Courtesy of Celanese Fibers Marketing Company.)

After curing, the fabric is sold to the sewn-goods manufacturer who cuts, sews and presses it (with a hot-head press) to heat-set the thermoplastic materials in the blend. Sewing with specially developed sewing threads that are sewn in the seams and in a relaxed tension can prevent seam puckering.

(c) Recured. As the fabric is being precured, as explained above, a chemical is applied to it which breaks down the molecules of the resin being applied so that the fabric is temporarily uncured. Further application of heat both recures the resin and heat-sets the thermoplastic (polyester) fibers. Thus, the durable press is accomplished in two different ways at the same time.

(d) No-cure. In this method neither resin nor chemical is used. A special hot-head press is applied to the finished garment to heat-set the thermoplastic fibers, which should be at least 90 percent of the total fabric.

Some Problems of Durable or Permanent Press. While durable press has been a great boon to the homemaker, it has had its problems. Here are some of them:

1. A strength loss and reduced abrasion resistance in cellulosic fibers when treated with the necessary amounts of resin to create durable press (DP). Rayon is also affected. Therefore, 100 percent cellulosic fibers are blended with thermoplastic fibers (usually polyester).
2. Frosting—a color change of a cotton/polyester blended fabric that has been subjected to abrasion at certain wear points, like the crease of pants, collar, and elbows. Since cotton weakens when resin treatment is applied for DP, cotton wears away before the polyester.
3. Repairs and alterations are difficult to make on DP garments, for example, lengthening hems of dresses or slacks and letting out seams.
4. Seam puckering of resin treated fabrics. (See Figure 16.2 for rating appearance of seams after laundering.)
5. Laundering—wrinkles may occur unless DP garments are removed when the dryer stops because heat and weight of the clothes in the dryer may cause wrinkles. Tumble drying is generally recommended. In lieu of a mechanical dryer, drip drying, with an occasional shake of the article, helps the garment keep its DP features.
6. Objectionable (fishy) odors of new DP fabrics may be overcome by a second laundering.

159

160

*Fabric
Construction
and
Buying
Motives*

7. Poor moisture absorptive quality of DP makes fabrics warm because hydrophobic fibers plus plastic resin are used.
8. Collection of soil, especially oily soils, on DP fabrics in ordinary home laundering. Soil release finishes have been developed.

SOIL RELEASE FINISHES

There are several types of soil release finishes, and their chief purpose is the same, namely to increase the absorbency of the fabric. In the previous section on problems of durable press, it was stated that lack of absorbency of hydrophobic fibers plus the plastic resin for DP were problems in stain removal. Hydrophobic fibers do not permit wetting thoroughly in laundering.

One type of soil release is said to have the following advantages:[25]

1. To allow the stain to leave the fabric faster.
2. To enhance wicking action for greater wear comfort.
3. To make the fabric dry-cleanable without appreciably affecting soil release properties.
4. To maintain the brightness of the fabric through repeated launderings.

[25] Trademark Visa by Deering Milliken, Inc.

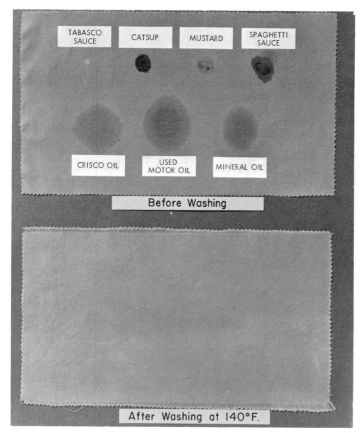

FIGURE 7.18. Acrylic Polymer Soil Release Finishes are neither hydrophobic nor oleophobic, but holds stains off the fiber. This soil release product is based on new fluorochemical technology developed by 3M. (Courtesy of *Textile World.*)

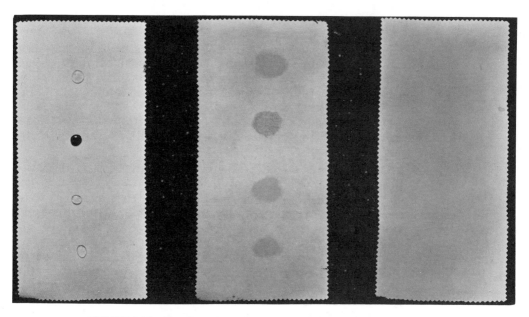

FIGURE 7.19. This Soil Release Finish is resistant to either oil- or water-borne stains, which were applied, rubbed in, and removed in one home laundering. The finish is chemical, using a modified fluorocarbon resin. (Courtesy of *Textile World.*)

WATERPROOFING AND WATER-REPELLENT FINISHES

The use for which a fabric is intended determines whether it should be waterproof, water-repellent, or stain-repellent. For umbrellas, galoshes, and raincoats, the fabrics should be waterproof. Waterproofing, done by several patented processes, closes the pores of the fabric. The most common processes consist of treatment with:

1. Insoluble metallic compounds such as aluminum soap, basic acetate of aluminum, mineral khaki, cuprammonium.
2. Paraffin or mixed waxes.
3. Bituminuous materials, such as asphaltum or tar.
4. Linseed oil or other drying oils.
5. Combinations of methods 1, 2, 3, and 4.

Treatment 1 (cuprammonium) is often used to make cotton mildew-resistant. But this treatment cannot be applied at home. Formulas for waterproofing and mildewproofing are given in the *Farmer's Bulletin* No. 1454.[26]

Water-repellent finishes do not close the pores of the fabric against air as does waterproofing. Hence, water-repellent fabrics are not so warm to wear as waterproofed fabrics; they can "breathe." The fabrics are treated to resist the penetration of water. The degree of resistance varies from a spot-proof or stain-repellent fabric to a showerproof cloth. To be

[26] *House and Garden Bulletin No. 42*, Consumer Service Dept. of U.S.D.A., Supt. of Documents, U.S. Government Printing Office, Washington, D.C. 20402.

showerproof, a cloth must resist penetration of water under considerable pressure.

Water repellents are surface finishes. Therefore, sizing, dirt, fats, and other foreign matter should be removed before finishing. Water-repellent fabrics are treated with wax and resin mixtures, aluminum salts, silicones, aluminum compounds, fluorochemicals, and others. Water-repellent finishes for polyester fabrics can be based on silicones or fluorochemicals. With proper preparation of polyester/cotton fabrics, water-repellent finishes can be applied in combination with cross-linking agents to give durable press rainwear.

There are two classes of water repellents:

1. Nondurable repellents. On the one hand these have excellent water resistance, are inexpensive, and are easy to apply. On the other hand, this class is nonlaunderable and nondry-cleanable and does not resist oily liquids. These repellents are used for tarpaulins, tents, and awnings.

2. Durable repellents are of several kinds. Some are developed for durability to dry cleaning only, others for durability to laundering only, while still others are durable to both dry cleaning and laundering. The fluorocarbon compounds are particularly resistant to oily stains. For instance, these fluorocarbon types used on wool resist oil as well as water.[27]

There are several standard test methods developed by the AATCC[28] and the ASTM. These tests require special laboratory equipment. A simple consumer-type test is done by spreading the fabric on a flat table top to determine whether it is water-repellent. Sprinkle droplets of water on the surface of the fabric. Wait a few minutes to see if the cloth absorbs the water or if droplets of water will remain on the surface of the fabric. If droplets remain, the fabric is water-repellent.

The AATCC devised a method for predicting, by means of an air-porosity test before a fabric is treated, whether it is suitably constructed for a water-repellent finish, and also the degree of protection that may be expected from this fabric when it has been treated.

[27] Scotchgard and Zepel.
[28] AATCC Standard Test Method 22-1952; ASTMD 583-54.

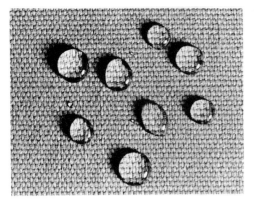

FIGURE 7.20. Water-repellent fabric. (Photo by Jonas Grushkin.)

The problem of water-repellent finishing is a difficult one because the fabric, to be comfortable, must be porous to allow circulation of air, and at the same time it must prevent water from leaking through. Consequently the fibers and yarns must be water resistant, and the construction must be well balanced and sufficiently close. In one test, two fabrics weighed the same number of ounces per square yard, the count of cloth was similar, the balance of the cloth was good, and it was adequate for the water-resistant finish; but the yarns in one sample were finer than the other, and the fabric with finer yarn showed leakage.

According to the results of this research, fabrics suitable for water-resistant finishing should have a combination of the following: (1) proper construction; (2) suitable permeability to air; (3) satisfactory water resistance of fibers and yarns.

Generally the label indicates whether the water-repellent finish can be dry-cleaned or laundered. Instructions on the label should be followed to insure the maximum service from such finishes.

SUMMARY

Fabric finishes vary in their effectiveness and durability. This means that the consumer who knows the difference between a water-repellent and waterproof garment will make a more appropriate selection of rainwear for a specific use. For example, for fishing or hunting in rainy weather, a waterproof raincoat would be essential because of the extensive length of time often spent in the rain. The informed consumer would choose a durable type water-repellent coat for short exposure to rain or snow.

Some of the finishing processes that have been discussed are mechanical in nature; this group includes those that employ rollers, steam, and pressure. The rest of the finishing processes are chemical in nature; they include weighted, mothproof, fire-retardant, crease-resistant, water-repellent, and mildew-resistant finishes; wash-and-wear; durable press; and bleaching, dyeing, and printing. These last two processes will be discussed in the next chapter.

REVIEW QUESTIONS

1. Why is a fabric not ready for sale to the consumer as soon as it is woven?
2. What is the purpose of finishing processes?
3. List and describe the finishing processes generally used for cotton broadcloth shirting.
4. (a) What finishes give luster to a fabric?
   (b) Describe each finish.
5. (a) What is sizing?
   (b) Why is sizing used to finish cotton fabrics? linen fabrics? silk fabrics?
6. (a) How may permanent creped effects be produced?
   (b) How is permanent embossing possible?
7. (a) What is calendering?
   (b) What textile fabrics are calendered?
8. When is it necessary to bleach a fabric?
9. (a) What is a permanent finish? a nonpermanent finish?
   (b) Give examples of each type.
10. (a) What is weighting?
    (b) When would it be used?
11. Give the provisions of the FTC ruling for shrinkage.

164

*Fabric
Construction
and
Buying
Motives*

12. Give the provisions of the Flammable Fabrics Act as last amended.
13. Compare durable press and wash-and-wear.
    (a) Give the methods of producing each.
    (b) What are the merits and drawbacks of each?
14. Define the following terms: moiré, crease-resistant, beetling, mercerizing, permanent finish, glazing, singeing, tentering, Sanforized, heat setting, embossing, sizing, rubberizing, piece dyeing, flame-resistant, water-repellent, waterproofing, mothproofing, preshrinkage, antistatic finish, antibacterial finish, abrasion-resistant, optical brighteners, soil release.

**EXPERI-
MENTS**

1. *Determining the permanency of finishing processes.* Before making any experiment, read the label or determine by any test previously outlined the kinds of fibers in the warp and filling of each sample:
   A. If the fabric is cotton:
      1. Rub your thumbnail over the cloth. Note whether little particles flake off the cloth. If so, the cloth is sized.
      2. If the fabric is colored, rub a white handkerchief briskly against it. Note whether some color is transferred to the handkerchief. If so, the cloth is heavily sized.
      3. Divide your sample in half. Take one half and tear it quickly. Note whether particles fly as the cloth is torn. If so, the cloth is sized.
      4. Wash a portion of the sample with warm water and soap. Dry and iron the sample and compare the washed and unwashed portions as to weight of fabric and crispness of finish.
         (a) For each sample, indicate which test or tests removed the sizing or finishing.
         (b) Were any finishes so tested permanent? How do you know?
   B. If the fabric is linen:
      1. Tear the fabric and notice whether particles fly as it is torn.
      2. Wash and iron part of the sample. Compare the laundered and unlaundered portions as to weight and luster.
         (a) Was the linen sized? If so, what do you deduce?
         (b) What finish or finishes were used? Were any of them permanent?
   C. If the fabric is rayon:
      Wash part of the fabric in warm water and soap flakes. Dry it and compare with the unwashed sample.
      (a) Was any of the luster or design removed by the washing?
      (b) Is the finish fast to washing?
   D. If the fabric is wool:
      1. Brush the back of the cloth with a stiff brush. Note whether short fibers come out.
      2. Rub two pieces of the cloth briskly together. Note whether the surface shines more after friction is applied. Was any nap removed?
      3. Cut the sample in half. Wash one half with warm water and soap. Dry and iron it; then compare the washed with the unwashed portion as to size, color, and softness.
         (a) Was the sample flocked? If so, did flocking affect the durabiility, weight, or warmth of the cloth?
         (b) Was the cloth tested fast to friction? Why?
         (c) Was the cloth fast to laundering? Why?
         (d) Would you consider the finish of a wool fabric permanent if it were fast to friction and to laundering? Explain.
   E. If the fabric is labeled durable press:
      Cleanse one half of the sample, following instructions for laundering or cleansing on the label. Note the appearance, smoothness, and hand after

cleansing, and compare with an unwashed sample.
Question: Does the sample require ironing? If yes, is the sample durable press?

GLOSSARY Absorbent finish—Chemical treatment of fabrics to improve their absorptive qualities.

Antibacterial finishes—See *Germ resistant.*

Basic finishes—Regular processes (mechanical or chemical) applied in some form to a fabric after it has been constructed.

Beetling—A process of pounding linen or cotton to give a flat effect. Beetling gives a linen-like appearance to cotton.

Bleaching—A basic finishing process to whiten fabrics. Different chemicals are used for different fabrics. Sun, air, and moisture are good bleaches for some materials, though bleaching by this method is slower.

Boardy fabric—A fabric which is too stiff. Maybe due to excessive amounts or improper application of chemical finishing materials.

Brushing—Removing short, loose fibers from a cloth by means of cylinder rolls covered with bristles.

Burling—Removing of irregularities, such as knots or slubs, with a small pick.

Calendering—A finishing process for fabrics that produces a shiny, smooth surface by passing the cloth through hollow, heated cylinder rolls or by running the cloth through a friction or glazing calender, as for chintz.

Carbonizing—A chemical treatment of wool to burn out vegetable matter.

Chemical finishing processes—Treatments with alkalies, acids, bleaches, starch, resins, and the like.

Crabbing—See Glossary, Chapter 12.

Crease resistant—A chemical finishing process to enable a fabric to resist and recover from wrinkling.

Creping—A chemical or embossing process that, when applied as a finish, gives a cloth a crinkled surface.

Decating—A process for setting the luster on wool, silk, spun silk, and rayons.

Degumming—A process for removing natural gum from silk by boiling it in a soap solution.

Dressing—See *Sizing.*

Drip dry—To hang up without wringing and let the article drip and dry.

Durable press—See Glossary, Chapter 3.

Embossing—A finish produced by pressing a raised design into a fabric by passing the fabric through hot engraved rollers. Permanent when heat-set.

Finishes—Basic or functional processes applied to a cloth after it has been constructed.

Fireproof—A fabric that is not affected by fire.

Fire resistant—A fabric treated to prevent the spread of flame.

Flammable Fabrics Act—A law passed by the Eighty-Third Congress and signed by President Eisenhower on June 30, 1953, prohibiting the introduction or movement in interstate commerce of clothing fabrics that are flammable enough to be dangerous when worn. Amended in 1967.

Flocking—Adding weight to woolens by steaming fibers into the back of the fabric; or sticking short fibers to a fabric base with an adhesive or by electrolysis.

Fulling—A shrinking process to make wool fabrics more compact and thicker. See *Felting*, Glossary, Chapter 2.

Functional finishes—Special finishes that contribute a specific attribute to the merchandise; for example, soil release, crease resistant, and water repellent.

Germ resistant—Fabrics treated with compounds to protect the wearer against fungi and germs.

Gigging—A process of raising fibers on the surface of a fabric to make it softer and to increase its warmth. It is done by teasels. See *Napping.*

Glazing—A finishing process consisting of treating the fabric with glue, starch, paraffin, shellac, or resin, and then moving it through hot friction rollers.

166

*Fabric
Construction
and
Buying
Motives*

Grey goods—See Glossary, Chapter 1.

Limp fabric—A fabric which is too soft due to inadequate amounts or improper application of finishing materials.

Mechanical finishes—Those finishing processes done by copper plates, roller brushes, perforated cylinders, tenter frames, or any type of mechanical equipment.

Mercerization—A treatment of cotton with caustic soda to make it stronger, more lustrous, and more absorbent, and to increase its affinity for dye.

Mildew resistant—Fabrics treated with metallic compounds and certain organic compounds. Waterproofed fabrics will also resist mildew.

Milling—See *Fulling.*

Moireing—A finishing process producing by engraved rollers a waved or watered effect on a textile fabric. Design permanent when heat-set.

Moth repellent—Fabrics treated with colorless chemicals, similar to dye-stuffs, added to the dye bath. Another method atomizes the fabric with mothproofing chemicals.

Napping—The process of raising short fibers of a cloth to the surface by means of revolving cylinders with wire brushes.

Nonpermanent finish—A finish that is removed when subjected to such agents as friction, laundering, light, and heat.

Permanent finish—One that will withstand whatever effects it in its particular use.

Permanent starchless—A process that impregnates a cloth with compounds that are not dissolved in laundering. When ironed, the cloth returns to its original crispness.

Plastic-coated fabric—A plastic film supported by a woven or knitted cloth.

Preshrunk—Fabrics that have been given a shrinking process before being put on the market. The percentage of residual shrinkage must be declared.

Residual shrinkage—The percentage of possible shrinkage remaining in a fabric after it has been preshrunk.

Scouring—A finishing process for removing oil, sizing, and dirt from fabrics.

Shearing—Cutting off excess surface fibers from a cloth.

Singeing—Removing surface fibers and lint from a cloth with hot copper plates or gas flames.

Sizing—A finishing process in which glue, wax, casein, or clay is added to the cloth to give it additional strength, smoothness, or weight.

Soil release—The ability of a fabric to permit the removal of water-borne and or oil stains by the usual laundering methods. These may be a special finish.

Special finishes—See *Functional finishes.*

Spot resistant—See *Water repellent.*

Stabilizing—Treating a fabric so that it will not shrink or stretch more than a certain percentage, perhaps 2 percent.

Starching—See *Sizing.*

Tentering—A basic finishing process done by a frame that makes the fabric even in width.

Wash-and-wear—Original chemically treated and cured (baked) fabrics. Often requires touch-up ironing.

Waterproofing—Treatment of fabrics to close the pores of the cloth.

Water repellent—A chemical treatment of a fabric to reduce its affinity for water. Pores of the fabric are open, and the degree of repellency varies.

Weighting—Finishing materials applied to a fabric to give increased weight.

Dyeing
and Printing

8

Mrs. Morris purchased a pair of shorts at her favorite sportswear department. When she reached home she hurriedly read the care label, noting that it said: This fabric is colorfast. That's good, she thought, and then cut off the label.[1] A few days later when the shorts needed laundering, she wondered if she should have them dry-cleaned or wash them in the washing machine. Should I use hot or warm water, and what setting? she thought. All these questions and more might have been answered on the label had Mrs. Morris left it sewn to the shorts.

COLOR-FASTNESS A distinction should be made between the two coloring systems used in textiles: *dyeing* (internal pigmentation) and *painting*, which includes printing (external pigmentation). In dyeing and staining, the coloring material penetrates the fibers and becomes an integral part of their structures. In painting, the pigment is applied to the fiber surface with a polymer binder between the fiber and the pigment; this is also called the pigment emulsion method. In general, the internal method of coloring is more fast to color than the external one.

SUITABILITY OF DYESTUFF

Perhaps if Mrs. Morris had carefully read the label on her shorts, she would have found not only instructions for laundering but also the information that the color was fast to sunlight—a characteristic so important in sportswear. The wise consumer considers, in addition to the qualities of the fibers, yarns, weaves, and finishing processes, the element of color—the suitability of dye to various uses. The buyer has a right to expect dyed fabrics to withstand the deteriorating elements or influences to which the finished cloth will be subjected—sunlight, perspiration, washing, and friction. Although most fabrics are not equally fast to all these destructive agents, they must be fast to those with which they will come in contact in their particular uses. For example, upholstery fabrics should withstand sunlight, but it is not so important that they withstand washing or perspiration. Summer furniture covers, on the other hand,

---

[1] See permanent care labeling, Chapter 1.

must be fast to sunlight and to laundering. An evening dress should be fast to perspiration and to dry cleaning, but it does not have to be fast to sunlight. Fabrics for sportswear should be fast to sunlight, to washing, and generally to perspiration. Dyes that are fast for the purpose for which the fabric is intended are termed *fast dyes.*

FASTNESS TO SUNLIGHT

Commercial testing agencies frequently use standard tests for lightfastness. A specially designed powerful carbon-arc lamp has the same effect as strong sunlight. Samples to be tested revolve around this lamp for a definite period of exposure.

Because consumers do not have access to standard laboratory equipment, some simple home tests are suggested in the following text. For comparison, commercial tests are briefly outlined.

Home Tests. Exposure to outdoor light: A 3-inch square of colored fabric is cut in half. One half is placed under a glass outdoors in a spot where it will get the maximum of hours of sunlight. After one week's exposure, the exposed half is compared with the other half, which has been kept in a box. Any change of color is noted. The same fabric can be exposed similarly for two weeks, and then for three weeks. Any change of color can be noted each time. If there is an appreciable change of color, the color is not fast to sunlight.

Commercial Tests. A. Sunlight method: Specimens are exposed against standards, on sunny days only, between the hours of 9 a.m. and 3 p.m.

B. Fade-Ometer[2] method: Colorfastness is rated in terms of number of "standard fading hours required to produce just appreciable fading" (change of color of any kind), when compared with unexposed samples.

[2] AATCC American Association of Textile Chemists and Colorists.

FIGURE 8.1 A Fade-Ometer measures a dye's colorfastness to light (Photo courtesy Celanese Fibers Marketing Co.)

C. Daylight test: Specimens are allowed to remain in a test cabinet for 24 hours a day. Specimens are also exposed to low intensity radiation (before 9 a.m. and after 3 p.m.), and on cloudy days, during which time the specimen temperature may be low and the moisture content high. Since the three tests may produce varying results, laboratories test a specimen under a variety of conditions simulating the performance from the fabric in a machine called a Weather-Ometer.

FASTNESS TO PERSPIRATION

Light-colored silks, especially those used for evening wear, should be fast to perspiration. Most consumers rely on the salesperson's advice concerning the fastness of a fabric to perspiration. In fact, some large department stores have their own merchandise testing laboratories, to which buyers may send new materials for testing fastness before instructions are given to the salespeople. Reliable manufacturers often provide the buyers with the same information. In buying yard goods, however, the consumer can usually obtain a sample of material, take it home, and test it before buying enough for her needs.

Home Test. It is best to subject the fabric to actual wear. A small piece of material may be worn in the sole of the shoe for a day. A quicker test is to sew a swatch of material to a white cloth of the same general texture, then immerse both for a moment in vinegar (not cider but synthetic vinegar), and let it dry. If stained, the sample is not fast to perspiration. Synethic vinegar is used because it comes closest to perspiration; both contain acetic acid.

Commercial Test (AATCC 15). Separate specimens are wetted out in alkaline and acid perspiration solutions. Fabrics are inserted in a perspiration tester; are subjected to a fixed mechanical pressure; and are allowed to dry slowly in an oven $10 \pm 2°$ F. for at least six hours. Bleeding, migration of color, or changes of dyed material are evaluated.

FASTNESS TO LAUNDERING

The best way to determine fastness to laundering is actually to launder a fabric. Ideally, the consumer should launder a small piece of material as many times as the fabric would be expected to resist laundering in actual use. Of course, this is too much to ask of the average consumer. Many testing laboratories do this very thing for the manufacturers and retail stores. For example, suppose that the specifications for a certain brand of sheet require that "the sheet must be fast to 20 washings in a reliable laundry and after these washings shall lose not more than 8 percent of its tensile-strength testing to make sure it is up to specifications."

Home Tests. A. Hand laundering: A 6-inch square of colored fabric should be cut into three equal parts. One of the parts is sewn to a 2-inch swatch of white cotton cloth of about the same weight and texture as the test cloth. It should be washed with warm water and strong soap, rinsed in clear water, and then dried. It should be ironed gently with little or no pressure, if necessary to make it smooth. The color of the washed and unwashed samples is compared, and the white fabric is examined for any

170

*Fabric
Construction
and
Buying
Motives*

discoloration. One or two washings with strong soap generally give the same result as many washings with a mild soap.

B. Automatic washing: A 2-inch white swatch is basted to a colored fabric. These fabrics are subjected to a normal washing cycle in an automatic washer with usual soap solution and water temperature. No chlorine is used. Washing of the test samples can be done with a regular load of colored clothes. If there is a change of color of the washed fabric or discoloration of the white fabric, the color is not fast to the test method used.

Commercial Tests (AATCC 61). A 45-minute accelerated test: Specimens are placed in stainless steel tubes or glass jars that revolve at a standard speed in a water bath that is thermostatically controlled. Metal balls are added to each tube to simulate washing action.

TABLE 8-1. Testing Methods

Test Number	Temperature	Soap (percent)	Sodium Carbonate (percent)	Available Chlorine (percent)	Time (minutes)
1.	$105°$	40	0.5	None	30
2.	$120°$	49	0.5	None	30
3.	$160°$	71	0.5	0.2	45
4.	$182°$	83	0.5	0.2	45

Tested specimens are evaluated for alteration in color by comparing them with the international Geometric Scale. Color staining is evaluated by comparison with the AATCC chart for measuring transference of color or the Geometric Staining Scale.

FASTNESS TO DRY CLEANING.

Home Test. The procedure for dry cleaning should be followed explicitly as given in the directions on any standard brand of dry cleaning fluid.

Commercial Test (AATCC 132-69). This is the standard test for commercial dry cleaning. While there are a number of solvents that may be used in dry cleaning, the one used almost universally in this country is perchloroethylene, which has the highest solvent power. Samples of the material are treated in a Launder-Ometer with a solvent and the tested specimen compared with the Gray Scale for Color Change. Problems are encountered when two or more pigments used to produce a color are differently affected. For example, a green may be produced by an application of blue and yellow pigments, but the yellow may be soluable in the dry cleaning solution and the blue colorfast. Thus, the green may be changed to blue. See Chapter 16 for a discussion of dry cleaning procedures.

FASTNESS TO PRESSING, WET AND DRY

Home Tests. To test fastness to pressing of cotton and linen fabrics, two samples, each $\times$ 4 inches, are used. One sample is covered with a wet piece of bleached, unsized cloth.

The sample is ironed for ten seconds at 350° F. The tested sample is placed in a dark room for about an hour to regain its natural moisture. The other test sample is ironed dry for five seconds at 425° F. and is then placed in a dark room. Cotton and linen fabrics pressed wet that show no appreciable change in color and no appreciable staining of the white fabric are considered colorfast to wet pressing. Similarly, cotton and linen fabrics that show no change in color after dry pressing are colorfast to dry pressing.

For testing fabrics other than cotton and linen and other than woolens and worsteds, pieces of white wool, silk, desized cotton, rayon, and acetate cloths are sewn to one test sample. For wet pressing, the test sample is wetted, the surplus water is shaken off, and the sample is placed face down on the dry-test sample. Then the fabric is allowed to rest for one hour. Another sample is tested for ten seconds with a flat iron between 275° and 300° F. Fabrics that pass both tests are colorfast to wet and dry pressing.

Commercial Test (AATCC 117). A piece of colored fabric is placed between two pieces of uncolored cloth (composite specimen). The fabrics are placed in a heating device or Scorch tester, German Precision Heating Press, or Molten Metal Bath for 30 seconds at one of the following test temperatures:

$$300° \pm 5° \text{ F.}$$
$$325° \pm 5° \text{ F.}$$
$$350° \pm 5° \text{ F.}$$
$$375° \pm 5° \text{ F.}$$
$$400° \pm 5° \text{ F.}$$

The composite specimen is removed from the heating device and evaluated for each component by comparing with the Gray Scale for Color Change and the Gray Staining Scale.

FASTNESS TO CROCKING

Fabrics used for street and business dresses must withstand a great deal of friction, that is, the color should not rub off, or crock, even though the fabric is not intended to be washable. Dyestuffs that crock are very likely to bleed or run. This is usually due to dyestuffs left in the surface of the goods after processing because of improper afterwashing following the dyeing. In washable fabrics crocking may be an indication that the colors are not fast to laundering. Furthermore, if a dye crocks badly, it may discolor fabrics rubbed against it.

Home Tests. A. Dry crocking: A 2-inch square of colored fabric is rubbed against a piece of white sheeting. Any discoloration of the white cloth should be noted. If there is any discoloration of the fabric itself, the color is not fast to dry crocking.

B. Wet crocking: A piece of white sheeting should be dampened and rubbed against a piece of the untested colored fabric. Any discoloration of the white cloth should be noted. If this occurs, the color is not fast to crocking.

172

Fabric
Construction
and
Buying
Motives

Commercial Tests (AATCC 8). A. Dry crocking: A test specimen is fastened to the base of the Crockmeter. A standard crock cloth is attached to the rubbing finger of the machine. The finger is lowered onto the test specimen, and by turning the crank the finger is caused to slide back and forth 20 times.

B. Wet crocking: Fabric squares are wetted in distilled water, then placed between two filter papers (like a sandwich). The "sandwich" is passed through a wringer. The transfer of color (both wet and dry) is evaluated by comparing with a chart for measuring transference of color or with the Geometric Staining Scale.

**DYEING
CLOTH**

Fabrics in colors such as blue, yellow, red, green, and their combinations are made by impregnation of the cloth with certain color substances called *dyestuffs.* The fastness of these colors depends on the chemistry of the dyestuff, the affinity of the dyestuff for the fabric, and the method of dyeing the cloth. If a color has a greater affinity for the fabric than it has for sunlight, perspiration, washing, or friction, the color will be fast to these influences.

SELECTION OF THE PROPER DYESTUFF

Until 1856 all dyestuffs were natural dyestuffs; that is, they were obtained from plants, shellfish, insects, and woods. Some of the most common natural dyestuffs are cochineal, made from the dried bodies of female insects found in Central America and Mexico, used to dye scarlet; logwood, taken from the brownish heart of a tree found in Central America; quercitron, which comes from the yellow inner bark of a large oak tree growing in the eastern part of this country; fustic, a light yellow dye coming from a tree growing in Mexico and the West Indies; and indigo, a blue dyestuff derived originally (by the Indians) from plants but now also made artifically.

Natural dyes were used in the early days of the Roman Empire—when so-called Tyrian purple was used for the ruling family. The substance that first produced the color purple was derived from a kind of snail. Pliny tells us that the art of dyeing yellow, green, and black was brought from India to Greece by Alexander the Great. In the Middle Ages, northern Italy was most skilled in the art of dyeing. The early explorers who came to American brought back many dyestuffs. Certainly dyeing is one of the oldest arts.

In oriental rugmaking a century ago, the modern commercial dyestuffs were unknown. Each family was skilled in making certain colors that would be fast to washing and sunlight. The secret formula for making a certain color from natural dyestuffs was handed down from one generation to another.

Obtaining natural dyestuffs and mixing them to obtain the desired color is a slow process compared with our present methods of commercial dyeing, in which all the dyes are synthetic or chemical. They are man-made by the mixing of certain chemicals whose bases are either salts or acids. At the present time synthetic dyes have practically replaced natural dyes.

The first synthetically made dyestuff was discovered by William Henry Perkin in 1856. He was experimenting with aniline, whose base is principally coal tar (a substance produced in the process of making coke), when he discovered the colored substance known as mauve. Later other coal-tar colors followed. But the great development in chemical dyestuffs in this country has come since World War I. During the war years 1914-1918, the dyed fabrics in the United States were of poor quality and not fast. The United States had to do much experimenting before it knew the secret of making fast synthetic dyes. Before and during the war Germany held that secret.

Dyestuffs may be classified according to their method of application to a cloth. The principal synthetic dyestuffs are (1) acid dyes; (2) mordant dyes; (3) basic colors, comprising most of the older aniline dyes; (4) direct dyes; (5) developed colors; (6) disperse dyes; (7) naphthol or azoic dyes; (8) pigments; (9) vat dyes; (10) fiber-reactive dyes; (11) metal complex dyes; (12) oxidation dyes.

ACID DYES

Acid dyes are essentially organic acids that are obtained by the dyer in the form of salts. They are applied to the fiber directly from solutions containing an acid, such as sulphuric, acetic, or formic acids. Acid dyes can be used on wool, acrylic, nylon and certain modified polyester fibers, and spandex and certain selected polypropylene olefin fibers.

Fibers sensitive to weak acid solutions and cellulosic fibers cannot be dyed with acid dyes. To dye vegetable fibers, a mordant is necessary. A *mordant* is a chemical that has an affinity for both the dyestuffs and the fabric and acts as a bridging agent forming a complex of dye and fiber.

When wet-treated, bright acid colors may not be colorfast. Acid colors are only fairly to poorly fast to washing; they vary in degree of colorfastness to perspiration; but they give good colorfastness to dry cleaning and to light.

Acid dyes are water-soluble and can be applied to silk, wool, casein, and nylon without a mordant. Acid colors can be applied to Orlon 42 and acetate fibers at high temperatures by a special method. At present, it is possible to obtain a larger range of dyes and better wet-fastness than previously. Dynel modacrylic and the older Acrilan acrylic fibers can also be colored by acid dyes.

MORDANT OR CHROME DYES

So-called chrome colors are made by mordant dyes in which chromium is used as the mordant to fix the dye on the cloth. Other metallic salts, such as iron, aluminum, or tin, may be used. These dyes are much more satisfactory on wool and silk than on cotton or linen. On cotton, these dyes usually fade when laundered; but on men's wool clothing, which is dry-cleaned rather than laundered, chrome colors are often used. Nylon colored with these dyestuffs gives good colorfastness.

Mordant or chrome dyes have properties in common with acid dyes. They are used to dye the same fibers. But the major difference lies in the fact that metal is added to the dye molecule. The metallic compound combines with the fiber and the organic dye and forms an insoluble color compound in the fiber.

174

*Fabric
Construction
and
Buying
Motives*

Some of the most commonly used mordants are salts of chromium, cobalt, iron, copper, and magnesium. Generally, the mordant is applied after the dyeing process, but in some cases the fiber substrate can be prepared with the mordant before dyeing. The dyestuff changes in shade after the metallic salts are applied, making color matching with these dyestuffs more of an art than a science.

BASIC OR CATIONIC DYES

These colors were the first synthetic dyestuffs to be discovered. Basic dyes are salts of colored organic bases. They may be called cationic because the colored portion of the dye molecule is positively charged (cationic).

Organic basic dyes are sometimes called aniline colors because the first few colors were made from aniline. Basic dyes can be applied to cotton, linen, rayon, silk, and wool for excellent color value and penetration. However, before the advent of synthetic fibers these dyes were not frequently used because of their poor light fastness on natural fibers. Medium and full shades of Acrilan 16 can be produced with basic dyes. When used on the older Acrilan, basic dyes are fast but are limited to pale and medium shades. Selected basic dyes may be used on the acrylic Orlon 81. To be used successfully on cotton or rayon they must be applied with an acid mordant, but wool and silk can be dyed directly. This class of dyes is chiefly used on cotton to brighten other, duller colors (these are "topped" with basic dyes). Basic dyes are seldom used on wool, because acid colors are generally more fast. For dyeing silk, basic dyes give brilliancy and depth of color. These colors are satisfactory for silks weighted with tin. Basic dyes are not fast to light or washing, and the method of dyeing is slow. For these reasons, basic dyes are not included in Table 8-2.

TABLE 8-2. Degree of Fastness to . . .

	Home Washing (AATCC #2)	Laundry (AATCC #3)	Light	Slasher Sizing	Chlorine	Cross Dyeing	Mercerizing
1. VAT	Excellent	Excellent	Excellent	Excellent	Excellent	Excellent	Excellent
2. NAPTHOL	Excellent	Excellent	Excellent	Excellent	Excellent to good	Excellent	Excellent
3. BONDED (Fiber-reactive)	Excellent	Very good	Fair to good	Excellent	Most dyes poor	Good	Excellent
4. DEVELOPED	Good	Fair	Fair to poor	Excellent	Poor	Good	Good
5. SULPHUR	Very good	Good	Good to fair	Excellent	Most dyes poor	Excellent	Excellent
6. DIRECT	Good in light shades of selected dyes	Fair in light shades	Excellent in selected dyes. Others fair to poor	Good in light shades	Poor	Poor	Some good

NOTE: This table is only a generalization. It refers to the relative fastness of the different dyeing methods as a class. It should be borne in mind, however, that there are exceptions within each class.

The numbers on the left indicate the price class, No. 1 being the highest priced, No. 2 next, and so on.

Reprinted courtesy of the Franklin Process Company, a division of Indian Head Yarn Company.

DIRECT OR SUBSTANTIVE DYES

These dyestuffs, like acid dyes, are salts of color acids. They are applied directly to cotton, linen, rayon, requiring no mordant. Shades so produced are duller than those colored by basic dyes, but they can be topped with basic dyes to brighten them. Direct dyes may be used for dyeing wool yarns used for knitting and weaving, for reused wool, and for casein fibers. These colors are generally not fast to washing. They are more fast to light when applied to wool than when used on cotton.

Direct colors may also be applied to silk, and shades so obtained are faster than they are on cotton. But these colors have normally been regarded as cotton dyes and have therefore not been used so frequently on silk and wool. When direct colors are used to dye nylon, the dye is usually applied from a bath set with either acetic or formic acid.

Direct dyes may be developed after application to the fabric. Naphtholic compounds are used as developers. A radical in the dye molecule reacts with the developer. Developed direct dyes may have excellent fastness to washing but a decreased lightfastness. (See *developed colors*, below.) Bright shades are obtained from both direct and developed direct dyes.

DEVELOPED COLORS

These are dyestuffs that may be applied directly to the cloth and may change to a new color on the fabric when treated with nitrous acid and certain chemicals called *developers*. The intensity of the color and the fastness of the dyestuff may be changed by this treatment. A dye that is navy blue when applied directly to a cloth may become a fast black when developed. Cotton dyed with developed colors may be washed satisfactorily at home but should not be sent to a commercial laundry.

Developed dyes may also be used on rayon and other man-made fibers when developed from disperse-dye bases. (See *disperse dyes*.) Developed colors are sometimes used for discharge printing. (See p. 183.)

DISPERSE DYES

These dyes were formerly called acetate dyes because they were originally used to dye acetate fibers. They are now used for coloring acetate, polyester, acrylic, and nylon fibers. The molecules of these dyes are small, and the dye is slightly soluble in water but is easily *dispersed* throughout a solution. The fiber's dye sites are made more accessible by swelling the fiber with wetting agents, heat, or such. The small particles are "inserted," and the water medium is evaporated by heat. This seals in the dye molecule. Ratings for colorfastness to light, washing, and dry cleaning vary depending on the fiber used. Fume fading, said to be caused by exposure to nitrogen in the air, remains a problem when disperse dyes are used on acetate. This problem is minimal when these dyes are used on nylon or polyester.

NAPHTHOL OR AZOIC DYES

Naphthol dyes are commonly applied to cotton piece goods and are used extensively in cotton printing. The cotton is first impregnated with beta-naphthol that has been dissolved in caustic soda; then it is immersed in basic dye. Naphthol colors are fast to washing and to soaping when properly applied. The application of this type of dye requires a good knowledge of organic chemistry, and failure to follow directions for its application may result in poor colorfastness to crocking and washing. Fast bright scarlets and reds can be obtained at a fairly low cost. A naphthol dye can produce a green or blue-green shade on polyester fibers.

For the dyeing of acetate, certain of the insoluble compounds of azoic dyes are used. These compounds are treated with sulfonated oil or soap. By this treatment, a stable suspension for dyeing acetate is possible.

Azoic dyes can be applied to nylon by methods similar to those used for acetate; however, the colors are not as brilliant as on cottons. By first impregnating nylon with Naphthanil, then immersing in a second bath containing hydrochloric acid, and finally developing in a sodium-nitrite-acid liquor, strong, bright, well-penetrating colors with fastness to crocking are possible. Azoic dyes may be applied to the older Acrilan acrylic fiber by the use of a modified technique. Insoluble azoics dye polyester fibers well.

PIGMENTS

Pigments are by definition insoluble in their dyeing vehicle, although a few are soluble in certain solvents. Usually they are utilized in dispersed form as microvisible particles. They are fixed to the fiber with a binder since they have no inherent affinity for the textile fibers.

The use of pigments for coloring of textiles has been a comparatively recent discovery, because it utilizes the synthetic resins in the preparation of the dye emulsion. A common method of preparing the dye is to use fine synthetic pigment in a solution of synthetic resins in an organic solvent. Water is stirred in with a high-speed mixer. The resin serves to bind the pigment to the fibers. Usually the dye so prepared is padded or printed onto the cloth. (See *pad dyeing*, p. 181.)

Pigment colors are used mostly on cotton, acetate, rayon, cellulose/polyester blends, and glass. Almost all types of fibers and blends can be colored by pigment dyeing or printing.

When properly applied, pigment prints excel in lightfastness. With the proper binder and application, such prints have acceptable washability. Abrasion may remove color as surface fixing agents wear away, making the color vulnerable to crocking.

VAT DYES

The name originated in the making of the old indigo dyes, when the dyestuff had to steep for some days before it could be used. There are three classes of vat dyes: (1) indigo, indigoids, indigosols, and algosols; (2) anthraquinoids; (3) sulfur.

Modern indigo is perhaps the most famous vat dye, because of its fastness to light and washing. Increasingly important in this group are the indigosols (colorless dyestuffs), which are being used for dyeing wool. The wool or silk is saturated with dye, and color is later developed. The indigoids are a group of vat dyes that have pigment-bearing sacs similar to indigo.

The anthraquinoids are the fastest of the vat dyes. They are especially suitable for cotton and can be applied to acetate. In this category are the indanthrene dyes, which are extremely fast.

Sulfur colors are used on cottons and vegetable fibers. Although the colors are dull, they have good fastness to light, washing, and crocking, and are relatively inexpensive. Sometimes sulfur black dye attacks and weakens the fiber, because the oxidation of the sulfur gradually develops sulfuric acid.

Probably the reason for the increased importance of the vat dye is that it possesses a higher degree of fastness to washing, light, bleaching, cross-dyeing, and mercerizing than do the other dyes. (See Table 8-2.) As a class, then, vat dyestuffs are particularly fast when applied to cotton. They are used to produce fast colors in cotton dress fabrics and in shirtings. Vat dyes can also be used for dyeing silk, linen, rayon, and wool. They can be used for acetate, but many dyers consider them unsuitable for silk. The dye bath must be strongly alkaline, and so must be weakened to prevent the alkali from attacking the silk fiber. Vat colors on nylon possess all the characteristics of these dyes on other fibers with the exception of fastness to light. For improved color value and penetration, vat dyes can be applied at high temperatures to Orlon 81 and to Acrilan. When similarly applied to Orlon 42, bright shades of excellent fastness are possible. This high-temperature dyeing technique has been successfully adapted for the processing of cotton sliver containing an appreciable amount of dead fibers.

Probably the most interesting and technical part of dyeing with vat colors is the dyeing of one shade to match another. The difficulty of matching colors lies in guessing what the final color will be after the fabric is dried, because the action of air on the newly dyed cloth changes the hue. (See *computer processes in shade matching*, p. 191.)

FIBER-REACTIVE DYESTUFFS

In general, all classes of dyestuffs are fixed to the fabric by means of physical absorption or mechanical retention of an insoluble pigment by the fiber. In both cases, the color appears to be a part of the fiber.

Fiber-reactive dyestuffs, however, couple the color to the fabric by a reaction with the hydroxide (OH) group of the cellulose molecule. In this reaction the dye molecule becomes an integral part of the cellulose. It is because of this chemical integrity that reactive dyes possess excellent wash-fastness and dry-cleaning properties.

Most reactive dyes are fixed to the fabric by a system that employs an alkali as a catalyst. This alkali promotes the transfer of electrons, which causes the color to be integrated with the cellulose. Of the many alkalies (electrolytes) used, the most common are sodium carbonate, sodium bicarbonate, and caustic soda.

In practice, the fabric would first be padded with the dye, then dried. The fabric would then undergo a second padding containing the alkali. Once this is completed, the fabric would be exposed to extreme heat, steam, or air.

Fabrics such as wool or silk can be dyed in this fashion. However, the best results are obtained on cotton. This system has obvious labor- and time-saving advantages. These are brought to light in a consideration of

178
*Fabric
Construction
and
Buying
Motives*

the time it takes to fix a dye in a system that fixes only when an exchange between dye and fabric comes to an equilibrium. An example of this is exhaustion dyeing. The time element here may be from ten minutes to hours. Today, some reactive dyes can be fixed in thirty seconds.

METAL COMPLEX DYES

The metal complex dyes are closely related to the mordant dyes. This class of dyestuffs is ionic and premetallized, thus eliminating the need for a mordant. Metal complex dyes are suitable for wool, silk, and polyamides. In addition to the salt formation of the dye with the amino groups found in these types of fibers, complex formation of the dyes with the substrate takes place. The exact chemical structure of these dyes is not known. However, wash and light fastness ratings are generally high for this class of dyestuffs.

OXIDATION DYES

Like azoic dyes, oxidation dyes are formed in the fiber substrate. Their salts are water soluble. They are applied to the fabric as an oxidation base in the form of water soluble salts and thereafter oxidized to a pigment. A well-known example of this is the aniline black process. In this process the aniline salt solution is applied to cotton in the presence of a catalyst and then submitted to air oxidation, thus fixing the dye. Similar processes are used for dyeing animal fibers and human hair. Hydrogen peroxide is often used as the oxidizing agent.

DYEING OF BLENDS

The problem of dyeing textiles has never been an easy one if the selection of the dyestuff and its application is adequate to give the performance in use expected by the consumer. With the advent of the newer synthetics, and with the increasing use of blends, the problem has become even more complex. To cite one example, consider the dyeing of a blend of Dynel modacrylic (not less than 25 percent and not more than 30 percent) and rayon. Dynel is described in Chapter 14 as a partially acrylic fiber that is sensitive to heat at the normal textile dyeing temperatures of 240° to 250° F.; unless the fabric is put in tension, it will shrink enough to make the cloth feel firm. However, the problem is being surmounted by heat treatment before dyeing in order to shrink the fiber and to reduce the tendency to feel firm after dyeing. Selected dyestuffs for acetate and regular rayon dyestuffs can be used, but, again, application of heat over 250° F. is necessary. Consequently, neutral, premetallized dyestuffs are used to give lightfastness superior to acetate dyestuffs.[3]

Ciba-Geigy Corp., Basel, Switzerland, has developed a one-bath process to dye 50 percent wool/50 percent cotton blends. The process begins with an acid dyebath to which a wool-immunizing agent is added to keep direct color off the wool. Another ingredient is added to alkalinize the dyebath as the dyeing progresses. The fabrics are brought to a boil in thirty

---

[3] Premetallized dyestuffs are those that are chemically coupled with nickel, copper, and cobalt salts to make the dye on the fiber.

minutes and boil for one hour. A typical dyebath would consist of 100 units of fabric; 4,000 units of water; 6 units of 40 percent acetic acid; and 40 units Glauber's salt; and 13 units immunizing agent. Color shades are made in the usual way, and excellent cross-dyes are possible.

These are only two of the many possible blends that a dyer may encounter. Percentages of each fiber as well as the kind of fibers and the number of different ones included in a blend are considerations in the proper selection and application of a dyestuff for a blend.

METHODS OF DYEING FABRICS

When the proper type of dyestuff has been selected, the textile can be dyed by one of the following methods:

(a)

(b)

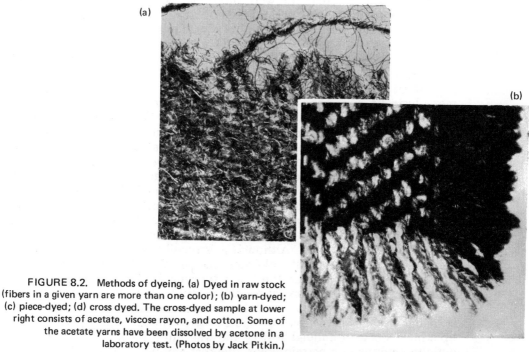

FIGURE 8.2. Methods of dyeing. (a) Dyed in raw stock (fibers in a given yarn are more than one color); (b) yarn-dyed; (c) piece-dyed; (d) cross dyed. The cross-dyed sample at lower right consists of acetate, viscose rayon, and cotton. Some of the acetate yarns have been dissolved by acetone in a laboratory test. (Photos by Jack Pitkin.)

(d)

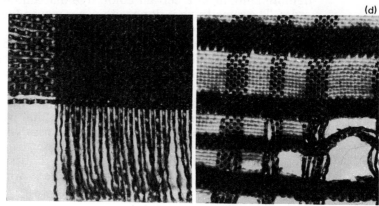

(c)

180

*Fabric
Construction
and
Buying
Motives*

1. *Dyeing the raw stock.* This method is very common in dyeing wool. "Dyed in the wool" is a familiar expression; it means that the wool fibers were dyed before they were carded or spun. This method enables the dyestuff to penetrate the fibers thoroughly, so that the color is likely to be fast. Interesting mixtures can be made by mixing two or more colors of raw stock. This method is more costly than other methods of dyeing textile fabrics. The favorite mottled gray flannel suiting is dyed in raw stock. Solution-dyed fibers also come in this category. Rayon, acetate, and Dynel may be solution-dyed.

2. *Dyeing the slub.* When the fibers have been carded and combed preparatory to spinning, they lie in the shape of a smooth slub, sliver, or rope. This sliver can be printed with dye at the desired intervals. By drawing and spinning the yarn, interesting mixtures may be obtained. This method is also common for wool mixtures. The dyestuff penetrates the fibers easily, thus ensuring permanency of color.

3. *Dyeing the yarn.* One of the best selling points a salesman has for textile fabrics is the term *yarn dyed.* This means that the yarns were dyed before the fabric was woven. (See *space-dyed yarns.*) Because the dyestuff penetrates the yarns to the core, a yarn-dyed fabric is faster than a piece-dyed fabric; and a yarn-dyed fabric usually has a deeper, richer, and more lustrous appearance. In speaking of hosiery, the term *ingrain* is synonymous with *yarn dyed*; the term *dip dyed* has the same meaning as *piece dyed.* Plaid ginghams, shepherd checks, and denims are yarn-dyed fabrics. An important method of dyeing yarn is called *package dyeing.* Yarn is wound around a cylinder known as a *package.* It is approximately six inches long by five and one-half inches in diameter. Dye packages are placed in the dyeing machine—a stainless steel cylinder (like a pressure cooker) with vertical spindles fastened to the bottom or to a removable carrier. The packages are placed on the spindles and the lid is closed. The dye is pumped through the packages from the inside out.

4. *Dyeing in the piece.* Although it is possible to make fast colors by piece-dyeing, the dyer must make sure that the cloth is covered evenly and that the dye has penetrated the fibers thoroughly. Piece-dyeing is done a great deal, for it is economical for the manufacturer—especially in fabrics such as hosiery, whose style in colors changes rapidly. Another advantage is that any shade can be dyed on short notice. The knitting mills can make up a huge stock of undyed hosiery and wait until the demand comes for a definite amount in a certain color, dye that amount, and wait for another order. The same thing is done with other woven fabrics.

Since not all dyestuffs have an equal affinity for both vegetable and animal fibers, very interesting mixtures and frosted effects are produced by *cross dyeing.* For example, when a cloth contains both vegetable and animal fibers, a dyestuff may be used that colors the animal but not the vegetable fibers.

Rayon and acetate mixtures can be dyed with a dyestuff that takes on the rayon but is resisted by the acetate. Blue wool suiting with a white cotton hairline stripe can be made by cross-dyeing. The dyestuff colors the wool blue but does not color the cotton stripe. Similarly, the acrylics Acrilan and Acrilan 16 can be cross-dyed. If basic dyes are applied under strong acid conditions, Acrilan 16 is dyed, whereas the older Acrilan resists the dye.

Acrylic blend of Acrilan and Orlon 42 is also being cross-dyed. Acid dyestuffs applied to the blend leave Orlon relatively undyed and Acrilan in color. A two-tone effect can be obtained by first dyeing the cloth with basic dyestuffs to get the required shade on the Orlon and then dyeing the blend with acid dyestuffs in the same bath to get the Acrilan component in the desired shade.

Another type of piece-dyeing is called *pad dyeing*. This cloth is passed through a trough containing the dyebath. It is then squeezed between heavy rolls to remove excess dye. This is a very quick method of applying the dye, but unless there is some aftertreatment the colors are not usually so fast as in other methods of dyeing. Pad dyeing is frequently chosen to produce lighter shades.

Still another method of piece-dyeing is called *jig dyeing*, because the cloth is passed through a jig-dyeing machine that consists of a large tub holding dye and rollers that guide the cloth through the dyebath. A great number of yards of cloth can be dyed at once by this method. Jig dyeing is used particularly for dark, direct dyes.

A reel-dyeing machine, consisting of a dye tub with a reel that lifts the fabric into the dyebath, is used for lightweight fabrics that cannot stand tension in dyeing. Heavy crepes are dyed in this way, because this method does not flatten the creped surface.

When great quantities of one fabric have to be dyed, the continuous dyeing process is a definite timesaver. Previous to this discovery, dyeing was all done on comparatively small batches of cloth. The dyeing operation had to be stopped after each operation to transfer the cloth from one machine to another machine that might be in a different location. Now, all dyeing and subsequent operations can be done in one continuous process. Disadvantages of this method lie in the fact that it does not, without difficulty, dye cloth in deep shades, and it is not economical for dyeing short lengths of cloth. Du Pont has overcome these disadvantages with a process called the Pad-Steam Continuous Dyeing Process. By this process coat dyes can be applied to a cloth in about one-tenth the time required for the old type of dyeing in batches. Another Du Pont invention, called the Multilap Continuous Processing Machine, enables dyeing of lightly constructed fabrics by continuous processing without stretching or distorting them.

The process of dyeing blends in one dyebath is both time- and labor-saving. Alexis Massainoff of Lake Arrowhead, California, has patented a multiple-color process for any type of fabric. Only one dipping of the fabric is required.

PRINTING CLOTH

Fabrics with colored figures stamped on them are known as printed cloths. The design in this case is not woven into the cloth but is printed on after the cloth has been woven. If the background of the fabric is to be white, the cloth is usually bleached before it is printed.

The printing of fabrics represents an important part of the textile industry. (See *dyeing of wool and cotton blends*, p. 178.) It is interesting to note that printed goods are often bought on impulse by the consumer because a particular pattern, design, or color combination in a dress, sport shirt, or blouse appeals to him or her. To retain this market, the print

182

*Fabric
Construction
and
Buying
Motives*

industry and those involved in the textile business face a major problem of meeting competition and maintaining price levels in the face of increasing raw material and labor costs. To alleviate this problem, chemists have developed new methods. One that seems to give promise is an emulsion (oil in water or water in oil) print paste that can be used on any regular printing machine with conventional engraved rollers. Color effects unobtainable with old paste methods are possible with emulsion printing. Also, procedures may be simplified and cost of printing cut.

STEPS IN PRINTING

First, artists submit their designs to manufacturers. Out of an assortment of designs submitted, a great number are rejected. The few accepted ones are then printed on samples of fabrics. Some of these may be scrapped. The design is next enlarged so that flaws may be detected and corrected. On this large scale, the design is carved on a zinc plate. Each color in the design appears clearly on this plate. A *pantograph* transfers the design from the zinc plate to the copper rollers (a different roller for each color) and at the same time reduces the design to its original proportions. Thus we see that when a particular design contains red, yellow, green, and black, four distinct rollers must be used—one for each color and all of the same size. The design scratched on the copper rollers is then treated with nitric acid, which eats out the design as it would an etching. The etching of fine parallel lines inside the design proper serves to hold enough of the dyestuffs to penetrate the cloth as it is printed. Rollers may also be engraved by hand or by a photo-chemical process that reproduces the shading and detail of a photograph. The actual printing is done as the cloth passes over a series of rollers that revolve in a vat of dye. Each roller retains its particular color in the etched design and prints it on the fabric.

Dyestuffs used for printing are the same as those used for piece-dyeing or yarn-dyeing, except that dyestuffs may be thickened with starch, gum, or resin to prevent a color from bleeding or running outside the outline before it is dry. When they are dried, printed cloths are passed over hot rollers and then steamed so that the colors are set. Any excess dye is removed by a washing after the steaming. Colors carefully printed can be fast to both light and washing. It has been found that mercerization of the grey goods before printing results in a brighter, stronger colored print.

KINDS OF PRINTING

There are many different ways of printing fabrics. The chief ones are as follows:

1. *Direct or roller printing.* This is the simplest method and probably the most used. The cloth is passed over a series of rollers (as already described), the number of rollers depending on the number of colors in the design. As many as 16 colors can be printed at the rate of up to 200 yards a minute. Almost any textile fabric can be printed in this manner. Printed percale, printed dress linen, printed rayon and silk crepes, and printed wool challis are generally printed by this method.

A design may be printed on the warp yarns before the cloth is woven. When so printed, the fabric is called *warp printed.* The designs may appear

FIGURE 8.3. Fabric being roller (direct) printed. (Photography courtesy of Cranston Print Works Company.)

grayed and their outlines may be hazy. This is because the filling yarns are usually a neutral shade—often white. *Vigoureux printing* is a variation of warp printing that is used on wool. Before the yarn is spun, color is applied to the wool tops or slubbing in the rope form. A variation of the roller method applies the colors in horizontal or cross-striped designs. When the wool is spun into yarn and woven into cloth, the stripes are broken into colored flecks. This type of printing is also called *mélange*.

2. *Discharge printing or dyeing.* When the design is to contain not more than two colors, the method called *discharge* is often used. The whole cloth is dyed a solid color first; then the design on the roller is covered with a chemical, which, when it is applied to the cloth, discharges (removes) the color from it in those portions that correspond to the design on the roller. The background is left colored and the design is white. The same depth of color appears on both sides, because the colored portion was piece-dyed first. Likewise, the color in the background can be discharged if the background is printed with chemical so that the design is left colored. Usually, however, the background is darker than the design. Polka dots and the figures in the foulards are often printed in this manner.

183

FIGURE 8.4. a. Roller (direct); b. Discharge. Right sides are shown at the top; wrong sides in the turned-up portions at the bottom. (Photos by Jack Pitkin.)

3. *Resist printing or dyeing.* In this method the design is printed first with a chemical paste so constituted that when the cloth is dyed the parts covered by the paste resist the dye and retain their original color. Batik work is an excellent example of one type of resist dyeing. The portions of the fabric that are to resist the dye are covered with paraffin. The whole cloth is then dyed and, when dried, the paraffin is removed. At times the paraffin cracks during the dyeing, so that little runs of color appear in the resisted portions. Often the resisted portions are painted by hand in different colors.

Sometimes certain yarns are chemically treated to resist dye before they are woven. When the cloth is piece-dyed, the yarns so treated do not take the dye. Accordingly, stripes and checks appear in piece-dyed goods.

Another type of resist dyeing is called *tie dyeing.* In certain seasons tie-dyed scarfs and other accessories are very stylish. Pieces of string are tied around bunches of cloth where the dye is to be resisted. The fabric is left tied in many little bunches while immersed in the dyestuffs. When the fabric is dry, the strings are removed, and very interesting sunburst designs appear. Parts of the fabric may be tied in different proportions and dipped in more than one color. It is possible to produce a varicolored design in this way. Still more complicated designs can be made by stitching the design areas rather than by tying.

Another type of resist dyeing is *stencil printing,* which is done by hand. Paper or metal is cut in the desired pattern and is placed over the fabric where the pattern is to be resisted. The parts that are covered do not take the dye.

4. *Hand block printing.* Before the method of direct roller printing was discovered, fabrics were printed by hand. The method is very similar to rubber stamping. A wooden block with a portion of the design carved on it is inked with dyestuff and stamped on the cloth by hand. The number of blocks used corresponds to the number of colors in the design. Great skill is required to stamp each portion of the design accurately so that all designs will be clear in outline and proportionate without a change in depth of color. Hand blocking gives a greater variety of designs and color effects, for the regular repetition of a pattern that is necessary in the roller method is not necessary in hand blocking.

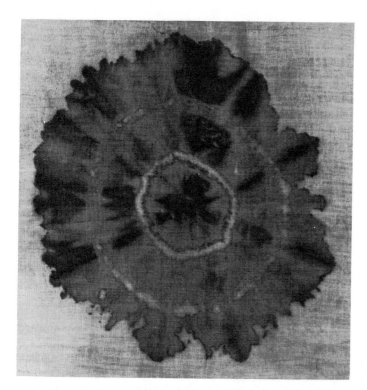

FIGURE 8.5. Resist (done by tie-dyeing). (Photo by Jack Pitkin.)

FIGURE 8.6. Hand-blocked wool challis.

185

186
*Fabric
Construction
and
Buying
Motives*

Linen is used quite extensively for hand blocking because it has the proper texture and quality. As hand-blocked fabrics are generally expensive, it does not pay to do such handwork on a poor grade of cloth. Real India prints are produced by hand block printing.

One way to detect hand blocking is to look along the selvage for the regularity of the repetition of the design. In roller printing, the design must be repeated at regular intervals. Not so with hand blocking. Another way to detect hand blocking is to look at the edges of the designs. Almost invariably one color runs into another in at least a few places. Also, the quality of workmanship may be determined by the clearness of each color, the sharpness of outline, and the regularity of the design.

5. *Duplex printing.* When a fabric is intended to be reversible, it is printed on one side, turned over, and then printed again on the other side so that the outlines of the designs on each side coincide. There is a special machine called a *duplex printing machine* that prints both sides of a fabric simultaneously. This method is called duplex printing. If it is done well, it gives the impression that the design is woven in.

6. *Flock printing.* The application of short, dyed cotton, rayon, or wool fibers to fabric or to paper is called flock printing. There are two methods of application: (1) The flock fibers are pressed into the resin substance, which has already been printed on the fabric. (2) The flock is applied to the resin-printed fabric by electrolysis. The second method produces a velvety surface.

7. *Painted design.* Hand painting is most effective on silks. The design is outlined on the fabric with wax and is filled in later by hand brushwork. Usually the wax is mixed with dye so that the outline appears a different color and so stands out from the background. The dyes may be thickened, as is done for roller or block printing, or real oil paint may be used for the design. Most hand-painted fabrics are expensive because of the great amount of artistic labor involved.

Another method is painting the fabric with mordants rather than with color. When the dyebath is applied, each mordant reacts differently to the

FIGURE 8.7. Duplex print. In order to determine a good quality duplex print, a pin may be used to pierce the fabric from the right side. The pin should appear at the same position in the design on the opposite side. (Photos by Jonas Grushkin.)

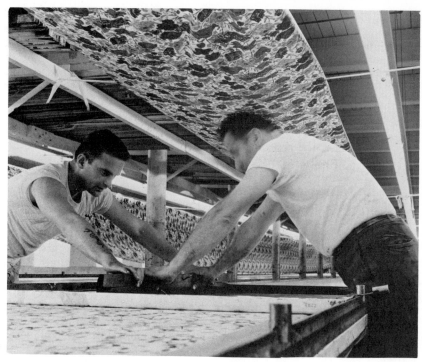

(a)

(b)

FIGURE 8.8. a. Hand screen printing; b. Automatic screen printing. (Photographs courtesy of Cranston Print Works Company.)

188

*Fabric
Construction
and
Buying
Motives*

same dyebath. For more complicated designs, mordant printing can be combined with the wax-resist process. A modern version of mordant printing is called *madder* printing, so called because a dye prepared from the madder plant was formerly used for painting fabrics. This natural dyestuff has now been replaced by a synthetic dyestuff. Mordants are printed on the fabric first, and different colors are developed from a single dyebath.

8. *Screen printing.* When a design called for delicate shading, the process originally employed to produce the pattern was similar to that used for reproducing photographs in newspapers. Today a photochemical process reproduces the design exactly as it was painted. Elaborately shaded effects can be printed exactly like the original and reproduced many times. The fabric is first stretched on a padded table. A printing screen, made of silk, nylon, or metal stretched on a frame, is placed over the fabric. The parts of the pattern on the screen that are not to take the print are covered with enamel or certain paints to resist the printing paste. The printing paste is poured on the screen and pushed through the pattern portion with a wooden or rubber paddle called a *squeegee*. When one section of a pattern has been finished, the frame is moved to the next section, and so on until the entire length has been completed.

For screen printing, a continuous operation has now been mechanized, so that several yards can be printed every minute. The fabric moves along a table, and the automatic application of the screens is electrically

FIGURE 8.9. Screen-printed fabric. (Photo by Jack Pitkin.)

FIGURE 8.10. Photographic printing. (Grant's Tomb.)
(Photo by Jonas Grushkin.)

controlled. An automatic squeegee operates electronically. Mechanized printing reduces costs appreciably for large batches. Whenever high-quality fashion prints on exclusive dress goods or intricate patterns and big repeats are requisites, screen printing is an important process.

Fabrics with large designs in limited quantities are frequently screen-printed by hand. Rayon jerseys, crepes, and other dress fabrics, luncheon cloths, bedspreads, draperies, and shower curtains are often screen printed. Although screen printing is a slower and more expensive process than roller printing, the pattern repeats can be large—up to eighty inches. Pigment colors are sometimes put on in layers to give a look of handcraftsmanship.

9. *Photographic printing.* A design is photographed and the negative is covered with a screen plate to break up the solid areas of the design. A light is then projected through the screen plate onto another film to make a contact print. This film is placed on a copper roller treated with sensitizing solution. A powerful arc light focused on the film affects the sensitized roller by baking the coating where the light passes through. The roller is then washed to take away the solution from sections that the light did not reach. These portions of the roller are etched away to form the pattern. The roller is then treated to remove the baked coating, and printing is done from the roller. This method provides fine designs for dress goods.

10. *Airbrushing.* Another method of producing shaded effects on fabrics employs a mechanized airbrush to blow color into the fabric. The hand guides the brush. This method is most effective on silk brocades and fabrics that are made in Jacquard or dobby designs.

11. *Heat-transfer printing.* In this technique the fabric is printed in color on large rolls of paper. This printed design is pressed against the fabric. When heat is applied, the design is transferred to the fabric and the

190
*Fabric
Construction
and
Buying
Motives*

color is set. This process is less expensive than roller or screen printing because the converter can buy rolls of printed paper cheaper than using the more costly copper engraved rollers or mechanized screens. It is claimed that up to six colors in about 2,000 color combinations are possible. The Sublistatic Corporation of America owns this process. Almost any kind of design may be printed by this method. The technique was first used on double knits and polyester/wool blends for men's wear.

12. *Polychromatic printing or jet printing.* This is a process of applying (squirting) dye on a continuous width of fabric. The movement of the various jets controls the design. Patterns in stripes of many colors are possible with this technique. Jeans, shirts, scarfs, and bathroom mats can be printed in this way. This process is sometimes called polychromatic printing because the fabric shows a variety of colors.

FIGURE 8.11. Polychromatic or jet printing. (Photo by Jonas Grushkin.)

DISTINGUISHING DYEING AND PRINTING PROCESSES

YARN-DYED AND PIECE-DYED FABRICS

Although raw stock and yarn dyeing usually produce the best colorfastness, depth of color, and luster, many piece-dyed fabrics are colorfast and equally attractive. Colorfastness depends on the degree to which the fibers have been penetrated by the dye. Since fibers and yarns are more easily penetrated before they are woven, a yarn-dyed cloth is more likely to be colorfast than is a piece-dyed cloth.

Of course, microscopic examination will reveal the degree of penetration of the fibers by dye, but the consumer does not usually have access to a microscope. A simple though not infallible test is to unravel yarns and untwist them. In piece-dyed cloths the core of the yarn may be white or a lighter color than the outer surface. This is especially true in piece-dyed linens and in cottons finished to resemble linens.

PRINTED AND WOVEN DESIGNS

Many consumers confuse a small, geometrical printed pattern with a dobby weave. But if the cloth is unraveled enough to include a portion of the design, an examination of the yarns may reveal a printed pattern. In a design printed on the cloth, the individual yarns will be in two or more colors where the design is present. For example, one yarn may contain white, yellow, and blue, and another yarn white and blue. Such a cloth is printed. In a woven-in pattern, individual yarns are the same color throughout their length. One yarn may be blue and another white, but from selvage to selvage a yarn is either all blue or all white.

COMPUTER PROCESSES IN SHADE MATCHING

In the dyeing industry, as in nearly every industry, there is an effort to computerize those processes that lend themselves to repetitive actions and inventory controls.

In short, what the computer does is to recreate a certain color by analyzing the information stored in the computer. The information is derived from machines that can break down the color constituents of a sample of fabric or liquid. This information is then put into terms of concentration of color, which colors are to be used, and the desired shade. In turn, all these earmarks of the specific color are translated into computer language to be stored and cross-referenced for later usage.

The most common devices used to find the fingerprints of a color are the spectrophotometer and the colorimeter. The spectrophotometer measures the amount of light reflected by a sample of colored material. The measurement derived is in the form of a graph that shows at what parts of the spectrum the sample reflects light, hence its color to the eye, and the intensity of this reflectance. Once it is known what colors the sample reflects—what it is made up of—then it is known what it takes to make the color.

In a somewhat similar way the COMIC (acronym for colorant mixture computer) is a device for shade matching. The colorimeter, of which there are only a few in the United States, takes the information derived from a spectrophotometer and establishes 16 points on the spectrum that, if matched, will yield the desired color. After the 16 spectral points have been fed into the colorimeter, the 16 points on the spectrum are established for the undyed substrate. At this point the dyer will select various "plug-in" boxes, each representing a certain dye that he feels will be useful in the match. By varying concentration dials for each of the dyestuffs selected to match the shade, the operator can line up the 16 points of the spectrum on an oscilloscope and obtain a prediction of how much of each dye should be used to match the standard.

In these systems a digital computer has a great advantage in speed. Once the colorist decides on the dyes he feels will make the shade, the 16 points for each individual dye used in the match, as well as for the unknown, are fed into the computer, which in turn prints out the formula for the match. The computer's large storage capacity and rapid calculating speed allow the computer to make formula selections. In this case, the colorist selects a range of colors—10, 15, or 20—which he feels will be suitable for matching all shades. For example: A colorist finds he needs 12 different dispersed dyes to make all the shades he comes in contact with on polyester fabric. The 16 points for the 12 dyestuffs have already been programmed into the computer at three or four different concentrations. When the complementary 16 points of the unknown are fed into the computer, it will search through all possible combinations along with their costs and change in shade from one source of light to another.

In general, it seems unlikely that the industry can ever be computerized in the same sense as those giant plants that need but a handful of men to run their computers. Indeed, the computer is a tool that narrows the field of dyestuff selection, checks over results, eliminates some of the trial-and-error methods, and keeps stock of what has been done. However, the matches the computer makes can never really be perfect. Variables such as substrate, dyeing procedure, auxiliaries, and even the devices used

192
*Fabric
Construction
and
Buying
Motives*

to check the result must all be constant in order to insure a precise match. In fact, the identical temperature and humidity on a particular day would help provide better results.

The experience of the dyer and colorist are essential. Although it is possible to quantify many of these variables, experience is still the greatest asset. The substrate's preparation for dyeing, the action of the dyes themselves and their interaction, the differences in machinery, and the end use of the fabric all must be considered in making a match. A computer could probably store the information if the Herculean task of programming it were ever undertaken. Yet, some of the factors that influence the dye match cannot be measured by machines. However, when two dyers get together they know exactly what they are talking about.

SUMMARY

The average consumer is becoming more conscious of the color of fabrics. Through the educational aid of intelligent salespeople and national advertising, the consumer is learning what colors and their combinations best suit certain types and is becoming more particular in selecting colors for the home. Furthermore, the consumer wants fabrics to perform satisfactorily in their intended use. She has learned how to care for fine fabrics to preserve their original beauty. For these reasons manufacturers must produce a variety of beautiful, and at the same time fast, dyes.

Prints have become classic with Americans and are here to stay. To be sure, some years are more definitely print years than others. But most women like the gaiety of at least one printed dress or other clothing article a year.

In conclusion, a fabric made from good raw stock, beautifully and strongly woven, can be enhanced manyfold by the application of the proper coloring. The reverse is also true—that good fibers and yarns, even if durably woven, can be ruined by the use of fugitive dyestuffs crudely applied.

REVIEW QUESTIONS

1. When is a dye considered fast? Explain fully.
2. Is there such a thing as an absolutely fast dye? Why?
3. Outline a method for testing the fastness of a color to light; perspiration; washing; friction; wash-and-wear.
4. When is a color considered absolutely fast to light? Moderately fast? Fugitive?
5. (a) What is meant by bleeding of colors?
   (b) What test can be used to determine whether or not colors will bleed?
6. (a) What is crocking?
   (b) What is a good test for crocking?
7. (a) Explain the difference between natural and synthetic dyestuffs.
   (b) Name some of the most important dyestuffs of each classification.
8. What are the advantages of synthetic dyestuffs over natural dyestuffs?
9. (a) What are basic dyes?
   (b) What are acid dyes?
   (c) To which fibers are basic dyes applied directly without prior chemical treatment?
10. (a) What is a mordant?
    (b) When is a mordant necessary?
11. (a) What are vat dyes?
    (b) Describe their method in application and use.

(c) What are pigments?

(d) When are they used?

(e) What are some of the more recent developments in the dye industry? Explain.

12. (a) Explain fiber-reactive dyes; metal complex dyes; oxidation dyes.

(b) How are they used?

13. (a) List the methods of dyeing cloth.

(b) Explain each method.

14. (a) What kinds of cloth are made from dyed raw stock?

(b) Name two fabrics that are usually yarn-dyed.

(c) When is cross-dyeing advantageous?

(d) List the different methods of printing cloth.

(e) Explain each method.

15. Describe the procedure for transferring the design from the original to the copper roller.

16. (a) How does resist printing differ from discharge printing?

(b) How is batik made?

17. (a) What are the selling points of a hand-blocked linen drapery?

(b) How can hand block printing be distinguished from roller printing?

(c) How can a duplex-printed fabric be distinguished from a woven cloth?

(d) Describe jet printing and the heat transfer technique.

18. What test is helpful in distinguishing yarn-dyed from piece-dyed fabrics?

**EXPERI-
MENTS**

1. *Determining the permanency of dye.* Samples of five different materials should be tested for both permanency of dye and method of dyeing.

A. Fastness to light:

Follow the instructions for *Home test*, p. 168.

(a) When did the fabric fade slightly?

(b) When did it fade appreciably?

(c) Is the dye fast? moderately fast? fugitive?

B. Fastness to perspiration:

Follow the instructions for *Home test*, p. 169.

Is the dye fast to perspiration? Why?

C. Fastness to laundering?

Follow the instructions for *Home test*, p. 169.

Is the dye fast to washing? Why?

1. Bast half of the fabric to a piece of white silk. Wash and dry.

2. Compare the washed colored fabric with the unwashed piece. Note especially, after the two washed fabrics are separated, whether the white silk has been discolored.

(a) Did the colors bleed?

(b) Are the colors fast?

D. Fastness to crocking:

Follow the instructions for *Home test*, p. 171.

Is the dye fast to friction? Why?

2. *Determining the method of dyeing.*

A. If the fabric is solid colored:

1. Untwist several yarns in both warp and filling.

2. Note the evenness or unevenness of color penetration.

Is the cloth piece-dyed or yarn-dyed? Why?

B. If the cloth is figured:

1. Unravel yarns in both warp and filling.

2. Note the color of individual yarns.

(a) Are individual yarns the same color throughout their length or are they of more than one color?

(b) Is the design printed or woven in?

194

*Fabric
Construction
and
Buying
Motives*

C. If the cloth is printed:
   1. Count the colors in the design.
   2. Note the shape, regularity, and order of the patterns.
      (*a*) Are there more than two colors in the design?
      (*b*) Are the designs small and geometrical?
      (*c*) Are the designs placed at regular intervals with regular repetition of the patterns?
      (*d*) Are the outlines clear?
      (*e*) Does one color overlap another?
      (*f*) By what method is the cloth printed?
      (*g*) Is the printing done well?

GLOSSARY Acetate dye—See *Disperse dye.*
Acid dye—A type of dye used on wool and other animal fibers. When used on cotton or linen, a mordant is required. It has poor color resistance to washing. A special method of application is required for acrylic fibers of Orlon 42. Dynel modacrylic fibers may be colored in light shades.
Airbrushing—Blowing color on a fabric with a mechanized airbrush.
Alizarin dye—A vegetable dye originally obtained from the madder root, now produced synthetically. It is best used on wool but can be used on cotton, particularly in madder prints.
Aniline dye—A term generally applied to any synthetic, organic dye. Any dye that is derived from aniline.
Azoic dye—See *Naphthol dye.*
Basic dye—A type of dye that will dye wool and silk directly without a mordant. It can be used on cotton with a mordant.
Batik—A kind of resist dyeing in which parts of a fabric are coated with wax to resist the dye. It is usually done by hand but can be imitated by machine.
Catalyst—A substance or agent that initiates a chemical reaction and makes possible for it to proceed under milder conditions than otherwise possible.
Chrome dye—See *Mordant.*
Crocking—Rubbing off of a fabric's color.
Crock meter—A standard device for testing a fabric's fastness to crocking.
Developed dye—A type of dye in which one color may be changed by use of a developer. The intensity of the color and the fastness of the dyestuff may be changed by this treatment.
Dip dyeing—a process of piece dyeing hosiery or other knitted goods after construction.
Direct dye—A type of dye with an affinity for most fibers. It has poor resistance to washing.
Direct printing—Application of color by passing the cloth over a series of rollers engraved with the designs. Developed direct dyes have good resistance to washing.
Discharge printing—A method by which the cloth is piece-dyed first and then the color is discharged or bleached in spots, leaving white designs.
Disperse dyes—Dispersions of colors or pigments in water. They were originally known as acetate dyes. At present these dyes are also used to color the newer synthetic fibers.
Dope dyed—See *Solution dyed.*
Duplex print--Method of printing a fabric on the face and then on the back.
Dyed in raw stock—See *Raw-stock dyeing.*
Dyeing—A process of coloring fibers, yarns, or fabrics with either natural or synthetic dyes.
Fade-Ometer--A standard laboratory device for testing a fabric's fastness to sunlight.
Fast dyes—Those dyes that are fast for the purpose for which the fabric is intended.

Fiber dye—See *Raw-stock dyeing.*

Fugitive dye—Those colors that are not fast to such elements as light, washing, perspiration, and crocking.

Hand-blocked print—Fabrics printed by hand with blocks made of wood or linoleum.

Heat-transfer process—See *Sublistatic printing.*

Indigo—A type of dyestuff originally obtained from the indigo plant, now produced synthetically. Blues are brilliant. It has good colorfastness to washing and to light.

Ingrain—A knitted or woven fabric made of yarns dyed before knitting or weaving.

Jig dyeing—Passing the cloth through a jig-dyeing machine (a large tub holding dye). It is used particularly for dark, direct dyes.

Launder-Ometer—A standard laboratory device for testing a fabric's fastness to washing.

Madder—See *Alizarin dye.*

Metal complex dyes—A class of dyestuffs that is ionic and premetallized (chemically coupled with nickel, copper, and cobalt salts to make the dye on the fiber).

Mordant—A substance that acts as a binder for the dye. A mordant has an affinity for both the dyestuff and the fabric.

Naphthol dye—Insoluble azoic dyes formed on the fiber by impregnation of the cotton fabric with beta-naphthol that has been dissolved in caustic soda and then immersed in a basic dye. It is used primarily on cotton and gives brilliant scarlet and red at relatively low cost.

Oxidation dyes—A class of dyestuffs formed in the fiber substrate. These dyes are applied to the fabric as an oxidation base in the form of water-soluble salts and thereafter oxidized to a pigment

Pad dyeing—A process of first passing the cloth through a trough containing dye, then squeezing it between heavy rolls to remove excess dye.

Photographic printing—Application of a photographic image to a fabric.

Piece-dyeing—A fabric dyed after weaving, knitting, or other method of construction.

Pigment dyes—Dye emulsion made with certain kinds of fine synthetic pigment in a solution of synthetic resins in an organic solvent; water is stirred in with a high-speed mixer. Often applied by pad dyeing. Good colorfastness to light, washing, acids, and alkalies. When resin binder is ineffective, dye may crock or have poor resistance to washing.

Polychromatic printing or jet printing—A process of applying (squirting) dye on a continuous width of fabric. The movement of the various jets controls the design.

Printing—Methods of stamping colored figures on cloth.

Raw-stock dyeing—Dyeing of fibers before spinning into yarn. It is synonymous with *fiber-dyed.*

Resist printing—Application of substances to a cloth to resist dyeing; the cloth is immersed in dye, the "resist" is then removed. See *Batik.*

Roller printing—See *Direct printing.*

Screen printing—Background of design painted on screen first. Dye is printed on exposed portions of fabric.

Slub dyed—Sliver dyed or printed.

Solution dyed—Man-made fibers dyed in the spinning solution.

Space-dyed yarns—Those yarns that have been dipped in dye or spotted in various places along the yarn.

Spun dyed—See *Solution dyed.*

Stencil printing—A type of resist printing where portions of the design are covered with metal or wood so the covered parts do not take dye.

Sublistatic printing—A technique in which the design, printed on rolls of paper, is pressed against the fabric. When heat is applied, the design is transferred to the fabric.

Substrate—An underlying support or foundation, for example, fiber substrate prepared with a mordant before dyeing).

196

Fabric
Construction
and
Buying
Motives

Sulfur dye—A dye derived from chemicals containing sulfur. It is used mostly for vegetable fibers. It has fair resistance to washing; poor resistance to sunlight.

Tie dyeing—A type of resist printing in which pieces of string are tied around bunches of cloth, or the fabric is stitched where dye is to be resisted.

Vat dyed—This process uses an insoluble dye made soluble in its application. It is then put on the fiber and is oxidized to its original insoluble form. Excellent colorfastness to washing and sunlight.

Warp printing—Printing of warp yarns with the design before weaving. A hazy grayed effect is produced.

Weather-Ometer—A device that can simulate weather conditions, such as sunlight, heavy dew, rain, and thermal shock. The deteriorating effects of these conditions on fabrics are the objectives of tests in this device. These effects can be determined in a few days.

Cotton
and the Consumer

9

Do you know what consumers look for first in their choice of clothing? According to a National Consumer Study by Opinion Research Corporation, the consumer's first concern is *comfort*. In fact, 85 percent of those in the study chose comfort. Cotton is a desirable fabric because it is, indeed, comfortable. Being a hollowlike fiber, it breathes like a person does. This means that cotton remains porous no matter how it is woven or knitted. These pores permit body moisture vapor and air to pass constantly and invisibly through the cloth. Consequently, it is comfortable. Cotton fabrics feel good against the skin regardless of the temperature and humidity.[1]

Comfort is a buying point for the consumer and a selling point for the salesperson to emphasize in selling. The salesperson should have a knowledge of the qualities of each of the textile raw materials: the kind of fiber used, the type and quality of yarn, the construction and finish. Such knowledge helps the salesperson assist a consumer in making a proper selection of fabrics for different uses.

From a knowledge of the qualities of the different textile raw materials, the salesperson should develop selling points.

This chapter will consider the physical and chemical characteristics of cotton fibers and how these factors contribute to buying points. The type of yarn, construction, finishes, and coloring of cotton and their specific contributions to buying points will be discussed.

HISTORY OF COTTON The history of cotton may go back 7,000 years. Even earlier than 2500 B. C., Egyptians were known to be wearing cotton as well as flax and wool. Through the ages cotton has clothed and sheltered man. In 1793 Eli Whitney's invention of the cotton gin revolutionized the processing of cotton and led to the Industrial Revolution.

Production processes which heretofore had been carried out in widespread locations were now centralized so that operations became more efficient. Upon the introduction of the power loom in 1884, cloth manufacturers could devote their energies to improving and varying the fabric itself.

[1] Pamphlet: "Sew Something Beautiful with Cotton the Natural Fiber," Cotton Incorporated.

197

Cotton is a white or yellow-white vegetable fiber grown in greatest amounts in the United States, the U.S.S.R., China, and India, followed in descending order of importance in cotton production by Pakistan, Brazil, Turkey, Egypt, Mexico, Iran, and the Sudan. Over 55 other countries produce lesser amounts. In this group, the larger producers include Syria, Peru, Columbia, Greece, Nicaragua, Guatemala, and Argentina.[2]

Cotton fibers come from a plant, related to the hollyhock, that ranges in height from 2 to 20 feet, depending upon the variety. The plant requires a warm climate with about six months of summer weather for full development. It blossoms and produces bolls, or pods, of cotton fibers. (See Figure 9.1.)

In the United States, cotton is grown in the so-called Cotton Belt, which covers roughly the southern and western states from the Carolinas to California.

Production methods differ in various parts of the Cotton Belt, according to the National Cotton Council of America. Such factors as types of soil, climate, moisture, growing conditions, and physical features of a locality determine the varieties of cotton to be poanted, crop income, size of farms, and yield per acre.

The chief steps in cotton production are as follows:

PREPARATION OF THE SOIL

Production of next year's crop generally starts right after the completion of harvesting in the fall. Old stalks are chopped and shredded by machine. The residue is plowed under, and the field is generally left rough until spring tillage.

Before planting, the soil is tilled to a depth of several inches. Smoothing and laying off in rows follows.

PLANTING

Machines plant cotton four, six, or eight rows at a time, usually with planters timed to drop about half a dozen seeds in a group the desired

[2] Rankings prepared with the assistance of the Cotton Council International.

FIGURE 9.1. Cotton bolls.

distance apart. In some areas, the seeds are planted in a thin, continuous row, but the practice of thinning by hand hoes has been discontinued except in rare cases.

CULTIVATING

A cotton grower has a wide choice of fertilizer, material, and equipment. Application of fertilizer may be made prior to, during, or after planting.

Pre-emergence weed control is carried out by applying a chemical herbicide to a 10- to 14-inch band over the drill area at the time of, or just after, planting. For a few weeks, this band is not disturbed. The chemical does not harm cotton seedlings, but it does kill germinating weed and grass seeds.

Post-emergence weed control consists of spraying an area six to eight inches wide on both sides of the plant. Weed and grass seedlings are killed without injury to the young cotton. Care must be taken not to kill the cotton by spraying chemicals on leaves or branches. Almost every acre of cotton is now treated at least once with weed control compounds, and most of the acreage is treated more than once.

Improved cultivators and rotary hoe attachments for cultivators also help keep weeds and grass under control. High-speed rotary hoes travel through the field at rates up to seven and a half miles per hour.

INSECT CONTROL

Losses due to insects amount on the average to about one bale out of every five to six bales. The boll weevil accounts for most of this damage. Insecticides are applied at various intervals during heavy infestation—either by airplanes, which can cover up to 1,500 acres a day, or by tractor-mounted ground rigs, which can spray several rows of cotton at one time.

Maturation of the Cotton Boll. The cotton plant first buds, and, about 21 days thereafter, creamy white to yellow flowers appear. These later turn red, and, after about three days, wither and drop from the plant, leaving the ovary on the plant. When the ovary ripens, a large pod, known as the cotton boll, is formed. Moist fibers growing inside the boll expand it until it is about 1 1/2 inches long and 1 inch in diameter. The boll opens approximately 1 1/2 to 2 months after the flowering stage.

HARVESTING

So that the bolls will open quickly and uniformly, before the fall rains damage fibers and seed, cotton plants are treated chemically to make them shed their leaves. This process, called *defoliation* or *dessication*, is important if cotton is to be picked mechanically. Furthermore, it is a method of insect control. Cotton is then ready for picking.

PICKING

Before the advent of the mechanical picker, cotton was picked by hand. The great labor shortage in the South was a major reason why mechanical pickers became so important. Smaller farms were consolidated into larger

FIGURE 9.2. Two-row mechanical cotton picker. (Photo courtesy National Cotton Council.)

farms as mechanical pickers were perfected. In the United States machine harvesting jumped from 32 percent in 1957 to virtually 100 percent in the mid-1970s.

To accompany this accelerated shift to mechanical harvesting, changes in ginning processes have taken place. An increasing number of gins are using multiple lint cleaners, and there is a marked increase in the use of stick- and green-leaf removing machines. Two types of machines harvest the cotton: the *picker* and the *stripper*. The picker has vertical drums equipped with spindles (barbed or smooth) that pull the cotton from the boll. This machine can harvest 5 to 15 acres a day depending on whether the machine does 1 or 2 rows at a time.[3] The stripper pulls the bolls off when they enter the rollers of the machine. Some strippers have mechanical fingers to do the job. This type of tractor-mounted machine can harvest 2 rows at once and 10 to 15 acres a day. To compare hand and machine picking: a single stripper can harvest as much cotton as 26 laborers hand-snapping the bolls.

PROCESS-ING OF COTTON

GINNING

After the cotton has been picked, the fibers are separated from the seeds by a process called *ginning*. The ginning is done by circular saws revolving on one shaft. The grower normally takes the cotton to the gin and pays for ginning. After the ginning, the cotton is packaged in bales of about 500 pounds each. At this point, the seeds and the fibers go separate ways.

PROCESSING THE SEEDS

Seeds go to the crushing mill, where they are *delinted* (fuzz is removed mechanically). The short fuzzy fibers so removed, called *linters*, are used in mattresses and other cushioning and in the making of plastics, fine paper, and other products.

[3] Cotton Council International.

Hulls are next removed from the delinted seed. The hulls serve as cattle fodder or as the source of a chemical used in making synthetic rubber or plastics. Inside the seed is oil that can be pressed out in the crushing mill or removed by solvent extraction. This cottonseed oil is valuable in making cooking oil, shortening, salad dressings, and margarine. The meat of the cottonseed serves as feed for cattle.

A process developed by the United States Department of Agriculture makes it possible to extract high purity protein concentrates from the seed. The concentrates are for human food, and the first commercial plant for extracting protein from cottonseed has an ultimate capacity of 25 tons per day. It may be used to fortify cereals or meats, as a flour in baked products, or as a protein supplement in soft drinks.

BALING AND CLASSIFYING THE COTTON

Cotton is baled after ginning, and then it is classified by (*a*) staple length (fiber length), (*b*) grade, and (*c*) fiber character. Fiber properties measured are fineness, color, length, uniformity, and strength.

A practical but unofficial basis of classifying by staple length is as follows:

1. *Extra-short-staple cotton* (not over 3/4 inch). This length is not very suitable for spinning and is best used in batting and wadding.
2. *Short-staple cotton* (3/4 inch to 1 inch). This type is spinnable and is used for coarser, inexpensive goods.
3. *Medium-staple cotton* (1 inch to 1 1/8 inches). The United States produces the bulk of this variety for its own use and for export.
4. *Long-staple cotton* (1 1/8 but less than 1 3/8 inches). The United States produces the bulk of its own requirements. Imports are relatively small.
5. *Extra-long-staple cotton* (1 3/8 inches and longer). United States production is limited; we import from Egypt, Sudan, and Peru.

Long staples account for 1 percent of the domestic crop. Group 3 accounts for 75 percent, and group 2 accounts for 24 percent.

Classification by Grade. In the trade, American cotton is classified not only according to length of fiber, but also according to the condition of the cotton, on a basis called *middling*. Middling cotton is creamy white, with no evidence of dirt or gin cuts (fibers matted and cut) and with only a few pieces of leaf and immature seeds. The following grades and half grades are recognized:

1. Good middling
2. Strict middling
   Middling plus
3. Middling
   Strict low middling plus
4. Strict low middling
   Low middling plus
5. Low middling
   Strict good ordinary plus
6. Strict good ordinary
   Good ordinary plus
7. Good ordinary

FIGURE 9.3 (A). Blending cotton from several bales in opening room. (Photo courtesy National Cotton Council.)

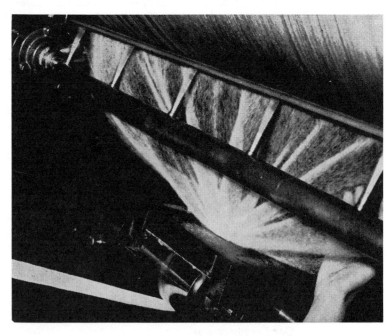

FIGURE 9.3 (B). Cleaning and separating individual fibers takes place in carding machine. The web of fibers is formed into a rope-like strand or "sliver." (Photo courtesy National Cotton Council.)

FIGURE 9.3 (C). Lap, composed of slivers, is passed through comb which combs out short fibers. Output of comb is formed again into sliver. (Photo courtesy National Cotton Council.)

FIGURE 9.3 (D). Lapping. (Photo courtesy Springs Cotton Mills.)

204
*Fabric
Construction
and
Buying
Motives*

FIGURE 9.3 (E). Finisher
drawing. Strands of combed sliver
are blended on finisher drawing
machines for still greater
uniformity and paralleling of the
cotton fibers. (Photo courtesy
Springs Cotton Mills.)

FIGURE 9.3 (F). Slivers are fed into
roving frame where cotton is
twisted slightly and drawn into a
smaller strand.

FIGURE 9.3 (G). Roving is fed to spinning frame where it is drawn out to final size, twisted into yarn, and wound on bobbins. (Courtesy National Cotton Council.)

FIGURE 9.3 (H). Several hundred warp yarns are rewound from cones or cheeses into large section beams (Courtesy National Cotton Council.)

FIGURE 9.3 (I). In slashing, threads are unwound from assembly of warper beams, immersed in sizing mixture, dried, and rewound on loom beams. (Courtesy National Cotton Council.)

FIGURE 9.3(J). Weaving room. (Courtesy National Cotton Council.)

FIGURE 9.3 (K). Inspecting. (Photo courtesy National Cotton Council.)

Good middling—the best—has lustrous, silky, clean fibers, whereas good ordinary contains leaf particles, sticks, hulls, dirt, sand, gin cuts, and spots. To indicate the degree of whiteness of the cotton, five distinct color groups are used: white, spotted, tinged, yellow-stained, and gray. Practically all the United States cotton falls below good middling.

SPECIES OF AMERICAN COTTON

Classification of American cotton according to length of staple is probably more logical than a geographical classification, because the length of staple and fineness of fiber are criteria in judging the quality of cotton.

PIMA

That the importance of fine long-staple cotton is realized by American cotton growers can be seen from the fact that an American-Egyptian type is being grown here, chiefly in the irrigated lands of Arizona, New Mexico, and around El Paso. This pima has an extra-long (1 3/8 to 1 5/8 inches) staple. Of the American cottons, pima ranks next to sea island in order of quality. It is used in sheer woven goods and in fine knitted fabrics.

Cotton farmers and the U.S. Department of Agriculture, in crossbreeding seeds of all kinds, were responsible for the producing of the silky, long-staple, lustrous, and strong *pima cotton*. They cooperated in development work and produced a superlative cotton fiber. Marketed under the trademark Supima, it is used in promoting garments and fabrics made from the pima variety. It is grown in Arizona, New Mexico, Texas, and California, where climate and soil are right for its growth. The staple is longer, finer, stronger than any other, takes colors well, and has a smooth silky hand. It can be woven from a sheer chiffon weight to a heavy broadcloth.

UPLAND (Gossypium Hirsutum)

The term "upland" originally denoted cotton raised away from the sea coast on higher land, as distinguished from cotton grown on the lowlands,

208
*Fabric
Construction
and
Buying
Motives*

the coastal regions. Now upland cotton is produced at all altitudes, from the foothills of the Ozark and Blue Ridge mountains to the Mississippi Delta. Sheetings, carded broadcloths, twills, drills, print cloths, and carded yarns for knitting are commonly produced from fibers of this class. Upland cotton constitutes over 99 percent of the United States production. It produces fibers ranging from 3/4 to 1 1/2 inches in length.

DELTAPINE

New varieties of cotton, called *Deltapine*, have spread from their original locale in the Mississippi Delta to the far West, particularly to the Imperial Valley of California and to the Salt River Valley of Arizona. The varieties owe their increased use to a high yield per acre, the ease with which they clean at the gins, and their comparative strength. In fact, many cotton varieties are shifting geographically across the country because cotton breeders are trying to meet the demands of increased mechanical harvesting and modern ginning practices. There are also newer varieties with improved fiber properties that make mechanical harvesting and modern ginning practices less harmful. Coker, Deltapine, Stoneville, Rex, Acala, and Dixie King varieties are providing growers with wider choices of the exact fiber properties, yields, and regional adaptation for best growth under the widest range of soil and weather conditions.

SPECIES OF FOREIGN COTTON

EGYPTIAN (Gossypium barbadense)

Egyptian cotton, next to sea island cotton, has the longest fiber. It can be made to look almost like silk by mercerizing. This type of cotton is grown along the Nile Delta. It is a light tan or brown in color and therefore must usually be bleached. Hosiery, knit goods, and underwear are often made of Egyptian cotton. It is only slightly shorter in length than the sea island variety, the former averaging mostly 1 1/2 inches or less. Other African production (except Egyptian) is in medium- and long-staple groups.

TANGUIS (Gossypium barbadense)

Tanguis cotton has fibers averaging 1 1/4 inches in length. It comes from Peru. Most Tanguis cotton fibers have a rough, harsh, wiry, woolly feel and a slight crimp. For this reason they are often mixed with short-staple wool. Such cotton-and-wool mixtures may be used for underwear, if knitted so that the cotton will be next to the skin and the harsher wool will be on the outside. Hosiery may be similarly made of this cotton.

INDIAN (Gossypium arboreum and Gossypium herbacium)
AND OTHER VARIETIES

India and Pakistan also grow the American upland type of cotton. The fiber length averages from 1 to 1 1/32 inches. China also grows cotton, but it has a yellowish-brown fiber and is not often exported. Israel grows the American-type Acala and fine pima cotton and has one of the highest average yields per acre of cotton fiber in the world.

**CHARAC-
TERIS-
TICS
OF
THE
COTTON
FIBER**

MICROSCOPIC APPEARANCE

When seen under the microscope, unmercerized cotton fibers resemble flat twisted ribbons. The unripe cotton fiber is a tubelike structure or canal (lumen). Within this tube is a cell protoplasm that either dries as the cotton ripens or shrinks back to the stalk of the plant. The disappearance of this substance causes the fiber to flatten and twist, so that under the microscope it appears like a twisted ribbon. The canal can be seen. (See Appendix A.) When cotton is mercerized by treatment with caustic soda, the twist comes out to some extent, depending on the degree of mercerization.

LENGTH OF FIBER

Cotton ranges in length of staple from 3/4 to 1 1/2 inches. Since the very short lengths are difficult to spin, they are not considered in the figures given here. Yarns made of shorter staple are more apt to be linty and fuzzy than are those of longer staple. For combed yarn, a long staple is advisable.

DIAMETER OF FIBER

The diameter of the cotton fiber ranges from .0005 to .0009 inch. The U.S. Department of Agriculture *Bulletin No. 33* places the range from .00064 (sea island) to .00844 (Indian) inch. Pima and Egyptian fibers have the smallest diameters and so can be spun into the finest yarns.

LUSTER

Untreated cotton has no pronounced luster. Therefore cotton fabrics that need to be lustrous to imitate silk must be mercerized to produce the desired result.

STRENGTH

Tensile strength is obtained on a small bundle of fibers. (ASTM [American Society for Testing and Materials] method D-1445.) A single cotton fiber will sustain a dead weight of two to eight grams. Such a fiber is not very strong, but the finished cotton cloth can be made very strong if tightly twisted, mercerized yarns are used in it. Mercerization adds both strength and luster. Through scientific breeding, cotton farmers are growing a better product—longer, finer, more lustrous, and stronger. With further developments in scientific breeding there are even greater possibilities of improving the value of cotton for the end uses the consumer wants.

ELASTICITY

In a study of the feeling of different textile fibers, it was found that cottons have more elasticity than linens but not so much as the animal fibers. The natural twist in cotton increases the elasticity and makes it easier to spin the fiber into yarn.

210

*Fabric
Construction
and
Buying
Motives*

HYGROSCOPIC MOISTURE

Hygroscopic moisture is not the water content of the raw material, but the moisture (water) held in the pores of the fiber and on its surface. It is not a part of the chemical constituents. Some scientists give raw cotton 5 to 8 percent of hygroscopic moisture, whereas others rate it as high as 7 to 10 percent. If the moisture in the air is great, the moisture content in the fabric is increased.

COMPOSITION OF FIBER

The chief constituent of cotton is cellulose (87 to 90 percent). Cellulose is a solid, inert substance that is a part of plants. The fact that it is the chief component of cotton fibers and is an inert substance explains cotton's characteristic feel. Water (5 to 8 percent) and natural impurities (4 to 6 percent) are the other components of a cotton fiber. The cellulose can be modified by cross-linking to give cotton the properties of wash-and-wear. (See Chapters 2 and 7.)

HYGIENIC QUALITY AND LAUNDERABILITY

Cotton is the whitest and cleanest natural fiber. It can be laundered easily, for it withstands high temperatures well (boiling water does not hurt the fiber), and it can be ironed with a hot iron because it does not scorch easily. A chemical process, called partial acetylation. gives cotton fabrics additional heat resistance. Cottons so treated make excellent ironing-board covers. Weak alkalies, such as ammonia, borax, and silicate of soda, and cold dilute bleaching agents, such as hypochlorites or chlorine bleach, are not detrimental to the fiber. Bleaching agents must be used only under controlled conditions, since too high temperatures and concentrations destroy the fiber. Treatment of cotton fabrics with resins improves crease resistance and crease recovery after washing.

ACTION OF STRONG ACIDS

Concentrated acids, such as sulfuric, hydrochloric, hydrofluoric, and nitric, destroy cotton fibers, if the latter are cooked in these acids for a few minutes. Dilute solutions of the acids may weaken a cotton fabric and may destroy it if it is allowed to dry without being rinsed.

ACTION OF LIGHT

If cotton is continuously exposed to sunlight, it loses strength. This fact is particularly true of curtains, which may appear in perfect condition when hanging at the windows but when taken down may fall apart in spots where sunlight has reached them.

AFFINITY FOR DYESTUFFS

Cotton takes dyes that are fast to washing and to sunlight. For a vegetable fiber, cotton has a fair affinity for dye. Vat dyes as a class are the fastest to all the elements listed below. Vegetable fibers do not take dye as readily as do animal fibers.

TABLE 9-1. Fastness of Dyes of Different Classes on Cotton Goods

Price class:	1	2	3	4	5	6
Color type:	Vat	Naphthol	Developed	Sulphur	Basic	Direct
Home washing	Exc.	Exc.	Good	Good	Poor	Good (light shades) Poor (heavy shades)
Laundry	Exc.	Exc.	Fair-poor	Fair-poor	Very poor	Poor
Light	Exc.	Very good	Poor	Good	Very poor	Some poor, some very good
Bleaching (Chlorine)	Exc.	Exc.	Bad	Bad	Bad	Bad
Cross Dyeing	Exc.	Exc.	Good	Good	Bad	Bad

NOTE: There are some exceptions to these general rules in each class.
Reprinted from *American Fabrics*, 52 (Spring, 1961) 74. (Reprinted courtesy of the Franklin Process Company, a division of Indian Head Mills.)

MILDEW

Cotton is subject to rotting caused by mildew, which is caused by fungi. Heat and dampness further the growth of mildew. Considerable research has revealed that a chemical compound produced by the fungi has the power of changing cellulose in the cotton to sugar. The fungi feed on the sugar. It was found that there is less rotting if the cotton is treated to make it fire-resistant and water-repellent. (See Chapter 7.) Hence, mildew can be prevented. Former attempts to protect cotton against mildew by treating it with fungicides proved ineffective under climatic conditions favorable to the growth of fungi. Cotton can be treated with a chemical called acrylonitrile. (See Chapter 7.) Such treatment makes cotton not only permanently resistant to mildew but also more resistant to wet and dry heat and gives it greater affinity for dyes.

COTTON YARNS

PREPARING THE COTTON

At the mill, cotton is unbaled and then pulled out in small tufts and beaten to remove impurities. The tufts are compressed into a sheet called a *lap*. Several laps may be combined into one.

CARDING

Cotton is not thoroughly clean until particles of leaf are removed. A machine called a *card* separates the matted fibers and removes leafy matter. In colonial times carding was done by hand with a pair of

212
*Fabric
Construction
and
Buying
Motives*

cards—rectangular pieces of wood with wire teeth on one side of each card and with wooden handles. The teeth were placed together, and the cotton was pulled and straightened between the teeth. Now this process is done by machinery. The carded cotton in lap form is drawn through an aperture and comes out in rope form called a *card sliver*. The short fibers that fall to the floor or cling to the machinery during the carding are never wasted, but are often used to make fabrics in which evenness and strength of yarn are not requisites.

DRAWING

If the yarn is to be fine enough for use in clothing, the diameter of the yarn must be reduced to a size appropriate to the particular fabric. Several card slivers may be fed between two pairs of rollers, the second of which revolves faster than the first. This operation draws out or stretches the sliver, thus decreasing its diameter. The sliver may be drawn three times and may be reduced further in size and given a slight twist by a process called *roving*. In this process, the sliver is passed through rollers and wound onto bobbins set in spindles. Improved carding devices, together with new and faster machinery for drawing, and new roving frames have increased production and decreased labor costs.

COMBING

This process is really a continuation and refinement of the carding process. Short fibers are eliminated from the sliver; fibers are laid more nearly parallel; and the filmy sheet of fibers is further attentuated. Cotton yarns for fabrics are carded, but not all are combed. On the other hand, some fabrics are made of yarns that have been combed several times. Combed yarns are even and free from extraneous material. Yarns that are merely carded are not so clean or so even as those that are given further treatment. Yarns can be made finer by combing; those used for fine-quality French voiles and batistes receive a good deal of combing.

FIGURE 9.4. Left: Carded cotton cloth. Right: Combed cotton cloth. (Photo by Jack Pitkin.)

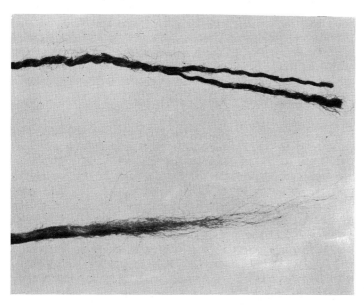

FIGURE 9.5. Top: two-ply yarn. Bottom: Single yarn. (Photo by Jack Pitkin.)

Yarns for coarse, unbleached muslins and unbleached duck are usually only carded. Even many good-quality fabrics are only carded.

SPINNING

The spinning process puts in the twist. Some yarns are loosely or slackly twisted, whereas others are tightly twisted. The more twists or turns to the inch, the stronger the cotton yarn.

WINDING

Yarns are wound on spools, on paper tubes, on double-headed bobbins, in skeins or hanks, in ball form, or on warp beams, ready for the weavers.

SINGLE AND PLY COTTON YARNS

Cotton yarns are made in singles or in plies. A tightly twisted cotton yarn may have a rayon yarn twisted loosely with it to form a two-ply yarn.

Ply yarns are ordinarily stronger than singles of the same diameter. Unique effects are produced in ply yarns by the use of singles with different degrees of twist. A ratiné or bouclé has a rough turkish-towel effect made by ply yarns in different tension. Slack-twisted yarns make soft fabrics that drape gracefully. Tightly twisted yarns make strong, hard-feeling fabrics.

The finer the yarn count, the higher the price. Also, two-ply yarns cost more than single yarns; combed yarns cost more than carded yarns; and yarns ready for use as warp cost more than yarns in skeins (used for filling).

SIZES OF COTTON YARNS

Most sewing cotton is marked 60 or 80. These numbers, as we have already mentioned, denote the fineness of the thread—80 being finer than 60. Accordingly, yarns used in fabrics are given numbers or counts to

214
Fabric
Construction
and
Buying
Motives

denote their weight and fineness. In size 10 yarn there are 10 × 840, or 8,400, yards to the pound. Size 10 in this case is the count of the yarn. A small "s" after the number means the yarn is single; that is, 10s, 20s, 30s. The notation 10/2 means that size or count 10 yarn is two-ply. Yarn spun in this country reaches as high as 160s; a medium count is 30s; Egyptian is 100; Brazilian, 40; Surat from India, 30; Peruvian, 30.

COTTON THREAD

American women have had cotton sewing thread only since 1840. This thread was first produced in 1812 in Paisley, Scotland (the small town where Paisley shawls were made), by James and Patrick Clark, who were searching for a new material for making the heddle eyes of the loom. The heddle eyes have to be smooth, for it is through these eyes that warp yarns are threaded into the loom. The Clark brothers perfected a cotton yarn smooth and strong enough to replace silk for this purpose. By chance, the yarn was found to be suitable for sewing. At first this yarn, called *thread*, was sold in hanks, but it was later wound on spools as it is today.

James Coats, who had also been associated with the manufacture of Paisley shawls, employed his knowledge of yarn making and weaving when he built a factory to make high-grade cotton thread. His factory, later owned by his sons James and Peter (J. & P. Coats), competed with the Clarks.

In 1840 Andrew Coats, a brother of James and Peter, came to America as a selling agent for J. & P. Coats of Scotland. A factory was built in Pawtucket, Rhode Island, and, in 1841, George and William Clark, sons of the third generation, came to the United States. Mills for making thread were built in Newark, New Jersey.

The O.N.T. so commonly seen on Clark's spool cotton stands for "Our New Thread." This softer, stronger thread was composed of six strands of cotton twisted together, instead of the usual three.

Cotton thread comes in sizes ranging from coarse to fine: 8, 10, 12, 16, 20, 23, 30, 36, 40, 50, 60, 70, 80, 90, 100. (See Chapter 3 for the differences between thread and yarn.)

WOVEN COTTON FABRICS

PLAIN WEAVES

Cotton can be made in all weaves and variations. The cotton fabric called *muslin* traces its name to the French *mousseline*, which in turn derived its name from the town of Mosul in Mesopotamia. Muslin is the generic name of cotton fabrics in plain weave ranging from the sheerest batiste to the coarsest sheeting. The lower counts, 48 square to 80 square (finished), are called *print cloths*, the higher counts in sheer fabrics are *lawns*, and the higher counts in sheetings are *percales*.

Cottons in the basket weaves include oxford 2 × 1, 2 × 2, 3 × 2, and monks cloth 4 × 4 and 8 × 8.

In rib variations of the plain weave, there is the poplin or popeline, first woven at Avignon, France, as a compliment to the reigning pope. Ribs are closely spaced next to each other fillingwise. Broadcloth is similar to poplin, with finer, closer ribs. Dimity is also a ribbed fabric, but the ribs are spaced at regular intervals either in warpwise strips or in crossbars. Numerous fabrics in plain weave will be described in Part II.

TWILL WEAVES

Denim (de Nimes), first woven in Nimes, France, and *jean*, first made in Italy, are typical twill weave fabrics. Another closely woven, wind-resistant cotton and rayon twill is used in ski suits, parkas, football and basketball uniforms, and rainwear. It is lustrous and durable.

SATIN OR SATEEN WEAVES

When the warp floats in cotton, the fabric is called *warp satin*. When the filling floats, which is more common, the fabric is called *sateen*, the suffix "een" meaning cotton. Cotton satin is often found in linings of men's clothing. Cotton sateen may be used for lining draperies.

FANCY WEAVES

Damasks for both dresses and tablecloths are illustrations of cotton Jacquards. Dobby appears in bird's-eye diaper fabrics and in huck toweling. White-on-white broadcloth or madras shirtings are Jacquard or dobby.

Terry cloth and turkish toweling are uncut looped pile. Velveteen is also pile weave.

Marquisette for curtains is made in leno. It may have embroidered effects. In fact, any cotton fabric may be embroidered or given an embroidered effect.

LACES

Cotton is currently used more than any other textile for laces. (See Chapter 19 for kinds of laces.)

NONWOVEN COTTON FABRICS A web of fibers held or bonded by an adhesive is called a nonwoven fabric. (See Chapter 6 for methods of bonding.) Articles such as disposable napkins, wallpaper backing, bandages, polishing cloths, tea bags, dish and guest towels, and tablecloths can be made of nonwoven fabrics. Perhaps the greatest potential for the nonwoven goods industry is in hospital and medical supplies.

KNITTED COTTON FABRICS A common weft-knitted cloth in stockinette stitch is cotton jersey, used in T-shirts and basque shirts. The tops of men's socks and the wrists of sweat shirts are commonly rib-knit. The purl stitch, called plain knitting by hand knitters, is used for scarfs, baby carriage covers, and pot holders.

The warp-knitted cotton fabrics in tricot and milanese are frequently used in fabric gloves. A modified tricot knit of fine cotton yarns sueded on one side is manufactured into gloves and sports jackets.

REGULAR FINISHES FOR COTTON FABRICS Improved finishes for cotton have been responsible in large measure for cotton's popularity. Among them are the resin and nonresin finishes that give cottons the same easy- or minimum-care features that man-made fibers possess. Advances in antibacterial, mildew-resistant, and flame-resistant treatments have improved the effectiveness of the performance

216
Fabric
Construction
and
Buying
Motives

of cotton in various end uses. Since the regular and special finishes have been described in Chapter 7, only those finishes applied to cotton will be considered here.

PRELIMINARY TREATMENT

This includes singeing or gassing to remove lint and loose yarn, which is followed by a chemical bath to desize the fabric. Kier boiling further removes foreign material, waxes, and sizings. A Kier is a vat used for boiling the fabric. Bleaching is then done if the fabric is to be white or if it is to have some further surface interest. Bleaching and kier boiling are now combined.

If a cloth is to resemble linen, it is beetled; if it is to be used for warmth, it is often napped. When surface irregularities appear, the fabric must be sheared by rotating spiral blades at various stages in finishing. Then the cloth must be dried.

MERCERIZATION

If a cotton fabric is to have a glossy surface, it is mercerized after it has been bleached. Sometimes the mercerizing is done in the yarn stage or possibly in the fiber stage, in which case the operation is not repeated in the finishing of the cloth.

The process of mercerizing was discovered by John Mercer about the middle of the nineteenth century. He happened upon it quite accidentally when he found he had left some cotton in a caustic soda solution and feared the treatment had been too long. Upon microscopic examination, he found the fibers had lost their natural twist, appeared structureless like silk, were shiny, and had increased in tensile strength. For about thirty years the discovery was practically forgotten, because the process was too expensive to be used commercially. Then, in 1890, Lowe of England patented a process by which the cotton fiber was made lustrous if held in tension in caustics. Improvements have been made in the combined methods of Mercer and Lowe, and now mercerization is used on a large scale.

Formerly, few mercerized cotton fabrics were available. Now we have many, including sateen, batiste, cotton satin, better grade of cotton broadcloth, cotton poplin, and knitted underwear.

For mercerizing, cotton of long staple (long fiber) gives best results. The fibers are carefully combed, and the cloth is singed and bleached before it is mercerized. Since most cloths are mercerized in the piece, this process is generally considered a method of finishing.

Mercerization gives cotton fabrics definite advantages. It makes them stronger, more elastic and pliable, more lustrous, and more absorbent, and it gives them a greater affinity for dyestuffs.

SIZING OR DRESSING

Mucilage, China clay, starch, flour, casein, or wax may be used as sizing. Sometimes oily or greasy substances, such as oil, tallow, or glycerin, are applied after the stiffening substance to soften the texture of the cloth. Because sizing makes a cotton more susceptible to mildew, antiseptics such as zinc chloride or formaldehyde are added to the sizing to prevent this growth. In sizing, the cloth is passed between two rollers, one roller dipping into the vat of sizing. The sizing process follows the singeing, bleaching, and dyeing, because subjecting cloth to liquids after it is sized removes the stiffening.

If a cotton is sized too heavily, the substance may crack and rub off with friction; a thumbnail, if rubbed over the cloth, causes little particles to flake off. Also, if the cloth is heavily sized, particles fly off the cloth as it is being torn. If a colored fabric that has been sized is rubbed briskly against a white handkerchief, the sizing may rub off onto the handkerchief. Washing generally removes sizing, and then any defects in the yarn or weave become noticeable.

Sized cotton cloths include organdy, costume cambric, sheeting, and mosquito netting. Other cloths, such as lawn, marquisette, nainsook, and dimity may contain small amounts of sizing to give them a fresh, crisp appearance.

STARCHING

(See *sizing or dressing*.)

DYEING AND PRINTING

Cotton may be dyed in raw stock, yarn, or piece. It may be printed by roller, discharge, resist, screen, hand-block, duplex, photographic, or jet methods.

CONDITIONING

After the fabric has been colored (dyed or printed), it is starched (sized) as a basic finish to give a hand to the cloth.

FIGURE 9.6. In vat dyeing, spun yarn is dipped into large vats containing coloring materials. In raw stock dyeing, the cotton fiber is packed directly from the bale into large kettle-like machines and dye is pumped through it. Dyeing of the fabric after it has been woven or knitted, however, is the most common method. (Courtesy of National Cotton Council of America.)

FIGURE 9.7. Machines for printing cotton cloth resemble those for printing newspapers. (Photo courtesy National Cotton Council of America.)

TENTERING

This process evens the fabric in the width.

CALENDERING

This process smooths the cloth by a series of rollers. Sometimes the rollers are engraved to give an embossing like the watered design of moiré or a crepey texture.

SPECIAL FINISHES FOR COTTON FABRICS

Probably more special or functional finishes are applied to cotton than to any other fibers. These finishes include crease, perspiration, mildew, flame, and stain resistance; also waterproofing and water repellency, shrinkage control, permanent glazing, heat setting, permanent starchless, absorbency, germ resistance, wash-and-wear, and durable press. (See Chapter 7.) In connection with cotton/polyester blends for durable press, it is not commonly known that it is the cotton that carries the durable press treatment. The polyester is added to overcome the strength loss that most mass production finishes cause in 100 percent cotton.

CONSUMER DEMAND FOR COTTON

Cotton is plentiful and economical to produce, and it has the inherent characteristics of easy care that consumers want. According to *Textile Organon*, the world output of basic textile fibers (cotton, wool, and man-made fibers) was 56.7 billion pounds in 1973. Of the total output, cotton accounted for 50 percent; wool for 6 percent; and man-made fibers for 44 percent. Silk was a nominal percentage of the total.[4]

To be sure, cotton continues to feel the competition of the man-made fibers that began to invade the market during the 1930s. Man-made fibers still present cotton and the other natural fibers with a challenge.

[4] *Textile Organon*, XLV-6 (June 1974).

Man-made fiber and yarn companies have spent huge sums of money on basic research, development, and promotion of their products. Despite increases in cotton's research and promotion expenditures in recent years, its total outlay in these areas is still much less than expenditures by man-made fiber producers. Their promotional efforts have been instrumental in capturing part of cotton's share of the fiber market, but in 1973 cotton remained the largest volume fiber consumed by United States textile mills, accounting for 30 percent of total pounds used. The remaining 70 percent was shared by a host of natural and man-made fibers. Data from the National Cotton Council indicate that cotton accounted for 39 percent of all fiber consumption in apparel; 25 percent in home furnishings; and 24 percent of all fibers consumed in industrial textile markets.[5]

The cotton industry is making every effort to meet this challenge through improvement of processing machinery, reduction of labor costs, and improvement and promotion of functional finishes for cotton fabrics to impart permanent press, flame retardance, and other desirable properties. Cotton growers finance much of this effort through contributions of $1 per bale into Cotton Incorporated, which carries out an intensive program of research and promotion.

What will happen? Eventually, there will probably be a balance between the use of natural and man-made fibers. Blends will maximize the advantages and minimize the disadvantages of each. Each fiber must continue to improve its quality, beauty, and suitability. None can remain static.

BUYING POINTS OF COTTON FABRICS

Table 9-2 presents consumers' rankings of fabric characteristics when buying apparel for themselves,[6] referred to at the beginning of this chapter.

Table 9-2.

	Men	Women	Teens
Comfort	1	1	1
Value	2	2	2
Durability	3	6	7
Shape retention	4	4	4
No shrinking	5	3	3
Feel of fabric next to skin	6	7	6
Ease of cleaning/ washing	7	5	Fashion a
Wrinkle free	8	8	

aNot significant

Ratings are in order of importance, from 1 (highest) through 8. (7) denotes that teenagers named durability as their seventh most important characteristic. Fashion ranked fifth.

[5] *Cotton Counts Its Customers*, National Cotton Council (June 1974).
[6] National Consumer Study by Opinion Research Corporation.

220
*Fabric
Construction
and
Buying
Motives*

Those are the buying points that consumers consider in buying apparel. Let us consider those points in relation to cotton.

COMFORT

Cotton conducts moisture away from the body and allows the cooler temperatures outside to reach the body, so it is a cool material for summer or tropical wear. But, since short cotton fibers nap easily, cotton fabrics can also be made warm when necessary. Knitted cotton underwear absorbs perspiration and keeps the wearer comfortable.

In the above study, better than half of the women and almost 60 percent of the men preferred cotton, in terms of the *feel of the fabric next to the skin*, over polyester and rayon.

VALUE

By *value*, we mean providing good quality for the money. Value was ranked second in consumer preference for apparel. In short, the consumer wants his or her money's worth.

In considering the price of cotton garments, the following factors are involved: (1) quality of fibers, (2) quality of yarn, (3) construction, (4) finishes, (5) style, and (6) workmanship.

DURABILITY

Durability refers to the length of time that a fabric will wear. Workmanship indicates the skill and care that is given to a fabric when it is manufactured. Cotton fibers are comparatively short; therefore one would expect them to produce a yarn that is fairly weak in tensile strength. However, a cotton fiber, because of its natural twist, spins so well that it can be twisted very tightly; hence, since tightly twisted yarns are more durable than those that are slackly twisted, cotton yarns are strong and fabrics made from them are durable.

Two-ply yarns are more durable than single yarns of the same diameter; so a turkish towel made of two-ply yarn will be stronger and more absorbent than one constructed from a single yarn. It is also important to remember that yarns of even and regular texture are usually stronger than irregular yarns of the same average diameter. Also, since cottons are temporarily stronger when wet than when dry, there is no need to worry about their breaking when they are in the wash.

Cotton yarns, then, can be given considerable tensile strength, and the cloth made from these yarns can be durable. It is the quality of the yarn, (in addition, of course, to weave and finish) that primarily determines the durability of the cloth.

There is little need for the consumer to fear that a guaranteed colorfast cotton fabric will fade if hung as a window drapery. It is not likely that the hand laundry or the household automatic washer will remove color from table damasks, dresses, or colored domestic cotton. There is still some danger that an unreliable commercial laundry will use bleaches under poorly controlled conditions and consequently cause fading of color. Any good detergent may be used. Cottons resist the alkali of which some soaps are made.

Cotton can be pressed with a hot iron; its scorching point is high. Since cotton fiber is fairly inelastic, most cotton fabrics wrinkle easily, and hence, unless they are finished for crease resistance, need frequent pressing. But cottons require no particular care in pressing. Unless they are treated for mildew resistance, they should not be folded and kept on shelves where there is dampness. Moths, however, will not attack cottons.

SHAPE RETENTION

An innovation in fabric finishing has provided the first wash-and-wear cloth for men's and boy's casual slacks. It is a resin finish called Koratron that imparts permanent crease and shape to a garment. After cutting, the fabric is heat-cured to "bake in" the resin. Fabrics so finished are wrinkle- and crease-resistant, and should not require ironing. The shape of the garment is thus retained permanently.[7]

RESISTANCE TO SHRINKAGE

One of the chief objections to cotton was its danger of shrinkage. A generation ago, consumers allowed a whole size for shrinkage of a shirt after laundering. Shrinkage-control treatments can now be applied to cottons so that not more than 1 percent residual shrinkage remains to be taken into account. (See Chapter 7.)

FEEL OR HAND

This characteristic is related to how the cotton fabric feels next to the skin. In the consumer survey, almost 60 percent of the men associated cotton specifically with comfort and *feel of the fabric next to the skin*. Cotton ranked over polyester by more than two-to-one.

Cotton fibers feel cool, smooth, and soft. When cotton is processed into fabric, the feel or hand can be changed by the type of yarns, construction, and finish applied.

EASE OF CLEANING/WASHING (Care)

The factors of light, laundering, ironing, and perspiration are the common considerations in colorfastness of cottons. Possibly dry cleaning should be added, but inasmuch as cotton per se is considered washable, it would be assumed that it is dry cleanable if colorfast. Some consumers will not purchase a cotton fabric if the label reads "Dry clean only."

In the discussion of physical characteristics of cotton it was stated that cotton takes dyes that are fast to washing and to sunlight. Standard Fade-Ometer tests appropriate to the fabric's end use can be made to determine the degree of colorfastness.

In resistance to fading by perspiration, cotton is considered good.

The fact that cotton fabrics with durable press finish can be washed, dried, and appear wrinkle free with no ironing required is an important reason for buying cotton articles.

---

[7] "Cotton Its Properties and Uses;" a pamphlet by the Canadian Cotton Council.

222
*Fabric
Construction
and
Buying
Motives*

FASHION RIGHTNESS[8]

The couturiers of New York and Paris have considered cottons glamorous enough for inclusion in their collections. Probably the special finishes have been largely responsible for the fashion rightness of cotton today. Then too, the textured effects obtained by blending cotton with other fibers in nubby, bouclé, and novelty yarns have glamorized cotton. Fabrics such as cotton brocades, tweeds, shantungs, and suitings have appeared. Staple fabrics, such as chambray, denim, corduroy, and jersey, have been restyled for the casual mode.

The National Cotton Council of American, the central organization representing all branches of the cotton industry, was instrumental in elevating cotton as a fashion fabric. Its work also is reflected in a wide array of developments that have increased cotton's value to consumers.

VERSATILITY

Cotton can serve for food (cottonseed products), for clothing, and for shelter. Cotton clothing can be worn around the clock. A single cotton fabric, piqué, can be used for a house dress, a sports dress, a summer business dress, a bathing suit, or a beach bag. It is particularly adapted to children's dresses. Cotton, then, is appropriate for wearing apparel, home furnishings, industrial uses, and military supplies.

IMPROVEMENTS IN FINISHES

The improvements in finishes have given newer and better uses to cotton. Other than the basic finishes, there are treatments for resistance to stains, water, flame, mildew, and germs; also functional finishes for permanent stiffness, crease resistance, crease retention, wash-and-wear, durable press, and embossed or heat-set patterns. (See Chapter 7 for a discussion of each process.)

SUMMARY Mistakes are frequently made by both the consumer and the salesperson because each fails to appreciate the inherent qualities of a fabric. The consumer will make a better buyer if he or she knows the *characteristics* of cotton and their *effect* on the finished fabric. Salespeople will improve their selling efficiency if they increase their technical knowledge of how cotton will best serve the customer; and they will be better equipped to answer customers' questions, such as, Will the fabric wash well? Will the material be suitable for an evening dress?

Satisfied customers are those who buy the fabrics best suited to their needs. These customers are assets to any store.

**REVIEW
QUESTIONS**
1. (*a*) Of what value to the salesperson is a knowledge of the qualities of cotton?
   (*b*) Of what value is such knowledge to the consumer?
2. (*a*) In what countries is cotton raised?
   (*b*) Which species of cotton has the longest fibers? Which cottons have the finest fibers?

[8] Fashion ranked fifth by teen-agers in a survey by the Opinion Research Corporation.

(c) Which kind of cotton is best for use in hosiery and knit goods? Which for mixing with wool?

3. (a) What advantages has the mechanical cotton picker?

(b) What are its disadvantages?

4. Explain the classification of upland cotton.

5. What effect have the fineness of the fiber and the length of the fiber on the finished cotton fabric?

6. Define: tensile strength, mercerization, hygroscopic moisture, cellulose, carding, count of yarn, ply yarn, combing, spinning.

7. (a) What effect on cotton have weak alkalies, such as borax, ammonia, phosphate of soda, and soap?

(b) How will this knowledge help the consumer in laundering cottons?

(c) What is the effect on cotton of strong, concentrated mineral acids such as sulfuric acid, nitric acid, and hydrochloric acid?

8. (a) Under what conditions does cotton mildew?

(b) How may mildew be prevented?

9. Describe the process of making cotton yarn.

10. Describe the effect of the following types of yarn on the finished cloth:

(a) slack-twisted yarns   (f) coarse yarns

(b) tight-twisted yarns   (g) fine yarns

(c) irregular yarns   (h) carded yarns

(d) even yarns   (i) combed yarns

(e) ply yarns   (j) low-count yarns

11. (a) In what woven constructions are cotton fabrics made? Give fabric illustrations in each construction.

(b) In what knitted constructions? Give fabric illustrations in each knitted stitch.

12. In what ways have finishes improved cotton fabrics?

13. What is meant by *versatility?* Illustrate the versatility of cotton.

14. (a) What qualities in the cotton fibers and yarns make cotton fabrics durable?

(b) Why does cotton launder easily?

15. What factors make for style in cotton fabrics?

16. Forecast the use of cotton in consumer goods.

**EXPERI-
MENTS**

(Tests to determine the effects of chemicals on cotton.)

1. *The alkali test.* Ordinary lye, which can be bought in the grocery store, may be used for this experiment. Boil several pieces of cotton cloth for 5 minutes in a 5 percent solution of lye. Remove from the fire and place what remains on a blotting paper. Describe the residue left after boiling. What was the effect of the lye on the cotton yarns? Boiling the test fabrics for 5 minutes in a 10 percent solution of sodium hydroxide is equally effective.

2. *The acid test.* An ounce of concentrated sulfuric acid will suffice for this experiment. Place the liquid in a beaker or a heavy, shallow/glass dish. Drop several cotton yarns into the acid, but do not boil them. Let the yarns remain in the acid for 5 to 10 minutes. Note any changes that take place during that time. Remove any residue and describe the result of this test. A 25 percent solution of aluminum chloride may be used instead of concentrated sulfuric acid. In this case, saturate the fabric thoroughly, then press the cloth with a very hot iron. Vegetable fibers scorch and pulverize when abraded between the fingers.

3. *The microscopic test.* This test is the most accurate of all for distinguishing one textile fiber from another. Consumers will have difficulty in obtaining a microscope, but college students can arrange to use the biology laboratory if they have no microscope in the textile laboratory. Unravel a cotton yarn and pull out one or two of the fibers. Put a small drop of water or glycerin on the glass slide. Place one or two fibers in the drop of water and cover all with a cover glass. Use the lower power first and note the general appearance of the fiber. Then, without

moving the slide, switch to the higher power. In your textile notebook draw the cotton fiber as seen through the microscope.

Sateen—Mercerized cotton fabric in (filling float) sateen weave.

Sea island cotton—A species of American cotton once produced off the coast of the Carolinas. Has the longest staple, averaging about 2 inches. Now produced on the Lesser Antilles—Montserrat, St. Kitts, Nevis, and St. Vincent.

Short-staple cotton—Fibers 1/4 to 15/16 inch long.

Stripper—A mechanical device that pulls the bolls off when they enter the rollers of the machine.

Tanguis—A species of cotton averaging 1 1/4 inches in length. Grown in Peru, which also grows other types of cotton, including pima and Egyptian.

Terry cloth—A cotton fabric with uncut looped pile, used in turkish toweling.

Thread—See Glossary, Chapter 3.

Upland—Cottons of the species *Gossypium hirsutum*. They usually produce staples from 3/4 to 1 1/2 inches.

Velveteen—A cotton pile-weave fabric in filling pile construction, with either a twill or a plain weave back.

Wash-and-wear—See Glossary, Chapter 7.

Linen
and the Consumer

10

The use of linen, or *flaxen cloth*, dates back to the European Neolithic people who lived before the appearance of metals—probably about 10,000 years ago. These people dressed in skins, but they made coarse cloth and fishnets from flax. Fragments of the cloth and nets have been discovered in parts of Switzerland, the home of the Neolithic Lake Dwellers.[1]

Fine linens have been the burial shrouds of the Egyptian pharaohs, the textile of Bible times, a fashionable and regal fabric of the Middle Ages, and the pride of the modern hostess.

Linen, then, has served man as a textile for thousands of years. It has been more important in the past than it is today. Flax lost much of its importance when the cotton gin was developed. More recently the emphasis on quality, high-fashion linen fabrics and blends for apparel and for the home has satisfied a traditional respect for and interest in linens. Even so, world production of flax fiber is only 1 percent of all fibers produced.

FLAX PRODUCTION

FLAX FOR FIBER

Flax is a vegetable fiber plant. When grown to full height it resembles golden-colored straw. The fibers for spinning are obtained from the outside of the straw.

Belgium, France, Holland, and the U.S.S.R. and its satellites are the principal flax producers. (Ireland, England, Germany, Sweden, and Italy discontinued production after World War II.) Belgium produces the tallest, best grade of flax, while the U.S.S.R. produces the greatest acreage— several million acres of shorter length. The United States raises low growing flax for seed. The Oregon flax industry partially attributes its growth to newer and better methods of harvesting. The cost of labor for cultivating, harvesting, and preparation of the fiber, added to a lack of suitable climatic conditions, has prevented flax production from becoming important in the United States.

[1] H. G. Wells, *The Outline of History* (New York: The Macmillan Company, 1921).

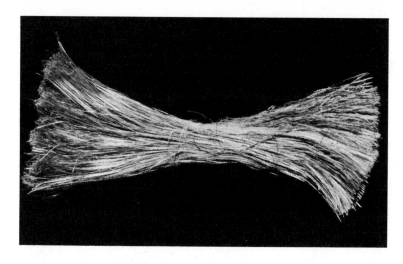

FIGURE 10.1. Flax.

FLAX FOR SEED

Flax for seed to be processed into linseed oil for paints and finishes is raised in Michigan, Minnesota, and the Dakotas. Flax plants raised for seed do not produce good fibers for spinning. Stalks of the straw are used as fodder for cattle. The best portion of the flax may be used for fibers, for twine, and for rope. Quality tow and line fibers are used to back upholstery and rugs, depending on the weave.[2] Linen fibers used as backings include those used for damask, velvet, satin, twill and plain weaves, and pile for woven rugs.

Argentina and Brazil rank high in flaxseed production in the southern hemisphere. India, Canada, Morocco, Lithuania, and Latvia produce flaxseed and hempseed.

FLAX CULTURE

A consistently moist but mild climate is necessary for the growing of flax for fiber. It requires more care than cotton before it can be made into cloth. A considerable amount of the labor in foreign countries is performed by hand—selecting, sorting, and grading. If climatic conditions are right, large quantities of flax for fiber can be produced. Great progress has been made in mechanizing the flax industry. Specially designed machines have now replaced many of the laborious hand operations. In northern countries flax is sown in the spring, like wheat and rye. The flax plant has an erect stem about three feet in height, toward the top of which are branches that carry blue or white flowers and later bolls of linseed. Flax fibers surround the pithy center of the stem. Little care is needed until harvesting time, which comes in late July or August. Large harvesting machines pull up flax plants by the roots when the stalks begin to turn yellow at the base and when the seeds are turning green to pale brown. This insures long, unbroken fibers that can be spun into yarn easily, and at the same time clears the field for the next rotation of crops.

---

[2] Short flax fibers.

227

FIGURE 10.2. Early in spring, flax seed is planted and grows to maturity about three feet high. Large machines harvest the plants by pulling. They are never cut. The stalks are bundled and threshing machines remove the seeds used for linseed oil. (Courtesy of the Belgian Linen Association.)

DRESSING THE FLAX

RIPPLING

Rippling is a process of removing the seeds. Today it is done by threshing machines that strip the seeds before tank-retting is undertaken. Bundles of flax are piled into wigwams in the fields to dry.

RETTING

Retting or soaking loosens the flax fiber from its inside straw. It is done by the following methods, either in natural water or chemicals.

1. Tank retting: The best grades of Belgian flax are retted in water from the River Lys. Bundles of flax are placed in huge concrete tanks with river water which is heated to 75° F. and gradually increased to 90° F. It requires four to five days and produces strong, lustrous, highest quality flax.
2. Dew retting: The object of this process is to let the dew loosen the fiber from the stalk. If the flax is dew-retted, the harvesting machine lays out small bundles of uprooted plants in orderly rows. The seeds are extracted by a special machine (rippling process). The bundles of flax are turned by a mechanical tedder to insure retting of the upper and lower layers. A great deal of flax seed is often wasted. Although dependent upon the weather, dew-retting is the most common method in use today and the most economical process. However it is difficult to control the quality uniformly. This process is used extensively in France, Belgium, and the U.S.S.R.
3. Chemical retting: Many processes have been tested but the use of this method is limited.

228

FIGURE 10.3. Here men are loading the bundles of flax into retting tanks filled with heated water from the River Lys. The soaking action loosens the outside flax fibers from the woody center stalk. (Courtesy of the Belgian Linen Association.)

FIGURE 10.4. Chapels of flax out to dry after soaking in retting tanks of heated water which separates outside fibers from the straw. (Courtesy Belgian Linen Association.)

FIGURE 10.5. Flax straws drying along the River Lys near Kortrijk, Belgium. (Courtesy Belgian Linen Association.)

SCUTCHING

After the flax has been thoroughly dried, it is run through a machine that breaks the wooden stalk by crumbling or crushing it. The flax is now ready for *scutching*—the removal of the fibers from the woody stalks. A machine with a series of fluted rollers beats the fibers free.

HACKLING

This process, sometimes called *combing*, corresponds to the carding and combing of cottons. The object is to prepare the fibers for spinning by laying them parallel with one another. On large machines a series of combs with iron teeth ranging from very coarse to very fine are used. The scutched fibers are pulled through each comb, beginning with the coarsest one. Some short fibers adhere to the teeth of the comb, become entangled, or drop to the floor. These short fibers, called *tow*, are used in yarns designed for draperies and upholstery, and in artistic effects found in table linens and dish towels. Such fabrics are called tow linens. The long, regular, even fibers, laid parallel in the hackling, are called *line*; they are used in fine tablecloths, handkerchiefs, and decorative dress fabrics. Tow is separated from line. Cotton or polyester may be blended with tow linen.

CHARACTERISTICS OF THE LINEN FIBER

MICROSCOPIC APPEARANCE

Linen fibers are round and at intervals have cross-markings (nodes or joints) that give the fibers the appearance of bamboo poles. There is evidence of a central canal, but it is not continuous like that of cotton. The nodes keep the fiber from collapsing. These round, jointed structures make linen harder to spin than cotton. The longer fibers are more resistant to discipline and for that reason tend to create a curly or wavy effect.

FIGURE 10.6. Emerging from the combing process, these long wisps of fiber have passed over the series of graduated metal pins of the combing machine. A man gathers the glossy flax which now resembles switches of human hair. (Courtesy of the Belgian Linen Association.)

FIGURE 10.7. In large mills spinning methods vary according to the type of yarn desired. Here fine linen threads are being spun for the weaving of sheer linens. (Courtesy of the Belgian Linen Association.)

231

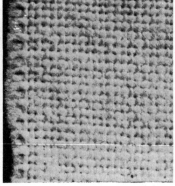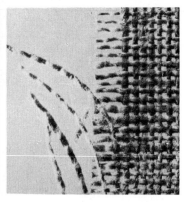

FIGURE 10.8. Left: Tow linen. Middle: Line linen. Right: A poorly hackled tow linen. (Photos by Jack Pitkin.)

LENGTH OF FIBER

Linen fibers are longer than cotton fibers. In fact, linen fibers used in fine yarns average eighteen to twenty inches in length. Consequently it is not so necessary to spin linen fibers tightly to hold the ends in as it is with cotton.

DIAMETER OF FIBER

Linen fibers range from .0047 to .0098 inch in diameter—the average breadth being greater than that of cotton. All cotton fibers are finer than the finest flax fibers.

LUSTER

Linen fibers have a characteristic silky luster, much more pronounced than that of untreated cottons. Linens are rarely mercerized. The natural look, cool hand, and textured appearance give it a unique quality.

STRENGTH

Linen is stronger than cotton, and its tensile strength increases when the fiber is wet. Overretting weakens the fiber appreciably.

HEAT CONDUCTIVITY

Linen is better than cotton as a conductor of heat. It carries heat away from the body faster. Hence, garments made of linen feel cooler than those of comparable weight in cotton.

HYGROSCOPIC MOISTURE

Flax fibers have about the same amount of hygroscopic moisture as cotton—between 6 and 8 percent. Linen fabrics, unless beetle-finished, absorb moisture quickly and dry faster than cotton. Linen dish towels will dry more dishes than cotton before feeling damp.

232

COMPOSITION OF FIBER

Like cotton, linen is composed chiefly of cellulose, but it has 15 to 30 percent more natural impurities. The chemical constituents are pure cellulose (65-70 percent); pectic substances—plant cells (20-25 percent); woody and cuticular tissue (4-5 percent); and ash (1 percent).

LAUNDERABILITY

Linen fiber is smooth; dirt and germs do not collect on it easily. Linen launders easily, but not so easily as cotton. However, since it tends to return to a natural twist with dampness, it either must be pressed when evenly damp or controlled with a blend of polyester which makes it no-iron.

ACTION OF STRONG ACIDS AND ALKALIES

Linens, like cottons, are vegetable fibers; hence acids have the same effect on linens as on cottons. Concentrated mineral acids, such as sulfuric, hydrochloric, hydrofluoric, and nitric acids, destroy linen fibers that are soaked in them for a few minutes. Dilute acids also affect linen and cotton similarly; they tend to weaken the fabric, but do not destroy it if it is not allowed to dry.

The flax fiber is attacked more readily by alkalies than cotton is. It is more difficult to bleach linen than cotton because of the natural impurities in its fibers. Weak alkalies, such as borax, ammonia, or phosphate of soda, do not injure linen.

ACTION OF LIGHT

Linens are much more resistent to the ultraviolet rays of the sun than are man-made fibers.

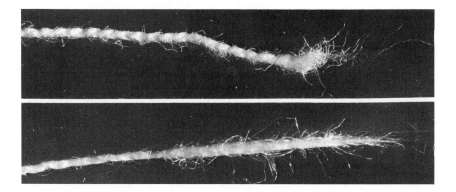

FIGURE 10.9. The breaking test, showing broken ends of two yarns. a. Cotton is brushlike; b. linen is pointed. This is a non-technical test that may be made by removing a yarn from a fabric and pulling it until it breaks. An all-linen yarn is more difficult to break than an all-cotton yarn. (Photo by Jack Pitkin.)

234
*Fabric
Construction
and
Buying
Motives*

AFFINITY FOR DYESTUFFS

Linen requires special dyes because of the hardness and less penetrability of the fiber. Its cells are held together with tissue that is broken down only under processing. Linen yarns often being of uneven thickness will dye somewhat unevenly and this fact gives linen its natural look of quality.

FIGURE 10.10. A vast amount of research has gone into the production of fast dyes. This picture shows the Moygashel fabrics going through the machine in the warm, damp atmosphere of the dyehouse. (Photograph courtesy of the Irish Linen Guild.)

**MAKING
LINEN
YARN**

PREPARATION

After the flax fibers have been sufficiently hackled or combed, the fibers go to the *preparing room*. The first machine, called the *spread board*, lays wisps of flax fibers parallel on traveling bands in continuous lines, with the ends of the wisps overlapping. These lines of fiber are then passed through sets of rollers that draw one fiber away from the other to produce a ribbon of fibers (sliver). Ribbons of sliver are drawn out longer and thinner until the last machine, the *roving frame*, puts in a loose twist. It is wound on large wooden bobbins that are mounted on the top of the spinning frame.

WET SPINNING

The roving on the bobbins is immersed in hot water, dried, and put on rapidly revolving spindles (2,000 to 3,000 revolutions per minute) that put in the twist. The twist or spin of the spindles is the operation of spinning the flax fibers into linen yarns.

WEAVING

Essentially the preparation and weaving of linen is not very different from that of wool, cotton, silk, and other textile yarns.

The manufacturer runs the cones directly onto the warp beam; several of these beams then go to the weaver's beam. The warps are set up in the loom, the filling shuttles are prepared with yarn, and weaving begins.

Plain Weave. Although very few linens are used for ready-to-wear, most of those available are plain weave. Sometimes there is a moderate texture created by rougher yarns.

A sheer linen in plain weave for handkerchiefs or fine blouses is called handkerchief linen, but in most cases it is superseded by man-made fibers of similar weave. Some slightly heavier linens for dresses or sportswear may be embroidered.

The greatest variety of weaves are created for home furnishings, although plain weaves of many weights are designed for colorful prints and are dyed very effectively. Schiffli embroidery is applied to the lighter weight for draperies and the heavier weaves for upholstery.

Plain weaves of different weight are widely distributed for embroidery of pictures and crewel pillows or other novelties. Basic weaves are also in demand as luggage and briefcase linings.

Novelty Weaves. The Belgians, who have produced fine linens for over a thousand years, create the most unusual weaves. From the sheer casements for large contemporary windows to drapery, slipcover, and upholstery weaves, the linen yarns are skillfully designed so nubs will repeat to create the desired effect. It is the thick and thin look, spaces, or twisted yarns that make the difference. This craft is so specialized that few others attempt it.

Twill Weave. Linen fabrics are far more numerous in plain weave than in twill. Twill weaves are sometimes seen in drapery and upholstery linens. Fine twills are used for crewel work, especially copying antique pieces, which revived in popularity in the 1970s.

Jacquard and Dobby Weaves. A limited amount of linen is at its best in beauty when woven in Jacquard as a table damask and in novelty dobby designs, giving a three-dimensional look: On the right side, the warp floats in a satin weave ground and the filling floats in the design.

VELVET (PILE) WEAVES

Luxurious linen-faced velvets are an important item, made of a pile construction. They include not only plain and antique velvets, but also crushed and printed colorings. Belgium is the main producer for the United States market. Velvet weaves are made in many colors, with the less expensive low pile and most expensive highest pile. The backing is cotton or man-made fibers.

FINISHING LINEN FABRICS

BLEACHING

In the past the snowy whiteness of linen was obtained by the centuries-old practice of *grass bleaching*. Grass bleaching produced beautiful color and

FIGURE 10.11. Grass bleaching flax in Ireland. (Photograph courtesy of the Irish Linen Guild.)

did not injure the strength of the fiber. But since this process required weeks or even months, much capital and land are necessary.

In today's modern bleaching processes, chemicals are used under carefully controlled conditions so that an even whiteness is achieved for dyeing light colors or printing. Important processes clean the fibers of impurities in large boiling tanks and only at the end of the process is the linen fully bleached.

REGULAR AND SPECIAL FINISHES

Regular finishes for linens have been discussed in Chapter 7, and may be referred to at this point.

There has been much discussion about flameproofing linens for contract use, about durable finishes, and about effects on the fiber after a period of time. A number of processes now used are successfully applied to linens. Flameproofing has the following additional features: (1) It may shrink fabric to the same degree as plain water. (2) It does not accelerate fading. (3) Water-repellent fabrics may be flameproofed with the durable types of flameproofing.[3]

Many cities and states have their own flameproofing regulations for fabrics used in public buildings—regulations that surpass the federal regulations.

Among the more recent functional finishes are permanent-press soil-release finishes for table linens. To make a table linen no-iron permanent press soil release, it is necessary to have a ration of 65 percent linen and 35 percent polyester in which the polyester controls the curl of the linen yarns and gives place for the finishing chemicals.

[3] "A Guide to Fabric Finishing, Flameproofing, and Service" (Perma-Dry Division, Kiesling-Hess Finishing Co., Inc., New York, Philadelphia, and Los Angeles).

FIBER IDENTIFICATION OF LINEN

Linen is a generic fiber name recognized by the FTC under the Textile Fiber Products Identification Act. Consequently, fabrics made of linen must be labeled with this generic fiber name and with percentages (over 5 percent) in order of predominance by weight of the constituent fibers in the textile fiber product, exclusive of ornamentation.[4] For example: 60 percent linen/40 percent cotton. The act states that "Fiber or fibers in an amount of 5 percent or less must appear last and be designated as 'other fiber' or 'other fibers,' as the case may be." A label might read, for example, 60 percent linen/36 percent cotton/4 percent other fibers. If the article is all linen, it may be identified by those words or by "100 percent linen."

In advertising, the percentages of the fiber need not be stated but simply listed in order of predominance by weight. The rule for fibers in an amount of 5 percent or less is the same as for labeling.[5]

Under the TFPIA, a retailer who imports linen products directly must assume full responsibility for the correct labeling of his product. Should he purchase an imported linen article from any person residing in the United States, he should obtain a guarantee issued in good faith by such a person. This rule applies to all imported textile fiber products.

SOURCES OF LINEN FABRICS

Belgium, Ireland, and Scotland are the principal exporters of linen to the United States. Smaller amounts are imported from other European countries and from Argentina, Brazil, and Japan.

The difference between the linen produced in Northern Ireland and Belgium is mostly a matter of specialization. Both produce the weaves they are most skilled at manufacturing, and each produces some of the same items as the other country—for example, oyster and plain linens used for table linen—in comparable quality. However, sheer handkerchief weaves, hemstitched linen, and damasks are mainly Irish, whereas the novelty weaves—textured and drapery weaves—are mainly Belgian. There has been a decline in sales of damask to the United States, owing to competition from Japan's rayon/cotton damask and the demand for no-iron tablecloths.

In the table linen area, Ireland produces more finished goods, while the greater part of Belgian linen enters the United States as grey goods, which are dyed, printed, trimmed, and finished here. Ireland and Belgium ship to Portugal and the Azores for hand-embroidered cloths, mats, napkins, and novelties.

In 1955 a New York center for the Belgian Linen Association was opened. Its activities include publicity, sales promotion, public relations, advertising, and education. Its blue and white shield is well known as it appears on tablecloths and drapery fabrics. The Linen Trade Association was organized by linen importers.

TRADE NAMES OF LINENS

Over the years, even for several generations, certain names on labels have spelled quality of linen fabrics to consumers. One such name is Moygashel,

---

[4] *Ornamentation* is defined as "any fibers or yarns imparting a visibly discernible pattern or design to a yarn or fabric."

[5] See Chapter 1 for a discussion of the TFPIA.

238
*Fabric
Construction
and
Buying
Motives*

from an old Gaelic castle in Dungannon. The making of linen fabrics at Moygashel goes back 1,500 years.

In 1953 Moygashel Ltd. was formed and became a public corporation, incorporating the interests of Stevenson & Sons, Ltd., and twenty-two other firms. In the spring of 1969, Moygashel Ltd. became a subsidiary of Courtaulds, Ltd.

Many of the old Irish firms have gone out of business. Belgian firms flourish from the sale of no-iron colored and embroidered tablecloths, and high priced and exclusive decorative fabrics.

CONSUMERS DEMAND FOR LINEN

At a time when there are copies of almost any weave or texture, it is interesting to speculate on why many consumers search for the natural linens woven of yarns spun from real flax. It is not so much the appearance, which is unique, as the way the light reflects from the more distinct fibers of its surface. The way in which linens take dyes or prints is another prime reason for their choice.

Many households have inherited fine table linens, damasks, or hand embroideries which have been handed down from mothers, grandmothers, or even great-grandmothers. For centuries—in fact, since the Egyptian, Greek, and Roman periods—linens have been cherished. Today, due to the faster pace of living, linens which are no-iron, soil release are used for every day, while others become part of special occasion settings.

Linens for home furnishings are a different matter. Department stores and decorating shops sell thousands of yards of printed fabrics for draperies, slipcovers, and upholstery which may contain no linen, but which, although cotton or a man-made fiber, are in demand because they have linen's textured look. It is easy enough to tell the fabrics which are 100 percent linen or have a high percentage of it. The hand is cool and the fabrics have a crisper look. For the most part linens for home decoration are ordered through interior designers, since such specialized work goes into them that prices are necessarily higher.

Of the many countries that have produced linens over the years, both by handweaving and by highly mechanized machines, the Belgians have been famous for intricate weaves since the eighth century. Today, these are mainly expressed in sheer casements. As they hang at the windows, open warp stripes, tied and knotted threads, colored yarns, and heavy nubby yarns contrasting with smooth light threads give a very special style. Other countries are now in this market, both in Europe and South America. One of the best things about such linens is that they are resistant to deterioration by the sun, as may not be the case with some fabrics of man-made fibers.

Of recent years velvets woven in Belgium have a linen pile and cotton back. Even strong dyes have a deep, not shiny, look of an almost antique patina. They are available in a wide spectrum of colors.

Above all, the natural undyed linens are in demand, from sheer fine weaves, to close weaves, to heavy nubby weaves. Most of them also come in bleached white, which is effective for contemporary rooms. In other markets, closely woven natural linen is made into shoes and handbags with leather trim. Highly prized are sets of luggage with linen on the outside, and briefcases with linen on the inside.

In aiding the customer to buy linen, the salesperson should stress the following features.

DURABILITY AND WORKMANSHIP

The durability of the cloth depends on the fibers and yarns of which it is made. Care in growth, harvesting, and dressing of flax affects the quality of the fiber. If flax is allowed to overripen, the fiber becomes too brittle to make good cloth. If fibers are overretted, they become too tender. If care is not taken in scutching and hackling, good-quality fibers may be broken or wasted. Consequently, the durability of linen cloth depends upon the degree of skilled workmanship. Since the linen fiber is longer and stronger than cotton of the same diameter, linen should be more durable than cotton, considering fibers alone. Linens and cottons are stronger when wet than when dry, so that washing does not weaken them. Weaving them together may create a more durable fabric.

The strength of linen yarn does not increase with the number of twists or turns to the inch, as does the strength of cotton. The linen fibers are sufficiently long and strong to require little twisting.

ABSORBENCY

Linen is absorbent because the flax fiber is hollow through the center, like bamboo. Since linen dish towels will dry more dishes than cotton before feeling damp, fewer dish towels are required. The consumer may not appreciate the absorbency of linen until after it has been laundered, for frequently linen's leathery beetle finish restricts absorbency.

Since linen absorbs moisture readily, dries quickly, does not "perspire" nor mold, it is well suited for drapery use in humid climates. Also, the absorptive nature of linen yarns contributes to sound deadening. For this

FIGURE 10.12. Some of the many uses of Belgian linen today. (Courtesy Belgian Linen Association.)

240

*Fabric
Construction
and
Buying
Motives*

reason, linen wall coverings are often selected—as in the Ford Foundation Building in New York City.

EASE IN CARE

Because flax fiber is inelastic, linen fabrics require frequent pressing to remove wrinkles, unless the fabric has been treated for crease resistance. It is best to sprinkle the fabric and to iron it while damp.

Linen does not get soiled as quickly as cotton because the fibers are longer, harder, and smoother. Hot water and soap will not injure the fiber, but care should be taken not to starch linens heavily (especially damasks), for there is danger of breaking the fibers under a heavy iron.

Washability of linen is a strong buying motive for any consumer. Household linen, handkerchiefs, and linen apparel (but be sure to check the label, since many articles require dry cleaning), all wash easily week after week, year after year. Linen is a clean, sanitary textile. White linens should be dried in the sun if they are to keep their whiteness. (For care of specific articles, the storing of linens, and stain removal, see Chapter 16.)

Generally speaking, dry cleaning is the recommended method for drapery and upholstery linens. Decorative linens should not be washed, unless labeled washable and preshrunk. Since linen does not have static properties, dust particles are not attracted and do not cling to the fabric, and therefore it may require less cleaning. The permanent press, soil release finishes are now used effectively only on 65 percent linen/35 percent polyester tablecloths, napkins, and mats.

**MINOR
NATURAL
FIBERS**

RAMIE

Ramie, or rhea, is a bast fiber that has often been sold as a substitute for flax. The fiber comes from within the upright five- to six-foot stems of a nettlelike East Indian shrub. It is also produced in Europe, China, and Egypt.

The first ramie plants were brought to the United States in 1855. Ramie grows best in a semitropical climate with abundant rainfall. The stems must be cut at maturity, because immature plants yield coarse, brittle fibers. The plants send up a new growth after each cutting. Hence three to five crops a year are possible.

Research on ramie by the U.S. Department of Agriculture has led to the growth of ramie in Florida. E. B. Elliot, president of his own outdoor advertising firm, is credited, on the basis of his personally financed research, with finding a method of recovering and refining ramie fibers on a large commercial scale. Experimental plantings of ramie in Savannah and New Brunswick, Georgia, southern Mississippi, Louisiana, Alabama, and Texas augured success. But it has not been possible for promoters to develop a process commercially.

The fiber ranges from 2 1/2 to 18 inches in length and from .002 to .003 inch in diameter (finer than flax), and it is very strong. One authority states that ramie is seven times stronger than wool and twice as strong as flax. Ramie is claimed to be stronger than flax when wet. Its smooth, lustrous appearance seems to improve with washing. Ramie fabrics keep their shape and do not shrink. They resist mildew, absorb more moisture than linen, and dry quickly. They dye easily, but fibers are brittle and have low twisting and bending strength. In the United States, processors experienced difficulty in spinning methods. Ramie is spun here on the worsted system, but to do so, fibers must be cut into staple lengths. The shortened fibers produce coarser fabrics. Finer fabrics would require the use of the full, lengthy ramie fibers. The countries of Europe find it practical to spin ramie on the silk system. By so doing, the whole length of fiber can be used. Ramie is also blended with wool and rayon in carpets.

JUTE

Jute is a bast fiber that comes chiefly from India, because the plant grows well in rich land, especially along tidal basins. India, through improved methods, financial aid, and greater acreage, has increased its production. There has been some attempt to raise jute along the Gulf of Mexico, but the cost of labor has been too high to warrant its cultivation.

The jute plant grows to a height of about twelve feet. It is cut off close to the ground when it is in flower. Like flax, it is stripped of its branches and leaves and put through a retting process to loosen the fibers from the stalk. After they are separated from the outer bark, the fibers are dried and cleaned.

Jute fibers are weaker than those of linen. The fibers are very short, but lustrous and smooth. Because jute is affected by chemical bleaches, it can never be made pure white. It is not very durable and is very much weakened by dampness. It is attacked by sunlight. Since alkalies used in the laundry weaken jute, neutral soaps containing no free alkali should be used. Jute can be distinguished from linen or cotton if the fibers are stained with iodine and then concentrated sulfuric acid and glycerin are applied. Jute fibers remain yellow; cotton and linen turn blue.

Jute is used chiefly for gunny sacks, burlap bags, cordage, and binding and backing threads for rugs and carpets. One company[6] finishes burlap with a flame-resistant finish for uses on walls of bowling alleys and night clubs with modern décor. The company also makes a rotproof finish that permits nurserymen to bury shrubs wrapped in burlap in the soil.

HEMP

It was explained in Chapter 2 that hemp is grown in the Philippines, Mexico, Central America, the West Indies, and India. The Manila variety is white; the outer fiber is used for cordage and the inner fibers can be woven into webbing and gauzes. The Central American variety is not so strong as Manila hemp and is used mainly in cordage. The Indian product is not so strong as the Central American and Manila varieties, but it can be used in cables and canvas. Hemp is stronger than flax, jute, or cotton. It is dark brown in color and cannot be bleached without an appreciable loss of strength. It is less elastic and harsher than linen, and so cannot be used extensively in woven cloth.

Hemp fiber has the microscopic nodes and joints of linen, but the central canal is wider. If the same test (sulfuric acid, iodine, glycerin) is

---

[6] Jonell Corporation, Bridgeton, Rhode Island.

applied to hemp, jute, linen, and cotton, hemp turns bluish green; jute, yellow; and cotton and linen, blue.

SUMMARY   Linen is a competitor of cotton and the man-made fibers for household use. But although it may be suited to almost as many uses as cotton, the cost of producing and manufacturing linen keeps the price of good, durable qualities higher. Now that a chemical treatment has been found to give linen and polyester tablecloths a no-iron, soil release finish, a wide market has opened up.

It is highly improbable that the United States will ever be able to compete with Ireland in the production of fine linen fabrics. Since we have to import most of our linen, the cost will doubtless exceed cotton. Although the initial investment in a linen article is high, its beauty and durability make the purchase less costly in the long run.

REVIEW
QUESTIONS

1. What are the chief physical and chemical characteristics of flax fibers?
2. Compare each of the above characteristics with the corresponding characteristic of cotton.
3. Describe flax production and culture.
4. (a) What are the different methods of retting flax?
   (b) Give the advantages of each method.
5. (a) How are linen yarns made?
   (b) How does this method differ from that for making cotton yarns?
6. Why does linen require more care in bleaching than cotton?
7. What is the law on labeling textile fiber products made of linen?
8. Write a label for a fabric that contains 20 percent cotton, 15 percent rayon, 65 percent linen.
9. Why do consumers buy linen fabrics?
10. (a) Why is linen suitable for dish towels?
    (b) Why is linen suitable for table coverings?
11. From your knowledge of production and manufacturing of ramie, what would you consider to be the future of ramie in the United States?
12. (a) For what purpose is jute used?
    (b) What are the advantages of hemp for use in cordage?

EXPERI-
MENTS

1. *Alkali test.* Use the procedure outlined for cotton, Chapter 9.
2. *Acid test.* Use the procedure outlined for cotton, Chapter 9.
3. *Microscopic test.*
   (a) Look at linen fibers through the microscope. Draw and describe their microscopic appearance.
   (b) Perform the same experiment on jute, hemp, and ramie. Describe the results of your tests.
4. *Test to determine the durability of yarns.*
   (a) Use yarns from three linen and two cotton fabrics.
   (b) Untwist each yarn and note:
        (1) Whether yarn is linen or cotton.
        (2) Amount of twist.
        (3) Evenness of yarn.
        (4) Construction (single or ply).
        (5) Amount of hackling or of combing.
        (6) Length of fibers.
   (c) Judging from the above factors, is the yarn durable?
5. Determine the construction and count of the fabric.
6. List the finishes applied to the fabric.

GLOSSARY Art linen—An ecru, white, or unbleached linen fabric in plain weave. It is used for embroidery, dresses, uniforms, and table linens.

Bast fiber—Fibers between the pithy center of the stem and the skin. Flax, jute, hemp, and ramie are the bast fibers.

Beetle finish—See *Beetling*, Glossary, Chapter 7.

Bouclé yarn—Linen yarn often plied with yarns of other fibers for textural interest. See Glossary, Chapter 3.

Butcher linen—A variety of plain woven crash originally used for butchers' aprons. All rayon or rayon and acetate blend in crash is often erroneously called butcher linen.

Crash—A coarse linen fabric made of thick, uneven yarns and having a rough, irregular surface. It may also be cotton, spun rayon, or blends. It is used for dresses, draperies, and table linens.

Damask—A glossy linen, cotton, rayon, silk, or mixed fabric. Patterns are flat and reversible. Linen and cotton damask are used for table coverings.

Dress linen—See *Crash*.

Embroidery linen—See *Art linen*.

Flax—Fibers of the flax plant, which are spun into linen yarns and woven into linen cloth.

Friction towel—A terrycloth made with linen pile. It may be made into a mitt used to develop friction after bathing.

Grass bleaching—Whitening fabrics by laying them on the grass in the sun.

Hackling—A process that prepares the flax fibers for spinning by laying them parallel. It may be done by hand or by machine and corresponds to the carding and combing of cottons.

Handkerchief linen—A well-hackled sheer linen fabric in plain weave that is used for handkerchiefs, blouses, summer dresses. It is synonymous with *lawn*.

Hemp—A plant grown in the Philippines, Mexico, Central America, the West Indies, and India. Outer fibers are used for cordage, inner fibers for cables and canvas.

Huck or huckaback—A honeycombed dobby face towel. It may be linen or cotton or mixtures with rayon.

Irish linen—Linen products that come from Ireland, mainly Belfast in Northern Ireland.

Jute—A bast fiber, chiefly from India, used mostly for gunny sacks, bags, cordage, and binding threads of rugs and carpets.

Lawn—A light, well-hackled linen fabric first made in Laon, France. Linen lawn is synonymous with handkerchief linen. Cotton lawn is a similar type of fabric. It can be white, solid colored, or printed.

Line—Longest flax fibers, used for fine, even linen yarns. Shortest flax fibers are called *tow*.

Linen—A vegetable fiber obtained from the inside of the woody stalk of the flax plant.

Moygashel—A trade name representing excellent quality in imported Irish linen.

Ramie or rhea—A bast fiber from a nettle-like East Indian shrub, also produced in China, Egypt, and the United States. It is used for shirts, suitings, automobile seat covers, table covers, and, in blends with wool, for carpets.

Retting—A process for loosening the flax fiber from the woody stalk. This may be done by several methods: pool, dew, tank, and chemical.

Rippling—Threshing of flax to strip the seeds or bolls from the plant. This process may be done by hand or by machine.

Roving frame—A machine that puts a loose twist in the drawn-out sliver.

Scutching—Removing the flax fibers from the woody stalk by a series of fluted rollers.

Sisal—A variety of hemp grown chiefly in Kenya, East Africa. It is used primarily for cordage but may also be used for millinery.

Spinning—The operation of putting the twist into linen yarn.

Spread board—A machine that lays wisps of flax fibers parallel on traveling bands in continuous lines, with the ends of the wisps overlapping.

Spun linen—Finest hand-woven linen fabric, used for handkerchiefs, women's collars, and so on.

243

244
Fabric
Construction
and
Buying
Motives

Suiting—A heavy, fairly coarse linen fabric in plain, twill, or herringbone weaves, used for women's and men's suitings. It is also made in cotton, spun rayon, or acetate.

Tow—Short flax fibers, separated by hackling (combing) from the longer fibers.

Tow linen—Fabric made of uneven, irregular yarns composed of the very short fibers.

Silk
and the Consumer

11

Overheard in the fitting room of a large department store: "I can't find anything but polyester dresses. There doesn't seem to be a single silk in stock."

"You're right," answered the saleswoman. "Silk is too expensive. Our customers don't have that kind of money."

"But I want silk," said the customer. "It's comfortable, lightweight yet warm, and beautiful and luxurious."

There is no doubt that many women, and some men too, still prefer silk. In this chapter, we shall discover why silk, through many centuries, has been the premier fiber for outerwear, underwear, and home furnishings, even though its sales volume is relatively very small.

SERI-CULTURE

HISTORY OF SILK CULTURE

Silk was used by the ancients. History records the Chinese as the first people who knew how to raise and manufacture it. About 1725 B.C. silk culture, sponsored by the wife of the emperor, was begun in China. Until the time of the Chinese People's Republic of 1958, the Chinese empress paid homage to the "Goddess of the Silkworms" on a special day each year by feeding the insects.

About 1765 B.C. the mulberry tree was cultivated to provide food for the silkworm. The secret of the cultivation of these worms and of the manufacture of their fibers into cloth was carefully guarded for about 3,000 years. Eventually, according to one story, two monks sent to China by the Byzantine Emperor Justinian stole mulberry seeds and silkworms' eggs. At the risk of their lives, they brought them back to Byzantium in their walking staffs. From these monks, Justinian learned of the Chinese sericulture. From this knowledge a large silk industry grew up in the Byzantine Empire. Rich fabrics woven of silk on imperial looms are still in existence there.

With the rise and spread of Islam, silk culture spread to Sicily and Spain with the Moslem conquests. After the Moslems withdrew from conquered soil, the art of silk weaving remained.

By the twelfth and thirteenth centuries A.D., Italy had become the silk center of the West. The art of weaving ecclesiastical and ducal silk fabrics

246

Fabric
Construction
and
Buying
Motives

was unexcelled. For over 500 years Italy was the leader in silk production. But by the seventeenth century, the French city of Lyons was vying with Italy for excellence and beauty in weaving silk.[1]

Parts of Japan had been raising silkworms as early as A.D. 300, when the Japanese had learned the secret of sericulture from four Chinese girls they had kidnapped. Still later, India learned this secret when a Chinese princess came to India to marry an Indian prince.[2]

England began to manufacture silk in the sixteenth century, when Flemish weavers fled to England from the Low Countries. In the seventeenth century Huguenot weavers settled in the vicinity of Spitalfields. The English climate was not suitable for sericulture, but silk weaving was extensive.

England showed interest in the silk industry and sponsored its introduction to the American Colonies about 1732. The Colonial government allotted grants to Georgian settlers on condition that they plant one hundred mulberry trees on every ten acres. Carolina also raised silk. In the eighteenth century Connecticut became the most important silk-raising section. The first silk mill in America was built in 1810 at Mansfield, Connecticut. Pennsylvania followed, and in 1838 New Jersey set up a silk mill in Paterson.

The cost of the labor needed for silk cultivation has done much to exclude the United States from importance as a silk-raising country. While the United States is not important in silk production, it is the largest importer of raw silk. Today some of the most beautiful silk fabrics in the world are woven on American looms.

LIFE OF THE SILKWORM

Silk is an animal fiber. It is the product of the silkworm, of which there are two varieties: the wild and the cultivated. The fibers of the wild silkworm are yellowish brown, instead of yellow to gray, and have a coarse, hard texture. This worm feeds on the scrub oak instead of the mulberry leaf. It grows in India, China, and Japan.

The cultivated silkworm requires a great deal of care. Quiet and sanitation are necessary. A whole scientific industry, that of raising mulberry trees for food for the worms, has grown up. The best mulberry leaves seem to come from plants that are the result of a combination of the tall mulberry tree and the dwarf or shrub mulberry tree.

Silkworms live a very short time—only about two months. During that period they pass through four stages of development: (1) egg, (2) worm, (3) chrysalis (pupa) or cocoon, and (4) moth. (See Figure 11.3.)

Eggs that have been kept in cold storage for approximately six weeks after they were laid are bathed in warm water and dried in the air. Then they are placed in incubators, where they remain until all are hatched (about thirty days).

A tiny white worm about 1/4 inch long is hatched from each egg. These worms are very delicate and require the utmost care. They are placed on bamboo trays covered with straw mats on which selected mulberry leaves

[1] *Silk*, a pamphlet of the International Silk Association (U.S.A.).
[2] *The History of Silk and Sericulture*, a pamphlet by John Kent Tilton, formerly Director, The Scalamandré Museum of Textiles, p. 4.

FIGURE 11.1. When the silkworms are ready to spin their cocoons, the farmers put them in a "mabushi," or bed of straw. In three days the worms will have spun their cocoons, which are then ready to be treated in the next stage of silk-making. The beds shown here are old-fashioned, but they are used by 20 percent of the Japanese silkworm-farming households. (Photograph courtesy of the International Silk Association, U.S.A., Inc.)

are laid. The worms are very greedy; it is estimated that each worm eats about 30,000 times its initial weight. During this stage the silkworm molts (sheds its skin) four times. At the end of about thirty days the worm ceases to eat, attaches itself to a piece of straw, and begins to spin its cocoon.

Two filaments are ejected from the mouth—one an almost invisible silk filament and the other a glutinous substance. The filaments merge and harden when exposed to the air. The worm covers itself with these filaments, completing the cocoon in about three days. The worm is then transformed into a moth in about eight days. One manufacturer estimates that 2,500 to 3,000 cocoons are necessary to make one yard of silk fabric. The color of the cocoon is either white or yellow, depending on the species. The color is not dependent on its feeding, and there is no difference in the quality of silk produced. However, the white cocoon silk does not have to be bleached.

If the moth is permitted to emerge from the cocoon, the silk filament is broken into many short pieces. Therefore the chrysalis (unless it is selected for breeding) is steamed or subjected to hot air to kill the larvae inside the cocoon. Long thin fibers can be reeled from the unpierced cocoons.

The moths that are reserved for breeding purposes emerge from cocoons creamy white. Three days after they have hatched, they mate, lay eggs, and die. Their cycle of life is complete.

SORTING

Cocoons most suitable for propagation of the species are separated from those to be used for weaving. For propagation, it has been found that

248

*Fabric
Construction
and
Buying
Motives*

cocoons with a "waist" are preferable. Elliptical or nearly round cocoons are used for reeling into yarn. The former type is sorted by sex. Cocoons pass along a belt that allows the heavier ones (males) to drop down into a container and the lighter cocoons (females) to continue on the belt.

REELING

The unpierced cocoons, whose larvae have been killed, are used for reeling. Cocoons are aired to dry the dead chrysalis. Then they are put in basins of hot water, to melt the gum, or sericin. Dexterous fingers must find the end of the silk filament that will unwind (reel). Filaments from five or six cocoons are reeled and twisted together into a strand finer than a human hair. Next, six to eight of these strands are attached to revolving reels that twist them into a stronger yarn. The resultant yarn is the product of thirty to forty-eight cocoons. This yarn is now ready for winding into skeins and packing into bales. In this condition the thread is too thin and weak to be used without further twisting (*throwing*) and doubling into strands of varying thicknesses. Throwing increases the strength of a yarn. However, a silk thread need not necessarily be thrown to make a yarn for weaving, thus differing from wool and cotton, which must be spun and twisted.[3]

Yarns made of reeled-silk threads twisted together are called *thrown silk*. These yarns are wound on spools or in skeins, ready for the weavers. To facilitate handling, oils may be added to the gum weight by the throwster. Up to this point, silk is lusterless and harsh to the touch. This is because the gum is still in it. Silk in the gum is called *raw silk*. To make it soft and lustrous, it is boiled in soap and water until the gum is removed.

[3] *What Is Silk?*, a pamphlet of the International Silk Association.

FIGURE 11.2. An up-to-date "apartment house" for cocoons. Separate living quarters ensure a finer gloss and more uniformity in the finished silk. (Photograph courtesy of the International Silk Association, U.S.A., Inc.)

MICROSCOPIC APPEARANCE

Under the microscope, cultivated silk fibers in the gum appear rough, like sticks of wood. Sometimes two fibers are held together by silk gum. After degumming, the fibers are structureless, transparent, and rodlike. The unevenness in diameter of the fibers distinguishes them from rayon. (See Appendix A) Wild-silk fibers are very irregular and resemble flattened, wavy ribbons with fine lines running lengthwise.

LENGTH

The silk fiber ranges from 800 to 1,300 yards in length. This characteristic—great length—aids the manufacturer because he can easily combine a number of the filaments, which require little twist to give them strength. Also, long fibers make more lustrous yarns than do short fibers.

DIAMETER

It is estimated that the diameter of silk fibers ranges from .00059 to .00118 inch. Longer fibers can be spun into finer yarns, and the resultant fabrics are sheer. Furthermore, many fibers can be combined in a fine yarn. The silkworm's fiber varies in diameter throughout its length, but the combination of several fibers to form a yarn equalizes the natural unevenness of the individual fibers.

COLOR OF FIBER

Cultivated silks are yellow to grayish white in color. The color of the wild-silk fiber is usually yellowish brown. The brown color is in the fiber itself, but the color of cultivated varieties is in the gum and so can be removed by washing.

LUSTER

Silk in the gum does not possess high luster, but after the gum has been removed silk has a soft, fine luster. This fact is important in the manufacture of satins, the beauty of which lies in unbroken sheen. Yarns of long reeled-silk fibers lie flat, lengthwise on the right side of the cloth, with only occasional interlacing with the filling or crosswise yarns.

STRENGTH

Silk is one of the strongest of the textile fibers—that is, of fibers of the same diameter. Silk is often compared with iron wire of the same diameter. Although it has only about one third the strength of good-quality iron wire, these fine fibers are very strong. Silk is weaker when wet than when dry, but, like rayon, its original strength returns when it dries.

A silk fiber can sustain a dead weight of five to twenty-eight grams before breaking. One silk filament is so strong that it will support the weight of a cocoon. However, hosiery made of silk snags if it is given a sudden, sharp pull. But silk will withstand even pulling better than it will a sudden, severe strain.

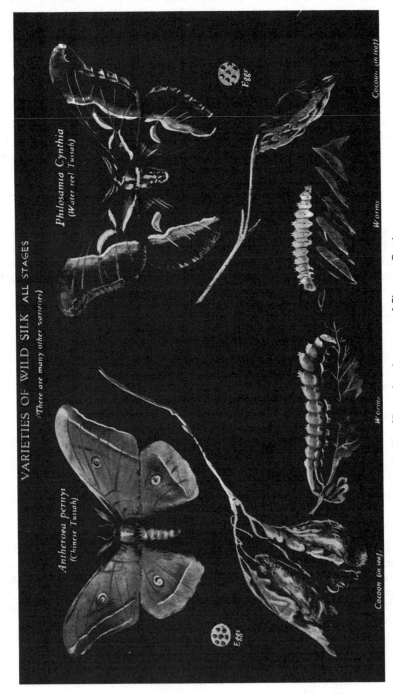

FIGURE 11.3. Varieties of wild and cultivated silks. (Reproduced courtesy of Cheyney Brothers, Inc.)

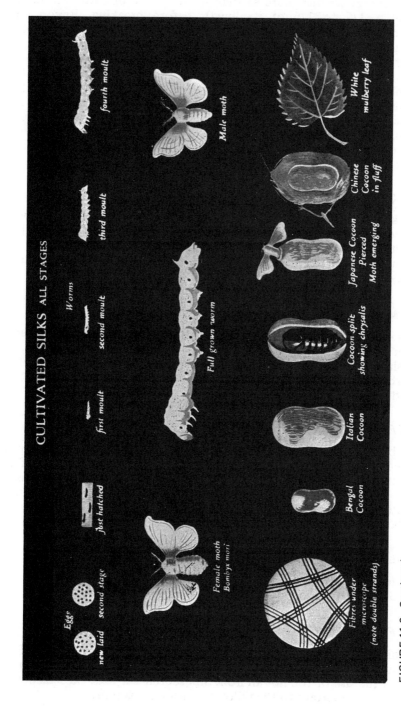

FIGURE 11.3. Continued.

ELASTICITY

Silk is very elastic—more so than linen, rayon, or cotton. In fact, silk will stretch 1/7 to 1/5 of its length before breaking. Rayon and other man-made fibers will elongate, but they may not return to their original length. Therefore, silk weavers prefer all-silk warp yarn to a synthetic warp in Jacquard weaving (see p. 98), for in this weave warp yarns are subjected to stretching due to the pull exerted on the yarn. Silk, then, is resilient (elastic); synthetics elongate. Silk's elasticity means that no loose threads will be evident on the finished fabric. One of the first questions a silk weaver asks the synthetic yarn manufacturer is, "How much will the synthetic yarn elongate?" On the basis of elongation a silk weaver can determine whether he can use the synthetic for warps. Garments made of silk keep their shape and do not wrinkle badly.

HYGROSCOPIC MOISTURE

Silk absorbs about 10 percent of moisture. It has a higher average for absorptive quality than cotton, linen, or rayon. The strange and important fact is that silk can absorb a great deal of moisture and still feel comparatively dry. Silk absorbs perspiration and oil from the skin, but it sheds dirt easily.

COMPOSITION

The chief constituents of silk are fibroin, the silk fiber, and sericin, the silk gum. Cultivated silk also contains small percentages of fats, waxes or resins, and mineral matter. The chemical constituents of fibroin are carbon (48.3 percent), hydrogen (6.5 percent), nitrogen (19.2 percent), and oxygen (26.0 percent). [4]

EFFECT OF LIGHT

Laboratory tests show that silk is not so resistant as cotton to strong light. And yet, when damask draperies made of a combination of silk and cotton were removed from the White House in 1953, the silk was in about the same stage of deterioration as the cottons. In this instance, silk and cotton had about the same degree of resistance to light. Heavily weighted silks are less resistant to light than pure silks.

MILDEW

Mildew is seldom found on silk. It is relatively resistant to other bacteria and fungi. Rot-producing conditions will decompose silk.

EFFECT OF HEAT

White silks turn yellow after fifteen minutes in an oven at 231° F. Cottons would not be affected at this temperature. Silk fabrics may turn yellow with the use of too hot an iron. Silk scorches if heat exceeds 300° F. This factor is important to the tailor who uses a steam press.

[4] George H. Johnson, *Textile Fabrics* (New York: Harper and Row, 1927), p. 64.

EFFECT OF ACIDS

Acids, such as sulfuric, hydrochloric, and nitric, do not injure silks if they are dilute. Silk is more resistant to acids than are the vegetable fibers, but concentrated acids destroy silk if it is soaked in them or if the acids are allowed to remain on the silk any length of time.

Formic acid and acetic acid (found in vinegar) have no injurious effect on silks. Oxalic, tartaric, and citric acids are not injurious if they are removed promptly.

EFFECT OF ALKALIES

Concentrated solutions of alkali, such as caustic soda or caustic potash, dissolve silks if the solutions are hot.

Weak alkalies, such as ammonia, phosphate of soda, borax, and soap, attack silk more quickly than they attack cotton or linen. It is therefore advisable to use a mild soap with no alkalies for washing fine silk fabrics.

ACTION OF BLEACHES

Chlorine or hypochlorites are not used on silk, because of their deteriorating effect. Hydrogen peroxide and perborate bleaches are used when silk requires bleaching. Care should be taken to control bleaching conditions. Many popular-priced printed silks develop holes because acid bleaches are too strong.

AFFINITY FOR METALLIC SALTS

As previously stated, silk has a great affinity for metallic salts; this characteristic is utilized in weighting silks. Silks are weighted either in the yarn or in the piece—that is, after the fabric has been woven. There is more danger to the wearing qualities of the fabric if it is weighted in the piece, for the following reason: The usual specifications for the weighting of yarn require sixteen ounces of weighting for warp (enough to replace the gum lost), and twenty-two ounces for filling (37½ percent of the weight of the raw silk in addition to the weight required to replace the gum). There can be no such discrimination in weighting if the whole fabric is immersed. If the whole fabric is weighted equally, the warp and filling carry equal loading; and if the amount of weighting is correct for the filling, it is too great for a durable warp. (For a discussion of silk weighting, see p. 255.)

AFFINITY FOR DYESTUFFS

Silk has a natural affinity for dye. Probably the chief reason is that silk fiber has good penetrability. Basic, acid, and direct dyestuffs are all used on silks. (For a description of these dyestuffs, see Chapter 8.) Cotton and linen do not have as good an affinity for dye as silk. Rayon has a good affinity for dye. Acetate requires the use of special dyestuffs.

KINDS OF SILK YARNS

REELED SILK

Thrown Silk. This is a single yarn made of several strands of reeled silk twisted together.

254

*Fabric
Construction
and
Buying
Motives*

Organzine. This is a ply yarn of the type that must be made if yarns are to be used for warp where strength is required, as in upholstery, drapery fabric, or sheeting. The twist of the ply is in the reverse direction to that of the singles, in order to give additional strength and hold in the twist. Organzine is the center section of the yardage reeled from the cocoon (500 to 1,000 yards).

Tram. Also made for fabrics requiring tensile strength, it, too, is a ply yarn, but the twist of the singles and the final twist are in the same direction. This yarn has a higher luster because it has a slacker final twist than the organzine (about two and one-half turns to the inch for tram and four and one-half turns for organzine). Generally, tram is used for filling yarns and organzine for warp, although this is not always the case.

Douppion. Derived from the Italian word *doppione*, it means double. Two silkworms (regardless of sex) have an affinity for each other and want to stay together, so together they spin one cocoon. It is difficult to reel filaments evenly from these cocoons, so that a knotted yarn results. This textured yarn is particularly suited to fabrics such as shantung and some of the contemporary draperies and upholsteries. Douppion can also be made into spun-silk yarns.

Tussah. This is wild silk reeled from cocoons of uncultivated worms that have fed on oak leaves. These rough, yellowish brown fibers are made into tussah silk yarns.

SPUN SILK

Before silk can be reeled from the cocoon, long, tangled ends must be removed so that an end can be found with which to start the reeling process. The tangled ends, called *floss*, are put aside because they cannot be reeled. Likewise, when most of the fiber has been reeled from a cocoon, there may be short lengths. Only about half of the silk of a cocoon is fit to be reeled, but the rest cannot be wasted; it is made into spun silk. All floss and silk from pierced and defective cocoons appear in spun-silk yarns. Spun silk requires more twisting than reeled silk, to hold in all the short fibers. Twisting decreases luster, so that spun silk appears less lustrous than reeled silk. It also has less tensile strength, less elasticity, and a rather linty, cottony feeling.

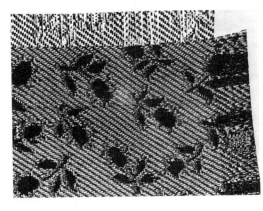

FIGURE 11.4. Reeled silk. Note how these long-fibered yarns shred apart. (Photo by Jonas Grushkin.)

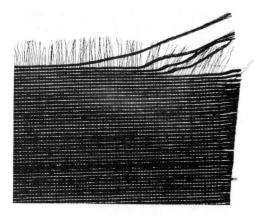

FIGURE 11.5. Spun silk. Note the yarn unraveled from the filling (top). Yarn is composed of fibers of varied lengths. (Photo by Jonas Grushkin.)

Spun silk is less expensive than reeled silk and is suitable for the crosswise or filling threads in a cloth. These threads do not have to be as strong as warp yarns. Plush, velvet, satin, lace, flat crepe, and silk broadcloth may have spun-silk yarns.

The silk to be used for this purpose is scoured, the gum is boiled off, and the fibers are dried. Then the fibers are combed in order to separate and straighten them and make them lie parallel. The filmy sheets of fibers are then drawn out between rollers several times. A slight twist is put in—called *roving*. A spinning frame, which winds and rewinds the yarn on spindles, puts in the twist. A tighter twist than that used for thrown silk is necessary.

NOIL SILK

In the processing of spun-silk yarn, there is a certain amount of waste called *silk noil*. According to the FTC Trade Practice Rules for the Silk Industry, such waste shall be labeled "silk noil," "noil silk," "silk waste," or "waste silk." Silk noil is used extensively for powder bags in artillery units. It can also be used in modern textured draperies and upholstery. Noil silk is dull, rough, and lifeless.

IDENTIFICATION OF REELED, SPUN, AND NOIL SILK

Long fibers of reeled silk lie parallel and are only slackly twisted together. The yarns are lustrous, and the fibers shred apart. If the fibers are short and of uneven length, generally in dull yarns, the yarns are spun silk. If the yarns are coarse and very dull and if the fibers are very short and very uneven, the yarns are noil silk.

Chiffon crepes look dull and sometimes cottony, but that does not necessarily mean that yarns are of spun silk; rather, the tightness of the twist—made tight to produce fine crepe—has decreased the luster.

WEIGHTED AND PURE SILK When yarns are prepared for weaving, the skeins of yarn are boiled in a soap solution to remove the natural silk gum, or sericin. The silk may lose 20 to 30 percent of its original weight as a result of boiling. Since silk has a great affinity for metallic salts, such as those of tin and iron, the lost weight is replaced through the absorption of metals. Tannin may also be used as weighting material.

255

256
Fabric
Construction
and
Buying
Motives

Thus a heavier fabric can be made. Heavily weighted silk may not wear as long as pure unweighted silk, because sunlight and perspiration weaken or destroy the fibers. Furthermore, heavy weighting causes silk to crack. The long treatment of silk in the weighting process may also have a weakening effect on the fibers. Silks can be weighted only about 1 percent in each application of weighting, which makes the process costly. There is no weighting done in the United States.

The burning test may be used to identify pure and weighted silk. If the yarns char but do not burn, they are weighted; if they burn slowly and leave a residue in the form of a gummy ball, they are pure silk.

According to the FTC rules, a weighted silk must be marked "weighted," with the amount of weighting indicated. A variation of five points from the stated percentage is tolerated to allow for unavoidable variations in processing, but not to allow for a lack of "reasonable effort to state the percentage of proportion accurately." For example, a weighted silk label may appear as "Silk, weighted 5 percent" or "Silk (weighted 25 percent) and rayon." The percentage of weighting may be disclosed as not over a certain percentage or as ranging from a certain minimum to a maximum figure.

Silk containing no metallic weighting may be called "pure silk," according to the FTC rules. The terms "all silk" or "pure dye silk" may also be used for fabrics whose fiber content is silk exclusively, with no metallic weighting. The rules for labeling and advertising as specified under the Textile Fiber Products Identification Act are required for silk textile fiber products. (See Chapters 2 and 10.) The FTC rules allow the finisher or the dyer to use special finishing materials, other than metallic weighting, that will make the fabric more useful—water-repellent finishes, for instance. The maximum percentage of the finishes present must be disclosed if such special finishing materials exceed 10 percent on colored fabrics and 15 percent on blacks.

SIZE OF SILK YARN

Sizes or counts of reeled-silk yarns, like rayon counts, are expressed in terms of denier (den'yer).[5] There are several methods of computing denier, all differing slightly from that used for rayon. The International Denier method uses 500 meters of silk yarn, weighted with a .05 gram weight. If 500 meters weigh .05 gram, the yarn is #1 denier. If 500 meters weigh 1 gram, the denier is 1 ÷ .05, or #20. The size of thrown silk yarn is also expressed as the weight (in drams) of a skein of 1,000 yards. The dram weight times 33.36 equals the size in deniers.[6]

Spun-silk sizes are computed in two ways: by the English and French systems. The English system sets 840 yards as equal to 1 pound (the same as with cotton). The yarns are designated as 20/1 or 20/2, meaning 20 single- or 20 two-ply. In a pound size of 20/2 there are 840 yards times 20 or 16,800 yards. The French system uses as its base the number of 1,000-meter skeins weighing a kilogram.

---

[5] Legal denier: When the weight of 450 meters is 0.5 gram, the denier is #1.

[6] See "Tex" system, Chapter 3.

PLAIN WEAVE

No matter in what construction silk is used, the fabric appears attractive. In plain weave, silk apparel dress fabrics include habutai, shantung, flat crepe, crepe de Chine, taffeta, pongee, ninon, organza, chiffon, and broadcloth. For men's wear there are silk broadcloth and habutai (shirtings). In ribbed variations there are several fabrics for both men and women: faille, moiré faille, grosgrain, bengaline, rep, poplin, and ottoman. (See Glossary, Chapter 16.) For home furnishings there are taffeta (pillow covers, bedspreads and curtains), voile and ninon (glass curtains), China silk, flat crepe, and pongee (lampshades).

TWILL WEAVE

There are not as many silk twills as there are satins or plain weaves, but the following twills are most common: silk serge, piqué, foulard, and surah. These fabrics can be used in dresses and men's ties.

SATIN WEAVE

Probably this is the most beautiful of the basic weaves to which silk is adapted. All varieties of satin, including dress, slipper, bridal, and upholstery satins, are made in this construction. Slipper and upholstery satins may have cotton backs. Antique satin has become very popular for draperies and upholsteries. Although this fabric is not always made of silk, some of the most beautiful and high-priced draperies are silk.

FANCY WEAVES

Silk, because of its natural beauty, is particularly suited to the fancy constructions. Jacquards, such as brocades and damasks, make luxurious draperies for formal traditional living rooms. (See Chapter 21.) Lamé and brocade make exquisite evening gowns. Small dobby designs are found in silk scarfs, linings, and men's tie fabrics. In pile construction, silk velvet, velour, and brocaded velvet are always considered luxury fabrics. Silk pile rugs are museum pieces. In leno weave, silk marquisette is suitable for evening dresses and glass curtains.

KNITTED CONSTRUCTION

Silk knitted jersey and bouclé are excellent fabrics for traveling because they are attractive and do not wrinkle when worn.

Some of the regular finishes applied to silk include the usual tentering and calendering (particularly for polished surfaces), dry decating to set the luster permanently, napping of spun silk to raise the fibers, shearing when needed to cut the surface fibers, steaming to shrink and condition certain spun silks, and weighting to give body. (See pp. 135 and 255).

Silk fabrics may be treated for fire resistance to comply with the Flammable Fabrics Act. They may also be given germ-resistant, moth-resistant, permanent starchless, and water-repellent finishes.

BEAUTY

No fabric is so luxurious in appearance as silk. It has a natural deep luster that makes it an aristocrat among textiles. Compare a Louis Quinze chair covered in silk damask (woven in floral design) with a similar chair covered with wool damask in the same design. The silk covering has a regal look; wool has a utility look.

A silk dress, whether it is a shantung for sport or an organza for evening, looks dressy. Similarly, silk draperies are more luxurious than the average cotton, linen, or wool. Cotton draperies are particularly suited to informal rooms, whereas silks in varied textures are appropriate in any room except possibly the kitchen and the bathroom.

Since silk fiber has a good affinity for dye, the colors found in silks are innumerable.

Fabrics of wild silk and douppion silk appear rougher, often gummier, and less lustrous than the cultivated or mulberry silks. Crepes made with tight-twisted yarns are less lustrous than satins made with loose-twisted yarns. Spun silks are soft, but less lustrous than thrown silks.

DURABILITY

Silk fiber is the strongest natural fiber. Consequently, silk fabrics can be made durable. If silks are pure and unweighted, they will last for years, as is evidenced by the perfect preservation of many silks worn generations ago. Overweighting weakens the tensile strength, decreases elasticity, and encourages quick deterioration from sunlight and perspiration. Weighted silks may shrink badly, lose shape, or crack in washing or cleaning; they cannot be called durable. At present, weighted dress silks are seldom found in retailers' stocks. Spun silk has a lower tensile strength and lacks the elasticity of reeled silk. It has short fibers, which, although twisted tightly, may work themselves loose and make a fuzzy, rough, uneven surface. Noil silk is inferior to reeled or spun silk, but it has textural interest when used for draperies.

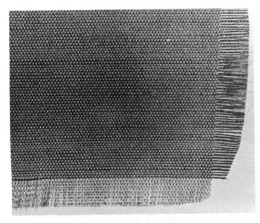 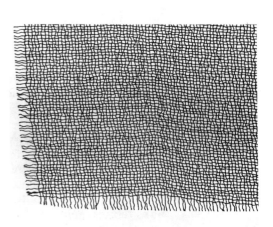

FIGURE 11.6. a. Silk pongee, made from wild silk; b. Silk chiffon, made from pure cultivated silk. (Photos by Jonas Grushkin.)

COMFORT

Silk, like other animal fibers, is warmer than rayon, cotton, or linen of comparable weights. Because silk is very absorptive, silk fabrics, when they become drenched with perspiration, do not feel so damp and clammy as do fabrics made entirely of hydrophobic fibers. Hence, underwear and blouses are appropriately made of silk.

Silks can be woven of very fine yarns in open weaves, a fact that makes silk fabrics feel cool in summer. Organza, georgette, net, and chiffon are illustrations of sheer silk fabrics. Silk is lightweight, a factor in traveling comfort.

Because of its elasticity, silk can be made up into accordion pleats that hold creases. One designer of exclusive misses' dresses who has used a pleated skirt successfully found that by starting the skirt's fullness below the hips, by pressing each pleat individually, and by stitching the pleats properly, the creases stayed. This same designer preferred silk and natural fibers for her line because they held their shape better. Pure silk ties also retain their shape better than rayon or acetate ties. Silk dresses are very serviceable for traveling. They can be packed in a small space; in dark colors they do not show dirt; and wrinkles in silk crepes will hang out especially well.

Silk mixes easily with rayon, adding the elasticity that rayon lacks. It also mixes with nylon and with Orlon acrylic in shantung.

SUITABILITY

The purposes for which silks are intended determine in a large measure the methods used in their manufacture. For example, long, reeled-silk fibers are used in fine silk yard goods, such as satins, crepe satin, and ribbons. Fine sewing thread is also made of reeled silk.

Silk thread comes in more than 300 colors, so that fabrics can be matched easily. For sewing lustrous fabrics, silk thread should be chosen to match the luster of the fabric. All-silk or all-wool materials should be sewn with silk thread because silk and wool are animal fibers and so react similarly to laundering or dry cleaning. Silk threads make smooth, flat seams. Spun silk is suitable for knit goods, such as sweaters, hosiery, and underwear; for embroidery silk, braids, bindings, laces, crochet silk, and crepes; and for the pile of plushes, velvets, and velours.

Some yarns are twisted more tightly than others, according to the type of fabric in which they are to be used. Creped yarns used crosswise of the fabric are twisted forty to eighty turns to the inch. Silk creped fabrics include, among others, flat crepe, satin crepe, chiffon, and crepe faille.

Warp yarns—those running lengthwise—should have a very slack twist, so that fibers lie on the surface of the fabric and do not break the sheen. Dress satin, satin crepe, and satin linings are made this way.

Fabrics that have rather rough, bumpy surfaces, dull luster, and a gummy feeling may be made of wild silk. Shantung and pongee are examples.

Since wild silk cannot be made a snowy white and since it is rougher than cultivated varieties, its uses are limited more to sports fabrics, underwear, and draperies. For the latter use, it is desirable to line silk with

260
*Fabric
Construction
and
Buying
Motives*

silk or cotton material, because a lined drapery hangs better. The lining should be placed next to the glass.

Pongee and shantung may also be made of douppion silk, which results when two or more worms cooperate in making a single cocoon. The fibers are very irregular and cannot be reeled in long, even filaments, but the irregularities of the fiber and resultant yarn make an interesting fabric quite suitable for modern textured draperies and for shantung. Douppion can be reeled or spun yarn.

Silk fabrics lend themselves to any style changes that may occur. At one time the mode for evening dresses may demand a firm fabric that can be tailored easily. In another season, evening dresses may have to be fluffy, ruffly creations. Silk faille, broadcloth, and shantung will suit the tailored mode, for these fabrics are dull, strongly constructed materials of plain weave. (See Chapter 4, pp. 77, 78.) Chiffon and marquisette give the soft, fluffy, feminine effect. Organza gives a bouffant effect.

Since silk fits into the mode for both tailored garments and the more feminine frills, the consumer should select the silk fabric with the purpose for which she wishes it clearly in mind. She should always consult fashion publications and advertisements of leading stores to be sure that she selects a fabric then in style.

Silk has a wide variety of uses, especially in the apparel, drapery, and upholstery fields. There is not an hour of the day when a silk dress is not appropriate. House dresses, however, are more often made of cotton, man-made fibers, or blends.

SENTIMENT

Silk, like linen, is sometimes purchased for reasons of sentiment. An old silk prayer rug may be bought because of associations it brings to mind or because of its rarity. Old silk damask hangings or silk laces may be bought for similar reasons. Works of art made of silk are bought by museums, collectors, and those who appreciate rare things. A living room may be furnished chiefly in silk damasks, satins, and brocades because its owner likes the elegance and luxury that silk reflects.

PRICE

If raw silk is selling at approximately $10 a pound and rayon yarn at 42¢, one can see there is a tremendous difference between the price of a finished silk article compared with a finished rayon article. Thus, high price may be a buying point for the affluent.

While silk is more expensive than any other fiber, it can be used in less expensive ways if:

1. Spun silk can be used one way of the fabric; reeled silk the other way.
2. Spun silk can be used entirely, instead of thrown silk.
3. Wild silk can be used instead of mulberry silk.
4. Rayon may be used one way of the fabric and silk the other.
5. Mercerized cotton can be used one way of the fabric and silk the other.
6. Spun douppion silk may be used one or both ways of the fabric.

SUMMARY Silk, as an animal fiber, is the product of two distinct varieties of silkworms: wild and cultivated. Wild silks, often called tussah silks, are gummy in feeling, dull in luster, and have rough, uneven yarns. From the cultivated silkworm's cocoon a fine, even, long fiber can be reeled.

There are several terms applying to raw or reeled silk that should be borne in mind. Raw silk is the fiber reeled in the gum from the unpierced cocoon.

Several strands of reeled silk are twisted together into a yarn called thrown silk. Two kinds of ply are made from the same yarn: a yarn for warps called organzine and a yarn for fillings called tram. Douppion silk comes from one cocoon spun by two silkworms. Yarns of douppion silk can be reeled or spun.

Spun-silk yarns are made from silk waste—the tangled fibers removed from the outside of the cocoon before the reeling; the short lengths of fibers from the inside of the cocoon; and the short fibers from the pierced cocoon. These fibers are usually twisted into yarn. They are duller in luster than reeled silk and weaker in tensile strength. Noil silk is the waste from spun-silk yarn manufacturing.

REVIEW QUESTIONS

1. What is the effect of the degumming process on the silk yarn?
2. (a) Explain the meanings of pure silk and weighted silk.
   (b) What effect has weighting on durability, versatility, launderability, comfort, and price?
   (c) What is the FTC ruling on weighted silk?
   (d) According to the TFPIA, how should an all-silk with no weighting be labeled?
3. Describe the life cycle of the cultivated silkworm.
4. What are the chief advantages of spun silk? The chief disadvantages? Its principal uses?
5. In what ways do the length and the fineness of silk fiber affect the appearance of the finished fabric?
6. (a) What are the chief characteristics of wild silk?
   (b) What are the uses of wild silk?
7. In what way does the elasticity of silk fiber affect the finished cloth?
8. (a) What is the TFPIA regulation on labeling silk mixtures and blends?
   (b) What is the FTC ruling on special finishing materials?
9. Outline instructions for laundering a pure-silk flat crepe.
10. (a) What texture in silk fabrics may become the matron with a mature figure?
    (b) What texture in silks may the young high school girl with a slender figure wear?
11. (a) What factors should be considered in determining whether or not silk yarn is durable?
    (b) How are sizes of silk yarns computed?
12. By what methods can the cost of a silk fabric be lowered?
13. Define the following: reeled silk, thrown silk, spun silk, wild silk, douppion silk, mulberry silk, weighted silk, tussah, chrysalis, noil silk, resilient silk, degummed silk, organzine, tram, raw silk.

EXPERIMENTS

1. Unravel silk yarns from each of five samples of silk material and place a few fibers of each under the microscope. Draw the fibers as you see them. Are the fibers mulberry silk or wild silk, silk in the gum or degummed silk? Give reasons for your answer.

262
*Fabric
Construction
and
Buying
Motives*

2. Burn yarns from each sample. Note the speed with which each yarn burns and describe the residue. Are the yarns weighted or pure silk? Give reasons for your answer.

3. Unravel yarns from each sample. Do the fibers seem about the same length? Are they long and parallel, or are they of different lengths and not parallel? Are the yarns reeled or spun silk? Why?

4. *Alkali test.* Prepare an alkaline solution of 10 percent sodium hydroxide. Boil a small piece of silk in this solution for five minutes. Note the results of strong alkali on silk.

5. *Acid test.* Dip a few yarns or a piece of silk in concentrated sulfuric acid for one or two minutes. Wash the residue with water and dry it on a clean blotter. Note the results of concentrated acid on silk. What is the effect of acid on an animal fiber? What is the effect of acid on a vegetable fiber?

GLOSSARY   Antique satin—See Glossary, Chapter 21.

Antique taffeta—A taffeta often woven of douppion silk (see *Shantung*) to resemble beautiful fabrics of the eighteenth century. It may be yarn-dyed with two colors to make an iridescent effect.

Canton crepe—A fabric heavier than crepe de Chine with a slightly ribbed crepe filling. It was originally made of silk in Canton, China. It is also made of the man-made fibers.

Chiffon—An extremely sheer, airy, soft silk fabric with a soft plain or rippled finish that is used for evening dresses and scarfs. It is made also in rayon and other man-made fibers.

Chiffon velvet—A lightweight, soft, usually silk fabric with a dense pile.

Chrysalis—The dormant silk larva within the cocoon.

Cocoon—A covering of silk filaments extruded by the silkworm.

Crepe de Chine—A very light, sheer flat crepe as now made. It was originally a pebbly, washable silk fabric, degummed after weaving.

Cultivated silk—Fibers from a silkworm that has had scientific care.

Damask—See Glossary, Chapter 10.

Douppion—Silk from two silkworms that have spun one cocoon together.

Faille—A soft, finely ribbed, glossy silk fabric. It may also be made in cotton or man-made fibers.

Flat crepe—A firm silk crepe with a soft, almost imperceptible crinkle. See *Crepe de Chine.* It may also be made of man-made fibers.

Floss silk—Tangled silk waste. Floss is also a twisted silk yarn used in art needlework.

Foulard—A fine, soft twill-weave silk fabric, often printed—used for neckties and dresses. It may be made in mercerized cotton, rayon, acetate, or thin worsted.

Gauze—A thin, sheer fabric in plain weave silk, rayon, or other man-made fibers. It is used for curtains and trimmings of dresses. In cotton, gauze is used for surgical dressings.

Georgette—A soft, sheer, dull-textured silk fabric with a crepy surface, obtained by alternating right-hand and left-hand twisted yarns.

Honan—The best grade of Chinese silk; a finer weave but similar to pongee.

Lyons velvet—A stiff, thick pile velvet; may be silk pile and cotton or rayon back. Lyons-type velvet may be 100 percent of man-made fibers.

Mousseline de soie (silk organdy)—A very sheer, crisp silk fabric.

Noil silk—Short fibers of waste silk produced in the manufacture of spun silk.

Peau de soie (skin of silk)—A reversible silk fabric in a variation of the satin weave with riblike fillings.

Piqué—A silk, rayon, or cotton fabric with raised cords or wales. In true piqué the cords run crosswise, but most of the piqués are now made like Bedford cord with warpwise wales.

Pongee—A light or medium-weight Chinese silk fabric made from wild silk. See *Tussah.*

Pupa—See *Chrysalis.*

Pure silk—Silk containing no metallic weighting. It is synonymous with pure-dye silk. See *Weighted silk.*

Raw silk—Reeled silk wound directly from several cocoons with only a slight twist.

Reeling—The process of unwinding silk from the cocoon onto silk reels.

Satin—A shiny, smooth fabric in warp satin weave. It may be made of acetate, rayon, or synthetic blends or mixtures.

Satin brocade—A satin with a raised woven-in design. It resembles a fine embroidered pattern.

Scroop—The rustle of crisp silk. See *Taffeta.*

Serge—Twilled silk or rayon commonly used for linings. It is also made of worsted.

Sericin—Silk gum extruded by the silkworm; it holds fibers together.

Sericulture—See *Silk culture.*

Shantung—A silk fabric with a nubby surface similar to but heavier than pongee. It was originally woven of wild silk in Shantung, China. Now made of almost any fiber, blend, or mixture.

Silk—The natural fiber that a silkworm spins for its cocoon.

Silk broadcloth—A soft spun-silk fabric in plain weave, used for shirts, blouses, and sports dresses.

Silk culture—The care of the worm that produces silk fiber, from the egg to the moth.

Silk illusion—A net similar to tulle but even finer in mesh, used primarily for bridal veils.

Spun silk—Either yarn or fabric made from short silk fibers that cannot be reeled.

Surah—A soft fabric, usually in a variation of a twill with a flat top wale (sometimes described as a satin-faced twill). It is used for neckties, mufflers, dresses, and blouses, is made in plaids, stripes, or prints, and is also made of man-made fibers.

Taffeta—A fine yarn-dyed, plain weave fabric (closely woven) with a crisp feel. The rustle of silk taffeta is called *scroop.* It is also made in rayon and other man-made fibers.

Throwing—See Glossary, Chapter 3.

Tissue taffeta—A crisp, lightweight taffeta.

Tulle—A very soft, fine, transparent silk net used for evening dresses and veiling. It may also be made of nylon or rayon.

Tussah silk—Fibers from the wild silkworm. Tussah is strong but coarse and uneven. Its tan color is difficult to bleach. Used in shantung and pongee.

Weighted silk—Fabric in which metallic salts have been added in the dyeing and finishing to increase its weight and to give a heavier hand. FTC ruling requires weighted silk to be marked and the amount of weighting indicated.

Wild silk—See *Tussah silk.*

Wool
and the Consumer

12

The herding of flocks of sheep was one of the earliest stages of man's cultural development between barbarism and civilization. In the Old Testament of the Bible, we read of sheep wandering "through all the mountains and upon every high hill." History records that in the fourth century B.C., when Alexander the Great conducted an expedition to India, he found that natives were wearing wool cloth. In A.D. 50, an Italian took sheep from Italy to Spain to be crossbred with the Spanish variety—the *merino*. In the thirteenth century, Spain was producing fine wool cloth. Later, France, Saxony, Germany, England, Austria, South America, South Africa, and New Zealand imported the Spanish merino for breeding. Beginning in 1810, Australia showed the best results in raising this variety of sheep. England was the only country that was unsuccessful; English sheep were primarily raised for mutton, and crossbreeding for the fleece-wool variety was not satisfactory. The United States imported Spanish sheep about 1810. They were first raised along the Atlantic seaboard. Later, sheep raising spread westward. In the Ohio Valley the merinos were crossbred with native sheep, with good results. The wool produced is called Ohio Delaine, and the fibers are the best quality of merino wools produced in this country.

WOOL PRODUC- TION
Merino wools come from Australia, South Africa, and South America. The best come from Australia (the world's largest wool producer), because better care is given the sheep there than in other places. The Australians use what is known as the *paddock system*, where the sheep are allowed to graze in large enclosed areas called paddocks.

Merino wool has shorter fibers than wool from native English sheep. Lincolnshire and Leicestershire raised the longest wool fiber. Carpet or braid wools are very coarse; they come from Turkey and Argentina.

The wool produced in the United States is classified according to the region in which the sheep are raised: (1) *domestic* wools, from the Eastern and Middle Western states; (2) *territory* wools, from the Rocky Mountain Plateau states; (3) *southwestern* wools, from Texas, New Mexico, Arizona, and Southern California.

The domestic wools are softer and finer than the territory wools. The southwestern states mentioned are great sheep-raising states but, since they usually shear their sheep twice a year, their wools are not classified as domestic or territory wools, which are usually clipped once a year. Texas wools have become finer and are more nearly like the merino. Boston is the largest wool port in this country, and, along with Philadelphia and New York, is a big wool marketing center. Since we cannot supply enough wool to meet domestic demands, we must import large quantities from abroad. In fact, all our carpet wool is imported.

As the Table 12-1 indicates, the world production of wool is slowly declining. Since population is growing rapidly and costs of production increasing, it is not surprising that wool is in relatively scarce supply.

The largest production countries are: Australia and New Zealand together with 40 percent of the world's production; the U.S.S.R. with 18 percent; followed by Argentina with 7 percent. About 76 percent of the entire production goes into the apparel market, with the rest into carpeting and other household products.

GRADING FOR MARKETING

For marketing purposes, wool is classified as merino (full-blood) and crossbreed. The latter are graded as 3/4 blood, 1/2 blood, 3/8 blood, and 1/4 blood, depending upon the proportion of merino blood in the sheep

TABLE 12-1. World Production of Raw Wool[1]

	Thousand metric tons		
	1969-70	1971-72	1973-74
	Greasy basis		
Commonwealth			
Australia	923	875	693
New Zealand	328	322	278
United Kingdom	48	47	48
India	33	35	35
Other Commonwealth	12	11	9
Total Commonwealth	1,344	1,290	1,063
Other countries			
Argentina e	202	189	180
South Africa	145	114	103
United States	88	82	72
Uruguay	80	54	60
Turkey	47	48	48
Other Asia (ex. China)	73	74	74
Other Africa b	38	37	37
Other America	77	78	74
Other Western Europe	127	123	120
Non-Communist Total	2,221	2,089	1,831
Soviet Union, China and Eastern Europe			
Soviet Union	390	429	428
Eastern Europe c	92	90	93
Other (primarily China)	78	81	82
Total	560	600	603
World Total	2,781	2,689	2,434

[1] "Wool Statistics" (for years indicated), International Wool Textile Organization and International Wool Study Group.

266
Fabric
Construction
and
Buying
Motives

producing the wool. In order to provide a more exact measure, there are also grades of fineness from under 40 for coarse wool to as high as 80 for very fine wool. The standard for full-blood is 64, with crossbreed lower. For example, 3/8 blood is graded from 50 to 58.

SHEEPSHEARING

Most sheep are shorn in the spring in the northern hemisphere, and in our fall in the southern hemisphere. Formerly wool was clipped from the sheep's body by hand, but now as many as two hundred sheep can be clipped in one day by machinery. In the United States, the fleeces clipped from sheep are usually all one piece. In Australia, separate fleeces are taken from the same animal—that is, fleece from the belly is kept separate from fleece from the sides. The Australian method is the better, because different grades of wool come from the same sheep. The fleece of the head, belly, and breech is inferior to fleece from the shoulders and sides of the sheep.

FLEECE WOOL VERSUS PULLED WOOL

The wool shorn from the live sheep is termed *fleece wool*. It is usually marketed to wool buyers before washing or scouring. Some sheep die from disease or are slaughtered. Their skins are wetted, treated with lime paste, and then "sweated." The fibers can then be pulled easily from the skin. This class of wool is called *pulled wool*. It is not so good a grade as fleece wool, but pulled wool can be blended with noils (short fibers separated from the long by combing) and with reprocessed and reused wool in very inexpensive suitings and blankets.

SORTING AND GRADING

Wool is graded by men who have developed an extremely keen sense of touch; they grade wool according to the fineness of the individual fibers. Each fleece is graded according to what the grader believes the majority of the fibers to be. The sorter shakes out each fleece and separates fibers from different parts of the body. The wool is then ready for the worsted or woolen goods manufacturer.

Australian wool is delivered to manufacturers sorted and graded. Actually, Australia uses some 5,000 classifications for grading. This practice lowers conversion costs.

The U.S. Department of Agriculture, in cooperation with experimental stations, is promoting the sorting and grading of our domestic wool before it is delivered to the manufacturer. It is felt that this will help the wool grower to get a better price for his product. The Department has set up standards for grading wool by fineness of diameters of wool fiber and "wool tops" (long combed slivers). The method followed is that prescribed by the American Society for Testing Materials (ASTM Designation D472-50T, issued 1947, revised 1950). Effort is being made to grade wool in the grease (before it is scoured) by this method.

FIGURE 12.1. Woolblend Mark symbol giving fiber content and care. (Reproduced courtesy of the Wool Bureau, Inc., photo by Jonas Grushkin.)

INTER-PRETA-TION OF THE WOOL PRODUCTS LABELING ACT

The Wool Products Labeling Act requires that all wool products that move in "commerce"[2] be labeled.[3] Prior to the Textile Fiber Products Identification Act, carpets and rugs containing wool were exempt. Labels shall indicate the percentage of total fiber weight, exclusive of ornamentation that does not exceed 5 percent of the total fiber weight, of each fiber amounting to 5 percent or more of the total.

The labeling law defines wool as new fibers (unused before in a fabric) from sheep, goats, and certain specialty fibers, such as camel's hair, alpaca, llama, and vicuña.

The labeling law sets forth three kinds of wool, depending upon the extent of its previous use in consumer goods:

1. *Wool:* refers to fleece wool being *used for the first time in the complete manufacture of a wool product.* The term "wool" may also include (a) new fleece wool that has previously been processed up to, but not including, weaving or felting, and (b) clips of knitted fabric made of new wool and not used or worn in any way. A fabric labeled "wool" may therefore contain certain wastes, resulting from carding, combing, and spinning, which have been recovered and processed again without being previously used.
2. *Reprocessed wool:* includes scraps and clips of woven and felted fabrics made of previously unused wool. These scraps or clips, never having been used by a consumer, are *garnetted* (shredded into fibrous state), and remanufactured into woolen fabrics. For example, cuttings from workrooms of garment manufacturers are a source of this class of wool.
3. *Reused wool:* old wool that has been woven, knitted, or felted into a wool product and, after having been used by the ultimate consumer, has been cleaned, returned to a fibrous state, then blended to make yarns for fabrics. Reused wool is also called *shoddy.*

If an article contains any fiber other than new wool, it must be labeled to show the percentage by weight of new wool, reprocessed wool, and reused wool. This provision has caused the retailer no end of problems. From the standpoint of accurate fiber identification, no one but the yarn manufacturer knows what percentage of fibers by weight goes into a certain yarn. When a wool fabric is old stock, it is very difficult to make this identification accurately. But law allows a product to be designated as reused wool if amounts of wool or reprocessed wool cannot be accurately determined. Some yarn manufacturers have pointed out that when they indicate the percentage of reused or reprocessed wool on the label, the

---

[2] The general meaning is interstate commerce.
[3] The TFPIA specifies that any product composed in whole or in part of wool or furs must be labeled by reference to the respective regulations on wool and furs issued under the Wool Products Labeling Act or the Fur Products Labeling Act, respectively.

268
Fabric
Construction
and
Buying
Motives

figure may not be accurate when the cloth is finished, as some of the fibers fall out in the finishing process.

Certain specialty names for fibers falling within the definition of wool may be used on a label instead of the term "wool." If desired, the terms "mohair," "cashmere," "camel hair," alpaca," and so on may be used instead of "wool." If the word "cashmere" or "mohair" is used in lieu of the term "wool," the percentage of each fiber must be designated. If these specialty fibers are reprocessed or reused, that fact also must be indicated.

If nonwoolen fibers amount to less than 5 percent each, they may be labeled as "other fibers"; for example, a fabric consisting of 55 percent wool, 30 percent reprocessed wool, 4 percent rayon, 4 percent linen, 4 percent silk, and 3 percent cotton may be labeled for fiber content as follows: "55 percent wool/30 percent reprocessed wool/15 percent other fibers." Preferably, fibers should be listed in order of predominance by weight.

If a fabric has fiber ornamentation (a stripe or woven figure, for instance) not exceeding 5 percent of the total fiber weight of the product, a phrase such as "exclusive of ornamentation" must follow the statement of other fiber content. Should the fiber ornamentation exceed 5 percent, the percentage must be included in the percentage statement of fiber content. A label might read: "50 percent wool/25 percent rayon/25 percent cotton (exclusive of ornamentation)."

All wool products imported into the United States, except those made more than twenty years before importation, are subject to the provisions of the act.

The retailer can secure a guarantee from a manufacturer that a specific wool product is not misbranded under the provisions of the act, or the retailer may secure a continuing guarantee filed with the Federal Trade Commission that will be applicable to all wool products handled by a guarantor. These guarantees must conform to the rules and regulations of the Commission. Such guarantees between manufacturer and retailer must be made in good faith.

Since the wool labeling law pertains to sales of wool products in interstate commerce, every retailer must actively and intelligently comply with its requirements.[4] Manufacturers, wholesalers, retailers, and consumers have a common interest in maintaining truthful merchandising practices.

The consumer is probably familiar with the term "virgin wool." The Wool Products Labeling Act does not define virgin wool, but the FTC has defined it. The term is applicable to fabrics or products that do not contain within them any wastes from preliminary processing of new wool. It should be remembered that wool wastes and reprocessed and reused wool can be used only in fabrics of woolen (as opposed to worsted) type. (See pp. 277 for a description of processing woolen yarn.) Thus, the reliable manufacturers of woolens are proud to identify their fabrics with their own brand names if their fabrics are made of 100 percent virgin wool. The improper use of the term "virgin wool" on tags or labels and in

---

[4] The retailer may also substitute his own label—revealing, instead of the manufacturer's name, the name under which he does business. He may employ a word trademark or housemark for this purpose if it has been registered with the U.S. Patent Office and if, prior to use, the FTC is furnished a copy of the registration.

PURE WOOL

Figure 12.2 The woolmark label is your assurance of quality tested products made of the world's best . . . Pure Wool. (Reproduced courtesy of The Wool Bureau, Inc.)

advertising of fabrics represents a deception of the consumer and therefore, under provisions of the Wool Products Labeling Act, constitutes an offense subject to corrective measures.

The consumer should bear in mind that this act is intended to inform him of the exact fiber content of a fabric containing wool from which garments are made. The consumer must also realize that the presence of reprocessed and reused wools does not necessarily make a fabric inferior in quality. The grade of the fabric depends upon the *quality* of the reprocessed or reused wool. Sometimes a mixture of new wool with reprocessed and reused wool is like a metal alloy—particularly strong and durable for the purpose for which it was made. In other cases, the use of reprocessed or reused wool does not have the effect of a strengthening agent, but makes it possible for a manufacturer to sell a garment at a price that would be impossible if first-grade new wool were used.

A manufacturer who has always made it his practice to use good-grade new wool in his fabrics will not suddenly change to using reprocessed or reused wool. Similarly, a manufacturer who has been making popular-priced clothing containing reprocessed or reused wool is going to keep on making that clothing. What the act has done is to make all manufacturers label their products as to fiber content. The fact that a garment is labeled "reused wool" doesn't mean that the consumer is not getting service commensurate with what he pays for the garment. Labels are merely a guarantee as to the content of the fabric.

**CHARAC-
TERISTICS
OF THE
WOOL
FIBER**

MICROSCOPIC APPEARANCE

Under the microscope, a wool fiber resembles a worm with horny scales. Wool fiber consists of three parts: (1) the medullary, (2) the cortex, and (3) the outside scales. The medullary is a honeycombed cellular section found in medium and coarse wools. Not all wool fibers have a medulla, and it is not necessary to the growth of the fiber. Its chief function seems to be "to increase the protective properties of the fiber by adding internal air spaces."[5] The cortex consists of cortical cells that are really bundles of

[5] Werner Von Bergen and Herbert Mauersberger, *American Wool Handbook*, 2nd ed. (New York: Textile Book Publishers, Inc.), pp. 133-34.

269

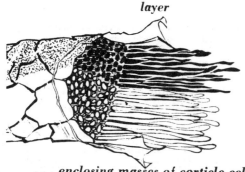

. . . encasing imbricated (overlapping) outer layer

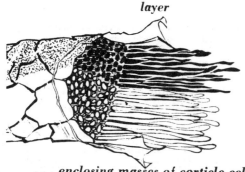

. . . enclosing masses of corticle cells

FIGURE 12.3.   a. Outerlayer of wool fiber. Microscopic view. b. Enclosing masses of corticle cells (Courtesy of The Wool Bureau, Inc.)

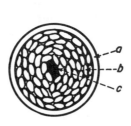

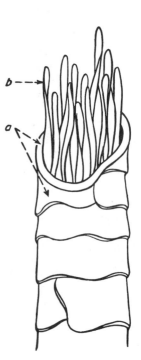

a – cuticle
b – corticle cells
c – medulla

FIGURE 12.4. Elements of the wool fiber. (Reproduced courtesy of the Wool Bureau, Inc.)

fibrils.[6] The outside scales have a protecting membrane called the *cuticle*. The scales overlap, and their free ends point toward the tip of the fiber. Hence the scales are partially responsible for the wool fiber's slipping and sliding more easily toward the root of the fiber. On the other hand, materials coming in contact with the fiber slip more easily toward the tip of the fiber. This difference in friction on a sheep's back causes burrs and dust particles to work their way out of the wool. This same frictional difference is a factor in giving wool its felting quality. When wool is wet, the fibers move and entangle as the wet cloth is manipulated mechanically (chemicals may or may not be used to cause felting). Excessive shrinkage occurs when felting is not controlled. (See *shrinkage control of wool*, p. 284.)

LENGTH OF FIBER

Wool fibers range from 1 to 14 inches in length, depending on the kind of sheep and the part of the sheep from which the wool is taken. Wool is a comparatively short natural fiber and is surpassed in length by silk and linen. The shorter fibers are used chiefly in woolens, and the longer ones are used primarily in worsteds. Fibers used for worsteds average 3 to 8 inches in length, whereas those used for woolens are 1 to 3 inches (usually 2 inches or less).

DIAMETER

The average wool fiber is coarser than rayon, silk, linen, or cotton fibers. The approximate diameter of wool fiber is .0005 to .0015 inch. Therefore, wool yarns are ordinarily not so fine as other textiles.

COLOR OF FIBER

Wool fibers range from whitish to gray, brown, and sometimes black. The color pigment is distributed through cells in the cortex and medulla. As in the case of human hair, it is easy to dye the scales and the cortex, but the dye rarely penetrates the medulla. Bleaching has a similar effect, although for all practical purposes bleaching with peroxide is permanent. Black sheep's wool cannot be bleached white.

LUSTER

Luster of wool will vary according to the origin and breed of the sheep and with climate. The luster is higher in poor-quality wools than in good grades. A poor-grade serge suit is more shiny when purchased and will show a greasy shine more quickly than a better-grade serge. Although luster is temporarily removed by a sponging with an ammonia solution, the shine will return. Dull wools are better buys in the long run with one exception—broadcloth, which is purposely steam-lustered in the finishing process to increase the luster and lay the nap.

[6] The nucleus at the center of each cortical cell is a granular structure. The electron microscope reveals still finer filaments than fibrils, called microfibrils, Ibid., p. 130.

272
Fabric
Construction
and
Buying
Motives

STRENGTH

A single wool fiber can sustain a dead weight of 15 to 30 grams. A silk fiber will break at 5 to 28 grams. But although wool fiber seems stronger than silk according to these figures, the diameters of the two fibers are usually quite different. Wool fiber is coarser than silk, so it is logical to expect greater tensile strength from wool; but if the five major fibers of equal diameter are compared, nylon ranks first, silk second, wool third, and then come rayon and cotton. There are so many different grades of each fiber that it is difficult to generalize.

Wool is stronger dry than wet. Vegetable fibers, with the exception of rayon, are stronger when wet. Rayon's wet strength has been improved appreciably.

ELASTICITY OR RESILIENCE

Wool is the most elastic of the natural fibers. It stretches 25 to 35 percent of its length before breaking.

Wool fiber possesses crimp or wave, the amount of crimp varying with the fineness of the fibers from almost no crimp to 22 to 30 crimps per inch.[7] The finer fibers have a pronounced crimp. This characteristic crimp causes wool fibers to repel each other when in fabrics. When a wool fiber is stretched, the crimp comes out, but when the fiber is released, the crimp returns—the fiber springs back. If masses of wool fibers are pressed together, they spring apart as soon as pressure is released. This quality is called resilience or elasticity. It is very important in wrinkle resistance and insulation of wool. Resilience is also a factor in tailoring. Wool tailors easily because it is a "live" fiber. Furthermore, it is easily shaped and steamed while parts of the garment are being put together.

INSULATION VALUE

Heat conductivity and insulation are not the same, although the terms are related. The insulation value of a fabric depends on the amount of air enmeshed within the fabric and on its surface. In this, the actual heat conductivity of the enmeshed or trapped air is important, rather than that of the fibers themselves. Trapped air is a nonconductor of heat. In wool fabrics, because of their porosity and the fact that by nature wool fibers stay apart (repel each other), about 80 percent of the entire fabric volume is air.[8] The air held closely against the fiber surfaces prevents heat loss by the body, thus keeping the body warm. Even when the wool is wet, its resilience remains, so its insulating trapped air remains. Hence, the wearer of wet wool garments does not chill suddenly.

Furthermore, a loosely twisted woolen yarn with varied lengths of nonparallel fibers can enmesh more still air than a worsted yarn with its long parallel fibers held in the yarn by twist. A porous plain weave would also serve to create air pockets. Woolen yarns, with their resilient fibers of

[7] Giles E. Hopkins, *Wool as an Apparel Fiber* (New York: Holt, Rinehart and Winston, 1953), p. 9.
[8] Ibid., p. 67.

varied lengths, lend themselves to napping, and napped fibers of varied lengths create more air pockets. Not only the repellence of fiber to fiber and resilience of the fiber, but also the type of yarn, weave, and finish are factors in heat conductivity.

MICROSCOPIC MOISTURE

Wool has a high absorptive quality, but it absorbs moisture in the form of water vapor very slowly. Observation of liquid spilled on wool garments shows that if the surface is slanted, the liquid runs off, but if horizontal, the liquid is absorbed very slowly. Wool is naturally water-repellent, because the membrane protecting the scales is nonprotein, so that liquid water is not attracted to the fiber's surface. However, water vapor can penetrate the fiber's interior, which has a strong affinity for moisture. This quality of wool explains why wool garments can absorb body moisture in the form of water vapor without feeling damp. This moisture from the body is then released to the atmosphere slowly, so that the body is not chilled.

Although wool can absorb a great deal of moisture, it does so slowly, and it dries more slowly than silk or linen. Wool can absorb much moisture before it feels damp.

COMPOSITION OF FIBER

Wool is the only fiber containing sulfur. Its chemical composition is carbon, hydrogen, nitrogen, oxygen, and sulfur. The wool fiber is composed of animal tissues, which are classed as a protein called *keratin.*

EFFECT OF LIGHT

Laboratory tests show that raw wool is about as resistant to light as cotton or jute. Dyed wool, used in woolen suits and hats, does not seem to lose so much strength in the same test.

MILDEW

Wool is attacked by mildew only if the fabric has remained damp for some time. Mildew-resistant processes may be applied in finishing wool goods.

EFFECT OF ACIDS

Dilute acids, even if boiling, do not injure wool. Highly concentrated acids, such as sulfuric, hydrochloric, and nitric, will destroy wool if the fabric is soaked in them for more than a few minutes or if the acid is allowed to dry in the fabric. Often raw wool is treated with dilute sulfuric acid to remove any vegetable matter, such as burrs, from the fibers. Formic and acetic acids are not detrimental to wool. Oxalic, tartaric, and citric acids are not injurious if the acid is not allowed to dry on the cloth. In fact, formic, acetic, oxalic, tartaric, and citric acids are less injurious than dilute sulfuric, hydrochloric, or nitric acids, given equal concentration.

274
Fabric
Construction
and
Buying
Motives

EFFECT OF ALKALIES

Weak alkalies such as ammonia, borax, phosphate of soda, and soap are not injurious to wool if care is taken to keep the temperature below 68° F. But boiling in a 5 percent solution of caustic soda (lye) for five minutes will completely disintegrate wool. Wool is sensitive to alkalies; therefore the use of neutral soaps with no free alkali is advised.

EFFECT OF BLEACHES

Chlorine bleach is ordinarily harmful to wool. The use, in the past, of a form of chlorine to shrinkproof or feltproof wool was very unsatisfactory, because it caused loss of strength and elasticity. Furthermore, fabrics so treated would still felt, and they did not have the durability of untreated wool. Now, however, the use of a chlorinating agent can be satisfactorily controlled so that shrinkage is prevented. (For a discussion of shrinkage control, see p. 284.)

Potassium permanganate, sodium peroxide, and hydrogen peroxide are used for bleaching and removing some kinds of stains.

AFFINITY FOR DYESTUFFS

Wool has a good affinity for dyestuffs. Its chemical structure enables the fiber to unite chemically with a wide variety of dyestuffs. Acid or basic dyes, chromes, indigo, and even vat types can be used for wool. Selected basic dyes can be used for dyeing wool and acrylic fiber blends and mixtures, but the cationic dyes, developed especially for acrylics, are better.[9] Deep rich colors and pale pastels are possible because of the wool fiber's affinity for dye.

MOTH DAMAGE TO WOOL

The larvae of the clothes moth feeds on wool. The female moth lays eggs in a dark spot such as the nap of a wool sweater, blanket, or rug. The moth larvae first eat the nap and then the ground yarns in a fabric.[10] Washing will kill moths and eggs. A reinfestation may be prevented by sealing the washed article in paper or cellophane. Moth-proofing techniques are described in Chapter 7.

MANUFAC-TURE OF WORSTED YARNS

Wool fibers can be manufactured into two kinds of cloth: worsteds and woolens. Worsteds are characterized by smooth surfaces, and they are harder to the touch than woolens. The weave or pattern is clearly visible in worsteds, and for this reason they are described as *clear finished.*

Worsteds are made from long wool fibers, usually two to eight inches in length. The English wools are often imported for worsted manufacture.

SORTING

When wool reaches the mill it is sorted; this process has been described earlier in the chapter.

[9] *Textile World,* CXII, No. 4 (April 4, 1962), 82.
[10] IFI Bulletin Service, Textile Notes #26.

Chapter 12

OPENING

After sorting, the wool is put through a machine, called an *opener* or *breaker*, containing a tooth cylinder, the purpose of which is to remove all loose dirt and sand and to separate the whole fleece into small sections.

SCOURING

Since wool contains grease, dirt, and other substances, the fibers must be washed or scoured. A mild alkaline solution of soap or soda ash is the most usual method of removing grease and swint (perspiration). Other methods include *swint washing* (wool is steeped in water, and the swint liquor, after removal of sand and dirt, is used for scouring); solvent scouring (with white spirit and chlorinated hydrocarbons) followed by water; refrigeration processing (wool grease is frozen and removed as powder by treatment in a dusting machine); and scouring by using soda ash to remove free fatty acid oils and an emulsifier and synthetic detergent to remove mineral oils.

WOOL DRYING

The wet scoured wool is dried in a machine that provides a gentle flow of air and heat.

CARDING

The carding of wool is similar to the carding of cotton. Large revolving cylinders with wire teeth all running at different speeds lay the fibers in a filmy sheet, or sliver. Carding partially straightens the wool fibers and lays them in one direction. The carded wool sliver is then made even.

COMBING

Worsted cloths show the woven pattern clearly, so that any unevenness in the yarn is noticeable in the finished cloth. The carded slivers are run through a combing operation to (1) remove the short fibers from the sliver; (2) straighten the remaining fibers and make them parallel; (3) remove any foreign matter, such as straw, burrs, or dirt. Combing adds to cost but is essential if felting is not desired.

The short fibers are called *noils*—corresponding with *tow* in linen. The long fibers lying parallel in the sliver are called *tops*. (See specifications and methods of test for determining fineness of wool tops, p. 266.)

Slivers of tops are combed and drawn out. This drawing process is called *drafting*. Slivers are drawn out narrower and narrower until the desired thickness is reached. A sufficient twist is put in to prevent further drafting (*drawing*). The combed top can now be dyed, because the color can penetrate through the fibers at this point in the process better than it can after the cloth is woven.

SPINNING

Spinning puts in the required twist. Spools holding slivers are arranged horizontally to revolve on a frame. From these spools the slivers are carried to another series of spools, arranged vertically on another frame.

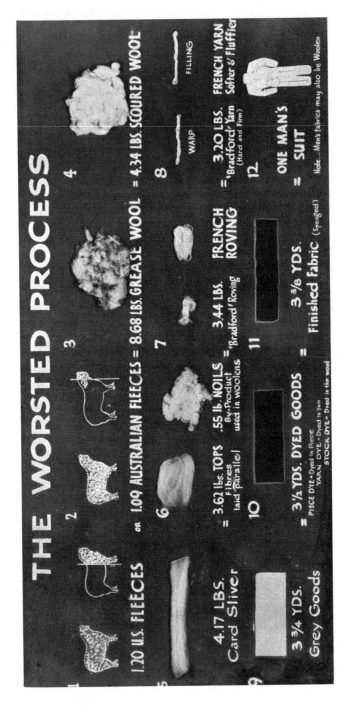

FIGURE 12.5. The worsted process. (Reproduced courtesy of Industrial By-Products & Research Corp.) "Bradford" yarn has largely been replaced in the United States by "American Ring System" which is faster and abbreviated over the "Bradford System." "French Yarn" is also declining in use in favor of the "American."

The speed and tension of winding are so regulated as to twist the yarn as it is wound from one spool to the other. Worsted yarns are usually more tightly twisted than woolen yarns. (See Figure 12.5.) The yarns are sold to the weavers on these spools, or in skeins or hanks.

TWISTING

Twisting is spinning two, three, or four yarns together (plies). Two-ply yarns are generally used for weaving and machine knitting, and three- and four-ply are sold for hand knitting.

REELING

Worsted yarns are then reeled into skeins.

INSPECTION

Inspecting the skeins and putting them into bundles of about 40 pounds each completes worsted yarn manufacture.

SIZES OR COUNT OF WORSTED YARNS

The size of worsted yarns is determined by the number of hanks of 560 yards weighing one pound. If one 560-yard hank weighs one pound, the count or size is #1. If 5,600 yards weigh one pound, the count is #10, and so on. Yarns numbered 5s to 10s are very coarse and used for heavy sweaters; 10s to 30s are medium; 40s to 60s are fine. Worsted yarns are two-ply, three-ply, and four-ply, as well as single. (See Tex System, Chapter 3.)

QUALITY OF WORSTED YARN

The quality of worsted yarn depends on the grade of the fibers used, the amount of carding and combing, the skill applied to these operations, and the regularity of the spinning.

Fabrics made of worsted yarn include tropical worsted, unfinished worsted, worsted flannel, worsted cheviot, worsted covert, sharkskin, and gabardine.

MANUFAC-TURE OF WOOLEN YARNS

SELECTING THE FIBER

Fibers averaging less than two inches in length are customarily selected for woolen yarns. Short-fiber merino wool is especially good. Since the beauty of a woolen lies in its softness and warmth, this type of cloth lends itself more to adulteration than does worsted. The woven pattern is usually indistinct and often obliterated. The felting, or shrinking, of wool goods after they are woven makes it possible to conceal many varieties of fibers.

For woolen yarns, then, short fibers of new or virgin wool can be used, as well as reprocessed or reused wool. If any reprocessed or reused wool is used, the percentage of each by weight must appear on the label. Blends of wool with other natural or man-made fibers are becoming more prevalent.

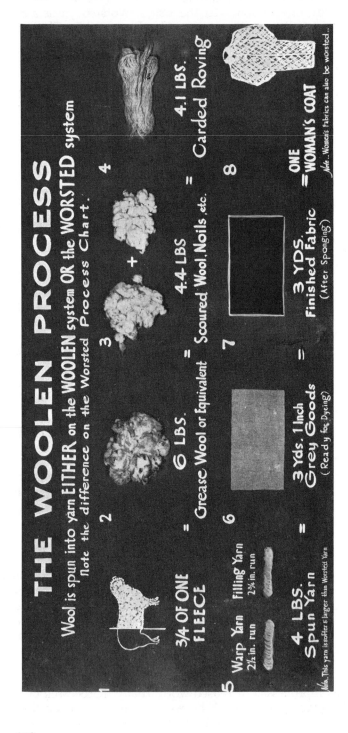

FIGURE 12.6. The woolen process. (Reproduced courtesy of Industrial By-Products & Research Corp.)

PROCESSES PRELIMINARY TO CARDING

The processes of preparing wool for carding are similar to those used in preparing wool for making worsted yarn.

CARDING

The purpose of carding woolen yarn is to make it fuzzy enough to allow a nap to be raised later. The process is more violent than that used for worsteds; rollers with wire teeth revolve in opposite directions, whereas for worsteds they revolve in the same direction. Woolen yarn may be carded several times, but it is not combed since felting is desired. Short fibers are not taken out of the sliver as they are for worsted yarn. Like worsted yarn, it is drawn out and twisted. Woolen yarn has a slacker twist than worsted yarn. (See Figure 12.6.) It is then wound on bobbins and rewound on spools or made into skeins. Woolen yarn may be dyed before it is woven, and when that is done the cloth is said to be yarn-dyed. Sometimes the wool stock is dyed before carding. In this way it is possible to produce heather and melange effects.

SIZE OR COUNT OF WOOLEN YARNS

There are two methods of computing sizes of woolen yarn: one method, the American *run count*, will be discussed here. If 1,600 yards weigh one pound, the count or size is #1. This yarn is very coarse and is used for overcoats and blankets; #3 and #4 yarns are medium; and #6½ to #10 yarns are fine. (See Tex System, Chapter 3.)

Fabrics made of woolen yarn include homespun, tweed, wool flannel, wool cheviot, wool covert, wool shetland, and wool broadcloth.

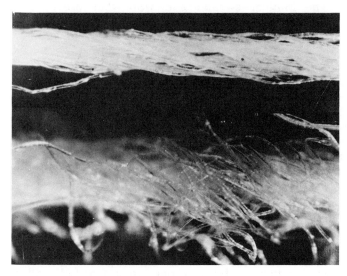

FIGURE 12.7. Photomicrograph of woolen (bottom) and worsted (top) yarns. (Photo courtesy of The Wool Bureau, Inc.)

WEAVING
AND
KNITTING
WORSTED
AND
WOOLEN
FABRICS

PLAIN WEAVE

Although more men's suitings are made in twill than in plain weave, the plain weave is popular where porosity, softness, and sponginess (in women's wear) are factors. Men's and women's suitings and coatings in this construction include homespun, donegal tweed, and tropical worsted. Women's dress fabrics include wool crepe, batiste, nun's veiling, poplin, faille, and some flannels and tweeds.

TWILL WEAVE

The twill is a durable construction and therefore particularly suited to men's suitings and coatings. Kersey (heavy felted overcoating), cheviots, coverts, tweed, broadcloth, flannel, whipcord, and serge are made in twill for men's wear. Women wear most of the fabrics listed, but the weight is lighter and the finish usually softer.

PILE WEAVE

Many fabrics are made in pile construction to imitate fur. Some fleeces, double-cloth coatings, velours, velvets, friezés, and plushes are made in this manner. Velour, velvet, and plush are upholstery fabrics in pile weave. Rugs with wool pile include Wilton, Axminster, tufted, and velvet. (See Chapter 20 for construction of rugs.)

DOBBY WEAVE

The very durable elastique and cavalry twill, originally for uniforms for the armed forces, is dobby weave and is particularly appropriate in civilian jackets and trousers when durability is a major factor.

KNITTED CONSTRUCTION

Jersey blouses, wool basque or polo shirts, some fleeces, and bouclé dresses are knitted. The familiar sweater and wool sock are of this construction. Wool's resilience, bulk, and ease in handling make it most appropriate in knitted goods. (See Chapter 5.)

FINISHES
FOR
WORSTED
AND
WOOLEN
FABRICS

Worsteds look more ready for sale than woolens when they come from the loom, because their attractiveness depends on their even yarns and structural design, whereas much of the attractiveness, softness, and often the warmth of the woolen depends on its finish. Usually woolens are more heavily felted than worsteds. Woolen and worsted fabrics are given one of two finishes: (1) clear or hard finish; (2) face finish.

The clear-finished fabric, which includes most of the worsteds, has a smooth, even surface with the weave clearly visible. For clear finishes very little, if any, fulling is done. (See p. 283.) A slight fulling of a worsted would produce a good, firm hand.

The face finish has either a pile or a nap on the surface, which almost, if not entirely, obliterates the weave. Considerable fulling is done, and a nap is raised. The nap may be pressed in one direction, as in broadcloth. Sometimes the finisher produces a fuzz or nap on a worsted, called *unfinished worsted.* Then again he may make one side of the fabric *clear finished* and the back *face finished* with a nap.

PERCHING OR INSPECTING

All fabrics must be subjected to this visual examination. (See *inspection*, Chapter 7.) Inspection is done both before and after finishes have been applied.

BURLING[11]

For inspection the cloth is laid over a smooth, sloping table. The inspector or burler first examines the back of the cloth to detect and remove snarls, slubs, and straws. All thick warp and filling yarns are opened with a pick called a *burling iron.* The burler next examines the face of the cloth for irregularities. All imperfections are pushed through to the back of the cloth so that the right side of the fabric will be smooth.

MENDING

This is a finishing process in which weaving imperfections, broken yarns, or tears are repaired before further finishing.

BLEACHING

Wool is frequently bleached in the yarn, but it can also be bleached after weaving and scouring.

Natural wool fibers are slightly yellowish, black, or brown. The yellowish color predominates. As the amount of deeply colored wool is small, these wools are rarely bleached. The yellowish tinted wool can be whitened by (1) tinting, (2) sulfur dioxide, or (3) hydrogen peroxide.[12]

Tinting is not a bleach but a dyeing of the wool with violet or blue to neutralize the cast of the natural pigment and change the tint to gray. There is no destruction of the natural pigment, and the gray tint is so slight that the eye perceives the wool as white.

The sulfur dioxide bleach is an older method of bleaching, but it is less permanent than the hydrogen peroxide bleach. In the sulfur dioxide method the cloth is subjected either to a sulfur dioxide gas or to an acidified solution of bisulphite.

In the third method of bleaching, the well-scoured fabric is saturated and steeped for about twelve hours in a bath of hydrogen peroxide made slightly alkaline with sodium silicate or ammonia. A thorough rinsing in dilute acetic acid removes bleaching chemicals. To cheapen the bleaching process and to provide a milder bleach, stabilized hydrosulfite compounds are used. Frequently this method is combined with the peroxide method.

SCOURING AND CARBONIZING

Both of these processes are preliminary cleaning processes. Scouring removes oil, dirt, and sizing from wool, cotton, linen, and rayon fabrics.

[11] Von Bergen and Mauersberger, *op. cit.,* pp. 809-10.
[12] Ibid., pp. 791-94.

282
Fabric
Construction
and
Buying
Motives

Carbonizing frees wool of burrs and vegetable matter by the use of an acid solution and heat. A rinse is an alkali that neutralizes the acid. When the wool is dry, the carbonized matter "dusts off."[13] This process can be done in the fiber stage, but the purpose is the same when done as a finishing process.

BRUSHING AND SINGEING

These processes, described in Chapter 7, remove short, loose fibers and lint from wool.

SHEARING

To cut off excess surface fibers and to even the pile in length, wool fabrics may be sheared.

CRABBING[14]

This operation is a permanent setting of the weave in order to prevent uneven shrinkage, which may develop in crimps, creases, or cockles when the fabric is fulled. The process consists in passing the fabric in full width around a series of rollers and immersing the cloth in a number of tanks. Each tank is equipped with steam pipes and cross sprays. At the end of the machine there are two rollers that squeeze water from the fabric. This equipment is used not only for worsteds but also for wool and rayon blends.

DECATING (Dry and Wet)

Wool is dry-decated to set the luster and wet-decated to add luster.

1. *Dry decating* (often called semidecating).[15] The operation consists of applying hot steam to a dry cloth wound under tension on a perforated roller. The roller is not really sealed, but merely contains the steam and allows the steam to escape through the perforations and hence through the fabric.

Then the process is reversed by forcing steam through the cloth from the outside to the inside. The cloth is then removed from the tank and is cooled by air.

2. *Wet decating.*[16] If the finished wool fabric must have luster and a more permanent setting of the fibers, the fabric is wet decated. For this process, heat, moisture, and tension are needed. The cloth is wound in tension around a perforated metal cylinder that is placed in a trough of water 140° to 212° F. The five- to ten-minute treatment consists in circulating the water from the tank through the fabric into the cylinder, and vice versa. Hot water plus steam will make the process more effective. The fabric is then cooled with cold water or cold air.

---

[13] *Dan River's Dictionary of Textile Terms*, 10th ed., Dan River Mills, Inc., p. 17.
[14] Von Bergen and Mauersberger, *op. cit.* pp. 813-14.
[15] Ibid., pp. 860-61.
[16] Ibid., pp. 837-38.

FULLING

If wool is to be made more compact and thicker, the fabric is placed in warm soapy water or a weak acid solution, where it is pounded and twisted until it has shrunk a desired amount—10 to 25 percent. This process may last two to eighteen hours and is called *fulling*, *felting*, or *milling*. The secret of fulling lies in the structure of the wool fiber. The scales of the fiber swell in the warm water, and the pounding and twisting cause them to entangle or interlock with one another. When the fabric is dried, the fibers stay massed together—they are felted. Worsteds are fulled to close the weave and to soften the cloth. Slight fulling of a woolen will give it compactness and softness.

GIGGING

The raising of a nap on a wool fabric may be done with teasels—burr-like plants one and one-half to two inches in length.[17] The teasels are set in rows in frames mounted on revolving drums. As the cloth comes in contact with the teasels, the fibers are untangled and lifted. It is wise to use worn teasels first, so that fibers will not be torn out. New teasels are sharper and are best introduced gradually until the desired nap is raised. Gigging is also used for spun silk and spun rayon.

NAPPING

Those woolen fabrics that are to have a fuzzy surface are fulled a great deal more than the others, because the more the short fibers of wool are massed together the thicker will be the nap. After they are fulled, woolens are washed, dried, and tentered (evened in their width). The cloth is then passed over cylinders whose surfaces are covered with wire bristles. When teasels are used, the process is called gigging. The teasels make a more natural nap and are not so rough on the cloth as the wire bristles. But where fibers have formed a felted surface, napping is necessary to untangle them. The nap is then sheared to a certain length.

STEAMING[18]

This operation, when applied after drying, partially shrinks and conditions the fabric. After the cloth has been decated, steaming takes off unsightly glaze. The fabric is run over a steam box with a perforated copper cover, and the steam is passed through it. While this process is not essentially for shrinkage, it does have that effect. Silk and spun rayons may also be steamed.

WEIGHTING OF WOOLENS

To make a firmer, more compact cloth, manufacturers steam fibers (obtained by shearing a cloth) into the back of a fabric. Reused wool may also be used for this purpose. Men may have discovered little rolls of wool in the pockets of their overcoats. This is *flocking*. Its presence can be

[17] Ibid., p. 839.
[18] Ibid., p. 870.

284
Fabric
Construction
and
Buying
Motives

detected if the back of the cloth is brushed with a stiff brush to see whether short fibers come out. If the manufacturer uses a good quality of wool fiber for flocking and does not use it merely to cover defects in weaving, the practice is considered legitimate.

Unscrupulous manufacturers may take advantage of the absorptive qualities of wool and treat fabrics with magnesium chloride so that the cloth may absorb more moisture than it naturally would. This practice is called *loading*. It gives the buyer a good percentage of water with his purchase.

SHRINKAGE CONTROL

Great strides have been made in overcoming objectionable shrinkage of wools. Although such finishes as steaming, fulling, and decating help to lessen wool shrinkage, these finishes do not insure fabrics against progressive shrinkage in washing.

It is estimated that there are hundreds of shrinkage-control processes for wool. Four of the methods in current use in this country are (1) chlorination (either dry or in neutral or acid solutions). (2) resin treatment; (3) combination of alkaline hypochlorite and permanganate; (4) combination of very mild chlorination plus a resin addition.

These chemical methods cause the wool to resist felting and hence to resist shrinkage. Chlorination consists in subjecting wool tops, yard goods, or garments to a chlorine agent. The chlorination process modifies the fiber structure of wool. Under the microscope the scales of treated fibers may appear less clear or may disappear substantially. Since the treatment prevents felting shrinkage, directional frictional effect (discussed earlier as fiber slippage from tip to root and root to tip) is diminished, and that reduces resilience. It has been found that chlorination may reduce washfastness of the dyes.

Application of melamine formaldehyde resin masks the scale structure but does not modify that structure. Essentially the process deposits resin on the surface of the fabric. One scientist compares resin's action to spot welding of the fibers—an action preventing movement of the scales and hence preventing felting. This method, although it is effective in preventing shrinkage, causes fabrics to lose wool-like hand because of fiber-bonding and increase in fabric weight.

Acrylic resins stabilize wool and avoid the undesirable effects on secondary fabric properties from which other commercial treatments suffer.[19]

The third method has enjoyed considerable commercial success. When applied to grey goods, decreased affinity for dyes and uneven dyeing have been drawbacks. Also there have been few dyes that maintain their shade and fastness if applied before this treatment. The fourth method uses a much reduced level of chlorination in which virtually no fiber scales are damaged or removed. Following this mild treatment, resins of the nylon and acrylic type are found to spread and permanently adhere in an ultra-thin layer on each individual fiber in the treated structure. Dyeing is not impaired and the hand is not changed.

[19] Trade names for this technology are Dylan GRB and Superwash.

Present industrial shrink-resistance treatments are capable of preventing any wool fabric from felting in any washing machine. However, there may be disadvantageous side effects, such as loss of strength and woollike hand, change in appearance, and possible stretching of the treated fabric when given a mild laundering. (For brand names of finishes for shrinkage control, see Chapter 7.)

WASH-AND-WEAR

In the previous discussions of wash-and-wear, particular emphasis has been placed on the cellulosic fibers, cotton and linen. After laundering, such characteristics as smoothness of the surface of the fabric, wrinkle resistance dry and wet, and shrinkage control were considered. Wool, by nature, is elastic and therefore wrinkle resistant, and wrinkles tend to hang out. Therefore the major problem in making wool fabrics wash-and-wear are those of shrinkage, felting, and fuzzing in laundering. The shrink-resistant finishes are being improved to the point where wash-and-wear wools may become commonplace.

Heat-set treatments have become a boon to the man-made fibers and to cottons in permanent pleating of fabrics. Now a process for improving the permanence of pleating in wools has been developed by Unilever, Ltd., of Great Britain. In this pretreatment process, the salt linkages in the keratin are partly broken, after which the fabric is steam-pressed.

TENTERING

Evening a wool fabric in its width is especially important. (For a description of the tentering process, see p. 140.)

PRESSING

Pressing accomplishes the same result for wool that calendering does for other fibers. Calendering is really a pressing process, but the term is not applied to wool.

To press wool, the fabric is placed between heavy, electrically heated metal plates that steam and press the fabric. Another method is to wind the fabric around a cylindrical unit that dampens the fabric and then presses it. The latter method can be used not only for woolens and worsteds but also for spun rayons and silks.

FIRE-RESISTANT FINISH

Some fire insurance companies recommend wool blankets for smothering fires. Why? Laboratories have found that wool absorbs about twice as much moisture as cotton and that moisture absorption is a factor in reducing flammability. The chemical nature of wool also contributes to its natural flame resistance. Even when forced to ignite, wool has a very low temperature of burning; thus there is reduced hazard of flash burning. Another factor involved in flammability is the construction of a cloth. A flame must have sufficient heat concentration and new fibers to consume, plus enough oxygen to keep burning. If a flame is applied to an all-wool fabric, it is slow in ignition, and, if the material is dense enough, the fire will often go out when the flame is removed. It may be deduced that

286
Fabric
Construction
and
Buying
Motives

flammability is not a problem in 100 percent wool fabrics. However, blends, depending on the nature and percentage of other fabrics, may create a flammability problem. Also, if flammable finishing materials are used in sufficient amounts, flammability must be reckoned with under the Flammable Fabrics Act.

OTHER FUNCTIONAL FINISHES FOR WOOL FABRICS

Wool is not subject to mildew unless it is allowed to remain damp for some time; however, wool may be given a mildew-resistant finish. (See Chapter 7.)

The attack on wool by moths is always a worry to a consumer. Again a proper moth-repellent finish done by the finisher or by the consumer can be adequate to prevent eating by moths. (See p. 155 for chemicals used in this finish and common trade names for this type of finish.)

Wool fabrics for rainwear are treated for water repellency. The degree of repellency and the length of time the treatment will last after dry or wet cleaning depends on the nature of the finish. Trade names of water-repellent finishes for wool include Cravenette, Wat-a-set, Neva-Wet, Rainfoe, Zelan, and Zepel (spot- and stain-repellent).

BUYING POINTS OF WOOL FABRICS

APPEARANCE

The attractive appearance of a wool fabric lies partly in its natural low luster for good-grade wools or in its steam-lustered finish for fabrics like wool broadcloth. But the rich coloring of wool fabrics is probably more important to the fashion-minded consumer. Colors can be soft and muted or high in intensity, with depth and permanence. The depth and softness of a woolen pile, the nap of a woolen, and the intricacies of weave in a worsted have an eye appeal. A fabric that drapes and fits well always presents a good appearance.

EASE IN CARE

Wool's elasticity is responsible for its wrinkle-resistant quality, a particularly important factor in suits and coats that have almost daily wear. The ability of worsteds to take and hold a crease is also important, particularly in men's slacks. Wools are slow to show soil because of the fiber's resilience. Since moisture is absorbed slowly, many liquids can be sponged from the fabric before it dries, thereby taking the soil particles with the liquid. It has been explained that the covering of the scales makes the fiber naturally water repellent; hence, liquid will run off the fabric if it is slanted. Wool's low static quality is also a factor in resisting soil. Once soil becomes embedded in the fabric, it can generally be removed by washing or dry cleaning. Improvements in shrinkage control and resistance to felting will make laundering of wool easier. (See Chapter 16 for simple rules to follow in the care of wool.)

The Wool Bureau, Inc., has been instrumental in perfecting and introducing to the trade a permanent creasing (and pleating) process for all-wool garments. Known as the WB-4 process, it is a chemical add-on which imparts a "memory" to the wool fiber, helping it to keep its crease throughout the life of the garment.

HAND

The soft, springy, warm feel (hand) of wool is pleasing to the buyer of wool fabrics. To be sure, the softness or stiffness of a fabric is controlled not only by the choice of fibers but also by the kind of manufacturing processing they receive. In general, large-diameter fibers produce a stiffer hand than fine fibers. Large slub or nubbed yarns present a more bumpy surface texture than smooth, even yarns. A woolen usually has a more hairy surface than a worsted, which has had the short fibers removed from the yarn. Therefore, woolen feels warmer, generally softer, less firm, and less smooth than a worsted. The amount of other fibers mixed or blended with wool may affect the hand.

COMFORT AND PROTECTION

Why wool is warm and therefore comfortable, particularly in cold weather, has been explained. The same principle of trapped air is applicable to napped wool blankets And yet wool fabrics can be woven or knitted so that they are so loose and porous that air transmission is good. The wearer is protected from sudden chill by the wool fabric's natural water repellency and slow absorptive quality. The fact that wool is slow to ignite protects the user of wool pile rugs and wool blankets.

SUITABILITY

Wool fabrics are made in many weights, from the filmiest sheer veiling to the heaviest overcoating.

Sheer fabrics, such as wool georgette, voile, featherweight tweeds, lightweight crepes, and some sheer wool meshes, can be worn by the woman with a full figure. The stout woman may feel that wool jersey is too stretchy. She may have had jerseys that bulged at the elbows and knees. But this objection can be overcome by lining or bonding a knitted garment by the fabric-to-fabric method.

Certain fabrics, such as checked or plain tweeds, are adapted to sports clothes, depending on the climate. Smooth, luxurious flannels and broadcloths are suitable for dress wear for men, again depending on the style and the time of year and climate. Women can look as trim and tailored as men, because men's suitings (some in lighter weight) are being used extensively for women's suits. Wool or blends with wool make warm, comfortable sweaters.

The hard-finished worsteds are good for the tailored woman, because these fabrics tailor easily, hold their shape, and press better than woolens. A woolen in men's suiting requires frequent pressing, since creases do not stay long in the cloth. As a class, worsteds are more durable than woolens, and they are generally more expensive. (For a more complete discussion of men's suitings, see Chapter 18.)

MINOR HAIR (SPE-CIALTY) FIBERS

Hair fibers classed with wool as specialty fibers by the FTC include various breeds of goats and camels. In addition, less-used hairs from the cow and horse, fur from rabbits, and feathers from the duck, goose, and ostrich are not to be overlooked. (See the requirements of the Wool Products Labeling Act, p. 267.)

288
Fabric
Construction
and
Buying
Motives

Microscopically, the medullas show in hair fibers and differ from wool. (See Appendix A.) In some, hair scales are faintly visible; in others they are not.

A list of hair fibers and their most common uses follows.

TABLE 12-2. Hair Fibers and Their Common Uses

Fiber	Animal	Major Source	Uses (alone and in blends)
Mohair	Angora goat	Asia Minor (Turkey) and the Cape Colony, Texas	Upholsteries, draperies, spreads, linings, braids, men's suits, riding habits, brushed-wool sweaters, gloves, mittens, socks, imitation astrakhan, plush
Alpaca	Camel-like ruminants	South America (Peru)	Men's coat linings, women's furlike fabrics, dress goods, linings
Llama	"	South America	Dress goods, sweaters
Vicuña	"	South America	Sweaters, fleece fabrics, coats (very rare)
Cashmere	Cashmere goat	Himalaya Mountains, Tibet, Kashmir	Shawls, sweaters, coats
Camel's hair	Camel	Asia, Africa, China, Russia	Oriental rugs, sweaters, blankets, coats, gloves, piece goods
Horsehair	Horse	South America	Braid, upholsteries, fur
Rabbit hair	Angora rabbit	Turkey	Felt, knitted garments

MOHAIR

Mohair is obtained from the Angora goat, which is raised in the southwestern United States, South Africa, and Turkey. The United States is producing good grades domestically.

Mohair comes in different grades. Adult and kid hairs are the broad classifications. Kid hair, clipped twice a year, is the finest grade; adult hair, very strong and resilient, is the lowest grade.

The fiber, which ranges from six to twelve inches for a full year's growth, is smooth and lustrous, because the scales scarcely overlap.[20] Since mohair has fewer surface scales and less crimp than sheep's wool, it is more lustrous, smooth, and dust-resistant. The bundles of fibrils in the cortex are similar to wool, and the cells in the medulla are few in a good grade fiber. Chemical properties are similar to those of wool.

Mohair can be used alone or blended with wool and other fibers. It is desirable for men's suitings, women's dresses, coats, and sweaters, net and braid trimmings, the pile of rugs, automobile and furniture upholstery, draperies, lap robes, and stuffing around the springs in furniture.[21]

[20] Von Bergen and Mauersberger, *Wool Handbook* p. 221.
[21] "Mohair, Distinguished Fiber of Unlimited Uses," a pamphlet by the American Wool Council, Inc.

FIGURE 12.8. The Kashmir goat provides the fleece for cashmere fabric.

CASHMERE

Those who have worn cashmere sweaters or coats appreciate its warmth and lightness. The fleece is grown on a small, short-legged animal of the high plateaus of central Asia in Chinese Mongolia, Soviet Outer Mongolia, Iran, and Afghanistan.[22] The finest and most expensive fibers come from the Mongolian regions. These fibers are used mostly in sweaters. The coarser fibers from Iran and Afghanistan are used in woven cloth for coats and sports jackets.

We read of Kashmir shawls by the Roman Caesars, woven of cashmere from the Vale of Kashmir. Actually, very little cashmere now comes from the state of Kashmir, India.

Cashmere is naturally gray, brown, or white (white is very rare). Fleece of the animal is never shorn but is plucked or combed out by hand. When the animal molts, it rubs itself against the shrubs to relieve itself of itching. The fibers adhering to shrubs are picked off and used.[23] In handpicking, much long hair from the animal's outer coat is mixed with the soft inner fibers. These coarse outer fibers can be removed by special machinery.

Fibers range from 1 1/4 to 3 1/2 inches long. The scales are hardly visible under the microscope. The diagonal edges of the scales are more or less sharply bent. The cortical layer is striated and filled with color pigment. Some medullas are continuous. Chemical properties of cashmere are similar to those of wool.

[22] *New York Times*, February 2, 1973.
[23] *Cashmere* (New York: Bernhard Ulmann Co.).

290
Fabric
Construction
and
Buying
Motives

The amount of fibers from a single animal is very small: A male produces about four ounces and a female about two ounces per year. It is estimated that fleece of from four to six animals would be needed for a sweater.[24] Small wonder, then, that articles of 100 percent cashmere must be high priced.

CAMEL'S HAIR

There are two types of camels: the dromedary, which is not heavy enough to produce usable fiber for cloth manufacture, and the Bactrian, the heavier, two-humped, pack-carrying species whose hair is suitable for cloth. This animal lives in all parts of Asia, from the Arabian Sea to Siberia, Turkestan, Tibet, Mongolia, Manchuria, and to all parts of China.[25]

The camel has a fleece with an outer layer of coarse hair and an inner layer of finer hair like a cashmere goat. The inner fibers, called *down*, run 1 to 5 inches, whereas the outer fibers range up to 15 inches. Down is used for clothing. The camel is never sheared or clipped like sheep. At certain seasons, when the warmth of the body expands the skin, the animal sheds his hair. The hair is gathered from the ground. Only when soft under-fibers or down is desired must the camel be plucked.[26] A combing process separates the down from the hair. Wool is often added to camel's hair to give it strength in spinning into yarn. However, the more wool added, the coarser the fabric becomes. Polo cloth, by the Worumbo Manufacturing Company, is an illustration of a fine camel's hair and wool blend. Also, the camel's natural pale tan hair is sometimes blended with clear white cashmere, llama, or some of the fine, rare wools for the purpose of obtaining light-colored fabrics. Camel's hair can also be blended with cheaper grades of fibers to bring down the cost. One of the most common uses of camel's hair is in men's and women's coats, because it has a high insulation quality and wears satisfactorily. It may also be found in oriental rugs, blankets, and sweaters.

THE LLAMA FAMILY

This family is large and may be called "the camel of South America." A few members of this family are: the alpaca (the closest relative to the llama), the huarizo and misti (hybrids of the llama and alpaca), and the guanaco and vicuña. The family inhabits the heights of the Andes Mountains. These animals have some of the characteristics of the camel, yet there is no real proof that the camel and llama have the same origin.

The llama and the alpaca are domesticated members of the family, and the guanaco and vicuña are the wild members. Most scientists believe the llama and alpaca to be direct descendants of the guanaco, and the vicuña to be a distinct species.[27] Until shearing time, alpacas roam the range during the day and return to primitive corrals at night. November and December, the spring in llamaland, is shearing time. This is done by hand,

[24] Ibid.

[25] *The Story of Camel Hair* (New York: S. Stroock & Co., Inc.), p. 3.

[26] Ibid., p. 11.

[27] *Llamas and Llamaland* (New York: S. Stroock & Co., Inc.).

half a fleece at a time. Sorting and baling follow. Fleeces of llamas are fine and lustrous but not curly, and the fiber is strong in relation to its diameter. Scales of the fiber are only partly visible and, like the camel's hair, the fiber has a medulla down the center.

The alpaca fibers are white to black in color, and are 8, 12, 16, or even 30 inches in length. Llama fibers are black to brown, the guanaco is reddish brown, and the vicuña cinnamon brown (generally used in natural color because of its resistance to dye). Since the vicuña has only recently been domesticated, in small numbers and under government control, production of the fiber is limited. These animals live at great heights, and are found in Peru, Chile, and Bolivia.[28] The vicuña, which produces the world's most valuable specialty fiber known, is protected by law. Only the most opulent consumer can buy a coat of vicuña. Knitting yarns and knit goods are possible uses.

Llama fabrics include women's coats, suits, and dresses; men's summer suits, topcoats, and overcoats.

MUSK OX

The federal government is protecting a herd of musk ox, similar to the bison, which is being raised in Alaska. One domesticated breed, the white-faced, has soft, fine, grayish colored fleece similar to cashmere.

MISCELLANEOUS HAIR FIBERS

Cow hair, obtained from our own slaughtered animals and from Japan, England, Canada, and Spain, is used for rug cushions, felts, and coarse rugs.

We import *horsehair* from Argentina and Canada. Horsehair is used principally in interlining for men's suits and coats, and as a stuffing for upholstered furniture.

The *Angora rabbit's fur* has proved very popular for knitting. It can also be blended with wool for filling yarn of a fabric. Such a cloth will feel soft and luxurious. The United States, England, the Netherlands, and Belgium raise the Angora rabbit.

Common rabbit's hair is used for felt hats. The most desirable is the white-faced rabbit, found on this continent and in Europe, parts of China, and Japan. The cheaper gray, wild rabbit's fur, from New Zealand, Australia, and Great Britain, is also used.

FEATHERS AND DOWN

Goose and duck feathers and down have always had considerable use for stuffing pillows, comforters, and upholstery. Sometimes down is blended with wool to produce a luxurious effect in fabrics.

SUMMARY The consumer who selects a wool fabric should be willing to pay for wearing quality, if that is the major factor governing the decision. A good-quality wool is not cheap, and prices are tending to rise. A good

---

[28] *Vicuna, The World's Finest Fabric* (New York: S. Stroock & Co., Inc., 1946).

292
Fabric
Construction
and
Buying
Motives

grade of reprocessed or reused wool, however, is sometimes superior to a poor grade of new wool. Blends of wool with man-made and natural fibers have grown in importance. The consumer should read the percentages of each fiber and any selling points on the label. His or her own judgment and that of the salesperson will help to decide whether the particular blend will satisfy his or her needs.

REVIEW QUES-TIONS

1. (a) What is the definition of wool as given in the Wool Products Labeling Act?
   (b) What are "specialty fibers"?
2. (a) What is the difference between *domestic* wool and *territory* wool?
   (b) In what respects is Australian wool superior to wool grown in the United States?
   (c) What is the difference between Australian merino wool and English Lincolnshire or Leicestershire wool? For what purposes is each used?
3. (a) Tell the differences between new wool and reused wool.
   (b) Define reprocessed wool.
   (c) How does reprocessed wool differ from new wool? From reused wool?
4. What factors determine the grade or quality of wool fiber?
5. (a) How do worsteds differ from woolens in manufacture?
   (b) What are the chief characteristics of worsteds?
   (c) What are the chief characteristics of woolens?
6. (a) Name five fabrics made of woolen yarn.
   (b) Name five fabrics made of worsted yarn.
7. In what ways do the length, diameter, and strength of the wool fiber affect the final cloth?
8. What part do the scales on the fiber play in the manufacture of wool goods?
9. What factors should be considered in judging the durability of wool yarn?
10. (a) For what purpose is reused wool important?
    (b) If a label reads "all wool," what should the consumer infer?
11. Why are wool fabrics comfortable?
12. What laundering instructions should a salesperson be able to give a purchaser of a wool fabric?
13. Define mohair, alpaca, cashmere, fleece wool, pulled wool, merino wool, noils, scouring, tops, yarn dye.

PROJECT

Make a tabular presentation comparing the physical and chemical properties of the four major natural textile fibers. Use the following form:

Physical Characteristics	Cotton	Linen	Silk	Wool
Microscopic appearance				
Length of fiber				
Diameter				
Color				
Luster				
Strength				
Elasticity				
Heat conductivity				
Hygroscopic moisture				

EXPERI- MENTS	1. Examine a wool fiber under the microscope. Draw the fiber as you see it.

EXPERI-
MENTS

1. Examine a wool fiber under the microscope. Draw the fiber as you see it.
2. Boil several wool yarns or a sample of wool fabric in a 10 percent solution of sodium hydroxide for five minutes. Describe the result.
3. Boil a wool-and-cotton fabric for five minutes in a 10 percent solution of sodium hydroxide. Describe the result.
4. Place several wool yarns in concentrated sulfuric acid for five minutes. Note the result.
5. Unravel yarns both ways from the fabric. Untwist the yarn. Is it loosely or tightly twisted? Are the fibers parallel, or do they run in every direction? Are the fibers less than two inches or more than two inches in length? Are the fibers all about the same length? Is the yarn a worsted or a woolen?

GLOSSARY

Alpaca—Domesticated member of the llama family, species of "South American camel."

Breaker—A machine containing a tooth cylinder used to remove all loose dirt, sand, and the like, and to separate the whole fleece into small sections.

Camel's hair—Fibers from the Bactrian, a two-humped, pack-carrying species.

Carding—A process of opening and cleaning the fibers and putting them in a sliver or web preparatory to spinning.

Carpet or braid wool—Very coarse wool from Turkey, Siberia, China, and South America, primarily used in carpets; not suited for clothing.

Cashmere—Fleece from the cashmere goat of Tibet, Mongolia, China, Iran, India, and Iraq.

Cheviot—A woolen or worsted fabric in twill weave originally made of wool from sheep of the Cheviot Hills along the English-Scottish border. It has a slightly rough, napped surface and is used for men's and women's coats and suits.

Chlorinated wool—Woolens chemically treated to decrease shrinkage and to increase affinity for dyes.

Clips of knitted fabric—New wool; never used or worn in any way.

Combing—Removing short wool fibers from the sliver and making the fibers parallel.

Cortex—Cortical cells in the wool fiber consisting of bundles of fibrils.

Covert—A woolen or worsted coating or suiting in twill weave made with two-ply yarns. One of the yarns in the ply may be white and the other colored. This gives a flecked appearance. Covert has recently been made in solid color. It is very durable and is also made in cotton fabrics for work clothes.

Crimp—Natural wave of a wool fiber.

Domestic wools—From the eastern and middle-western states.

Donegal tweed—Originally a thick woolen homespun tweed woven by hand by Irish peasants. Now it refers to a tweed in plain weave characterized by colorful slubs woven into the fabric.

Drawing—Attenuating a sliver till it becomes narrower and narrower. Drawing is synonymous with *drafting*.

Dry decating—A process of setting the luster of a wool fabric.

Finished worsted—Fabric with a softened finish. It is synonymous with *semifinished*.

Flannel—An all-wool fabric of woolen or of worsted yarns, finished with a soft snap that practically obliterates the weave. It is also made in cotton.

Fleece wool—Wool shorn from the live sheep. It is superior to *pulled wool*.

Gabardine—A tightly woven twilled worsted with a raised diagonal wale on the right side. It can also be cotton, rayon, and blends or mixtures.

Garnetting—Shredding wool fabrics into a fibrous state, prior to remanufacture into woolen yarn.

Gigging—Raising nap by means of teasels.

Grading—Determining by touch the fineness of the diameters of individual fibers. *Wool tops* are graded in this fashion. Efforts are now being made to grade wool in the grease by this method.

293

294
Fabric
Construction
and
Buying
Motives

Grease—Natural grease adhering to the wool fiber, which must be removed by scouring.

Guanaco—A wild animal of the llama family. See *Llama family*.

Hard-finished—A term applied to woolen, worsted, and cotton fabrics that are finished without a nap. Synonym: *clear-finished*.

Homespun—A coarse, nubby woolen in plain weave.

Horsehair—Fibers for the most part from Canadian and Argentine horses.

Jersey—A wool fabric, usually in stockinette stitch, used for blouses, dresses, and basque shirts. See Glossary, Chapter 6.

Kemp—Short-fibered, harsh wool, used principally in carpets.

Keratin—A protein substance that is the chief constituent of the wool fiber.

Lamb's wool—Soft, resilient wool from lambs seven to eight months old. It is used in fine-grade woolen fabrics.

Llama family—A large family of "South American camels." It includes the llama, alpaca, huarizo and misti, guanaco, and vicuña.

Medulla—Honeycombed cellular section found in medium and coarse wools.

Merino wools—From merino sheep of Australia, South Africa, and South America.

Mohair—Hair fibers from the Angora goat.

Napping—Raising nap by means of wire bristles.

New wool—Wool not previously woven, knitted, or felted into a wool product.

Noils—Short wool fibers separated from the long fibers by combing.

Opener—See *Breaker*.

Paddock—A large enclosed area for sheep grazing. The paddock system is common in Australia.

Perching—Visual inspection of wool fabrics.

Polo cloth—Trade name for a fine camel's hair and wool blend by the Worumbo Manufacturing Company.

Pulled wool—Wool taken from pelts of dead animals by means of chemicals.

Rabbit hair—Fur from the angora rabbit.

Reprocessed wool—Includes scraps and clips of woven and felted fabrics made of previously unused wool. It must be labeled "Reprocessed wool."

Reused wool—Old wool that has been made into a wool product and used by consumers, then cleaned, garnetted, and remade into merchandise. It must be labeled "Reused wool."

Scales—Protective covering of the wool fiber.

Scouring—The process of freeing wool from dirt, grease, and swint.

Serge—Worsted fabric in even twill with the wale showing on both sides. It is piece-dyed to a solid color. It may be cotton, rayon, or silk.

Sharkskin—A wool fabric in twill weave, originally made of yarns of two colors; it is so-called because of its resemblance to sharkskin leather. Used for men's and women's suitings and slacks, it comes in a clear or semifinished worsted. Patterns include plaids, stripes, nailheads, and bird's eye. It is made also in man-made fibers and blends.

Sheared wool—See *Fleece wool*.

Shoddy—See *Reused wool*.

Sorting—Separating wool fibers by touch according to fineness of fibers.

Southwestern wools—From Texas, New Mexico, Arizona, and southern California.

Specialty fibers—Hair fibers from various breeds of goats and camels. Also included are cow- and horsehair, fur from rabbits, and feathers of the duck, goose, and ostrich.

Swint—Perspiration on the wool fiber.

Territory wools—From the Rocky Mountain plateau states.

Tops—Long wool fibers in the combed sliver.

Tropical worsted—A lightweight, plain weave suiting for men's and women's summer wear. To be labeled "tropical worsted," it must be all-wool worsted. It is made in a variety of fiber blends and mixtures.

Unfinished worsted—A worsted fabric finished with a nap.

Vicuña—Wild member of the llama family. It produces the world's most valuable specialty fiber.

Virgin wool—A term applicable to fabrics or products that have not used any wastes from preliminary processing of new wool.

Wash-and-wear—A wool fabric that is shrink-resistant, will not felt or fuzz in washing, has good wrinkle resistance and recovery, and has good tensile strength. See *Wash-and-wear*, Chapter 7.

Wet decating—A finishing process to add luster to wool fabrics.

Whipcord—A twill-weave worsted fabric with a pronounced diagonal wale on the right side, more pronounced than in gabardine. It may also be made in cotton. It is used for riding habits and outdoor wear.

Wool—Fibers from lambs, sheep, and other animals that are used for clothing. It is unlike carpet wool, which is much coarser and unsuitable for clothing. "Wool" refers to fleece wool used for the first time in the complete manufacture of a wool product.

Wool Products Labeling Act—A law requiring that all wool products moving in "commerce" shall be labeled. Carpets, rugs, and upholstery fabrics containing wool come under the TFPIA.

Wool rugs—A wool floor covering made of carded yarn.

Woolen—A class of wool fabrics made of short-staple carded yarns.

Worsted—A wool fabric made of long-staple combed yarn.

Rayon and Acetate

and

the Consumer

13

Mrs. Greene went to her favorite department store in response to an advertisement for acetate satin and Avril rayon twill by the yard. She knew that satins and twills were often used for coat linings, and she needed a new one for her wool tweed coat. When she saw both twills and satins, she was in a quandary. The acetate satin was heavier and somewhat stiffer than the Avril rayon twill. Which fabric should she buy? Both were the right color, and at a price Mrs. Greene was willing to pay. She looked at the care labels attached to the bolts. They read "Dry-clean only," so the labels didn't help her decide which fabric to buy. However, a well-informed salesperson helped her to make a decision to buy the Avril rayon twill rather than the acetate satin because Avril rayon fibers are high tenacity—stronger than acetate—and the fabric is made in twill weave—stronger than satin weave.

RAYON   *HISTORY AND PRODUCTION OF RAYON*

Rayon is a generic name of a man-made fiber, coined in 1924 at the National Retail Dry Goods Association (now the National Retail Merchants Association) to replace the names "artificial silk, fiber silk, and glos." These terms had been applied to the man-made fiber since its discovery in 1884 by Count Hilaire de Chardonnet, who dissolved nitrocellulose in alcohol and ether in the hope of producing silk. He made a vegetable fiber, not an animal fiber as is silk. But his discovery led to the making of a fiber by the nitrocellulose process, one which is no longer used in the United States. The fibers were highly flammable and especially weak when wet. By 1924 there were other methods of making this man-made fiber, but the term "rayon" was intended to apply to all methods then used. For making each type of rayon, cellulose, the fibrous substance of all forms of plant life, was the basic ingredient. The cellulose was derived from either cotton seed after the long fibers have been removed by ginning or from spruce and other soft woods. Today the cellulose used comes almost entirely from the latter source.

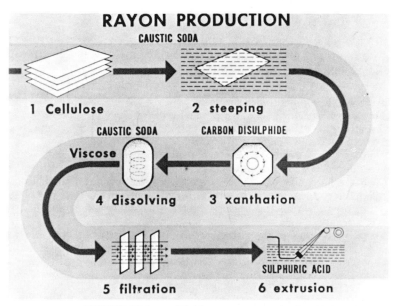

RAYON PRODUCTION

CAUSTIC SODA

1 Cellulose

2 steeping

CAUSTIC SODA

CARBON DISULPHIDE

Viscose

4 dissolving

3 xanthation

SULPHURIC ACID

5 filtration

6 extrusion

FIGURE 13.1. a. (1) Viscose rayon production begins with cellulosic sheets. (2) The sheets are steeped in caustic soda. (3) After a given period of time, the excess caustic soda solution is pressed out and the sheets are shredded into fine crumbs. After the crumbs have aged, they are chuted to tumbling barrels where carbon disulphide is added and a chemical reaction takes place. This is called the xanthation ("zanthation") process. (4) The crumbs are then fed into viscose dissolvers where they are mixed with weak caustic soda and stirred to form a viscose solution. (5) The viscose solution is filtered. (6) It is then pumped to a spinneret for extrusion into a sulphuric acid bath. (Courtesy of Man-Made Fiber Producers Association, Inc.)

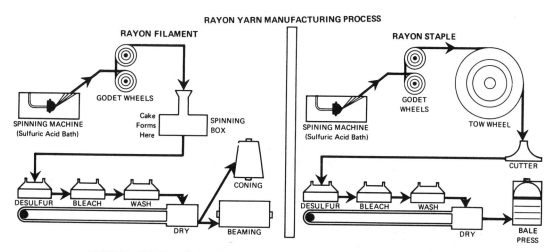

RAYON YARN MANUFACTURING PROCESS

RAYON FILAMENT

GODET WHEELS

Cake Forms Here

SPINNING BOX

SPINNING MACHINE (Sulfuric Acid Bath)

CONING

DESULFUR BLEACH WASH

DRY BEAMING

RAYON STAPLE

GODET WHEELS

TOW WHEEL

SPINING MACHINE (Sulfuric Acid Bath)

CUTTER

DESULFUR BLEACH WASH

DRY

BALE PRESS

FIGURE 13.1 (cont.). b. From the spinning machine or spinneret (step 6) the rayon filament passes into a spinning box as described in the text and then is desulfured, bleached, washed, dried, and stored in cone or beam form ready for marketing or weaving. For rayon staple, the filament goes to a cutter where it is cut into short lengths, called *tow*. This is then desulfured, bleached, washed, dried, and baled, ready to be spun into various types of yarn by the same processes used for natural fibers. (Courtesy FMC Corporation.)

297

298

*Fabric
Construction
and
Buying
Motives*

THE VISCOSE PROCESS OF MAKING RAYON

Three English chemists, Cross, Bevan, and Beadle, discovered this process in 1892, but commercial production did not begin until after the turn of the century. The steps in the process follow:

1. Bleached sulfite wood pulp is cut into sheets.
2. The sheets are steeped in caustic soda; the product is called *alkali cellulose.*
3. It is treated with carbon disulphide; the product is *cellulose xanthate.*
4. It is treated with a weak solution of caustic soda.
5. The honey-colored solution is forced through a spinneret into sulfuric acid, which generates the cellulose in a continuous filament.
6. While the fibers are hardening or after they are hardened, they are stretched to (*a*) reduce the diameter of the fiber, (*b*) to arrange the molecules in the fiber in a more orderly fashion, (*c*) to permit the fiber to stretch without breaking, and (*d*) to increase tensile strength.
7. (*a*) For filament yarn, most of the viscose rayon fiber is twisted into yarn by the *box method.* Here a container, called a box, revolves, and centrifugal force throws the group of filaments to the side of the box, putting in twist at the same time. The yarn emerges from the box in hollow form resembling an angel cake. It is then reeled into skeins, washed, bleached, and dried.
   (*b*) For tow, large bundles of monofilament yarn are assembled without twist. This is cut or broken up into desired lengths (up to 8 inches) called "staple fiber" to be spun like natural fibers.

The term *viscose process* is derived from the syrupy, honey-like viscous solution that is extruded through the spinneret. Modifications and improvements have been made and will be discussed later in this chapter. Most rayon is made by the viscose process.

THE CUPRAMMONIUM PROCESS OF MAKING RAYON

Louis Henri Despaisses developed this process in France in 1890, and the process was later improved. The following steps are necessary:

1. The purified cellulose is dissolved in copper oxide and ammonia.
2. The dark blue solution is forced through spinnerets.
3. Filaments (fibers) are hardened in mild sulfuric acid.
4. They are stretched as in the case of viscose.
5. (*a*) For filament yarn, most of the cuprammonium rayon is twisted into yarn by the continuous spinning method. Several filaments passing through the spinneret are grouped together, the number depending on the size of the yarn

FIGURE 13.2. Spinneret. (Photograph courtesy of FMC Corporation.)

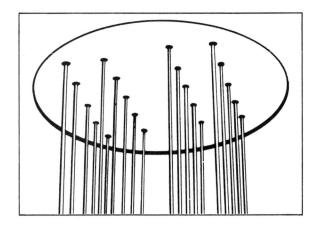

FIGURE 13.3. Man-made fibers are created by forcing melted polymers through small holes in a disc called a spinneret. The molten polymer emerges from the holes as bundles of smooth, strong filaments. They are then set by a heat treatment. These are called filament yarns. Nylon, polyester, and triacetate are often used in filament form. (Courtesy Celanese Fibers Marketing Co.)

required. These grouped filaments are wound on spools and then rewound on other spools as they are being twisted. They are then wound onto bobbins for weaving.

(b) Tow and staple fiber are produced as in the case of viscose.

Viscose and cuprammonium rayons are regenerated rayons because their basic material is cellulose and the final product is vegetable fibers. In other words, the reconversion of the soluble compound to cellulose causes rayon to be referred to as a regenerated cellulose fiber. The Federal Trade Commission uses the term "regenerated cellulose" in its definition of rayon: "Rayon is a manufactured fiber composed of regenerated cellulose as well as manufactured fibers composed of regenerated cellulose in which substituents have replaced not more than 15 percent of the hydrogens of the hydroxyl groups." This definition of the generic fiber rayon conforms to the authority given the FTC by the Textile Fiber Products Identification Act.

FIGURE 13.4. Extrusion of viscose fibers into a hardening bath. (Photograph courtesy of FMC Corporation.)

Rayon fibers are *wet spun*, meaning that the filaments extruded from the spinneret pass directly into chemical baths for solidifying or regeneration rather than being solidified in the air.

MODIFIED RAYONS

Basic technical developments in the field of cellulosic fibers have caused rayon to achieve renewed importance to the consumer. These developments include high-tenacity rayon, which has increased its durability in apparel; rayon fibers with permanent crimp, which are adaptable to fabrics of a bulky texture; cellulosic-based fibers with a basic inner structure similar to the natural cellulosic fibers; and dry spinning, which results in a fiber that has an extremely high tensile and wet strength.

HIGH-TENACITY RAYON

Viscose rayon filaments can be "modified" by chemical treatment while they are in a plastic state to give them high tenacity. (See Chapter 2.) Trademark names of high-tenacity modified rayons are Cordura and Avril.

The cross-linking method, also described in Chapter 2, produces another high-tenacity rayon, which, although it has dimensional stability, has a tenacity that is not so high as the high-wet-strength type discussed later. This product, Corval, is made by Courtaulds North America, Inc. It shows greater dimensional stability in washing than regular rayon.

CRIMPED-FIBERED RAYON

Crimped (viscose process) rayon is achieved by several different processes, each of which modifies the internal structure of the fiber. In one method the crimp is due to an asymmetry in the molecular structure of the fiber. The crimp is permanent because it is an integral part of the fiber itself. Crimped Fibro by Courtaulds, Ltd., is produced by this method. Crimped fibers when used in dress goods are warm and soft, and may be solid-colored or printed.

HIGH-WET STRENGTH RAYON

This type of modified rayon has been commercially available since 1961. In a study of the natural cellulosic fibers, it was found that these fibers are characterized by a very fine fibril structure and that the molecular orientation is very regular. Scientists know that natural cellulosic fibers like cotton have increased tensile strength when wet, a low swelling factor, and good dimensional stability. So they directed their efforts to develop man-made cellulosic fibers whose structure would be similar to the natural cellulosics. On the other hand, a study of the properties of man-made cellulosic fibers has contributed to the improvement of the natural cellulosic types.

This type of fiber—referred to as a high-wet modulus rayon—is sold under the trade names Avril, Nupron, Xena, and Zantrel.

A 50/50 blend of high-wet strength rayon and carded cotton produces a fabric with the esthetic quality, the hand, and appearance of 100 percent combed cotton at a lower price. Hence, style can be added to a cotton fabric, and at the same time carded cotton can be upgraded to the combed category. Furthermore, to enhance their beauty, these fabrics can be mercerized, because they are more resistant to caustic soda than regular rayon. Fabrics can be stabilized by compressive shrinkage (as is the case with cotton) and treated with resins for minimum care.

SAPONIFIED RAYON

Saponified rayon is made by converting cellulose to cellulose acetate (see below), which is dissolved in an organic solvent for extruding. The extruded filaments of cellulose acetate are reconverted to cellulose. This chemical regeneration process is called *saponification.* Saponified rayon has exceptionally high strength, good shape retention, fine textures in lightweight fabrics, and good dimensional stability. Its fibers when treated are known as regenerated cellulose, yet its yarn can be finer than silk. It does not shrink or stretch; it is easier to dye because the fiber is saponified; and it resists sunlight and chemicals. Since it feels a bit clammy, it is not used for apparel. It has been used in blends for curtains and draperies.

ACID-DYEABLE FILAMENT AND STAPLE

The acid-dyeable filament and staple rayon products developed by American Enka have all the physical properties of regular rayon. In addition, they can be dyed with acid and premetalized dyes as well as those generally used on regular rayon. Probably the greatest advantage of these products is the possibility for new styling.

ACETATE AND TRI-ACETATE   Acetate is the generic name of a man-made fiber whose basic ingredient is also cellulose. The acetate solution was discovered by Maudin and Schutzenburger in 1869, but it was not used for spinning commercial fibers until after World War I. The British Cellulose & Chemical Manufacturing Company had utilized this method to make dope for airplane wings. Dope prevented the fabric from deteriorating in the ultraviolet rays of the sun. A coating of varnish was the necessary weatherproofing. After World War I, the factories that had made this material would have closed had it not been for the discovery of a method of making yarn by a similar process.

PRODUCTION PROCESS

Briefly, the steps are as follows:

1. Wood or cotton linters are treated with a solution of acetate anhydride in glacial acetic acid to form cellulose acetate.
2. The ripened product is plunged into cold water, where the cellulose acetate separates into white flakes.
3. The flakes are washed and dried.
4. They are then dissolved in acetone into a liquid solution and mixed.
5. The syrupy solution, either colorless or dope dyed, is forced through the holes of a spinneret and hardened by the evaporation of the acetone in warm air (dry spinning) to form a vegetable and chemical fiber.
6. (*a*) The hair-like filaments are then stretched and twisted into filament yarn and wound on a bobbin by means of the continuous spinning method (used for cuprammonium rayon).
   (*b*) Instead of twisting the continuous filaments into yarn, they may be assembled as tow and cut into controlled lengths of staple fiber.

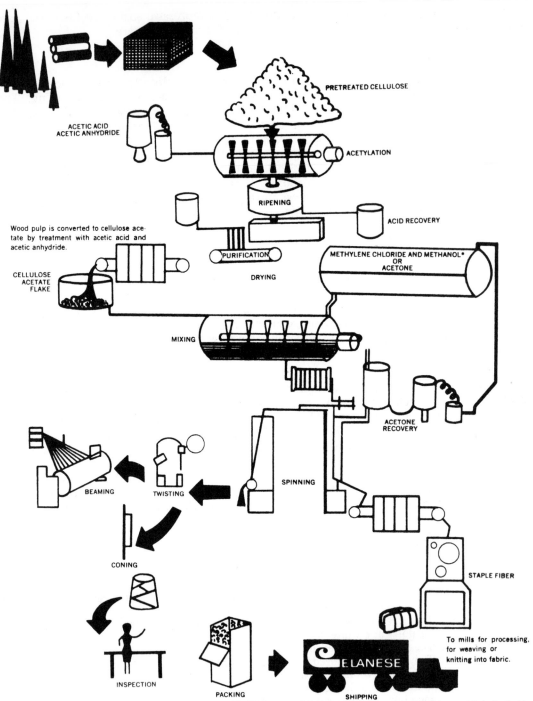

PRETREATED CELLULOSE

ACETIC ACID
ACETIC ANHYDRIDE

ACETYLATION

RIPENING

ACID RECOVERY

Wood pulp is converted to cellulose acetate by treatment with acetic acid and acetic anhydride.

PURIFICATION

DRYING

METHYLENE CHLORIDE AND METHANOL*
OR
ACETONE

CELLULOSE
ACETATE
FLAKE

MIXING

ACETONE
RECOVERY

BEAMING

TWISTING

SPINNING

CONING

STAPLE FIBER

INSPECTION

PACKING

SHIPPING

To mills for processing, for weaving or knitting into fabric.

FIGURE 13.5. Acetate and Triacetate Manufacturing Process. (Courtesy Celanese Fibers Marketing Co.)

*NOTE: Acetate and triacetate are both derived from cellulose by combining cellulose with acetate from acetic acid and acetic anhydride. However, in forming acetate, the cellulose acetate is dissolved in acetone for spinning; in forming triacetate the cellulose acetate is dissolved in a mixture of methylene, chloride and methanol for spinning. Triacetate fibers contain a higher ratio of acetic acid than do acetate fibers (92%, as against 80% in acetate).

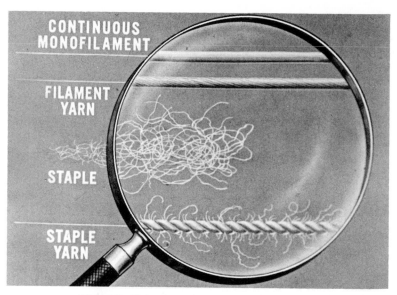

FIGURE 13.6. Forms in which fibers are utilized, in varying deniers, are (1) Continuous monofilament: single filament. (2) Filament yarn: continuous strands of two or more monofilaments which have been twisted together. (3) Staple: discontinuous lengths of fibers which have been cut or broken from large bundles of continuous monofilaments. (4) Spun staple yarn: staple fiber which has been aligned, combined, and twisted into continuous lengths. About half of the man-made fibers used in the United States are in the form of continuous monofilaments or filament yarns, and the remaining half are used in the form of staple. (As in the case of yarn spun from staple, continuous monofilaments and filament yarns are utilized in weaving and knitting fabrics.) Courtesy of Man-Made Fiber Producers Association, Inc.

Since both filament yarns and staple yarns can be produced in any desired weight, size, length, and color, they have a uniformity not found in cotton, wool, and flax.

Filament yarns are used to make sleek, smooth textures such as satins, chiffons, taffetas, and moirés. Staple fibers are used to produce spun yarns for fabrics such as gabardines, challis, and crash in clothing and for a variety of fabrics used for upholstery, draperies, and bedspreads. Staple fiber cut in short lengths produces a fabric that looks like cotton, whereas in long lengths the fabric looks like worsted.

VARIATIONS

Acetate can be modified to give the fibers special characteristics. As we have seen, they can be saponified to become high-tenacity rayon. They can also be crimped by fusing with heat. A permanent crimping process has been developed that can be used in blends with wool in cotton skirts, dresses, and shirtings.

PRODUCERS

Acetate fibers were first commercially produced in the United States in 1924 by the Celanese Corporation. Today, other producers include Du Pont, Eastman, American Viscose, American Enka, and Courtaulds. Trade names include Chromspun, Eston, Acele, Avicolor, and Celaperm.

304
*Fabric
Construction
and
Buying
Motives*

TRIACETATE

One of the consumer's objections to acetate was that it fuses when pressed with a hot iron. Triacetate was the answer to that problem. It was first produced by the Celanese Corporation in the United States in 1954.

Like acetate, triacetate is derived from cellulose by combining cellulose with acetate from acetic acid and acetic anhydride. Then the cellulose acetate is dissolved in a mixture of methylene chloride and methano (for spinning). The solution is extruded from the spinneret and the solvent is evaporated in warm air (dry spinning). Triacetate fibers contain a higher ratio of acetate to cellulose than do acetate fibers. Once classed as a modified acetate, now the FTC permits the use of triacetate as a generic name of the fiber provided "not less than 92 percent of the hydroxyl groups are acetylated." This means that triacetate is a thermoplastic material that contains three acetate components.

We are all familiar with 100 percent Arnel triacetate jersey—its minimum-care characteristics; its good colorfastness to light and washing; its basic stability in washing; its relatively low cost; its ability to be pressed at a much higher temperature than regular acetate; its permanency in holding pleats. Yet, even Arnel is not perfect in all respects. It has relatively limited abrasion resistance and tensile strength. But it is the modified rayons and acetates that have helped rayon and acetate to compete with other man-made and natural fibers.

**CHARAC-
TERISTICS
OF RAYON
AND
ACETATE
FIBERS
AND TRI-
ACETATE**

MICROSCOPIC APPEARANCE

Under the microscope, viscose rayon has even, rodlike fibers. Small, lengthwise striations, like shadows, are distinguishing features of bright or lustrous viscose. In viscose rayon that is made dull, the fibers become specked as with pepper.

Under the microscope, acetate fibers also appear even and rodlike. In cross section the fiber is similar to the clover leaf. The lustrous type does not seem so glossy as do the regenerated rayons. There are heavy grooves or line marks running the length of the fiber. (See Appendix A.) Arnel's lengthwise microscopic view is much like regular acetate, but its cross-sectional view has less distinct cloverleaf configurations.

Cuprammonium rayon fibers are even in diameter and rodlike, but with no lengthwise markings. When delustered, the surface of the fiber is covered with fine pigment. Under the microscope the fiber looks peppered. (See Appendix A.)

The modified rayons Avril and Zantrel are cylindrical in cross section. Other characteristics of rayon and acetate appear in Table 13.1.

**RAYON,
ACETATE,
AND
TRI-
ACETATE
YARNS**

KINDS

The kinds of yarn can be classified as follows:

1. Filament rayon, acetate yarns are made of continuous filaments grouped together so that they lie parallel. Because they are all long, only a very slight twist is needed to hold the fibers together.

TABLE 13-1. Characteristics of Man-Made Cellulosic Fibers

Length of fiber: Continuous, staple controlled to any length desired.

Luster: Normally bright but may be delustered by adding mineral oil or insoluble white pigment to the spinning solution.

Strength: Fairly strong but not as strong as many of the noncellulosic fibers. Normally stronger dry than wet (opposite of cotton and linen). Rayon may be made in four degrees of tenacity: regular, medium, high, and high-wet modulus. The last three are generally stronger than acetate.

Resistance to:

mildew—Fair; acetate more than rayon.

heat—vicose more resistant than cuprammonium or acetate. Acetate shines when pressed at 270° F. Rayon may be ironed at 300° F, or even higher in certain types.

acids—tend to weaken and concentrated acids to destroy; but formic and acetic acids, while injuring acetate, do not injure rayon.

alkalies—potassium permanganate bleach weakens rayon, and ammonia, borax, and phosphate of soda deaden luster of acetates.

light—rayon much the same as cotton, acetate more resistant, triacetate still more.

gas fading—acetate, when solution dyed, is resistant to atmospheric fumes.

moisture aborption—rayon about the same as cotton, acetate somewhat less, triacetate very little.

affinity for dyestuffs—rayon very good with the same dyes used for cotton; acetates require other types of dye.

Thick and thin and slub yarns vary in diameter because they are made of continuous filaments that vary in diameter.[1] Such yarns are novelty yarns. Another type of novelty yarn is made by flattening the yarn so that it has the gleam of crystal. Other novelty yarns include textured and spiral yarns.

2. Filament high-strength yarn is made of a continuous filament chemically or mechanically while in the plastic state. These yarns may be used in hosiery, sports clothes, shirtings, towelings, sailcloth, draperies, filter cloths, football uniforms, belts, tire-cord fabrics, and coverings for elastic yarns. (See p. 300.) The high-wet strength modified rayons are good blenders (with cotton in particular). Minimum-care finishes employ resins in these rayons much the same as in all-cotton.

3. Spun yarn is spun from staple fibers. Such fibers are sometimes combined with one or more of the natural or newer synthetic fibers. This mass of short fibers gathered together has to be straightened before being twisted into yarn. Spun yarns are tightly twisted to hold the short fibers together. The ends of the fibers project from the yarn to make a fabric with a fuzzy surface.

4. Combination yarns can be made with rayon and acetate yarns combined in ply form (often in different degrees of twist), or with rayon yarns combined with yarns of another fiber. It should be remembered that filament or spun yarns can be composed of fiber blends.

5. Textured and novelty rayon yarns can be made. The bulky types are used in pile fabrics particularly. Skyloft is a bulked continuous filament rayon yarn by Enka; Loftura is a slub voluminized filament acetate yarn by Eastman.

---

[1] Spun yarns may also be made thick and thin and slubbed.

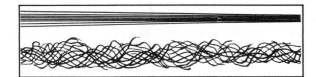

FIGURE 13.7. Flat filament, compared with textured filament. (Courtesy Celanese Fibers Marketing Co.)

FIGURE 13.8. The two cones of bulk-textured filament yarn on the left side of the scale are the same weight as only one cone of non-textured filament yarn on the right. (Courtesy of Man-Made Fiber Producers Association, Inc.)

FIGURE 13.9. After leaving the man-made fiber producing plant, staple is spun into yarn basically the same as the natural fibers are spun. The compressed bale being opened here contains many millions of the precisely cut short fibers called staple. (Courtesy of Man-Made Fiber Producers Association, Inc.)

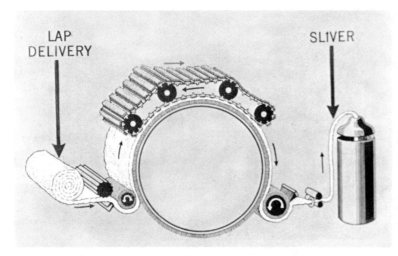

LAP
DELIVERY

SLIVER

FIGURE 13.10. The staple fibers are formed into a compact roll called a lap. The lap is delivered into a carding machine where the fibers are straightened and assembled into a rope-like strand called a "card sliver" ("slyver"). (Courtesy Man-Made Fiber Producers Association, Inc.)

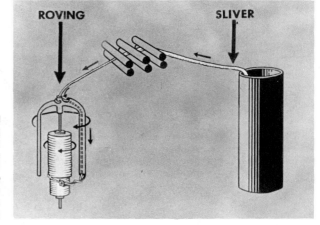

ROVING

SLIVER

FIGURE 13.11. A blended sliver is fed into a roving frame which draws it down in size and at the same time gives it a small amount of twist. The strand is now called "roving." (Courtesy Man-Made Fiber Producers Association, Inc.)

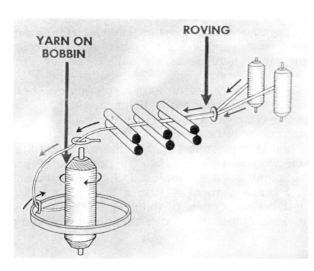

YARN ON
BOBBIN

ROVING

FIGURE 13.12. The spinning operation is the final step in spun yarn production. Two packages of roving are feeding into a spinning frame which draws the material down still further and completes the twisting of the finished yarn. A winding machine will re-wind the yarn onto packages which meet the requirements of manufacturers of fabrics and other articles. (Courtesy of Man-Made Fiber Producers Association, Inc.)

FIGURE 13.13. Blended yarn is made by combining two or more types of staple fibers, either natural or man-made. Here are acetate staple, rayon staple, and the yarn made from them. (Courtesy Man-Made Fiber Producers Association, Inc.)

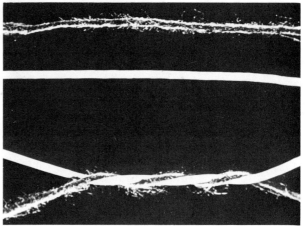

FIGURE 13.14. A combination yarn is formed by twisting or plying together a staple yarn (shown at top) and a continuous monofilament or a filament yarn. (Courtesy Man-Made Fiber Producers Association, Inc.)

SIZES OF RAYON, ACETATE, AND TRIACETATE YARNS

The size of filament rayon and acetate yarn is computed on the denier basis. (See Chap. 3.) Rayon yarns average between 100 and 200 denier, with 150 the usual. The coarsest yarn is 2,200 denier. Fifteen denier would be considered a fine yarn. There are 1-, 1¼-, and 1½-denier Avril rayon staples made by the American Viscose Division of the FMC Corporation, which makes possible finer, softer, spun-rayon fabrics. These fine rayon fibers can also be used in blends with pima and Egyptian cotton, fine wools, and silks. Acetate yarns have similar deniers.

The sizes of spun-rayon yarns may be computed on the same basis as cotton (840 yards to the pound for count #1), but the woolen (1,600 yards to the pound) and the worsted (560 yards to the pound) bases are also used, depending on the spinning system employed. Single rayon yarns range approximately from a coarse yarn of #10 to a fine yarn of #80, with an average of #30 on the cotton system of spinning. The same sizing system is also used for the noncellulosic fibers discussed in the following chapters.

CONSTRUC-
TION OF
RAYON,
ACETATE,
AND TRI-
ACETATE
FABRICS Since rayon, acetate, and triacetate can be made to resemble cotton, linen, silk, or wool textures, the choice of fiber (staple or filament), type of yarn (filament, spun, combination, or novelty), construction, and finish will be determined by the appearance and the desired use of the resultant fabric.

The fabric constructions considered here have application also to the noncellulosic fibers discussed in the next two chapters, so much of this information will not be repeated.

IN PLAIN WEAVE OR ITS VARIATIONS

In the cotton-like textures, rayon and/or acetate may be made in gingham, seersucker, poplin, and sharkskin (for blouses). A cotton and rayon blend may be used in ottoman for dresses and suits. One of the most popular textures, made to resemble linen, is rayon and/or acetate butcher, used in sportswear. To resemble wool, there are challis, some flannels, some bouclés, and crepe, used in clothing. A few of the silk-like textures in plain weave are rayon or acetate shantung, faille, taffeta, moiré, flat crepe, chiffon, and bengaline used in dresses, and ninon or voile in curtains, and shantung in draperies.

IN TWILL WEAVE OR ITS VARIATIONS

A good rayon twill may be used for linings in mens' and womens' coats. Serge in polyester and Avril rayon are suitable for sportswear. Many tweeds, most flannels and gabardine, and many sharkskins (suiting) are twills. In silklike textures, there are foulard and surah.

IN SATIN WEAVE

Satin in dress, bridal, slipper, or drapery weights is frequently made of these fibers and resembles silk in construction.

IN JACQUARD AND DOBBY

Rayon and/or acetate necktie fabrics in Jacquard or dobby are silk like in texture. Brocades, damasks, and tapestries for draperies and upholsteries may be made in part or entirely of rayon or acetate.

IN PILE WEAVE

Probably the best-known pile fabric in these fibers is transparent velvet. Brocaded velvets frequently are made with the pile designs of rayon for evening gowns and upholstery. Furlike fabrics made to simulate broadtail, beaver, mink, and Persian lamb may be partially of rayon, for winter coats. There are a few novelty terry cloths made with rayon pile, for robes and towels.

IN LENO WEAVE

Marquisette for glass curtains and dress fabrics is always made in leno weave, no matter what fiber is used.

FIGURE 13.15. Embossed transparent velvet, 100 percent rayon. Pile weave. Fabric is passed between steaming rollers that "emboss" the design on the fabric. It is used for pillows and evening wear. (Photo by Jonas Grushkin.)

IN KNITTING

The webbing of foundation garments may be knitted acetate. Tricots for dresses and blouses are often made of triacetate. Ready-made knitted slipcovers have the advantage of stretching to fit a chair, for example. Pleated knitted garments are wrinkle-resistant and hold their pleats when made of triacetate. Machine-made laces, produced on a tricot or raschel knit machine, can be of rayon or acetate.

RAYON, ACETATE, AND TRIACETATE FABRICS: REGULAR FINISHES

BLEACHING

Although rayon is usually bleached in the yarn or skein, the finisher may bleach rayon fabrics. To do so, he uses sodium hydroxide, sodium perborate, and hydrogen peroxide. Sodium hypochlorite is used for acetate cloth. A wool-and-acetate blend is generally bleached with hydrogen peroxide.

BRUSHING

To remove short, loose fibers, brushing is important.

DRY DECATING

When a rayon is made to resemble wool or when rayon is blended or mixed with wool, dry decating is done to set the luster permanently. (See p. 282.)

NAPPING

Again, when a fabric is to resemble wool, it is napped. (See *gigging* and *napping*.)

SINGEING AND SHEARING

Both processes are needed to remove surface fibers and lint. Even though a fabric has been singed, fibers may become raised as the cloth passes through various finishing processes, and may have to be sheared. Pile is shortened by shearing.

SCOURING

This process is applied to most fabrics to remove oil, sizing, and dirt.

SIZING

Sizing increases weight and crispness of a fabric.

SHRINKAGE CONTROL

Shrinkage of rayon in width and in length can now be controlled— stabilized to repeated launderings. (See Chapter 7 for shrinkage control finishes.) When the fabric is resin-treated, the stability is good. The new modified rayons have greatly improved stability over the regular type. Cotton and rayon blends are stabilized with mechanical compressive shrinkage procedures similar to those used on all-cotton fabrics. There is less loss of strength in the new modified rayon than in the cotton component. Acetates normally have good dimensional stability, and have fair stability after repeated launderings.

INSPECTING, TENTERING, AND CALENDERING

All fabrics must be visually inspected and then tentered in order to even them in the width. The calendering finish smooths, glazes, moirés, or embosses. On acetate and triacetate, a slight fusion by heat embosses or moirés a fabric permanently.

RAYON, ACETATE, AND TRI-ACETATE FABRICS: FUNC-TIONAL FINISHES

ABSORBENT

Since foundation garments and underwear are required to absorb moisture, an absorbent finish is used for these fabrics.

CREASE-RESISTANT

Synthetic resins give additional resiliency. Tebelized is a trademark of the T. B. Lee Company, indicating a fabric's ability to hold a press. Prestwick, by Courtaulds North America, Inc., is a familiar crease-resistant finish. (See Chapter 8.)

FIRE-RESISTANT

Vegetable fibers, such as cotton and rayon, burn much more rapidly than wool. The speed of burning depends not only on the fibers but also on the twist of yarn, construction, and finish. Napped or so-called brushed rayon is highly flammable unless treated for fire resistance. Trademark finishes in this field include Pyroset, by American Cyanamid Company, and Flamefoil, by Philadelphia Textile Finishers, Inc.

GERM-RESISTANT

Fabrics to be made germ-resistant, such as linings in slippers, are treated with germicides-fungicides.

312
*Fabric
Construction
and
Buying
Motives*

STARCHLESS

Bobbinets, glass curtainings, and organdies are fabrics in which stiffness and crispness are characteristics. Wat-A-Set is a durable, washable finish that may be applied in manufacture. It is used particularly for curtains to keep them crisp. This is a trademark of the Mount Hope Finishing Company.

MINIMUM CARE

Since modified rayons can be treated for crease resistance, can be shrinkage controlled, and have good tensile strength when wet, these rayons are used particularly in blends with cottons, polyesters, and acrylics. A successful durable press item is a polyester/rayon blend which is chemically treated and cured.

WATER REPELLENT

Most consumers, and servicemen in particular, are familiar with the permanent Zepel finish by Du Pont for rayon, acetate, cotton, and blends. (For the method of treatment for water repellency, see p. 161.) The Cravenette Company has several water-repellent finishes: (1) a nondurable wax finish, (2) a semidurable wax finish called Long Life, and (3) a durable Super Silicone finish. These finishes are used on apparel, slipcovers, draperies, and curtains. Impregnole, by Warwick Chemical Company, Inc., is made in both nondurable and semidurable types. A professional laundry or cleaner will use another nondurable type to reapply to cleaned articles. Permel Plus, manufactured by American Cyanamid, is a durable water-repellent finish. Hydro-pruf, by the Arkansas Company, is a durable silicone finish for water repellency.

**DESIR-
ABILITY
OF
THE
CELLULO-
SIC
MAN-MADE
FIBERS**

Rayon, acetate, and triacetate quickly appealed to consumers because they incorporated many desirable characteristics in use. They were (1) *economical*, especially when compared with wool and silk; (2) *attractive*, with permanent luster in bright, semibright, and dull shades; (3) *versatile*, suitable for most types of clothing and many home furnishings (also for tires); (4) *comfortable*, absorbing moisture readily (hydrophillic), except for triacetate, and feeling cool in summer if made from filament yarns, and warm in winter if made from fuzzy/spun yarns; (5) *durable*, especially if made from high-tenacity and high-wet modulus fibers but tending to slip at the seams unless substantial allowance is made and the tension and length of the stitches properly regulated; and (6) *easy to iron* if properly heat controlled. Rayon can withstand higher temperatures than acetate. (See Table 13.1.)

Nevertheless, the newer noncellulosic fibers and fabrics to be discussed in the next two chapters also have most of the above characteristics except for ready absorbency, and they have other important advantages as well.

TRENDS IN THE OUTPUT OF THE CELLULOSIC FIBERS

Historically rayon and acetate are tremendously important, representing a great breakthrough in technology that until then had depended on the natural fibers for textile products. But they are no longer keeping pace because of the broad acceptance of the noncellulosic man-made fibers. It is true that the world production of rayon and acetate filament yarns and staple increased nearly 10 percent from 1966 to 1973, but their percentage of world production declined in the same period from 18 percent to 14 percent while noncellulosic fiber production more than doubled in percentage of the whole, from 13 percent to 29 percent.[2]

In the United States, the trends away from the cellulosic man-made fibers has been even more pronounced. Actual production declined about 10 percent from 1966 to 1973, whereas the noncellulosic fiber production has nearly tripled. Rayon production is about double that of acetate when both filament yarns and tow are included. But the production of acetate filament yarns exceeds that of rayon filament. Most of the tow yarn is rayon, not acetate; in fact, very little tow acetate yarn is produced in this country. The demand for a silk-like luster and hand coupled with greater stability (than rayon) probably accounts for the importance of acetate filament yarns.

SUMMARY

Of all the synthetic fibers, rayon is the oldest. Although its original creators were trying to make silk artificially, they actually discovered a new and distinct fiber more versatile than any natural one. Rayon can be made to imitate cotton, wool, silk, and even linen, and it can produce effects not possible with these fabrics. The availability of the raw materials from which rayon is made and the cheapness of its production process have assured the consumer of an ample supply at moderate prices. Acetate, another of the oldest man-made fibers, has properties different from rayon. These properties must be considered in the end uses for acetate and in its care. (For the care of rayon and acetate, see Chapter 16.)

However, the preeminence of rayon and acetate has been challenged by nylon and the other newer synthetics. Each of these fibers has properties peculiar to itself, and all possess certain properties in common. There is a place for all these fibers in consumer goods. The problem lies in the proper selection of fibers to give the best service in end uses.

REVIEW QUESTIONS

1. (a) Who was the father of the rayon industry?
   (b) What method did he use to make artificial textile fibers? What was its chief disadvantage?
   (c) Is that method used today?
2. When was the name rayon coined?
3. (a) What is the present federal law on labeling and advertising of rayon and acetate fibers?
   (b) How does this law protect the consumer?
   (c) Is the present TFPIA adequate? Explain.

[2] *Textile Organon* (June 1974). Olefine and glass fibers are excluded in worldwide figures since accurate data are not available.

314
*Fabric
Construction
and
Buying
Motives*

4. (*a*) Outline briefly the most important steps in the making of rayon by the viscose and cuprammonium processes.
   (*b*) Explain the differences between rayon and acetate fibers.
5. (*a*) How are dull rayon yarns made?
   (*b*) How would you identify filament rayon yarn, spun-rayon yarn, and combination yarns?
   (*c*) How is high-strength rayon yarn made? Give its uses.
   (*d*) How does high-tenacity rayon yarn differ from high-wet strength yarn? Give the selling points of the latter.
6. (*a*) Which type of acetate fiber has the strongest tensile strength?
   (*b*) Which is the strongest when wet: cotton, regular rayon, regular acetate, or linen?
7. By what process or processes do the following companies manufacture rayon or acetate?
   (*a*) E.I. Du Pont de Nemours & Company
   (*b*) Celanese Fibers Company
   (*c*) American Viscose Division, FMC Corporation
   (*d*) Beaunit Corporation, Fibers Division
   (*e*) Courtalds North America, Inc.
   (*f*) Eastman Chemical Products, Inc.
8. In what ways do the following characteristics of rayon and acetate affect consumer demand?
   (*a*) Length of fiber
   (*b*) Microscopic appearance
   (*c*) Strength of fiber
   (*d*) Elasticity
   (*e*) Hygroscopic moisture
   (*f*) Effect of light
   (*g*) Composition of fiber
   (*h*) Heat
   (*i*) Effect of acid and alkali
   (*j*) Affinity for dyestuffs
9. Describe briefly the differences between the continuous spinning and the box methods of spinning rayon yarn.
10. (*a*) How are the sizes of rayon and acetate filament yarns computed?
    (*b*) What is the range of denier in rayon yarn?
    (*c*) Give the denier number of a coarse yarn; of a fine yarn. What is the aerage denier?
11. (*a*) List the uses for rayon
    (*b*) List the uses for acetate
    (*c*) In what constructions are rayons and acetates made? Name a fabric to illustrate each construction.
12. (*a*) List the finishes that would be applied to a rayon blanket.
    (*b*) When would a water-repellent finish be considered durable? Give two trade names of durable water-repellent finishes.

**EXPERI-
MENTS**

1. *Alkali test.* (*a*) Boil some rayon yarns for about five minutes in a concentrated solution of caustic soda (lye). Describe the effect of strong alkali on rayon. (*b*) Make the same test with acetate yarns. Describe the effect of strong alkali on acetate.
2. *Acid test.* (*a*) Place a few rayon yarns in concentrated sulfuric acid for five or ten minutes. Describe the effect of strong acid on rayon. (*b*) Make the same test on acetate yarns. Describe the effect of strong acid on acetate.
3. *Microscopic test.* Examine a rayon fiber under the microscope. Draw the fiber as you see it. How does its appearance differ from that of cotton and linen? Examine and draw an acetate fiber.

Abraded yarn—A two-ply combination yarn, of which one ply is abraded and the other is filament viscose rayon.

Acetate—Man-made fibers or yarns formed by a compound of cellulose and acetic acid that has been extruded and hardened.

Acetate process—Method of making man-made fibers derived from cellulose. See *Acetate*.

Arnel—See *Triacetate*.

Bright yarns—Made with rayon or acetate fibers of high luster.

Brushed rayon—A rayon fabric that has been heavily napped. This type of fabric is highly flammable and must be treated for fire resistance.

Chardonnet, Count Hilaire de—Made the first synthetic fiber by dissolving nitro-cellulose in alcohol and ether.

Combination yarn—A ply yarn in which each ply is composed of a different fiber; for example, one-ply acetate, one-ply rayon.

Cuprammonium—Fibers or yarns made by dissolving cellulose in ammoniacal copper oxide, extruding the solution, and hardening.

Delustered fibers—Those permanently dulled by incorporating mineral oil or micro-scopic solids in the spinning solution. When delustered, fibers are said to be pigmented; for example, pigment taffeta.

Dimensional stability—Ability of a fabric to keep its shape and size.

Dope dyed—See *Solution dyed*.

Dry spinning—A derivative to be spun is dissolved in a solvent that can be evaporated, leaving the desired filament to be hardened by drying in warm air.

Filament—A fiber of indefinite length (continuous). This term is applied to the continuous synthetic fibers.

Filament yarn—Yarns made of continuous filaments.

Gas fading—Change of color of some acetates when exposed to nitrogen in the air.

Groove markings—Rather heavy line markings running lengthwise of the acetate fiber; a mark of identification.

High tenacity—See *Modified rayon* and *Modified acetate fibers*.

Hydrophillic—A fiber that has a high affinity for water.

Hydrophobic—A fiber that lacks affinity for water.

Jersey—Weft-knitted rayon, acetate, or two-bar tricot-knitted rayon or acetate used for slips, gowns, and blouses. Jersey is also made of wool, cotton, silk, nylon, or blends with the newer synthetics.

Linters—Very short fibers that cover the cotton seeds after the long fibers have been removed by ginning. Linters are a source of cellulose for rayon and acetate.

Marquisette—A sheer fabric in leno weave used for glass curtains. It is made of cotton, rayon, acetate, nylon, polyester, acrylic, glass, silk, or mixtures.

Modified acetate fibers—Stretching the fibers and then treating them with alkali. See Chapter 2.

Modified rayon fibers—Chemical treatment while fibers are in the plastic state to give them high tenacity (high strength). Changes in the molecular structure of the fiber have been made.

Nitrocellulose rayon—The first type of synthetic fiber discovered—no longer made in the United States. This type of rayon is made of a solution of nitrated cellulose solidified into filaments.

Pigmented fibers—White or colored pigments added to a fiber-forming substance before spinning.

Rayon—See Glossary, Chapter 2.

Solution dyed—Dyestuff is put into the spinning solution, and the color is "locked in" as the fiber is coagulated. Synonymous with *spun dyed* and *dope dyed*.

Spinneret—A jet or nozzle containing very fine holes through which the spinning solution is forced (extruded).

316

*Fabric
Construction
and
Buying
Motives*

Spun dyed—See *Solution dyed.*

Spun yarn—Yarn made of staple.

Striations—The many fine microscopic lines extending lengthwise on the viscose rayon fiber; a mark of identification.

Thick-and-thin yarns—Yarns made of fibers of varying diameters.

Tow—See *Staple.*

Trade names of rayon and acetate fibers—See Table, Chapter 2.

Transparent velvet—A sheer cut-pile velvet usually all-rayon or with rayon pile, suitable for evening dresses, wraps, and millinery.

Triacetate—A thermoplastic fiber classified under the generic name of *acetate.* It does not dissolve in acetone, and it can be ironed with the heat set for linen.

Viscose process—A method of making rayon fibers from purified cellulose.

Wash-and-wear—See Glossary, Chapter 7.

General Purpose
Noncellulosic Fibers
and the Consumer

14

Consumers may be satisfied that they are acquainted with rayon, acetate, and polyester. They may think they know how these fabrics will perform and how to care for them. But do they? As stated in the previous chapter, improvements in rayon and acetate may change a consumer's image of these fibers if he or she purchases a newly manufactured rayon or acetate article. The noncellulosic fibers such as nylon, polyester, acrylic, and modacrylic are also undergoing improvements to meet the needs of consumers.

Before the mid-twentieth century, chemists made a great discovery. To get textile fibers, it was not necessary to depend on natural fibers or on man-made fibers derived from plants or animal protein. Chemists discovered that elements from the mineral world could be subjected to chemical synthesis and could produce fibers with desirable characteristics not found in the natural ones or in those with a cellulosic or protein base.

Thus, the great noncellulosic man-made industry was born, one that included a wide variety of chemicals and fibers, each with varying use characteristics.

With a plethora of brand names attached to these newly created fibers, the Federal Trade Commission was authorized under the Textile Fiber Products Identification Act to set up generic names for the varying types, so that the consumer could come to know the characteristics of each class. Unfortunately, perhaps, the classes were not based on performance but rather on the different chemical compositions of each. Starting with generic classes for noncellulosic man-made fibers, the Commission now recognizes the seventeen listed in Table 14-1. It also recognizes acetate, including tricetate, and rayon as man-made fibers of the cellulosic type.

The average consumer, not familiar with the chemistry of the fibers and deriving very little clarification from the FTC's definitions of generic classes, must rely on labels that give information on performance and care. As we have seen generic names on labels leave much doubt in the consumer's mind. We have also seen that ideally the salesperson could be an excellent source of merchandise information. But salespeople, too, require knowledge about performance of the various classes of fibers to enable them to answer customers' questions intelligently. Fiber and yarn manufacturers are good sources of information of this type and the permanent care labels referred to in Chapter 1 provide consumer guidance.

318
Fabric
Construction
and
Buying
Motives

In this chapter, we shall discuss the composition and the advantages and drawbacks in performance of the four general purpose generic fiber classifications. The remaining thirteen may be thought of as special purpose fibers and will be considered in the next chapter. Within a classification, of course, there may be certain brands of fibers and yarns that vary slightly in their plus or minus qualities from characteristics of the generic classifications. But discussion will necessarily be limited to the general classification.

TABLE 14-1. Generic Names of Noncellulosic Fibers

acrylic	metallic	polyester
anidex	modacrylic	rubber (includes lastrile[a])
aramid	novoloid	saran
azlon[a]	nylon	spandex
glass	nytril[a]	vinal[a]
	olefin	vinyon[a]

[a]Not currently produced in the United States.

NYLON

Some of the registered brand names (trademarks) under which nylon fiber and yarn of various types are marketed include:

Allied Chemical's Caprolan (type 6), Source (for carpets).
American Enka's Crepeset (knitting yarn), Enka Nylon (type 6 carpets), Enkasheer (hosiery).
Beaunit's Blanc de Blancs (foundation garments), Qulon (type 6)
Celanese's many numbered types
Dow Badische's Zefran (type 6).
Du Pont's Antron (many numbered types), Cordura (industrial twine), Cantrece (hosiery), Nomex (industrial goods and clothing used at high temperatures), Qiana (high quality, silklike), and many other numbered types.
Firestone's Nytelle (filament yarns).
Monsanto's Blue "C" (many type varieties, also used for polyester), Cadon and Cumuloft (both for carpets).

According to the Federal Trade Commission rules, as indicated in Chapter 2, these brand names may not be used alone on labels and in advertising but only in close conjunction with nylon and in no larger or more prominent type.

PRODUCTION OF NYLON

While it is popularly said that nylon is made from coal, air, and water, the major contributors of raw materials have been the carbon obtained from petrochemicals and natural gas, also nitrogen and oxygen and water (hydrogen). While hydrocarbons can be obtained from coal, costs have been considerably lower when they have been derived from petroleum or natural gas. Furthermore, much of the energy needed for chemical synthesis has been derived from the same sources. There are two major types of nylon that vary with the chemical composition of the ingredients: nylon 66 and nylon 6. The first was created by Du Pont in 1939 and is now also made by Celanese and Monsanto in the United

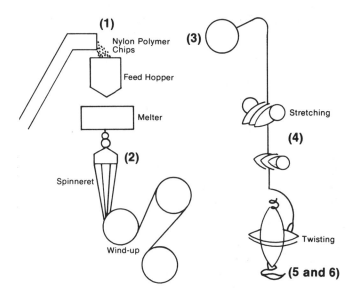

1. The production of nylon fibers begins with hard white fragments called nylon polymer chips.

2. The chips are melted and the fluid is pumped to a spinneret where it is extruded and solidified to form continuous mono-filaments.

3. Assembled continuous monofilaments are taken up on a bobbin.

4. The bobbin is transported to another area where the nylon is stretched. Stretching allows molecules within the continuous monofilaments to be arranged in a more orderly pattern.

5. The assembled continuous monofilaments are twisted into yarn.

6. The yarn is then wound onto bobbins and is ready for shipment.

FIGURE 14.1. Nylon production. (Courtesy Man-Made Fiber Producers Association, Inc.)

States and by many others abroad. It involves treating hydrocarbons to yield the compounds adipic acid and hexamethylene diamine. These are treated under pressure in an autoclave, something like a pressure cooker. The acid molecules hook up with the diamine molecules to form new larger molecules in a molecular chain called a polymer. The polymer in viscous state leaves the autoclave through a slot at the bottom and is poured over a rotating wheel, where water hardens it into a translucent, ivory-colored ribbon. A rotary cutter processes the solid into chips or flakes.

Type 6 nylon was first produced in America by Allied Chemical and American Enka. Now made by others as well, it accounts for nearly half of the nylon produced in this country. It is made from caprolactam, which in turn is derived from cyclohexanone or hydroxylamine.[1] The manufacturing process is very similar to that of type 66. The Dow Badische Company is the largest producer of caprolactam in this country.

Type 66 dyes lighter and melts at a higher temperature than type 6. Type 6 has a softer hand and stains slightly with certain direct dyes. Both have a wide variety of uses.

THE NYLON FILAMENT

The flakes or chips created by the chemical reaction and treatment of either the chemicals used for type 66 or 6 are melted and extruded through a spinneret, a perforated plate with tiny holes, into nylon filament fiber. This method is called melt spinning. The extruded strands of nylon can be stretched again to three or four times their original length. This stretching improves strength and elasticity. Nylon is made both in

---

[1] The reactive groups of the lactam are at opposite ends of the carbon chain; a ring of six carbon and one nitrogen unit is opened up and polymerized into nylon 6.

320

*Fabric
Construction
and
Buying
Motives*

filament and in staple fibers. Single filaments (monofilaments) are made into such items as sheer hosiery, blouses, gowns, and veils.

CHARACTERISTICS OF NYLON FILAMENTS

Under the microscope, nylon filaments appear either bright or dull. Bright filaments closely resemble the filaments of cuprammonium rayon. Their diameters are even and the surfaces smooth and structureless, like glass rods. There are no crenulations (fine notches) such as there are in most rayons. (See Appendix A.)

The dull nylon filaments show pigmentation of titanium oxide, similar to that of medium-dull rayon, but the pigmentation of nylon is more sparse and looks more like pockmarks than specks.

Nylon is a chemical compound that reacts to mineral acids by losing strength or even dissolving. An example of this occurred when several women shoppers suddenly discovered that holes were forming in their nylon stockings. It was found that when sulfur-dioxide and sulfur-trioxide gases, produced by combustion of low-grade industrial fuels in factories, meet moist dust and dirt particles in the air, sulfuric acid is formed on the particles. Since nylon stockings are in tension on the leg, these tiny specks are sufficient to start runs.

Because nylon may be destroyed by acids, an accepted test to separate nylon from wool and vegetable fibers, for fiber identification, is to immerse a yarn or fabric in a solution of one part concentrated hydrochloric acid to one part distilled water for sixty minutes at room temperature. The nylon is dissolved. Nylons can be bleached with an oxygenated bleach, available in some stores. While clorox may be used, it tends to yellow nylon ultimately.

Table 14-2 presents the characteristics of nylon important to the consumer and the fabric manufacturer.

Certain premium types of nylon provide other special qualities. For example, a silklike quality is now available from several companies. One, called Ultron, is produced by Monsanto. It is antistatic and has good moisture transport properties for use in sleepwear, lingerie, and other intimate apparel. Another is Du Pont's Qiana, which also has silklike properties combined with ease in care.

Another Du Pont fiber, trilobal in cross section, provides a delustered yarn called Antron, used for women's jersey blouses. A special type of Antron has antistatic properties, while still another contains a microscopic structure specifically for use in carpets.

A more recent nylon fiber modification is the development of different dye levels which produce various color effects in a single dye bath. Through the chemical modification of the fiber, striking two- and three-color patterns can be achieved without the cost of yarn dyeing. Cross-dyeable nylon yarns and cross-dyed garments are now widely marketed by major producers.

Monsanto has developed a continuous filament cross-dyeable yarn for heather effects, designated Type Z01. Before its introduction, nylon yarns for heather effects were generally spun from blends of dissimilar dyeing nylon staple fibers. Unfortunately, the differential-dyeing nylons did not always have the required matched physical properties and the staple yarns did not fare too well in the tortuous piece-dyeing step. The finished garments were also plagued with pilling and other assorted ills associated with high-strength staple yarn products. Type Z01 filament nylon provides high performance pill-resistant heather products at moderate cost.

TABLE 14-2. Characteristics of Nylon

Tensile strength: Strongest of the textile fibers, except for a high-tenacity type of anidex. Wet strength only 15 percent less than dry strength.

Luster: Bright and smooth but may be modified for dullness by adding pigments to the polymer solution.

Affinity for dye: Can be dyed in a broad range of colors and be colorfast. But in the solution, the yarn or the fabric dyeing of blends that contain nylon may prove difficult.

Blending: Staple nylon blends well with wool since the nylon contributes strength, abrasion resistance, and dimensional stability in washing.

Crimping: Staple nylon fiber crimps well, a factor important in spinning for use in sweaters, socks, flannels, rugs, and blankets.

Resistance to:
    abrasion—high, many times that of wool.
    heat—safe to iron at 300°F-350°F, depending on type.
    sunlight—as in the case of cotton, may be injured by strong or long sun exposure, but virtually all commercial nylons are now treated with a sun-resistant agent.
    soil—does not soil easily since filaments are smooth and nonporous.
    insects—not vulnerable to moths, silverfish, mildew, and fungi.
    chemicals—resists damage from alkalies and oil, but mineral acids in the air or water may weaken and even dissolve it.
    water may weaken and even dissolve it.

Absorption of perspiration: Poor, because nylon is hydrophobic. Hence, a clammy feeling in clothing of filament nylon. It dries quickly since it is nonabsorbent.

Dimensional stability: Excellent stability to repeated laundering and holds it shape if heat-setting has been properly done.

Elasticity: High. When a filament stretches 20 percent, recovery after first stretch is 95 percent and thereafter 93 percent. Also returns to original form after compression.

YARN MAKING

After the nylon fibers have been extruded from the spinneret, they are hardened, grouped together in a strand, and wound into a "cake" or spinning bobbin preparatory to stretching. A series of rollers revolving at different speeds stretch the fibers. The operation arranges the molecules in an orderly fashion, parallel to the axis of the filaments. Polymerization merely links the molecules together at random. The stretching adds both strength and elasticity to the yarn.

Nylon is made in both multifilament (yarn) and monofilaments (single filaments). (See Chapter 3.) Throwsters twist the multifilament yarn to give it tensile strength, snag resistance, and durability, and spinners spin or twist nylon staple into yarn, much as cotton and wool are spun. Most nylon yarns are made in the multifilament type and are used in dresses, hosiery, blouses, lingerie, shirts, upholstery, and carpets. Monofilaments are used in such items as sheer hosiery and various tricot garments.

The sizes of filament nylon yarns are figured on the denier basis, similar to rayon. Spun nylon yarns are on a count basis, like spun rayon.

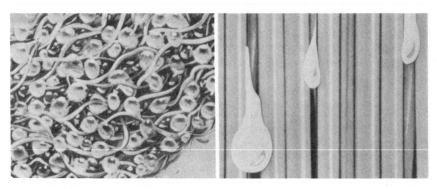

FIGURE 14.2. Left: Garment woven of spun yarn does not dry rapidly because each of the air spaces fills with water. Right: Garment woven of continuous filament nylon has practically no air spaces to trap moisture. (Reproduced courtesy of E.I. DuPont de Nemours & Company, Inc.)

Spun yarn is made of either 100 percent nylon or blends of staples. Nylon staple is cut in different lengths, 1½ to 8 inches, depending upon the spinning system being used—cotton, woolen, worsted, silk, or other. Spun yarn is light, soft, and springy and is very popular in wool-like textures and blends, especially in socks and sweaters.

The making of bulky yarns was described in Chapter 3. By combining different deniers and plies of looped, curled, and crimped varieties of yarn, it is possible to obtain a great many new textures from continuous-filament nylon. Stretch yarns were also discussed in Chapter 3. Improvements in the luster of yarn have occurred, as evidenced by Du Pont's Sparkling Nylon in 1959 and a nylon jersey of Antron trilobal multifilament yarn with a certain type of delusterant chemical in 1960.

TEXTURING NYLON YARNS

The comfort factor in nylon clothing can be improved by texturing. (See Chapter 3.)

TEXTURED YARNS

1. Combine the high abrasion resistance, strength, toughness, and ease-of-care properties of nylon or polyester with stretch, bulk, superb hand, and more rapid wicking of perspiration for greater wearing comfort.
2. Permit simulation of some of the better characteristics of fabrics made from spun yarns while permitting new and novel approaches to styling and fashion.
3. Have better drape and greater cover and opacity.
4. Texture and hand can be varied at will depending on the method and conditions under which the yarn is textured.
5. In many cases their use enables garment manufacturers to produce stretch-to-fit items in a smaller number of sizes that span the complete size requirements.

Because it is thermoplastic, nylon yarn, like some other noncellulosics, can be textured to impart loft, bulk, stretch, and a drier hand than "flat," or nontextured, filament yarns. In texturing the yarns are coiled, crimped, or the filaments are entangled by a number of different processes. (See Chapter 3.)

322

The first type 66 nylon was essentially concentrated on fashion uses in intimate apparel, both in knitting and weaving. Continuous filament nylon is important for basic knit construction in foundation garments, lingerie, and women's and men's hosiery. In 1957 Du Pont introduced Tissue Tricot, and in 1960 Tricot Satinette. These constructions of warp knitting were achieved through the trilobal modification of the fiber's cross section by combining special yarn denier and fabric finishing.

American Enka produces physically modified crepeset monofilament yarns that can be knitted on tricot machines to obtain fabrics with a definite, permanent crepe effect for lingerie and blouses. (See *warp. knitting*, Chapter 6.) Stretch fabrics can be both knitted and woven. Bulky-knit sweaters, either hand- or machine-made, are popular for sports and casual wear. Special types of nylon and other noncellulosic fibers may be molded. Bras are often made by this process. A molded bra is comfortable because it has no seams; it keeps its size and shape permanently after machine washing and drying; it is durable; and it has an esthetic appeal.

A nylon monofilament straw, made by a process developed in Switzerland and marketed by Scheuer Associates of New York, is sold under the name of Yuva. It can be woven or knitted into shoes, belts, hats, handbags, lampshades, curtaining, and automobile fabrics.

Any type of weave—plain, twill, satin, or fancy—can be made in 100 percent nylon or in blends or mixtures. The principal constructions are hosiery, tricot slips, gowns, shirts, and blouses. Nylon fleeces, furlike pile fabrics, and rugs are popular, as well as laces and nets.

FINISHES FOR NYLON FABRICS

Nylon fabrics can usually be bleached safely with sodium chlorite without risk of tendering, but certain types of nylon require special bleaching methods and the manufacturer's recommended instructions should be closely followed. All nylon fabrics are subjected to heat-setting conditions, which must be carefully controlled. All parts of the fabric must be subjected to setting, and excessive time at high temperatures must be avoided. Setting is a matter of degree, but an unset finished cloth would not be stabilized; it would not be smooth; and it would wrinkle easily.

To make a durable stiff finish, a melamine resin is used that cannot penetrate but polymerizes on the surface. Nylon taffeta petticoats are finished in this fashion. Thiourea-formaldehyde resin flameproofs nylon nets and laces. Nonslip finishes do not penetrate the fabric either, but they bond the warp and filling yarns to make a firm hand. A resin polyethylene oxide is claimed to eliminate fiber static. Some fabrics are calendered. (See Chapter 7.) Piece dyeing is a method of coloring nylon after construction. (See Chapter 8 and page 320 for dyeing of nylon.)

WHY CUSTOMERS BUY NYLON FABRICS

Customers buy nylon for durability, suitability, ease of care, and versatility as explained on page 324.

FIGURE 14.3. Uses of nylon. The strength of nylon is seen in the top photograph. Pantyhose, as shown in the lower photograph, are made of a combination of nylon and spandex biconstituent fiber (Monvelle) by Monsanto. Nylon is used for sheerness and durability and spandex for stretch and recovery. (Courtesy of Monsanto Textiles Company.

Durability: The plus characteristics of nylon have been given in the Table 14-2 on page 321. From a consumer's point of view, these provide the following advantages: The wearing quality of nylon fabric depends on the tensile strength of its fibers and yarns. This exceptional strength and the recovery from small stretching forces and resilience, coupled with lightness in weight, make very desirable sheer fabrics. Nylon also resists abrasion, another factor in durability.

Suitability: The engineering of various types of nylon for specific end uses widened the market for the product. The resilience and strength of nylon make it suitable for hosiery and underwear. Stockings do not become baggy at the knees, because nylon's resilience brings the stocking back to shape. In pile velvets of nylon, the pile is not deformed when crushed.

Ease in care: Heat setting makes embossing of fabrics permanent and sets permanent pleats. Heat setting also keeps a fabric from shrinking or sagging noticeably. Nylon fabrics are easy to wash, many of them can be hung to drip dry, and many need no ironing. Nylon dries very quickly, and filament nylon dries faster than spun nylon. The consumer will never need to mothproof 100 percent nylon fabrics. Nylon is not adversely affected by water, perspiration, or dry-cleaning agents. However, mildew might discolor nylon.

Versatility: The versatility of nylon seems limitless, particularly in blends with other fibers. When nylon and rayon are blended, nylon adds strength, abrasion resistance, and stability in washing and wearing. A nylon/rayon blend makes a fine-count, strong yarn for lightweight washable fabrics. When nylon and cotton are blended, nylon again contributes its strength, abrasion resistance, and dimensional stability, as well as better resistance to perspiration, a softer hand, better elasticity, and quick drying qualities. Nylon combined with acetate or acrylic fiber adds strength and wearing quality. Nylon staple is particularly suitable for reinforcing socks, anklets, sweaters, swimsuits, undershirts, dress flannels, upholstery, tufted rugs, industrial fabrics, and sewing and darning threads, and is frequently used in 100 percent form in lingerie. Some of these same properties make nylon an excellent material for woven and tufted carpets used in homes, institutions (schools and hospitals), and commercial enterprises (restaurants and airports). Nylon is also used for nontextiles such as bristles and films, which are characterized by toughness, elasticity, and strength. With the development of textured yarns, it is possible to produce nylon fabrics that are more comfortable because of their stretch properties. (see *textured yarns*, Chapter 3.)

LIMITATIONS OF NYLON

Research has been responsible for the great strides in the uses for nylon. Early consumer objections to faults such as pilling (the forming of little balls on the surface of the fabric), development of static electricity, graying of white nylon, and clamminess of 100 percent filament nylon, all have been alleviated to varying degrees by active research programs.

Both Enka and Du Pont produce antistatic nylon for women's lingerie. These yarns are chemically modified so that the antistatic properties are inherent and last for the life of the garment.

Some fabrics may always retain one or more objectionable features. There is no one perfect fiber for all purposes. If the fiber possesses all the minimum requirements needed to perform satisfactorily in a given end use, there should be no customer objections. However, in order to meet price competition, certain treatments necessary for satisfactory performance may be omitted by the fabric manufacturer. As a result, the consumer may have legitimate grounds for dissatisfaction with a fiber.

THE POLY-ESTERS

Polyester,[2] a chemically created fiber with properties differing from those of the other man-made fibers, has shown the greatest growth potential of all man-made fibers. It is widely believed that polyester will ultimately become the world's most important fiber. Consumption in the United States was estimated at 3.5 billion pounds by 1976, exceeding that of any other fiber, man-made or natural. This figure already accounts for over half of all the yarns consumed—spun and filament—in men's, women's, and children's tailored knitted outerwear. Polyester fibers have enjoyed a phenominal growth in double-knit fabrics, especially for both women's and men's apparel. Currently, however, these fabrics have, at least temporarily declined in fashion acceptance perhaps because of the weight of the fabrics. This has led to excess productive capacity and lowered prices for polyester yarn. The growth is reflected in the home sewing market and is likely to continue rapidly in this field.

DEVELOPMENT

Some years ago, British chemists developed polyester and called it Terylene. Their work was based on the research by Du Pont that resulted in nylon. Du Pont and the British group effected a licensing agreement that permitted each company to pursue parallel commercial development programs. Thus, in 1953 Du Pont opened its first polyester plant in Kinston, North Carolina, and became the first commercial producer.

Du Pont named its fiber Dacron, pronounced dācron not dăcron, and it quickly achieved wide consumer acceptance. Today, a score of other companies are producing polyester in America. The product is made available in bright, semibright, and dull lusters and in varying tenacities (strengths). And many companies produce other varients for special uses. As in the case of nylon, selection of the appropriate type for an intended use is important.

The well-publicized brand names under which polyester is available, in addition to Dacron, are the following:

Avlin (American Viscose Co. of the F.M.C. Corp.)
Blue "C" (Monsanto—also applied to nylon)
Encron (American Enka)
Fortrel (Fiber Industries)
Kodel (Eastman Chemical)
Spectran (Monsanto)
Sitraline (American Enka)
Trevira (Hystron)
Vycron (Beaunit Fibers)

---

[2] Polyester is defined by the Federal Trade Commission as a manufactured fiber in which the fiber-forming substance is any long chain synthetic polymer composed of at least 85 percent by weight of an ester of a substituted aromatic carboxylic acid, including but not restricted to substituted therephthalate units, and parasubstituted hydroxybenzoate units.

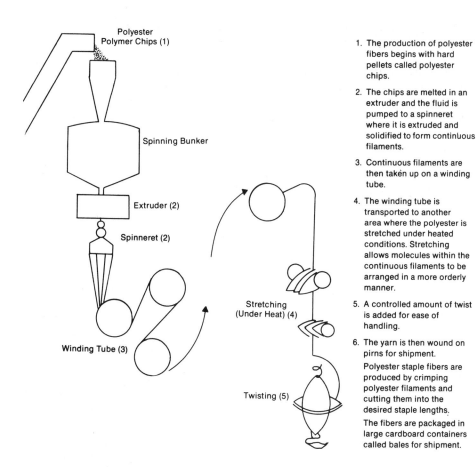

Polyester Polymer Chips (1)

Spinning Bunker

Extruder (2)

Spinneret (2)

Winding Tube (3)

Stretching (Under Heat) (4)

Twisting (5)

1. The production of polyester fibers begins with hard pellets called polyester chips.

2. The chips are melted in an extruder and the fluid is pumped to a spinneret where it is extruded and solidified to form continuous filaments.

3. Continuous filaments are then taken up on a winding tube.

4. The winding tube is transported to another area where the polyester is stretched under heated conditions. Stretching allows molecules within the continuous filaments to be arranged in a more orderly manner.

5. A controlled amount of twist is added for ease of handling.

6. The yarn is then wound on pirns for shipment.

Polyester staple fibers are produced by crimping polyester filaments and cutting them into the desired staple lengths.

The fibers are packaged in large cardboard containers called bales for shipment.

FIGURE 14.4. Polyester Production. (Courtesy Man-Made Fiber Producers Association, Inc.)

PRODUCTION OF THE FIBER AND THE YARN

The process of producing polyester fiber is an intricate one. Basically, the raw materials are petroleum or natural gas and air and water. There are two different combinations of chemicals that produce virtually identical fibers. One is a combination of dimethyl terephthalate and ethylene glycol, "cooked" at high temperatures. The other combines terephthalic acid and ethylene glycol. The result of both chemical processes is solid, hard, porcelainlike chips that are melted (melt-spun) into a honeylike liquid and then extruded through a spinneret and solidified to form continuous filaments. These are taken up on a winding tube and then stretched to many times their original lengths and twisted together to form filament yarns to add strength and elasticity. The number of filaments and the amount of twist determines the size and texture of the yarns. For staple yarns, filaments are crimped and cut into desired lengths.

Smooth filament yarns are used for taffetas, glass curtains, satin, and lightweight apparel fabrics for both men and women.

327

328
*Fabric
Construction
and
Buying
Motives*

Textured polyester filament yarns, made today by the false-twist method, are used extensively in both men's and women's knitted slacks and suits.

Spun yarns are used in fabrics whose texture is cotton- or wool-like, since they produce softer, bulkier yarns. Stuffings of spun polyester for pillows, comforters, sleeping bags, upholstered furniture, mattresses, and auto cushions do not mat and are lightweight, comfortable, and nonallergic.

Modifications in polyester fibers and yarns are continually being made to make the product more suitable for specific uses. For example, American Enka produces a thick and thin yarn called Sitraline, that gives a linenlike appearance with a differential dyeing look to knitted and woven

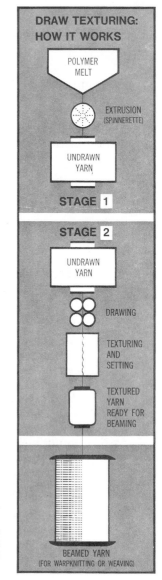

FIGURE 14.5. Draw-texturing polyester yarn. The conventional process for texturing filament yarns has three stages: (1) yarn is extruded through a spinneret and wound; (2) it is then unwound, drawn out through heated stretchers and wound a second time; (3) it is unwound again and processed through a texturing machine. (Courtesy FMC Corporation.)

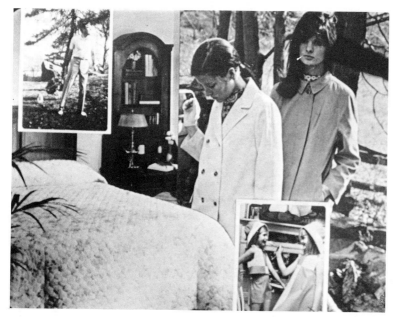

FIGURE 14.6. a. Uses of polyester. Polyester fibers are ideally blended in durable press merchandise. The outstanding characteristics of the fibers are resilience, strength, and resistance to stretching and shrinking. Polyester also provides a soft filling material for such items as pillows and comforters. (Courtesy of Man-Made Fiber Producers Association, Inc.)

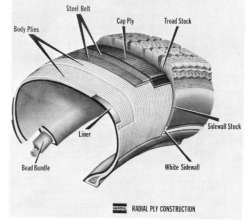

FIGURE 14.6. b. An important use of polyester, and of nylon as well, is in the construction of automobile tires. In this radial ply construction, the body ply and the cap ply are made of polyester. (Courtesy of Uniroyal, Inc.)

fabrics. This company produces another filament yarn used to make fabrics that have a silky touch and improved drapability.

BLENDS

Polyester yarns are especially appropriate for blends. A polyester and cotton blend 50/50 percent (50 percent polyester and 50 percent cotton) has become popular in minimum-care men's shirtings, women's blouses, dresses, slacks, knitted T-shirts, uniforms, and sportswear. A polyester and acrylic blend (50/50 percent) was introduced in 1960 for men's summer suitings; it is also used in slacks, sportswear, and dresses. A blend of polyester and worsted (55/45 percent) is used for men's regular suiting. Men like this fabric because it holds its press and resists wrinkles, and because wrinkles tend to hang out. It is lighter in weight than 100 percent

330

Fabric
Construction
and
Buying
Motives

worsted and tailors beautifully. Nevertheless, the high cost of wool has led to a great increase in all polyester suitings. Another satisfactory blend is polyester and rayon 65/35 percent to 50/50 for dresses.

Polyester/cotton blends are finished differently from 100 percent cotton. The cloth is singed before scouring and heat-set after finishing. To obtain dimensional stability, these blends must be given a compressive shrinkage treatment. Polyester/rayon blends are treated with resins for shrinkage control. However, the polyester/modified rayon blends do not require resin treatment.

CHARACTERISTICS OF POLYESTER

Polyester has established itself as an all-purpose fiber, suitable for a great many uses, on the person, in the home, and in industry. It blends well with many other fibers and yarns, which makes a variety of effects possible.

From the consumer's point of view, it is prized for its ease in care, reflected in its wrinkle resistance, its stability in repeated washings, little or no ironing, and its affinity to permanent heat setting to control shrinkage and sagging and to retain pleats. It is resistant to most outside elements, such as sunlight, acids in the air, bleaches, and dry cleaning solvents. Originally high in price, volume production has made its price moderate, lower at times than cotton.

The standard commodity product has distinct limitations in dyeability and printability because carriers are generally required for coloration. Serious pilling problems in staple constructions are largely overcome by the use of special low-pilling grades or by the use of filament polyester,

TABLE 14-3 Characteristics of Polyesters

---

1. **Tensile strength:** Very strong, but not as strong as nylon or aramid, and very durable.
2. **Luster:** Either bright or dull depending upon the chemical solution.
3. **Affinity for dyes:** Easy to dye fast colors with acetate dyes; newer types can be dyed with basic and disperse dyes.
4. **Blending and Crimping:** May be combined with other fibers and yarns, especially with worsted suitings, but with special yarn treatments makes a good and inexpensive substitute for worsted woolen suits.
5. **Resistance to:**
   abrasion—Tends to pill.
   heat—will not dissolve; can be ironed at 300°F to 400°F.
   sunlight—equal to nylon but better for curtains since windowglass screens out wave lengths harmful to polyester.
   insects—moths do not consume it.
   chemicals and fungi—not affected by dilute acids, cleaning solvents, and microorganisms.
   soil and stains—readily removed except for oil-based stains; tends to grey; picks up soil from the skin ("ring around the collar"). Newer types are overcoming this problem.
6. **Effect of perspiration:** Like nylon, does not absorb but dries quickly.
7. **Dimensional stability:** Resists shrinkage, stretching, and wrinkling. Easy to wash with little or no ironing; keeps shape and can be heat-set for permanent press; does not mat.
8. **Elasticity:** Superb hand, resilient.

---

which is generally also textured for comfort. Stains, particularly oily stains, frequently cannot be satisfactorily removed, and resoiling is often a problem. Difficulties with static electricity have resulted in the development of a wide variety of industry and home finishes, which generally are only partially successful.

Table 14-3 summarizes the chief characteristics.

IMPROVED POLYESTER YARNS

Polyester yarns have now been produced that improve upon the standard product. An example is Spectran® polyester.

Spectran® polyester, by Monsanto, is similar to conventional polyester in its round cross section, disperse dyeability, and excellent strength, but in other qualities it is quite different from conventional polyesters. It offers a warm soft hand, greater bulk, and supple drape.

It can be dyed with disperse dyes without carrier at atmospheric pressure. With pollution problems mounting, dyeing polyester without carrier is certain to become more important. Printing yields good results on fabrics of Spectran® polyester—both woven and knitted. It can be used in 100 percent form or in blends with acrylic and wool fibers in jersey constructions.

Stain release properties of Spectran® are superior to those of regular polyesters. In particular, release of oil-based stains, such as motor oil, butter, mayonnaise, hand cream, and mineral oil, is improved over that of regular polyesters in normal laundering.

Regular polyester fabrics have a persistent tendency to grey upon repeated laundering because they tend to act as scavengers for oils, grease, and particulate matter in the wash water. In contrast, fabrics of Spectran®, because of their inherent resistance to soil redeposition, clean up better and retain a satisfactory appearance longer.

Likewise, Spectran® polyester/wool blend fabrics have been developed. The hand of these styles is soft—almost cashmerelike—and pleasantly different from the somewhat harsh, unyielding hand of regular polyester/wool blend construction.[3]

THE ACRYLICS

PRODUCTION

Acrylic fibers are made from a chemical compound called *acryl*onitrile (the italicized letters of the compound indicate the derivation of acrylic fiber).[4] It is derived from chemicals taken from coal, petroleum or natural gas, and from air, water, and limestone. After a series of complicated chemical reactions (often combined with other chemicals to improve dye absorption), the solution formed is extruded through a spinneret. The

[3] A leatherlike fabric has recently been developed. One variety is called "Ultra-Suede." It consists of 60 percent polyester fiber and 40 percent non-fibrous polyurethane. Another variety is made of ultra-fine nylon fibers of 0.001 to 0.01 denier. With the feel of leather but only two-thirds its weight, this costly fabric is being used for dresses and coats.

[4] Acrylic is defined by the Federal Trade Commission as a manufactured fiber in which the fiber-forming substance is any long chain synthetic polymer composed of at least 85 percent by weight of acrylonitrile units.

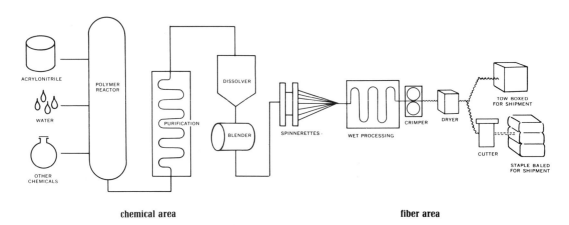

chemical area   fiber area

FIGURE 14.7. How Creslan® acrylic fiber is made. (From Creslan® pamphlet, American Cyanamid Co., center spread.)

extruded filaments are dried and stretched to improve the strength and elasticity of the fiber. The fiber may be either wet spun or dry spun. (See Chapter 13.) Acrylic fibers are produced only in staple-fiber form in this country, and are used in sweaters, hand-knitting yarns, carpets, and pile fabrics, and in blends with other staple fibers for weaving and knitting of apparel fabrics. In solution form, acrylic is important in the manufacture of paint, a nontextile.

Bicomponent acrylics, available from several companies, are permanent-crimped fibers. The shape of the crimp is comparable to the spiral of a reversible corkscrew. The fiber is not a conventional type but is made of two components, each of which differs from the other in molecular structure. Because of this unique structure, the fiber develops a three-dimensional spiral crimp when the fabric is processed. This fiber has been responsible for new style developments in knitwear because of its esthetic appearance and wool-like resilience. Bicomponent acrylics, such as *Orlon®* Sayelle by Du Pont and *Acrilan®* Types B-57 and B-94 by Monsanto, are widely used in sweaters and other outerwear, hand-knitting yarns, and carpets.

Acrylics have served well in 100 percent acrylic-fibered sweaters and blankets and in blends of 50/50 percent acrylic/cotton (or acrylic/rayon) for men's hosiery. Raschel-knit fabrics in 50/50 percent blends of acrylic/cotton improve resilience and reduce the shrinkage of cotton. Acrylic/nylon blends are found in fancy yarns (slub and textured) for knitwear that is washable and lightweight. Commercial acrylic blends are used for men's suitings, women's dress fabrics, slacks, sportswear, and carpeting.

Acrylics are readily and inexpensively dyed to almost any color, from subtle earth shades to bright hues. Colorfastness is good in all but fluorescent shades.

DEVELOPMENT

The first major acrylic fiber was Orlon. Preliminary work on it was started in the pioneering Research Division of Du Pont's Textile Fibers Department as early as 1940, but the fiber was not available commercially until 1948. Others entered the field and now there are several brands of acrylic fiber in addition to Orlon, among them:

Acrilan (Monsanto)
Creslan (American Cyanamid)
Sayelle (DuPont)
Zefkrome (Dow Badische)
Zefran II (Dow Badische, formerly Dow Chemical)

They are made in a variety of types.

CHARACTERISTICS OF ACRYLIC FIBERS

The acrylics are soft, since virtually all in the United States are made in staple form, and although they are bulky, they are light in weight. Acrylics are not as strong or as resistant to abrasion as nylon. Excellent resistance to sunlight, to pressed-crease retention, and to moths is important to the consumer. Finishing acrylics presents no particular problem. Acrylics have moderate to good resistance to pilling. They are subject to the same problem of static electricity as other noncellulosic man-made fibers, but this is generally overcome by application of selected antistatic finishes.

The chief characteristics that knowledgeable consumers have in mind when selecting acrylics in 100 percent form or in blends depend upon end use. For outer clothing, this fiber holds its shape well, resists abrasion, washes easily, dries quickly, and needs little or no ironing. It avoids crushing and mussing in travel. For coats it is fluffy and light. For carpeting, acrylics provide a luxurious texture and ease in cleaning.

Table 14-4 summarizes the characteristics of this fiber.

TABLE 14-4. Characteristics of Acrylics

1. **Tensile strength**: Fair in spun form but durable.
2. **Weight**: Light and soft, fluffy and bulky in fabric form.
3. **Affinity to dyeing**: Many types can be dyed in bright colors. If solution dyed, fast to perspiration (as well as sunlight).
4. **Blending**: Adds above characteristics to blends.
5. **Resistance to:**
   Abrasion: Good, but to pilling moderate.
   Heat: Holds heat, warm.
   Sunlight: Colorfast if solution dyed.
   Soil: Easy to wash, quick to dry.
   Insects: Moth-resistant.
   Chemicals and microorganisms: Excellent
6. **Absorption and perspiration**: Poor; hydrophilic like nylon and polyesters.
7. **Dimensional stability**: Excellent crease retention, resistance to wrinkling, sagging, shrinking, and stretching; withstands repeated laundering (wash-and-wear).

FIGURE 14.8. Typical use of
acrylic fibers in Nordic sweater
and scarf. (Courtesy of E.I.
DuPont de Nemours & Company,
Inc.)

THE MOD-ACRYLICS   The modacrylics, which have been in the marketplace for many years, were once simply called "acrylics," a term used to describe almost any fiber containing acrylonitrile. Under the Textile Fiber Products Identification Act of 1960, acrylics are officially described as containing at least 85 percent acrylonitrile. Fibers containing 35 to 84 percent acrylonitrile are described as "modacrylic" fibers, when the acrylonitrile is a minor component and, for example, polyvinylchloride is the major component. These chemicals are derived from elements in natural air, salt, and water. True, these modacrylics rendered excellent service in industrial and certain apparel and home furnishings end uses, but they could more realistically be described as polyvinyl chloride fibers and their properties mirrored their makeup. Other modacrylics did have acrylonitrile as a major component by a narrow margin, but they had serious deficiencies that limited their use.

As more emphasis was placed on flame retardancy and other built-in pluses mentioned below, the fraction of additives in premium acrylics rose steadily until the 15 percent limit was exceeded and these precisely engineered fibers became modacrylics. These acryliclike modacrylics are one of the fastest growing segments of the textile market, as their use, in

VEREL® Modacrylic Fiber

How it is Made at Tennessee Eastman Company, in Kingsport, Tennessee

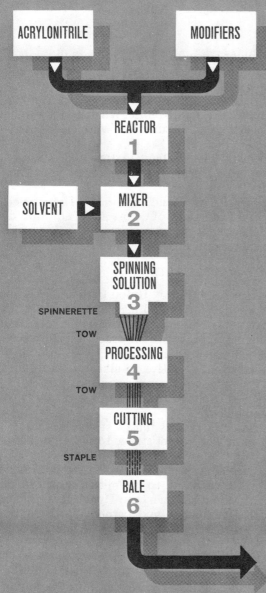

Man-made fibers have been assigned eighteen generic names by the United States Federal Trade Commission under authority of the Textile Fiber Products Identification Act. A modacrylic fiber is defined as follows: "A manufactured fiber in which the fiber-forming substance is any long chain synthetic polymer composed of less than 85% but at least 35% by weight of acrylonitrile units $(-CH_2-CH-)$."
$$\qquad\qquad\qquad\qquad CN$$

1 POLYMERIZATION IN REACTOR: The production of VEREL modacrylic fiber begins in a polymerization reactor where acrylonitrile and certain modifiers are combined into long chain-like molecules called **polymer. The type of modifier used helps give VEREL fiber properties which are distinctive from other modacrylic fibers.**

2 MIXING: A suitable solvent and the polymer are placed in a tank where they are stirred together until the polymer has dissolved and the mixture has a consistency similar to molasses.

3 SPINNING:
- This mixture, called **spinning solution,** is forced through the microscopic holes of the **spinnerette** . . . a device similar to a miniature shower head . . . forming thin, continuous strands of solution.
- The solvent is removed leaving the **polymer.**
- The strands are gathered into bundles of continuous fibers called **tow,** which looks like untwisted rope.

4 PROCESSING THE TOW:
- The tow is moved to the processing area where it is treated to make it resist shrinking or stretching.
- Lubricating oils are added to aid in spinning yarns.
- A crimp (like a permanent wave) is added to give texture and bulk.

5 CUTTING: The tow now moves to a cutting machine where the continuous strands are cut into short lengths called **staple fiber.**

6 BALING: The staple fibers, looking very much like wool, are compressed into bales and wrapped for shipment.

SHIPPING: The VEREL fiber is shipped to textile mills where it will be spun into yarn and woven into fabric.

Tennessee Eastman Company produces the VEREL modacrylic fiber. It does not weave fabrics or make garments or home furnishings.

FIGURE 14.9. Production of modacrylic fibers. (Courtesy Tennessee Eastman Company.)

336
*Fabric
Construction
and
Buying
Motives*

many instances, meets legislative requirements for flame retardancy without sacrificing the superb aesthetic properties of the acrylics. Moreover, these modacrylics are engineered to perform well in both wet and dry processing, and specific products are tailored to meet the precise needs of each market.

MAJOR CHARACTERISTICS

Compared to the acrylic, the major advantage of the modacrylic is its high flame resistance. It is difficult to ignite when exposed to flame and is self-extinguishing. But it has a lower melting point and will soften at a lower temperature. This feature makes it possible to mix fibers that shrink in different amounts in the surface of a pile fabric. When applied to heat, the surface takes on the appearance of natural fur, with both long and under hairs.

Modacrylics also have a specially soft resilient texture and a warm and luxurious hand. While hydrophobic, drops of water on a coat can be shaken off, leaving the coat dry.

Like the acrylics they resist acids well and have a good resistance to abrasion. They can be dyed in a wide range of colors and if solution dyed are colorfast and resistant to sunlight, perspiration, and wetness. They may be heat set for shape resistance and shrinkage control.

BRANDS AND THEIR SPECIAL CHARACTERISTICS

Dynel is an early modacrylic fiber produced by Union Carbide. This fiber, made from a combination of vinyl chloride and acrylonitrile, is resistant to flame, water, microorganisms, and insects. Because of its good flame and sunlight resistance, the fiber is appropriate for draperies; and because of its resistance to nearly all chemicals but acetone, it is suitable for industrial filter cloths. It is somewhat sensitive to alkalies. Its resilience makes the fibers particularly well adapted for use in pile construction to resemble fur. The fiber is also used in the manufacture of wigs, along with the newer modacrylics discussed below.

Dynel can be safely ironed at 225° F.; its tensile strength is poor; its stability to repeated launderings is fair; its resistance to pilling is fair; and its abrasion resistance is fair.

Another early modacrylic is Verel, produced by Eastman Chemical Products, Inc. Like Dynel, it is resistant to chemicals, resilient, and nonflammable. It has better abrasion resistance than Dynel. It is primarily used for furlike fabrics, apparel, draperies and carpets. Both of these modacrylic fibers come only in staple form and have limited use at present.

Verel can be dyed in a variety of shades and cross-dye effects. The neutral dyeing premetallized dyes are usually best for fastness to light and washing. For most purposes Verel does not require bleaching, because it is unusually white. Should bleaching be desired, sodium chlorite and formic acid are used.

ACRYLIC-LIKE MODACRYLIC FIBERS

A series of new acrylic-like modacrylic fibers are being marketed by Monsanto, primarily to meet needs for reduced flammability. One, used to

FIGURE 14.10. Coat, showing typical use of modacrylic fibers. (Photograph courtesy of Eastman Chemical Products, Inc., a subsidiary of Eastman Kodak Company.)

make Elura® wigs, combines many of the aesthetic and performance characteristics of human hair with certain advantages of man-made fibers—good resistance to flammability and to damage from heat. (Some wig's frizz when hit with a wave of heat from opening an oven door.) Professional stylists find Elura® wigs can be restyled and otherwise handled much like wigs of human hair.

Monsanto modacrylic for Elura® wigs is producer-colored in a score of carefully selected wig shades. The different deniers available permit control of wig softness.

Another acrylic-like modacrylic fiber produced by Monsanto is SEF®. It has a semidull luster and can be dyed in a variety of colors. Properly constructed and finished apparel fabrics of SEF® modacrylic fiber will extinguish when the source of ignition is removed, and they meet or exceed recognized standards, such as the U.S. Department of Commerce Standard (DOC-FF3-71) for the flammability of children's sleepwear.

Several companies have marketed various types of children's sleepwear made from SEF® fabrics. Woven and knit fabrics, including warp knits,

338
*Fabric
Construction
and
Buying
Motives*

are used to make flame-retardant garments in virtually all the favorite styles, including the popular fleece types. Other sleepwear, institutional garments, and dresses with SEF® are also marketed. Fully as important as the safety features are the comfort factors.

Flame-retardant draperies and casement fabrics, tufted scatter rugs, and bath mats and sets made of SEF® modacrylic fiber and its blends are being marketed by many companies. These fibers are well suited for bedspreads and upholstery too.

SUMMARY   Consumers are more aware of the fiber content of their garments since the TFPIA has required that all fibers be labeled by generic names as specified by the FTC. Previous to the enactment of this law, consumers had become familiar with trade names such as Orlon, Dacron, Acrilan, and Dynel. But with the new generic names such as acrylic, modacrylic, and polyester, the consumer not only has to learn what these terms mean but also has to learn the characteristics of each of these new classes of fibers and how to care for them. If informative labels are adequate, learning is relatively easy. Also, if the consumer associates a trade name with the generic class to which it belongs, she will be able to differentiate these generic names. For example, if she remembers the phrases Orlon acrylic fiber, Acrilan acrylic fiber, Dacron polyester, and Fortrel polyester, she will probably remember the characteristics of each generic classification.

By and large, the man-made fibers with noncellulosic bases—nylon, polyester, acrylic, and modacrylic—have the following plus qualities (unless the structure of the fiber is modified):

1. Dimensional stability (when properly heat-set).
2. Strength and durability (long wear).
3. Ease of care (ease in washing, quick drying, little or no ironing, durable pleats and creases).
4. Resiliency (wrinkle resistance).
5. Elasticity (comfort and fit).
6. Resistance to moths and mildew.

Although pilling and static electricity may still exist, ways have been found to overcome or to lessen these objectionable features.

**REVIEW
QUESTIONS**

1. (*a*) What is the major difference between rayon and the noncellulosics?
   (*b*) What is the major difference between acrylic fibers and nylon?
   (*c*) What is the major difference between polyester fibers and nylon?
2. Define the following:
   (*a*) polymerization
   (*b*) melt spinning
   (*c*) stretch spinning
   (*d*) curing
   (*e*) pigmentation
3. (*a*) Name two solvents for nylon.
   (*b*) How can nylon be identified chemically?
4. (*a*) List the important physical properties of nylon.
   (*b*) List the important chemical properties of nylon.

5. (*a*) Give ten specific uses of nylon.
   (*b*) Why do consumers buy nylon?
6. (*a*) Why is Dynel considered a modacrylic fiber?
   (*b*) How does Dynel differ from Orlon chemically?
   (*c*) What specific advantages does Orlon have over Dynel?
7. (*a*) For what purposes is Verel modacrylic suited?
   (*b*) What is an advantage of Orlon acrylic over nylon for a girl's sweater?
8. How does Dacron polyester differ physically and chemically from Orlon acrylic?
9. (*a*) What can be done to overcome static electricity?
   (*b*) What can be done to prevent pilling?
10. (*a*) Why do consumers like Dacron polyester?
    (*b*) For what uses is Kodel polyester most popular?

EXPERI-MENTS

1. *Alkali test.* Take yarns or small pieces of fabric constructed from the four fibers discussed in this chapter. Boil for five minutes in 10 percent solution of sodium hydroxide. Describe the effect of strong alkali on each fiber.
2. *Acid test.* Place as many of the yarns from these fabrics as possible in concentrated sulfuric acid for five or ten minutes. Describe the effect of strong acid on each fiber.
3. *Microscopic test.* Examine the nylon fiber under the microscope. Draw the fiber as you see it. Examine and draw as many of the newer synthetics as possible. Note the similarities between some of these fibers and the difficulty in identifying them by microscope.
4. *Absorbency test.* Cut strips eight inches by one inch in both warp and filling directions of the following fabrics: nylon, polyester, acrylic, and modacrylic. Brush water-soluble red ink lightly onto the strips to serve as an indicator. Support each strip above the beaker of water (80°F.) so that the edge of the sample is just one inch below the surface of the water. Measure the height to which the water rises at one minute, five minutes, and ten minutes. Rate the fabric as follows at the end of ten minutes:

5 to 6 inches	Excellent
4 to 5 inches	Very good
3 to 4 inches	Good
2 to 3 inches	Fair
1 to 2 inches	Poor
0 to 1 inch	Very poor

(Weirick Method, Sears, Roebuck and Company.)

PROJECT

What fabrics would you advise for the different articles in a wardrobe for a two-week winter cruise to Puerto Rico and the Virgin Islands; a trip on which there will be limited laundry facilities?

GLOSSARY (See Chapter 15.)

Special Purpose
Noncellulosic Fibers
and the Consumer

15

In addition to the four main classes of man-made noncellulosic textile fibers—nylon, polyester, acrylic, and modacrylic—that can be thought of as all-purpose fibers, others excel in filling special purposes and needs. They may be grouped as follows:

To reduce flammability: glass, aramid, and novoloid.
To resist heat, wetness and sunlight: olefin and saran.
To stretch and provide permanent stretch: spandex and rubber, including lastril and anidex.
For esthetic effect: metallic.
For bonding: vinyon.

All of the above fibers are chemically derived except for natural rubber, glass, metallic, and azlon, which are derived from non-fibrous sources. See Table 2-1.

These special purpose fibers will be discussed in the order indicated above.

Three other special purpose fibers—azlon, nytril, and vinal—are not produced in the United States and are of little importance in American consumption.

GLASS FIBERS
The generic name "glass" is defined by the FTC as a "manufactured fiber in which the fiber-forming substance is glass." Its mill consumption in pounds is the largest of the special purpose fibers discussed in this chapter. The process of making glass into fiber was discovered by research engineers of Owens-Illinois Glass Company at Newark, Ohio. The product called Fiberglas was first produced commercially by Owens-Corning Fiberglas Corporation in 1936. Thus it is the first of the noncellulosic fibers produced, but not the first made by chemical synthesis—that was nylon in 1939. These fibers have had a phenomenal development, and their future looks bright. Other producers of glass fibers are PPG Industries, Inc. (formerly the Pittsburgh Plate Glass Co.), Ferro Corporation, Johns-Manville, and others.

FIGURE 15.1. Hallway entrance to the Metropolitan Opera's executive office area. Window draperies are made of a medium weight, open weave fabric of Fiberglas, "Fresco." (Photograph courtesy of Owens-Corning Fiberglas Corporation.)

PRODUCTION

Glass marbles five-eighths of an inch in diameter are melted in an electrically heated furnace that has a V-shaped bushing made of a metal with a higher melting point than glass. Molten glass enters the top of the bushing and is drawn downward by gravity. It emerges through orifices at the bottom of the bushing. Each hole makes a long continuous filament, and these filaments are combined to make one strand. Then the strands are wound on spools that put in the twist. The winder revolves faster than the molten glass flows, and the resulting tension draws out the filaments. The yarns and cords are then processed on standard textile machinery.

The diameter of the fiber can be controlled by regulating (1) the viscosity of the molten mass through temperature control, (2) the size of the holes through which the glass flows, and (3) the rate of speed at which fibers are drawn.

To make staple fiber, jets of compressed air are used to draw the molten glass. The molten glass flows through orifices at the base of the furnace. Compressed air, or steam jets, break up the filaments into lengths varying from 8 to 15 inches. The staples so made are drawn upon a revolving drum in the form of a cobwebby ribbon. This web of fibers is gathered into a sliver and wound in such a way that the fibers lie parallel lengthwise. These slivers can be made smaller in diameter and then twisted

342
*Fabric
Construction
and
Buying
Motives*

or plied into yarns by the same type of machinery used to process other long-staple fibers.

Two general types of finishes are employed on Fiberglas, depending upon its end use as an industrial fiber or as a decorative fabric. We are concerned here with the decorative type, with such fabrics as marquisettes and casement cloth, and fabrics that are to be screen-printed. A basic finishing process subjects the fabric to high temperatures to release the stress developed in the yarns during twisting and weaving. This treatment gives fabrics principally a good hand, wrinkle resistance, and durability. Then fabrics are treated to relubricate the filaments. Color can be applied, and a protective agent may be administered to improve abrasion resistance. Coronizing, a finish of Owens-Corning, is a combination of (1) heat-setting to relax the fibers, to crimp the yarn permanently, and to set the weave; (2) finishing with resins to produce resistance to abrasion, color retention, water repellency, and launderability. It has been found that a Coronized glass fabric treated with a special chemical solution improves the hand and its dyeability.

Fiberglas can be yarn dyed or printed, with good resistance to crocking. Pigmented resins are applied in the same manner as in the pigment printing or dyeing of cottons and rayons.

CHARACTERISTICS

The outstanding characteristic of glass fiber is that it is fireproof. Glass fiber will not burn and will not melt below 1500°F. It has very great tensile and bursting strength; resistance to microorganisms, moisture, and sunlight; and it provides electrical insulation. But glass fiber is attacked by hydrofluoric and phosphoric acids and by hot solutions of weak alkalies as well as cold solutions of strong alkalies. The fiber will not shrink, stretch, or sag.

The fibers, which under the microscope resemble translucent rods, will not absorb moisture, and a wet surface of the fabric will dry quickly without affecting the strength. While glass fabrics will not crock, when dyed they do not resist abrasion, a major shortcoming.

MAJOR USES

The fire-resistant quality of glass fiber and its resistance to sunlight deterioration make it admirably suited for curtains and draperies in the home, theater lobby, public commercial building, and also for fireproof and waterproof wallpaper. Since glass fibers will not shrink, stretch, or sag, accurate measurements for curtains and draperies are possible. Glass is also used for reinforcements for molded plastics in boats and airplane parts and as batting for insulation in buildings, boats, and railway cars.

Fiberglas is well suited for nonallergic pillow stuffing, ironing board covers, and interlinings for women's and men's wear. Fiberglas yarns suitable for wearing apparel are being developed by Owens-Corning.

Some homemakers who have had trouble sewing glass-fibered fabrics might avoid future difficulties by the following procedures:

1. Use a good quality, fine cotton mercerized thread.
2. Use a longer stitch.

3. Use looser tension top and bottom threads.
4. Lighten pressure of the pressure foot.
5. Use a sharp needle.

Furthermore, the sewing machine should be guided rather than pushed or tugged. Only washable drapery heading should be used with Fiberglas, and Fiberglas ought not to be lined.

Glass fibers can be easily washed by hand and drip-dried. Cloths of glass fibers should not be ironed. They are not machine washable or dry cleanable. Because glass fibers are easily abraded, they should not be allowed to blow in the wind at open windows, where they could be badly damaged.

ARAMID

Aramid is the name given by the Federal Trade Commission in 1974 to a class of aromatic polyamide fibers, distinctly different in properties from the more conventional aliphatic polyamides, or nylons. On an equal weight basis, the high tenacity aramid fibers have greater strength than any other fiber, although nylon is as high as other aramid types. The aramids perform well at highly elevated temperatures, and can be made with a high "modulus," or resistance to stretch, that makes them especially well suited for industrial applications.

There are two commercial aramids, both products of Du Pont. One is Nomex, a high temperature-resistant fiber used in protective clothing for fire fighters; race car drivers; industrial workers exposed to heat, flames, and corrosive chemicals; and by the military forces. Under most circumstances Nomex does not support flame but merely chars at temperatures in the range of 1800 to 1850°F.

The other newer aramid is Kevlar, whose major use is for tire reinforcement where its great strength (five times that of steel on a weight basis) and resistance to stretch is most valuable to tire performance. There are two other types of Kevlar in use. Kevlar 49 is used as a reinforcing fiber for plastic composites in aircraft, high pressure vessels, sporting goods, and boat hulls. Kevlar 29 is used in cables and ropes. Kevlar is being studied by the National Institute of Law Enforcement and Criminal Justice, a division of the Department of Justice in Washington, D. C. The fabric may serve as armor to protect policemen from bullets and knives. In future years it may become standard for the policeman's uniform, lightweight and flexible.

NOVOLOID

Novoloid is the generic name for a noncellulosic man-made fiber derived from phenol, a chemical acidic compound of carbon, hydrogen, and oxygen. The U.S. Carborundum Company produces it under the brand name of Kynol. It is highly flame resistant. It is also lightweight, resilient, and unaffected by many acids. It is used for felting, batting, and flame resistant clothing.

OLEFIN

The generic name "olefin" denotes fibers with paraffin bases and is defined as a manufactured fiber. At least 85 percent of the fiber-forming

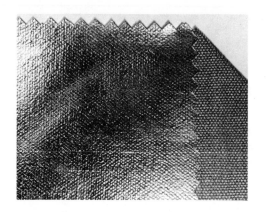

FIGURE 15.2. Flame resistant aluminized fabric of Kynol filling and Nomex (nylon) warp. Fabric produced by the Carborundum® Co., Niagara Falls, N.Y. (Photo by Jonas Grushkin.)

substance must be a long chain synthetic polymer composed of at least 85 percent by weight of ethylene, propylene, or other olefin units.

Polyethylene is a resin that is formed as a result of polymerization of ethylene under heat and pressure. This resin is melted, extruded, and cooled in continuous monofilament form. The polyolefin fibers so formed still have a waxy hand, low heat resistance, a fair-to-good average strength (depending on the type), fair abrasion resistance, and floating ability. Such characteristics appear to render these fibers unsuitable for use in apparel. But because of their good resistance to sunlight, they have found uses in drapery and upholstery fabrics. Since these fibers have excellent resistance to chemicals, they can be used in fiber cloths, braids, cords, ropes, and webbings. Considerable research and development may bring new uses for them.

Du Pont's product, Vexar, is a polyethylene netting made by extruding the polymer directly into net form. Diameter, size, design, and color of each filament can be controlled. Vexar has the usual properties of polyethylene resins: flexibility and resistance to moisture, chemicals, rot, and mildew. Hercules Inc., produces a plastic netting called Delnet®. Propylene, based on propylene gas, was first produced for textiles in Italy by Montecatini in 1951. Today it is produced by several United States companies as well as firms in Europe and Japan. It is a paraffin-based fiber and therefore is classed under the generic name of olefin. Propylene's advantages over ethylene are that it is lighter, stronger, and less sensitive to heat, and it does not have the undesirable waxy hand. It is also quite inexpensive and has excellent resistance to chemicals, excellent strength, good resistance to sunlight (in special light-stabilized grades), and very good abrasion resistance. Its chief drawbacks have been its low melting point (326° to 333°F.). Montecatini has developed the first commercial polypropylene fiber that is dyeable. It is a chemically modified type that can be dyed in raw stock, yarn, or piece, alone or in blends. Acid, premetallized, chrome, vat, and reactive dyestuffs may be used.

More recently, fiber producers have used various means to add a dye receptor to the fiber by incorporating nickel or aluminum salts to provide dye sites for metallized disperse dyes. An acid dyeable polypropylene fiber is being developed.[1]

[1] "Chemistry in the Economy" (ACS, 1973), p. 97.

Significant developments in dyeability of fibers which previously resisted available dyes are accelerating the use of olefin in apparel and home fashions. Both solution-dyed and dyeable forms are offered commercially.

MAJOR USES

The largest single application of polypropylene is in carpeting. Carpets made from this olefin are used in homes and in nonresidential installations (hotels, schools, offices, and stores). In addition to conventional carpet pile, polypropylene olefin is used in nonwoven felts for outdoor purposes. The durability of polypropylene olefin has made it a dominant fiber for indoor-outdoor carpeting, where weather resistance, good cleanability, strength, and resistance to moisture, mildew, and rot are important factors. Upholstery fabrics are another important polypropylene product. The fabrics are generally plaids and stripes, but subdued colorations are also being offered.

One hundred percent polypropylene olefin and polypropylene olefin in combination with other fibers are used in hosiery, ties, undergarments, sweaters, pile fabrics, and sportswear. Olefin contributes comfort, shape retention, long wear, and easy maintenance to apparel.

Olefin fibers, both the woven and nonwoven forms, are extensively used in industry for filter fabrics, industrial felts, laundry bags and dye nets, rope and cordage, sewing thread, and sandbags. This fiber has a dominant position in backing fabrics for tufted carpets.

Wool and polypropylene (30/70 percent and 35/65 percent) have been blended, as well as cotton (35/65 percent). Accordingly, polypropylene has possibilities for an increasing market in a number of fields.

Producers of polypropylene fibers in the United States include Hercules Inc., Phillips Fiber Corporation, Exxon Chemical Corporation, and Patchogue-Plymouth Co.

FIGURE 15.3. Use of olefin fibers. Because of their low specific gravity, olefin fibers provide bulk with a minimum of weight. Since olefin does not absorb moisture, it is highly stain resistant. The fibers are used extensively in carpeting. (Courtesy of Man-Made Fiber Producers Association, Inc.)

FIGURE 15.4. Outdoor chair, showing typical use of saran. (Photograph courtesy of Firestone Tire & Rubber Company, former manufacturers of saran.)

SARAN

"Saran" is the generic name for vinylidene chloride and vinyl chloride (at least 80 percent by weight) copolymer resin and yarns extruded from it.[2] It was first introduced as a fiber in 1939 by the Dow Chemical Company, now Dow Plastics of North Miami, Florida.

Like nylon, polyester, and other fibers made from synthetic polymers, saran is thermoplastic. Its basic raw materials are petroleum and salt. Ethylene is made from the petroleum and chlorine from the salt. These two chemicals combine to form another, which is converted into vinylidene chloride. The chemical is easily polymerized. Resin is supplied to the manufacturer in powdered form. The powder is heated to form a fluid, which is forced through a spinneret. The filaments are hardened in water, stretched, and wound on spools.

A large proportion of the yarn is monofilament, although a limited amount of staple is produced. Because it is a stiff, plastic-type yarn and resistant to sunlight, it is good for screening and outdoor furniture. It has good resistance to chemicals and is nonflammable. Colorfastness of saran is excellent when dyed with disperse dyes in pigment-spun colors; stability to repeated launderings is good; and abrasion resistance is good. However, it has low tensile strength; the hand is stiff and plastic; and safe ironing temperature is low—150° F. It is more expensive than olefin fibers.

MAJOR USES

Saran is used for trolling lines, fishing leaders, tennis racket strings, laundry nets, and suspenders. Originally made in monofilament yarn for outdoor furniture, seat covers for automobiles and buses, and upholstery, it is now also used for drapery fabrics, sheer curtaining, rugs, and doll's hair. Saran is appropriately used where colorfastness (color is "built in"), easy cleaning, quick drying, and resistance to mildew, moths, soil, grease, chemicals, and abrasion are requisites.

[2] Defined by the FTC under the TFPIA.

346

SPANDEX "Spandex" is the generic name of synthetic fibers derived from a chemical substance known as segmented polyurethane (which must comprise at least 85 percent of the long chain synthetic polymer). Plastic foams of this kind suitable for lamination were discussed in Chapter 6. Spandex fibers are known for their excellent elongation and nearly instantaneous recovery. They are not rubber and are superior to it in resistance to sunlight, abrasion, oils, and oxidation. Garments of spandex fit, control, and wear well. However, they do discolor, and the spandex industry is trying to correct this fault.

One of the best-known trade names is Lycra by Du Pont, which has been most successfully used for foundation garments, support hosiery, tops of socks, and elastic tapes. Lycra threads may be covered or uncovered. Uncovered Lycra has the outward appearance of unsupported, white rubber yarn. Uncovered Lycra yarns are more sheer, thinner, and lighter than covered yarns. Warner Brothers Company, makers of foundation garments, claims that covered spandex adds weight and opacity to an article but does not add control power. Some garments contain spandex as well as nonspandex elastic in waistbands, closures, and panels. This factor may affect both the fit and wearing qualities of the garment. Other companies making spandex are Ameliotex, Inc., Numa and Globe Manufacturing (Glospan), and Union Carbide (Unel).

Consumers like spandex for foundation garments because of its elasticity and comfort. It gives satisfactory control without boning for the small and average figures. With appropriate boning, spandex garments have excellent control. Garments of spandex are light in weight, cool (the skin can "breathe"), and washable in an automatic washer. Spandex dries

FIGURE 15.5. Typical use of spandex. Spandex fibers are noted for their great elasticity, light weight, strength, and durability. (Courtesy of Man-Made Fiber Producers Association, Inc.)

348
*Fabric
Construction
and
Buying
Motives*

quickly. Foundation garments are made with spandex by many well-known national manufacturers.

NYLON/SPANDEX BICONSTITUENT FIBER

A fundamental re-examination of the properties needed for a more satisfactory hosiery product resulted in the spandex biconstituent fiber by Monsanto Textiles Company. Trademarked Monvelle®, the fiber combines the strength and sheerness of nylon with the resilience, power, and stretch of spandex.

The nylon and spandex segments are extruded side-by-side so that they are joined along the entire length. By decree of the FTC, this structure is properly labeled a "biconstituent" fiber.

The two components in Monvelle® are so dissimilar that drawing develops an intense crimp. The crimp causes the fiber to coil like a spring and the entire "cylinder" of coils even starts to coil if completely unrestrained. This tight crimp is produced by the rubber-band nature of the spandex, which causes it to try to return to its original length after drawing, but it is restrained by the drawn nylon. With one side of the fiber contracting and the other not, tremendous crimping force is built into the

FIGURE 15.6.   a. With the acid dyes used to color the fiber, only the nylon portion is dyed and the transparent spandex portion blends with the skin coloration—another reason for the extra sheer appearance of Monvelle® support hosiery and pantyhose.

FIGURE 15.6 (cont.).   b. The smooth extension of the Monvelle® coils with gradually increasing pull is the reason that support hosiery and pantyhose made with this pioneering product give measured control over a broad range of elongation. This means better fit for women of all sizes and shapes, not just those ideally proportioned ones of the four or five standard sizes. (Courtesy Monsanto Corporation.)

fiber. Just like a spring, the fiber coil extends smoothly with increasing pull, which is an excellent way to get desired force levels over a wide range of elongation. This combination of an elastomer (spandex) and a thermoplastic (nylon) in a single filament leads to several properties which are important to the consumer as well as the manufacturer. First it provides excellent balance of properties essential to comfortable support panty hose and hosiery. Second, fabrics of Monvelle® with their snug cling and higher denier per filament tend to prevent formation of loops and loose filaments which would promote snagging, picking, pulling, and running. They provide snug comfortable fit, no bagging, and fine sheerness. Third, Monvelle® garments, because of their acid-resistant urethane (spandex) content, do not fail as quickly as their nylon equivalents in acid-polluted atmospheres.[3]

RUBBER

"Rubber" is the generic name of man-made fibers in which the fiber-forming substance is comprised of natural or synthetic rubber.

FIBERS FROM NATURAL RUBBER

The core of fibers is made with natural rubber. (Natural rubber is made of a milky fluid called latex, which is tapped from the bark of the Para rubber tree.) The latex fluid is forced through tiny holes the diameter of the thread desired and is hardened in a solidifying bath. Then the thread is vulcanized, and ammonia is added to preserve it. Round threads retain their elasticity longer than strips cut from sheets, because round threads can have their surface completely vulcanized, whereas strips cut from sheets necessarily have two unvulcanized edges. This latex elastic rubber fiber is covered with cotton, silk, wool, or rayon to form a yarn that can be woven or knitted into cloth for clothing.

Lastex is a trademark for a combination yarn produced by UniRoyal, Inc. The core of the yarn is covered with cotton, silk, wool, rayon, or nylon to make a yarn that can be woven or knitted into cloth or webbing. As webbing, it is used for foundation garments, shoes, garters, suspenders, tops of shorts and briefs, wristlets and anklets, tops of hosiery, shoelaces, and surgical bandages. In cloth, it is used for riding breeches, bathing suits, nets, and laces. Lastex yarns can be used for gathering the tops of blouses and to stabilize the ribbing of nylon sweaters.

The chief advantage of Lastex is enduring elasticity. Lastex garments shape themselves to the figure of the wearer and hence fit well. The Lastex garment should be laundered frequently with lukewarm suds for best service. Firestone also produces a covered yarn called Contro.

FIBERS FROM SYNTHETIC RUBBER

Chemists have succeeded in creating synthetic rubber that has much the same qualities as natural rubber. It has both textile and nontextile uses. For consumer goods it is used for a variety of knitted and woven fabrics, either covered or uncovered, where stretch is important.

[3] As reported in *Knitting Times*, November 5, 1973.

350
*Fabric
Construction
and
Buying
Motives*

There are actually three varieties that differ in their chemical composition. One is made from chemicals that produce hydrocarbons which are chemically very similar to natural rubber. Another is a polymer of acrylonitrile and butadiene units. This type may properly be called "lastrile" as a generic name, but is not manufactured in the United States. The third is a chemical composition that contains at least 35 percent chloroprene as the fiber-producing substance.

ANIDEX "Anidex" is the generic name of a man-made fiber in which the fiber-forming substance is any long chain synthetic polymer composed of at least 80 percent by weight of one or more esters of a monohydric alcohol and acrylic acid.[4]

The fiber was first produced in 1969 by Rohm and Haas Co., under the trademark Anim/8. Anidex is neither spandex nor rubber but is a monofilament elastomeric acrylate fiber. The fiber can be used in the ways that spandex yarns are used, for example, uncovered, wrapped, and core-spun forms.

CHARACTERISTICS

Permanent stretch and recovery are the most important characteristics of anidex. While Anim/8 can be dyed with both disperse dyes and basic dyes, fastness to light is not as good when dyed with basic dyes as with disperse dyes. Foundation garments and hosiery made with anidex have improved fit, comfort, and appearance. Since this fiber has resistance to gas fading, oxidation, sunlight, oils, and chlorine bleach, it can be used in sportswear, athletic wear, career apparel, and upholstery.

METALLIC The FTC defines the generic term "metallic" as "a manufactured fiber composed of metal, plastic-coated metal, metal-coated plastic, or a core completely covered by metal."

Real gold and silver are seldom used for textile yarns, but their effect can be duplicated by the use of aluminum in combination with man-made substances and produces a pleasing esthetic effect.

[4] Definition by Federal Trade Commission.

FIGURE 15.7. Typical uses of metallic fibers for evening gowns and home furnishings. (Photo by Jonas Grushkin.)

A common process for producing metallic filaments is to coat one or both sides of aluminum foil with adhesive to which coloring matter has been added. To each side of the adhesive coated foil a sheet of transparent plastic film is applied. The resultant product is then slit into narrow widths.

The advantages of coated metallic filaments are that they are nontarnishable, can be either dry-cleaned or washed, and can be ironed at a low setting. Metallic yarns are frequently used in combination with other yarns for draperies, upholstery, place mats, tablecloths, evening gowns, sweaters, blouses, ribbons, trimmings, fashion fabrics by the yard, and knitting and crocheting yarns. Steel yarns are used in making tires.

An important producer of metallic yarn (Lurex®) in the United States is the Dow Badische Company.

VINYON

The basis for the generic class of fibers called "vinyon" is polyvinyl chloride, whose basic materials are found in salt water and petroleum. In order to be generically classified as vinyon the FTC has specified that the fiber be composed of not less than 85 percent of polyvinyl chloride.

Vinyon was first commercially produced in the United States in 1939 by the American Viscose Corporation—now the FMC Corporation. It is now also made by the Voplex Corporation's Plastic Division.

Vinyon has poor tensile strength, shrinks at 150°F. and melts at 260° F., but has good resistance to chemicals, bacteria, and moths and can be dyed with (dispersed) acetate dyes. It is used largely for industrial purposes as a bonding agent for nonwoven fabrics and products.

NONCELLU- LOSIC FIBERS PRODUCED ABROAD

AZLON

Azlon as defined by the FTC is "a manufactured fiber in which the fiber-forming substance is composed of any regenerated naturally occurring proteins."[5] Azlon, then, includes fibers derived from plant and animal proteins. Natural sources of raw materials (for these fibers are proteins) are milk curd (casein), peanuts, cottonseed, cornmeal (zein), egg white, soybeans, and chicken feathers. Azlon has been blended with wool for suits, coats, and knitted outerwear.

NYTRIL

Nytril is a man-made fiber composed largely of a complex chemical substance known as vinylidene dinitrile (where the vinylidene dimitrile content is no less than every other unit in the polymer chain),[6] derived from ammonia and natural gas.

Until 1962, this fiber, under the trade name Darvan, was made in this country by Celanese Fibers Company, a division of Celanese Corporation. Early in 1962, however, Celanese reached an agreement with Farbwerke Hoechst of Germany to build a jointly owned plant in Europe for the

[5] See FTC definition of this generic fiber, Chapter 2.
[6] Ibid.

352
*Fabric
Construction
and
Buying
Motives*

production and marketing of Darvan. (In Europe the fiber is known as Travis.) Its uses include sweaters, suits, and coats. The United States has not produced nytril fibers since 1961.

Nytril's properties resemble those of the acrylic fibers, although it is weaker, harder to dye, and slightly more sensitive to heat than either the Orlon or Acrilan acrylics. Nytril fibers are suitable for articles that need no pressing, such as pile fabrics and blends with wool. Nytril can be permanently pleated and has an excellent soft, woolly hand. It has good colorfastness, excellent sunlight resistance, good stability after repeated launderings, fair tensile strength, and fair resistance to pilling.

Available in staple form, its uses are in sweaters, suits, coats, and a variety of other products.

VINAL

"Vinal" is the generic name for man-made fibers in which the fiber-forming substance is any long chain synthetic polymer composed of at least 50 percent by weight of vinyl alcohol units and in which the total of the various acetal units is at least 85 percent by weight of the fiber. This class of fibers was developed in Japan.

Vinal is claimed to have very good strength and abrasion resistance but does not match nylon in these qualities. Vinal fibers soften at low temperatures but have good chemical resistance. Colorfastness can be achieved in vinal with vat dyes. For apparel uses, its poor dry-wrinkle resistance is a drawback. It is made in filament, staple, and water-soluble forms. There are two types of vinal: One type is made by a system that approximates rayon technology in its sequential stages of coagulation, drawing, heat treatment, and formalization to develop and harden the fiber structure. With certain modifications, this fiber has been the chief commercial type. Its high strength and its abrasion and weather resistance have made it useful in products in which cotton is traditionally used. The second type of vinal, used for tire cord, is a highly crystalline form of pure polyvinyl alcohol.

**THE
FUTURE
OF
MAN-MADE
FIBERS**

The table below prepared by the textile analyst of a leading fiber manufacturer, shows the current predominance of man-made fibers over natural fibers and the estimate for 1979.

Many technologists believe it is unlikely that the next few years will see the emergence of a "new" generic fiber—at least not by today's definition of what constitutes a new generic. What we will see are fiber variants, many of them of sufficient magnitude to at least claim separate generic status. Basically, the variants will fall into the following broad classifications known as second and third generation fibers.

The second generation of man-made fibers evidenced modifications made to alter the fibers' physical appearance and esthetic properties to suit a particular end use or need. Variations occur in fiber cross sections, luster, crimp, strength, dyeability, and flame-resistance.

The third generation of man-made fibers is characterized by the engineering of a group of more sophisticated and custom-tailored items,

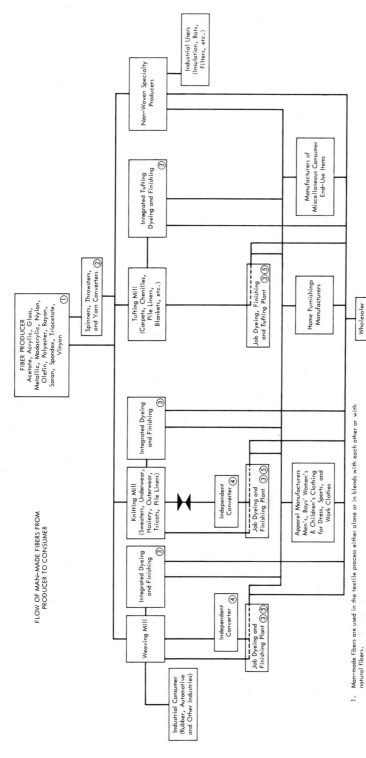

FIGURE 15.8. Flowchart of man-made fibers. (Courtesy Man-Made Fiber Producers Association, Inc.)

TABLE 15-1.   U. S. Mill Consumption—Millions of Pounds

		1965		1973		1979
NATURAL FIBERS(a)		5,026		3,824		2,900
MAN-MADE:		3,557		8,722		13,400
Cellulosic(b)	1551		1406		1,100	
Noncellulosic(c)	1639		6041		10,300	
Other(d)	367		1275		1,900	
TOTAL		8,583		12,546		16,300
% NATURAL		58.6		30.5		17.8
% MAN-MADE:		41.4		69.5		82.2
Cellulosic		18.1		11.2		6.9
Noncellulosic		19.1		48.1		63.4
Other		4.2		10.2		11.9

(a)Excludes silk, linen, and hard fibers (sisal, jute, etc.)
(b)Rayon, acetate, triacetate—filament, staple, and tow
(c)Nylon, polyester, acrylic—filament, staple, and tow
(d)Textile glass, spandex, olefin, rubber thread, steel (tires), spunbonded products, minor noncellulosics (vinyon, saran, etc.)

such as bicomponent and biconstituent fibers and textured filament yarns for specific markets in response to consumer desires.[7] There appears to be no end to the creations and variations that can come from the man-made fiber producers.[8]

The future of blends also seems limitless. Any fiber is a potential contributor to a blended fabric. Testing goes on constantly to find out what the best fiber blends are and what percentages are best adapted to certain uses. The results of tests so far show that no fiber can be ignored as a tool in a blend. But to get the maximum of one quality, such as abrasion resistance, another quality may be sacrificed. If the sacrificed quality is not important in the fabric's use, it will not be missed. All fibers are complementary and supplementary to one another.

Second- and third-generation fibers that meet special requirements without blending are already on the market. Antron nylon, Spectran polyester, various flame-retardant fibers, and many similar advanced products offer properties significantly different from the conventional generic fiber, and even more revolutionary variations are virtually certain to come into the marketplace at a greater and greater rate.

None of these man-made fibers is an all-purpose fiber. Technical changes are continually taking place, so it is not possible to associate any particular advantages for long periods with any particular fiber.

REVIEW
QUESTIONS

1. (a) Describe the manufacture of glass fibers.
   (b) What are the chief advantages of glass fibers?
   (c) What are this fiber's limitations?
   (d) For what purposes are glass fibers used?

[7]See Chapter 2 and Glossary.
[8]Man-Made Fiber Fact Book, Man-Made Fiber Producers Assn., Inc., 1974.

354

2. What are the techniques and uses of the flame-resistant fibers, aramid and novoloid?
3. (*a*) Name the olefin fibers.
  (*b*) In what ways is polyethylene similar to polypropylene?
  (*c*) In what ways are they different?
4. (*a*) Describe the production of natural rubber yarn.
  (*b*) List the chief uses of natural rubber yarn.
  (*c*) How does Lastex differ from Helanca yarn?
  (*d*) What is spandex?
  (*e*) How does spandex differ from natural rubber fibers?
5. (*a*) What is anidex?
  (*b*) For what purpose may it be used?
6. (*a*) What is the chemical composition of metallic yarns?
  (*b*) List the uses of metallic yarns.
  (*c*) What are the chief advantages of these fibers and yarns?
7. (*a*) What is vinyon?
  (*b*) What are its advantages?
  (*c*) For what purposes is vinyon used?
  (*d*) What are its limitations?
8. (*a*) How do azlon fibers differ from nylon, polyester, and acrylic fibers?
  (*b*) Name and describe the fibers in the azlon family.
  (*c*) Where is azlon used?
  (*d*) What are the advantages and weaknesses of these fibers?
9. (*a*) What is nytril?
  (*b*) For what purpose may it be used?
10. (*a*) What is vinal?
  (*b*) For what purposes is vinal used?
  (*c*) What are the advantages of vinal?

**EXPERI-
MENTS**

1. Obtain as many samples as you can of fabrics made of the following: glass fiber, anidex, novoloid, olefin, and saran.
2. Try to ignite each piece with a match or lighter. Report on your results in detail.
3. Wet and rub dirt into each fabric and then dry. Wash or rinse out in cold water. Compare your results.
4. From these tests, can you come to any conclusions as to the best end uses for the different materials? Explain.

PROJECTS

1. Collect magazine advertisements featuring glass fiber, olefin, saran, spandex, rubber, and possibly other special purpose fibers. Obtain a sample of each, and classify it by group origin. Indicate its most appropriate uses (give reasons for your choice). Check veracity of advertisement claims by your own original test or tests.
2. (*a*) What advice would you, as a salesperson, give a consumer on the choice of fabric for automobile seat covers?
  (*b*) How would you advise a consumer to choose fabric for an outdoor American flag? Carpeting for a patio? Lawn chair? Support hose? Webbing for belts Trimming on an evening jacket? Draperies?

GLOSSARY

Acetate—See Glossary, Chapter 13.
Acrylic fibers—The generic name of fibers made from acrylonitrile.
Acrylic resins—Thermoplastic in nature, of synthetic type. These resins are polymerized from acrylic and methacrylic acid.
Acrylonitrile—A chemical compound from which acrylic fiber is made. This compound is made by the reaction of ethylene oxide and hydrocyanic acid.

356

*Fabric
Construction
and
Buying
Motives*

Anidex—A generic name for an elastomeric fiber.

Antistatic finish—A chemical treatment applied to noncellulosic synthetic fibers in order to eliminate static electricity.

Aramid—Generic name for a noncellulosic man-made fiber. A class of aromatic polyamide fiber differing from nylon's polyamide fiber.

Ardil—A fiber derived from protein in peanuts; it is made in England. A type of azlon.

Autoclave—A vessel similar to a pressure cooker in which a chemical solution is heated under pressure.

Azlon—A generic name for man-made textile fibers made from protein, such as casein, zein, soybean, and peanut.

Bicomponent fiber—A combination of two types of the same generic class.

Biconstituent fiber—A physical combination or mixture of two generic fibers.

Blend—See Glossary, Chapter 2.

Bright yarn—High luster yarn.

Carrier—An agent which swells fibers to improve the diffusion rate of disperse dyes into the fiber. Widely used in the dyeing of conventional polyester.

Casein—A protein compound found especially in milk. Synthetic fibers can be derived from this protein.

Conjugate-spun fiber—Distinct polymer compositions in a specific configuration, for example, side-by-side, sheath-core.

Coronizing—A finish for Fiberglas that heat-sets the fibers, crimps the yarn, wets the weave, and produces abrasion resistance, color retention, water repellency, and launderability.

Count—Size of a spun synthetic yarn. See Glossary, Chapter 3.

Denier—Size of a nylon or any other synthetic filament yarn. See Glossary, Chapter 3.

Dimensional stability—See Glossary, Chapter 13.

Dye Carrier—See *Carrier.*

Ester—A technical chemical term for a compound formed by substituting a hydrocarbon radical for the hydrogen of an acid.

Filament yarn—See Glossary, Chapter 13.

Fleece—Fur-like pile fabrics made of Orlon acrylic, nylon, Verel modacrylic, Dynel modacrylic, Dacron polyester, or other synthetic pile.

Glass fibers—Very fine flexible fibers of pure glass.

Heat-set finish—The stabilization of synthetic fabrics to ensure no change in size or shape. Methods of setting fabrics of nylon and polyester fibers, for example, including (1) treatment of fabrics at boiling or near boiling temperatures one-half hour to one hour; (2) treatment with saturated steam; (3) application of dry heat. Heat setting also secures maximum dimensional stability of acrylic fibers.

Hexamethylene-diammonium-adipate—A solution of a salt that is polymerized and hardened into a solid and cut into flakes, then melted and extruded into nylon fibers.

Hydrophillic fiber—An absorptive fiber, with a great affinity for water.

Hydrophobic fiber—A nonabsorptive fiber, with no affinity for water.

Metallic—The generic name of a man-made fiber composed of metal, plastic-coated metal, metal-coated plastic, or a core completely covered by metal.

Mixture—See Glossary, Chapter 2.

Modacrylic fibers—The generic name of man-made fibers composed of less than 85 percent but as least 35 percent by weight of acrylonitrile units.

Monofilament—A single filament.

Multifilament yarn—Continuous strands of two or more monofilaments that have been twisted together.

Novoloid—A generic name for a noncellulosic man-made fiber made from a cross-linked polymer derived from carbon, hydrogen, and oxygen.

Nylon—A man-made polyamide fiber derived largely from petroleum, chemically combined with air and water.

Nylon-spandex biconstituent fiber—A conjugate spun filament having nylon and spandex segments joined along its entire length.

Nytril—A generic name for a noncellulosic man-made fiber made from a polymer derived from ammonia and natural gas.

Pigmented fibers and yarns—Delustered or, occasionally, producer-colored with pigment to a desired hue. See Glossary, Chapter 13.

Pilling—Fibers of certain synthetic spun yarns form little balls or pills on the surface of the cloth.

Polyamide—A chemical rearrangement of atoms to form a molecule of greater weight. A resin made by condensation. Nylon is a polyamide.

Polyester fiber—The generic name of a man-made fiber made from a chemical composition of ethylene glycol and terephthalic acid.

Polymer—A large molecule produced by linking together many molecules of a monomeric substance.

Polymerization—The way in which certain small molecules combine into fiber-forming molecules.

Rayon—See Glossary, Chapter 13.

Rubber—The generic name of man-made fibers in which the fiber-forming substance is natural or synthetic rubber.

Saran—The generic name of vinylidene chloride fibers.

Soybean—A small herb of the bean family of India and China; source of protein for certain man-made fibers.

Spandex—The generic name of man-made fibers derived from a chemical substance called segmented polyurethane.

Spinneret—See Glossary, Chapter 13.

Spun yarn—See Glossary, Chapter 13.

Static electricity—Stationary electric charges caused by rubbing an article or exposing it to abrasion. Static electricity attracts small particles to the object.

Synthetic fiber—A man-made fiber produced by chemical synthesis.

Thermoplastic—A fiber that has the property of softening or fusing when heated and of hardening again when cooled.

Vinal—The generic name of a man-made fiber derived from polyvinyl alcohol.

Vinyon—The generic name of a man-made fiber made from polyvinyl chloride, a derivative of natural salt, water, and petroleum.

Zein—Cornmeal from which protein is derived for synthetic fibers.

Care
of
Textile Fabrics

16

For Christmas, Mrs. Frank's daughter had given her a pale blue polyester crepe cocktail dress. When it became soiled, Mrs. Frank checked the care label. Located at the top on the inside back of the neck, the manufacturer's label read:

Machine wash: Garment can be washed by machine or by hand
Warm: Water temperature "Warm setting" about 90° F - 100° F
No bleach: None to be added
Gentle: Machine set for delicate fabrics
Tumble dry low: Dryer set for low heat or drip dry
Cool iron: Low or wash-and-wear setting

Mrs. Frank knew what the terms listed on the label meant; she could care for her dress properly at home. The Care Labeling Act, explained in Chapter 1, gave the consumer information on the proper care of the dress. A garment that is properly cared for may be expected to last considerably longer than one that is not cared for adequately, and it will look better all through its wear-life. Care includes three elements which the consumer may accomplish at home: cleaning, refreshening, and storage.

WASHING CLOTHING AND HOUSE-HOLD TEXTILES
Cleaning is usually a more technical and more involved process than storage or refreshening. It involves both overall cleaning and spot removal, both of which are considered in this chapter. There are two major overall cleaning methods: washing and dry cleaning. Washing may be either hand washing or machine washing. For either process there are variations in the required water temperature, the nature of the detergent used, the use of bleach, the length of sudsing time, the length of soaking and agitation time, the method of moisture removal, and the method and amount of pressing required.

HAND LAUNDERING

Primitive peoples washed their clothes by hand in the water of a stream or lake. Today, those who live in developing countries or in inaccessible and rural parts of the world may still wash clothes on stones in running water. In early times a tub was used to collect rain water. The soiled articles were

CARE INSTRUCTIONS

Wash by machine or hand using any good soap or detergent. Avoid the use of chlorine bleach. This garment can go through the full washing machine cycle. When home dryers are used, best results will be obtained by using the low temperature setting. If automatic dryer is not used, lay garment flat to dry. If touch-up ironing is desired, use a press cloth and a warm iron (low or synthetic setting). Store garment flat. If dry cleaned, make certain dry cleaner is advised of fiber content.

This fabric is made in America by American craftsmen

L-1100-19

FIGURE 16.1. Care instructions appearing on the back of a hang tag to be attached to a fabric of stretch corduroy made of 62½ percent cotton and 37½ percent Helanca nylon. (Reproduced courtesy of Cone Mills, Inc.)

placed in the tub and agitated by a smooth wooden pole. A tub of clear water was used for rinsing. In later years the pole was replaced by the corrugated tin (later wood and glass) washboard. Soil and stains were removed from cottons and linens by rubbing the article on the washboard with a strong alkaline bar soap. To whiten fabrics, bleaching powder was used in a metal wash boiler (a tub of boiling water) placed on the coal stove or gas range. A smooth stick or pole was used to turn the wash occasionally. Another method of washing, in the early twentieth century, took place in two soapstone adjoining tubs set on iron legs. One tub contained soapy water and the other clear water drawn from a tap. When the washboard and soapy water had cleansed the article, the laundress "fed" the wash through a wringer consisting of two rollers to squeeze out the soapy water and to drop the articles into the second tub of clear rinse water. Hand rinsing followed and another wringing. The laundry was hung out-of-doors to dry, weather permitting.

General Procedure for Hand Laundering. Although most of today's fabrics are either machine washable or dry cleanable, hand washing continues to be important, not only for small washes but also for certain materials. In general, silks, sheer fabrics, knitted woolens, and curtains of glass fibers should be washed by hand. Fabrics in which the fastness of color is uncertain should also be washed by hand.

Following are some guides for hand laundering:

1. Launder fabrics before they become too soiled.
2. Examine the fabric thoroughly for spots, small tears, or holes.
3. Mend all tears or holes, and mark the spots with thread so that they may be specially treated before or during washing.
4. Remove any accessories that are not washable.
5. If there is any question whether the dye is fast, wash an inconspicuous part of the fabric first. A small piece of fabric can be clipped from one of the seams. Dry it and compare the washed with the unwashed part. If there is fading or streaking, the cloth should be dry-cleaned.
6. For delicate fabrics use a soap with no strong alkali, such as Lux, Ivory Snow, Ivory Flakes, Woolite (especially for wool and wool blends).
7. With a cupping of the palms of the hands in lukewarm water and soap, the soap solution should be forced through the fabric. Exceptionally dirty spots must have additional soaping. Several soapy waters may be used—as many as are needed to cleanse the fabric.
8. Several rinses of water of the same temperature as the soapy water should follow.
9. Roll the fabric in a terry towel and squeeze out excess moisture. Gently pull the fabric to shape and throw it over a line or chair. Do not use clothespins, especially

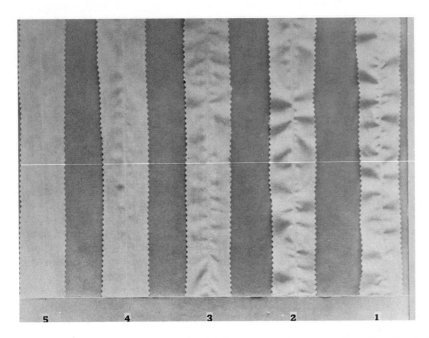

FIGURE 16.2. a. A.A.T.C.C. photographic comparative ratings for single needle seams. This test method is designed for evaluation of the appearance of seams in wash-and-wear fabrics. Seamed fabric specimens are subjected to procedures simulating home laundry practices. Evaluation is performed by using the overhead lighting procedure and comparing the appearance of specimen seams with the standard photographs. Five appearance classes are recognized.

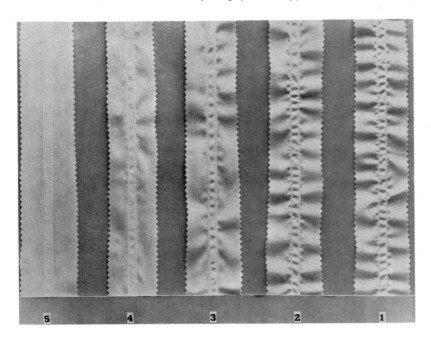

FIGURE 16.2. b. A.A.T.C.C. photographic comparative ratings for double needle seams. (Photos reproduced courtesy of the American Association of Textile Chemists and Colorists.)

360

on knitted goods, for the weight of the fabric may start a runner. Since rayon is not very elastic, knit goods of rayon should be laid flat on a table or board, eased to shape, and left to dry. If knit garments are hung, they may dry in longer and narrower proportions than existed before the washing.

WASHING BY MACHINE

Most washing today in the United States is done by washing machines, the great majority of which are the automatic types that carry a wash through the following cycles:

1. Soak.
2. Wash.
3. Two or more rinses.
4. Wring after each wash and rinse. Water temperature and load capacity can be controlled.

Most modern machines can be adjusted for the following:

1. The capacity claimed by manufacturers of automatic washers ranges from 12 to 18 pounds per load (a few are larger). Clothes should be put in loosely.
2. Temperature, speed, and time are indicated, as well as water temperature—hot, warm, or cold wash; warm or cold rinse; normal or slow wash and spin speeds; controlled long or short wash periods. There is great flexibility in controlling water temperature, speed, and time. A short time cycle should be set for wash-and-wear and for durable press.
3. Water levels can, in most machines, be set for both wash and rinse. Most machines permit a partial wash fill.
4. An automatic safety feature locks the lid automatically during the spin. Or, if the lid is opened during the spin cycle, a switch shuts off the machine.

Selecting and Using an Automatic Washer. In selecting an automatic washer, the following are important considerations for the customer:

a. Clothes capacity, depending on family size.
b. Space available for the machine.
c. At least two speed variations for different fabrics.
d. Three water temperatures.[1]
e. Pressure control rather than time control for filling.
f. More than one fill level to handle a small load.
g. Moderate use of electricity (kwhr per load low).

There are certain cautions to observe in using an automatic washer:

1. Turn off the water supply when the machine is not in use, to prevent the hose from rupturing.
2. Remove all articles from the clothing pockets before washing.
3. Keep hands out of the washer when it is in operation.
4. Don't overload the machine. Distribute the loads evenly. Should the machine vibrate or bang, turn it off at once. It is off balance.

---

[1] Since heating of water takes more electricity than machine operation, rinsing in cold water is recommended.

362
*Fabric
Construction
and
Buying
Motives*

Procedure for Home Laundering by Machine. All soiled clothes should be stored in a well-ventilated hamper. If fabrics are badly stained, they should be treated for stain removal as soon as possible, because the stains are more easily removed soon after they have been made. Although each homemaker has pet ways of doing laundry, a few general rules may prove helpful.

Sorting. Separate all colored clothes from the white clothes. Use a table or counter for this purpose to avoid bending over. If there are any colored clothes that have doubtful colorfastness, put them to one side to be washed by themselves, or try a wash test on an inconspicuous part of each garment before mixing it with other clothes. To make a wash test, place the sample in a jar with detergent and water at the same temperature that will be used in regular washing. Let it stand for a few minutes; then shake the jar. If the water is discolored, or if color is transferred to a white paper or cloth when the fabric is pressed, then it should always be washed separately. An article marked "bleeding Madras" is expected to bleed or run and should not be laundered with other clothes.

It is not necessary to make one wash load completely white clothes and another load completely colored clothes. Certain combinations of articles launder and dry well together.

Combination loads that wash and dry well together:[2]

1. White and colorfast sheets, pillowcases, table linen, hand towels, tea towels, men's shirts, white gloves, and pajamas.
2. Heavy bath towels and mats, underwear, light-colored shirts and socks. (Nos. 1 and 2 can be combined if not enough for two loads.)
3. Lightweight colored cottons—dresses, aprons, shirts. Select water temperature by colorfastness.
4. Sheer white and colorfast cottons—organdy, batiste, voile, lawn, and dotted swiss. White and colorfast rayons.
5. Acrylics, acetates, nylons, and other man-made fiber fabrics. Silk.
6. Extra-soiled, heavier, and darker cotton pants, overalls, play clothes, socks.
7. Wash separately: shag rugs, pillows, quilts, blankets, slip covers, draperies, curtains.

All torn or frayed fabrics should be put aside to be mended before they are washed. Infants' clothes and those from a sickroom should be washed separately. If garments are stained, put them aside and treat stains before laundering. (See p. 376 for stain removal.)

Preparation of the Automatic Washer. Automatic washers may have accompanying instructions about how many garments or pounds constitute a load. However, it is better to underload than to overload a washer, because clothes get cleaner when they can tumble about freely in the wash water.

The amount of detergent or soap should be carefully measured, and the dial should be set to hot (160°), medium hot (120°), or warm (100°), depending on the fiber content, sheerness, construction, finish, and degree of soil.

A general rule is to wash white and colorfast cottons and linens with proper finish in hot water (160°) for a short time. Lightly soiled lingerie

[2] *All about Modern Home Laundering,* a pamphlet by Ruud Manufacturing Company, p. 41.

How to do the laundry

Sort Clothes

By color:

| WHITE | COLORFAST | NONCOLORFAST |

If colors bleed dye, wash these items alone or with the same colors.

By type of fabric and construction:

| COTTONS & LINENS | WASHABLE WOOLS | DELICATES | PERMANENT PRESS & MAN-MADE FIBERS |

By amount and kind of soil:

| HEAVY | NORMAL | LIGHT |

By size:

Heavy, bulky items — blanket, bedspread or slipcover — should be washed alone.

Check Clothes

Close zippers, fasten hooks.

Empty and brush out pockets.

Take off pins, ornaments, heavy buckles. Mend rips, tears.

Remove spots and stains (see stain removal chart).

Loosen ground-in dirt by making a paste of detergent or soap and a little water or use a liquid laundry detergent or bar soap.

Dampen the soiled area and gently rub in the solution. Use on collars and cuffs, feet of socks and knees of pants.

Measure and Add Washing Products

Read and follow package directions.

Size of the washing machine.

Kind of water. If water is hard, use more detergent. Soft water may require less, depending on amount and type of soil.

Put Clothes in Washer

Mix small and large pieces together.

Don't overload the machine.

Set Washer

Turn on both hot and cold water faucets.

Select wash and rinse temperatures.
    Different kinds of clothes require different water temperatures.

Set water level control if there is one.

Select the cycle for the correct wash action.

Start Washer

KNOW YOUR WASHER AND HOW TO USE IT.

WASHER CONTROLS DIFFER SO READ AND FOLLOW THE DIRECTIONS IN YOUR WASHER MANUAL.

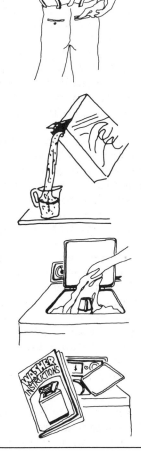

FIGURE 16.3. How to wash by automatic washer. (*From Housekeeping Directions—A Simplified Guide*, Soap and Detergent Association.)

364

*Fabric
Construction
and
Buying
Motives*

and pastel sheets and other colorfast fabrics can be washed in medium hot water (120°) for four to six minutes.

For the general family wash, consisting largely of sturdy colorfast cottons such as dish towels, sheets, night clothes, blouses, shirts, underwear, and play clothes, hot water (160°) should be used with a synthetic detergent or built soap, and the machine should be run ten to fifteen minutes. (See p. 372 for choice of detergents.) Bleach should be diluted and added to the water before articles are immersed. If the articles are badly soiled, they should be prewashed for five minutes at 160° with detergent or built soap (special alkalies added).

Sheer cottons, nylon, rayon, acetate, washable silks, and acrylic fibers can be done in an automatic washer with warm water (100° to 120°) with a three-to-five minute washing period. Gentle hand-washing is often preferable. No chlorine should be used in washing garments containing Lycra spandex, since this bleach can discolor the fabric permanently.

Woven and knitted woolens and polyester fibers can be washed in warm water (100°) with mild soap or synthetic detergent for three to five minutes. Unless the woolen has been treated for shrinkage control, it may shrink if agitated too long. Blankets may also be washed in this manner. (See specific instructions for laundering blankets, Chapter 19).

Cottons and linens used by those who have common illnesses should be laundered for fifteen minutes in water 160° with a synthetic detergent or heavy-duty soap.

For home washing, a reliable supply of hot water at the right temperature and in the right quantity is advisable. Authorities recommend a temperature of 140° to 160° in the automatic washer itself, for white and colorfast cottons, linens, and rayons. Such a tub temperature, of course, calls for a higher temperature in the water heater to offset piping and other temperature losses.

The necessary quantity of hot water is determined by the design of the individual automatic washer and varies greatly from one make to another. Modern practice is to provide an automatic water heater with a hot water delivery that will supply the washer on a consecutive, load-after-load basis. Experience has proved that, in most homes with one bathroom, such a water heater will supply not only the washer but bath, kitchen, and all other requirements as well. Quick-heating, laundry-rated gas water heaters have proved very popular.

In the late 1960s, detergent producers began to advise consumers to use cold water with a heavy-duty detergent that gets out the worst kind of dirt in cold water. Since a bacteriostat is added to the detergent, it actually germproofs as well as cleans. It is claimed that cold-water washing leaves woolens softer and fluffier than does hot water. Danger of shrinkage is minimized. It is estimated that a family might save $50 a year by using cold water instead of hot. This treatment is recommended for acrylics, polyesters, and nylon. Even permanent press garments come clean with this treatment. Familiar trade names are Cheer, Tide, and Liquid All.

Washing Durable Press. Durable press garments are primarily intended for home laundering, but good results can be obtained from the commercial laundry and from dry cleaners. In case the home washer is

FIGURE 16.4. To get best performance from durable press shirts, remove them from dryer as soon as tumbling stops and hang them up. (Photo reproduced with permission. Copyright by Consumers Union of U.S., Inc., a nonprofit organization.)

used, follow any special washing instructions that come with the garment. General instructions follow:

1. Use the wash-and-wear or durable-press setting.
2. Use cool water for less chance of wrinkling.
3. Use your regular laundry detergent.
4. Don't overcrowd the washer; use several small loads.
5. Tumble-dry and remove from the dryer soon after it stops. If you have no dryer, remove from the washer before the spin cycle, and drip-dry.
6. Hang on nonrusting hangers immediately after drying. Slacks should be hung on spring-clip hangers.
7. If touch-up ironing is desired, a steam iron on a "low" setting is best.
8. Wash durable press garments frequently, since heavy stains are difficult to remove. Use soap or detergent on stains, and cleaning fluid on greasy stains prior to washing.

DRYING FABRICS The old-fashioned method of drying was to remove excess water by hand wringing followed by laying the goods flat in the sun or hanging them on a line. Later, the wringer, consisting of two rubber cylinders, replaced much hand wringing. When operated by electricity, the wringer was very dangerous. In today's machines excess water is removed automatically. Those homemakers who do not have combination washers and dryers often have companion dryers that complete the drying operation quickly and easily. Temperature selections in dryers may be low (140° F.), medium (158°F.), or high (172°F.). The time control often allows

366
*Fabric
Construction
and
Buying
Motives*

automatic settings up to 120 minutes with a 5-minute cooling period at the end of the drying stage. Since such drying equipment uses considerable gas or electricity, the control should not be set for a longer period than is necessary. Do not use a dryer for articles cleaned with a dry cleaning solution or for knitted woolens. Do not overload the dryer because clothes need room to tumble in order to dry more quickly. Clothes should be taken from the dryer before they are "bone dry" to avoid wrinkling, stiffness, or shrinkage. To drip-dry fabrics, instead of placing them in a machine, smoothe them out while dripping wet and hang neatly in a place where drippings will cause no water damage. Unless marked "durable or permanent press," some ironing may be desirable. Woolens and leather articles should be dried on a clean flat surface and away from direct heat. Woolens should be blocked and dried on a flat surface. If an item is to be dried on a line, the line should be wiped clean; clothes should be shaken and smoothed out as they are hung; all seams should be straightened; articles should be hung with clothespins and removed from the line before they are fully dry in order to avoid dampening and insure ease in ironing.

**PRESSING
AND
IRONING**

Before the advent of durable press, most articles needed some pressing after cleaning to restore them to their original appearance. In those clothes requiring pressing, fibers are affected differently by heat and steam; therefore it is important to know how to iron the goods. The seller's care instructions are the best guide. Unless the laundered article is marked "durable press," it may need a certain amount of ironing—perhaps a little "touch-up" to improve its appearance. The modern electric iron has a dial by which one may select the amount of heat needed. In general, silks and man-made fibers need low heat, while cottons and linens require higher heat. If the right heat is dialed, clothes will not be scorched and wrinkles will come out. A good rule is to iron articles that require low heat first, then those that require more heat, then those that need low heat—after the heat is turned off and the iron is cooling.[3]

It is difficult to state an exact degree of heat needed to iron a given fabric because (1) finishing and dyeing processes may increase or decrease safe ironing temperatures of a fabric; and (2) safe ironing temperatures do not necessarily apply to blended fabrics. For example, a blend of a low-heat-resistant fiber and a high-heat-resistant fiber will assume a resistance to heat that is somewhere between the heat resistance of the two original fibers.

**REFRESH-
ENING**

Some garments, particularly those of wool fiber, require frequent refreshening in order to maintain freshness and appearance.

Brush wool fabrics at frequent intervals, especially before wearing them. Since wool absorbs oil from the skin, any dirt coming to the fabric

---

[3] "Housekeeping Directions: A Simplified Guide," The Soap and Detergent Association, New York, N.Y., p. 59.

FIGURE 16.5. Spraying garment to stop perspiration stains and odors. (Photo courtesy Kleinert.)

mixes with the oil, and a greasy stain is the result. Neckbands, collars, and the portions under the arms of garments should have special brushing. Wool gets dirty slowly, but once it becomes soiled it is more difficult to clean than cotton, linen, or silk. Pile fabrics, however, should not be brushed when wet. When dry, they should be brushed lightly against the pile, and then brushed several times in the direction of the pile.

Blankets, bedspreads, and woolen clothing should also be refreshened by an occasional airing. Hang in the fresh air—in sunlight, if possible.

Fabrics that wrinkle easily often need refreshening long before cleaning is necessary. Pressing between usage is a common practice. In the case of velvets, corduroy, and other pile fabrics, wrinkles are best removed by hanging the garments over a bathtub filled with steaming hot water. In ironing flat goods that require creasing, there should be as few creases made as possible, and folds should be even.

STORAGE In general, after an outer garment has been worn, it should be brushed lightly and promptly hung on a hanger in such a way that it hangs naturally and is not crushed by other garments on the rack. Good ventilation should be provided to remove dampness, perspiration, and odors. If woolen goods are to be stored for some time, such as through the summer, mothballs should be put in the storage bag, or a similar naphtha preparation should be sprinkled or sprayed on the garments. If the storage space is subject to dampness, goods should be sprayed with a compound to prevent mildew. In the fall, bathing suits should be rinsed in fresh water and thoroughly dried before packing away.

Knitwear, underclothing, domestics, and draperies should be stored flat in drawers, chests, and closet shelves, preferably in the dark, since light deteriorates some fabrics. Hangers should be particularly avoided for

367

368
Fabric
Construction
and
Buying
Motives

knitwear. Nearby steam radiators and hot-water pipes should be avoided, particularly in the storage of silks, wools, and acetates. The chief requirement is that the merchandise be folded carefully so that it is ready for use without further pressing. A cedar chest or naphtha flakes are recommended for woolens. Fiberglas does not need to be stored, since it is resistant to light, moths, moisture, fire, and fumes. It is best left hanging at the windows.

Some homemakers roll linen in colorfast blue paper before storage to prevent yellowing. It is also desirable to wash new linens before storage, for the starch or dressing plus dampness may promote mildew.

The storing of floor coverings and upholstery will be discussed in Chapters 20 and 21.

DRY CLEANING[4]   In general, any article of clothing or household use not specifically made for washability must be cared for by dry cleaning methods. Solvents as the washing medium in dry cleaning machines, which operate much like laundry machines, minimize shrinkage, fabric distortion, and seam puckering, and are safe for water-soluble dyes and finishes. Unless the label warns against dry cleaning, all washable articles are considered dry cleanable under the FTC Permanent Care Labeling Regulation Rule for Wearing Apparel and under the two national, recommended practice, labeling standards in support of the regulation.[5]

Dry cleaning may be done professionally as a full service treatment (removal of lint from cuffs and articles from pockets, cleaning, stain removal, retreatment as for water-repellency in rainwear, steam finishing, and pressing). Or it may be carried out in coin-operated, self-service machines usually operated as part of a self-service laundry or multiple-housing laundry facility. The service is suitable for draperies, slipcovers, blankets, sweaters, skirts, and other items that require little or no pressing or finishing. Water-soluble stains do not come out unless treated separately with water before or after cleaning. Most stores are attended by knowledgeable people who can be consulted for assistance in processing questionable items, such as leather- or fur-trimmed apparel, real and imitation suede and leather articles, obviously fragile materials, and items that might better be given professional attention.

The machines used in both services are engineered to recover and keep solvent clean and to protect against fumes. By far, the most common solvent worldwide is nonflammable perchlorethylene, a completely manufactured chlorinated hydrocarbon. Refined petroleum solvents are still common, but only where flammable solvents are permitted. An example of a more recent solvent is Valclene, a Du Pont product closely related to the fluorocarbon refrigerant called Freon. In Europe, fluoro-

[4] Prepared especially for this book by Albert E. Johnson, Seal and Trade Relations, International Fabricare Institute, Textile Approval Division, 350 Fifth Ave., New York, N.Y. 10001.

[5] These standards are D3136-1972, American Society for Testing and Materials, and 128.1, American National Standards Institute.

carbon solvents are popularly called Solvent 113.

Dry cleaning at home (except localized spot removal) requires extreme care because of flammability or toxicity of solvents. Instructions on the container should be followed carefully when using any such solvents.

The International Fabricare Institute, formerly the National Institute of Drycleaning and American Institute of Laundering, tests articles for resistance to dry cleaning in full-scale machines. The item is run for three or more cycles, after which it is measured for dimensional change (shrinkage or stretch), change of appearance (color, pilling), and change of hand (softness or stiffness).[6]

The FTC labeling rule makes necessary the use of these test and performance standards for determining correctness of dry cleaning instructions on apparel. Household furnishings are not as yet covered by the rule.[6]

In self-service equipment, one must be sure to remove all articles from pockets, as well as buttons, belts, and other trimmings if they may be harmed by the process. For maximum cleaning efficiency, underloading the machine is advisable. Garments needing pressing can be steam ironed at home unless store facilities are available. Some dry cleaners do "cleaning by the pound" at prices comparable to self-service. In either case, cleaning of general soil is the same, provided good solvent condition is maintained.

STAIN REMOVAL IN DRY CLEANING

Ninety percent of all stains (food oils, wet paints except lacquers, greases, beverages) respond to either proprietary cleaning fluids or water and should be applied in that order. All chemical stains (perfumes, dried paints, lipstick, inks, polishes) should be only treated by professional dry cleaners. "Rings" form easily on smooth, light colored fabrics and are difficult to prevent without the special equipment that dry cleaners have. Solvent-formed rings come out in regular dry cleaning. Water-formed rings must be "feathered" out with a "steam gun."

STANDARD CLEANING PROCEDURES

The International Fair Claims Guide for Consumer Textile Products of the International Fabricare Institute is the standard reference used by dry cleaners, Better Business Bureaus, and others for settling questions of responsibility for damage claims, definitions of terms related to fabric care, and adjustment values.

---

[6] Standard laboratory tests include American Association for Textile Chemists and Colorists Test #132-1973 for colorfastness using a Launder-Ometer, and AATCC Test #86, Durability of Applied Designs and Finishes. American National Standard L22 (transferred to subcommittee D13.56 of the American Society for Testing and Materials) specifies minimum performance requirements for essential properties of consumer-type textiles, including dry cleaning. ANS L24, sponsored by the American Hotel and Motel Association, covers institutional textiles. ASTM Test #D3135-1972 specifies requirements for launderability and dry-cleanability of bonded fabrics. All dry cleaning test methods specify perchlorethylene because any material that withstands this solvent is dry-cleanable in the other solvents, whereas there are many exceptions to the reverse of this rule.

370
Fabric
Construction
and
Buying
Motives

A. Hard Finished Woolens and Worsteds

Solvent—Perchlorethylene
Time Cycle—15 minutes
Solvent R.H.[7]—70% at room temperature
Drying—Tumbler, 155°F.
Finishing—Utility press (padded)

B. All Soft Finished Woolens and Knits

Solvent—Perchlorethylene
Time Cycle—5 minutes
Solvent R.H.—60% or less
Drying—Tumbler, 135°F.
Finishing—Utility press or steamer

C. Household Products

Solvent—Perchlorethylene
Time Cycle—10 minutes
Solvent R.H.—No moisture
Drying—Tumbler, 135°F.
Finishing—Hot head, drapery press, or steamer

**D. Woven or Knitted Dress or Sportswear
    (Synthetics or Cellulosics)**

Same as A. See B for woolen knits.

E. Fragile (Sensitive to normal dry cleaning)

Solvent—Perchlorethylene
Time Cycle—5 minutes (article processed)
Solvent R.H.—60% or less
Drying-Tumbler, in net bag (or air dry), 135°F.
Finishing—Utility press (padded)

**F. Heavily Soiled Articles
    (Rainwear, work clothes, etc.)**

Solvent—Perchlorethylene
Time Cycle—15 minutes
Solvent R.H.—70 to 75%
Drying—Tumbler, 155°F.
Finishing—Hot head press

**LABELS
AS
GUIDES
TO
CLEANING**

MANDATORY GARMENT CARE LABELS

As already explained, the FTC requires that labels in regard to care be permanently attached to most apparel, with the exception noted on page 11. The care information refers primarily to washing and cleaning.

The wording used on most labels and their meanings in reference to machine washing are given in the following list.

Labels most commonly used are:

1. Machine Wash Hot (Regular Cycle[8] 130°-150° F).
2. Machine Wash Separately Hot (one article at 130°-150° F).

[7] Solvent relative humidity—represents moisture added to represent room temperature up to 90° F.
[8] Regular Cycle encompasses other terms that may appear on some washers and dryers, such as Automatic Dry, Timed Dry, Special, Normal.

3. Machine Wash Warm (Regular Cycle 90°-100°F).
4. Machine Wash Warm (Regular Cycle 90°-100° F). Line Dry.
5. Machine Wash Warm, Gentle⁹ (Regular Cycle 90°-100° F). Tumble Dry Low Heat.
6. Machine Wash Separately, Warm (Regular Cycle 90°-100° F).
7. Machine Wash Separately, Warm (Regular Cycle 90°-100° F). Line Dry.
8. Machine Wash Separately, Warm, Gentle Tumble Dry Low Heat.
9. Hand Wash Line Dry.
10. Hand Wash Dry Flat.
11. Hand Wash Separately Line Dry.
12. Hand Wash Separately Dry Flat.
13. Dry Clean Only.
14. Wipe with Dry Cloth Only.

In all instances the garment manufacturer is responsible for providing the proper care procedure to the consumer.

With any basic label, additional terms may be combined such as:

1. Do not bleach.
2. Do not use chlorine bleach.
3. Do not twist or wring.
4. Do not iron.
5. Do not dry clean.
6. Wash separately.
7. Remove trim.

The labels recommended come in any of four forms and are attached securely, such as under the waistband, at the back of the collar, or under the lower front flap of the coat. If labels are printed, they must remain legible for the wear-life of the garment.

The size of the label depends on the detail of the instructions. Obviously, the more detail, the larger the label. Should the label not contain enough details, the consumer may assume that:

1. White fabrics are bleachable.
2. Colored fabrics should be washed separately and should *not* be bleached.
3. All fabrics can be ironed using heat setting for that fiber or fiber blend.
4. If the above assumptions are inapplicable, the label must say so.
5. If label is incorrect, the store, where merchandise was purchased, should be informed.

The chief consumer objection to present labels are: (1) they are too brief; (2) the space on the label is too small for detailed instructions; (3) the manufacturer recommends dry cleaning if he is not sure of safe washing.

FIBER MANUFACTURER'S VOLUNTARY INSTRUCTIONS FOR CARE

It is customary for the processors of natural fibers and the man-made fiber manufacturers to make more detailed labels with care instructions than are required by the FTC. If this detailed label and the FTC garment care label are both on a garment, sometimes there is confusion because the two

---

⁹Low-speed agitation and shorter washing periods, durable press setting on dryer.

372
Fabric
Construction
and
Buying
Motives

labels may not agree on care. For example, one label may say *Dry Clean Only*, while the other may say *Hand Washable in Cold Water*. The consumer must decide whether to chance hand washing or pay a higher cost for dry cleaning.

It may be that fiber information on care will help in determining suitability of an item for a given end use rather than in determining its care.

PRODUCTS USED IN LAUNDERING

The chief objective in laundering an article is to get it clean—to release soil from the fabric. This can be done by soaps and by synthetic detergents.

SOAP

This product is the result of the reaction of soda and a fat. Soap is by far the oldest of the cleaning agents, going back at least to the days of the early Romans. Some historians claim that when sacrificial animals were burned on altars to appease the gods, the accumulated fats were mixed with ash. Rain leached alkali from the ash and the water carried it through the clay soil. The resultant soapy substance was later found to make washing easier. This, some say, was the origin of soap. With the exception of the clay ingredient, the formula for soap hasn't changed basically from Roman times.[10] To be sure, soap has been greatly improved through the ages. Modern soaps are purer in ingredients and mildness. From the crude bar soap of yesteryear, we have progressed to refined bars, from coarse chips to delicate flakes, from coarse powders to blown granules.

There are numerous laundry soaps on the market. Ivory is the only one distributed nationally. Other brands are restricted primarily to soft water areas. This is the reason—soap has one drawback. It combines with minerals in hard water to form a curd called *lime soap*, an insoluble, sticky, soft material that gathers soil from the wash water and sticks to whatever it contacts (clothes, the washing machine, skin). Briefly, soap and hard water are responsible for this objection to soap, which caused the search for synthetic detergents.[11]

SYNTHETIC DETERGENT

Synthetic detergents are organic chemicals whose preparation is complicated because of the nature of the process involved. There are several types of synthetic detergents:

Light Duty. First to come on the market in the early 1930s. They did not combine with hardness minerals to form precipitates as the soaps had done, but cleaning power was limited, so there was need, and still is, for hand dishwashing. This type is inadequate for general laundering. Comes in liquid or granules. Some examples are Lux, Joy, Ivory, Vel, Chiffon, and Trend (granules).

Heavy Duty. First "built" synthetic detergent, appeared in 1946, composed of complex phosphates. Now represents 95 percent of the

[10]"Detergents-in Depth," A Symposium Sponsored by The Soap and Detergent Assn. p. 2.

[11]Ibid.

laundry products sold. It works in hard water and cleans various types of soil well.

1. *High sudsers*—granular and liquid products. Well suited to top-loading automatic washers and wringer washers. Examples are granular Tide and Wisk liquid.

2. *Low sudsers*—this type is suitable for front-loading, tumbler-type automatic washers when there is danger of excess suds interfering with the machine's cleaning action. Can be used in all types of automatic washers. Low sudsers come in liquid and tablet forms. Examples of controlled types of sudsing include Cold Power, Bold, All, Dash, and Drive.

3. *Normal and intermediate sudsers*—lighter in weight, more concentrated. Less detergent is needed: 3/4 to 1 cup in a top-loading machine, ¼ to ½ cup for liquid type. Examples include Dreft, Oxydol, Cheer, Rinso, and Tide.

Because manufacturers may change the composition of their various brands, the classification of brands by degree of sudsing may change.

In all cases, the consumer should carefully read the package recommendations for the product's use in order to ensure maximum performance of the product. Legislation has banned (or limited to less than 9%) phosphate-type detergents in some localities for ecological reasons (pollution of the water supply). Nonphosphate formulas have been developed, but these detergents should be handled carefully because they may irritate the eyes, nose, and throat, and may nullify the flame-retardant treatment of children's sleepwear. This is particularly true if sodium carbonate is used as a builder.[12] The U. S. Department of Agriculture suggests that to avoid damage caused by chemical deposits left on laundered sleepwear, a cup of white vinegar should be added to the rinse cycle.

All major brands of detergents are labeled on the package as to phosphorous level and some brands, such as Tide, have a phosphate version and a no-phosphate version. Generally, the statement will be found on the side panel of the container. Examples of nonphosphate detergents include Dreft, Oxydol, Cheer, Tide, Rinso (normal sudsing types); Drive, Punch, Bold, All, Dash, Ajax, Cold Power (controlled sudsing types); and Wisk, All, and Era (heavy duty liquid types).

ADVANTAGES OF SYNTHETIC DETERGENTS.

1. They wash satisfactorily in hard, soft, and sea water without leaving deposits on garments or washing utensils.
2. They are effective on colorfast woolens.
3. They have excellent grease-removing properties.
4. They have an antistatic effect on the noncellulosic man-made fibers.

PRESOAK PRODUCTS

Presoak products are not complete detergents but are very effective for use along with the detergent to provide an additional cleaning agent for stubborn soils. The presoak products contain enzymes and are used in a

---

[12] *Consumer Reports,* 1975 Buying Guide Issue, Consumers Union, 256 Washington St., Mt. Vernon, N. Y. 10550, p. 68.

374
Fabric
Construction
and
Buying
Motives

prewash soak. Usually half an hour soak in warm water with an enzyme presoak is effective and safe on many difficult stains and soils. For old and persistant stains, a two to three hour, or an overnight, presoak will suffice. Examples of presoak products include Axion, Biz, and Irizyme.

OTHER PRODUCTS USED IN LAUNDERING

Water Softeners and Conditioners. Water softeners, which prevent the formation of soap film or curd that tends to gray the fabric, are necessary only in localities where the water is hard with lime deposits. There are two general types of packaged water softeners—precipitating and non-precipitating. Both kinds are chemical compounds that are added to the rinse water, or to both the soap and the rinse water if the water is very hard.

1. *The precipitating type* of water softener combines with lime in the water to form solid particles that do not dissolve in the water. If the recommended amount of softener is added to the soapy water, the cleansing action begins immediately, because the alkalinity helps to remove grease and dirt from very soiled articles. The directions should be following exactly, because if an insufficient amount is used, the soap will combine with the remaining lime that has not combined with the softener to form soap film. Some familiar names of this type of softener are Borateem, Borax, Sal Soda, and washing soda.

2. *The nonprecipitating type* is a conditioner for making the water normally soft. The purpose of this type is to prevent the formation of lime. When the correct amount of softener is added to the water and the soap is put in, suds appear immediately. No soap film appears. If the amount of softener is inadequate, soap film will form; however, the film will dissolve when more softener is added. The advantage of this type of softener is that it is mildly alkaline and does not change the color of the fabric or irritate the skin. However, it is more costly than precipitating softeners. Brand names of this type of softener include Calgon and Oakite.

In some homes the cost of water-softening equipment may be considerably less than the cost of soap plus softener for laundering.

Bleaches. A fabric that has yellowed with age or has grayed from soap film due to incorrect washing requires bleaching. Occasionally bleaching is advisable for a routine removal of stains. But authorities agree that bleaching is not a substitute for correct washing, because it does not remove soil and its whitening power is limited.

There are liquid (so-called chlorine) bleaches and powder (sodium perborate) or oxygen bleaches. The liquid or chlorine type, which is most popular, is stronger and quicker but requires more careful adherence to instruction so that fabrics are not damaged by it.

Chlorine bleach can be used on white and colorfast cottons, linens, man-made fibered fabrics, and permanent press articles. Chlorine should not be used on wool, silk, mohair, and some types of spandex, and flame-retardant treated cottons. It is important to measure liquid bleach carefully and add it to the wash water before the clothes are put in. When diluted with a quart of water, it may be added to the load after the wash action starts. Brand names of chlorine-type bleach products include Clorox and Action; oxygen-types are Snowy and Clorox 2. *Caution:* Do not pour the liquid bleach or the powder directly on the fabric.

Disinfectants. For antibacterial action in washing of diapers and articles from the sickroom, Borateem is frequently used. Diaper White is intended for diapers. Different types of disinfectants include liquid chlorine bleach, phenolic, and pine oil.

Bluing. Bluing, used mostly on cotton and linen and seldom on fabrics of man-made fibers, makes clothes look whiter but has no real whitening or cleansing action. Comes in liquid or in little bags of powder. Since most synthetic detergents have a fluorescent dye in them that serves the purpose of bluing, the practice of bluing white clothes is decreasing in importance.

Starches. Starches make clothes stiffer, crisper, and shinier. There are two general types of starch: vegetable (made of a white vegetable and corn mixture) and plastic (made of resins). The plastic type is of comparatively recent origin, and is sometimes considered a starch substitute.

The vegetable starches attach themselves to the fabric by covering its pores and by making the surface smooth, which prevents soil from collecting. When soil does collect, it adheres to the starch and is removed easily with the starch in laundering. This type of starch is sold in dry or in liquid forms. Dry starch must be cooked or mixed with water before using. Liquid starches are precooked but are mixed with water before using.

In contrast to the vegetable starch, the plastic type impregnates the fiber, rather than just covering the surface of the fabric. It is therefore more permanent and will withstand more than one laundering.

Starch in aerosol spray cans has proved popular, since the homemaker can easily spray it on the garment just before ironing rather than having to prepare a solution in which to wet the garment. However, it is relatively expensive. Brands include Salina, Reddi-Starch, and Easy-On.

Fabric Softeners[13] The purpose of fabric softeners is to make washable fabrics softer, fluffier, and less likely to wrinkle, and to make ironing easier. When used on man-made fabrics, softeners are said to cut down on static electricity (clinging of the fabric).

While many different fabric softeners are available, most of them come in liquid form. One type of softener is added to the final rinse water, whereas another type is to be put into the water along with the detergent. With the latter type, it is important to follow instructions carefully lest the softener and detergent interact, causing an insoluble precipitate that is difficult to remove. There are also products in aerosol spray form that work only in the dryer. Again, one should follow instructions carefully. Some fabric softeners are Nu Soft, Downy, Sta-Put, and Final Touch (rinse added); First In (wash added); and Free Soft and Bounce (dryer added).

[13] *Consumer Reports*, p. 6.

Every consumer is occasionally plagued by a spot or stain on a garment or household article. Prompt and proper treatment will save a great deal in dry cleaning bills. Fortunately, some clothing today is treated with a finish that repels stains. A process called Scotchgard, which is indicated on the labels of numerous articles—raincoats, men's and women's suitings, tablecloths—makes the fabric resistant to both water and oil stains when new and even after a few dry cleanings.

The problem of spot removal is complicated because there are two variables involved: (1) the nature of the foreign agent causing the stain; and (2) the nature of the fabric to which it adheres. The chances of successful spot removal are best with washable fabrics and rough-finished dry-cleanable ones. The first rule is prompt treatment before the stain "sets." Cool water is generally the best treatment for nongreasy stains, and particularly for dye stains such as one might get from colored paper napkins. Some fresh grease stains can be removed by absorbent powder such as talcum or cornstarch, or by an absorbent powder mixture. On a dark article, however, this method may lead to the additional problem of removing the white powder. Cleaning fluid will remove grease from colored washables and dry-cleanable fabrics.

If the fabric is washable and colorfast, soaking of a stain in a detergent is helpful in any type of stain removal. Soaking in an enzyme product for thirty minutes (or overnight if necessary) will break down or digest by chemical means the various kinds of organic matter, protein, starch, or

FIGURE 16.6. Removal of fresh grease stain by application of absorbent powder. (Photograph courtesy of Consumers' Research, Inc.)

FIGURE 16.7. Removal of fresh grease stain by application of cleaning fluid. (Photograph courtesy of Consumers' Research, Inc.)

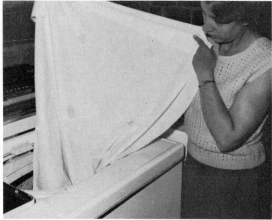

FIGURE 16.8. Durable press sheeting stained for Consumers' Research test of enzyme-active home laundry products. (Photos and caption courtesy of *Consumer Bulletin*, Washington, New Jersey.)

whatever into very small particles. This is a technique of soil release for polyester/cotton blends with durable press finishes. (See Chapter 7, p. 160.)

Table 16-1 shows some treatments for removing common stains from washable fabrics. It should be pointed out that success of stain removal depends on following the procedures, but that some stains cannot be removed.

When using any stain removal material, read and follow instructions carefully. Some products may be inflammable or toxic. Follow all safety suggestions. Work where there is plenty of fresh air.

TABLE 16-1[a]

Type of Stain	Treatment
Blood	Soak in warm water and an enzyme presoak product. Launder as usual.
Chewing Gum	Put ice on gum to harden it. Take gum off fabric with a dull knife. Place fabric face down on paper towels and sponge with a dry cleaning solvent. Launder.
Coffee or Tea	Soak in enzyme presoak product or oxygen bleach. Use hottest water safe for the fabric. Then wash. If stain remains, use chlorine bleach if safe for the fabric.
Cosmetics	Dampen stain. Rub with bar soap. Then rinse and wash.
Deodorants, Antiperspirants	Rub liquid detergent on light stain and wash in hottest water safe for the fabric. For heavy stains, place garment face down on paper towels and sponge back of stain with dry cleaning solvent, rinse. Rub with liquid detergent and rinse. Launder in hottest water safe for fabric.

TABLE 16-1 (cont.)

Type of Stain	Treatment
Fabric Softener	Dampen stain and rub with bar soap. Rinse and repeat if necessary. Then wash.
Grass	Soak in enzyme presoak product. Then wash. If still stained, use chlorine bleach if safe for fabric, and launder.
Greasy Stains (car grease or oil, butter, margarine, lard, salad dressings, cooking oils)	Place stain face down on paper towels. Put dry cleaning solvent on back side of stain. Brush from center of stain to outer edges with a clean white cloth. Dampen stain with water and rub with bar soap or liquid detergent. Rinse and launder.
Ink, Ballpoint	Place stain face down on paper towels. Sponge back of stain with dry cleaning solvent. If some ink still remains, rub with bar soap. Rinse and wash.
Lipstick	Place stain face down on paper towels. Sponge back of stain with dry cleaning solvent. Move fabric to clean area of towel frequently to take out more of the color. Dampen stain with water and rub with bar soap. Rinse and wash.
Mildew	Wash the detergent and chlorine bleach if the fabric can be bleached, If not, soak in an oxygen bleach, then wash.
Milk, Cream, Ice Cream	Soak in warm water with an enzyme presoak product. Wash as usual.
Paint, Water-Base	Rinse fabrics in warm water while stains are still wet. Then launder. Once paint is dried, it cannot be removed.
Oil-Base Paint, Varnish	Use the solvent that the label on the paint can tells you to use as a thinner. If can is not available, use turpentine. Rinse and rub with bar soap. Rinse and wash.
Perspiration	Dampen stain and rub with bar soap. Soak in an enzyme presoak product. Launder in hot water and chlorine bleach if safe for fabric. If color of fabric has changed, use ammonia for fresh stains and vinegar for oil. Rinse and launder in hottest water safe for color.
Rust	A few spots can be removed with a rust stain remover. Rinse and wash. If a full load of white items shows rust, use a fabric color remover. Launder.
Scorch	Soak in an enzyme presoak product or oxygen bleach. Then launder. If stain remains, use chlorine bleach if safe for fabric and launder again using hottest water safe for fabric.
Shoe polish[b]	Sponge with liquid detergent followed by cleaning fluid. Rubbing alcohol, diluted, is often effective.
Urine, Vomit, Mucous[b]	Soak in an enzyme presoak product. Launder using a chlorine bleach if safe for the fabric or an oxygen bleach.
Wine, Soft Drinks[b]	Soak in an enzyme presoak product, bleach using hottest water safe for fabric. If stain remains, launder again using chlorine bleach if safe for the fabric.

[a]"Housekeeping Directions," pp. 53-54.
[b]Added by the author.

**SPECIFIC
CLEANING
AND
DRYING
REQUIRE-
MENTS
OF THE
VARIOUS
FIBERS**

Even though special finishes and mixtures make it dangerous to assume that a knowledge of the fiber reveals the best way to clean it, the following summary may be of some value.

COTTONS

Washable in hot water with a heavy-duty detergent; can be pressed with a hot iron. Unless treated, they wrinkle easily and need frequent pressing.

LINENS

Washable in hot water with a heavy-duty detergent. Heavy starching should be avoided; it tends to break the fibers under heavy ironing. Table linen is best ironed damp on both the right and the wrong sides, moving the iron across the cloth from selvage to selvage. This method brings out luster.

SILKS

Unless labeled "washable," silks should be dry cleaned. If washable, they are best done by hand with lukewarm, mild suds. Remove excess water by rolling the article in a towel, and iron it while damp, on the wrong side. Wrinkles are best removed by placing a damp cotton cloth over the fabric and steaming. Soiled silks should be cleaned at once, since perspiration weakens the fabric.

WOOLS

Washable in warm water, not hot, with a mild neutral soap, mild synthetic detergent, or cold water soap such as Woolite. Use several soapy waters; rinse at the same temperature, but do not remove all the soap, since this prevents felting. Dry slowly away from heat. Knitted fabrics should be pulled into shape while wet and should be dried on a flat surface. It is desirable to measure the original dimensions of the garment before washing and to pull the garment back to these measurements while wet. Liquid or powdered soaps that make suds in cold water are good for hand laundering of wool fabrics. Brand names of cold water soaps are Woolite and Cool Magic. Wools should be ironed, preferably on the wrong side, with a steam iron or damp cloth. To retard shine, two pieces of cheesecloth may be placed on the right wide of the garment when it is pressed on the wrong side. Dry cleaning is often preferable to washing.

RAYONS[14]

For items labeled "washable," use mild, lukewarm suds. Squeeze gently through the fabric and rinse in lukewarm water. Do not wring or twist the article. Smooth or shake out article and place on a nonrust hanger to dry. Fabrics containing rayon can be bleached. Some finishes are sensitive to chlorine. Press article on wrong side. Iron should be at a moderate setting. Use a cloth if pressing is needed on the right side.

[14] *Man-Made Fiber Fact Book*, Man-Made Fiber Producers Assn., Washington, D.C., pp. 15-24.

380
*Fabric
Construction
and
Buying
Motives*

ACETATE AND TRIACETATE

Most acetate articles should be dry cleaned, but if labeled *washable*, then hand wash in warm water with mild soap. Garment should not be twisted or wrung. Neither should colored items be soaked. Press article on the wrong side while damp, with a cool iron. Use a cloth if pressing is to be done on the right side. Only most frequently used man-made fibers are covered. Triacetate, if used in pleated garments, is best hand laundered. Most other 100 percent triacetates can be machine washed and dried. For ironing, a medium to high setting may be used since triacetate resists higher temperatures than acetates.

NYLONS

Most nylon can be machine washed and tumble dried at low temperature. A fabric softener may be added to the final rinse cycle. A warm iron should be used if ironing is needed. Articles should be removed from dryer as soon as tumbling stops.

POLYESTERS

Most polyester fabrics can be machine washed and dried. Warm water plus a fabric softener added to the final rinse cycle is recommended. The dryer should be set at a low temperature, and articles should be removed from dryer as soon as tumbling stops. For any pressing needed, use a moderately warm iron. Dry cleaning is satisfactory except for pigment prints usually applied to polyester double knits.

ACRYLICS AND MODACRYLICS

For washable items, machine wash in warm water, and add a fabric softener during the final rinse cycle. The dryer should be set at low heat and articles removed as soon as tumbling has stopped. The low setting—never hot—should be used on the iron. Dry cleaning or a fur cleaning process is recommended for deep pile fabrics.

OLEFINS

Items containing olefin may be machine washed in lukewarm water with a fabric softener added to the final cycle. A very low setting should be used on the dryer and all articles should be removed when the tumbling cycle stops. Gas dryers and those of the laundromat type must be avoided. Olefin fibers in blends should be ironed (touch-up) with an iron set at the lowest heat; 100 percent olefin fibered fabrics should not be ironed. With tissues, stains on olefin fibered carpets may often be blotted away.

GLASS

Wash by hand in hot, sudsy water; do not scrub. Rinse in clear, warm water; do not wring. Hang over shower rod or clothesline to drip. Rehang damp without ironing. Do not machine wash, and avoid dry cleaning.

SARAN

Does not absorb moisture and is used mostly for upholstery, so it can be wiped clean with a damp cloth. Brushing with soapy water removes stains.

For instructions in the care of draperies and curtains, see Chapter 21. For instructions in the care of soft floor coverings, see Chapter 20.

SUMMARY

The manufacturer's informative label is the consumer's best guide for the care of fabrics, especially with blends. If, however, there is no label giving instructions for care, then the consumer should clean the blend according to the method required for the fiber that needs the most special care.

Fiber content is one criterion for the kind of care that should be given a fabric to insure proper satisfaction in use. The type of yarn, closeness and firmness of construction, the nature and permanency of finish, and colorfastness are also important factors in determining the proper care for a fabric. But the best criterion is the mandatory care label permanently attached to or printed on the merchandise.

REVIEW QUESTIONS

1. To ensure proper care of textile fabrics, what three elements must be considered? Explain.
2. Give briefly the historical background of washing.
3. What features should one consider in buying an automatic washer?
4. (*a*) What fabrics are best washed by hand?
   (*b*) Explain the procedure for hand washing a wool scarf.
5. Describe the procedure for laundering household fabrics such as sheets, pillow cases, and towels.
6. (*a*) Which articles would you wash together: men's colorfast cotton pajamas, women's blue jeans, men's white cotton T-shirts, women's cotton lawn blouses, men's white polyester/cotton shirts, women's nylon slips, tea towels, white nylon gloves, women's colorfast cotton shorts?
   (*b*) Describe the method of washing for each lot.
   (*c*) Describe how each item should be ironed, if ironing is necessary.
7. (*a*) When should an article be hand washed?
   (*b*) What fabrics are best cleaned by hand washing?
8. Describe the method of removing ballpoint ink stains from (*a*) white cotton, and (*b*) colored linen.
9. (*a*) What treatment would you recommend for the cleaning of an acetate crepe blouse?
   (*b*) How would you clean a polyester knitted dress?
   (*c*) How would you clean a 100 percent acrylic baby blanket with rayon satin binding?
10. A white cotton blouse has become gray from soap film. How would you restore its original whiteness?
11. (*a*) Why is it inadvisable to dry-clean rayons at home?
    (*b*) Why is it inadvisable to use acetone or chloroform on acetate?

EXPERI-MENTS

Select as many of the following fabrics as possible for this experiment: white nylon tricot jersey, pure silk shantung, colored dress linen, colored cotton broadcloth, white polyester/cotton shirting, 100 percent polyester, or polyester/cotton crepe.

Experiment 1. Follow the instructions for either home automatic washing, p. 364, or the durable press instructions, p. 362. Analyze the results of each test.

Experiment 2. Evaluate the results of the test by stating the purpose for which the fabric is best used. Give reasons for your decision. What instructions should the consumer be given for laundering the fabric?

PROJECT   Write a manual of instructions for the consumer on one of the following topics:

   (a) Care of men's suits
   (b) Care of women's pantsuits
   (c) Care of men's and women's hosiery
   (d) Care of household textiles (rugs, draperies, and curtains)
   (e) Care of men's and women's sweaters
   (f) Care of men's shirts (dress and sport)

GLOSSARY   Bluing—A liquid, bead, or flake type tint that makes clothes look whiter but has no real whitening or cleansing action; used mostly on cotton or linen.

Builder—An ingredient in a detergent that reduces hardness in wash water, provides the proper alkalinity, and helps keep the soil from being redeposited on clothing.

Built soap—Has a builder, such as phosphate, added.

Chlorine—A quick liquid type of bleach.

Cold water detergent—An agent that cleans and germproofs in cold water.

Completely washable fabric—A fabric washable by machine in water hot enough to clean the fabric efficiently (160° in the tub).

Detergent—An agent or solvent used for cleansing fabrics. The term was originally applied to soap, soap savers, and soap softeners. At present the term connotes washing products called *synthetic detergents*, which are organic chemicals.

Dressing— See *Starch*.

Drip dry—A method of drying a fabric without wringing or squeezing it. After a garment has been cleansed and rinsed, it is hung directly on a hanger. Every care is taken not to wrinkle it so that it will drip and dry with no wrinkles, thus reducing ironing to only a touch-up.

Dry cleaning—The removal of soil from fabrics by means of a solvent.

Durable press—See Glossary, Chapter 3.

Enzyme—Organic catalyst used to speed soil removal from a fabric and to speed decomposition of starch during desizing of fabric preparatory to dyeing or finishing.

Fabric softeners—Chemical solutions added to the final rinse to improve the hand of terry cloths and infants' fabrics.

Fine fabric—A fabric that usually requires hand washing or dry cleaning.

Heavy-duty soap—Pure and mild but has special alkalies added to improve its cleaning power.

Heavy-duty synthetic detergent—One that has a builder for improved cleaning power. A suds-making ingredient is added primarily for automatic washers. A low-sudsing detergent is often recommended for the front-loading type of automatic washer.

Hydrophillic fibers—Fibers that absorb water readily, take longer to dry, and require more ironing. See *Hydrophobic fiber*, Glossary, Chapter 14.

Informative label—Factual information about the goods. See Chapter 1.

Laundry soap—A heavy-duty soap with special alkalies added to improve its cleaning power.

Load—The number of garments or pounds that can be put into an automatic washer at one time.

Neutral soap—A mild soap that has no alkali.

Pure mild soap—All soap with nothing added. See *Soap*.

Soap—A cleansing agent produced by the action of caustic soda and a fat.

Sodium perborate—A bleach in the form of powder (an oxygen bleach).

Soil release—See Glossary, Chapter 7.

Sorting—Separating colored clothes from white clothes so that there will be no danger of colored ones bleeding onto the white ones.

Starch—A white, odorless dry or liquid vegetable compound used for stiffening fabrics. Plastic starch is made of resin (plastic) that can permanently stiffen a cloth.

Unwashable fabric—A fabric that should not be washed by hand or by machine. Such fabrics are usually labeled "dry-clean only."

Washable fabric—A fabric that can be washed. The method of washing (by hand or machine) may not be designated.

Wash-and-wear—See Glossary, Chapter 7.

Wash-fast fabric—One that will not fade or shrink excessively in laundering.

Wash test—A trial washing of an inconspicuous part of a garment to determine if the color is fast to washing.

Water softener—A chemical compound added to the rinse water or to both the soap and the rinse water if the water is very hard. Its purpose is to prevent the formation of soap film that tends to gray the fabric.

Selection
of
Appropriate Fabrics

PART TWO

Women's and Girls' Wear

17

Costume planning and selection of clothing by the typical woman is the most creative activity in which she is engaged. Nearly every woman is attempting to express her personality and her sense of becomingness as reflected in her various moods.

How often do we hear the word "relax"? Most of us hear it frequently. We want to go home to relax after a hard day's work at the office; we want to relax as we sunbathe by the pool; we want to relax after a strenuous game of tennis. With the stress on the desire for relaxation or relief from tension, apparel is being designed in "relaxed types." What article of clothing could feel more relaxing than a loose flowing kaftan or a tent chemise? A knitted dress or pants with stretch moves with the body (called action stretch) and does not constrain bodily movements.

When speaking of "relaxed styles" in dress, we mean that women are wearing many types of garments in a variety of combinations for the same occasion. For example, for a cocktail party in winter, a long velvet skirt with a blouse of sheer crepe, a velvet suit with pants or skirt, a crepe de chine dressy dress, a matte jersey long dress with a metallic knitted sweater would all be appropriate. The combinations are almost limitless. There is no longer one type of garment for a given occasion. Therefore, the salesperson can help the customer by showing the various combinations possible.

Just as there is no longer one style for a particular occasion, there is no longer one fabric that surpasses all others for that occasion. In fact, many men's wear fabrics have become popular for women's wear. For example, a Harris tweed coat is suitable for both sexes. Home furnishing fabrics have also entered the women's wear field. Chintz, especially popular for slipcovers and curtains, is now frequently found in women's summer dresses, skirts, and aprons. In short, certain fabrics are no longer exclusively confined to women's, men's, or home furnishing categories.

Of course, differences in weight automatically limit some fabrics to particular seasons and uses. In summer the weather calls for thin materials, such as voile, eyelet batiste, sheer crepes, and chiffons; in winter, for heavier materials, such as wool tweeds, homespuns, velveteen, velvet, corduroy, and furlike fabrics. Some stiff fabrics look better when a crisp appearance is required; soft and clinging fabrics are appropriate when a slinky, draped effect is desired; rich and luxurious fabrics look best in the

387

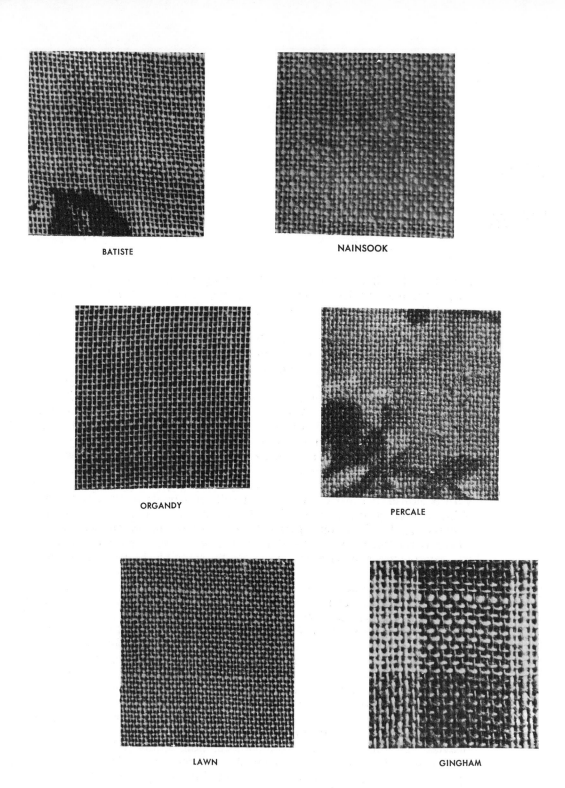

BATISTE

NAINSOOK

ORGANDY

PERCALE

LAWN

GINGHAM

FIGURE 17.1. a. Dress fabrics in plain weaves. (Photo by Jack Pitkin.)

388

RAYON BUTCHER

COTTON POPLIN

SILK SHANTUNG

RAYON FAILLE

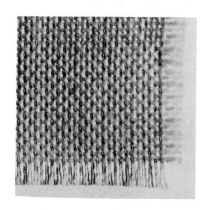

2 x 1 BASKET (OXFORD)

COTTON BROADCLOTH

FIGURE 17.1 (cont.). b. Dress fabrics in plain weaves. The butcher and shantung have slub (uneven) yarns. Others are ribbed except for the oxford. (Photos by Jack Pitkin.)

evening; washable fabrics appear to advantage when worn in the house, in the garden, and for sports.

STYLES AND FABRICS IN WOMEN'S AND GIRLS' OUTER APPAREL

It is estimated that more than 50 million women in the United States are sewing at home, and the number is growing.[1] With home sewing so important, the problem of selecting the proper fabric for the particular purpose has become a major one. Therefore, the first part of this chapter will be devoted to helping the home sewer select the appropriate style and fabrics for a particular use. Fabrics for outerwear may be grouped under the following classification of occasions for which they are worn: (1) daytime wear, (2) active sportswear, (3) evening wear.

To list all fabrics is impossible, because names change and some fabrics temporarily go out of style. Staple names rather than brand names will be used. After the study of styles and fabrics is presented, points for selection of garments for women and girls will be considered.

STYLES AND FABRICS FOR DAYTIME WEAR

The 1970s have become the "pants era." No longer are pants confined to the young living in suburbia. Women of all ages, in town and country, wear them for street and business, classes in schools and colleges, housework, baby tending, gardening, food marketing, and parties. Pants are suitable for any and all daytime activities.

Pants are made in many styles: high-waisted, natural waisted, and hip-huggers that ride the hips below the waistline. They may fit snuggly or loosely. Pant legs may be straight, tapered, or flared.

Skirts are alternatives to pants in A-line, pleated, gored, and wrap-around in a variety of lengths.

Tops for both pants and skirts include shirts (woven or knitted), vests, blouses, sweaters, and suit-type jackets to match the pants—an ensemble called a "pants suit."

One-piece dresses in shift, chemise, or coat style, or traditional shirtwaist with a straight, gored, or gathered skirt can be worn.

For spring, summer, and early fall, cotton, man-made fibers, and blends are important. For skirts, pants, and dresses, woven cotton fabrics such as denim, gingham, gabardine, and sailcloth are popular. Double knits and 100 percent acrylic knits backed by acetate tricot with luxurious acetate quilt linings with polyester fluff are both light and warm for coat and pants. Heavier fabrics, such as polyester/wool blended flannel, 100 percent polyester double knit, woven textured polyester, velveteen, and corduroy are suitable for fall and winter.

Both woven goods and knits are used for tops. Woven fabrics include crepes, triacetates, acetates, polyesters, and blends found in blouses, shirts, and jackets. Sweaters and vests are usually knitted of acrylic or man-made fibered yarns and wool blends.

Tops, pants, and skirts (called "separates," because each article is sold separately) are made of all-wool melton, wool/nylon, polyester/wool, wool/rayon, 100 percent acrylic. The familiar jeans are made of polyester/cotton denim in fall and winter weights.[2]

[1] *Consumers Research Magazine*, Handbook of Buying Issue (October 1974), p. 54.
[2] For definition of fabrics used in women's wear, see Glossary at end of this chapter.

390

FIGURE 17.2.   An all-polyester knit
pantsuit.

Suits.   Suits are worn the year round, with darker colors in the fall and winter. Among many other fabrics, they may be made of tweed textured fabrics in the fall and winter and of shantung, lightweight flannel, or ribbed fabrics in the spring and summer.

Suits may be classified as boxy or fitted. The boxy suit hangs straight from the shoulders and is not fitted at the waist. The fitted suit, often called tailored, fits the figure as a man's suit does.

A good fit in a coat or suit means that the style is cut full enough so that the arms can be raised above the head without pulling at the seams. This fit requires large armholes and curved underarms—a feature especially important for girls' wear and for active women. The fabric in the body and sleeves should be cut with the grain of the fabric, and the bottom of

COTTON GABARDINE RAYON TWILL 2 x 1 TWILL DENIM

FIGURE 17.3. Dress fabrics in twill weaves. (Photos by Jack Pitkin.)

RAYON SURAH WOOL FLANNEL

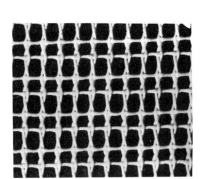

RAYON MARQUISETTE

FIGURE 17.4. Dress fabrics in fancy weaves. (Photos by Jack Pitkin.)

BROCADE (SILK WITH METAL THREADS)

RAYON MATELASSÉ   RAYON ROUGH CREPE   RAYON ALPACA

RAYON CREPE ROMAINE   FLAT CREPE   CHIFFON

FIGURE 17.5. Crepes. (Photos by Jack Pitkin.)

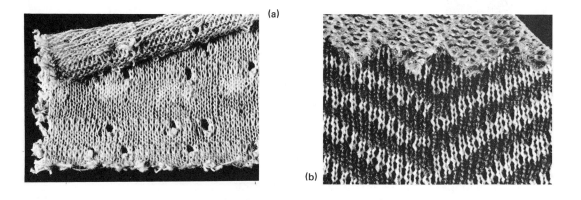

(a)

(b)

FIGURE 17.6. a. A cotton openwork jersey, single knit. b. Double knit with herringbone design. (Photos by Jonas Grushkin.)

FIGURE 17.7. Shirt and pants set.

FIGURE 17.8. Knit suit.

the coat or suit should hang evenly. An outer garment should have smooth shoulders that are the right width. Seams should be adequately wide, even, and pliable so that they will not pull out. Reinforcements should be found at points of strain, buttons should be sewn firmly, and buttonholes or loops should be made evenly and strongly sewn.

If the coat has a collar, it should fit the neck snugly. Lapels should be the same width and should roll back smoothly. A belt ought to be stitched firmly at the sides of the coat or be run through slides.

STYLES AND FABRICS FOR ACTIVE SPORTSWEAR

The nature of the sport generally governs the type of garment to be worn. For spectator sports any garment style suitable for daytime wear is appropriate. Inasmuch as space will not permit a discussion of all types of active sports, tennis, swimming, skiing, and golf will serve as examples.

For tennis, women usually wear a one-piece dress consisting of bodice and very short skirt over panties. Some dresses are tailored while others may be embroidered. Billie Jean King wore an elaborate tennis dress with

FIGURE 17.9. Shirt and knit jumper.

FIGURE 17.10. Dress of double knit textured polyester.

sequins in her doubles match for the championship in Los Angeles, in December 1974.

For swimming, a suit that fits the body snugly but does not constrict its movements is desirable. A knitted stretch nylon and spandex is recommended because it has the desired features and dries quickly. A lightweight suit is preferable—one whose colors and finishes are not affected by salt water or chlorine in the swimming pool. A bra with a polyurethane foam or nylon lining is both comfortable and supporting. The crotch of the panty should be lined. The one-piece tank suit worn by competitive

FIGURE 17.11.   a. Swim suits. b. Little girl's tennis dress,
in polyester knit. Ric-rac trim and ruffled hemline, leg openings,
embroidered applique on bodice, zippered back.

397

swimmers is generally plain, while most one-piece swimsuits are pull-on styles with stretch straps and elasticized legs for comfort. Other styles may have skirts or cut-out sections. The two-piece bikini is very popular. It consists of a bra with adjustable straps and an abreviated panty of the pull-on type. After a swim, a terry cloth beach robe or shift with or without attached hood may be worn. A stretch polyester or terry knit is also serviceable for this purpose.

Skiing is a very popular winter sport. One should be dressed warmly but in lightweight clothing that acts as a windbreaker and is water-repellent. A nylon taffeta jacket and pants with quilted polyester or nylon insulation will suffice. A knitted acrylic cap or nylon hood with quilted lining will also meet the clothing requirements for ski wear because all these articles are lightweight, warm, strong, water-repellent, and quick drying. A wool shirt or sweater worn underneath the jacket adds another layer of clothing to trap warm air of the body, keeping the cold air out.

The golfer prefers casual attire that may consist of slacks, shorts, or skirts, of cotton or cotton/polyester gabardine twills, cords, denim, seersucker, or double knit in solid colors, plaids, or stripes. A knitted or woven sport shirt or a sleeveless V-neck acrylic knitted top may be worn sometimes with a white or colored Jacquard textured blazer with double rows of stitching, or a crocheted sweater or knitted cardigan. The traditional unlined nylon taffeta or polyester zippered golf jacket is usually a part of the golfer's clothing for cool weather.

STYLES AND FABRICS FOR EVENING WEAR

Women wear trousers to cocktail parties, dinners, the theater, nightclubs, and dances. However, the fabrics used in nighttime trousers or long skirts are more luxurious than those used for daytime wear. Velvet, velveteen, metallic knits, matte jersey, brocade, and satin are all suitable. For tops to the costume, a blouse or jacket may be made of the same fabric as the trousers or skirt, or a more sheer fabric, such as chiffon, voile, or crepe de chine, may be used. Metallic cloths (woven or knitted), satin, velvet, taffeta, and lace make exquisite formal evening gowns. For summer formals, sheer fabrics such as chiffon, organza, voile, and tulle may be worn.

COATS AND JACKETS

Coats and jackets are worn over dresses, skirts, and pants with tops. There are two kinds—dressy and casual.

Dressy Coats and Jackets. The dressy coat usually has a fitted line and generally covers the long or short dressy dress, or long skirt and blouse. Usually a dressy coat has a smooth or shiny texture. Hence it can be made of wool broadcloth, polyester/wool blends, furlike fabrics of acrylic or modacrylic fibers, and suede. Often cloth coats are trimmed with furlike fabrics to give a dressy, dramatic effect. In mild weather a velveteen or metallic cloth jacket or sweater can also serve as a wrap.

For formal evening wear, long coats or capes with or without hoods are appropriate. Wool flannel or wool blended with polyester or nylon,

FIGURE 17.12. Evening dress. The sleeves are tapered; zippered back, step-in style. Soft, printed polyester fabric.

FIGURE 17.13. A long flowing gown with full sleeves. Polyester, silk, or cotton. Originally popular in the Levant.

FIGURE 17.14. A dressy coat made of polyester.

FIGURE 17.15. Casual polyester double knit with suede finish. Fleece-look collar of polyester.

transparent velvet, crushed velvet, or velveteen are suitable. In mild climates, a silk or velvet jacket may be worn over a ball gown.

Casual Coats and Jackets. Casual clothes are garments with easy, fluid, flowing lines that present an uncluttered, fresh, relaxed appearance. Coats of the casual type may be worn over spectator sports dresses. Such a coat may be made of camel's hair. Short sports coats and car coats might serve as tops for pants or skirts. These garments may be made of machine-washable polyester blend pile with vinyl trim, cotton suede, cotton-backed rayon, or acrylic fleece or plush, cotton corduroy, polyester woven tapestry, or Loden cloth. Some jackets are tailored like a suit and are made of the same fabric as the pants, making what is termed a "walking suit." Pea jackets that are styled like the sailor's short coat are usually made of wool melton. Double knits of acrylic or polyester are found in shirt or sweater jackets and also in sweater coats. Sports jackets and blazers are made of wool flannel or wool-blend flannel, 100 percent polyester with a worsted texture, and polyester knits.

COLD-WEATHER COATS FOR WOMEN AND GIRLS

When women buy coats they look for style, color, fabric, fit, comfort, and price. To one woman, color and style may be most important; to another, comfort and price are paramount. And to still another, fabric, color, and fit may be the major considerations.

Because style in coats changes more or less from season to season, it would be inadvisable to stress current styles in this book. But there are styles—basic ones that do not change except for minor details—that are known as staple or classic styles. For example, in dresses we think of the shirtwaist as a classic style, because buyers must always have some in stock to satisfy customer demand.

There are classic styles in coats as well, in both fur and cloth. Since real fur is not a textile, cloth coats will be discussed here. The following terms for cloth coats are general categories, whether intended for winter, spring, or fall:

Polo coat: made of beige camel's hair or wool; generally double-breasted with tailored patch pockets and a tailored collar, with or without back belt.
Princess coat: fitted closely through the waist, with darts, and gored skirt that flares at the hem.
Box coat: straight-lined, full-length coat with a collar.
Reefer: a short or long double-breasted box coat.
Balmacaan: a loosely flaring coat with raglan sleeves and small collar. Made of cotton poplin with water-repellent finish or heavy, rough tweed.
Chesterfield: a single-breasted smooth wool coat cut straight or slightly fitted. Usually dark color or black, with a velvet collar.
Officer's, coachman's, or guardsman's coat: a heavy, fitted double-breasted coat buttoned up high on the chest. May have wide revers and big collar, a half-belt, and back pleat or flared skirt.
Tuxedo coat: an unfitted coat with a turned-back flat collar that forms a band down the front to the hem. When it has no front fastenings, it may be called a *clutch coat*.
Trench coat: a double-breasted wool, cotton gabardine, or covert, belted all around. It may have a lining.

Sport coats and jackets, although they come in all lengths, are usually worn to the hips or just below. The boxy type is generally water-repellent. The car coat typifies these lines, although it may be belted. Raincoats, which may be either straight or fitted, are waterproof or water-repellent and are sometimes reversible.

The popular all-weather coat, which may be tailored in balmacaan style with raglan sleeves, is commonly made of 65 percent polyester and 35 percent cotton in a permanent press poplin that is completely machine washable and dryable. A Scotchgard finish repels rain and stains. With a warm acrylic pile zip-out lining, such a coat can be comfortable in all kinds of weather.

Linings should be cut to fit the outer garment smoothly and should not strain at the armhole when the garment is put on. Seams should be stitched firmly and should not pucker. The linings in coats of good workmanship have loose stitching at the bottom, so that the lining will not show below the exterior of the garment.

FIGURE 17.16. Polyester raincoat. With zip-out acrylic lining, it becomes an all-weather coat.

Formerly there were only five size ranges in women's outer apparel. A young junior/teen replaces the former preteen and teen types. The long established ranges were found to be inadequate for pattern sizes because of (1) the great variation in body height that in the past made shortening, lengthening, and waist adjustment so often necessary; (2) the increasing demand for exact fit without alteration; and (3) the necessary catering to those with special needs, such as the very tall woman or the teen-ager.

The four major pattern companies (Butterick, McCall's, Simplicity, and Vogue) have cooperated toward a revision of size standards for patterns. They studied the size standards of the federal government and of the popular-priced ready-to-wear and mail-order garment industries. The object was to establish new standard body measurements for the pattern industry, in order to enable the home sewer to buy a dress, coat, suit, or sportswear pattern of the same size as specified for ready-to-wear.

These standards (see the chart of sizes) took effect in January, 1968. Now the homemaker is actually buying one size smaller by the revised size standard than she did before. Formerly, a size 34 bust (misses) required a size 14 pattern. In this standard, it calls for a size 12 pattern.

To determine the correct size, the figure type must first be determined. (See Table 17-2.) The correct pattern size should be based on the measurement of the bust, waist, hips, and back neck-to-waist length.

In ready-to-wear there are no size standards for ready-made dresses are not as exact as those for the pattern industry.

In response to these consumer demands the wholesale ready-to-wear market has both broadened the size ranges and added new ranges. Whereas misses' sizes used to run 10 to 20, they are now available in sizes 6 to 22; and juniors, once 7 to 15, are now available in sizes 3 to 17. To accommodate the short misses and junior figure, petite misses' sizes and petite junior sizes have been introduced. And for the tall miss, 5 feet 7 inches and over, a special tall size has been created. Similarly, to take care of the woman who is under 5 feet 3 inches, a short half-size has been added. With the regular half-size and the short half-size, it may not be necessary to make regular women's sizes available at all.

TABLE 17-1.   Sizes in Outerwear for Women and Teen-Agers

There are six sizes ranges in women's outer apparel, as follows:[3]

Misses	6-20
Women's	38-50
Half-size	10½-24½
Junior	5-15
Junior petite	3-13
Young junior/teen[4]	5/6, 7/8, 9/10, 11/12, 13/14

[3] See body measurement chart, Table 17-2.
[4] Vogue does not use this size range.

TABLE 17-2. Body Measurement Chart as Established by the Pattern Fashion Industry

MISSES'
Misses' patterns are designed for a well proportioned, and developed figure; about 5'5" to 5'6" without shoes.

Size	6	8	10	12	14	16	18	20
Bust	30½	31½	32½	34	36	38	40	42
Waist	22	23	24	25½	27	29	31	33
Hip	32½	33½	34½	36	38	40	42	44
Back Waist Length	15½	15¾	16	16¼	16½	16¾	17	17¼

JUNIOR
Junior patterns are designed for a well proportioned shorter waisted figure, about 5'4" to 5'5" without shoes.

Size	5	7	9	11	13	15
Bust	30	31	32	33½	35	37
Waist	21½	22½	23½	24½	26	28
Hip	32	33	34	35½	37	39
Back Waist Length	15	15¼	15½	15¾	16	16¼

YOUNG JUNIOR/TEEN
This new size range is designed for the developing pre-teen and teen figures, about 5'1" to 5'3" without shoes.

Size	5/6	7/8	9/10	11/12	13/14	15/16
Bust	28	29	30½	32	33½	35
Waist	22	23	24	25	26	27
Hip	31	32	33½	35	36½	38
Back Waist Length	13½	14	14½	15	15³⁄₈	15¾

WOMEN'S
Women's patterns are designed for the larger, more fully mature figure; about 5'5" to 5'6" without shoes.

Size	38	40	42	44	46	48	50
Bust	42	44	46	48	50	52	54
Waist	34	36	38	40½	43	45½	48
Hip	44	46	48	50	52	54	56
Back Waist Length	17¼	17³⁄₈	17½	17⁵⁄₈	17¾	17⁷⁄₈	18

HALF-SIZE
Half-size patterns are for a fully developed figure with a short backwaist length. Waist and hip are larger in proportion to bust than other figure types; about 5'2" to 5'3" without shoes.

Size	10½	12½	14½	16½	18½	20½	22½	24½
Bust	33	35	37	39	41	43	45	47
Waist	26	28	30	32	34	36½	39	41½
Hip	35	37	39	41	43	45½	48	50½
Back Waist Length	15	15¼	15½	15¾	15⁷⁄₈	16	16¹⁄₈	16½

JUNIOR PETITE
Junior Petite patterns are designed for a well proportioned petite figure, about 5' to 5'1" without shoes.

Size	3JP	5JP	7JP	9JP	11JP	13JP
Bust	30½	31	32	33	34	35
Waist	22	22½	23½	24½	25½	26½
Hip	31½	32	33	34	35	36
Back Waist Length	14	14¼	14½	14¾	15	15½

404

BUYING
YARD-
GOODS
AND
HOME
SEWING

PLANNING YOUR SHOPPING TRIP

Before you go to your favorite store for yard goods or an article of apparel, make a check list of the following:

1. Items of apparel you need most in your wardrobe.
2. Items of apparel you will wear together.
3. List of colors which will become you and your wardrobe needs.
4. Carefully consider your skill as a seamstress. (If you are a novice, choose a simple pattern and a fabric that is easy to handle.)
5. Consider how much care you want to give a garment and the cost involved in its upkeep. Dry cleaning bills can cut into the budget.
6. Estimate the price you wish to pay for the finished garment.

SELECTION OF PATTERN AND FABRIC

The home sewer can consult pattern books readily available in any store that sells yard goods for home sewing to select the style and size of the garment. However, she will want a pattern that will require as few adjustments and alterations as possible. To determine one's figure type and size, have someone take measurements of the bust, waist, hips, and back (from the base of the neck to the waist). When taking measurements, be sure the home sewer wears the same foundation garment she will wear under the outer garment she will make. At the pattern counter, the sewer should compare her measurements with those in the pattern catalog. The correct bust measurement is the most important for all garments except skirts and slacks, so she should select the pattern that has this correct measurement and if necessary alter the pattern in the waist or hip dimensions. The correct hip measurement should be selected for skirts and slacks. Alterations of waist size may be made if necessary.

At the yard goods counter, the salesperson can show the customer the fabrics best suited for the garment's intended use. With a knowledge of fibers, yarns, constructions, and finishes that are desirable in that use, fabric selection should be made easier. In any case, the customer should look at tags that give instructions for care. Usually a tag marked "machine washable" will ensure ease of care. Before she buys the fabric, she should be sure that the basic fabric lining and interfacing materials, tape, and/or decorative trim are compatible. For example, the lining of a jacket might shrink more than the outer fabric, resulting in an ill-fitting garment after washing.

A final decision on buying fabric should be made only after a thorough examination of the cloth. The customer should look for loose threads, miss-weaves, overaccentuated slubs, uneven selvages, and poor dyeing. For example, friction in wear will make slubs weaker and often unsightly.

While the home sewer is at the store, she should make sure she has the necessary sewing aids, such as thread, needles (rounded for sewing tricot and lightweight knits), tracing wheel or chalk for marking, sharp shears, dressmaker's pins, and pin cushion. It is assumed that she has a smooth table or cutting board, and a sewing machine in good condition with a machine needle of correct size—10 for lingerie, 11 or 14 for double knits.

CUTTING, SEWING, AND PRESSING [5]

Before the fabric is cut, it should be washed or dry-cleaned to preshrink it. The lining, zipper, and tape should also be preshrunk.

1. Press out the fold line in the yard goods.
2. Lay out the pattern on the fabric, following instructions.
3. The grain of the cloth should follow the line of dress design. Good fit is insured if the grain of the cloth (the warp) is straight vertically at the center of the bodice. An exception, of course, would be bias-cut blouses or dresses. For straight skirts, the side seams should be cut with the grain of the goods, leaving a slightly biased center seam. Since bias-cut skirts tend to sag, an allowance for sagging should be made in the pattern. Some dressmakers find that if the garment is allowed to hang for a few hours before it is completed, the sag can be adjusted.

Similarly, the lengthwise grain of the cloth (*warp*) should run straight from the shoulder seam to the back of the wristbone. The crosswise grain of the sleeves should then run similar to the crosswise grain of the blouse. The shoulder line will be smooth if the sleeve is eased into the blouse, rather than the blouse into the sleeve. Armholes, to fit well, should not be cut too low.

4. Seam and hem allowances should be adequate and workmanship should be neat.
5. Cut the fabric with sharp shears. Take long, keen strokes with the shears.
6. Edge-finish all pieces by overcasting, multiple zigzag, serpentine, or straight stitching (1/8" from cut edge) before beginning to assemble the garment. Handle man-made fibered fabrics as little as possible, and finish cut edges as soon as possible. Stitch length should be adjusted to 6 to 10 stitches per inch for heavy woven fabric, 10 to 14 for lightweight cloth. Probably 10 to 15 stitches per inch will be adequate for knitted fabrics. The machine instruction manual will tell how to adjust the tension so that stitches look the same on both sides.
7. A trial seam should be made and then checked for smoothness. Seams will be flatter if pressed immediately after stitching.
8. Garments to be backed with any type of material should have each garment piece pinned to backing not more than 2½ inches apart (pins perpendicular to cut edge).
9. Stitch the backed pieces of the garment (backing on top of garment) as described in step 6. Plain-stitch center of darts before asembling.

GUIDES TO SEWING CERTAIN FABRICS

Inasmuch as space does not permit instructions for each woven fabric, we will examine a few of the most problem-causing fabrics for the home-sewer—crepes, permanent press, and textured woven fabrics made of man-made fibers and yarns.

Crepes.[6]   Since crepes are usually woven of tightly twisted yarns, they

---

[5] Adapted from pamphlet "Sew On and Sew Forth," by Celanese Fibers Marketing Co.
[6] Ibid.

are susceptible to shrinkage. Hence the following precautions should be taken:

1. Preshrink basic fabric and findings.
2. Pin fabric on grain of goods. Don't stretch.
3. Use 100 percent spun polyester thread on polyester fabrics or cotton-covered polyester thread.
4. Use a sharp fine #9 needle and 10 to 12 stitches to the inch.
5. Loosen tension on machine.
6. Stabilize edges by stay-stitching curves and other off-grain edges while pattern pieces are being joined.
7. Select a lining fabric and tape that are compatible with the crepe fabric.

Permanent Press Woven Fabrics. If you are sewing a permanent press garment at home, be sure to:

1. Choose a pattern with straight lines and a minimum number of seams, fullness, and frills.
2. Use cotton-covered polyester thread (if all-polyester fibers are present or blended with cotton).
3. Have zipper, tape, and interfacings preshrunk.
4. Loosen tension on machine to prevent seam puckering when laundered.
5. Gently guide fabric through machine with hands at both the back and the front of the pressure foot.
6. Ease zipper in carefully and avoid puckering.
7. Iron seams with as hot an iron as can be used without fusing or harming the fabric. Make a test to determine this.

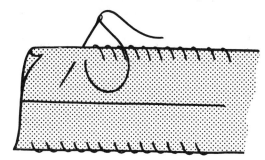

Overcasting Seam Edge

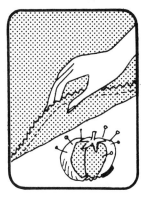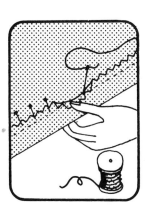

Hemming Knitted Fabrics

FIGURE 17.17. Sewing aids. a. Over-casting seam edge. b. Hemming knitted fabrics.

Textured Woven Fabrics. In the discussion of textured yarns in Chapter 3, it was pointed out that textured filament yarns are more bulky than untextured filament yarns. Textured filament yarns may also have stretch for comfort and ease of care and may be found in gabardines or crepes.

The home sewer can follow the guide for working with crepes, with a word of caution on pressing. To avoid glazing, these fabrics should be pressed on the wrong side.

Knitted Fabrics. There are two basic methods of constructing knitted fabrics, weft knitting and warp knitting. The reader will recall that weft knits stretch in both length and width and include single- and double-knit fabrics. Most warp knits stretch only in the width, and include tricot and raschel.

In making any knitted garment, a home sewer should choose a fabric with a minimum of crosswise seams, because the greatest amount of stretch is crosswise and any puckering of seams is difficult to control. As in woven goods, the basic knitted fabrics and the findings should be preshrunk before cutting.

Double Knits.

1. Pin the pattern on the grain of the goods. Use sharp dressmaker pins.
2. Use ballpoint or sharp needle (#9 to 11) and 8 to 10 stitches to the inch.
3. Sew with cotton-covered polyester thread with polyester or acetate knits. Use 100 percent polyester thread for polyester fabric.
4. Adjust tension of the machine so that the stitch looks the same on top and underneath. Use two thicknesses of fabric when making this adjustment. Gently guide fabric under pressure foot.
5. Press all seams open with light steam pressure. Move iron lengthwise, lifting the iron occasionally to prevent stretching.
6. To hem, make a single row of stitching ½″ from the bottom edge. Pin up the hem. Hold back top edge and loosely catch the machine stitching by hand to the fabric opposite. The hand stitching will not show on the right side of the garment.

Single Knits, Jerseys, and Tricots.[7] These knitted fabrics are relatively lightweight and come in triacetate, acetate, polyester, or nylon. They are popular in both casual and dressy wear.

The home sewer should follow the steps for sewing polyester and acetate double knits, with the following additional steps for lightweight materials.

1. Make all pattern adjustments before cutting the fabric.
2. Use ballpoint pins and needles.
3. Stay-stitch curves and other off-grain edges while pattern pieces are being joined.
4. Reinforce buttonhole areas with lightweight interfacing.
5. Stabilize waistline, shoulder seams, and stress points with woven seam tape.
6. Adjust tension of machine so that it makes loose stitches. Stitch two thicknesses of fabric to check this adjustment.

Stretch Fabrics.[8] The popularity of stretch fabrics for women and girls

[7] Adapted from "Sew On and Sew Forth."

[8] Adapted from *Fiber and Fabric Facts*, Beaunit pamphlet no. 2 of a series of Beaunit Textiles. a division of Beaunit Corporation.

has necessitated that home sewers learn special methods in cutting and sewing these fabrics. A few suggestions:

1. A simple pattern with few seams and a minimum of buttonholes should be selected.
2. The fabric should be placed on a flat surface to "relax" for twenty-four hours before cutting.
3. The pattern should be placed so that the stretch goes crosswise on skirts, bodices, and jackets; either way for pants.
4. Sharp shears should be used to cut the fabric with long, even strokes. The fabric must not be allowed to hang off the cutting table.
5. Seams should preferably be stitched with small zigzag stitches (14 to 16 stitches per inch minimum), with a slightly looser tension than for regular sewing.
6. To check the tension of the machine, two pieces of fabric may be stitched together in the direction of the stretch. The seam should be pulled to see if the thread breaks before the cloth reaches its maximum stretch. Should a break in the thread occur, adjustment of the tension should be made according to the machine's instruction book.
7. Regular interfacing may be used in collars and cuffs, but no rigid underlinings for bodice or skirt. Lightweight stretch or tricot, running with the fabric grain, should be used for a jacket or swimsuit.
8. At raw edges, hems may be turn-stitched or overcast. No seam tape should be used for the hem.

Bonded Fabrics.[9] Bonded fabrics are easy for the home sewer to handle, provided she follows these suggestions:

1. The pattern should be placed on the right side of the fabric where the grain line shows.
2. The lengthwise grain or rib of the fabric should be followed when cutting.
3. Pins and chalk are better than a tracing wheel for transferring pattern markings to the wrong side of the fabric.
4. Thread suitable for the outer fabric should be selected.
5. Pinking is sufficient for the seam finish, since cut edges of bonded goods do not ravel.
6. No separate underlining is required when a tricot backing is used.
7. Before pressing, a small sample of fabric should be tested. In pressing, the setting of the iron should be suited to the fiber on the side being pressed.

GENERAL REQUIRE-MENTS FOR SERVICE-ABILITY OF OUTER APPAREL

In the previous sections of this chapter suggestions have been made to the home sewer in choice of fabrics for various occasions. Whether the consumer is buying ready-to-wear or yard goods to sew at home, the requirements for garment serviceability are similar.

In workmanship, the consumer should look for:

(a) Colorfast, strong thread darker than the fabric.
(b) Smooth seams.
(c) Pinked seams for firm fabrics.
(d) Overcast seams for pliable fabrics.
(e) Seam binding for hem without showing stitches on right side of hem.

Dressmaking details should meet these standards:

[9] Ibid., pamphlet no. 3.

(a) Fitted darts should be straight and smooth, inside and outside the garment.

(b) Placket closing should be one continuous, lengthwise seam.

(c) Front facing should be turned over the hem. Bias facings should be cut on a true bias.

(d) Pleats are usually made on the lengthwise grain of the fabric, and the underfold of the pleat should be deep. Pleats should be pressed straight.

(e) Pockets should be sewn onto the garment to appear either functional or decorative. Pockets should be reinforced by tape stitching at points of strain.

POINTS FOR SELECT- ING WOMEN'S AND GIRLS' READY-TO- WEAR

In the previous section, emphasis was placed on pattern and fabric selection and tips for the home sewer. Now we will consider the important points when buying ready-made dresses, tops (sweaters, vests, shirts, and blouses), bottoms (pants, slacks, and skirts), and sportswear.

DRESSES

1. Make sure the dress style and color fit into the needs of your wardrobe. (It was previously suggested that you preplan a shopping trip.)

2. Always try on the dress before you decide to buy it.

3. Check the fit of the dress while you have it on by noting whether: [10]

   (a) Wrinkles appear in front of the shoulder seam or crosswise on the front of the bodice along the armhole. If so, the inset-sleeve shoulder is too loose.

   (b) Crosswise wrinkles appear below the shoulder dart in a raglan sleeve shoulder near the arm. If so, the shoulder is loose.

   (c) Crosswise wrinkles appear below the shoulder seam in a kimono sleeve. If so, the kimono-sleeve shoulder is loose.

   (d) In inset-sleeve shoulder, the shoulder seam feels too snug. If so, wrinkles appear just below the shoulder near the armhole.

   (e) In raglan sleeve shoulder, the dart feels taut. If so, vertical wrinkles appear below the shoulder dart near the arm.

   (f) In a kimono sleeve, if the fabric binds the shoulder near the upper arm and if vertical wrinkles appear below the shoulder point, the kimono-sleeve shoulder is tight.

   (g) The neck seam lies away from the base of the neck—the neckline is too loose. If the neck is tight in front, back, or both, the fabric bunches, and small crosswise wrinkles appear below the neck seam line, the neckline is too tight.

   (h) The back of the bodice feels snug over the shoulder; stands away from the back of the neck; wrinkles radiate from the upper back toward the armholes. If so, the upper back is too tight.

   (i) Wrinkles appear across the top of the sleeve along the armhole seam. If so, the sleeve top is loose in the inset sleeve. In the raglan sleeve, the wrinkles appear at the top of the arm. In the kimono style, the sleeve droops from the shoulder over the arm and wrinkles appear at the top of the arm. If the inset-sleeve top is tight, the top feels tight around the upper arm and wrinkles radiate from the armhole on both the sleeve top and the shoulder. A too tight raglan sleeve will bind over the shoulder and down the top of the arm. The kimono style will have wrinkles radiating from the natural shoulder point.

   (j) A high, narrow bustline needs adjustment. If so, the underbust dart angles inward and ends less than an inch below the forward point of the bust.

   (k) A low wide bustline needs adjustment. If so, the underbust dart angles outward and ends more than one inch below the forward point of the bust.

---

[10] Time & Life eds., *The Custom Look*, one of the series of illustrated books, *The Art of Sewing* (New York: Time & Life Books, 1973).

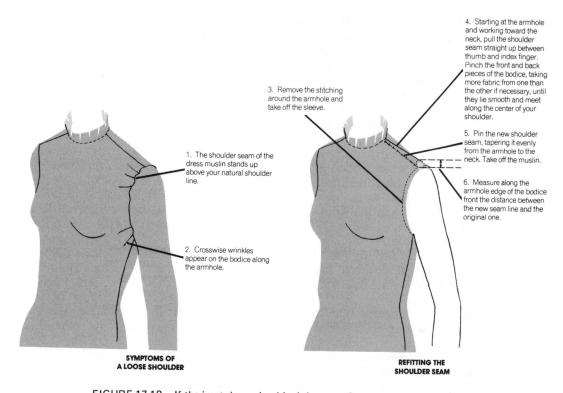

3. Remove the stitching around the armhole and take off the sleeve.

1. The shoulder seam of the dress muslin stands up above your natural shoulder line.

2. Crosswise wrinkles appear on the bodice along the armhole.

4. Starting at the armhole and working toward the neck, pull the shoulder seam straight up between thumb and index finger. Pinch the front and back pieces of the bodice, taking more fabric from one than the other if necessary, until they lie smooth and meet along the center of your shoulder.

5. Pin the new shoulder seam, tapering it evenly from the armhole to the neck. Take off the muslin.

6. Measure along the armhole edge of the bodice front the distance between the new seam line and the original one.

**SYMPTOMS OF
A LOOSE SHOULDER**

**REFITTING THE
SHOULDER SEAM**

FIGURE 17.18.   If the inset-sleeve shoulder is loose: a. Symptoms of a loose shoulder. b. Refitting the shoulder seam. (Courtesy of TIME-LIFE Books, from *The Custom Look,* drawing by Gale Gustofsen © 1973, Time, Inc.)

(*l*) A too rounded bustline is present. If so, diagonal wrinkles form in the fabric below the side-bust dart and radiate down from the armhole toward the center of the bodice.

(*m*) The bustline is too flat. If so, diagonal wrinkles form below the forward point of the bust and radiate down toward the side seams.

(*n*) The skirt front is tight if the skirt feels snug across the abdomen and wrinkles radiate from the abdomen toward the side seams.

(*o*) Crooked side seams are present if the side seam fails to run vertically from armhole to hem. It may be curved in one or more places or it may veer diagonally forward or backward.

(*p*) Consider the length of the skirt and sleeves. Should adjustment be needed, can it be done at home?

4. Consider the cost of alterations as estimated by the fitter. The cost may bring the price of the dress above your budget.

5. If possible, ask the advice of a third party (other than the salesperson) before you buy the dress.

6. Read the care label carefully to see how much the maintenance of the dress will cost in light of the amount of service it should give.

APPAREL TOPS

When pants or trousers became suitable for all occasions, a change in women's and girls' outerwear occurred. This change emphasized the importance of "tops," including sweaters and vests, shirts and blouses.

411

Women's and Girls' Sweaters and Vests. The sweater, a knitted garment for the upper part of the body, has long been a staple for both casual and dressy wear. There are two main or classic types: the pullover or slip-on and the cardigan. Either type may have long or short sleeves, and either type may be in a classic or contemporary style. The classic sweater, not usually bulky, has a round neck without a collar. Contemporary styles are often bulky and may be made in cable stitch and turtlenecks or crew necks.

A variation of the sleeveless pullover sweater is the knitted vest. It is worn over a shirt or under a long-sleeved cardigan. The vest goes well with either pants or skirts. In some instances, the sleeveless vest may be lengthened, buttoned down the front with patch or flap pockets. Such a garment when worn by women or girls with a skirt or pants makes an attractive ensemble. Another variation of the long pullover-style sweater is the long-sleeved sweater that looks like the sweatshirt with a stand-up collar and trim.

Until the development of the noncellulosic man-made fibers, wool was the major fiber used for sweaters, with cotton an important fiber for children's wear. But today the acrylics are in first place, with blends second and wool third. The reason for the great popularity of the man-made fibers is that they can be cleaned in the home laundry machine at the setting for fine or delicate fabrics, and they need no reshaping. Wool sweaters, unless labeled "machine washable," should be hand washed in cold water detergent, reshaped, and dried most carefully. Also man-made fibers are usually less expensive than comparable wool products, and are better than wool in resistance to abrasion. The degree of softness of sweaters made from man-made fibers depends on the fiber denier (weight and fineness)—the finer the denier, the softer the fabric.

The acrylics can provide a wool-like bulkiness that resembles wool fibers. Thus they provide more warmth than nylon. Nylon is less bulky, has a smoother texture and a slightly shiny surface. It is more readily distinguishable from wool than is acrylic fiber.

Acrylic fiber pills more than nylon in laundering and more particularly in rubbing against other garments or furniture. On the other hand, nylon is more easily snagged by sharp objects and fingernails. Sweaters are also made of 100 percent polyester.

Sweaters are made from many varieties of wool (particularly Shetland), wool and nylon, and mohair blended with wool and polyester. The finer sweaters are cashmere, noted for great softness and lightness.

Some suggestions for evaluating sweater construction:

1. For good fit, look for full fashioning where panels are individually knit and where lines of knitting at the seams are turned parallel.
2. Examine seams and buttonholes for finishing; avoid buttons snagged in buttonholes and ribbed neckbands with crooked or uneven seams.
3. Make sure buttons and buttonhole tabs are securely attached.
4. If possible, try on the garment to note the set of the shoulders.
5. If the sweater is long-sleeved, be sure there is a long-ribbed cuff, well finished on the reverse side to allow turning up.
6. Where trying on is not possible, buy a size larger than dress size. Women's sweaters run from size 32 to 42; larger sizes, 44 to 48. A woman wearing a size 18 dress would be well advised to buy a size 40 sweater. Children's sizes run 2 to 10, and a 4-year-old would probably wear a size 6.

FIGURE 17.19. Women's sweater styles. a. V-neck cardigan. b. mock-turtleneck pullover. c. V-neck vest. d. polo-style pullover.

(a)

(b)

(c)

(d)

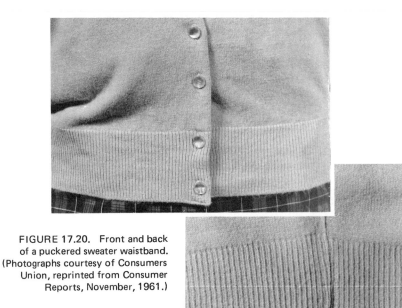

FIGURE 17.20. Front and back
of a puckered sweater waistband.
(Photographs courtesy of Consumers
Union, reprinted from Consumer
Reports, November, 1961.)

Shirts and Blouses. A shirt may generally be described as a tailored garment with or without sleeves that covers the torso from the neck to below the hips. A long shirt that extends to and fits the crotch with elasticized leg openings is called a body shirt. Shirts often have pointed collars. They may be worn inside or outside pants or skirts and may be woven or knitted. They may be worn inside a vest or sweater or may be covered by a blazer or shirt jacket with pointed collar, drawstring waistline, buttoned front closing, and buttoned cuffs.

Blouses are tops that usually have a less tailored appearance than shirts. For example, a neckline may be scooped, ruffled, or lace trimmed. The waistline and wrists may be elasticized. Cuffs may consist of ruffles edged with lace or embroidery. Also, in general, shirts are made of less luxurious fabrics than blouses, such as broadcloth, knits, poplin, and heavy crepe. Blouses may be made of chiffon, satin, tricot metallic cloth, velvet, or lace.

Durable press shirts and blouses are important in any woman's wardrobe. Fabrics that resist wrinkling are those made of the acrylics, polyesters, triacetates, and blends of cotton and man-made fibers.

When you select a blouse or shirt:

1. Try it on to be sure it fits your figure. See the section on dresses, p. 410.
2. Look at the facing of the collar. Be sure the facing is smooth and even, with medium to fine stitches.
3. See if the seams are smooth, even, and adequate in width.
4. Look at the buttons to see if they are smooth, of uniform thickness, and well fastened. Avoid buttons with plastic tops or bottoms because they might fuse or drop off in cleaning.
5. Examine buttonholes for loose threads and insecure stitching. Buttonholes should be cut on the grain of the goods.

FIGURE 17.21. Crepe blouse and double knit
polyester skirt.

Sizes in women's blouses are not standardized. Misses' sizes are usually less full through the bust, waist, and hips than women's sizes. Women who wear half sizes, juniors, or talls may have a problem in fit because blouses are not sized to particular figure types.

APPAREL BOTTOMS

Pants and Slacks. Probably the most popular of garments worn as bottoms of a costume are jeans. Jeans are trousers worn not only for

FIGURE 17.23. Polyester/cotton classic jeans.

FIGURE 17.22. Polyester double knit
pants and pullover style top.

work, play, and sport, but also for casual wear by both sexes and all ages.
They are made of the classic fabric jean, denim, twills, and double knits in
solid colors, plaids, and stripes.

Jean, the fabric, until recently was an all-cotton cloth, made of carded
yarns in a 2 × 1 twill construction with colored warp (and generally blue)
and white filling. Now the fabric is made of cotton and man-made fibers
such as nylon and/or polyester. This combination of fibers adds resistance
to wear, and durable press ensures abrasion resistance and no-ironing as
well. In fact, an entry describing this blended fabric in a mail-order
catalogue stated that the fabric jean is so rugged that a child's tampoline
was made of it. (See Chapter 18 for a more thorough discussion of jeans
and jean suits, p. 437.)

Slacks are trousers that may be dressy, tailored, or casual, fitted or elasticized at the waist, cuffed or uncuffed. Styles are similar to men's and boys. Fit is as important in women's wear as it is in men's wear. (For guides to fit, see Chapter 18, p. 462.) Slacks are often worn with sports jackets or blazers.

Skirts. Women's skirts are cut on the straight, the bias, or circularly from the same fabrics that are used for dresses and suits. The fit or, more particularly, the hang of a skirt is important. A skirt should not wrinkle below the waistband and should be even at the hem. The aspects of garment construction (cuffing, sewing, and pressing) on p. 409 should be checked by the consumer. Sizes for juniors are 5 to 15; misses, 8 to 18; women, 34 to 44. Size may be stated by waist measurement.

The principles for selection of appropriate outer garments for adults are essentially the same for girls.

SPORTSWEAR

Since sportswear is designed for the kind of sport in which the wearer participates, suitability is an important factor in selection. The wearer usually wants a comfortable garment made of a smooth fabric with flat seams that will not irritate skin made sensitive by the sun. Fabrics that are attractive and stylish yet require minimum care are most serviceable. Spot-resistant, crease-resistant, water-repellent finishes and durable press are a great boon to the sportswear business.

Active sportswear can be classified as garments for summer sports and garments for winter sports.

Some of the styles and fabrics for active sportswear were discussed earlier in this chapter.

Styles and fabrics in coats and jackets are discussed earlier in this chapter.

UNDER-WEAR

STYLES AND FABRICS

Styles in the cut of undergarments vary, as do the types of materials used. Nylon underwear is important because it is soft, lightweight, comes in attractive colors, is easily laundered by hand or machine, is quick drying, and needs no ironing. Other underwear fibers are cotton, acetate, and rayon for panties and briefs, and blends of cotton and polyester for slips.

Underwear garments include slips and half slips, panties and briefs, body suits, and bras (brassieres). Peignoirs, robes, lounge wear, and bed jackets may also be included in the underwear classification.

SLIPS

Slips are either one-piece dress-length undergarments with shoulder straps or half-slips (garments extending from the waist to slightly above the hemline of the dress). In many instances, slips are trimmed with nylon lace, embroidery, or applique. (See *embroidery and lace*, Chapter 19.) The amount, type, and quality of the trimming accounts for some of the differences in the prices of slips.

Slips may be knitted or woven. Knitted constructions predominate

FIGURE 17.24. Both of these slips were marked "Medium." (Photographs courtesy of Consumers' Research, Inc.)

because they cost less to produce; they are elastic, porous, resilient, crush-resistant, and easy to launder, and they require no ironing as compared to woven fabrics.

The TFPIA requires the fiber identification of fabrics used. But there are other considerations in the selection of a slip besides fiber, yarn, construction, and finish of the fabric. The following points should receive attention:

1. Garment construction. Seams should be overcast to protect the cut edge of the fabric if knitted (pinked if woven).
2. Close, firm stitching. Lace should be attached firmly with close, zigzag stitches, and straps or elastic waistbands should be firmly attached.
3. Residual shrinkage in percent stated on the label.
4. Garment measurement. The garment should be measured against the customer or tried on in the store to be sure it fits.
5. Laundering instructions. Instructions for laundering should be stated on the label.

Regular slip sizes run according to bust measure: 32, 34, 36, 38, and so on. Extra sizes are: 46, 48, 50, 52. A person who wears a size 14 dress should select a size 34 slip; one who wears a size 16 dress, and size 36 slip; a size 18 dress, a size 38 slip. The Commodity Standards Division of the U.S. Department of Commerce suggests that half slips are mostly made for younger figures. Therefore, misses standard sizes are more important than women's sizes, 34, 36, 38, and so on.

PANTIES AND BRIEFS

A panty is a garment with legs cut longer than a brief. It may have straight or flare legs. Briefs are very short, close-fitting, waist height garments with elasticized waist and leg openings. Some leg openings are made with bands.

The sizes of panties are governed by hip measurements. For example, a hip size of 33″ to 34″ would require a size 4 panty, 35″ to 36″ would take size 5, and so on up to 49″ to 52″ for size 11.

TIGHTS AND BODY SUITS

Tights are snug-fitting garments usually knitted of stretch nylon, in black, white, and colors. They are often sold in either the underwear or hosiery departments. The size ranges are shown in Table 17-3.

TABLE 17-3. Sizes in Underwear

| | Children's | | Women's | |
Size	Underwear Size	Size	Height	
Small	4-6	A	5′ to 5′4″	
Medium	7-10	B	5′5″ to 5′8″	
Large	12-14	C	5′8″ to 6″	

Body suits are one-piece garments that cover the torso and have elasticized leg openings and a snap crotch. They are often made of nylon or polyester rib knit, short or long sleeves, ribbed neck or turtleneck. The body suit is often worn with jeans. It is a versatile garment because it can serve as outerwear or underwear;[11] it moves with the body and is therefore comfortable.

[11] See body shirt in section on apparel tops.

FIGURE 17.25. Body suit of polyester/cotton. Has pointed shirt-type collar, elasticized leg openings, and snap crotch closing.

Sleepwear includes nightgowns, pajamas, and sleep sets (consisting of a coat and gown, tunic pajamas, or sleeveless nightgown and coat with elbow-length sleeves—a peignoir set). The lines, designs, and colors vary with fashion. Some common fabrics for gowns and pajamas are fleece, nylon tricot, flannelette, batiste, stretch nylon, terry cloth, brushed nylon knit, chiffon, and challis.

FIGURE 17.26. Permanent press button-front robe.

Dainty gowns may be trimmed with lace, embroidery, appliqué, or contrasting bindings. (See *embroidery and lace*, Chapter 19.)

Sizes of gowns and pajamas are determined by bust measure. The length of these garments depends upon the style.

Garments related to the sleepwear category, and the fabrics in which they are made, are the following:

Robes and lounge wear: wool flannel and blends, all-cotton blanket-type robing, velour, fleece, brushed knits, quilted fabrics, terry, corduroy; also cotton crepe, cotton broadcloth, and chiffon (for summer).

Bed jackets: knitted wool or acrylic, quilted cotton or man-made fibers, brushed textured fabrics, and cotton or rayon challis.

Peignoirs and travel sets (coat-and-gown or coat-and-pajamas): spun rayon, acetate or nylon crepe, tricot, brushed knits, all-over lace, trimmings of satin ribbon, lace, fur, metal threads, embroidery, and self-bindings.

HOW TO SELECT UNDERWEAR, SLEEPWEAR, AND LOUNGEWEAR

In buying these garments, the customer wants apparel that is comfortable—soft and lightweight—and will conform to body lines yet not constrain bodily movements. The garment should neither irritate the skin nor cling to outer garments.

The garment should require a minimum of care. This means fibers that can be washed by machine, dry quickly, and require no ironing, or merely touch-up ironing. Velour and velvet should be dry-cleaned.

Underwear and lounge wear come in pastel shades and prints, and some articles are trimmed with lace or embroidery. Trimming should be of good quality and should be sewn on evenly. Seams and hems should be even, narrow, and smooth. These are marks of good workmanship. In addition, buttonhole bindings should cover all cut edges. No threads should trail from any part of the garment.

INTIMATE APPAREL

This classification includes bras, girdles, corsets, panty girdles, and garter belts. There are various styles in each of these articles. (Definitions for these items will be found in the Glossary.)

Women are conscious of the lines and fit of their outer apparel, but comparatively few women realize that the fit of a dress can be improved by a perfect-fitting foundation garment. The items of apparel that control and support the figure are specially classed as foundation garments. A girdle of webbing made of spandex or rubber yarns gives a limited amount of support. With additional heavy woven fabric over the abdomen and buttocks, the garment gives improved support and figure control, and with varied amounts and weights of boning, the figure can be well controlled. A professional corsetiere should be consulted in the fitting of a corset. It is advisable to try on girdles, particularly the boned ones, to insure proper fit and the desired support and control.

Garments that are intended for support are made with at least a portion of webbing of rubber or spandex. Some girdles are made entirely of spandex or power net (nylon, or acetate and spandex). Girdles with legs are called *panty girdles*. A girdle with bra attached may be termed *all-in-one*. Fabrics used for foundation garments include nylon and spandex power net, panels of brocade or satin elastic (acetate, cotton, polyester, or spandex), trimmings of elasticized lace, and nylon tricot for panel linings and crotches. Abdominal support belts have light boning at the front, sides, and back. They may be made of knitted elastic (cotton, rayon, rubber). Panty girdles come in small, medium, large, and extra-large sizes. A small size should fit a size 12 or under; medium, a size 14; large, a size 16; and extra large, a size 18.

Bras, styled for various figure types in length, size of bust, and features for control and slimming, are either separate items of apparel or part of a corset. They are made with or without adjustable shoulder straps of corded or satin ribbon of cotton, acetate, or nylon, or they may be elastic. Bust measurement in inches denotes the size, and cups are designated as A, small; B, medium; and C, large.

The frame and cups may be made of power net, nylon lace, tricot, embroidered nylon, or polyester/cotton. Linings may be cotton or taffeta tricot; padding may be spun polyester or polyurethane.

Garter belts, designed to hold up stockings, may gently firm and control the younger figure (usually under a 29-inch waist). Sizes are small, medium, and large.

**HOSIERY
AND
PANTY
HOSE**

While cotton hosiery (especially lisle) and wool hosiery are worn for sports, children's, and men's wear, the great majority of women today wear nylon most of the time mainly in panty hose form.

Cotton, acrylic and stretch nylon, cotton and spandex, and 100 percent stretch nylon are used for women's and girls' socks, and for boys' and men's socks as well.

STRETCH YARN

To an increasing extent nylon hosiery and panty hose are being made from stretch textured yarns that are fluffy and have great permanent elasticity. This nylon is made from a continuous-filament fiber and should not be confused with spun nylon made from short lengths of fiber. Because of their stretching property, stretch nylons will adjust themselves to the size of the foot. Thus, three sizes are all a store need carry: small fits sizes 8 to 9; medium, 9½ to 10½; and large, 11 to 12.

One of the principal advantages of stretch nylon socks for children is that youngsters do not outgrow a pair so fast. Mothers with several small children can buy the same socks for all and keep them together in one drawer. This hosiery has been found to fit snugly and to be fast-drying and comfortable. However, some wearers object to a tight fit at the tip of the toes. In addition, if the sock is too snug, it may develop a hole. Stretch nylon yarn has been modified to create a leg with elastic-support properties; one such garment is marketed under the name of Supp-hose. The manufacturer claims that these stockings alleviate "tired legs," and it is implied that they take the place of surgical rubber stockings used for varicose veins. Although the support stocking probably is not an adequate substitute for the surgical rubber type, many women who are on their feet a great deal feel more comfortable with the right support provided. Support stockings are now made of a combination of nylon and spandex.

TYPES OF HOSIERY

There are two types of hosiery: full-fashion knit and circular knit. Full fashioned hose are knitted flat. Stitches are taken off (two stitches are knit as one to decrease the number) so that the fabric is narrowed at the ankle. The two edges of the fabric are sewn together, which provides a real seam from toe to heel and up the back. Two machines may make full-fashioned hosiery: one, called the *legger*, makes the leg; another, called the *footer*, makes the foot. There are also single-unit machines. On either side of the back seam, over the calf, small dots are visible. These dots, really double loops, are the points where stitches are decreased to make the hosiery narrower. They are called *fashion marks*. They are also visible on either side of the seam under the arch of the foot.

Circular-knit hosiery is commonly called *seamless*, because no back seam is present. In this type, the tension of needles is tightened at the time of knitting to shape the stocking below the calf of the leg. Thus, there are the same number of wales at the ankle as farther up the leg. In circular-knit hosiery a seam appears about one inch from the tip of the toe rather than at the toe as it does in full-fashioned hosiery.

Full-fashioned hosiery, a better-fitting fabric than circular knit, retains its shape better during wear and after washing. However, the overwhelming majority of women today wear seamless stockings. They eliminate the problem of crooked seams and fit smoothly on the foot. In a recent price list of six offerings by a mail order house, five were for seamless and only one for those with seams.

PANTY HOSE

Until the advent of the mini skirt, the standard length of women's regular nonstretch knit hosiery was 30 inches from the heel to the top of the garter welt. With the much shorter skirts, longer lengths of hosiery were required. Thus, thigh top and a hip length with opaque panels that hook to an elasticized waistband were made to meet consumer demand. Panty hose appealed to the consumer, and the sales now exceed that of conventional hosiery, including socks and knee-high varieties, in the ratio of 3 to 1. This change has been a major one, for hosiery sales have declined and panty hose have taken its place.

The consumer is assured of a smooth, snug-fitting garment from toe to waist. The stocking section can be patterned in variegated-size mesh, polka dot, point d'espirit, rib, cable, lacy, and crochetlike textures. Panty hose can also give mild support if the panty is knitted of nylon and spandex.

STANDARDS AND SPECIFICATIONS FOR HOSIERY AND PANTY HOSE

Grades. Hosiery and panty hose are classified first-quality, irregulars, seconds, and thirds. A stocking may be marked "irregular" if there are irregularities in dimensions, size, color, or knit, without the presence in the hose of any mends, runs, tears, or breaks in the fabric, or any substantial damage to the yarn or fabric itself. Seconds and thirds include hosiery that contains runs, obvious mends, irregularities, substantial imperfections, or defects in material, construction, or finish. Irregulars can be marked seconds or thirds if they have runs, mends, defects, and the like, but seconds and thirds cannot be marked irregulars according to government standards.

Foot Size. Except for stretch socks, the foot size of hosiery is measured in terms of inches. For instance, a size 9 1/2 stocking should fit an average foot 9 1/2 inches long. The standard size scale is 8 1/2 to 11 in 1/2-inch intervals. The relation to shoe size is given in Table 17-4.

TABLE 17-4. Stocking Chart.—Order Only Sizes Listed Each Item

If shoe size is	3	3½-4	4½-5½	6-6½	7-7½	8-9	9½-10	10½-11	over 11
Hose size is	8	8½	9	9½	10	10½	11	11½	12

To facilitate fitting, most salesmen have access to a foot size chart that shows the stocking size needed. As already indicated, if stretch yarn is used, three sizes may prove adequate for most customers, greatly simplifying stock problems.

Length. Hosiery is available in four lengths—ankle or calf, knee-high, over-the-knee, and thigh high, in addition, of course, to panty hose. Spandex knitted into the top band commonly holds the garment in place.[12]

Mesh knit, as compared to plain knit, has such great stretch that a single foot size will fit most women from 5' 2" tall to 5' 8", but two or three length variations are provided. Better hosiery may be length-sized to shape. For example, Sears provides in some styles:

Petite: for a person up to 5" 2" tall, with short legs and weight up to 120 lbs.
Shapely: 5' 2" to 5' 9" tall, average length slender legs, weight 95 to 140 lbs.
Classic: 5' 2" to 5' 9" tall, average length full legs, weight 120 to 170 lbs.
Tall: 5' 6" to 6' 3" tall, long, full legs, 160 to 200 lbs.
Statuesque: 5' 5" to 6' 3" tall, extra long and full legs, 180 to 260 lbs.

Where garter belts or foundation garments are worn, it is especially important to buy the correct length, which in conjunction with the fullness of the leg may be determined by measuring from the heel to the garter button.

To provide well-fitting stretch panty hose, a mail-order house gives the following size lengths.

TABLE 17-5. Sizes in Panty Hose

Size	Height	Weight
A (petite)	5 ft. to 5 ft. 3 in.	95 to 115 pounds
B (average)	5 ft. 3 in. to 5 ft. 7 in.	115 to 135 pounds
C (tall)	5 ft. 7 in. to 5 ft. 9 in.	135 to 160 pounds
D (large)	5 ft. 7 in. to 5 ft. 11 in.	160 to 180 pounds

Order next larger size if weight exceeds that shown for height.

[12] Over-the-knee hose and thigh-high hose are commonly called *stockings* as distinct from socks.

Gauge. This term refers to the degree of closeness of knitting, especially in full-fashioned hosiery. The closer the knitting, the higher the gauge number, the stronger the fabric, and the greater the snag resistance. Gauge is determined by the number of wales to an inch or the number of stitches to an inch and a half. The number of needles per inch is two-thirds the gauge number. For example, in a 45-gauge knitting machine, there are 30 needles to the inch. This 45-gauge machine knits a fabric 14 inches wide, so this machine would use 30 X 14, or 420 needles.

In seamless (circular knit) stockings and panty hose, the term *needle count* rather than gauge is often used. For example, 60 gauge is equivalent to 40 inch. If a circular knit measurement is 14 inches, a total of 420 needles (30 needles to the inch) is equivalent to 45 gauge. Sometimes the manufacturer does not put into operation all the needles on the machine. In the example above, he may not use all the 420 needles and erroneously call his product 45 gauge.

Denier. Hosiery and panty hose are often classified as sheer, semisheer, and service weight, with most today in the sheer and semisheer classes. The degree of sheerness is determined partly by the gauge but primarily by the denier. This is the weight of the yarn as indicated by a standard numbering system. (See Chapters 11 and 13.) In the wholesale trade, nylons are classified by denier. The designation 30s and 40s means 30- and 40-denier. The higher the denier number, the coarser, heavier, and stronger the yarn. For instance, 30 denier is twice as heavy and twice as strong as sheer 15 denier. Today the consumer may have a choice of several deniers, 10 to 50.

While panty hose may be made entirely of sheer 15-denier yarn, they may also be made of two denier sizes—a sheerer denier for the stocking and a coarser one for the panty. For example, regular-knit hose may be 28

FIGURE 17.27. A plain knit, very sheer nylon with nude thigh and sandal-foot for shoes with open toes or heels.

denier knitted into a 40-denier panty; a sheer seamless 21 denier (3 threads of 7 denier twisted together for strength) may be knitted onto a 50-denier opaque panty.

Through the years, hosiery has become more and more sheer. Before World War II, 30 denier was the sheerest; today we have 10, 12, and 15 denier. And then consumers ask: "Why don't my nylons wear the way they used to?" Obviously, since they are much more sheer, they are not so strong.

When an advertisement refers to nylon stockings or panty hose as 12/.66s, it means that the stockings are made of 12-denier nylon yarn with 66 stitches to 1 1/2 inches of fabric measured around the stocking.

Reinforcements. Reinforcements, by means of extra yarns, are commonly placed in the toe, heel, sole, and crotch in the case of panty hose, in direct proportion to the weight and style of the stocking. Nylon is so sturdy that it will stand a lot of abrasion, so some sheer hosiery styles are not reinforced. Frequently nylon yarns are used as reinforcements in wool and cotton socks.

Splicing styles (reinforcements above the heel) change from season to season. One style may call for a short, wide splicing; another may require a narrow, high splicing; another may feature a triangular effect. Whatever form splicing may take, it should be symmetrical for each stocking. Nylon seamless stockings do not necessarily have splicing above the heel.

Stretch. The stretch crosswise at the top of the garter welt in women's medium-length hosiery should be 12 to 13 inches when measured flat. Less than 12 inches is not sufficient stretch for comfort. If more than 13 inches, there is danger that the fabric will lose its elasticity and will not spring back to its original width. Such a fabric does not give the trim, snug fit desired. The elasticized waist and hips of panty hose should stretch to nearly double their unstretched measurement.

The stocking should stretch to 7 or 7 1/4 inches at the instep. To determine this measurement, grip the fabric at the instep and the point opposite on the sole and stretch the cloth. The attempt to make narrow heels may cause some manufacturers to narrow the width of the reinforcement on the sole. Then, when the stocking is worn, too much strain is put on the fabric at the instep. Holes may consequently appear at the point where splicing and sole reinforcement meet.

Color. Hosiery is dyed in the yarn before it is knitted or in the piece after it is knitted. Hosiery that is dyed in the yarn is called *ingrain* hosiery, whereas that dyed in the piece is called *dip-dyed* hosiery. The former has a more even, richer, deeper brilliance than the latter.

From the standpoint of economy, the manufacturer prefers to dip-dye his hosiery. He can knit a supply in natural color and dye the fabrics later as the style demand arises. An overstock of ingrain hosiery in an unpopular color may prove difficult to sell to the retailer.

SUGGESTIONS FOR HOSIERY SELECTION

Many women who have worn the patterned mesh hosiery seem to enjoy not only its attractive appearance but also its serviceability.

The shorter the skirt length, the greater is the focus on hosiery. A variety of fashion colors have appeared, and interesting patterns have been knitted into the stockings. Hosiery has become a fashion item.

Some suggestions for hosiery selection follow:

1. If durability is important, avoid very sheer, low-denier hosiery.
2. If you buy panty hose, be sure to consider your shoe size, your height and weight, and your leg contour. A stocking may fit perfectly, but the panty section may not fit ill-proportioned hips.
3. For children, buy cotton lisle, cotton mixtures, or stretch nylon.
4. Buy wool hosiery a size larger than normal, unless drying forms are used or the label is marked "preshrunk, residual shrinkage less than 3 percent."
5. For durability, look for a reinforced heel and toe, a special toe guard, a wide garter welt, and a run-stop below the garter welt.
6. Ingrain hosiery is normally to be preferred to dip-dyed; it is likely to retain its color better.

SELECTION OF CLOTHING ACCESSORIES

In addition to underwear and negligees, which are sometimes classed under accessories, there are many small items of clothing or personal adornment that are made of textiles.

NECKWEAR AND SCARFS

Neckwear may include collars, cuffs, and stoles. Since these pieces, with the exception of stoles (made of wool or acrylic knitted goods and furlike fabrics), are made of the same materials as dresses, they need no further description. The same is true of scarfs. They are commonly made of silk, rayon, acetate, acrylic, nylon, wool, cotton, or mixtures of these materials. Typical fabrics include twills, satins, foulard, crepes, and knitted goods. Scarfs may be square, $23'' \times 23''$ or $27'' \leqslant 27''$; oblong, $11'' \times 36''$, $15'' \times 44''$, or $14'' \times 64''$; or cravat-shaped. The neckwear department often carries small capes and short jackets as well.

ARTIFICIAL FLOWERS

Many artificial flowers are made of nontextiles such as paper, glass, plastic, and wax, but flowers are also made of velvet, velveteen, taffeta, satin, lace, chiffon, and organdy. Very often flowers on coats and dresses are made of the same material as the coat or dress.

HANDKERCHIEFS

There are different types of women's handkerchiefs for different occasions. Handkerchiefs for everyday wear may be all white, pastel, or printed—with or without monogram, lace, or other ornamentation. These handkerchiefs are made of handkerchief linen, batiste, lawn, and washable silk. A silk handkerchief may be used to tie around the neck to ornament a sweater or jersey blouse. For evening, filmier and larger handkerchiefs are worn. They may be monogrammed, lace-trimmed, or plain with a hand-rolled hem. Chiffon and lace are common materials used for evening.

When buying a handkerchief, consider the following points:

1. General appearance
2. Wearing quality or durability
   (*a*) Grade of fabric
   (*b*) Workmanship
   (*c*) Quality of trimming, embroidery, and design
3. Purpose, or suitability for its use
4. Price

General appearance may include style. If colored borders or printed all-over designs are a style note, they should certainly be considered in the selection.

With respect to durability, the buyer should know that a good grade of linen will outwear the average cotton. White linen will appear fresher and more lustrous after laundering. Thin silks and rayons appear to advantage for evening or occasional wear if frequent laundering is not essential.

Hems rolled and sewed by hand are considered better than those that are machine-stitched, because they do not pucker and because the stitching, if well done, is not so noticeable. The firmness and quality of the hemstitching or other embroidery are important. If lace or other trimming is used, the sewing that attaches it to the handkerchief should be firm, even, and fine.

The careful buyer selects a handkerchief for a particular occasion. For example, if it is to appear from the pocket of a dress, the color of the dress and the occasion for its use should be considered. Handkerchiefs are made for special occasions, with hearts for Valentine's Day, poinsettia prints for Christmas, and shamrocks for St. Patrick's Day.

Price can be very important. If a woman needs a handkerchief for actual use rather than for show, she may select an inexpensive one. If she has a particular fondness for fine linens with real lace trimmings, she must be willing to pay the high prices.

MILLINERY

Styles. As one woman said to a friend who was considering wearing a hat to a luncheon, "You are dated if you wear that hat. Only old women wear hats. This is a hatless era." There has been and still is a strong trend to hatlessness. But some women wear hats to accent their outfits, to protect the head from winter's cold and summer's sun, to add height if the woman is short, or to flatter the face.

The trend toward hatlessness has caused manufacturers to exert efforts to create new colors, lines, and sizes of hats. Both styles and materials change from season to season.

Fabrics. Felts are made of either fur or wool. The former is more luxurious, softer, and more expensive than the latter. A velour is a fur felt with a long silky pile. In a discussion of felting, it was stated that pounding and steaming locks the wool fibers together. Staple polyester fibers can be felted by heat setting.

Both natural and synthetic straw is used for hats. Natural straws are made from grasses, rice shoots, stems, and leaves. Synthetic straws are made from nylon, modacrylic, rayon and cellophane.

Steps in the manufacture of natural straw include:

1. Bleaching to make the straw white or cream colored.
2. Weaving into a rough form; for example, panama, baku, leghorn, toyo; or braided into narrow strips sewn together into a desired shape.
3. Blocking by steaming and drying on a form.

Synthetic straws are made in different widths and colors. Their prices range from inexpensive to moderate.

Fabric hats are made of nylon and polyester velvet, cotton, acrylic, or modacrylic furlike fabrics. These materials are often draped over a frame of buckram. Real fur and leather are also used, but these materials are nontextiles and so will not be discussed here.

Trim. Hats are often trimmed with ribbon, flowers made from textile fabrics, feathers, felt, or leather; and novelty ornaments such as buckles, stones, and beads. One of the common ribbon fabrics is grosgrain, a heavy, fillingwise-ribbed rayon, acetate, or nylon material. The ribs may have a cotton core. There is quite a bit of body to the material and it wears well. Taffeta, moiré, velvet, velveteen, satin (both single-faced and double-faced), metal cloth, and novelty weaves are other common ribbon materials. Acetate moiré taffeta has become popular for ribbons because the fabric can be woven wide and cut into ribbon width, and the cut edges can be fused by heat. This method makes the ribbon inexpensive. Velvet ribbons with cut instead of woven edges can also be used for inexpensive trimmings for millinery. The velvet with cut edges ravels easily, and hence is not too satisfactory.

In selecting becoming hats, the style, suitability, shape-retaining quality, colorfastness, and finish are the important factors.

GLOVES

Although formerly most gloves were made of leather, many are now made of knitted and woven goods. Fabric gloves may be made of cotton, wool, acrylic, rayon or nylon tricot mesh, crocheted cotton, and woven goods such as lace and dress fabrics.

HANDBAGS

Comparatively few handbags are made of textile fabrics. Most of them are made of leather or a substitute. Faille, tapestry, double-woven stretch nylon, furlike fabrics, and fabrics to match a coat may be used for everyday wear. For evening, metallic fabric on acetate backing, peau de soie, cotton velveteen, satin, and brocade are appropriate. For summer handbags, the fabrics used include linen crash, homespun, the fabric of the dress being worn, straw, and nylon knits or crocheted materials. Linings include rayon and nylon satin, rayon faille, crepe, and printed cottons. Large beach bags for swimsuits or for knitting may be made of crash, homespun, string, canvas, sailcloth, or cotton tapestry. They may be waterproofed.

WOMEN'S AND CHILDREN'S SHOES

Most shoes are made of leather, but fabric shoes have become popular for specific occasions: for beach wear, beach sandals made of webbing, canvas, cotton crash, or cretonne; for street wear, canvas or crash; for evening, brocades, metal cloth, satin, faille, moiré, or taffeta.

The uppers of sneakers are textiles made of polyester/cotton poplin, cotton army duck, cotton canvas, or denim. Slippers for summer can be corduroy, terry, or nylon tricot; for winter, cotton velour with nylon or acrylic lining, rayon or acetate plush, quilted cotton, acrylic pile on cotton knit, acrylic and modacrylic blends, cotton knit backed with polyurethane foam.

**INFANTS'
WEAR**

Certain articles, such as sacques, bootees, dresses, shirts, blankets, diapers, and bonnets, are always essential for infants. The styles in length, type of yoke, and trimming of babies' wearing apparel may change slightly, but the general silhouette does not alter. Infants' clothing is sized according to age: 6, 12, 18, 24 months.

Toddlers' sizes 1 to 4 are designed for tots whose figures still retain the rounded contours of infancy. Coat and dress lengths are short; legs and seats are cut full to accommodate diapers. Height of the child is most important in determining size. For the child who is losing the roundness of infancy, a more fitted style is appropriate (sizes 2 to 6x). Again, height is a most important factor in determining size.

Materials for babies' clothing are, generally speaking, cotton, man-made fibers alone or in blends. A 50 percent cotton, 30 percent polyester, 20 percent nylon blend has the softness and absorbency of cotton, and the strength and durability of nylon; therefore is well suited for underwear. It is machine washable and dryable. All children's sleepwear (sizes 0 to 6X) must pass a standard test for flammability set by the U. S. Department of Commerce.

The department or specialty store saleswoman can recommend a choice of layette. In some instances, stores have made up suitable lists of layettes at various prices.

Two of the most important items in a layette are diapers and pads. Should the mother decide to use a diaper service or disposable diapers, she may not need to buy any diapers, although a few for emergency are desirable. For traveling, the throw-away, nonwoven type are convenient. Diapers are made of gauze, flannelette, knitted and bird's eye in rectangular or fitted types. Gauze, which allows air to circulate, is

FIGURE 17.28. Flame retardant sleepwear
for infants to 17 pounds.
This gown has snap fastener front closure
and a drawstring bottom
to keep the infant's feet warm.

comfortable and easy to wash and dry. Flannelette is soft but bulky. Pinked edges are more comfortable than hemmed ones. Cotton bibs, pads, and diapers that are double woven allow air to circulate between the layers to dry the material much faster and make it more comfortable.

The double-woven pads are more absorbent than quilted pads. As soon as the moisture hits the absorbent pad it spreads out as if it were on a blotter. On the quilted pads the water stays in one spot and then slowly spreads out. Plastic-coated and rubber pads are waterproof but are hotter in summer because they lack porosity.

SUMMARY This chapter shows the possibilities that a person faces in choosing clothing fabrics for different uses, and sets forth the points for selection of yard goods and ready-made apparel for women and girls. No one becomes expert in judging fabrics until he or she is willing to study their characteristics thoroughly, a pursuit that requires patience, time, and practice. To this end, the glossary below will describe fabrics used in women's and girls' clothing.

PROJECT 1. From the articles of apparel listed here, select one garment for study: Nightgown, robe, shorts, slacks, baby's bonnet, child's pajamas, head scarf, raincoat, pants suit, body suit, fur-like fabric coat.
Write up the information in the form of a merchandise manual to include:
(*a*) Where found in a store
(*b*) Fabrics of which it is made
(*c*) Size range
(*d*) Selling points
(*e*) Instructions for care
(*f*) Retail price range

GLOSSARY[13] Batiste—A very sheer, combed, mercerized muslin identified by streaks lengthwise. Better grades are highly mercerized. It is also made in spun rayon, wool, or silk and is used for summer dresses, blouses, lingerie, infants' dresses and bonnets, handkerchiefs.

Bias cut—A fabric cut diagonally across the warp and filling yarns. A true bias is cut on a 45° angle from the lower left to the upper right of a cloth.

Bouclé—See Glossary, Chapter 3.

Brassiere or bra—An undergarment that covers the bust and may extend to the waistline.

Brief—A short panty. See *Panty.*

Broadcloth—A plain-weave cotton fabric, with fillingwise rib finer than poplin. Best grades are made of combed pima or Egyptian cotton. It is used for women's blouses, tailored summer dresses, men's shirts. It can also be made of silk and polyester and cotton blends. See *Wool broadcloth*, Glossary, Chapter 18.

Brocade—Fabric with slightly raised Jacquard designs that may have gold or silver threads. It is used for formal dresses, blouses, evening wraps, and bags. See Glossary, Chapter 21.

[13] Since all apparel fabrics cannot be defined in a glossary, for those omitted see *Calloway Textile Dictionary* (Calloway Mills, La Grange, Georgia), *Dan River's Textile Dictionary* (Dan River Mills, New York), or *Fairchild's Dictionary of Textiles,* Fairchild Publications, Inc. (New York).

Brocatelle—See Glossary, Chapter 21.

Butcher—A coarse rayon or rayon and acetate blend made to resemble the original butcher linen used for the butcher's apron.

Cambric—A muslin that is lightweight, sized. Very low count, heavily sized glazed cambric is used for costuming.

Canton crepe—Thick, slightly ribbed crepe, heavier than crepe de Chine. It may be silk, rayon or acetate and is used for business and afternoon dresses.

Challis—A very lightweight plain-weave wool, spun rayon, or mixed fabric usually printed with small floral designs that is used for dresses, blouses, scarfs, infants' sacques.

Chambray—A plain-weave cotton fabric with colored warp and white filling that may have woven-in stripes. It is used for women's and children's summer dresses and blouses and men's shirts.

Chenille—A fabric woven from fuzzy caterpillarlike yarns. Usually the filling is the chenille yarn and the warp a regular textile yarn.

Cheviot—See Glossary, Chapter 18.

Chiffon—A sheer plain weave crepe fabric in silk, rayon, or nylon with either soft or stiff finish. It is used for formal dresses, scarfs, and evening handkerchiefs.

Chinchilla—Heavy twill-weave coating that may be all wool or mixed with cotton. Little nubs or tufts of nap make the characteristic surface to resemble chinchilla fur. It is used for coats and jackets.

Corduroy—Heavy cotton or rayon pile fabric. The cut pile forms wales warpwise. It is used for dresses, coats, sports jackets, slacks, and draperies.

Corselet—A type of girdle, with a boned front, that extends from above the bust to below the buttocks. Bras may hook onto girdle.

Corset—A heavily boned foundation garment for the torso.

Covert—See Glossary, Chapter 18.

Crash—A coarse linen, cotton, or rayon fabric with uneven yarns woven in plain weave. It is used for dresses, suitings, table linens, draperies.

Crepe—A fabric with a crinkled surface that may be made by several methods.

Crepe de Chine—Originally made in silk with the fabric degummed to produce crinkle. As made now, it is a sheer flat crepe in silk or man-made fibers. It is used for lingerie, dresses, and blouses.

Damask—A reversible Jacquard fabric. The designs are not raised as in brocade. It is made of almost any fiber or blends. It is used for afternoon and evening dresses, table covers in linen, draperies and upholsteries in heavier fabrics. See Glossary, Chapter 20.

Dart—A tapering fold that is stitched in a garment to improve its fit.

Denim—A heavy strong, twill-weave cotton fabric woven with colored warps and white fillings. Originally blue or brown, denims are now also made in stripes and figures. They are used for jeans, work clothes, overalls, draperies, and bedspreads.

Dimity—A sheer cotton with corded stripes or checks—used for children's summer dresses, bedspreads, curtains, and blouses.

Donegal tweed—See Glossary, Chapter 18.

Dotted swiss—Sheer, crisp, plain-weave cotton fabric with either clipped spot or swivel dots, colored or white. It is used for children's party dresses, women's summer dresses, lingerie, and curtains.

Dress linen—See *Crash.*

Embroidery—Ornamental needlework done on the fabric itself.

End use—Intended use by the consumer.

Faille—A flat, crosswise, ribbed fabric with more ribs to the inch than bengaline. It is made of rayon, acetate, cotton, wool, or mixtures and is used for tailored dresses, coats, suits, and draperies. Tissue faille is a lightweight faille.

Faille crepe—A silk, rayon, acetate, or other man-made fibered dress fabric with a decided wavy (crepe) cord fillingwise. It is used for negligees, blouses, daytime and evening dresses, handbags, and trimmings.

Flannel—Originally an all-wool fabric of woolen or worsted yarn with a soft napped finish. Now often a rayon or cotton fabric slightly napped on both sides to resemble woolen or worsted. It may be twill or plain weave and is used for coats, suits, dresses. Viyella flannel is a Williams, Hollins and Company trade name for a cotton and wool flannel made in England.

Flannelette—A lightweight cotton flannel napped on one or both sides, which may be printed. It is used for sleeping garments and sports shirts.

Flat crepe—A medium weight crepe with creped fillings alternating with two S and two Z twists. The surface is fairly flat. It is used for dresses, negligees, and blouses.

Fleece—A fabric with a deep, thick-napped surface that may be of wool, cotton, acrylic, nylon, or other man-made fibers.

Foulard—A lightweight, soft, twill-weave silk, cotton, or rayon fabric that is often printed with small figures on light or dark grounds. It is used for spring and summer dresses, scarfs, robes, and neckties.

Furlike fabrics—See Glossary, Chapter 5.

Gabardine—A tightly woven, steep twill with rounded wales and a flat back. Made in wool, cotton, rayon, polyester, or mixtures. It is used for suits, coats, tailored dresses, and slacks.

Garter belt—A fabric belt to which garters are attached.

Gauze—A sheer, open, plain-weave cotton fabric used for diapers and surgical dressings. It can also be made of silk or man-made fibers for use in curtains.

Georgette crepe—A sheer, dull crepe. The texture is obtained by alternating right and left twist yarns in warp and filling. It is used for summer and evening dresses.

Gingham—A yarn-dyed plain-weave cotton fabric with woven-in plaids, checks, or stripes. It is used for women's and children's dresses, blouses and men's sport shirts.

Girdle—A foundation garment extending from the waist or bust to below the buttocks. It has all-elastic webbing or inserts of webbing and fabric, with or without bones.

Gros de Londres—Ribbed or corded fabric. The flat, fillingwise cords alternate wide and narrow. It is used for dresses and millinery.

Grosgrain—A heavy ribbed fabric in ribbon width, made in silk or rayon warp with cotton cords. The cords are round and firm. It is really a bengaline in narrow goods and is used for ribbons, neckties, and lapel facings.

Honan—A heavy silk pongee, originally the product of wild silkworms of Honan, China. Honan has slub yarns in both warp and filling and may be made with synthetic fibers.

Jean—A solid-colored or striped twill-weave cotton fabric, softer and finer than denim. It is used for work shirts, girls' pants and shorts, and children's overalls.

Jersey—See Glossary, Chapter 13.

Lace—An openwork fabric made by looping interlacing, or twisting thread. For kinds of laces, see pp. 484-90

Lamé—Brocade, damask, or brocatelle in which flat metallic yarns are woven in warp and filling for a luxurious effect. Metallic yarns may be used in the main construction. Also a trademark term for a nontarnishable metallic yarn. It is used for evening dresses, blouses, and trimmings.

Lawn—A cotton muslin fabric generally more sheer and with a higher count than nainsook. It may or may not be sized.

Lingerie crepe—Formerly called French crepe because it was originally made in France. The creped surface was made by embossing (pressing cloth over a fleece blanket). Since it is no longer pressed, it is not a crepe. It is used for lingerie and spring and summer dresses.

Loden cloth—A fleecy coating woven of coarser grade of wool in the Austrian and German Tyrol. Since the wool has some grease, it is naturally water-repellent. Generally a soft wood green.

Marquisette—See Glossary, Chapter 13.

Matelassé crepe—A double cloth with quilted or blistered appearance that is used for afternoon, dinner, and evening dresses and trimmings.

Melton—A heavy woolen with clipped surface nap; somewhat feltlike in feeling; lustrous like a dull broadcloth.

Mesh—Any woven or knitted fabric with an open mesh texture. It is used for foundation garments and hosiery.

Moss crepe—A type of crepe woven and finished to have a mossy look.

Muslin—Any plain-weave cotton cloth ranging in weight from the sheerest batiste to the coarsest sheeting. Muslins include such fabrics as voile, nainsook, lawn, and percale.

Nainsook—A cotton muslin fabric heavier and coarser than lawn. In better grades it may be polished on one side. When well-polished, it is sold as polished cotton.

Negligee—A loose, robe-type garment, worn in the boudoir, made of sheer fabric and often lace or fur trimmed.

Net—A silk, rayon, nylon, or cotton mesh fabric. The size of the mesh varies as well as the weight of the net. It is used for veils, evening dresses, and trimmings.

Ninon—A voile with warp yarns grouped in pairs. It is made of rayon, acetate, silk, or man-made fibers and is used for dresses and curtains.

Nun's veiling—A sheer, worsted, silk or mixed fabric that is dyed black or brown for religious garb and dyed in colors for dresses.

100-denier crepe—A 100-denier viscose rayon yarn made in a flat crepe construction.

Organdy—A thin, stiff transparent cotton muslin used for summer dresses, neckwear, and trimmings. Permanent starchless finishes do not lose their crispness in laundering.

Organza—A thin, stiff, plain-weave silk or rayon fabric used for formal dresses, trimmings, and collars and cuffs. See *Organdy*.

Ottoman—A heavily corded silk or rayon fabric. The cords are heavier than bengaline and are widely spaced. The cords usually are cotton or wool.

Oxford—A basket-weave cotton fabric (2 × 1, 2 × 2, or 3 × 2) used for sport dresses, blouses, and shirts.

Pants suit—A two-piece garment consisting of jacket and long pants.

Panty—A woman's or girl's undergarment, with an elastic waistband, that is bound, scalloped, or lace-trimmed at the bottom. A panty girdle is an elasticized, form-fitting panty.

Panty girdle—A foundation garment with legs attached. See *Girdle*.

Panty hose—Stockings and panty knitted as one garment.

Peau de soie—See Glossary, Chapter 21.

Pebble crepe—Usually woven of abraded yarns (rayon and acetate) warp and filling. It is a plain weave with skips of warp over two fillings and two fillings over two warps at intervals, to give pebbled surface.

Peignoir—A loose robe worn in the boudoir or a coat worn over a bathing suit at the beach. It is often made of terry cloth to absorb water after bathing.

Percale—A medium weight muslin similar to cambric but dull in finish. It is generally printed for apparel. Heavy grades in higher counts are used for sheeting. Dress percale runs 80 square or 160 yarns to the inch, whereas percale sheeting is 180 or 200 yarns to the inch.

Piqué—A fabric with warpwise wales made in cotton, rayon, or other man-made fibers. In honeycomb design it is called waffle piqué; in diamond pattern, bird's-eye piqué. It is used for dresses, collars, cuffs, and shirts.

Placket closing—A narrow piece of material used to finish an opening made in a fabric to enable the wearer to put on the garment with ease.

Plissé or crinkle crepe—A crinkled, striped, or blistered pattern produced on a cotton, rayon, or acetate fabric by treating parts of the fabric with caustic soda to shrink certain areas.

Plush—See Glossary, Chapter 21.

Pongee—Fabric originally made in China of tan-colored tussah silk. It is plain or printed for summer dresses and suits and is lighter and less slubby than shantung.

Poplin—A crosswise-ribbed cotton fabric similar to cotton broadcloth but with a heavier rib. It may be of rayon, silk, wool, nylon, polyester, or combinations of these fibers. It is used for dresses, coats, jackets, and snowsuits (water-repellent).

Printcloth—Term applied to carded, plain-weave cotton fabrics with single yarns with counts 30s and 40s. Finishes may vary to produce cloths like lawn, percale, cambric, and longcloth. For longcloth, see *Muslin sheeting*, Glossary, Chapter 18.

Rep—A silk, rayon, cotton, wool, or mixed fabric in rib construction, heavier than poplin. It is used for draperies and men's ties, and in lighter weights for blouses and trimmings.

Romain crepe—A semisheer fabric of abraded yarns in warp and filling. It is made of rayon and acetate or wool and is used for street and dressy dresses.

Rough crepe—A heavy fabric of rayon, acetate, or mixtures made with alternately twisted fillings, two right and two left (2 × 2).

Satin crepe—A heavy reversible fabric with satin on one side and crepe on the other side. It is used in fall and winter dresses and linings.

Seersucker—A cotton, silk, or man-made fibered fabric made by alternating plain and crinkled stripes. It is used for summer dresses, boys' shirts, shorts, men's summer suits, and bedspreads. See *Woven seersucker.*

Serge—An even twill-weave worsted fabric with the diagonal wale showing on both sides of the cloth, used for men's and women's suits, coats, and dresses. It is made in cotton or rayon for linings.

Shantung—A plain-weave fabric woven with slub filling yarn made in silk, rayon, cotton, the man-made fibers, or wool. It is used for dresses and suits.

Silhouette—The outline of a garment.

Slipper satin—A heavy rayon, acetate, or silk satin usually with a cotton back. It is used for bedroom and evening slippers.

Staple fabrics—Those cloths which, over a period of years, have a steady sale or demand. Such cloths as muslins, flannels, broadcloth, shantung, and taffeta are staples that have to be kept in stock.

Staple names—Name of staple fabrics. See *Staple fabrics.*

Surah—A soft twilled fabric made of silk, rayon, or acetate woven in plaids, stripes, solid color, or print. Since the diagonal of the wale has a flat top, it may be described as a satin-faced twill. It is used for dresses, blouses, trimmings, and neckties. Foulard is often sold as surah.

Taffeta—Plain-weave, smooth, stiffened fabric in silk, rayon, cotton, or man-made fibers, solid colored or printed. It is used for dresses, blouses, and ribbons.

Terry cloth—See *Terry method*, Chapter 5.

Texture—See Glossary, Chapter 3.

Tights—Skintight garments closely fitting to the figure and extending from the neck down, or from the waist down.

Tricot—See Glossary, Chapter 6.

Tweed—A rough-surfaced woolen, usually yarn-dyed and often made in two or more colors. In women's wear, a tweed may look rough but feels soft or even spongy. It may be nubbed or slubbed. It is all wool unless otherwise indicated. Now cotton, linen, rayon, synthetics, or blends may be made to resemble wool tweed.

Unbleached muslin—Printcloths in grey goods and lightweight sheetings.

Unfinished worsted—See Glossary, Chapter 19.

Union suit—A one-piece knitted undergarment extending from the neck to the knee or longer.

Velour—See Glossary, Chapter 21.

Velvet—Silk, rayon, or nylon cut pile fabric made with extra warp yarns. Types of velvet include chiffon, Lyons, transparent, and uncut velvet.

Velveteen—A cotton fabric with a filling pile made to look like velvet. It has a cut pile with plain or twill back and is used for dresses, coats, jackets, millinery, and suits.

Viyella flannel—See *Flannel.*

Voile—A low-count, sheer muslin with a thready feel. In better grades, voile is made with ply yarns in counterclockwise twist. It is also made in wool, silk, or rayon and is used for summer dresses and curtains.

Whipcord—A twill-weave wool or cotton fabric resembling gabardine. The wale is more pronounced on the right side. It is used for riding habits and uniforms.

White-on-white—Fabric with a white dobby or Jacquard design on a white ground, common in madras, broadcloth, or nylon. See *Madras*, Glossary, Chapter 18.

Wool crepe—Made of either woolen or worsted yarns. The crepe texture is produced by keeping the warp yarns slack.

Woven seersucker—A crinkled, striped cotton fabric made by weaving some of the yarns in tighter tension than others. See *Seersucker*.

Men's and Boys' Wear

18

Through the years, certain fabrics have remained classic. One of these is jean. The French used to identify Genoese sailors by their heavy trousers, which they called *gènes* (after the French *Gènes* for Genoa). The word dungaree (so the story goes) is derived from the Hindustani word dungri. Sailors wore a garment by the same name. Denim, like jean and dungaree, is related to seafaring. The word denim, a contraction of "de Nimes," was named after the French city of Nimes, where the fabric was made for sailcloth.

One of the reasons why jean has been a classic fabric over the years is that it has withstood resistance to wear.

Jeans have now become a fashion not only for sports but also for casual wear for both sexes. Consequently, we now have jean the fashion garment and jean the fabric.

Jean, the trouser and more recently the suit, is made not only of the fabric jean, but also of sateen, denim (sometimes with brushed surface), twills, double knits in solid colors, plaids and stripes. Jean the fabric until recently was an all-cotton cloth, made of carded yarns in a 2 × 1 twill construction with colored warp (generally blue) and white filling. Now the fabric is typically made of cotton and man-made fibers such as nylon and/or polyester. This combination of fibers adds resistance to wear and durable press ensures abrasion resistance and no-ironing as well. In fact, an entry describing this blended fabric in a mail-order catalogue stated that the fabric jean is so rugged that a child's trampoline was made of it. However, not all jeans wear equally well. Generally, the higher the ratio of man-made fiber to cotton, the more durable the fabric.

Originally jean was used primarily for work clothes and children's play clothes. Now jeans are popular for almost any informal activity. In fact, the term "jean" was often used interchangeably with "denim," as for example, the use of the term "blue jeans." Today we are more likely to use the term "jeans" to refer to a trouser or a suit, and "denim" to refer to a popular fabric used for jeans.

Even in such a popular fabric as jeans, the consumer should carefully select items of clothing, not only for the end use but also for appropriateness in dress, whether for business, leisure, sports, or the college campus. Accessories, too, should be carefully selected in order to create a harmonious ensemble.

FIGURE 18.1. Growing into his father's clothes. (Photo courtesy Men's Fashion Association of America.)

SELECTION OF MEN'S AND BOYS' FURNISHINGS

Men's wear may be classified as (1) men's clothing and (2) men's furnishings. A similar division may be made for boys' wear. Work clothing is often treated as a separate classification.

Men's and boys' furnishings are composed of similar articles, the chief of which are shirts, sleepwear, underwear, hosiery, robes, ties, handkerchiefs, belts, suspenders, garters, mufflers and scarfs, sweaters, and swimwear. Men's jewelry (nontextiles), such as cuff links, studs, tie clips, and stickpins, are also commonly included in the classification.

Men's clothing includes garments such as suits, topcoats, overcoats, jackets, and slacks. Boys' clothing includes suits, topcoats, overcoats, jackets, and raincoats. With the emergence of fashion as a selling force, there are now more divisions of men's and boys' sections in department and specialty stores. Teen sportswear and furnishings departments have often become individual shops or boutiques—that is, sweater, slacks, swimwear, shirt shops.

SHIRTS

Shirts may be classified according to the occasion for which they are worn: (1) dress (tailored garments worn with a necktie for business, street, and semiformal wear), (2) work, (3) sports, and (4) formal.

Dress shirts are usually all white, solid colored, striped, or figures. For work shirts or one-piece work suits, khaki, dark blue, or color coordinated to pants are common. Sports or leisure shirts may be white, solid colored, plaids, stripes, checks, or figures.

438

TABLE 18-1. Color Coordinator for Men's Clothing[a]

Color of Suit	Shirt	Tie	Socks	Shoes & Belt	Square or Scarf	Hat	Outercoat	Gloves
Gray	Blue	Blue	Navy	Black	Blue/white	Medium Gray	Black	Gray
	Yellow	Black/Gold	Black	Black	Black/Gold	Black	Gray	Black
Natural	Blue	Black/Blue	Black	Black	Black/Blue	Gray	Navy	Navy
	Yellow	Navy/Gold	Black	Black	Navy/Gold	Gray	Black	Gray
Blue-Black	Red/Pink	Red/Blue	Black	Black	Red/Blue	Gray	Gray	Gray
	Gray	Blue/Green	Navy	Cordovan	Blue/Green	Brown	Tan	Brown
Green	Tan	Green/Gold	Brown	Brown	Green/Gold	Bronze	Natural	Brown
	Green	Blue/Green	Green	Olive	Blue/Green	Brown	Brown	Brown
Brown	Red/Pink	Red/Brown	Brown	Brown	Red/Brown	Brown	Brown	Natural
	Blue	Blue/Brown	Brown	Brown	Blue/Brown	Medium Brown	Camel	Brown

[a]Produced by the American Institute of Men's and Boys' Wear.

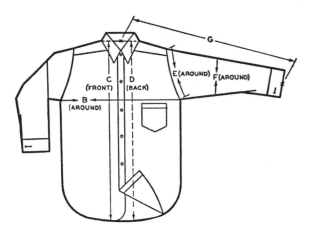

FIGURE 18.2. Commercial standards for men's shirt sizes call for minimum dimensions in five areas that are important for comfort and appearance. (Reproduced courtesy of Consumers' Research, Inc.)

Sizes in Dress Shirts. Men's dress shirt sizes run 14 to 17 (neckband measurement). Men who cannot wear standard sizes should buy custom-made shirts. Sleeve lengths come in sizes 32 to 36. Boys' sizes run 3, 4, 5, 6, and 8, 10, 12, 14, 16, 18, 20. Sleeve lengths are usually identified as long or short.

Cotton shirtings come under FTC rules for shrinkage. (See p. 143.) That is, if the words "preshrunk" or "full-shrunk" are used, they mean that the fabric will not shrink further. If there is a possibility of residual shrinkage, then the percent to be expected must be stated. It is advisable to buy a half size larger shirt if the residual shrinkage is over 1 percent. For shirts marked "Sanforized" this advice is unnecessary.

Standard commercial sizes for men's shirts, as agreed upon by the trade and published by the National Bureau of Standards, are found in Table 18-2.

TABLE 18-2. Standard Minimum Measurements for Men's Shirts

(All Measurements Are in Inches)

Stamped neckband sizes	(A)	14	14½	15	15½	16	16½	17
Chest, total circumference	(B)	42	44	46	48	50	52	54
Front, length of	(C)	33	33	33	33	33	33	33
Back, length of	(D)	33	33	33	33	33	33	33
Armholes, length around curve	(E)	19½	20	20½	21	21½	22	22½
Sleeve, width around	(F)	14¾	15¼	15¾	16¼	16¾	17¼	17¾

Styles in Dress Shirts. Collars in spread, long, or medium point are attached to the body of the shirt.[1] Shirts may have a single or a pleated closing that buttons down the front. Cuffs may be single (barrel) or French (double). The latter style has buttonholes for cuff links.

Fabrics for Dress Shirts, Including Formal Shirts. All-cotton or polyester/cotton blends are commonly used for dress shirtings. Broadcloth and polyester/nylon are popular for dress and knitted shirts. Best-quality domestic broadcloth is made of 2 X 2 combed pima cotton with a count

[1] See collar styles in illustration, Figure 18.3.

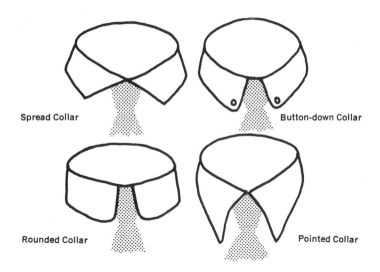

Spread Collar

Button-down Collar

Rounded Collar

Pointed Collar

FIGURE 18.3.   Basic collar styles. (Courtesy Celanese Fibers Marketing Co.)

FIGURE 18.4.   A polyester and cotton plaid dress shirt. (Photo courtesy Men's Fashion Association of America.)

of 144 × 76, mercerized, and shrinkage controlled. Poorer grades may have the following weaknesses: 2 × 1 (two-ply warp and single filing) or single carded yarns in both warp and filling; a count as low as 100 × 56; little or no mercerization; preshrunk fabric with residual shrinkage declared.

Chambray, a staple yarn-dyed fabric with colored warp and white filling, is also suitable for dress shirts. In better grades are found yarns single and combed, a balanced count 84 × 76, and shrinkage control. Tricot is a knit in 100 percent polyester or 80 percent polyester/20 percent cotton that is quick drying and has minimum-care properties. There is also a stretch-woven fabric that is comfortable, neat looking, and easy to care for.

Shirts for formal wear are usually pleated or plain, with a starched or soft bosom depending on the current mode. Fabrics include piqué, batiste, broadcloth, silk or man-made fibered crepe, and blends.

Requirements for Good Workmanship. To ensure good wearing quality, a dress shirt's seams should be stitched firmly but should not pucker (14 to 18 close, even stitches to the inch). Buttons (ocean pearl in better grades because they do not melt as plastic buttons do) should be stitched firmly; buttonholes should be evenly cut and firmly bound; collar points should be even, sharp, and neatly sewn. Double needle (two rows of stitching) is stronger than single needle.

Appearance and Comfort. In addition to size and good workmanship, the careful buyer is generally interested in the appearance of the shirt, its comfort, durability, launderability, and suitability. The customer looks for style, color, and cleanness (even the neatness of the cellophane wrapping). A shiny cotton surface created by mercerization is more attractive and easier to care for than a dull fuzzy surface. For comfort, a shirt should be cut full across the chest. Boys and stout men, especially, need full-cut shirts and correct size of collar. Length of sleeves and size of armholes also affect comfort.

Men are frequently exasperated because shirts do not stay tucked in after they have been washed; the shirt tail has shrunk. Shrinkage, already discussed in connection with size, is a major consideration if a garment is purchased for comfort.

Men's dress shirts are now durable press. The 100 percent cotton DP shirts have an advantage over blends in that white cotton shirts, being opaque, are whiter; they are also more comfortable, since they absorb perspiration more readily. However, cotton DP white shirts are subject to yellowing; they also have reduced wear qualities owing to the loss of tensile strength and abrasion resistance caused by the DP treatment.

One manufacturer objects to cotton DP shirts because they are too heavy for his specifications. On the other hand, the cotton/polyester DP shirt is subject to oil staining and odor absorption. The odor of perspiration may dissolve in the man-made fiber and be difficult to remove. Oil staining is a problem because polyester has an affinity for oil and does not release it readily. Soil release finishes have been discovered but have not proved as important in the clothing category as they have in home furnishings. Frequent laundering of the DP shirts with oil stains is necessary.

For young boys, a long shirt that will stay tucked into the pants is appropriate. School-age boys should wear shirts with tails or polo shirts sufficiently long to allow an active child to bend over easily. Convertible collars and open-neck styles with short sleeves are appropriate for a growing boy.

Boys' shirt sizes 6 to 20 are usually tailored like men's, with similar-style collars, tailored fronts, fullness at center back, and barrel-style cuffs. A few details in tailoring may be omitted from these shirts. Suitability of material and style of cut determine the use of a shirt.

Body shirts styled for the teen-age male are shaped for close, body hugging fit. The wide chest tapers down to suppressed sides and long shirttails, worn with jeans and often with a sleeveless pullover rib knitted sweater.

Work shirts, for utility wear, are made of sturdy fabrics, such as mercerized cotton/polyester and 35 percent cotton chambray, all-cotton chino, 65 percent polyester and 35 percent combed cotton gabardine, all-cotton denim, and all-cotton drill. The emphasis in selecting work shirts should be suitability rather than style. Nowadays the work shirt is not unattractive, because collar styles may be those of the dress shirt or convertible sport shirt with lined collar. The work shirt with the collar

FIGURE 18.5. Casual shirts for father and child. (Photo courtesy Men's Fashion Association of America.)

style of a dress shirt may be worn with a tie. For comfort, shirts usually have long tails that stay tucked in. Sleeves may be long or short, and sizes are based on the necksize.

Styles in Sport Shirts. Although sport shirts vary in style, a common feature is that they are made to be worn without a tie. They may or may not have a collar and may have either short or long sleeves. Since sport shirts are intended for active sports and for casual wear, a comfortable, easy-to-care-for fabric is suitable. In general, sport shirt fabrics are classified as knitted or woven. Knitted constructions include jersey and various types of fancy knits and meshes of cotton, polyester, acrylic, nylon, and blends. Woven fabrics may include cotton jean, flannel (wool or cotton and blends with man-made fibers), cord, chambray, gingham, broadcloth, corduroy, woven stretch and blends of polyester and cotton, cotton and rayon, polyester and rayon, and others. Sizes include small (14 to 14½-inch neck), medium (15 to 15½), large (16 to 16½), and extra large (17 to 17½).

Sweat shirts, with or without hoods, may be classified as a kind of sport shirt that is pulled on to protect the body from sudden chill. They may be

FIGURE 18.6. A geometric print sports shirt. (Photo courtesy Men's Fashion Association of America.)

pullover or jacket style, of fleece lined cotton knit or double or triple knit nylon. Cardigan and sweater shirt sets, sweat shirts and jackets, or sweat pants are worn for sports. The terry-cloth lined gingham jacket or double knit polyester beach jacket and trunks may constitute a set of jacket and shorts worn on the beach. Trunks of this set, which may match or contrast with the jacket, may be made of spandex, nylon stretch yarn, polyester double knit, and polyester/cotton poplin.

Durability of Shirts. The durability of a shirt is determined by the grade of fabric (judged according to the quality of the fibers, yarns, weaves, and finishing processes).

Workmanship also affects durability. Stitching aud buttons have been discussed under requirements for good workmanship. In addition, the following tips will help the consumer find satisfaction in purchasing shirts:

1. Stripes or patterns in sport shirts should match at seams.
2. A center pleat ensures a good anchorage for buttons.
3. A shirt with six or seven buttons stays tucked in better than one with five.
4. A band inside the collar is highly desirable.
5. Thread should match the predominant color of the shirt.
6. Wide seams and reinforcements increase the length of life of a shirt.
7. Everyday shirts and work shirts for men and boys should be made with a button fastening at the cuff to avoid the inconvenience of cuff links.
8. The lining materials should be shrunk to the same extent as the shirt fabric so that the collar will stay flat after laundering.

Ease in Laundering. Ease in laundering is also a factor in durability. Single-cuffed shirts are easier to iron than those with double cuffs, but the latter are usually more durable. For traveling, the polyester/cotton durable press or the knitted polyester shirts are popular among men. They can be washed at night, hung to drip dry, and worn without ironing the next morning. (See Chapters 7 and 16.) Since the collars and cuffs of shirts of polyester/cotton blends soil more quickly than the body of the shirt, a small nail brush can be used effectively to apply a liquid detergent to soiled areas. Sometimes a ring around the collar cannot be entirely removed by this method. One needs a soil-release technique with polyester/cotton blends with durable press finishes. As recommended in Chapter 16, soaking the shirt in an enzyme product for thirty minutes or overnight will break down or digest into small particles (by chemical means) the various kinds of organic matter—protein, starch, or the like.

Brands. Some men prefer to buy a shirt of a familiar nationally known brand. Although there may be a lesser-known brand that is more suited to their needs, some men refuse to switch from a brand to which they have become accustomed. Among the national brands are Arrow, Van Heusen, Manhattan, Marlboro, Truval, National, A.M.C., Towncraft (J.C. Penney), Hathaway, and Pilgrim (Sears).

Price. With the escalation of prices in the 1970s, price became an important factor in the purchase of a shirt. If the consumer knows that a dress shirt to his liking may cost $10 to $15, he expects comfort, dimensional stability, attractiveness (neat and style-right appearance), as well as ease of care and durability.

There are two main styles in men's ties: the formal and the informal. Formal ties include the bow ties, which may be tied by hand or ready-tied, long ties, and Ascots or scarf ties, the ends of which, being tied once, are crossed in front and fastened with a scarf pin. The bow tie is worn for formal occasions with dinner jackets and with full dress, and also with business attire. When fashion decrees, ascots are for formal or semiformal morning or afternoon wear with a cutaway or frock coat. Informal ties are usually the long type with pointed or straight ends.

In addition to the style and suitability of a tie, the durability of the material and the workmanship are important. The fibers, yarns, weave, and finishing processes affect the wearing quality.

As for workmanship, the two types of construction are resilient and rigid. The tie with resilient construction is sewn by machine with long, basting-like stitches that allow greater elasticity in tying than do the short, rather tight machine stitches of the rigid construction. The rigid type are inexpensive ties. To determine whether a tie has a resilient construction, grasp it with thumb and forefinger of each hand, pull it gently in opposite directions along the length of the tie, and note whether it gives. Other

FIGURE 18.7. Brown and white polka dot silk ascot to complement a linen-look shirt. (Photo courtesy Men's Fashion Association of America.)

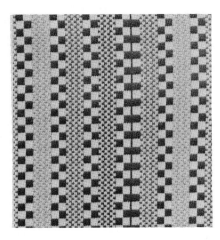

FIGURE 18.8. A fabric for a polyester tie. (Courtesy *America's Textiles Reporter/Bulletin, January 1972.)*

points to consider in workmanship are the stitching along the edge and the evenness of the hems.

A tie made of a fabric cut on the bias will hold its shape better than one cut on the straight of the material. If the outer fabric is cut on the bias, the lining should be cut on the bias too. Also, a tie that is lined with wool has greater elasticity and therefore holds its shape longer than one that is lined with cotton. A well-made tie has four or five folds at the broad end. A tie with facing at the ends has an improved appearance because no stitching shows.

Ties made from woven goods stay tied better than those made from knitted fabrics. There is less slippage of the knot. Knitted ties wear well and do not wrinkle.

Acetate, cotton, and weighted silk wrinkle badly, and the wrinkles do not hang out. Wool and pure silk are excellent as tie fabrics, because they are wrinkle-resistant and resilient. Polyester, which is both resilient and spot-resistant, makes a good woven or knitted tie fabric.

SWEATERS

Many customers are interested in style when they buy a sweater. The two classic styles for men as well as women are the pullover, which pulls over the head and generally has no buttons but may have a short zipper, and the cardigan, which fastens down the front, generally with buttons or a zipper. The pullover without sleeves is popular because it is more comfortable under jackets or coats. Necklines of the pullover may be V-shaped, round, boat, turtle, or crew. Sizes are 36 to 46. The cardigan may be made with or without shawl collar and two lower pockets.

Sweaters are made in smooth and in bulky, shaggy, hairy, nubbed, and linenlike textures. The smooth type is more comfortable under a jacket, whereas the others are particularly suited to sportswear.

Patterns in sweaters are created by variations in the knitted stitch and by color contrast in body, collars, and cuffs. The three classic stitches for sweaters are (1) jumbo, a coarse stitch with large, heavy yarn; (2) gauze, a close stitch with fine, thin yarn; and (3) shaker knit, a weight between jumbo and gauze. Other knitted stitches include interlock, links, cable, waffle, pineapple, fisherman's knit, and bulky rib. Sweaters are made of

FIGURE 18.9. A cardigan
sweater with polyester/cotton
slacks. (Photo courtesy Men's
Fashion Association of America.)

all wool or all-cashmere, acrylic, polyester nylon, and blends. (See women's sweaters, Chapter 17.)

UNDERWEAR

Garments sold in men's and boys' underwear departments include T-shirts, undershirts, drawers, shorts, briefs, and union suits (knitted one-piece garments with sleeves and legs in varied lengths). The most popular styles in underwear for men and boys are athletic or T-shirts and athletic shorts or briefs.

For boys, T-shirts or athletic shirts come in sizes 2 and 4 and in sizes small (6 to 8), medium (10 to 12), and large (14 to 16). Some size ranges run to 20. T-shirt and undershirt sizes for men are small (34 to 36), medium (38 to 40), large (42-44), and extra large (46-52).

Drawers come in mid-length and long-length. See Figure 18.10.

Men's underwear is the latest convert to style, color, and pattern. Until 1935, the drop-seat style predominated. Now styles range from an all-in-one stretch mesh union suit to a modified G-string known as "jock sock." Bikini styles have arrived. While they may seem uncomfortable and impractical for men who are overweight and over 25 years old, there is a trend away from loose fitting garments to those that hug the body closely and smoothly. For example, there are:

1. A-line undershirts and bikini outfits.
2. Brief and top combinations in colorful cotton blends.

Selection. While these styles may not appeal to the masculine consumer, he should buy for:[2]

1. *Comfort* by checking the length, width, size of neckband and armhole opening; seams smooth next to the skin.
2. *Cleanliness* in keeping outer clothes clean.
3. *Durability* by having taped or overcast seams to resist snagging.

Styles in men's woven shorts are (1) boxer, which has an all-around elastic waist and (2) yoke, which has a snap fastener and elastic inserts in the waist. Sizes, based on waist measurement, run in even numbers 28 to 44. These garments are commonly made of cotton or cotton and polyester blends in broadcloth or percale. Many fabrics are durable press.

Briefs are knitted articles of underwear of rib-knitted cotton or polyester and cotton flat knit. A nylonized finish on combed cotton adds strength and wear; a sanitized finish gives hygienic protection. The better qualities are made of cotton yarns like Durene, which is combed, two ply, mercerized for strength and luster, highly absorbent, and sanitized to check perspiration odor and to arrest growth of bacteria. A durable blend is 80 percent cotton and 20 percent nylon.

Support briefs may be made of 94 percent combed cotton and 6 percent spandex, with a belt of 64 percent acetate, 28 percent rayon, and

[2] "Moneysworth," vol. 4, no. 8, January 21, 1974.

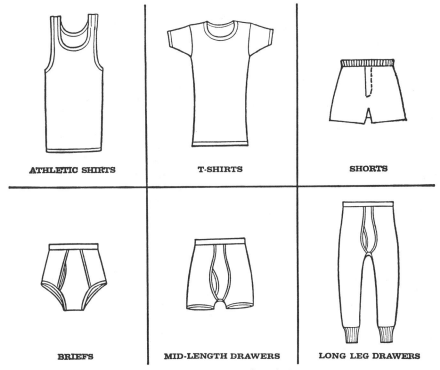

FIGURE 18.10. Major styles in men's underwear.

FIGURE 18.11. Nylon briefs with an athletic shirt with trim to match briefs. (Photo courtesy Men's Fashion Association of America.)

8 percent spandex. A reinforced double crotch and front-panel reinforced seams, nonbinding bound elasticized leg openings, and elastic waistband are considerations in comfort and wear. Sizes in briefs are also by waist measurement.

Probably the most comfortable underwear is made of a knitted fabric, because it gives with movements of the body, ventilates the skin, keeps the body warm in winter and cool in summer, is easily washed, and needs no ironing. It is especially suitable for athletics. Some men prefer a short cap sleeve in knitted undershirts to protect the outer shirt from perspiration. Since cotton absorbs perspiration better than silk, rayon, or nylon, many men prefer cotton for underwear in all climates. Both woolen and worsted yarns can be used in knit underwear. The woolen yarn is soft and pliable and makes a good napped or fleecy surface. Worsted yarn is smooth and lustrous and makes a fine, even, smooth-knitted structure. Wool knitted underwear is very warm.

Nylon yarns, which are often used in combination with another textile, may be used alone in lightweight underwear. These yarns, incidentally, are most attractive in white and pastel shades. One hundred percent nylon knitted underwear, although it is very strong and quick drying, does not absorb perspiration. Nylon or polyester thread can be used for sewing seams of underwear because of its strength. A knitted fabric made of a mixture of cotton (75 percent) and Merino wool (25 percent) is comfortable. Since the wool, buried between two layers of cotton,[3] does not touch the skin, the underwear does not cause itching.

[3] This fabric is Innerwool by the William Carter Company.

In winter, quilted or thermal Raschel knits are often worn for sports. The quilted type may consist of jacket and drawers made with a cotton shell, modacrylic batting, and cotton interlining. This set is made flame-retardant. The Raschel knits are 100 percent cotton, or 75 percent cotton/25 percent Acrilan acrylic. Heavy stretch thermal knits may be 94 percent cotton/6 percent spandex.

Launderability is an important factor in underwear. Both wash-and-wear cotton and the noncellulosic man-made fibers are easy to care for and require little or no pressing. The trademark Sanfor Knit assures the consumer lasting comfort and fit. The man-made fibers have the added advantage of drying quickly, but some men say that their fibers feel clammy because they do not have the absorptive quality of cotton.

HOSIERY

Men want socks to fit well and to wear well. A comfortable sock is soft, fits smoothly over the instep, ankle, and heel, does not pinch the toes, does not slip or roll down, and is smooth on the sole of the foot. There are three main styles in men's socks: (1) dress for street wear, (2) casual socks for sport, and (3) work socks. Each style comes in lengths from over the calf (executive length) and mid calf to just above the ankle. The sock for street wear, which is more conservative than the sports type, usually comes in solid colors in stockinette or rib knit. Clocks and small patterns often enhance it. Sport or casual socks are intended to be worn with a sport jacket and slacks or sweater and slacks. They can be made cushion soft by using 70 percent acrylic bulky textured yarn, 20 percent cotton, and 10 percent nylon. A kind of casual sock in white with colored stripe top, called a "crew sock," may be made of bulky textured acrylic 69 percent, stretch nylon 29 percent, and nylon reinforcement 2 percent in toe and heel. A second type of casual sock is the argyle with the familiar Jacquard plaid pattern. A third type is novelty, with varied designs and colors, and a fourth type is thermal for winter, made of stretch nylon outside (lined with 50 percent olefin/50 percent cotton), or 80 percent worsted wool/20 percent stretch nylon.

For comfort and wear, a sanitized finish inhibits germ growth, which helps feet to stay fresh longer.

Ingrain-dyed (yarn-dyed) color is a selling point. Bulky acrylic blends that feel woolly and are shrink-resistant are suitable for sportswear. Also, a 50 percent lamb's wool and 50 percent nylon blend and an 80 percent wool and 20 percent stretch nylon are appropriate. (See *stretch yarn*, Chapter 3.)

Tops of socks are frequently made of spandex yarn in rib knit. Since these yarns keep the sock from slipping, the wearer need not use garters. When labeled antistatic it means the socks have been finished to keep them from clinging to the trouser legs and from collecting lint. An acrylic/stretch nylon blend insures a good fit. A 100 percent stretch nylon or textured nylon/spandex blend with an elastic top is called "support hosiery."

Work socks are intended to be long wearing—suitable for workmen, school boys and the home owner who "does it himself." A sock made of 95 percent cotton/5 percent spandex with nylon reinforcements is durable and suitable for hard wear. Also the all-cotton sock with reinforced heel and toe are popular. For absorbency and softness, the sole of the sock may be made of terry cloth. For cold weather, wool may be blended with nylon. For extra support some work socks have a support section in the calf area. The tube sock with no heel in cotton/stretch nylon with elasticized top is said to be comfortable no matter which way they are put on.

Men's hosiery sizes run from 9 to 13. Three stretch sizes will cover the entire size range. Boys' sizes commonly come in three sizes: medium to fit little boys' shoe size 9-2; large to fit boys' sizes 1½-8½; and extra large to fit men's sizes 9-12.

SLEEPWEAR

Just as men seek comfort in underwear, they also want comfort in sleeping garments. If a garment feels smooth and soft, if it is easy to put on and take off, and if it has a full cut and smooth seams, it will generally prove comfortable.

Probably the next most important consideration in sleepwear is durability, which includes launderability. Shrinkage of less than 5 percent is considered satisfactory. Durable press is a valued selling point. For some men the appearance of the garment is more important than comfort or durability. In such cases, decoration, trimming, or quality of workmanship are noticed.

Pajamas generally include a coat-style, or pullover top with or without collar, and pants. Small children often wear the same styles as grown-ups, or they may wear one piece, sometimes with feet attached. The separate coat is buttoned down the front, whereas the pullover needs no front closing. The pants are fastened at the waist with an elastic band or drawstring. For summer, short-length pajama pants and short sleeves are comfortable. For winter, two-piece pajamas made in ski-suit style (with elastic waist and fitted wristlets and anklets) are warm. Other styles may include the cossack, with stand-up collar; the tunic, with shaping at the waist and a slight flare at the bottom; and the long knitted or woven nightshirt.

Pajamas are made of the following materials:

Balbriggan (See Glossary, Chapter 15)	Knitted jersey
Broadcloth	Tricot knit
Chambray	Percale
Cotton crepe (for young boys)	Pongee
Flannelette	

The sizes in men's pajamas are indicated by the letters *A, B, C, D.* These sizes are limited because pajamas do not have to be so form-fitting as underwear. Size *A* generally fits a 34 or smaller; *B,* a 34 to 36; *C,* a 38 to 40; and *D,* a 42 to 44. Size *E* is an oversize. In sizes *B, C,* and *D* extra lengths can be procured. Boys' and students' sizes run 8-20.

In more recent years pajamas have become popular for lounging. The lounging type, generally made of luxurious materials such as silk, rayon, or the man-made fibers, has more ornamentation than the sleeping pajamas. Such fabrics as satins, corduroy, Jacquard, nylon or silk tricot, and crepe are also used.

FIGURE 18.12. Polyester and cotton searsucker robe with chambray rayon pajamas with white piping. (Photo courtesy Men's Fashion Association of America.)

LOUNGING ROBES, JACKETS, AND BATHROBES

If a man is interested primarily in appearance as opposed to comfort, he will generally purchase a lounging robe rather than a bathrobe. Both garments serve almost the same purpose. In a lounging robe a man expects a good-looking fabric, the latest style of cut, rich coloring, and excellent workmanship. Lounging robes are usually made of plush velour, brocade, or flannel, trimmed with the same fabric in a contrasting color, a cord, braid, or satin. Jackets, shorter than robes, are made of the same fabrics as lounging robes. Most bathrobes are made of terry, flannelette (especially for boys), and corduroy. The sizes in robes run small, medium, large, and extra large.

ACCESSORIES

Handkerchiefs. Handkerchiefs for men may be classified as monogram, plain white, and fancy (colored handkerchiefs with patterns). High-quality handkerchiefs that are made of pure linen (Belgian or Irish) and have fine line yarns are called *linen lawn* or *handkerchief linen*. The count of cloth is high and well balanced (sometimes as high as 1200). The hems are usually hand-rolled (hand-stitched). A handkerchief may be labeled "pure Irish linen," yet may not be the best quality from the standpoint of yarn, weave, and workmanship. (It may be hemstitched instead of hand-rolled.) Linen (55 percent) and cotton (45 percent) in a blend, or 65 percent polyester/35 percent cotton, are commonly used for handkerchiefs. If fibers, yarns, construction, and workmanship are good, the article may be higher quality than a poor grade of all linen. The United States imports cotton handkerchiefs from Switzerland that are long-stapled Egyptian cotton, combed yarn, closely woven, and mercerized with hand-rolled edges. They can be sold at the same retail price as pure Irish linen that is not of the best grade. Some handkerchiefs are made of combed domestic cotton yarn that is sent to the Philippines to be woven, finished, cut, and sewn, and then shipped back to this country. Such merchandise constitutes the low end of the price scale for serviceable goods. Pure Italian silk handkerchiefs are sold for decorative use only. They are more expensive than a good grade of pure linen.

Sizes of handkerchiefs vary from 17-inch squares to 19-inch squares. Bandanas (vivid printed cottons) are generally 18-inch squares, or 24 by 22 inches.

Belts. Although most belts are made of leather or a nontextile plastic, some are made of a heavy cotton called *belting*, which is made with very heavy fillingwise ribs or cords. Belting may also have silk or nylon running one way to cover the cords. Fancy belts are made of cord in knitted or crocheted effects. Some belts are made of the same material as the slacks.

Belts differ in the kind of material used and also in length, width, shape (some are curved at the side), color, and design (of buckle as well as material).

Neckwear and Gloves. The scarf, thrown around the neck and crossed at the front, is worn under the coat. Scarfs may be long and narrow or square. For formal wear, luxurious fabrics of silk, acetate, nylon, and polyester are used. Wool flannel, knitted wool, cashmere, and blends are warm for winter wear. Lighterweight scarfs are made of surah, twills, and crepe in silk or man-made fibers.

When buying a scarf, a man thinks of warmth and weight, color and design, grade of material, workmanship (including hemming, fringe, and embroidery), size, and use.

Cotton and wool knitted gloves are suitable for sportswear when warmth is important. They come in varied colors, in sizes small, medium and large. While leather is more popular than fabric for gloves, sometimes fabric (acrylic/nylon) is combined with leather in gloves used for driving. A wool knit may line a leather glove. Work gloves are comfortable and economical when made of cotton flannel, cotton canvas, fleece-lined cotton, and nylon jersey. Mittens, sized like gloves, are in much less demand in men's wear but are particularly suited for small children.

Hats. For men who wear hats, fur felt made with wool is the traditionally accepted material for everyday wear. (See *felting*, Chapter 6.) Fur felt is made of Australian rabbit, nutria, and beaver blends. Widths of the brim and bands, the height and width of the hat, and the tapering of the crown vary according to style.

Straw is traditionally worn during the summer months. While for formal wear a man may wear a Homburg, bowler, or derby, a top hat is seldom worn except for very formal state occasions. For casual country wear, there has been considerable use of fabric hats of tweed, velour, corduroy, or blend or 90 percent wool/10 percent nylon knit. The visored cap of tweed, corduroy, flannel, or twilled cotton is adapted to sightseeing and to sportswear.

Very small boys wear brimmed fabric hats of wool or cotton with or without earlaps. For play in mild weather boys may wear cotton caps with or without visors, and for dress-up they may wear a flannel Eton style. Older boys often go hatless except in cold weather, when they may pull the hood of a parka or jacket over the head or may don a bulky knitted cap.

Men's hat and cap sizes run $6\frac{3}{4}$, $6\frac{7}{8}$, 7, $7\frac{1}{8}$, $7\frac{1}{4}$, $7\frac{3}{8}$, $7\frac{1}{2}$, $7\frac{5}{8}$, $7\frac{3}{4}$. To determine a boy's hat size, one should measure straight around the head above the ears, see Table 18-3.

TABLE 18-3. Boys' Hat Sizes

If Head Measures	Boy Wears Size
$19\frac{1}{8}$ "	$6\frac{1}{8}$ "
$19\frac{1}{2}$ "	$6\frac{1}{4}$
$19\frac{7}{8}$ "	$6\frac{3}{8}$
$20\frac{1}{4}$ "	$6\frac{1}{2}$
$20\frac{3}{4}$ "	$6\frac{5}{8}$
$21\frac{1}{8}$ "	$6\frac{3}{4}$
$21\frac{1}{2}$ "	$6\frac{7}{8}$
$21\frac{7}{8}$ "	7
$22\frac{1}{4}$ "	$7\frac{1}{8}$
$22\frac{5}{8}$ "	$7\frac{1}{4}$

SELECTION OF MEN'S AND BOYS' OUTERWEAR

SUITS

Although men may buy their suits, women often have much to say when a selection is made, and women do most of the buying of boys' clothing. Yet the average woman does not know a tweed from a gabardine, a woolen from a worsted.

Suit Styling. In general, today's suit can be defined as a garment composed of two matching pieces—a jacket and tailored trousers for everyday business wear or jeans with matching short jacket for casual or leisure wear. Sometimes a suit includes three pieces—a vest (often of another color and fabric) or an extra pair of pants.

One who is fashion conscious will notice that designers may change from time to time either/or both the style of the jacket and/or the trousers. The style of the jacket may be changed by:

1. Shortening or lengthening.
2. Varying the widths of the collar and lapels—notched, peaked, or L-shaped.
3. Shortening or lengthening the sleeves (two or more buttons on cuff).
4. Using natural or padded shoulders.
5. Changing the waistline (loose or fitted).

6. Making the jacket with straight or flared lines.
7. Making the front a straight line or rounded closing.
8. Using single- (2 or 3 buttons) or double-breasted closing (4 to 6 buttons).
9. Slanting the two front pockets or making them straight—with or without flaps—breast pockets (0, 1 or 2) 1 or 2 inside breast pockets.
10. Using one center back vent or two side back vents.

The designer may change the style of the trousers by:

1. Making them with or without cuffs.
2. Fitting the legs and buttocks tightly or loosely.
3. Making a high or low rise (the measurement extending from the crotch to the waist or above—low or high rise respectively).
4. Varying the size, depth, and number of pockets.[4]

Table 18-4 gives the specifications of the three recognized suit styles.

TABLE 18-4. Types of Men's Suits

	American	International (Continental)	Natural (Shoulder)
Shoulder	Lightly padded	More heavily padded	Unpadded and unconstructed
Waistline	Follows body line	Tapered	Straight
Vents	Center or side	Deep side, resulting in flared effect	Center
Closures	Two or three	One, two, or three	Three
Trousers	Cuffed, straight leg	Cuffless, tapered leg	Cuffed, straight leg

A knowledgeable clothing salesman will direct his customer's attention to changes in style. He will also emphasize color, price, and weight since these three factors are usually the main considerations in selecting suits and jackets.

Fibers and Fabrics in Suits. Two weights of suits are usually carried by retail stores located in the same latitude as the Middle Atlantic States—a lightweight for spring and summer and a regular weight for fall and winter. The summer weight is generally 4 to 5 ounces and is minimum care, made of polyester and blends with cotton or other man-made fibers. The heavier weight is about 7 ounces and may be all-wool or blends of wool and polyester.

Both natural and man-made fibers are used for suits and jackets. Cotton and wool are the most frequently used natural fibers. Cotton is both comfortable and absorbent, while wool is warm and long-wearing.

As mentioned previously, there are two main types of all-wool yarns and wool fabrics—woolens and worsteds. (See Chapter 12.) Generally speaking, woolens are made of fibers of varied lengths averaging less than two inches. The yarns are carded and are rather rough, and the finishing is customarily done by fulling and then brushing up a nap (it may be

[4] May have two side pockets—one may have a button closing. Possible change pocket at right front waistline.

FIGURE 18.13. A spring and summer dress suit of polyester with diagonal stripes. (Photo courtesy of Men's Fashion Association of America.)

FIGURE 18.14. A fall and winter three-piece woolen dress suit, continental style. (Photo courtesy Men's Fashion Association of America.)

sheared). Worsteds are usually made of fibers more than two inches long (all the short fibers have been removed). The yarns are carded and combed, and are even and smooth; the finishing consists of mending, scouring, shearing, and pressing. (See Figures 12.5 and 12.6.) Only unfinished and semifinished worsteds are fulled and slightly napped.

The man-made fibers used alone or in blends for man's suitings, both woven or knitted, are polyester, acrylic, nylon, and triacetate. When polyester is used alone or blended with cotton, wool, or other man-made fibers, it has wrinkle resistance, strength, crease retention, and durability, and requires minimum care. The blending of polyester staple with wool or acrylic makes fabrics with a worsted appearance. When blended with cotton or rayon, a cotton look and hand is produced. Acrylic fibers produce light weight, brilliant colors, bulk, and softness. Triacetate used alone or in blends is found in knitted jackets, blazers, and shirts that are cool and comfortable.[5] Fabrics made of man-made fibers are generally washable. However, one should always consult the care label.

Suiting fabrics appropriate for the four seasons appear in Table 18-5:[6]

TABLE 18-5. Fabrics for Men's Clothing

Spring and Summer	Fall and Winter
1. Cords	Cheviot
2. Gabardine (cotton or blend)	Double knits
3. Knits	Flannel
4. Linen and silklike textures	Gabardine
5. Poplin	Serge
6. Seersucker	Sharkskin
7. Sharkskin	Shetland
8. Tropicals	Tweed

Sizes and Fit of Suits and Jackets. Criteria for determining size are chest, waist, and height measurements. The following chart is taken from the mail-order catalogue of Sears, Roebuck and Company. Measurements needed to order a man's suit are given.

For boys' and girls' clothing, the U.S. Agricultural Research Service has done some research on sizes. From this study the United States of America Standards Institute has formulated standard sizes of clothing for boys from kindergarten to junior high school. To arrive at these standard sizes the committee of the Institute chose height and hip measurements. The committee felt that (1) hips are better than the chest as an indicator of the other girth measurements, (2) the hips can be more accurately measured than the chest, and (3) a tape measure is the only equipment needed to make these two measurements.

Table 18-6 gives seven standard body sizes as set up by the U.S.A. Standards.

TABLE 18-6. Standard Body Sizes

Height (inches)	Girth (Hips) (inches)	Average Age (years)
43	22½	5½
45½	23	6½
47½	24	7½
50	25	8½
52	26	9½
54½	27½	10½
57	28½	12

These standard sizes should make shopping easier for parents and should lessen the number of return goods. Manufacturers should find them advantages in making better-fitting children's garments. Mail-order catalogues give measurements of height in inches, and average, slim, and husky chest and waist measurements to facilitate ordering the proper size to fit. (See *infants', toddlers', and tots' sizes,* Chapter 17.)

[5] "Today's Fashions in Men's Wear," a pamphlet by Celanese Fibers Marketing Co., Consumer and Retail Information Dept.

[6] See Glossary for definitions of fabrics.

Proper fit of a suit or jacket is a must for the wearer. To ensure proper fit a consumer should notice whether the shoulder is wide enough to allow for comfortable movement. The collar should be flat against the neck and lapels should lie smoothly against the chest. Jacket should cover the seat; sleeves should end near the bend of the wrist so that part of the shirt cuff shows.

There are three basic cuts to high fashion styling as seen in the table below.[7] High fashion styling may add half belts, safari or shirt details, knickers or "jean" trousers.

FORMAL EVENING WEAR

The traditional tuxedo, appropriate when the occasion calls for "black tie," has a black jacket with satin or faille lapels, black cuffless trousers with satin or faille stripes along the outer seams, and a cummerbund. The current tuxedo is made of colorful and fancier fabric, such as brocade and satin. Trousers need not match the jacket material. The evening shirt styles have already been discussed.

[7] Ibid.

FIGURE 18.15. Spring and summer formal wear. (Photo courtesy Men's Fashion Association of America.)

FIGURE 18.16. Fall and winter formal wear. (Photo courtesy Men's Fashion Association of America.)

For very formal evening wear, a jacket with tails, and a white, rather than black, tie are required.

CASUAL WEAR

Garments designed for informal use are known as "casuals." A kind of casual is the so-called coordinate or separate that consists of two or more items of apparel with the same or contrasting fabrics, colors, patterns, and trimmings which are grouped together for joint sale. For instance, jackets and pants, shirts and jeans, shirts and pullovers may be coordinated. A heather blue jacket may be coordinated with a blue and white striped shirt, a solid blue tie, and grey trousers. The store may coordinate these pieces of apparel for ease in customer selection or leave it to the customer to do his own coordinating in the store.

Coordinates first appeared in casual sportswear. Today the blazer or sport jacket and slacks are a perennial outfit for casual and business wear. The popularity of this attire has cut down on the number of suits in a man's wardrobe. Likewise, the jean suit has become an outfit for casual warm weather wear. The leisure suit is so called because the male customer creates his own relaxed suit, which is a separate or coordinate. The suit may consist of a safari jacket with epaulets, patch pockets, button cuffs, and belted. The jacket may be made in twill of polyester and

FIGURE 18.17. A casual suit of donegal tweed. (Photo courtesy Men's Fashion Association of America.)

FIGURE 18.18. Casual wear: polyester double knit plaid blouse jacket with coordinated check slacks and an acrylic donegal tweed turtleneck sweater. (Photo courtesy Men's Fashion Association of America.)

cotton. The trousers may be flare bottom jeans of polyester and rayon in navy blue or tan. Table 18-7 is a chart for jean size:

TABLE 18-7.   Jean Sizes

				Waist				
Inseam	32	33	34	36	38	40	41	44
29		X	X	X	X	X	X	
30	X	X	X	X	X	X	X	X
31	X	X	X	X	X	X	X	
32	X	X	X	X	X	X	X	X
34	X	X	X	X	X			

A word of caution in selecting the correct size for double-knit and permanent press garments: Be sure the garment is comfortable. If it is not, select a larger size because when man-made fibers are heat-set for DP, a crease mark will remain when seams are let out.

Fabrics for casual slacks can be woven or knitted. Woven types include blends of polyester and cotton, nylon and cotton, or 100 percent cotton. For winter, the fabric may be a blend in which there is some wool. Double knits of textured polyester are used for both tailored and casual slacks, including jeans. Tailored slacks are intended for dress and casual for sports and leisure wear.

Men like polyester and wool worsted blends because these blends have inherent wrinkle-resistant properties, durability, and hold their shape well. When acrylic fibers are blended with wool, the acrylic gives strength, crease and shrink resistance, minimum-care properties, and dimensional stability. Nylon when blended with wool for boys' pants gives increased strength and abrasion resistance.

Boys also wear slacks and sports jackets. Madras, seersucker, and cords are appropriate for summer, whereas flannel and tweed are typical winter materials. The toddler wears overalls of corduroy, cord, denim, or seersucker. For rough play the older boy wears jeans like his father's.

Fit of Slacks.   No matter whether slacks are tailored, casual, hip-fitting, fitted at the waist, cuffed, or uncuffed, they will fit properly and be comfortable if there is:[8]

1. Accurate sizing at the waist.
2. Proper length of inseam and outseam.
3. No puckering in the cuff.
4. Correct length (touch top of shoes for straight pants and top of heel for flared pants), proper fit by hanging straight from the hips.
5. Correct depth of crotch for comfort.
6. Room for uninhibited movement and for sitting comfortably.

ACTIVE SPORTSWEAR

The word "active" as used here means that the man is to be a participant in a sports event. However, there are so many active sports in which men

[8]"Today's Fashions in Men's Wear."

FIGURE 18.19. Nylon swim suit with matching T-shirt. (Photo courtesy Men's Fashion Association of America.)

and boys participate that a discussion of each one and the attire appropriate for it would be impossible. Accordingly, only the attire for the following sports will be considered—swimming, golf, and skiing.

Swimming. Swim trunks are shorts in varied lengths. Men's and boys' styles are similar.[9] They may be boxer style with belt, zip front with tab closing, and have a drawstring or stretch waist. A loose style is most comfortable. Many styles have an inside lining and tricot knit supporter. A fully lined trunk wears longer and keeps its shape after swimming. Fabrics for men and boys are similar: polyester 65 percent/35 percent stretch knit nylon, and 100 percent polyester double knit. These modern fabrics are considered machine washable in warm water and tumble dried.

The swimwear garment should not cramp the swimmer's movement, yet should give support; it should dry quickly and have colors that are fast to light, to salt water, and to chlorine in pools. Sizes of trunks are based on waist measurements. Consult the care label for washing instructions.

Golf. Slacks in woven or knitted stretch, and sport shirt and/or sweater are comfortable for this sport. A snap or zip front flannel lined or unlined nylon taffeta jacket is worn in colder rainy weather. A solid color polyester blazer with plaid or checked pants is also appropriate. Shorts may be worn instead of slacks during the summer.

Skiing. This winter sport has become so popular that proper equipment and attire are essential. On the slopes, a water-repellent jacket with a bonded polyester lining or a quilted taffeta with polyester fiber filling is both lightweight and warm. Hoods may snap on or be concealed in the collar of the jacket. Separate knitted caps or ski masks may substitute for the hoods. The same fabric used in the jacket may also be used in the pants. Some skiers prefer a double-knit fabric backed with polyurethane foam. A lining of tricot gives resistance to wind and weather. Some pants have an inside storm cuff of nylon, and elastic fits over the boot to keep out snow and cold. Good fit is ensured if the waistband is elasticized. "Warm-up" ski pants are very popular as they have zippers on the sides

[9] The surfing trunk has already been mentioned.

FIGURE 18.20. A golf outfit: Polyester mesh knit shirt with alpaca cardigan linen-look slacks. (Photo courtesy Men's Fashion Association of America.)

that can be opened at the top or bottom. This feature makes them easy to put on or take off.

WORK CLOTHES

For hard work, men prefer overalls or jeans (sometimes with pockets to match). Since the prime requisites of these garments are durability and comfort, fabrics such as cotton/polyester twill and cotton/polyester denim (usually navy blue warps and white fillings) are used. Denim overalls with bibs are specially designed for painters, carpenters, iron workers, and welders.

For less arduous work, a work shirt of luster twill described previously may be matched to heavy pants of the same material. Stretch fabrics of 65 percent polyester/35 percent cotton are used for both the work shirt and the pants. A one-piece, long-sleeved work suit is both comfortable and absorbent when made of all cotton or cotton/polyester. This garment may be worn over shirt and pants.

Overalls and jeans are measured by the size of the waist and inseam. For the one-piece garment, often called a coverall, the chest measurement should be added to that of the waist and inseam. The waist is measured over the pants without a belt; the inseam is the measurement from the crotch to the desired length.

FIGURE 18.21. A sports outfit
for bicycling. (Photo courtesy
Men's Fashion Association of
America.)

SCHOOL CLOTHES

For the schoolboy who gives his clothes very hard wear and the young man who works his way through college, sturdy tweeds, sharkskin, or worsteds (cheviot, covert, or serge in all wool or blends with polyesters and acrylics) are appropriate, for they give him his money's worth in service and comfort. Poplins, cotton twills, corduroys, and denims are also durable fabrics.[10]

OUTER COATS AND JACKETS

For outerwear, men and boys wear coats or jackets in various styles.

Topcoats. A topcoat, which is generally worn in fall and spring, and in warm climates all winter, differs from the overcoat in the weight of the fabric used. The topcoat of 13 to 20 ounces per square yard has virtually replaced the heavier 23-ounce cloth. With a zip-out lining of 70 percent acrylic/30 percent modacrylic, or 50 percent polyester/35 percent rayon, this coat can be worn as an all-weather coat for at least three seasons of the year in a moderate climate. The coat proper may be made of water-repellent poplin, gabardine, 100 percent polyester with acrylic-coated inner surface, 50 percent polyester/50 percent cotton, or 80 percent polyester/20 percent combed cotton. Actually, the all-weather coat with an acrylic zip-out lining has virtually replaced the topcoat. Little boys and youths also wear the all-weather coat. It may be in the Balmacaan style with raglan sleeves or the double-breasted trench style with belt.

[10] See Glossary.

FIGURE 18.22. A boy's cotton/polyester corduroy jacket and overalls. (Photo courtesy Men's Fashion Association of America.)

FIGURE 18.23. A casual wool overcoat with raccoon collar. (Photo courtesy Men's Fashion Association of America.)

Overcoats. An overcoat is usually identified with cold-weather wear. Cashmere (100 percent) or cashmere and wool, camel and wool, fleece, heavy tweeds, reversible double cloth, worsted covert, and melton are found in men's overcoats. Furlike fabrics may be used for the outside or as collars and for linings. The length of a topcoat or overcoat depends on the weather conditions in which it will be worn and how it becomes the wearer.

Overcoats vary little in styling, color, and fabric from season to season. The sport coat such as the duffle coat is made of rainwear and overcoat fabrics, and in many cases replaces the overcoat in male attire.

Rainwear. Probably the all-weather coat should be considered the most popular garment for men's rainwear, with water- and stain-repellent finishes. Since these finishes differ in efficiency, one should read the label carefully for specific data on performance. The familiar finishes like Scotchgard and Zepel are chemical finishes given the fabric before the garment is constructed. Such treatments retain their repellency through several washings or dry cleanings. Liquids that are water or oil based can often be blotted off the fabric. They leave no mark. Water or cleaning solvent will often remove a stubborn stain without leaving a ring. One should realize that fabrics so finished are water-repellent and not waterproof. The former type has the pores of the weave open so the skin can "breathe." The latter type has closed pores and is, therefore, hot.

Boys and students wear vinyl parkas for rainwear. They may have adjustable drawstring hoods. Since these raincoats are waterproof, air holes under the arms provide ventilation. A waterproof suit with hood can

FIGURE 18.24. A rain suit. (Photo courtesy Men's Fashion Association of America.)

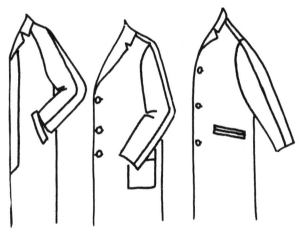

Raglan Sleeve   Set-in Sleeve   Split-raglan Sleeve

FIGURE 18.25. Sleeve types in rainwear and outerwear. (Courtesy Celanese Fibers Marketing Co.)

be worn for work or sport. It may be nylon with polyurethane coating that makes it lightweight and stronger than rubber or neoprene-coated rainwear. It resists both oils and chemicals, and won't stiffen in cold weather. Its seams are electro-thermo welded.

Knitted fabrics of 100 percent textured polyester are comfortable, wrinkle-resistant, and durable for rainwear.

Casual Coats. These are leisure types of coats suitable for all occasions. They are more casual than a sport coat, dressier than a jacket. This type of coat may be worn with a turtleneck or sport shirt and tie for summer. A cotton and acetate seersucker or a textured polyester is appropriate.

For cool weather, the rugged "bush coat" in western style resembling an old rancher's jacket may be worn. It may be made of stitch-trimmed cotton sateen in waist or hip length. It usually has flap patch pockets with buttons, and a snap front with shirred elastic waist in back. Another ranch style may be made of sweded split leather (nontextile) with leather buttons and an acrylic pile body lining; sleeves lined with acetate over fiber batting; collar of acrylic pile on a cotton back. A variation of the ranch style coat is the split cowhide shirt jacket with nylon body and sleeve lining. Trimming may consist of white stitching around the collar, a front snap closing, cuffs, and patch pockets.

Outer Jackets. Most of these jackets consist of a nylon shell (outer fabric) that may be coated for water repellency and lined with a deep acrylic pile. Polyester/cotton in chambray with a denim look on one side is reversible. A nylon quilted to a polyester fiber-filled inner lining is on the other side.

Sizes are:

Regular	5'7" to 5'11"
Tall	5'11" to 6'3"
Extra tall	6'3" to 6'7"

A waist-length, pile-lined, or unlined jacket of denim with or without a pile-lined vest can top jeans in a western style outfit.

Windbreakers, battle, or bomber jackets are usually made from rainwear or skiwear fabrics.

Fitting Overcoats and Outer Jackets. Rainwear and outerwear are easier to fit properly than are suits and jackets. A good rule is to have adequate room in the shoulders when worn over other garments. When the buttons are closed, there should be no strain on the fabric. Sleeves should cover the jacket sleeves.

Linings. Linings for suits, overcoats, all-weather coats, and jackets must be durable, attractive, and easy to slip on. Fabrics in satin weave with short floats or twill constructions in rayon, acetate, silk, nylon, or polyester offer attractive appearance and slip on easily. An acetate warp and rayon filling is a relatively inexpensive lining. Due to abrasion, this fabric often wears out before the suiting proper. Satins, sateens (cotton), brocades, and twills are common lining materials. For rainwear, a water-repellent shell with polyester lining is serviceable. All-weather and ranch style coats often have zip-out acrylic pile linings. Suit pockets are usually lined with a closely woven cotton twill (not heavily sized in good grades). All cotton linings should be preshrunk and colorfast.

Interfacings for suits and coats are, for the most part, shrinkage controlled, and some are machine washable. Better suits have coat fronts

FIGURE 18.26. A reversible outer jacket of wool plaid and nylon poplin. (Photo courtesy Men's Fashion Association of America.)

lined with a good quality of hair canvas. The shoulders are lined with a fine haircloth covered with flannel or thin felt. Interlinings for collars are made of firm linen. Armholes are taped with thin, strong, preshrunk tape. Fine, soft, flexible padding that does not feel bulky composes the shoulder padding.[11]

Canvas interfacing for sportswear is sheer and may be made of 60 percent cotton, 40 percent spun rayon. A nonwoven fabric can be obtained in several weights for this purpose.[12] There are also iron-on interfacings that are both woven[13] and nonwoven.[14]

Since interlinings are intended to give warmth to the garment, an all-wool woven fabric is highly desirable.

WHAT TO WEAR WITH WHAT

To assist men in the selection of colors for business wear, the American Institute of Men's and Boys' Wear has formulated the following dress-up selector:

TABLE 18-8. Color Selector. This dress-up selector offers two alternative color schemes. If you elect to use color scheme #1, follow #1 all the way down from top to bottom and the same applies to color scheme #2.

Suit	Grey	Blue	Brown
Shirt Solid or Stripe	1. Blue 2. Off White/Yellow	1. Blue 2. Off White	1. Tan 2. Off White
Tie	1. Red/Navy . Black/Gold	1. Red/Gold 2. Blue/Yellow	1. Brown/Red 2. Brown/Yellow
Socks	1. Navy or Gray 2. Black	1. 2. } Navy	1. 2. } Brown
Shoes	1. Cordovan 2. Black	1. Black 2. Cordovan	1. Brown or 2. Cordovan
Pocket Square or Scarf	1. Blue 2. Black/Gold	1. Red/Gold 2. Yellow	1. Red 2. Yellow
Hat	1. Medium Gray 2. Black	1. Gray 2. Brown	1. Brown 2. Green
Outercoat	1. Gray or Black 2. Black or Covert	2. Gray 2. Tan	1. Brown, Tan or 2. Charcoal
Gloves	1. Gray Suede or 2. Black Capeskin	1. Gray Fabric or 2. Brown Cape or Mocha	1. Brown Cape 2. Natural Pigskin
Jewelry	1. Silver Finish 2. Gold Finish	1. Silver Finish 2. Gold Finish	1. 2. } Gold Finish
Belt	1. Cordovan 2. Black	1. Black 2. Cordovan	1. Brown or 2. Cordovan

Courtesy of American Institute of Men's and Boys' Wear, Inc.

[11] "A Man's Guide to Good Clothes," a pamphlet by British Woolens. (Printed in the United States.)
[12] An example is Pellon by Pellon Corporation.
[13] An example is Staflex by Staflex Corporation.
[14] An example is Pellomite by Pellon Corporation.

SUMMARY The increasing use of blends in men's and boys' wear has changed the fabric picture in this area. When wool was plentiful at a moderate price, suits, jackets, slacks, and overcoats were made of all wool. As a general rule, one finds summer clothing made of the man-made fibers, often blended with cotton. For winter, nylon, acrylic, and modacrylic furlike fabrics are to be found almost exclusively in sportswear. An acrylic sweater is the rule rather than the exception. Even in winter suits, sports jackets, and slacks, one finds polyester, acrylic, nylon, and triacetate often blended with wool.

Since knitted fabrics are comfortable because of their stretch, wrinkle resistance, and ease of care, the knitted construction has become popular, often replacing the traditional woven fabrics for men's suits, coats, jackets, and slacks. Knitted fabrics when made of man-made fibers do not stretch out of shape when washed or dry-cleaned.

It is advisable to save the care label attached to the garment in case the article does not perform in use as claimed. The garment should then be returned to the store.

PROJECTS
1. Plan a complete wardrobe for a boy of 10 who is going to a summer camp in New England. Give names and quantities of the articles needed, the fabrics of which each item is made, and approximate retail prices of each.
2. Assume you are planning a weekend skiing outing. You will stay at a ski lodge for two nights.
   (a) List the articles of apparel in the quantities that you would need to take with you.
   (b) Give the names of the fabrics used in each garment and the approximate retail prices.
3. Plan a wardrobe for a male college student who is going to attend a small campus college in Minnesota.
   (a) List the article of apparel in the quantities that will be required.
   (b) Give the names of the fabrics used in each garment and approximate retail prices.

GLOSSARY Balmacaan—(named after an estate near Inverness). Swagger-style coat with slash pockets and no belt. It has a raglan sleeve and military collar. Fabrics used are gabardine, tweed, and cashmere (in solid colors for dress).

Barathea—A silk, rayon and cotton, or rayon and wool mixed fabric with a pebbly texture in a fine woven design resembling a brick wall. It is used for ties, women's dresses, and trimmings.

Batiste—A very sheer muslin used for men's summer shirts. See Glossary, Chapter, 17.

Belting—A heavy cotton, rayon, silk, or mixed fabric with large fillingwise ribs. It may be knitted. See *Webbing*.

Blazer—A casual sport-type jacket with metal pearl or leatherlike buttons on the front closing and cuffs. Suede or flannel are popular fabrics.

Box coat—A single- or double-breasted straight-hanging coat with notch or peak lapels. It generally has a regulation sleeve. Occasionally it is half-belted in back.

Broadcloth—See Glossary, Chapter 17.

Brocade—Used for ties, lounge wear, vests, and robes. See Glossary, Chapter 17.

Burlap—A coarse rough fabric often called gunny sacking, made of jute, hemp, or cotton. It is used as interlining in men's suits. This is a poorer fabric than hair canvas for the purpose.

Camel's hair—The soft lustrous underhair of a camel. Light tan to brownish black. Often combined with wool or acrylic fibers.

Canvas—A firm, heavy cotton or linen fabric. The unbleached fabric is used for coat fronts, lapels, and linings of men's suits. Hair canvas for interlinings is made of goat's hair and wool.

Cashmere—A fabric made of soft fibers of the Indian Cashmere goats that may be combined with sheep's wool. It is used for men's sweaters, scarfs, and coats. See Chapter 12.

Cavalry twill—See *Elastique.*

Challis—Lightweight wool or man-made fibers for a tie. See Glossary, Chapter 17.

Chambray—See Glossary, Chapter 17.

Chesterfield—(adapted from the style worn by Lord Chesterfield). It has a very long skirt, single- or double-breasted, with or without a velvet collar.

Cheviot—A woolen or worsted with a slightly rough texture in a twill weave. It is used for suits and coats.

Chinchilla—A men's overcoating. See Glossary, Chapter 17.

Chino cloth—A twill-weave cotton originally used for slacks, sport shirts, and summer army uniforms. It is made of two-ply cotton combed yarns, is of vat-dyed khaki color, and is mercerized and Sanforized.

Corduroy—A pile fabric with wales warpwise used for jackets, slacks, sport shirts, and bathrobes.

Covert—A medium-heavy cotton or wool fabric in twill weave. It originally had a flecked appearance because one of the ply yarns was white and the other one colored; now it is generally made in solid color (in wool or mixtures). Wool covert may be used for suits, topcoats, raincoats and uniforms; cotton covert is used for work clothes.

Crochet knit—Machine-knitted tie fabric made to resemble hand knitting.

Cummerbund—A wide fabric belt that fastens in the back, worn with a tuxedo evening suit.

Denim—See Glossary, Chapter 15.

Drill—A heavy, durable twilled cotton suitable for slacks, uniforms, overalls, and work shirts.

Dungaree—A heavy, coarse cotton or blended twill fabric woven from colored yarns. Heavier than jean.

Elastique—A firmly woven, clear-finished worsted with a steep double twill that is used for riding breeches, army uniforms, and slacks. It is similar to cavalry twill.

End-to-end—A colored warp yarn alternating with a white warp yarn; fillings are white. There is end-to-end broadcloth and end-to-end chambray, which is frequently sold as end-to-end madras. It is synonymous with *end-on-end or end-and-end.*

Faille—A tie fabric with fillingwise ribs. See Glossary, Chapter 17.

Fedora—A soft felt hat with crown creased lengthwise.

Flannel—See Glossary, Chapter 17. Also see *Flannelette.* See *Outing flannel* in this glossary.

Foulard—Soft, lightweight silk, mercerized cotton, or rayon fabric in fine twill weave used for men's ties and women's dresses. It is frequently sold as surah.

Gabardine—Steep-twilled wool, cotton, or rayon mixed or blended fabric, on which the back is flat. It is used for sport shirts, slacks, coats, and suits.

Haircloth—A stiff, wiry cloth of cotton with a mohair or horsehair filling. It is used for interfacing and stiffening.

Harris Tweed—Fabric identified by the label "Harris Tweed" which is required as a protective device by the British association of that name. Originated in the Isle of Harris and other islands of the Hebrides group. Originally, hand-woven and dyed with color pigments that were cooked over peat fires by cottagers—hence the distinctive odor.

Jean—See Glossary, Chapter 17.

Jersey—See Glossary, Chapter 13.

Macclesfield—Hand-woven silk or rayon fabric with small overall Jacquard patterns. Macclesfield, England, is the town of origin. See *Spitalfields*.

Madras—A muslin shirting with a woven-in pattern or stripe in balanced count. The designs may be dobby or Jacquard. White-on-white madras has a white figure on a white ground. Indian madras has rather subdued colors, usually in plaid design.

Melton—See Glossary, Chapter 17.

Mesh—Used for summer sport shirts and underwear. See Glossary, Chapter 17.

Mogadore—A corded silk or rayon fabric with wide ridges and often with wide stripes that is used for ties.

Moleskin finish—A cotton fleece-lined with close, soft, thick nap that is used in underwear for cold climates.

Outing flannel—A lightweight, soft plain- or twill-weave cotton fabric generally napped on both sides, often with stripes. It is used for pajamas, interlinings, and diapers.

Oxford—See Glossary, Chapter 17.

Percale—A muslin used for inexpensive shirts, shorts, and pajamas. See Glossary, Chapter 17.

Piqué—Used for shirts. See Glossary, Chapter 17.

Plush velour—A pile weave fabric with especially long shaggy pile, used for robes and lounge wear.

Pongee—Suitable for scarfs, sport shirts, and pajamas. See Glossary, Chapter 17.

Poplin—Used for shirts, ski jackets, and sports jackets. See Glossary, Chapter 17.

Raincoat—A water-repellent or waterproof coat of poplin or gabardine.

Rep—A heavily ribbed fabric in silk, rayon, cotton, wool, or a mixture. Fabric may be solid or striped. It is used for ties, robes, drapery, and upholstery.

Sateen—A cotton fabric in which the fillings float. It is usually mercerized and is used for linings, draperies, comforters.

Satin—Silk or man-made fabric sometimes made with a cotton filling. It has a smooth, lustrous surface, because the warp floats. It is used for linings of coats, jackets, facings, and ties.

Serge—Used for men's suits and slacks. See Glossary, Chapter 17.

Shantung—See Glossary, Chapter 17.

Sharkskin—A worsted fabric originally made in two colors. It is so called because it resembles leather sharkskin in durability. Now made in glen plaids, stripes, bird's-eye, and nailhead patterns; it is used for men's and women's suits, coats, and slacks.

or jacket. It is suitable for women's wear. It is also a type of knitting yarn.

Spitalfields—An English town, home of Huguenot weavers, now a lace-making center. In this town, the hand-woven Jacquard silk Spitalfields tie originated.

Tank Top—A snug-fitting, knitted garment, styled like a man's T-shirt. It may be worn as a top with pants. Named for tank suit or swim suit.

Trench coat—The officer's coat worn during World War I. It is double-breasted and belted. It has a high-closing collar and shoulder flaps.

Tropical—A plain-weave, lightweight summer suiting in worsted or blends with man-made fibers; it is also used for women's suits.

T-shirt—A knitted cotton undershirt with short sleeves that may be worn for sports or work without an outer garment.

Tweed—A rough-surfaced woolen, usually yarn dyed. It is generally twill or a variation in men's wear and is used for coats, suits, jackets, and slacks.

Unfinished worsted—A suiting fabric in twill weave, finished with a nap longer than that of other worsteds.

Webbing—A strong, tightly woven narrow fabric for straps or belts.

White-on-white—A fabric in any fiber mixture or blend that has a white woven-in design on a white background.

Wool broadcloth—A smooth, silky napped woolen in twill weave. Nap obliterates the weave. It is used for men's dinner jackets and formal evening wear—also for women's coats and suits.

Woolen—A class of wool fabrics made of short fibers of varied lengths and carded yarns.

Worsted—A class of wool fabrics made of long fibers and combed yarns.

Worsted flannel—See *Flannel,* Chapter 17.

Household Textiles 19

Household textiles, also called linens and domestics, are fabrics that serve the home. They dry dishes and hands and cover beds and tables.

In smaller stores, one buyer generally has charge of all home furnishing textiles. Larger stores have two buyers, one for domestics and linens and another for blankets, comforters, and bedspreads, while even larger stores have three departments—linens, domestics, and blankets. A typical merchandise classification follows:

LINEN CLASSIFICATION

1. Towels (bathroom, beach, kitchen, and kitchen accessories)
2. Shower curtains
3. Bathroom ensembles
4. Table linen (cloths and sets, place mats, doilies, runners, napkins)
   a. Damask
5. Embroidery and lace

DOMESTIC CLASSIFICATION

1. Sheets and pillowcases, yard goods (most stores no longer stock sheeting)
2. Mattresses and pillows
3. Blankets
4. Comforters and quilts
5. Bedspreads

THE LINEN CLASSI-FICATION

TOWELS

Towels, which make up a large category, are an essential part of any linen closet and should be chosen with the same care as sheets, pillow slips, and other household textiles. (Towels will be discussed according to the above linen classification.)

Bath Towels. Bath towels come in terry cloth, made of all cotton, or a tri-blended fiber mix (cotton, rayon, and polyester) to produce unusual textures and decorative effects. Terry cloth is characterized by looped-pile surfaces. This pile construction increases the absorbency; the more loops there are, the more absorbent the towel. (The actual meaning of the term "terry cloth" and its construction are explained in Chapter 5.) The construction, when on the loom, consists of a setup of ground warps in tension, arranged alternately with pile warps that form loops as their tension is released. By removing pile warps from a section of the cloth, the ground weave is discernible. In a three-pick towel, the filling yarns are grouped in threes, because two fillings are shot through the same shed and one filling is then shot through to interlace with the ground warps. This construction of fillings grouped in threes denotes a three-pick terry cloth. Fewer than three picks gives a minimum of contact between the pile warp and the ground warp. Hence, most towels are three-pick and are of medium grade. One- and two-pick towels are poor; towels of more than three picks are better than average. The quality of a terry cloth depends upon the following factors:

1. *Number and length of the pile loops.* The purpose of pile loops is to increase the surface area and thereby increase the absorptive power of the towel. For this purpose loops should be reasonably close together, soft, and not too tightly twisted.

In more expensive towels, pile loops are longer. Long loops in double-thread construction improve absorptive quality, but they catch and pull out easily. (For an explanation of double thread, see *strength of yarns.*) On the other hand, too short loops do not increase the surface area sufficiently. A loop about 1/8 inch deep seems to be generally the best.

So-called "friction towels" are made with all-linen pile or a row of linen pile alternating with a cotton pile.

2. *The tightness of the weave.* Some loops pull out very easily in laundering and in use, so that the towel becomes unattractive and weak. The greater the pickage, the less likely are loops to pull out. A groundwork of twill weave is more durable than a groundwork of plain or basket weave. A tight weave with balanced count is important.

3. *The strength of the yarns.* The tensile strength of the ground warp should be great enough to withstand the tension of the loom and the strain met in use; so the better towels are made with ground warps of ply yarns. Proper balance in tensile strength between ground warps and fillings is equally important. Poorer towels are made by the *single-thread* method, better grades are made by the *double-thread* method, in which each loop is made of two parallel threads not twisted together. These two threads come out of the same space between two filling threads. Double threads make for durability and, particularly, absorbency.

A more recent development has been the addition of polyester yarns in the warp direction, thereby increasing the overall durability of the towel, especially in the towel selvage. (Not all manufacturers have converted to polyester warps, particularly since the polyester market experienced increased prices and attendant shortages in the 1970s.)

4. *The selvage.* It should be firm and even. It is important that filling yarns bind in the warps used for the selvage. Sometimes only one filling out of three goes out to bind the edges of the fabric. Since yarns used in towels have to be loosely twisted to be absorbent, it is imperative that all fillings continue out to, and loop around, the very edge.

5. *Workmanship.* The hems at both ends of the towel should be even (all raw edges should be turned under at least one-quarter inch), carefully sewed with comparatively short, regular stitches, and finished at the sides so they will not pull out.

Although a consumer cannot mutilate a towel to determine pickage, number of threads, and strength of yarns, she can observe the closeness and length of the loops, the tightness of the weave, the firmness and evenness of the selvage, and the workmanship. Features such as pickage, double thread, ply ground warp, and twist of yarn are important specifications for a retail store buyer to understand. A project to determine these features can be carried out by students who have access to a textile laboratory.

The attractiveness of a bath towel has been greatly enhanced by the introduction of interesting solid colors, prints, and sheared loops on one side of the towel. When so done, the fabric is called *velour terry* or a sheared towel. Towels may be monogrammed in schiffli embroidery. After many years of all-white and color-bordered towels, solid colors appeared, followed by gaily printed fabrics and elaborate Jacquard woven designs. Solid colors that mix or match with prints and two-tone effects are featured. All-white towels, however, are still an important part of basic stock.

Bath towels are made in a range of sizes to please any personal taste. Medium sizes for the bath are 20 X 40 and 22 X 44 inches; the largest are 24 X 46 and 32 X 64, although beach towels, which come in solid colors and Jacquard prints, are even larger. Probably the largest volume of business is done in the 20 X 40 and 22 X 44 sizes, because medium-sized towels are less expensive than the large size, lighter in weight, and easier to manage. Heavy towels weigh more, and thereby increase the drying time. Also, small- or medium-sized towels are easiest for children to manage. Baby's bath towels come in size 36 X 36 inches and washcloths in sizes 9 X 9 inches.

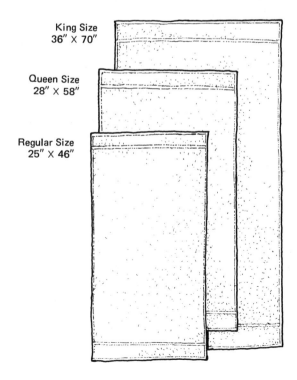

King Size
36" X 70"

Queen Size
28" X 58"

Regular Size
25" X 46"

FIGURE 19.1. Sizes of bath towels: regular, queen, and king.

The consumer should be warned of possible shrinkage before she considers what size towels to buy. Shrinkage occurs for the most part in the first five launderings; after that, it is negligible. For many towels residual shrinkage is as much as 10 percent, so that a size that seems adequate when new may be entirely too small after the first five launderings. Plenty of warm soap-suds or detergent should be used, followed by two rinses in clear warm water. Fabric softeners used to increase the softness of hand should be sparingly used, as they tend to reduce absorbency with overuse. Towels should be shaken before they are hung out to dry, preferably on a windy day; tumble drying improves absorption by fluffing the loops.

Hand Towels. Terry cloth is also a popular fabric for the smaller hand towels. They appear in sizes 16 X 26 and 18 X 36 inches, and in fingertip size 11 X 18 inches. When made in colors and patterns that match bath towel, washcloth, and bath mat, they compose a useful set. Huck face towels may be made wholly of cotton, wholly of linen, or of cotton warp and linen or rayon filling. Cottons and mixtures are less expensive than linens but are more apt to become linty after several washings.

The huckaback or honeycomb weave is done on the dobby loom. The grade of the fabric is determined by the quality of the fibers used, the quality of the yarns, and the construction. At present there are very few stores that carry huck towels, and 100 percent linen hucks are imported.

Washcloths. Since the primary purpose of a washcloth is to give friction for the purpose of cleansing the skin, a terry cloth with loops on both sides is better than a knitted back. Knitted washcloths are softer than woven ones, but they are more likely to stretch out of shape, although a locking stitch will prevent this problem. (Knitted washcloths are good for infants.) Durability depends upon a firm, even weave and firm stitching of edges so that corners will not fray or stitching unravel. Washcloths are 12 X 12 or 13 X 13 inches.

Dish Towels. Regular dish towels may be made of (1) cottonade, a coarse, heavy cotton resembling woolens and worsteds in weave and finish; (2) crash, a rough-textured cotton or linen in plain weave with novelty yarns; (3) damask, a cotton fabric in Jacquard pattern; (4) glass cloth, a cotton fabric with smooth, hard-twisted yarns that do not lint; (5) Osnaburg, a plain, strong cotton fabric with a crashlike appearance, having very coarse yarns in both warp and filling, and made of low-grade, short-staple cotton; (6) linen crash, a rather heavy, plain-weave linen made from tow yarns, and (7) terry cloth. Kitchen towels may be a two-fiber blend of linen and rayon or linen and cotton, or a three-fiber blend of cotton, rayon, and linen in terry cloth.

Crash is excellent for dish and glass towels, for, although it has a hard texture that prevents it from linting, it is still rough enough to be absorbent. Linen crash is preferable to cotton for dish towels because it does not lint so badly, does not seem wet so quickly, and dries faster than cotton. Linen crash towels are generally made of rather poorly hackled tow yarns. These yarns are naturally coarse and bumpy; hence they give the desired texture. Cotton crash is also made of irregular, coarse yarns, which are spun so as to resemble linen. Short fibers are singed in the finishing process to prevent linting as much as possible. Beetling is also used to make cotton resemble linen. An attractively printed linen crash makes an effective "show towel" (one to be seen but seldom, if ever, used).

A fairly high, well-balanced count—comparable to terry cloth in tensile strength of warp and filling—and workmanship are important for dish towels. Although the designs of crashes are not so intricate as those of terry towel fabrics, almost any color desired can be found to harmonize with a kitchen ensemble. Crash toweling can be purchased by the yard in some stores and by mail order. Ready-made crash dish towels come in sizes 15 × 30, 17 × 32, and 18 × 32 inches.

Pot holders of terry cloth and quilted cottons, and quilted mitts for handling hot dishes are usually found in the store near the dish towels.

Glass Towels. Glass towels are intended for drying glasses and thus should be free of lint. They are lighter in weight than regular dish towels. An all-linen crash makes a satisfactory glass towel. Usual sizes of Irish linen glass towels are 20½ × 31½ and 22½ × 33 inches. Glass toweling is also sold by the yard.

SHOWER CURTAINS

Since the fashion of having color in the bathroom has become important, shower curtains have been very prominent and colorful. They can be obtained in solid hues, stripes, or figures. The patterns and designs are nearly as varied as designs in draperies. At present, there is a trend to coordinate shower curtains with towels. In so doing, care should be taken not to create a busy, unaesthetic effect. Some fabrics of which shower curtains are made are taffeta, satin (in acetate, rayon, nylon, silk), moiré taffeta, and novelties such as a polyester schiffli-embroidered marquisette curtain over a plastic liner.

Fabrics for shower curtains may be either water-resistant (water-repellent) or waterproof. All-plastic sheet curtains (nontextile), plastic-coated fabrics, and cloths with plastic liners are waterproof.

Shower curtains in regular sizes are 68 × 72 inches and 72 inches square.

BATHROOM ENSEMBLES

Face and bath towels, washcloths, tank toppers, lid covers, window and shower curtains, and bath mats are sold separately or in sets. A smaller set may include bath and face towels, washcloths, and a bath mat. Bath mats are made of terry cloth (pure cotton or cotton with rayon pile), chenille, modacrylic, or rubber. Bath rugs are made of nylon in solid colors with etched or carved patterns. A dense plush nylon pile is locked with rubber coating to a cotton duck back to hold the pile tufts in place and to make the rug skid-resistant. Wall-to-wall nylon carpeting is gaining in popularity for bathroom floor covering.

TABLE LINEN

People often speak of their "table linen" and their "bed linen," although actually much of it is cotton and blends of cotton, rayon, and polyester. Yet linen is used extensively for dining tablecloths because (1) it looks

FIGURE 19.2. Shower ensemble. A multi-color coordination of 50/50 polyester/rayon consisting of shower curtain, window curtain, waste basket, and covered tissue box.

FIGURE 19.3. A bathroom ensemble.

clean; (2) it is somewhat lustrous; (3) stains can be removed from it easily; and (4) it wears and washes well, retaining its luster and beauty after many washings.

Cloths for Dining Tables. Cloths for dining tables include dinner cloths, banquet cloths, luncheon cloths, dinette and tea sets, place mats, napkins, table pads (made of felt of baize—a loose, plain-weave, napped fabric in imitation of felt—or a quilted material similar to that used for mattress covers), and hot spots (heavy, novelty mesh or doily material placed over pads of cork or silver).

The chief selling points for the cloths and sets mentioned here are appearance, suitability, serviceability, durability, minimum care, and size. For example, if a customer wants a cloth for a dinette where small children have their meals, the salesperson might show her a screenprinted, cotton woven cloth covered with a coat of vinyl plastic that can be wiped off, or a 65 percent polyester/35 percent cotton that is machine washable and durable press. In some instances, a soil-release finish lets stains wash out quickly and thoroughly. A small square cloth, 54 × 54 or even 45 × 45 inches, might suffice. A vinyl-faced laminated cloth would be equally suitable. Place mats of plastic-coated fabric might also be suggested. (One hundred percent plastic mats are also appropriate, but they are non-textiles.)

Place mats have become varied and imaginative in design. For a patio or barbecue pit, the homemaker might want a light, bright, gay, carefree touch. For indoor dining, she might prefer a richer, more elegant, quieter mat. Juvenile place mats should have a design that appeals to the child.

Table covers for outdoor dining are frequently made of laminated rayon, cotton terry, flannel-backed polished cotton in solid color, gay prints, checkerboards, and stripes. For informal dining indoors, a solid or printed cotton, rayon and cotton, all-linen crash cloth, or Fiberglas Beta (no-iron, soil-release), with or without napkins, are appropriate. Sizes are 54 × 54, 54 × 72, or 63 × 80 inches.

Luncheon and bridge sets, doilies, runners, and napkins are often made of linen crash cloth:

1. Smooth yarns of even diameter.
2. Count and balance: excellent grade, 80 yarns per square inch; medium grade, 64 inches per square inch; poor grade, 55 yarns per square inch.
3. Dyes fast to sunlight and to washing.
4. Hems evenly turned and firmly stitched.
5. The amount of sizing. Although good-quality linens are not heavily sized, a little starch may be added in the finish to give the leathery stiffness common to new linens. Flimsy cotton crash is often heavily sized to resemble heavy linen. The friction test will reveal the presence of excessive sizing.
6. Amount of bleaching. Although snow-white linens are beautiful, it is often advisable to buy linen cloth that is not fully bleached when it is purchased. Each time a full-bleached linen is laundered, the chemical bleaches used by the laundry overbleach the cloth, thereby tendering it. To ensure long service, linen cloths should be oyster-bleached (slightly bleached) or silver-bleached (deep cream color) when purchased.
7. Minimum-care finishes, such as durable press and soil release.

FIGURE 19.4. Lace cloths of 100 percent Dacron polyester for oblong, oval, and round tables. Photograph courtesy of the Quaker Lace Company.)

For cocktails, small napkins about 5 × 8 inches or 7 inches square are used. These may be of linen, cotton crash, handkerchief linen, or man-made and natural fiber blends; corners or edges may be embroidered.

Textiles Used for Table Linen. With the advent of improved minimum-care finishes, the tablecloth has become more popular for informal as well as formal dining.

For formal dining, a lace cloth of cotton, polyester, or nylon, or a cloth of embroidered linen or linen damask is appropriate. Machine-made lace cloths in ivory, ecru, white in venetian motifs, filet, and novelty patterns can be used. A discussion of laces of various types is to be found at the end of this section.

Damask. Damask tablecloths come in standard sizes, and the choice of size depends on the number of people to be seated at the table. A damask cloth 72 × 90 inches comfortably seats eight people, and a cloth 82 × 108 inches seats twelve. Banquet cloths are 60 × 116, 72 × 126, or 72 × 144 inches. Dinner napkins generally match the tablecloth and may be 18 or 22 inches square.

Table damasks are pure linen, pure cotton, or mixtures of these fibers. Sometimes rayon is included to make the design more prominent and lustrous. Damasks are made in Jacquard weave with a warp satin design and a filling sateen ground, or the reverse. The twill weave is sometimes used for the design and the satin weave for the ground.

From the standpoint of construction there are two types of damask: simple or single, and compound or double. Both types are woven single; the same applies to the type of weave. Single damask has a four-float construction, whereas double damask has a seven-float construction. The count of cloth of double damask is higher than that of single damask (some authorities say double damask should have a count of 180 with at least 50 percent floating yarn).

Quality of Damask. To judge the wearing quality of a damask, the following factors should be considered:

1. *The length of the fibers.* Since damasks are woven in a satin construction necessitating floats, long fibers do not pull out and fuzz as quickly as short ones; and, since linen fibers are generally longer than cotton fibers, they are more adaptable to satin weaves.
2. *The evenness of yarns.* If yarns are unevenly spun, then the cloth will be thick and thin in spots. Such a cloth presents a poor appearance and also gives poorer service.
3. *The closeness of the weave.* A loose weave is a weakness in a damask because it allows yarns to slip and thereby wear out the float. A close, firm weave is necessary if a damask is to be durable.
4. *The length of the floats.* Floats in this construction may pass over four to twenty yarns. A float that passes over four yarns is considered short. Although they will

FIGURE 19.5. Linen damask table-cloth. (Photograph courtesy of the Irish Linen Guild.)

wear well, short floats do not give a lustrous surface. The longer the float, the greater the light reflection and the more beautiful the cloth. For elaborate leaf and floral designs, a long float (eighteen or twenty yarns) is necessary. Long floats allow a great amount of yarn to be exposed to friction on the surface. Consequently, long floats are not durable.

EMBROIDERY AND LACE

Not only are laces and embroideries used for apparel, but they are also used for the table covers, doilies, scarfs, and trimming of household textiles.

Embroidery. Embroidery is ornamental needlework done on the fabric itself, whereas lace is a fabric created by looping, interlacing, braiding, or twisting threads. Embroidery can be done by machine or by hand. The latter method, if the work is done well, is preferable but generally more expensive than the machine product. Machine embroidery is often rather coarse, and the wrong side may not be well finished. A few common types of embroidery follow:

1. Japanese hand embroidery—large designs
2. Philippine embroidery—very small designs
3. Mexican drawnwork—lacy, spiderweb effects
4. French embroidery—silky looking with small designs
5. Madeira—floral patterns with punchwork
6. Appenzell—Swiss embroidery in geometrical punchwork designs

FIGURE 19.6. Machine embroidery with punch work. (Photograph courtesy of Max Mandel Laces, Inc.)

Much of the eyelet all-over embroidery and edges for trimming on tablecloths, curtains, spreads, dresses, lingerie, and blouses is embroidered by a machine called the Schiffli. This machine can embroider almost any design on either woven cloth or net. The machine itself is a double-decker about fifteen yards long. It is equipped with boat-shaped shuttles ("schiffli" means little boat) and needles, and it operates somewhat like a sewing machine. The design is controlled by punched Jacquard cards. Eyelets are punched by a separate operation.

Batiste, lawn, organdy, nylon sheers, cotton piqués, edgings, and flouncings are but a few of the fabrics that may be schiffli embroidered. Since schiffli designs are more intricate than swivel, clip spot, or lappet, they are also more expensive.

Lace.[1] This is an important trimming, for it is used for tablecloths, curtains, handkerchiefs, dresses, and underwear. Lace consists of two

[1] See "Lace," *Fairchild's Dictionary of Textiles* (New York: Fairchild Publications, Inc., 1967).

elements: (1) the pattern, flower, or group, which forms the closer-worked and more solid portion, and (2) the ground or filling, which serves to hold the pattern together. The two main types of laces are "real," or handmade, and machine made. Linen thread is usually used for real lace, but cotton, rayon, nylon, or silk may be used for machine lace. The former is softer, more irregular in mesh and pattern, and more expensive. There are five kinds of real laces: (1) needlepoint, (2) bobbin (pillow), (3) darned, (4) crocheted, and (5) knotted. All of these patterns are also made or imitated by machine.

1. *Needlepoint lace.* The design for needlepoint is drawn on parchment stitched to a backing of stout linen, and the lace is made by filling in the pattern with buttonhole stitches. When the lace is completed, the parchment is removed. Two of the most common needlepoint laces are Venetian and Alençon. See the illustrations.

2. *Bobbin lace.* Sometimes called pillow lace, the lace design is drawn either on a pillow or on a paper that is placed over the pillow. Small pegs or pins are stuck into the pillow along the design, and a large number of small bobbins of thread are manipulated around the pegs or pins to produce the lace. As the lace is completed, the pins are pulled out and the lace is removed from the pillow. Making pillow lace requires great skill and dexterity, for as many as three hundred bobbins may be needed to make some patterns.

3. *Duchesse.* Because of its exquisite large, clothy design, duchesse is the queen of the bobbin laces. Other bobbin laces are Binche, Val, Chantilly, Torchon, and Cluny. (See the illustrations and accompanying descriptions.)

4. *Darned lace.* When made by hand, the design of darned lace is sewn with thread and needle passed in and out of a square mesh net.

5. *Crocheted lace.* When handmade, this is made with a crochet hook, working usually with specially twisted cotton thread. It is a comparatively inexpensive heavy lace. Irish crocheted lace (not necessarily made in Ireland) is typified by a rose or shamrock design that stands out from the background.

6. *Filet lace.* Characterized by a flat, geometrical design, this lace may be either crocheted or darned. It is very common for household use, particularly for doilies, runners, antimacassar sets, and tablecloths. It may also be used for dress trimming.

7. *Knotted lace.* This is made by twisting and knotting thread by means of a shuttle. When made by passing a shuttle in and out of loops in a thread, it is called *tatting*. It is identified by a circle-like motif and picots around the edge of the motif.

8. *Machine-made laces.* Nearly all the laces classified as "real laces" can be duplicated by machine with slight variations and simplifications.

   Machinery for making looped net was invented about 1764. But the forerunner of the present lace machine, the bobbinet machine, was patented by John Heathcote in the early 1800s and was later modified by several other inventors, one of whom was John Levers, whose name has come down to us via the Levers machine we now use.

9. *Bobbinet.* The design is embroidered on a plain hexagonal mesh cotton or rayon net. The embroidery is done primarily by the Levers machine, but the Schiffli machine may be used for certain types, and the net is sometimes embroidered by hand. Bobbinet, which comes in wide widths like dress goods, is often imported from France. Bobbinet is sold by the hole count. To compute hole count, count the actual number of holes to an inch in a straight line, then repeat the count of the last hole and count the holes on the diagonal to an inch. Multiply the first figure by the second figure. (See Figure 19.8.) The greater the hole count, the finer the quality. Bobbinet, when stiffened, is used for veiling, evening gowns, and dress linings. Nylon bobbinet has become popular.

10. *Tulle.* This is similar to bobbinet but is made in silk, rayon, or nylon and has a

Carrickmacross, an Irish appliqued lace with a floral design. The pattern of handmade Carrickmacross is cut from fine cambric and appliquéd to the ground by point stitches. The pattern and ground of machine-made Carrickmacross are made at the same time.

Alençon, a needlepoint lace. Fine loops of thread form the background and produce a double-thread. Natural floral patterns are outlined by heavy threads.

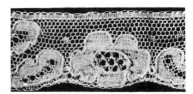

Breton, embroidered net. The design is made of heavy thread embroidered on net. This lace is used for trimming women's underwear.

Chantilly, a bobbin lace made of silk. The pattern is usually a rather simple branch design, but sometimes Chantilly has vine or spray motifs. It usually comes in white or black. This lace has long been a favorite trimming for bridal veils.

Cluny, a rather geometric bobbin lace. The design is so open that the finished product is light and pleasing. Cluny is used to trim dresses, luncheon sets, and so forth.

FIGURE 19.7. Types of laces.

Duchesse, an exquisite
bobbin lace. The design is
large and clothy. Brides, or
threads, join the various
parts of the design. The lace
is usually made in wide widths.

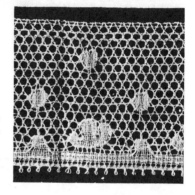

Binche, a bobbin lace. Real Binche is
made by appliquéing the flat sprig-like
design to a rather coarse net ground, the mesh
of which resembles a cane chair set. The design
and background of machine-made Binche are made
at the same time.

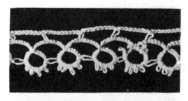

Tatting, a knotted lace. The knots are made
by passing a shuttle in and out of loops in the thread.

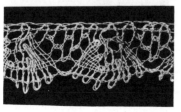

Torchon (beggar's lace), a coarse pillow lace made
with a loosely twisted thread. A shell pattern is
a common design. It is an inexpensive, common
lace—hence the name *beggar's lace.* Machine-made
cotton torchon laces are quite durable, and they
wash well.

FIGURE 19.7. (Continued)

487

Val (Valenciennes), a flat bobbin lace with a diamond or lozenge-shaped mesh ground. The lace is worked in one piece, and just one kind of thread is used for the outline of the design and every part of the fabric. The pattern is usually sprig-like or floral. Val comes in narrow widths for trimming babies' garments.

Irish, a fine crocheted lace with rose or clover-leaf patterns that stand out from the background. It is a heavy lace that is comparatively inexpensive. Irish crochet lace is easily made by hand.

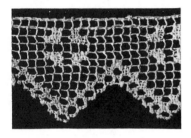

Filet, a darned lace with a square mesh. It is made by darning the thread in and out of the meshes. The pattern and background of machine-made filet are made in the same operation. Filet comes in narrow widths for trimming, and is also made in large pieces such as table covers, runners, and bedspreads.

Point d'esprit, an embroidered tulle or net used to trim evening gowns. The dots or small squares are closely set at regular intervals.

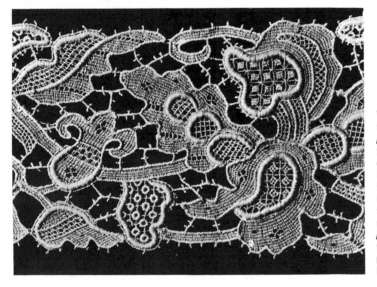

Venetian point, a needlepoint lace that is sometimes known as *raised point* because the design is thrown into relief by a sort of embroidery or buttonhole stitching. The pattern, in the form of flowers, is rather large, and is united by brides, or bars. When the pattern is in the form of a rose, the lace is called *rose point.* Venetian point is usually wide and quite heavy. In all-over patterns it makes very attractive blouses.

FIGURE 19.7. (Continued)

higher hole count. Tulle is stiffened. The nylon tulle, very sheer and rip-resistant, can be made fireproof, permanently crisp, and resistant to steam or rain.

11. *Point d'esprit.* Point d'esprit is an embroidered tulle or net. When made by hand, the dots or squares are embroidered into the net with point stitches. Point d'esprit (machine-made) is usually higher priced than bobbinet of the same grade.

12. *Breton.* A heavy thread is used for the design of this embroidered net. When embroidered by hand, the net is sold as *hand run*. This net is used for trimming slips and nightgowns.

13. *Princess.* Although real princess lace can be made by bobbins, it is usually an embroidered net made on the Schiffli machine. As an embroidered net, it can be used for bridal gowns and veils, and is comparatively inexpensive.

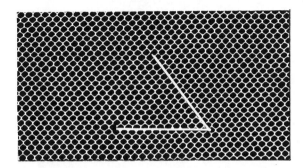

FIGURE 19.8. In bobbinet, there are thirteen holes to the inch horizontally and sixteen holes to the inch (counting the corner hole twice) on the diagonal. Therefore 13 × 16 = 208 hole count.

Some of the most common laces, both machine- and hand-made, are illustrated on the preceding pages.

Uses of Laces. Laces are made in different widths for different uses. For example, a narrow lace with a scalloped edge is used for trimming a baby's dress; a lace with slits or eyelets is so made that ribbon may be run through it. There are seven uses of laces:[2]

1. *All-over laces.* An all-over lace is a fabric up to 36 inches wide with the pattern repeated over the entire surface. The fabric is cut and sold from the bolt like woven dress goods. The dressmaker cuts it to pattern and makes it up into formal evening, dinner, and cocktail dresses and blouses.

2. *Flouncing.* Flouncing applies to laces 18 to 36 inches wide with a plain edge at the top and a scalloped edge at the bottom of the fabric. It is used for wide ruffles or flounces. Often these flounces are arranged in tiers to form a skirt.

3. *Galloon.* A galloon is a lace up to 18 inches wide with a scalloped edge at top and bottom. It may be used as an insertion between two cut edges of fabric, or it may be appliquéd to a fabric in bands or as a border.

4. *Insertion.* Insertion is a band of lace sewn between two pieces of fabric or on a fabric at the straight top or bottom edges. A variety of insertion is footing, which has a straight edge at top and bottom but no pattern. Footing is often used at the bodice or at the bottom hem of a slip.

5. *Beading.* Beading has slots through which ribbon may be run. These slots may be found in edgings or galloons but are much more common in insertions.

6. *Edging.* An edging is a lace never more than 18 inches wide that is straight at the top and scalloped at the bottom. It is sewn to the edge of a dress, gown, blouse, or handkerchief.

7. *Medallion.* A medallion is a lace in a single design that can be appliquéd to a fabric ground for ornamentation. It is sometimes used in the corners of napkins or as an ornament for a dress.

[2] The first six classifications and their descriptions are adapted from *Lace*, pamphlet by Max Mandel Laces, Inc.

FIGURE 19.9. Uses of laces. (a) all-over lace; (b) flouncing; (c) insertion; (d) galloon; (e) edging; (f) beading; (g) medallion. (Photographs courtesy of Max Mandel Laces, Inc.)

SHEETS AND PILLOWCASES

The word "muslin," as we have noted, is derived from the French word *mousseline*, which in turn originated with the city of Mosul in Mesopotamia. We often hear of *mousseline de soie* (silk muslin), which is a very thin, crisp silk organdy. Muslin is the name commonly applied to various cotton cloths in plain weave ranging in weight from thin batiste and nainsook to heavy sheetings, such as longcloth and percale. The lightweight muslins, called print cloths, have been discussed in Chapter 17 under fabrics for women's apparel; the heavier, sheeting-weight muslins will be discussed here.

Although we speak of "bed linen," it would be difficult to find a home using real linen sheets or pillow slips. Most sheetings sold are cotton muslins or blends. There are also nonwoven (disposable) and rubber sheetings, often with a cotton back, for babies and the sickroom; acetate satin; and cotton flannel sheets (used for cold climates and for light summer blankets). Rayon satin sheets as well as cotton and polyester blended knits have a wide range of colors that give them gift appeal. Pillowcases with nylon face and slip-resistance back of no-iron polyester, nylon, and cotton reduce the hair-do problem. All cotton sheets have virtually disappeared from the market. The exception is 100 percent cotton, 200 count.

There are two kinds of sheets—muslin and percale. Percale is the better grade and has the higher count. It is known that the typical consumer buys her sheets and pillow slips without first consideration of durability. A no-iron finish, size, price, brand, and general appearance are considered, however. In fact, many women know very little about sheets—younger customers especially. For example, few women are aware that the standard twin-bed sheet is usually 72 × 104 or 72 × 108 inches. When 5- to 6-inch hems are made (3 inches at the top, and 2 at the bottom) the finished size of the 72 × 104 is 72 × 98. Most mills are now packaging their sheets with the finished size marked rather than the "torn" (unfinished) size.

Nowadays sheets are sold primarily on the basis of the no-iron feature rather than durability. The consumer wants a sheet that is smooth and nonwrinkled after washing and drying. She also wants a colored sheet fast to repeated washings. Consumers' Research (CR) believes that the wise customer would do well to take into consideration the construction and probable life of a sheet.

How long will a sheet last? The life of a sheet is related to its breaking strength. The USA Standard L22.30.8 calls for a minimum breaking strength of 55 pounds for the 180 (B-grade) and 200 (A-grade) percales.

This standard for new sheets has been lowered from 60 pounds minimum breaking strength to 55 pounds. There is some question whether this standard is too low, if consumers are interested in durable sheets. However, it should be noted that CR found, in some cases, that a sheet can increase in breaking strength as much as 15 percent after 20 launderings. In other cases, a sheet may lose as much as 10 percent in one direction. But in the CR test of 13 brands of polyester/cotton blends that originally met the standard of 55 pounds minimum for new sheets, no sheet fell below the standard.

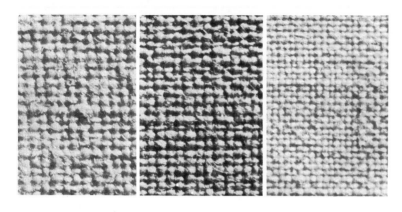

FIGURE 19.10. Sheetings with grades.

TYPE 128   TYPE 140   TYPE 200

Wearing Quality of Sheets. Two sheets of different brands may be purchased at the same time and be given the same number of washings; yet one sheet may outwear the other. A study of the fibers, yarns, weave, and finish will reveal the reason.

1. Cotton fibers should be of good quality and as long as possible if they are to be spun into regular, even, strong yarn. The best sheets contain cotton fibers at least one inch in length. An even yarn will stand washing better than an uneven one. A bumpy yarn may protrude on the surface, and, besides making an unsightly appearance, will be subjected to more friction and wear than would an unprotruding yarn. Uneven yarns are apt to break in laundering and so make a hole in the cloth.

2. To be durable, yarns should be spun tightly. Since most sheets contain fibers which are comparatively short, a tight twist will keep the fibers from pulling out with wear. The tensile strength of tightly spun yarns is greater than that of loosely spun yarns.

3. To be considered "first" or "standard" quality, a sheet should be free from imperfections in the weave, such as thick and thin spots due to uneven yarns. *Run-of-the-mill* means that the defects are due either to imperceptible uneven threads or to little oil spots that occurred in the manufacturing process. These defects do not affect the wearing quality of the sheet. Sheets are marked "seconds" if there are some defects in weave or imperfections in the yarns. Each manufacturer has his own rule of what constitutes a second. If a manufacturer's standards are high then slight flaws will not seriously affect the durability. Such a second, sold at a lower price than first quality, may be an economical purchase.

4. The count is also important. The number of warp and filling yarns to the inch determines the count of the cloth; the proportion of warps to fillings indicates the balance. A high-count cloth with a good balance will generally outwear a low-count cloth with poor balance. To illustrate: a high-count sheet of good balance would be 108 × 104; a low-count sheet with poorer balance would be 76 × 60. In each case the warp yarns are expressed first. Counts may vary from 54 × 47 for a sleazy sheet to 109 × 97 for a very fine one; the average count is 73 × 62.

492

USA Standard specifications for bleached bed sheets and pillowcases (L22.30.8) appear in Table 19-1.[3]

TABLE 19-1. Standards in Bed Sheets and Pillowcases

	Type 200[a] Combed Yarn	Type 180 Combed or Carded Yarn	Type 140 Carded Yarn	Type 128 Carded Yarn
Combined thread count warp and filling (per inch square)	200	180	140	128
Warp breaking strength (pounds)	60	60	70	55
Filling breaking strength (pounds)	60	60	70	55
Maximum added sizing (percent)	1	2	4	6
Weight (ounces per square yard)	3.6	3.6	4.6	4.0

[a]"200" and other numbers represent types or grades (by counts) of the U. S. Bureau of Standards and L22.

5. Tensile or breaking strength is an important factor in durability. The number of pounds required to break a strip of cloth an inch wide is called the *tensile strength* of that cloth. Since the warp is usually stronger than the filling, it has a slightly higher breaking strength. If in one sheet warps break at 62 pounds and fillings at 56 pounds, that sheet will wear better than one whose breaking strength is 47 pounds for warp and 34 pounds for filling. Furthermore, a sheet may have a well-balanced count and still have a low breaking strength. The two factors, count and tensile strength, must be considered separately. In general, sheets with satisfactory thread counts have been found to have good tensile strength, and vice versa. Polyester adds additional tensile and breaking strength.

6. When sheets were made primarily of cotton, they often had a great deal of sizing. Sizing in the form of starch or China clay was commonly used for finishing poor quality sheets. Sizing makes the finish appear smooth; seems to give weight to the cloth; and covers up imperfections in construction. However, after a heavily sized sheet has been washed, it looks flimsy and fuzzy. With the polyester/cotton blends, sizing is not present in appreciable amounts. In all 13 brands tested by CR, sizing amounted to less than 4 percent, the maximum sizing permitted by the industry standard. The chemicals applied in durable press treatments do not wash out because they become a part of the fabric.

Sheets vary in weight. According to industry standards, a Type 180 percale sheet should weigh a minimum of 3.6 ounces per square yard. The Type 140 muslin weighs 4.6 ounces per square yard. Most all-cotton sheets shrink somewhat in laundering. Loosely woven sheets shrink more than closely woven ones. Unless shrinkage-controlled, an allowance of 4½ to 5 percent should be made for shrinkage. There was no appreciable shrinkage (1.5 percent) in the CR tests cited.

Consumers have discovered the comfort of smooth durable press sheets. These sheets make a more tailored-looking bed, and they dry wrinkle-free with little or no ironing needed.

[3] All standards are minimum specifications, with the exception of sizing, which is maximum.

Determining Quality. To be sure, a consumer cannot use a tensile tester or a counting glass, but laboratory tests can be made by any testing bureau for the benefit of the store's buyer.

Most national and private brands of sheets now bear informative labels that specify size, thread count, tensile strength, weight, and percent of shrinkage. But what does a thread count of 128 mean to the consumer? She must be able to interpret that figure to know whether it specifies a grade A or a grade B muslin.

The appearance and feeling of the sheeting can be noted easily by the consumer. She can detect bumpy yarns at a glance. By holding the cloth to the light, she may notice any streaked effect. If there is a predominance of warp, there will be a heavy, warpwise streaking. She may also notice the closeness of weave. The closer the weave, the higher the count and, other factors being equal, the stronger the cloth.

If the sheet is hemmed, the stitching should be noticed. A fairly short, even machine stitch is preferable to a long or an uneven stitch. A minimum of 14 even stitches per inch is recommended.

Strong thread should be used, and the ends of thread should be fastened securely. Evenness of hems is insured if the sheeting used has been torn and not cut into lengths. Furthermore, if hems are to be even, they should be folded on the thread of the material. Hems with closed ends are to be preferred.

The selvage should be examined carefully, because it may be the first place to show wear. The edge should be firm, with all the yarns caught in securely. The taped selvage is recommended for added wear.

Sizes, Serviceability, and Comfort. The choice of size is really dependent on individual preference. But, largely through ignorance, many customers buy their flat sheets too short. If a bed is about 6 feet long, the customer is apt to think that a 90-inch sheet allows ample coverage. A standard mattress is 74 inches long and 5 inches thick. Therefore 10 inches should be allowed to cover the mattress at head and foot. In addition, tests show that the average all-cotton sheet shrinks 4½ percent after seventy-five washings.[4] If shrinkage-controlled, the sheet will shrink 2 percent or less. A 108-inch sheet, then, would shrink about 5 inches. This shrinkage should be considered in deciding size. Hems are generally 3 inches at the top and 2 inches at the bottom. Also, some allowance should be made for tucking in at top and bottom—about 7 inches. Accordingly, 74 inches (mattress) plus 5 inches plus 5 inches (thickness of mattress at both ends) plus 5 inches (allowance for shrinkage) plus 5 inches (for hems) plus 7 inches plus 7 inches (tuck-in allowance for both ends) equals 108 inches. The sheet required here is the 108-inch length (108 inches is the torn length before the sheet is hemmed). Since a polyester/cotton blend's shrinkage is negligible, the 104-inch length would be adequate.

To make flat sheets wear evenly, some buyers prefer hems of the same width at top and bottom; either end may be used as the top. Others prefer a wider hem at one end to distinguish top from bottom.

The lower and top sheets are the same size. The lower sheet should be long enough to tuck in at the head and foot and thus cover the whole

---

[4] Tests of forty-five sheets of different brands were made in a laundry under methods approved by the Laundry Owners' National Association.

mattress. The top sheet should tuck in 6 or 7 inches at the end and should fold back over the blanket about half a yard. The following sizes of flat sheets are sold in most stores:[5]

TABLE 19-2. Sizes of Flat Sheets

Type of Bed	Size of Sheet (inches)
Crib	42 X 72
Youth bed	63 X 104
Twin bed or three-quarter bed	66 X 104
Double bed	81 X 104
Queen size	90 X 110
King or Hollywood size	108 X 110

Fitted or contour sheets make bed-making easier. West Point-Pepperell, Inc., lists the following selling points of their fitted sheets: (1) they will not wrinkle; (2) they do not toss and turn with you; (3) beds need no remaking; (4) a perfect fit is assured by the Sanforized label; (5) corners slip on quickly and easily; (6) they need no ironing; (7) mattress lifting is eliminated; (8) they hold mattress pad in place; (9) they require less space in washer; (10) they come in hard-to-find sizes; (11) an exclusive seaming process makes fitted sheets one-third stronger at the corners.

Bottom-fitted sheets come in the following mattress sizes:

TABLE 19-3. Sizes of Bottom Fitted Sheets

Type of Bed	Size of Sheet (inches)
Cot	30 X 75
Youth or Day	33 × 76
Single	36 × 76 or 39 × 76
Three-quarter	48 × 76
Extra large twin	39 × 80
Queen	60 × 80
King	78 × 80

Top-fitted styles have two slip-on corners with "kick-room" allowance. Usual sizes are twin and full (double).

An improvement over the fitted sheet is the one with stretch around the corners. It gives the consumer ease of bed-making without reducing the strength of the corners of the sheet.

Color. Solid colors and prints have brought fashion to an otherwise uninteresting staple bed sheet. In addition to the bleached white staple, there are solids in virtually every color that can be coordinated with printed sheets. There are stripes and florals and combinations of these designs. There are also embroidered sheets and pillowcases, sold separately or in sets.

Brands. Some customers say, "I know what brands are good, so I buy one of them. If I can afford to pay more, I select *X* brand; if I cannot, I

[5] Top sheet sizes were reduced recently by practically every producer.

buy *Y* brand." These buyers are doubtless buying satisfactory goods. The best standard brands are backed by years of reliable service and sustained high standards of quality. Probably many customers do better if they buy by brand than by quality, because many of them do not know the factors determining wearing quality.

Some of the large department stores have their private brands that they wish to sell in preference to the nationally advertised brands; and many of the reliable stores do have a product as good as those nationally advertised and possibly cheaper. If the customer is able to judge quality, she may get a bargain in the private brand.

The intelligent consumer should learn how to judge quality and other factors making for value in use and thus choose the brand, style, or line number that best suits the combination of personal requirements.

Sheeting by the Yard. Most customers prefer made-up sheets, so the sale of sheeting by the yard is negligible. Pillow tubing and ticking is also sold by the yard in a few major department stores.

Linen Sheets and Sheeting. Although there is almost no demand for linen sheets, there are some distinct advantages in buying them. Linen sheets of good grade outwear cotton of good grade, but the cost of linen is considerably higher. After a linen sheet has served its life as a sheet, it may be cut up into doilies, hand towels, and dress trimmings. Even if linen is old, it has a rich brilliance that an old cotton does not have.

The wearing quality of linen sheeting is determined by the grades of fiber, yarn, weave, and finish. A sheeting should wear well if it has long, even fibers of good tensile strength; well-hackled, even yarns; a close, firm weave; and a smooth beetle finish—and if it is not overbleached. Hems should be even and hemstitching of good quality. Finished sizes are 72 X 108 for twin and 90 X 108 for double beds.

Pillowcases. Most pillowcases are made to match the sheet and usually are packaged two to a set. The two may be bought in attractive packages, and make desirable gift items. Bolster pillows, when in style, lead to sales of pillow protectors and bolster pillowcases.

Pillowcases should be about 10 inches longer than the pillow and about 2 inches larger around. The following chart shows the size of the pillow and the appropriate size for a pillowcase. The length is the torn length before hemming.

TABLE 19-4. Pillow and Pillowcase Sizes

Size of Pillow (inches)	Size of Pillowcase (inches)
Standard 20 X 26	22 X 36
Queen 20 X 30	22 X 40
King 20 X 36	22 X 46

The same points to be considered in judging the wearing quality of sheets should be applied to the selection of pillowcases and bolster cases. The hems should be 3 inches wide, straight and even. Seams should be firmly and evenly stitched (14 stitches to the inch) and finished to prevent raveling.

Disposable pillowcases and sheets are made of Kaycel, a fabric that looks like cloth but has strong yarns bonded between layers of cellulose wadding. For hygienic utility in hospitals, sickrooms, and clinics, these pillowcases have proved acceptable. They can also be used as laundry and shoe bags and as wastebasket liners. They come in white and a few colors.

Obtaining Longer Wear from Sheets and Pillow Cases. Many times customers complain that sheets in service only three or four months show signs of wear. The customer blames her laundry, and the laundry claims the fault lies in the poor quality of the sheet. It is difficult to determine which is at fault. Accordingly, salespeople should give customers a few hints that will help to get longer wear from sheets.

1. Sheets wear out where shoulders rub. Experiments made in hotels show that most sheets wear out first at this point. If the sheets have hems of the same width at both ends, head and foot can be reversed to equalize wear. If hems are wider at the top, the lower sheet may be turned head to foot.

2. A sheet that is the right size for the bed will wear longer than one that is too short or too narrow. Sheets too small for a bed are subjected to unnecessary strain.

3. Bedsprings, splinters, and nails on the bed may snag a sheet. A loose nail may work its way through the covering of a box spring; a projecting sliver of wood may catch a sheet when it is pulled off; the threads may become weakened and a hole may consequently appear. In short, a bed may be giving a sheet harder wear than the laundry.

4. Mattress pads or covers prolong the life of both the sheet and the mattress.

5. Sheets and cases will wear longer if all holes and tears are mended before they are laundered.

6. Whether sheets and cases are laundered at home or by a commercial laundry, strong undiluted bleaches should not be used because they weaken the cloth.

7. Folds of sheets and pillowcases should not be ironed. It weakens the fabric. No-iron sheets obviate this problem.

8. The bed should be made with a light touch rather than with force.

9. Laundries may wear out sheets and cases by putting them through the ironer too fast. As a result the selvage may roll or fold. Continued mangling in this manner may wear the sheet out along these folds in the selvage before the body of the sheet shows wear. Shrinkage is minimized if sheets are ironed or mangled at home. Shrinkage may also be cut down somewhat by varying the method of mangling. If the flat sheet is inserted in the mangle from selvage to selvage, it grows shorter and wider. The shrinkage takes place in the length. If the sheet is run through the mangle in the other direction, the shrinkage in length may be lessened.

10. Sheets should be rotated. Discarded sheets should be replaced immediately. By so doing, the homemaker will get better wear than to continue to use a smaller and smaller number of sheets until they are all worn out.

MATTRESSES AND PILLOWS

Mattresses. Although most housewives buy mattresses only a few times in their lives, when they do buy they want a mattress that is comfortable and durable. Probably comfort in some minds is associated with softness. Certainly in the days of feather beds softness and warmth were considerations. But there is much to be said for the firm, level mattress that does not let the sleeper sink down deeply into it and that provides good support for the body. This type will buoy up the small of the back and will be apt to keep the spine in a straight line rather than a sagging one. Beds that are too soft often restrict the normal body movements of a sleeper; beds that are too hard do not permit perfect relaxation and often restrict circulation.

Health experts say that a mattress should be adjustable; that is, the mattress should adjust itself to various degrees of pressure from different parts of the body. The body should not be required to adjust itself to an unyielding mattress.

The filling is largely responsible for comfort and durability. Probably the inner-spring mattress retains its resiliency longest (with the exception of the foam rubber). In the inner-spring or polyurethane plastic foam mattress there are approximately 200 to 850 coil springs mounted in a steel-wire frame. This spring unit is contained between two layers of padding (generally cotton) and insulating materials consisting usually of fiber pads. All these units are encased in a ticking. The durability of the inner-spring mattress depends, in a large measure, on the quality of steel used in the springs. A large number of springs is not necessarily a measure of good performance. A smaller number of well-designed springs, suitably tied and combined with padding and insulation, should give comfort, firmness, and good performance.

The majority of these mattresses have their coil springs tied with twine, wire, or metal clips in a manner to permit individual springs to move independently up and down. This movement helps the mattress to conform to and support the human body. The most popular bedsprings are box springs, in which the springs are stapled to wooden slats that are tied together at the top and fastened to an outer frame. In good-grade mattresses the springs are wrapped in muslin to prevent the wear of friction and also to eliminate creaking.

Mattresses without inner springs are filled with horsehair, kapok, polyester batting, felted cotton, loose cotton, or foam rubber. South American horsehair is the most durable, most resilient, and most expensive. Cattle hair is considered next best to horsehair. Kapok is less resilient than horsehair but is well suited to damp climates, because it throws off moisture and dries quickly. Felt fillings of combed cotton felted into strips and laid in layers are slightly less resilient than kapok. Loose cotton, which is often used for inexpensive mattresses, becomes lumpy in time.

Ever since the 1940s, foam rubber mattresses have been used in homes and hospitals. They are simpler in construction than inner-spring mattresses—just a rectangular slab of foam encased in ticking. A foam rubber mattress conforms to the contour of the body and supports it at all points, even the small of the back. These mattresses are about half as heavy as inner springs and never should be turned. They are expensive, but they have the advantage of being nonallergenic and not unduly hot in summer or cold in winter. They do not mildew or harbor insects; there are no buttons or tufting. Since foam rubber tears easily, any moving of the mattress should be done by its cover, the ticking. Foam rubber should never be soaked to clean it. Removing the ticking and washing the rubber with a dampened cloth is sufficient. The mattress should not be exposed to the sun, because the ultraviolet light deteriorates it.

The plastic polyurethane foam mattress, which is light and less expensive than foam rubber, assures firm, healthful support. It is very light (only 15 pounds) compared with foam rubber or inner-spring mattresses. The homemaker can easily lift it.

The mattress covering or bag that holds the filling is called *ticking*. It comes in twill weave, with variations of herringbone and Jacquard, and less frequently in sateen and satin weaves.

The color of the covering may sell the mattress to the woman who must have a harmonious color scheme in her bedroom. Drill—a stout, medium-weight twilled cotton—and cotton and rayon mixed fabrics are used. A slightly undersized ticking is preferable with the foam rubber filler in order to keep the filler from spreading.

Tufting, a brushlike button of clipped cotton yarn, appears at regular intervals on some mattresses. These buttons, or tufts, are the ends of yarns that are drawn straight through the mattress to prevent the filling from slipping or becoming lumpy. In a good mattress, tufts are directly opposite each other on either side and are about twelve inches apart. Deep indentations at the point of tufting are noticeable. Tufts that are merely sewed on the surface of the ticking are found in the poorer grades of mattresses. Handles on either side of a mattress facilitate easy turning.

Air mattresses for station wagons and for camping are made of double-coated, rubberized woven nylon or cotton, often with built-in pillows. Also, they may be made of embossed vinyl plastic (nontextile), water-repellent poplin, or vinyl-plastic-coated cotton sheeting. Liners are cotton broadcloth, cotton flannel, or oxford. Sleeping bags may be filled with layers of polyester or goose down and polyester for insulation.

Another requisite of a good mattress if a firm edge that will hold its shape. Felted cotton used as the core of a cord stitched around the edge of the mattress insures firmness. Better grades may also have the sidewalls reinforced with filling and cloth stitched together. A selling point of the inner-spring variety is the small, screened, hole ventilator. The air drawn into the mattress every time weight is removed keeps it sanitary and prolongs its life. A cloth tape is frequently bonded to the foam rubber edges to add strength. A zipper or chain-stitched seam permits removal of ticking for cleaning.

A cover protects the mattress and also keeps sheets and blankets from soiling if the mattress is dusty. Mattress covers come in all mattress sizes. They are made of muslin (unbleached, printed, or in pastel shades), taffetized 100 percent vinyl plastic, cotton muslin bonded to foam rubber, and bleached white cotton quilted pads and polyester/cotton blends. The plastic-foam-filled quilted mattress pad is easy to care for, nonallergenic, mildewproof, and fire- and liquid-resistant, and it will not sag because it has a strong, elasticized tuck-under to prevent slipping. It may fit over the mattress with elasticized corners or around the entire mattress surface with a zippered or snapped closing.

Although mattress covers should not be used primarily to cover a dirty mattress, they can often be used to cover an old, faded one. Covers should be removed and laundered at regular intervals. At this time a thorough vacuum cleaning will help keep the mattress completely dry and will prolong its life. Vacuum cleaning is even more essential when covers are not used.

Pillows. The factors of comfort and durability considered in buying a mattress are also considered in purchasing pillows. Some people prefer loosely filled pillows in which the head sinks deeply; others feel smothered by a soft pillow and prefer a thin, hard one. But most people seem to prefer a soft, plump one that is very resilient and light in weight.

The kind of filling used determines the comfort, wearing quality, and price. Fillings may be graded in order of excellence, beginning with the best: (1) down from the breasts of geese or ducks, (2) goose feathers, (3) duck feathers, (4) kapok, (5) fine chicken and turkey feathers, (6) mixed feathers, (7) acrylic or polyester staple fibers, and (8) foam rubber.

Of the feathers, white ones are considered best because they are apt to be finer, softer, and lighter in weight than dark ones. Down from the breasts of geese or ducks is very light, soft, spineless, and resilient. A pillow plumply stuffed with crushed goose down is a real sleep inducer. It is most expensive, however. Goose or duck feathers with quills are heavier and less resilient than down. They can be felt through the pillow casing if it is not of close construction. Turkey and hen feathers are about twice as heavy as down and are stiffer, less soft, and less buoyant. Different kinds of feathers may be mixed in the same pillow. Hen feathers are comparatively inexpensive but, like goose and duck feathers, they may come through the casing if it is not sufficiently close in weave.

Kapok and foam rubber are real boons to sufferers from asthma or hay fever. Feathers often irritate people with these diseases, whereas kapok (a vegetable fiber) or foam rubber does not. Kapok is also suitable for pillows used at the seashore, since it does not feel damp quickly, and, if it becomes wet, it dries in a short time. Cushions for canoes, cruisers, and yachts are satisfactory when stuffed with kapok, because if they fall into the water they float. Kapok-filled pillows are inexpensive, but they mat or become lumpy in time.

Synthetic staple fiber fill is nonallergenic, buoyant, odorless, and moth- and mildewproof. Better qualities of bed pillows are covered with tightly woven ticking in floral, stripes, or all-over printed patterns. Medium and poorer covers are made of percale. Any cover should be closely woven and seamed, so that stuffing does not come through. Corded edges make for durability. Separate zippered pillow protectors can be purchased to protect covers.

Foam latex pillows are springy and durable, cool for the summer months, and nonallergenic. Urethane foam is a synthetic material available in one piece or chopped form.

The following list should serve as a guide in buying pillows:[6]

1. Balance the pillow on the hands. The lighter pillow is the better choice.
2. Press both hands into the center of the pillow. When the hands are lifted, the pillow should spring back.

[6] Anne Sterling, *Buying and Care of Pillows.* American Institute of Laundering, Joliet, Ill. Merchandise bearing the seal of this organization has passed extensive tests for washability and wear.

3. Hold one end of the pillow and shake it vigorously. Filling should not shift easily and pack at one end.[7]
4. Pound the pillow with the fist to see if dust emerges or lumps appear. These are undesirable features.
5. Sniff the pillow for odor. If there is odor, do not buy it.
6. Notice whether the cover is closely woven and seams are welted for durability.

A few suggestions for the care of pillows follow: [8]

1. All rips and tears in a pillow ticking should be repaired immediately to prevent loss of filling.
2. All pillows should be cleaned after an illness.
3. Should a pillow sag when placed over one's arm, it needs cleaning and professional renovation.
4. Soiled tickings soil pillowcases. The use of a washable, zippered pillow cover is suggested.

BLANKETS

Blankets, like sheets, are an essential item of bed covering. Although blankets are purchased less frequently than sheets, the consumer is just as anxious to get her money's worth when she does buy.

Blankets may be made of 100 percent wool, cotton, rayon, acrylic, nylon, and polyester fibers, or blends of these with other man-made fibers. Wool and cotton, longtime blanket fabrics, now meet competition from the man-made fibers and blends. In 1967 an all-Dacron polyester unnapped Fiberwoven blanket appeared in Chatham Manufacturing Company's line followed by West Point-Pepperell's nylon flocked polyurethane core blanket in the late 1960s.[9]

A polyester blend or 100 percent Sanforized cotton in flat or fitted styles is commonly used for the dual-purpose sheet blanket.

The following points will guide the consumer in buying a blanket.

Warmth. The weight of a blanket is not a true indication of its warmth. Blankets average three to five pounds in weight, but very lightweight wool blankets may be just as warm as, or warmer than, heavy, tightly woven felted ones. The lighter the blanket, the more comfortable it is as a bed covering. The warmth of a blanket is determined largely by its thickness and nap, not by weight and fiber content. Since a closely napped cloth traps more still air than an unnapped cloth, it should be warmer. Pockets of still air act as insulation against cold air.

---

[7] According to Cameron A. Baker (research director of Better Fabrics Testing Bureau, New York), pillows properly selected don't need to be punched and tucked under for individual comfort. He has developed a device to measure filling materials, which enables a manufacturer to standardize production methods with the result that gives consumers the degree of firmness or resiliency they prefer. It is possible that performance evaluation will appear on a tag or label. The best fillers, according to Mr. Baker, are Polish goose down and Taiwan duck down (both expensive). Other fillers include chicken and turkey feathers, solid and shredded foams and rubber, man-made fibers, cotton batting, and kapok. From *Consumer Bulletin* (January 1969).

[8] Sterling, *Pillows*.

[9] Fiberwoven is the registered trade name of a process that converts fiber into fabric, thus eliminating yarn-making and weaving.

Loosely twisted filling yarns can be more successfully napped than tightly twisted yarns. The amount of twist in the filling yarns is a factor in warmth. To improve the napping of a cloth without jeopardizing durability, the core of the filling yarn may be tightly spun and the fibers then twisted loosely about the core. Cotton blankets may feel damper and therefore colder than wool if they are used in damp climates, especially at the seashore. Cotton holds moisture on the surface and therefore feels damp more quickly than wool, which can absorb much moisture before it begins to feel wet.

After several washings cotton blankets may shrink or felt to such an extent that they feel heavy, but they are no warmer than they were at first. A "pouflike" finish can be applied to blankets of 100 percent Acrilan acrylic, rayon, and blends in order to keep them from shedding, pilling, and matting. It is claimed that softness and loft are retained after repeated washings.[10]

If one is looking for a very lightweight, durable, lint-free covering, then a thermal-weave blanket should be considered. Many of these blankets are full of holes and look like the afghans of Grandma's day.

FIGURE 19.11. Thermal blanket fabric of acrylic fiber in leno weave. (Photo by Jonas Grushkin.)

In winter, a cover is placed on top of the blanket so that air warmed by body heat is trapped between the yarns. In summer, the cover is omitted and body heat is permitted to escape through tiny "air cells." Consumers' Research tests revealed that the thermal weave blankets with a cover were not as warm as a heavy wool blanket (4½ pounds). All the thermal-weave blankets tested with a cover were as warm as, or warmer than, a lightweight (2½ pounds) acrylic blanket.[11] Furthermore, all the thermal-weave blankets without a cover were cooler than the woven wool blanket, but only five of the nine brands tested were cooler than the woven acrylic blanket. In this CR study, the napped blankets lost lint in laundering, but not enough to affect their original weight. Blankets were rated good to fair after three launderings. Some of these thermal weaves are known to withstand 200 launderings.

Attractiveness. Color, design, and the finishing of the edges make for attractiveness. Blankets are made in solid colors, plain white, plaid,

[10] This protective finish is Nap-Guard, by West Point-Pepperell, Inc. and Neva-Shed by Fieldcrest Mills, Inc.

[11] *Consumer Bulletin* (December 1965).

checks, novelty color combinations, and with colored borders. If a blanket is to be used as an extra "throw" (folded on the bed during the day), the color selected should harmonize with the furnishings in the room. Even if blankets are covered by a bedspread, the color-conscious consumer will want the colors in blankets to be harmonious. The edges of blankets may be whipped (a kind of scalloped machine embroidery), or bound with cotton, acetate, or nylon bindings.

Blankets with a soft texture are usually the most attractive. If wool fibers are fine, of sufficiently long staple, and smooth, the blanket is sure to be soft. Acrylic fibers have an almost cashmere-like softness, while some of the newer flocked blankets have velvety suedelike textures.

Durability. Whether a blanket is wool, cotton, acrylic, rayon, or a blend, certain factors are important in judging the wearing quality:

1. *Length of the fibers.* Long fibers do not pull out or slip so readily as short fibers. If fibers are too short, they often pull out in the napping process, thereby weakening the yarn. The quality of the fibers is also important.

2. *Tensile strength of the fibers.* If fibers in a yarn are weak, the yarn is correspondingly weak. Therefore the first requisites for a long-wearing blanket are good-quality fibers sufficiently long and strong to make strong yarns.

3. *Tensile strength of yarns.* It is particularly important that warps have sufficient strength to withstand the tension in the loom and also to bear the weight of water in washing. Fillings are generally spun more loosely than the warps in order that fibers may be brushed up for the nap. Some manufacturers, however, sacrifice durability for appearance by spinning fillings too loosely and by making too thick a nap. Ply yarns usually have greater tensile strength than single yarns and so are often used for warp.

4. *Construction.* This factor depends upon the balanced strength of warp and filling—that is, a balanced count together with firm, even weaving. In considering the proportionate strength of warp to filling, it should be understood that the warp must be stronger than the filling in order to withstand the friction and tension of the loom. But if fillings are spun too loosely, they may be proportionately so much weaker than the warps that the blanket may split or shred when it is washed. This shredding occurs when strong cotton warps are used with short-staple filling fibers made of slack-twisted yarn. A well-balanced count insures an even distribution of warps and fillings, and longer wear. Most blankets for home use are twill or a variation of the twill. This construction throws more filling to the surface for the purpose of napping.

One of the best ways to test the uniformity of the weave is to hold the blanket to a strong light. Thick and thin spots indicate poor construction. If there is a border, the weave should be the same in the border as in the rest of the blanket. A difference in closeness of the weave in the border may result in ripples or puckers after laundering.

When the blanket is held toward the light, one can see whether it has been cut straight. The ends of the blanket should run parallel to the filling yarns.

A process of tufting blankets has been developed that may, in time, compete costwise with woven blankets. (For tufted bedspreads, see *tufted fabric*, Glossary, Chapter 19. For tufted rugs, see Chapter 20.)

Nonwoven constructions are later innovations in blankets. One process, called Fiberwoven, converts fiber directly into fabric. Invented by Dr. Alexander Smith, a former professor at the Massachusetts Institute of Technology, the process is conducted by interlocking many loops of fibers, shaped or entangled by fast-moving rows of barbed needles. Blankets so constructed are claimed to be warm and strong, to shrink less, and to last longer than commercially woven blankets.

One nonwoven blanket is produced by West Point-Pepperell, Inc., under a patented process called "Vellux." The blanket is built around an inner core of man-made foam that has special thermal qualities that trap warmth despite the lightness of the fabric. Nylon fiber is electrostatically bonded permanently to both sides of the core. The fabric is claimed to be soft, warm, lightweight, velvety, and luxurious. It will not shrink when laundered and is very durable; it is moth-resistant; it comes in solid colors and prints; and it can be reversed. Carved dimensional effects are available in a luxury blanket.

5. *Amount of nap raised.* As has been stated, a heavy nap of short fibers pulled out from loosely twisted yarn decreases durability. If filling yarns have sufficient tensile strength and fibers are long, a moderate nap makes a blanket attractive and warm and does not affect durability. To determine the durability of the nap, rub the surface of the blanket. If little balls of fiber roll up, the nap is made of too-short fibers, and the blanket will lose its warmth. Nap should be uniform in thickness and in coverage of the surface. Another way to test the durability of the nap is to take a pinch of it between the thumb and forefinger and lift the blanket slightly. If the nap does not pull out, the fibers are long and well anchored in the yarn.

6. *Bindings and finishes of the ends.* These should be neat and strong. Bindings should be eased onto the edge of a blanket and should be firmly stitched with two or three rows of parallel stitching or with close featherstitching. Some blanket corners fit closely like fitted sheets. Nylon makes a durable binding. Rayon and acetate are very attractive but have to be replaced sooner than nylon. Cotton sateen is inexpensive and usually wears well.

AUTOMATIC BLANKETS

When a person is asleep, he or she is unable to adjust to the loss of body heat by putting on more blankets, changing the room temperature, or exercising. Accordingly, uniform sleeping comfort can best be provided by an automatic blanket. There are three kinds: the thermostat blanket, the automatic sheet, and the solid-state blanket.

1. The thermostat blanket consists of four units:
   (a) the blanket unit that has a fabric woven so as to provide many small lengthwise channels. A network of parallel heating wires are shuttled through these channels. The wires terminate in a male plug at the bottom of the blanket. Double-bed blankets may be provided with dual controls to heat each side separately.

(b) A heater element consisting of conductor wires around a fiber core of polyester yarn. The core and wires are insulated and protected with vinyl plastic.

(c) A number of protective thermostats to prevent overheating. Even with excess folding or bunching, at least one or two of the elements will operate.

(d) A control unit that maintains the desired temperature, which is set manually by operating a dial. Somewhat like a home furnace control, a heater coil accentuates a bimetal switch.

2. The automatic sheet is similar in operation to the thermostat blanket, but it is lighter and the wires are not set in channels in the fabric, but rather are covered with tapes sewn to the sheet. These take less wattage than the blankets, yet with average room temperature provide adequate heat.

3. The solid-state blanket differs from the thermostat blanket in that electronic components modulate the energy, somewhat as a light dimmer switch does. It substitutes precise electronic elements for the manually adjusted bimetal switch. This assembly eliminates bimetal clicking and produces more uniform temperature than the thermostat.

COMFORTERS

Comforters are stuffed or quilted bed coverings. In parts of New England, a soft, lightweight, very resilient comforter is called a *puff*.

A consumer may be attracted to a beautiful brocaded satin comforter; the covering is all that she knows or cares about. It will look attractive in her room; her friends will admire it; so she buys it. But, although the covering is an important consideration, this customer has neglected a vital factor from the standpoint of comfort and wear—the filling. Just as in mattresses and pillows, the filling can make the comforter light or heavy, soft or hard, resilient or not. No one wants to be weighed down with heavy bed coverings that are hard and possibly lumpy. Heaviness does not necessarily make the comforter warm, for a resilient comforter, like a blanket, enmeshes air to retain warmth.

To test the amount of resiliency or buoyancy of a comforter, put one hand on the top and the other hand on the bottom of the comforter and press them together. Note how much it can be compressed and how fast it returns to its original shape. If it does not spring back to shape, there is a good chance of its becoming bunchy and misshapen in a comparatively short time when in use. If two comforters of the same thickness are compared, one may compress greatly and spring back quickly, whereas the other may compress very little and return to shape slowly. The former is usually the lighter in weight and will retain its resilience longer while in use.

Fillings. Fillings for comforters can be made of cotton, acetate and cotton, wool, down, feathers, acrylic, and polyester fibers. Long-staple cotton of good grade is resilient and wears well. Short-staple cotton, a coarser and poorer grade than the long-staple, is the second-best type of cotton filling. Short fibers, because they do not cling together as well as long ones, lump or bunch more readily. Cotton linters are poor because they do not have sufficient resiliency. Excellent grades of cotton are superior to poor grades of wool.

Fine, long-staple Australian wool makes a soft filling. The first shearing from the lamb is particularly fine and soft. The better-grade fillings are made of carefully scoured and carded wool. Poorer grades are grayish in

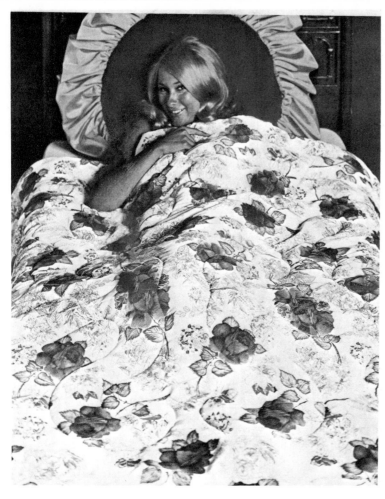

FIGURE 19.12. A light-weight comforter of acetate with polyester fiber fill that will not become matted down.

color, poorly scoured, poorly carded, and less soft. Often poor scouring leaves burrs and foreign substances in the filling, which in time may work their way through the covering of the comforter. Short ends removed from the sliver in the carding of wool are often used for poor-grade fillings. These short fibers are wool waste and are often coarse. Reused wool may also be used. As with cotton, long, well-carded fibers are necessary if a filling is to cling together and not lump.

Down and feathers are also used for filling. The former is the softest, lightest, most expensive filling. It is very resilient and warm. Down from the breast of the goose or duck is good, but down from a large sea duck, the eider, is even better. As a substitute for down, chopped chicken feathers are often used. But despite careful chopping, the quills can usually be felt if the comforter is pressed from above and below. Quills may work their way through a covering and shorten the life of the comforter. To prevent this, a covering should be closely woven, or two thicknesses of covering should be used. Man-made fibers are being used in comforters to replace down. The fiber fills of acrylics or polyesters are moderately priced, allergy-free, snow white, mildewproof, odorless. Their resiliency has been greatly improved.

Coverings. Comforter coverings should be soft and pliable, with good draping qualities; that is, they should cling to the other coverings on the bed and not look too bulky. A stiff, harsh material makes a cover that is hard to quilt—that is, to sew in a pattern or design. Corners may also appear bulky if the covering is too stiff.

Some fabrics slip easily, and no matter how well they are tucked in they do not seem to adhere to the bed. Rayons made in long-float satin weave have this undesirable characteristic. In fact, any satin of silk, acetate, or rayon will slip more than a fabric with a ribbed or dull surface. A closely woven nylon taffeta is both attractive and durable, but it too may slip. A fabric made of tightly twisted yarns in a firm weave is best. Brocaded satins are luxurious in appearance and adhere better than plain satins. Sateen and polished cotton are both practical and less expensive. Cotton corduroy and percale can also be used for less expensive coverings. A wrinkle-resistant fabric is desirable for a covering. If washable, a durable press fabric is desirable.

Coverings should be made with finishes permanent enough to dry clean or launder. A homemaker should save and follow instructions for care given on the attached label.

Quilts. Quilts are thinner and less expensive than comforters. Antique patchwork quilts, pieced by hand, in some instances are works of art. Artistic, well-made ones are collectors' items and, if in good condition, are expensive. Favorite designs were the star, wedding ring, or conventionalized florals. Frequently the maker made her own designs. She cut her own pieces, sewed them together in blocks or motifs, and sewed the blocks together to form the top covering of the quilt. Generally these covers were bright-colored solid or printed cottons, occasionally silk. When the covering was finished, a fabric the exact size for the back was cut and made ready for the next step, quilting. Cotton batting was placed between the covering and the backing. Then great-great-grandma was ready for her quilting party. Friends came in for the afternoon to help her sew the three layers (cover, batting, and back) together. Geometric or floral patterns were made with fine quilting stitches. Quilting was done on a frame to keep the fabrics smooth and in shape. The edges of the fabric were bound with bias-cut strips of cloth.

There are no standard sizes for antique patchwork quilts. Size was governed by the size of the bed to be covered and by the pieces of fabric available for the purpose.

Designs of modern patchwork quilts are frequently copies of old designs. Modern quilts may not have the sentiment connected with the old quilts, but their colors are faster. The machine stitching makes them firm, yet gives the homemade effect. Some so-called patchwork quilts have covers made of one piece of cloth printed to resemble small pieces sewed together. They are quilted or tufted. This type of quilt is quite inexpensive. Filling may be cotton or polyester.

Modern cotton patchwork quilts can be laundered at home or can be sent to the laundry. Antique quilts should be dry-cleaned, because there is no assurance of the fastness of the colors. Furthermore, the fabric may have tendered with age.

BEDSPREADS

One who is beginning to furnish a new home decides what type each room is to be—formal or informal—and what period or periods are most appropriate to each room. She usually buys large pieces of furniture first. The accessories, such as bedding, curtains, and pillows, come next. Although the average consumer may not think of style or appearance first when she buys pillows or a mattress for a bed, appearance is the first consideration in purchasing a bedspread. The intelligent buyer tries to visualize the bedspread in its intended setting. She asks herself, "Will it harmonize with my curtains, rugs, and upholstered chairs?" Fortunate is the woman who has this power of visualization.

Principles of Selection. A few simple principles will guide the consumer in the selection of bedspreads:

1. Materials should be of a texture that will not wrinkle or crush easily. This is particularly important when beds are to be used as seats during the day.

2. Materials should be cleanable by automatic washing or dry cleaning. Preshrunk fabrics that require no ironing are desirable.

3. The spread should be large enough for the bed. If pillows are to be covered so that they give the effect of a bolster, the length should be 105 or 108 inches. The sizes (without flounce ruffles) stocked in stores are shown in Table 19-5.

TABLE 19-5. Sizes of Bedspreads

Type of Bed	Size of Spread (inches)
Bunk	63 X 100
Twin	76 X 105, 79 X 108
Double	88 X 105, 96 X 108
Queen size	102 X 120
King size	120 X 120

4. The spread should be cut and sewed so that it has a trim appearance, whether tailored or boxlike. Flat spreads often have rounded corners. A spread of heavy material generally fits better if the corners are cut out for a fourposter bed. It is not so important to cut out corners if the material is light. Split corners and corner inserts help to give a good fit.

5. In tailored spreads, double interlocked seams and cord welt edges ensure serviceability. Matching the bedspread with draperies, upholstered chairs, or cushions makes a pleasing effect, provided the colors do not become monotonous. The modern homemaker considers the design as well as the function of bedroom and bathroom, and she chooses her draperies, curtains, bedspread, blankets, sheets, towels, and accessories accordingly. Cooperation of manufacturers in ensembling their related products makes shopping quick and easy.

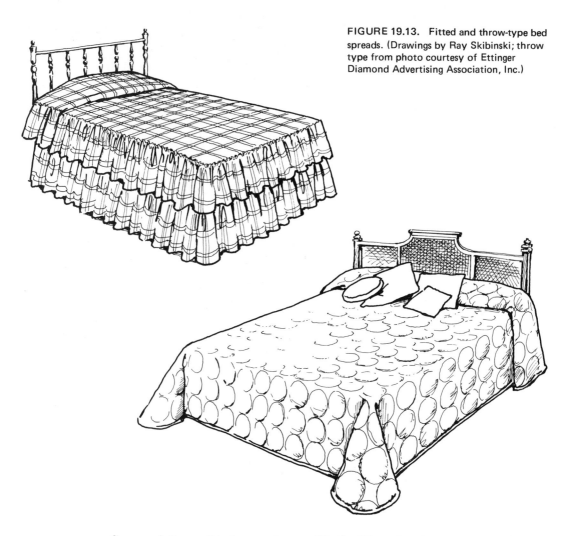

FIGURE 19.13. Fitted and throw-type bed spreads. (Drawings by Ray Skibinski; throw type from photo courtesy of Ettinger Diamond Advertising Association, Inc.)

Some of the quilted spreads are filled with polyester or acetate fibers.

Flounce ruffles, pillow shams, and draperies may be made of the same fabric as the spreads. These items can be purchased separately as well as in ensembles.

The following fabrics are used for bedspreads:

Washable corduroy
Loop woven cotton Jacquards with
  knotted fringe
Candlewick (cotton)
Broadcloth (cotton/polyester)*
Chenille (cotton, rayon)
Embroidered fabrics
Polished cotton*
Regular sheeting fabric

Cotton sailcloth
Quilted rayon, acetate, nylon
Textured cotton and blends
Tufted cotton (see Glossary)
Embossed cotton*
Crocheted lace
Taffeta (rayon, acetate, nylon)
Elaborate Jacquards (Old World look)

*Particularly well suited for children's spreads.

509

FIGURE 19.14. A cover-
let in authentic patchwork
quilt design.

SUMMARY   Bed coverings, towels, and table coverings are a very important part of home furnishings. Now that dyes are fast, printing more attractive, and woven designs more varied, fashion has really entered the domestic field. Some department stores feature ensembles for the bathroom in a special department, or bath shop. In short, a consumer should give as much consideration to the assembling of bed and table coverings and towels as she does to the buying of her personal wardrobe. Care in selection and proper care in use insure the durability and long life of domestics.

PROJECTS   1. Plan a color-coordinated ensemble for a bathroom that has one window, beige tile walls, pink fixtures and red wall-to-wall carpeting.
    (a) List all the household textiles you will need in this room for a family of two adults and two children (aged four and six).
    (b) Include the names of each fabric, its size, color, and design.
    (c) In a few paragraphs, give the reasons for your choices.
    2. Plan the household textiles of either a college girl's or a college boy's bedroom.
    (a) Accurately describe or draw a floor plan of the room.
    (b) Accurately describe fabric or include swatches of fabric that you would suggest for bedspread, curtains or draperies, and accessories.
    (c) Draw or accurately describe the style and size of each item.
    (d) In a few short paragraphs, give the reasons for your choices.
    3. Plan a table setting for a Sunday dinner for a family of two adults and four children of high school and college age.
    (a) Describe the table covering and napkins with regard to fabric name, texture, size, color, and price.
    (b) List and describe the household textiles used for the occasion.

4. (a) Make a count of colors, sizes, and prices of terry cloth bath towels sold in three retail stores.
   (b) Tabulate the results of your findings.
   (c) Analyze your data, and come to some conclusions as to how well these stores are meeting customer demand in the community.

GLOSSARY Bath rug—Usually a comparatively small rug with cotton, rayon, or nylon pile suitable for a bathroom.

Bed linen—Any cotton, linen, or nylon sheeting for use on a bed.

Blanketing—A heavily napped fabric of wool, cotton, or man-made fibers in blends or mixtures, woven 60 or 80 inches or more in size in plain or twill weave.

Bolster—A long, rectangular pillow the width of the bed.

Candlewick—See *Tufted fabric.*

Cheesecloth—A sheer, very low count, slackly twisted, carded cotton fabric.

Chenille—See *Tufted fabric.*

Chintz—See Chapter 21.

Comfortable—Synonym for *comforter.*

Comforter—A quilted bed covering made with a layer of stuffing between two fabrics of taffeta, brocaded satin, sateen, or printed muslin.

Contour sheets—See *fitted sheets.*

Crash—A linen, cotton, or mixture suitable for dish, glass, and kitchen towels. Better grades may be used for luncheon sets, doilies, and bureau scarfs. See Glossary, Chapter 17.

Cretonne—See Glossary, Chapter 21.

Crocheted lace—For bedspread or table cover. See *Lace.*

Damask—A fabric for table cloth and napkins in Jacquard weave. The pattern is reversible. Linen, cotton, rayon, or a combination of fibers are made in double or single damask.

Dimity—See Glossary, Chapter 17.

Domestics—A classification of textile merchandise that includes towels, table covers, and all bed coverings.

Embroidery—Ornamental needlework done on the fabric itself.

Felt—Used for table covers. See Chapter 12.

Fitted sheets—Those whose corners are made to fit the mattress. Both bottom and top fitted sheets are available.

Gingham—Used for bedspreads. See Glossary, Chapter 17.

Glass towels—Towels made of linen crash, cotton, or mixtures suitable for drying glasses because they are lint free.

Guest towels or finger-tip towels—Lightweight and smaller than hand towels. They are made of lightweight linen crash, huck, damask, terry, in white, solids, and designs.

Huck towels—Cotton, linen, or mixtures, occasionally with rayon in honeycomb dobby weave. They may have Jacquard borders. Face or hand towels in white or colors are made.

Lace—A fabric created by looping, interlacing, braiding, or twisting threads.

Longcloth—Synonym for *muslin sheeting.*

Muslin—See Glossary, Chapter 17.

Muslin sheeting—A carded muslin for bed sheets in white or colors made in types 140 (A grade), 128 (B grade), and 112 (C grade).

Patchwork quilts—Made of small pieces of cotton or silk fabric cut in various shapes and sewn together to form patterns. They are quilted on a frame when done by hand. Modern patchwork quilts may be printed to resemble the hand-sewn.

Percale sheeting—A combed muslin (may be carded in poorer grade) for bed sheets, in white or colors, made in type 200 (A grade) and 180 (B grade). See *Percale* for dresses, Glossary, Chapter 17.

Pickage—The number of fillings that pass between two rows of pile yarns plus the number of fillings under the pile loops. Two fillings shot through the same pile shed and one filling shot through to interlace with the ground warps (2 + 1) equals 3 picks.

Plastic-coated fabric—Used for shower curtains and dress covers. It is a plastic film supported by fabric or coating covering a textile fabric. See Chapter 6.

Puff—Synonym for a resilient comforter.

Quilt—A bed covering, usually thinner and less resilient than a comforter, made of two thicknesses of printed cotton muslin with cotton, wool, or polyester batting between. Fabrics and batting are sewn together with fine quilting (running) stitches.

Seersucker—Used for bedspreads. See Glossary, Chapter 17.

Silence cloth—A padding placed under the tablecloth on a dining table.

Table linen—Any fabric, regardless of fiber content, that is suitable for a table covering.

Taffeta—Used for bedspreads and shower curtains. See Glossary, Chapter 17.

Tapestry—Used for table covers. See Glossary, Chapter 21.

Terry cloth—A cotton pile fabric commonly made with uncut or cut loops on one or both sides of the fabric. It may have linen pile in a "friction" towel. It is used for bath and face towels, face cloths, bath rugs and beach robes. See Chapter 10.

Thermal woven—A porous cloth so constructed that air warmed by the body is trapped between the yarns. First used in underwear, now also used for blankets and the reverse sides of comforters.

Thread—In towels (double or single). In double thread, each loop is made of two parallel threads not twisted together, and these threads come out of the same space between two fillings. Single thread is made of a single yarn and is less durable and absorbent.

Ticking—A heavy, tightly woven carded cotton fabric in alternate stripes of white and colors, suitable for pillow and mattress covers. It is usually twill but may be sateen weave.

Tufted fabric—A fabric ornamented with soft, fluffy, slackly twisted ply yarns (usually cotton). Most tufts are inserted by needles into a woven fabric like unbleached muslin, textured cotton, and rayon plain-weave cloth. When tufts are spaced (as coin dots), the bedspread is called *candlewick*; when placed in close rows, the fabric is *chenille*. "Loom tufted" means tufts woven in as the cloth is woven. Tufted fabrics are used for bedspreads, mats, and robes. See *Rugs*, Chapter 20.

Tufting—A brushlike button of clipped cotton yarn that appears at regular intervals on mattresses.

Turkish towel—A bath towel, face towel, or washcloth made of terry cloth.

Unbleached muslin—A cotton plain-weave fabric used for ironing board covers, dust covers, and dustcloths. See Glossary, Chapter 17.

Period Styles in Home Furnishings and in Rugs

20

If a room is to be newly furnished, decide what sort of atmosphere you wish to create—formal or informal. Consideration should also be given to the various roles the room will assume in the life of the family.

CREATING AN ATMOS- PHERE The living room is what the name implies—a place to live. It should be warm, comfortable, and hospitable—an appropriate background for entertaining guests or for normal household life.

Rooms that are used less frequently may be a little bold or dramatic. Foyers, halls, and dining rooms come under this description. A bedroom should be serene and restrained; a child's room, restful but bright; a dinette, inviting and cheerful; a kitchen, efficient and colorful.

In decorating, it is helpful to be familiar with period furnishings, not to reproduce exactly the era desired, but rather to convey the spirit of the period while designing a room that is appropriate to its particular purpose and up-to-date in comfort and style. Different periods of furniture can be used together effectively. This avoids the monotony of everything looking alike and endows the room with the unique personality of the homeowner. An occasional traditional piece mixed with modern furniture lends warmth and a sense of heritage. Oriental antiques or reproductions mingled with contemporary furnishings suggest sophistication and elegance. This juxtaposition of styles calls for taste refined by exposure to a variety of settings. In choosing to mix periods, the combined styles should have some similarity or they should be very different. This eclectic decorating trend has no hard and fast rules, but rather, pieces are selected to complement each other, to soften hard modern lines, to dramatize beauty or individuality, and to offset and differentiate the ordinary.

The use of the room must be considered in the light of the kind of atmosphere the owner wishes to create: formal or informal, elaborate or simple. There are a few other points to be considered, however.

Massive furniture makes a small room seem smaller, whereas a few pieces of small furniture and small designs make a small room seem more spacious than it really is. In short, furniture and designs should be in proportion to the size of the room. (See Chapter 21 for other factors in creating a harmonious ensemble.)

An awareness of the history of furniture and an appreciation of design ingenuity and craftsmanship will pay dividends in the perceptive selection and enjoyment of such furnishings. Although furniture is not a textile, and so does not technically come within the scope of this book, it is helpful to be able to recognize the most common styles in order to select appropriate fabrics for draperies, upholsteries, and rugs.

PERIOD FURNITURE AND DESIGN

There are many long-standing styles in furniture and home furnishings that are in use today: Italian, Spanish, French, English, American, Modern, Contemporary, and Oriental. If all decorators do not agree to such a general classification, each style group may be subdivided into periods named for the king, queen, or cabinetmaker whose style in furnishings typified those times. See Appendix E for appropriate period styles in woods, rugs, upholstery, and drapery fabrics.

ITALIAN STYLE

Large, massive furniture ornately carved—with vivid, striking designs in upholstery, hangings, and draperies—is characteristic of the Italian style in general. Luxury and magnificence controlled the furnishings and the fabric decorations in the days of Italy's grandeur. The Italian Renaissance (1400-1643) marked the revival of the classic arts.

Woods used for the furniture were dark finish with geometric carvings. The designs in fabrics were large, raised, and impressive, consisting of flowers in vases or baskets, or the fluorescent artichoke or pineapple motifs, and clusters of round dots. Brocades, damasks, velvets, and velours are all suited to the Italian style. Fabric colors were dark green, burgundy, cream, and gold.

This style requires large, preferably formal, rooms. An upholstered sofa and a Jacobean chair would harmonize with the Italian style, for these pieces have a quality of massiveness. Venetian style favored painted finishes and mirrored walls. Decorative fringes were used.

SPANISH STYLE

The days of Queen Isabella, Columbus, and the Invincible Armada (1451-1504) are reproduced in the Spanish decoration of today. Designs are large, bold in outline, and often a combination of the Moorish and the Italian. Like the Italian, Spanish interiors should be spacious, since furniture and designs tend to be large, striking, and imposing. Adaptations of ship designs and appropriate white scrolls and motifs similar to the Italian types are used. Fabrics suitable for a Spanish-style room include leathers, damasks, and velvets. Fringes and nailheads frequently serve as decorative elements. For an informal room, printed linens or coarse cottons in colorful stripes or Spanish motifs are suitable. Off-white walls with green and/or orange furnishings are often seen.

FRENCH STYLES

The accepted French periods of decoration are: French Renaissance (latter half of the fifteenth century); Louis XIV (1643-1715); Louis XV (1723-74); Louis XVI (1774-93), Directoire (1795-99), and Empire (1804-25).

FIGURE 20.1. a. An ornate lampas, which is a silk, rayon, cotton, wool, or mixed-fiber fabric similar to satin damask. Lampas has two sets of warps and one filling. The heraldic influence is seen in the architectural motifs consisting of castles. Italy, early 16th Century.

FIGURE 20.1 (cont.). b. A modern composite American design based mostly upon the Italian Renaissance. Note the parapeted castle treated in the modern manner by placing it on the bias and forgetting all the rules of gravitation. The slender, needle-like tower is inspired from the "Trylon," the theme motif of the New York World's Fair. The ever-popular tulip motif has been utilized together with stylized Persian cone motifs. (Photos courtesy The Scalamandré Museum of Textiles.)

French Renaissance. The Renaissance was an intellectual movement with a revival in the arts. It marked the transition from medieval to modern times. In Italy, Renaissance architecture and art succeeded the Gothic, and spread to France during the latter half of the fifteenth century. It was expressed in great castles, such as Chambord and Fontainebleau, and in the interior decorations French furniture showed a marked Italian influence.

Louis XIV. So far as the cultivation of the arts is concerned, the Grand Monarch, Louis XIV, is the most important of the French kings. Furniture of the time was in a grand style called *baroque*. Massive and

515

symmetrical, the woods were carved, gilded, inlaid with tortoise shell or metals, and ornamented with marquetry.

During the reign of Louis XIV, renewed interest was taken in the arts and fabric weaving. The silk industry at Lyons flourished under the patronage of the king, and France became a producer of fine fabrics. French brocades and damasks were known for their fine quality throughout Europe. Probably the artistic interest of Louis XIV was fired by the woman whom he was courting, Louise de la Valliére, the woman who had called his hunting lodge crude and bare. In reply to this jibe. Louis built the palace of Versailles.

Louis himself loved brillance and so was often called *le roi soleil*—the Sun King. He preferred very large designs, such as flowers in baskets, immense fleurs de lis, feather and flower motifs. Rich colors borrowed from Italy—dark red, blue, dark green, and old gold—were his favorites. But a woman's choice again influenced color preference, and new, delicate colors such as yellowish pink (called aurora), plum, yellow, and flame appeared.

In the French furniture of this period, flat, boxlike lines of the sixteenth century were replaced by framework with rounded contours, characterized by much ornamentation, such as elaborate scrolls, engraved white metal ornaments, inlays of tortoise shell, and mountings in bronze. André Charles Boulle (1642-1732) was the outstanding furniture maker of the time.

Louis XV. During the reign of Louis XV, the king's favorites, Madame Du Barry and Madame Pompadour, were responsible for the ornamentation characteristic of all decorating of this period. Early Louis XV was called *regence* and was based on symmetrical patterns. Guilded wood continued to be used a great deal, and the Chinese influence began to show itself in imitations of Chinese lacquer for commodes, bookcases, and cabinets. There were *bambé* (convex) fronts and sides on cabinets and chests. Many more pieces of small-in-scale furniture were used in this period, and fabric decoration favored realistic flowers, scrolls, and chinoiseries. Beauvais tapestry was frequently used for upholstering fine sofas and chairs. Later Louis XV, called *rococo*, was extravagant in detail—not balanced or symmetrical. The two famous furniture makers of this period, who continued to be famous during the reign of Louis XVI, were Jean Riesener (1734-1806) and David Roentgen (1743-1807).

Louis XVI. The reign of Louis XVI is marked by less ornate design, more delicate and refined treatment. Designs of this period were copied from furniture and murals excavated at Pompeii and Herculaneum. The lines of Louis XVI furniture and designs are straight and right angles. Chair legs are usually straight and fluted longitudinally like columns, tapering to the base. Ornamentation was of classical Greek influence and was used to emphasize beauty of line.

Marie Antoinette, wife of Louis XVI, was interested in a rural life. Pastoral scenes, interlocked rings, musical instruments, turtle doves, bowknots, and gardeners' tools were popular motifs for upholstery and hangings. Bows of ribbon often surmounted furniture panels and chair backs. Brocade, satin, damask, and *toile de Jouy* prints were common upholstery coverings and draperies. More background and less design is shown in this period. The Jouy prints were the first roller prints (made by direct printing) and became so much the vogue that they rivaled the brocades of Lyons.

The Directoire Period. This era was a transition in design from Louis XVI to Empire. Napoleon emerged as the central figure after the French Revolution ended the monarchy. He admired Rome and so had the French palace redecorated in formal styles. The bee and the butterfly were his symbols. Designs were rich in color and perfectly balanced. Motifs were classical, from Roman influence and the Egyptian campaign. Stripes, medallions, cornucopias, circles, and squares were typical designs. Napoleon preferred golden yellow, red, and green; his wife, Josephine, liked pale blue, white, yellow, mauve, and gray. Woods commonly used in furniture were ebony, mahogany, and satinwood. For upholstery, heavy brocades, silks, and satins were evident. Military objects such as drums, stars, and wrought iron trimmed with bronze were popular.

The Empire Period. Furniture became more massive and heavy, and was frequently ornamented with brass or bronze mountings. Mahogany, ebony, and rosewood, often inlaid with ivory, were used for furniture. Tables had marble tops and metal feet; chair legs were fluted in front, somewhat like the Louis XVI type, but they were heavier. The back legs were curved in the classic mode. Some legs were made in the form of bundles of arrows, or fasces. Laurel wreaths, torches, eagles, lions, and sphinx served as ornamentation. Upholstery was heavy, consisting of damasks, velvets, and prints. A simplified Empire style, suited to the less pretentious life of the provinces, is called *Biedermeier* in Germany. Usually furniture combined two tones of wood.

French Provincial. The style of the furniture and furnishings that the French nobility created to simulate rustic simplicity in the provinces was copied for American households, using lighter caramel-color wood, and called French Provincial. This style makes an interior warm, informal, gay, and inviting. The designs are soft and curved. The furniture is made of hardy woods, usually maple, and can be combined very well with Early American styles. Chairs are comfortable with wide rush seats and padded backs, and tables are spacious. Floral or pastoral designs in chintz, cretonne, linen crash, and rough-textured peasant linens are in good taste. *Italian Provincial* is a more formal adaptation of the French style, with straighter lines and geometric designs of triangles and squares.

ENGLISH STYLES

The periods of English decoration may be separated into four main classifications: Early English, Georgian, Regency, and Victorian.

Early English. These styles may be subdivided into Jacobean (1603-88), William and Mary (1689-1702), and Queen Anne (1702-14).

During the Tudor days, when Henry VIII reigned, portable furniture and decorative refinements were rare. Cushions and fragments of cloth were used for decoration, if any cloth was used. But when Elizabeth I became queen in 1558, she encouraged all forms of needlecraft and weaving. Velvets and tapestries were imported. She had walnut trees planted abundantly so that succeeding generations might profit and not be dependent upon oak for furniture. So, although the Jacobean style of decoration did not begin until 1603, the foundation was laid in Elizabeth's time; her interest in window, bed, and wall hangings spurred textile imports and encouraged weaving and needlework at home.

Elizabeth's successor, James I, furthered the new movement by interesting himself in embroideries and tapestries; the result was that handsome designs prevailed in Jacobean hangings and upholsteries. The Jacobean floral is the characteristic design of the period. It is a rather large pattern full of gorgeous colors that emphasize movement and rhythm. English traders were bringing fabrics home from the Far East, especially India—fabrics which English designers copied. The Indian tree design and crewel embroidery were introduced into England in this manner. Heraldic insignia were important patterns for wall hangings.

Lines in furniture were straight or coldly curving, with vigorous scroll work and trimmings; pieces were consequently sturdy and heavy and often massive. Geometric paneling and furniture with stubby feet and turned legs were used. Oak and some walnut were popular. Embroideries, printed fabrics, needlepoint, brocade, velvet, and leather comprise the leading upholstery fabrics.

The next important period in Early English styles is that of William and Mary.[1] The ruggedness of Jacobean styles was modified by a Dutch influence that lent a more homelike and cheerful effect. Straight lines changed to sweeping curves; ball or bun feet and slender legs; stretcher connectors; caning; teardrop pull hardware; and finer proportions. Walnut was the principal wood used in furniture. Needlework, chintz, damask, and leather were the common upholstery fabrics.

The period called Queen Anne was not influenced much by Queen Anne herself, for history records that she possessed little originality or taste. It was a time of great commercial activity—a get-rich-quick era when gambling, dueling, and drinking were pastimes. It forms a period of transition from the massive furniture of the Early English style to the more delicate Georgian type.

Rooms of that time were spacious, sometimes with ornamented ceilings. The furniture does show a marked tendency toward comfort. The "easy chair" came into use; one type is the wing chair. These chairs were upholstered and often overstuffed. Love seats also came in. Common upholstery fabrics were petit point, needlepoint, and gros point. The period marked the popularity of the highboy (made in two sections for convenience in moving), the kneehole desk with hidden drawers, writing tables, secretaries, curved cabriole legs ending in pad feet, and decorative fan or sunburst embellishments.

For hangings, Chinese embroideries and India prints were popular, and chintz in oriental designs was used for window draperies. Some authorities credit Queen Anne with originating the fashion of covering furniture entirely with fabric. At any rate, the idea was a good one. A customer who wishes to cover a Queen Anne chair for the living room should consider fabrics having sturdy textures and well-defined yet small patterns in appropriate colorings that harmonize with other furnishings.

[1] Some authorities place the elegant, gay Carolean style between the Jacobean and the William and Mary.

The Georgian Period. This era (1710-1806) was marked by the expert craftsmanship of a new group of cabinetmakers: Chippendale, Hepplewhite, Sheraton, and the Adam Brothers. During this period, as was true in France at the time of Louis XV, rooms became smaller, less like Roman temples, and pieces of furniture became more numerous. This was an era of chairs. Whereas chests, benches, and stools were sufficient as seats for lesser members of a household in earlier days, chairs now became essential for all. This demand for chairs afforded Chippendale an opportunity to express his ability. Mahogany supplanted walnut and oak. Some of Chippendale's furniture stressed the Chinese influence, but he also utilized Gothic and French styles. Chippendale was the chief exponent of eighteenth-century English rococo expressed by naturalistic motifs, curves, and scrolls. Characteristics of Chippendale style are cabriole leg, claw and ball foot, serpentine or ox-bow design.

One of the four Adam Brothers (all architects) became interested in travel and studied Roman ruins extensively. He introduced the classical feeling later expressed in their work. He also created the interest in exquisitely decorated painted furniture and popularized the use (in England) of satinwood and inlay. The Adam Brothers are particularly well known for artistic chairs and sofas. They designed complete interiors with elaborate but symmetrical plaster ceilings and mantels. French brocades and moirés were favorite upholsteries. Colors were pale grey, blue, and white.

Hepplewhite and Sheraton were contemporaries of the Adam Brothers. Furniture became delicate in proportion, more slender and refined. Mahogany, satinwood, and rosewood inlay were used. Fabrics for the Hepplewhite period took on a French appearance. The French satin stripe became popular, together with silks and satins and designs of festoons, tassels, and ribbons. The designs that Sheraton approved were more conservative and classical than Hepplewhite's. Lightweight silks, damasks, and printed linens in designs of urns, musical instruments, and medallions were favored by Sheraton. He also favored tapering fluted legs and straight-back chairs. Hepplewhite used curved lines and designed shield chair-backs.

Regency Period. The Prince of Wales served as Regent for his deranged father, George III, from 1811-20, but the Regency era is listed as 1787-1880. The Brighton Pavilion, an extravagant resort palace, was built by the prince to reflect his interest in the Oriental and Indian decorative styles. Flamboyance became fashionable and there was considerable copying and borrowing from exotic sources. Bamboo furniture was introduced in England, and black lacquer was generously used with mother of pearl or gilt decoration. Eccentric shapes, contrasting textures, and richness of pattern abounded. Swagged draperies and shirred fabric tents contributed to the rich effect. The use of pattern that was popular in Victorian times began with George IV.

Victorian Period. Queen Victoria of Great Britain had the longest reign in English history. The Victorian era (1837-1901) was the day of the horsehair sofa, the very high architectural headboard on beds, wax flowers covered with glass, the parlor with its mantelpiece and whatnot covered with bric-a-brac, red plush seats in chairs and railroad coaches, and the

FIGURE 20.2.   The Green Room of the White House, early 19th Century.

FIGURE 20.3.   One of a pair of early 19th Century sofas covered in embroidered cotton of the period.

marble-top table, cluttered rooms, heavy draperies, large patterned wallpaper and rugs, oval or horseshoe-shaped chair backs. In short, there was much gingerbread work. Black walnut, oak, and mahogany were commonly used woods. Some of the architecture and furniture of the period borders on the hideous, it is true, but revivals of Victorian styles take the most attractive elements and eliminate the gewgaws. Victorian pink has been revived in dress and home furnishings. Many of the old horsehair sofas and chairs sell at a premium.

AMERICAN STYLES

American styles begin with Early American (1607-1725), the period of early colonization, and continue through the period 1725-90, often called Colonial. These two periods before the colonies became states will be discussed together.

Early American and Colonial. Much of the early furniture and furnishings used in America were essentially English styles: Jacobean, Queen Anne, Chippendale, Hepplewhite, and Sheraton. Some furniture was brought from England, and the rest was made here in reproduction of the styles with which the colonists were familiar. English oak and walnut were used, as were woods from native forests, such as maple, pine, cedar, cherry, ash, and hickory. The fact that the colonists were lacking in tools for making elaborate styles in furniture, and the great necessity for thrift, created a style that is plain and sometimes crude, yet individual. Chairs had wooden, leather, or rush seats with narrow vertical slats or horizontal ladder backs. Serviceability and sturdy construction were emphasized. Ingenuity produced many unusual pieces.

The first fabrics used in this country were imported from England, Italy, and France; it was not until the colonists had become fairly securely established that they began to make their own. In the first efforts of the colonial craftsman, present-day interior decorators find their models of Early American interiors. Homespun, damask, chintz in small designs, and quilted cottons were made. In the latter part of the eighteenth century more fabrics were imported from England and the Continent, with the result that homes became more elaborate, with silk damasks, brocatelles, Genoese velvets, and Chinese brocades. In general, Colonial styles were Georgian, Chippendale, Hepplewhite, and Sheraton.

Then came the Federal period, following the signing of the Constitution, made memorable with respect to furniture by our own great cabinetmaker Duncan Phyfe (fl. 1795-1847). He was often called "the American Sheraton." His mastery of carving and his skill in making curved lines did much to establish the Sheraton influence in America. Furniture became slender and graceful. Mahogany and walnut were the favorite woods. Striped brocades, satins, damasks, and haircloth were common upholstery fabrics.

Many of Duncan Phyfe's styles are reproduced in fine furniture of today. Some of the most common are the sectional dining table, each part of which, when not in use for dining, can be used as a separate table tilted back against the wall; and the lyre-back side chairs and sofas. The furnishings of the White House are typical of the early Federal period. (See Figures 20.2 and 20.3.)

American Victorian. In the 1850s, John Belter developed his process of lamination which made it possible to bend and shape wood and carve intricate designs. Wood was given a dark, almost black finish and upholstered in brilliant jeweltone velvets or tapestries. Light-colored marble table tops served as a contrast to the deep colors.

ART NOUVEAU

Originally developed as a renewed interest in the decorative arts, this period (1875-1900) gave rise to a rebellion against the stale copying of classicism and was based on natural growing forms and a shiplash curve. Furniture resembled flowers, trees, ferns, or animals. Wood appeared sculpted, combining light, dark, and painted finishes. Louis Comfort Tiffany (1848-1933), son of the famed American jeweler, was a profound influence on this era.

EARLY MODERN AND MODERN

A reaction against the Victorian ornamental excesses and the commercialization of the natural forms developed an impetus toward a simpler, more rational type of expression, known as Early Modern (1911-20s). As early as 1911 the Bauhaus school in Germany was applying an architectural approach to furniture. Straight lines replaced curves. In the United States, architects such as Louis Sullivan and later his star pupil Frank Lloyd Wright called for honesty in design, where extraneous details were eliminated and the simple utilitarian form was considered beautiful. Chairs, beds, couches, and storage units were slung close to the floor and appeared as architectural elements of the room.

Modern has gone through several periods of popularity since its inception. In the 1930s there was a resurgence of Art Nouveau, called Art Deco or Moderne. Geometric or American Indian patterns abounded. Colors were light, lots of mirrors were used, and lucite was introduced. Fabrics were smooth, soft, and shiny.

As the Bauhaus influence grew, the post-World War I furniture designers used such building materials as glass, chrome, and steel. Architects who also designed furniture that became modern classics were Mils Van der Rohe for his leather sling chair and Marcel Breuer for his cane and chrome chairs.

But to the average family, early modern was cold and bizarre looking. It took many years before the public accepted the modern credo that form follows function, that extraneous details are eliminated and beauty is the result of the innate qualities of the materials used and the clarity of design. Eventually modifications were made and modern pieces gained in popularity as buyers came to appreciate the comfort, simplicity, utility, and economy inherent in this furniture.

In the 1950s Scandinavian designers developed a lighter modular look with pieces that could be easily reassembled if the homeowner moved. Wood was light in color, of bleached mahogany or limed oak. Fabric was heavily textured wool or cotton and rayon.

In the 1960s, with technological advancements, plastic came to rival wood in furniture construction. New production techniques encouraged ingenuity and innovation. Charles Eames designed a lightweight, plastic-coated, bucket-seat chair that could be readily mass-produced. Eero Saarinen developed a line of pedestal tables and chairs that has become a design classic. In fabrics, textures have predominated—rough linen weaves, wool and man-made fiber blends, velvets, modern tapestries, and tweeds. Patterns involved mechanical symbols, simple geometrics, and later bolder free forms and florals. As more window was exposed, textured but translucent casement cloth was used as a simple window treatment, eliminating heavy, ornate hangings.

CONTEMPORARY

But modern was not, and is not, to everyone's taste, and so contemporary furnishing has proven a safe haven for those looking for a more traditional appearance. Period styling has been adapted to modern comfort and convenience. Heavy features have been lightened, scaled down in size and simplified. A hint of an era is sufficient to recall the past and warm the future.

FIGURE 20.4. Contemporary style in home furnishings, exemplifying some of the uses of Belgian linen. (Courtesy Belgian Linen Association.)

Since the time of Marco Polo, almost every period of furniture has responded to the exotic inspiration of drawings, screens, and chinaware that were exported from China and much later from Japan. Furniture makers usually borrowed Oriental details that could easily be transposed to the traditional period desired. Chippendale, in the 1750s, used fanciful chinoiseries to lend a sophisticated flavor to his designs. Pogodas, Chinese latticework, and lacquer finishes were used extensively.

Today, there is a greater appreciation for the structural beauty of Chinese furniture. The classical serenity, simplicity of line, and flawless proportions are especially suited to contemporary furniture. The integration of detail and sparse decoration within the furniture have provided particular inspirations to modern designers.

Japan, where comparatively little furniture is used, has lent an air of spaciousness and lightness to design. A room divider, whether a low squarish chest or an arrangement of shelves, allows a flexibility of use derived from the Japanese.

**SELEC-
TION OF
FLOOR
COVER-
INGS**

Textile floor coverings are broadly classified as rugs and carpets, although in common parlance the two words are used synonymously.

Rugs are soft floor coverings of a specific size, laid on the floor but not fastened to it. A rug does not usually cover the entire floor. Scatter rugs are small rugs, about 2 × 6 feet, which can be placed in front of doors, couches, and stairs. Usual sizes of rugs are 2¼ × 4½, 9 × 6, 9 × 10½, 9 × 12, 9 × 13½, 9 × 15, 9 × 18, 12 × 12, 12 × 13½, 12 × 15, 12 × 18, and 12 × 21.

A carpet is a soft covering that is sold by the yard. Wall-to-wall, stair, and hall carpets are examples.

A broadloom is a seamless carpeting of any weave or style, 6 to 18 (or more) feet wide. Most production today is in the form of roll goods that can be bought as wall-to-wall carpeting. Broadloom is also cut into rugs of all sizes and shapes.

Broadlooms are popular because there are no seams to break the attractive pile surface. A solid-color broadloom or one that has a two-tone effect will blend nicely with any period of furnishings.

A rug has often been called the heart of a room. If this is true, unusual care should be taken in its selection. Although today's homemakers tend to change their room decorations more frequently than the homemakers of a generation ago, a floor covering still usually represents an investment, and every consumer wants to get her money's worth in wear as well as satisfaction from her purchase.

There are several decisions a consumer has to make when a floor covering is selected—decisions as to color, design or pattern, suitability, quality, and price.

COLOR

Although the consumer often turns to the salesman for advice, choosing colors is really a personal problem. In general it may be said that colors harmonize if they have something in common. For instance, they may belong to the same hue or color family. Colors, like people, have personalities. Some colors are gay, light, and airy, whereas others are heavy and ponderous. It would therefore be inadvisable to introduce a delicate rose into a room with massive Italian period furniture and luxurious draperies in somber colors. A decorator might advise a middle-value green or rust to relieve this somber atmosphere. It should also be remembered that the extent to which colors are used and the way of using them are additional considerations. In some combinations, one color dominates but does not overpower the color scheme, because balance is emphasized by visualizing where the colors are to be used and the relative size of ceiling, floor, upholstery, draperies, and accents. Furthermore, there is a tendency today to stress those colors that emphasize informality and easy living. Home and women's magazines, furnishing displays in retail stores, home pages of newspapers, and salesmen's advice will help the homemaker answer her color questions.

DESIGN OR PATTERN AND TEXTURE

Floor coverings are solid-colored, two-toned, or varicolored, and are sometimes called *sculptured* or *carved.* The carved rug is made with different heights of pile; for example, the design might be deeper pile than the ground. Carved rugs have become popular in contemporary styles. The choice of design in a rug is contingent upon other factors, such as use and size of room, style of decoration, and colors and designs already present in draperies and upholstery. Generally speaking, solid-colored floor coverings show footfalls more than the two-toned or varicolored types.

Sometimes a pattern in a carpet is really not obvious, yet there may be a semblance of a pattern. Three of these types of carpets and rugs for contemporary décor have emerged: the shag, the plush, and the random-tip shear. The smart "shag look" is executed in nylon, wool, or a polyester pile. The pile is relatively long and loose, intended to provide a random-pile appearance. Shags are resilient. They come in tweed tones and high-fashion colors. Plush carpets have one level of cut pile made of soft twist yarn and also nubby and heat-set yarns. Random-tip shears have a high pile, sheared at random.

Wool Rya rugs come from Denmark. They are made of blended wools from New Zealand and Scotland in patterns suited to contemporary décor. The pile is thick and strong for luxury and wear. The designs are woven through to the back, achieving the effect of hand craftsmanship. Rya rugs are advertised as colorfast and mothproof.

A newer application of color to rugs is done by painting. This technique was introduced about 1968. At that time, one type of printing machine produced copies of linoleum patterns. Today, carpet printing can produce near perfect register for up to 10 colors. In 1973 about 25 percent of carpet square yardage was printed in exciting color patterns. By the late 1970s, perhaps 50 percent of floor coverings will be painted.

Fabrics that are printable are level loop pile, frieze, and shag in all types of fibers (acrylics, polyamides, and polyesters). In fact, the designs found in woven Axminster and Wilton can be reproduced in prints at appreciably lower prices. The homespun quality of authentic Colonial American patterns, colors, and designs have been adapted to room size as well as to wall-to-wall installations.

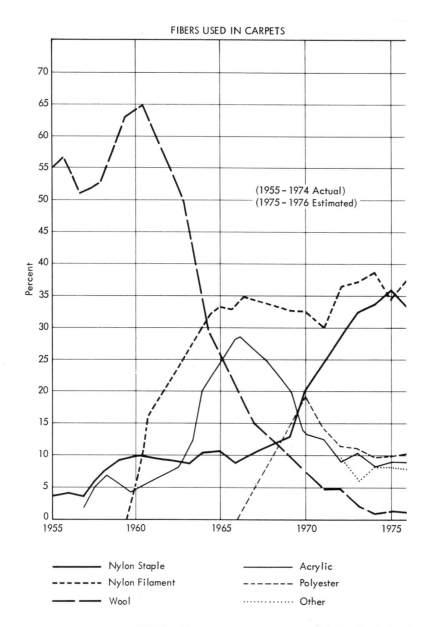

FIGURE 20.5. Fibers used in carpets. (Courtesy *Textile Topics,* Celanese Fibers Marketing Co.)

Improvements in printing machinery have increased speed, flexibility, and color changeover. Quicker drying dyes and improved shearing equipment are employed. The rotary screen technique has proved efficient and dominates the scene.[2]

[2] "America's Textiles Reporter Bulletin," September 1974.

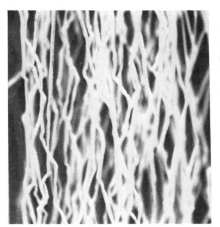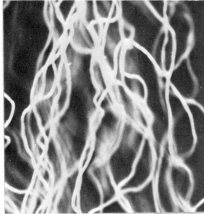

FIGURE 20.6. Enkaloft continuous filament nylon used in rugs. In this enlarged picture comparing strands of Enkaloft on the left with strands of another yarn on the right, note that the crimps in the Enkaloft yarn sample are orderly; they are in waves, and this gives clearer pattern definition. The other yarn has a random crimp—its curls are irregular. (Reproduced courtesy of American Enka Corporation.)

SUITABILITY

A salesman may ask his customer, "Do you live in the room or just walk through it?" If there is heavy traffic, as in an entrance hall, a durable floor covering that will not show soil should be selected. The salesman may show the customer a *twist*, a broadloom made with uncut pile, in which yarns of different colors may be twisted together to form the pile. The resultant blending of colors is attractive, and the carpet doesn't show footmarks so quickly. For a bedroom, where there is little traffic, a cotton rug or a hooked rug may be appropriate.

Carpets make suitable floor coverings because they virtually eliminate floor noises such as scraping of chairs and clicking of heels. They also absorb airborne noises and reduce incidence of slips and slides. Furthermore, carpeting is comfortable—it is soft, warm, and easy to stand on.

For institutional use, a careful selection should be made, since once installed the carpet may remain in use for years. Table 20-1 compares the wear-life and other factors of five carpeting fibers.

Indoor-outdoor carpets are floor coverings that are suitable both inside the house and outdoors—for example, carpets for boats, patios, terraces, miniature golf courses, kitchens, and bathrooms. They are made in tufted construction, of 100 percent olefin in dense pile plush-type or in a grasslike carpet. They are also made of acrylics.

One hundred percent cotton does not wear as well as wool; it is less resilient and therefore harder to walk on. It is inexpensive and can be found in interesting colors and varied textures. Preshrunk, colorfast, small-sized rugs with rubberized backing can be washed by machine. With the increasing use of man-made fibers, cotton as a pile surface for rugs has declined appreciably. Cotton yarns may be used for chain warps—those

527

TABLE 20-1   Comparative Behavior of Carpet-Type Fibers[a]

Factor	Wool	Nylon	Acrylic	Modacrylic	Polypropylene
Wear-life	High	Extra High	High	High	Extra High
Texture retention	Medium	High	Medium	Medium	Low-Medium
Compression resistance	Medium	Medium	Medium	Medium	Low
Resilience	High	Medium	High	Medium	Medium
Soil resistance	High	Medium	Medium	Medium	Medium
Stain resistance	Medium	High	Medium	Medium	High
Wet cleanability	Medium	High	Medium	Medium	Medium
Static generation	High	High	Medium	Medium	Low
Cost	High	Medium	Medium	Medium	Medium

[a]Original table provided by American Carpet Institute; revised by Mohasco Industries, Inc.

that bind the front and back of the rug together—and for filling in rugs. The price of silk makes it almost prohibitive for use in moderately priced rugs. Silk pile is exquisite in orientals but is not so durable as wool.

Fiber rugs are really made of tightly twisted strips of paper, often vinyl-coated to resist friction and moisture. They are quite inexpensive and are especially adaptable to use in summer cabins, sun porches, and so forth. Rugs of straw, sisal (often sold as hemp), and grass are suitable for the same purposes as fiber rugs.

The man-made fibers used in floor coverings were especially developed for the carpet industry and are not substitutes for, but permanent additions to, carpet raw materials. Carpet polypropylene, nylon, and acrylic fibers are the result of long years of research, and they are an answer to the limited world carpet wool supply.

It is estimated that 96.6 percent of all face fibers used in floor coverings produced in 1974-75 were man-made fibers.[3] These fibers help to keep our products within the consumer's budget as labor and overhead costs continue to rise.

In Table 20-2, total industry shipment of carpets and rugs are given in square yards. In 1973 yardage was up 10.1 percent from 1972. Tufted goods totaled 92.5 percent and all other carpets and rugs were 5.1 percent.

WEARING QUALITY OF FIBERS

Wearing quality of domestic floor coverings is based on (1) kind of fibers used, (2) quality of the yarns, (3) closeness of weave, (4) height of pile, and (5) construction of the back. (See Figure 20.7.)

Fibers for floor coverings should have resilience, luster, length, and strength. Wool, representing only 2.6 percent of face yarns, was once used for almost all floor covering, because it has all these properties and also absorbs noise.

Some rugs are made of wool; some are made of cotton, silk, paper, jute, straw, acetate, rayon, noncellulosic fibers, and blends.

[3] Carpet and Rug Institute, CRI Directory.

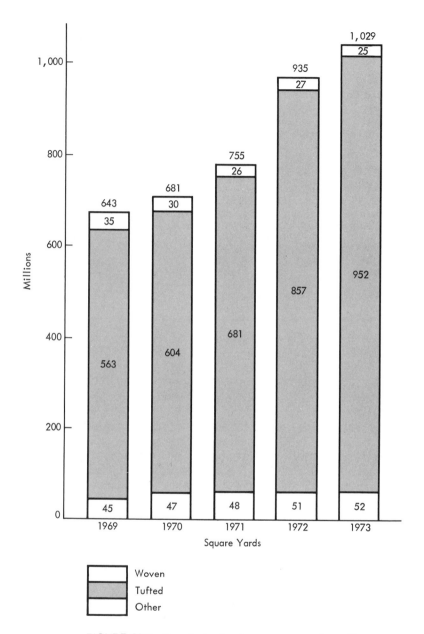

FIGURE 20.7. Bar chart of major rug constructions. (Courtesy The Carpet and Rug Institute, *Directory and Report,* 1973-74.)

The wool produced in this country is too fine and soft for use in textile floor covering. Carpet yarns are made instead from coarse, wiry, tough fleeces of low-grade wool. New Zealand and Argentina continue to be the major sources of our carpet wool imports. We also import carpet wool from the United Kingdom, Pakistan, Ireland, Iran, Italy, Iraq, India, and other countries.

529

TABLE 20-2. Major Rug Fiber Producers[a]

Manufacturer	Fiber Type	Reg Trade Name
Allied Chemical Corp.	Continuous filament nylon	Anso
American Cyanamid Co.	Acrylic staple	Creslan
American Enka Corp.	Continuous filament nylon	Enkaloft
	Nylon staple	Enkalure
Monsanto	Acrylic staple	Acrilan
	Continuous filament nylon	Cumuloft
		Cadon
Courtaulds (Alabama) Inc.	Rayon staple	
	Rayon staple (solution dyed)	Coloray
	Cross-linked rayon staple	Corval
	Cross-linked rayon spale	Topel
Dow Chemical Co.	Acrylic staple	Zefran
E. I. Du Pont de Nemours & Co.	Continuous filament nylon	Nylon 501
	Nylon staple	Antron
Eastman Chemical Products, Inc.	Modacrylic staple	Verel
Eastman Chemical Products, Inc.	Polyester staple	Kodel
Hercules Powder Co.	Continuous filament olefin	Herculon
	Olefin staple	
National Plastics Products Co.	Continuous filament olefin	Vectra
Union Carbide Corp.	Modacrylic staple	Dynel

[a]Original table provided by American Carpet Institute; revised by Mohasco Industries, Inc.

Early in 1962 polypropylene fibers appeared in the pile of carpets. Polypropylene was found to have a very high wear-life and stain resistance. See Table 20-1.

Olefin fibers are being used in indoor-outdoor "needle-punched carpets." (See definition in the Glossary.) The surface fibers are 100 percent Herculon olefin; they are interlocked and supported by a woven monofilament backing fabric. This construction is said to increase the depth of the wear surface by 50 percent; it makes a durable, stable carpet that lies flat and does not curl. Olefin is also used in automobiles. Yarns are bulked continuous filament, with no loose ends to cause fuzzing, pilling, or shedding.

The primary backings for carpets are about 100 percent man-made fibers. Cotton, jute, flax, and kraftcord (a tough yarn made from wood pulp) can be used, as are nonwoven man-made fibers and foams.

The first man-made fibered, primary carpet backing was Poly Bac (Patchogue-Plymouth), a woven fabric of polypropylene ribbon yarn. Then came Loktuft (Phillips Fibers Corp.), a nonwoven polypropylene-fibered web reinforced with cotton scrim. Vinyls have also come on the market. They are durable, nontoxic, and impermeable to moisture, and they have low maintenance cost. They are used for secondary backings. Another nonwoven polypropylene fabric is Typar, by Du Pont. Latex (styrene butadiene [SB] types) make durable, nonskidding backings and underlays. Natural latex is still used in contract carpeting, underlay mats, and scatter rugs. Urethane foams are important as underlay materials in contract carpeting; these foams are entering the market as a secondary backing for the needlepunched construction.

Quality of yarns is an important factor in considering wearing quality. Wool rugs are made from woolen yarns. The woolen fibers for rugs average three inches in length (for clothing, less than two inches). Wool fibers are purposely intertwined or interlocked in the carding process and are made into two-ply yarns. In wool rugs, the yarn weight (number of yarns per ounce) affects the density of the pile. Since density is a factor in wearing quality, weight of yarn is important.

Cotton yarns for rugs are made from one-inch staple and are used for the entire rug or for the base of the weave and to combine the surface yarns with cheaper jute yarns at the back.

Carpet yarns are made single-ply, two-ply, three-ply, and four-ply. Probably the major production is in two-ply and three-ply yarns. However, as far as wearing quality is concerned, a rug manufacturer claims that it makes no difference whether the yarn is two- or three-ply. For striated effects, three- or four-ply are used, and for very heavy fabrics three- and four-ply are necessary. Since most wear is on the pile yarn, these yarns must be of the right size and diameter, full, and lofty. They should be single or ply to give the best coverage to the surface, good appearance, and adequate tensile strength.

Bicomponent acrylic-fibered yarns, the texturized and bulky synthetic yarns, have afforded newer possibilities for styling in floor coverings. (See Chapter 2 for definition of bicomponent fiber.) Multiple random colors are possible with space-dyed yarns. (See Chapter 3 for description of space dyeing.)

CLOSENESS OF CONSTRUCTION AND KIND OF PILE

In general, the greater closeness of construction the better the wearing quality. Pile weight, pile density, and pile height are factors in determining the quality of a carpet. Pile weight would be governed by weight of the yarn while pile density would depend on the closeness of the tufts of yarn to each other. Pile height would signify the length of the yarn from the backing to the surface. The manufacturer decides what length to use. But, in general, high-pile rugs flatten and show footfalls more quickly than those with low pile (depending somewhat on the resiliency of the fibers). High piles are usually more difficult to clean.

CONSTRUCTION OF THE BACK

A strong backing supports the pile and forms the foundation of the carpet. A close constructed, firm back gives this support. Long wear, however, is not as important as it used to be in the selection of a floor covering, for modern homemakers are making more frequent changes in their furnishings than was done formerly. Lower-priced rugs fit into this picture.

PRICE

Many factors have made possible a general decrease in the prices of rugs. A process of construction called tufting has speeded up carpet construction and brought prices down. Man-made fibers, alone or in blends in a wide range of colors and textures, make tufted rugs popular. Very little cotton is sold today. The olefin fibers and polyesters have entered the market.

TYPES OF RUGS

Rugs may be broadly classified as domestic and imported. Or they may be divided into machine-made and handmade groups. Handmade rugs include hand-tied orientals and hand-hooked, hand-braided, and hand-crocheted rugs. Domestic and European oriental, tufted, Wilton, Axminster, chenille, and grass rugs are made by machine. Hooked and rag rugs made by machine also come under the latter grouping. Machine-made rugs are of four types: tufted, woven, knitted, and needlepunched (nonwoven).

In present-day advertising, probably much more emphasis is placed on the fiber content and brand name of a rug or carpet than on the construction. In former years rugs were sold on the basis of construction alone. Knowledge of the construction should be a great help to a consumer in getting her money's worth in wearing quality and in selecting an appropriate construction for a specific use.

Despite the wide variety of patterns and textures in modern carpeting, about 98 percent of all carpeting sold in the United States is made in tufted, woven, or knitted types.

TUFTED RUGS AND CARPETS

In the tufting process, pile yarns are inserted into a prefabricated backing by wide multiple-needled machines. A heavy coating of latex on the back of the carpet holds pile tufts of yarn in place. The more pile tufts to the inch, the denser the pile and the better the carpet. Owing to developments and variations in tufting construction, the tufted pile can be multilevel, cut or uncut. Carved and striated effects are made. Looped or plush textures are among those available. At mid-century there was no tufted carpet industry; now over 90 percent of the square yardage produced is

FIGURE 20.8. A tufted domestic carpet: 100 percent SPECTRODYE nylon 6 producer dyed, continuous filament pile yarns; double jute backing; random, multicolor pattern. (Courtesy of American Enka Corporation.)

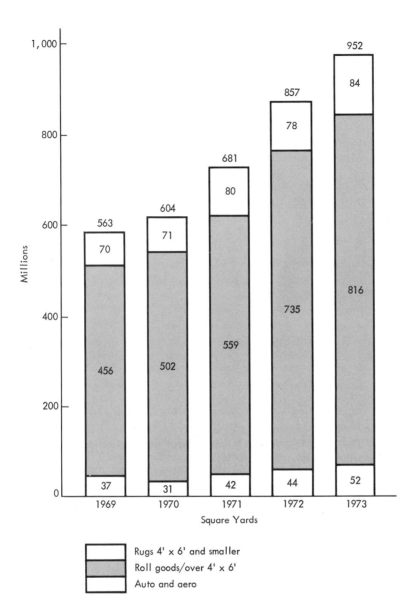

FIGURE 20.9. Shipments of tufted rugs by size. (Courtesy The Carpet and Rug Institute, Directory and Report, 1973-74.)

tufted. Woven, knitted, and needle-punched comprise the balance of carpet yardage. Tufting is faster than the woven method of producing carpet. A tufting machine produces two yards of 15-foot-wide carpet in one minute. It is therefore relatively inexpensive. Tufted rugs come in 7-, 12-, and 15-foot widths.

Notice that the accompanying bar chart (Figure 20.9) shows a marked rise in tufted shipments in carpets and rugs from 1971 to 1973. The largest shipments were in roll (yard) goods and rugs larger than 4 X 6 feet. A small percentage went into auto and aero carpets.

533

COMBINATION LOOP/CUT PILE

TUFTED

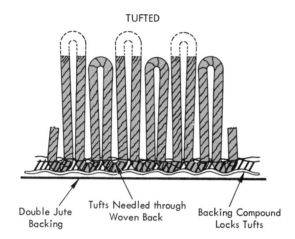

Double Jute
Backing

Tufts Needled through
Woven Back

Backing Compound
Locks Tufts

FIGURE 20.10. The tufting process.

WOVEN RUGS AND CARPETS

Wilton. As early as 1740 some weavers were brought from France to England, and a carpet factory was established at Wilton, England. In 1825 the Jacquard loom was adapted to Wilton carpeting. One color at a time is drawn up as pile and the other colors are buried beneath the surface. Buried yarn gives body, strength, and resilience to the carpet. The flat wires used to form the pile loops have knives on the ends that cut the top of each loop as the wires are withdrawn. The pile of a Wilton is therefore erect and cut.

Good quality Wilton rugs are long-wearing luxurious carpets with a wide range of solid colors, patterns, and textures. Very little Wilton production is available for domestic use. Almost all Wiltons are used in the contract business today. (See *Contract carpeting* in Glossary.)

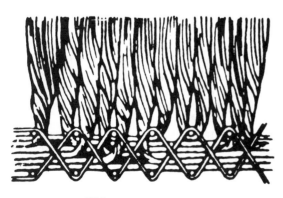

FIGURE 20.11. The Wilton process. (Reproduced courtesy of the American Carpet Institute Inc.)

Axminster. Although the Axminster loom was invented by an American, the name comes from a town in England. The special mechanism of this loom permits carpets of an unlimited number of colors and designs to be constructed on it. The pile yarns, all on the surface, are not concealed (buried) inside the rug as in the Wilton. These yarns are made of wool, man-made fibers, or blends; they are inserted in the fabric and held by binder yarns. When pulled out, pile yarns are V-shaped. The back of an Axminster is usually jute, is heavily ribbed, and cannot be rolled crosswise—only lengthwise.

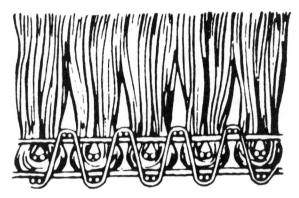

FIGURE 20.12. The Axminster process. (Reproduced courtesy of the American Carpet Institute Inc.)

Oriental Design Rugs. "Domestic orientals" is really a misnomer. They are machine-made domestic rugs with oriental designs and colors that are carefully blended to resemble hand-tied oriental rugs. They can be made in Wilton or Axminster construction. Washing or brushing in a chemical solution adds luster. Some of these rugs have the type of back found in domestics; others have the pattern woven through to the back, as genuine orientals have.

Good grades of oriental-type rugs will stand hard wear. They are moderately priced but average higher than the Axminsters. Their sheen makes them most suitable for living and dining rooms. These rugs have been a great boon to those who appreciate oriental designs and colorings but cannot afford the genuine articles.[4] The durability of the construction of the pile depends on the density of the pile and closeness of construction.

Velvet. The word "velvet" sounds rich and luxurious when applied to floor coverings, and the colors, range, and texture of these rugs are all that the word implies. A plush effect results when the pile is erect and is cut. Uncut looped pile gives a pebbly surface or may appear in distinct rows like friezé. Pile can be woven in different heights to form a pattern or hit-and-miss effects. For these varied textures, a velvet loom (not a Jacquard) suffices. When closely woven, velvet carpeting is durable and rich looking. Velvet carpets are almost all contract business. Few residential styles are available.

[4] Familiar brand names are Karastan, Karagheusian, and Gulistan.

FIGURE 20.13. The Velvet process. (Reproduced courtesy of the American Carpet Institute Inc.)

KNITTED

Like woven carpeting, the knitted type is made in one operation. But unlike the woven, the knitting process loops together the backing yarn, the stitching yarn, and the pile yarn with three sets of needles in much the same way as in hand knitting. Knitted carpeting is usually made with uncut loops, both single and multilevel. For cut pile, modifications must be made in the knitting machine. To give additional body to a carpet, a coat of latex is applied to the back. A second backing may be added. The quality of the carpet depends on the amount of pile yarn on the surface and the strength of attachment of the yarns.

NEEDLEPUNCHED AND FLOCKED[5] (NONWOVEN)

This is a nonwoven nonpile carpeting with a feltlike surface. A lap, web, or batt of loose fibers is created by needles having downward-facing barbs that entangle the fibers (mostly olefin). The primary use is for indoor-outdoor carpeting. When used indoors, a backing is sometimes applied.

Another type of nonwoven carpeting may be made of precut electrostatically charged fibers that are projected toward a backing fabric which has been coated with an adhesive. The appearance of the rug resembles flocked wallpaper.

OTHER MACHINE-MADE RUGS

This category includes rugs made of fiber, grass, sisal, and braided and rag rugs.

Fiber (paper). Made from fir or spruce pulp that is cut into strips, the strips are twisted into yarn and woven in plain, twill, and herringbone weaves. A vinyl coating is required for durability.

Grass. Cured prairie grass comes from the marshes in Wisconsin, Minnesota, and Winnipeg, Canada. The light yellow or greenish yellow straws are bound together into "ropes" or grass twine. These ropes are woven together. A pattern is stenciled on the rug after it is finished, or the rugs may be printed.

Rush is a tough reed that grows in sluggish waters of Europe and the

---

[5] "Handbook of Buying Issue" for use throughout 1975, *Consumers' Research*, pp. 44-47.

Far East. Japan and countries of western Europe produce it. Rush is often woven in one-foot squares, which can be pieced together into the desired shape.

Sisal. These rugs are made of a fiber from the leaf of a plant grown in Central America, Kenya, and the West Indies. Sisal rugs are more resistant to moisture than fiber rugs, but they are more expensive.

Braided. Usually made of mildew-resistant yarns covered with tubular braids electronically fused together, they may also be made of tubular braided outer surface yarns of olefin or nylon. The covered yarns are spot- and stain-resistant. The braids do not separate since they are fused together. These rugs come in round, oval or runner shapes and are suitable for porch, patio, or dining room.

Rag. When machine-made, rag rugs are produced with a cotton warp and rag filling. They often give a hit-or-miss effect and are quite inexpensive.

CARPET CUSHIONS

Carpet or rug cushions, sometimes called underlays, are made of hair, hair and jute, jute, foam rubber, and sponge rubber.

Hair. Made of felted cattle hair, these cushions are the most expensive of those listed above, but have been found most effective in increasing the wear-life of carpets.[6] They also have the greatest resistance to burning, but tear resistance is poor.

Hair and Jute. The proportion of hair to jute varies. Some have up to 80 percent hair (a factor in higher cost). The resistance to burning has been found acceptable. However, rubberized hair and fiber foam and fiber combinations were found to be unsatisfactory in this respect. Products in this category are poor in resistance to mildew.

Jute. These cushions are least expensive. When new they have resilience, but with wear, jute tends to bunch up and break down.

Foam Rubber. This makes for a "quiet" walk. Its natural thermal conductivity makes it good for covering floors that have embedded heating pipes. The wear-life of the carpet is not increased by the use of this kind of cushion. Foam rubber has fair resistance to mildew.[7]

Sponge Rubber. Sold in a number of thicknesses, some do not give sufficient support because the cushions are too light. Normal traffic areas should have 60- to 80-ounce weight. Sponge rubber insures a "soft" walk because it is resilient and it also has good heat conductivity. Slippage of the rug off the cushion is common unless the cushion has a scrim or mesh backing. Sponge rubber is flammable and may contribute to the spread of fire.

[6] From a study by the Institutional Research Council Consumer Bulletin, May 1971.
[7] Ibid.

JUDGING THE QUALITY OF DOMESTIC MACHINE-MADE RUGS[8]

In the store before purchase:

1. Look at the pile in the carpet sample. Bend the pile back on itself. The less backing you see, the denser the pile, and the better the quality. (This test does not apply to shags.)
2. Test the tufts by pulling a few to see if they are firmly anchored.
3. Examine the closeness of the weave in the backing.
4. Read the fiber content on the back of each label. See that brand name, name, or registered number of the manufacturer, pattern and color name, country of origin (if not in the United States) are given. The U.S. Government Standard for surface flammability of carpets and rugs (DOC FFI-70) became effective in April 1971. Therefore, no matter what type of rug a consumer selects, he or she can be sure that it has been tested and has passed the flammability test.

FIGURE 20.14. Two hand-hooked rugs.

HAND-WOVEN RUGS

The most exciting of all handwoven rugs are the orientals. Therefore, they are discussed separately following this section, according to place of origin, uses, design, color, prices, and selection.

HOOKED AND RAG RUGS

In the early years of American colonization, hooked and rag rugs were made by hand. They were popular as scatter rugs in New England and Nova Scotia.

[8] From data in "Handbook," *Consumers' Research*, p. 45.

For the very old handmade hooked rugs, a backing of linen was used; later burlap became common. The pile made of yarn or strips of cloth is pulled through the back by means of a hook. The resulting pile is sometimes cut.

Patterns in hooked rugs may be geometric or floral; animals, ships, and domestic scenes are depicted. The hooked rug made in New England in the early days is considered more valuable than the Nova Scotia rug because of its more intricate designs and more beautiful colorings. Many modern Nova Scotian rugs have geometric designs copied from current linoleum patterns. Japan is a source of many inexpensive hand-hooked rugs. Certainly many hand-hooked rug patterns are not beautiful and are even crude, but their very amateurish look is attractive to many people.

Most modern hooked rugs can be cleaned by shampooing, because the modern textiles from which they are made have generally fast dyes. Old hooked rugs should be sent to a reliable cleaner, for the burlap foundation may be weak and may fall apart when wet.

Hooked rugs are best suited to bedrooms and Early American interiors. They may be purchased in room size as well as scatter size. Old hooked rugs vary in size and shape, but large machine types are more or less standard.

Rag rugs are made of strips of twisted rags braided, crocheted, or bound together by cotton thread. Handmade rag rugs are less plentiful than handmade hooked rugs, even though they require less skill in the making and sell at lower prices. There are no particular patterns. Braided rugs are usually oval or round. Hit-or-miss rugs, made of many-colored twisted rags bound together, are generally oblong.

NAVAJO RUGS AND MATS

The Navajo Indian in the western part of the United States originally made blankets and mats for his own use, but now these are made commercially. The Navajo loom consists of warp yarns suspended between two horizontal sticks. The filling is passed over and under the warp yarns by means of a pointed stick on which the yarn is wound. At points where the design is to appear, another color is introduced. Designs are geometric, and favorite colors are bright red on a white or gray ground, or white on a red ground. Originally, the Navajos obtained wool for rugs and blankets from their own flocks, which were carefully tended. Now their fine blankets are made of Germantown wool yarn made ready for weaving.

Weaving by this method is slow. When weavers were more skilled than they are today, it took an expert weaver about a month to make a blanket 5½ × 6¾ feet.

ORIENTAL HAND-TIED RUGS

Hand-tied orientals come from three areas: Near East, India, and China. Although some hand-tied rugs are made in Europe, most of them come from Iran, Asia Minor, and the Caucasus region.

Oriental rugs are made on a vertical loom. The wool or silk yarns that form the pile are tied by hand and cut with a knife at the depth desired. Two kinds of knots are used: the Ghiordes (Turkish) and the Senna

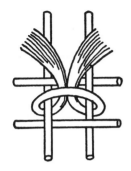

FIGURE 20.15. a. The Ghiordes knot. b. The Senna knot.

(Iranian).[9] In the Ghiordes the tufts of pile yarn come in pairs between two warp yarns; in the Senna the tufts pass singly between two warp yarns. (See Figure 20.15.) In both cases the pile does not stand vertically on the ground but rather leans toward the end of the rug first woven. The warp and weft are commonly made of cotton, but silk and wool are also used. In a few Anatolian rugs, the pile is also cotton. Rugs made from wool from hides (skin wool), rather than from live sheep, has a fraction of the strength of the usual wool. The fringe of the Oriental is the ends of the warp yarns; it is not sewed on separately unless the original fringe has been badly worn.

Some orientals are not made with a pile. Rather, a dyed filling thread is bound around the warp threads by means of a shuttle or needle. This makes the fabric look much alike on both sides. The construction is like that of tapestry. These coverings are called kilims (ghileems). While used in the Orient as floor coverings as well as spreads, they are not very satisfactory on the floors in this country. Heels and hard soles are likely to damage them, and they will slip unless backed with rug cushioning.

Dates on the origin of handwoven rugs cannot be stated exactly, but probably oriental rugs are as old as civilization and date back to 5000 B.C. Until we have further evidence, the date of origin must begin with the old Egyptian civilization. Later on, Assyria and Chaldea became the home of oriental rugs. The Persians, who were the master weavers, probably learned the art from the Babylonians. Some historians believe that the origin of the oriental rug antedates the early Egyptian times.

Oriental rugs may be classified according to their geographical origin and also as to use. (See Figure 20.16.)

IRANIAN

Rugs from Iran (formerly Persia) are perhaps the most sought after of the orientals because of their artistic, intricate designs and fineness of construction. It is said that the Italianesque touch in the design of some Persian rugs is traceable to the time of Shah Abbas, a Turkish ruler of the sixteenth century. He sent some young men to Italy to study art under Raphael, and it is through them that rugs reached their zenith of development. Designs of Persians are usually predominantly floral with now and then a depiction of animals or human figures. Straight fringes,

---

[9] There is a third knot—the Khorasson (Spanish)—that is tied around a single warp.

540

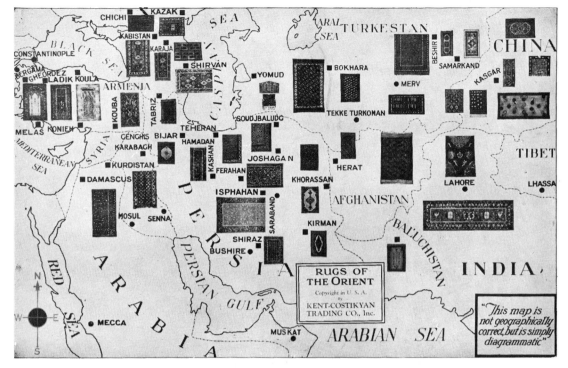

FIGURE 20.16. A rug map of the Orient. (Photograph courtesy of Kent-Costikyan, Inc.)

which are the actual continuation of warp yarns, appear at both ends. Sometimes fringes are braided or knotted.

The names of the rugs are derived from the towns where particular designs were first made. Some of the most common contemporary Persian rugs are: Bijar, Feraghan, Hamadan, Isphahan, Kashan, Kash Kai, Kirman, Qum, Sarouk, Saraband, Shiraz, Tabriz, and Teheran.

Nain and Qum rugs are extremely fine knotted constructions and sell at high prices. The popular Sarouk rugs are not produced in one town but in a district south of Teheran.

TURKISH

The patterns of Turkish rugs (Anatolian) are less intricate than the Persian, and they tend to be more geometric in design. The pile is longer than the Persian, and the rugs are somewhat coarser in construction. Some of the most common types are Bergama, Ladik, Ghiordes, Kulah, Milas, and Oushak.

CAUCASIAN

These rugs come from Caucasia and Transcaucasia on the Black and the Caspian seas. Characteristics are their geometric patterns with sharp outlines. Blues, yellows, and reds are favorite colors. These rugs seldom come in large sizes. It is said that Kazak rugs originated from the word

541

FIGURE 20.17. Persian (now Iranian) animal rug, Kurdistan; 18th Century. Animals and birds against a background design of trees and flowers, a type of composition derived from Persian court carpets of the classic period. Colors: field, red; animals, white, rose, light and dark blue; background pattern, white, cream, rose, reds, and blues; border, red and light blue on dark blue. $13_3''$ × 6" 67". (Collection of Mr. and Mrs. Arthur M. Brilant. Photograph courtesy of The Asia Society and *Antiques Magazine.*)

Cossack, the name of a nomadic people. The designs in this type of rug are more geometric and cruder than those made by other groups such as Chi-Chi, Dagestan, Kabistan, Karaja, Kazak, Kuba, and Shirvan.

TURKOMAN

Rugs from Turkestan, which is north of Iran and east of the Caspian Sea, are usually characterized by wide webbing at the ends. The designs in the center field are rows of octagonal medallions. Red, white, brown, and green are the principal colors. The most common Turkoman rugs are the

Bokhara, Beshir, Tekke Turkoman, and Samarkand. Pakistan is now making many Bokharas. Afghan rugs from Afghanistan, between Turkestan and Baluchistan, may be included.

BALUCHISTAN

Baluchistan is a section extending between Kirman on the west and India on the east, from Afghanistan on the north to the Arabian Sea on the south. Rugs from Baluchistan, often called *Baluchi*, have wide-webbed ends and are similar to the Turkoman. Vivid reds and browns predominate.

FIGURE 20.18. Turkish prayer rug, Anatolia, Ghiordes; first half of the 18th Century. A floral decoration takes the place of the mosque lamp in the mihrab, or niche; the stylized flowers in the border are derived from Turkish court rugs. Colors: niche, red; spandrels, light blue with yellow; border, dark blue with pattern in white, tan, green, red, and black. (The Metropolitan Museum of Art, Gift of James F. Ballard, 1922. Photograph courtesy of The Metropolitan Museum of Art, The Asia Society, and *Antiques Magazine.*)

FIGURE 20.19. Caucasian floral rug, Kazak; first half of the 19th Century. Modified cross in lobed floral medallion. Colors: field, red; border and background of medallion, white; pattern, yellow, rose, light and dark blue, black. Size: 7'2" X 4'10". (The Metropolitan Museum of Art, The Wilkinson Collection. Photograph courtesy of The Metropolitan Museum of Art, The Asia Society, and *Antiques Magazine*.)

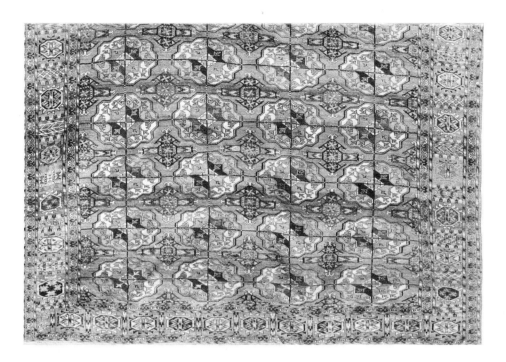

FIGURE 20.20. Turkoman geometrical rug, Tekke (called Bukhara); first half of the 19th Century. All-over pattern of roughly octagonal guls, or medallions. Colors: field, red brown; pattern, white, orange, dark blue, red. Size: 9' X 6'. (The Metropolitan Museum of Art. Gift of James F. Ballard, 1922. Photograph courtesy of The Metropolitan Museum of Art, The Asia Society, and *Antiques Magazine.*)

INDIAN

Indian rugs can be classified into three groups: hand-tied rugs, numdahs, and druggets. The hand-tied rugs come from the district around Lahore in the province of Punjab, and from Benares and Rajistan. The numdahs come from Punjab and Tibet. The druggets are made throughout India from the fleece of wire-haired sheep.

The numdahs come in different grades. They are made of felted goat's hair, not woven hair. Designs are embroidered by hand, the patterns being generally floral or vinelike. The *tree of life* design appears frequently. The usual dimensions of numdahs are 2 X 3, 3 X 4, and 4 X 6 feet. These rugs are comparatively inexpensive.

Druggets also come in different grades. The better ones are all wool; the poorer ones have a pile made of wool mixed with cow's hair. The groundwork of these rugs is jute. Patterns are usually very colorful and quite simple. Druggets are used on sun porches and in summer cottages.

Indian rugs should be dry-cleaned, not washed.

CHINESE

The pile is deep and rich. Blue and tan are common colors, Dragons and flowers in circles are characteristic motifs, although when modern furniture came into vogue, Chinese rug manufacturers had their designers create patterns to meet the style. Then, with the demand, they made them in plain colors. However, these rugs are not as durable as Persian and Turkish, and they require much care. Harder to keep clean, they show footprints easily. The political situation between the United States and China has long limited the supply to those few used rugs that are selling at auction and in stores selling old rugs.

ORIGINAL USES OF ORIENTAL RUGS

The artistic and poetic temperament of oriental peoples expresses itself in the beautiful pictures on their rugs. These designs have been copied by occidental peoples, but the latter have never really been able to duplicate the works of art handed down through the centuries.

Although our present-day rugs are used chiefly as floor coverings, room size, scatter size and mats, or hangings, the old oriental rugs were created for other purposes as well. These include *prayer rugs*, characterized by a design in the form of an arch directed toward Mecca during prayer; *hearth rugs*, often with a cypress tree design, once used for family prayers; *grave rugs*, used to cover the dead before interment and to cover the grave after burial; *dowry* or *wedding rugs*, considered part of a girl's dowry and woven by the bride herself; *mosque (Mecca) rugs*, taken to Mecca as a gift to the mosque; *saddle bags*, in the form of two pouches joined together by webbing used to transport merchandise—now often cut apart and used as couch pillows; *saddle covers*, to fit the back of the camel; *runners*, made to lay on couches—now used for halls and foyers; *hangings*, either silk rugs or Kilims (ghileems); *pillowcases*, now used also on tables and in front of doors; *bath rugs*, originally given to the bride by her parents on her wedding day; and *sample corners*, pieces about two feet square used to show the quality of weaving to wealthy buyers—very rare today.

Although it is romantic to think of the original uses of oriental rugs, it should be remembered that in our modern civilization the old uses have in many cases disappeared. In the selling or buying of rugs, then, the salesman or customer should try to visualize a rug in use in a home—not in a mosque in Turkey. Salesmen should remember that modern orientals are made solely "for the trade" and are not intended to be used in places of worship or for transporting merchandise.

DESIGN OF ORIENTAL RUGS

The geometric designs are the most primitive. Although they are not so complicated as the floral types, their simplicity makes them popular. Authorities on designs in rugs feel that geometric patterns originated with the rug itself. It must be remembered that the whole family used to weave rugs. The mother would tend the baby while weaving, and, to keep the child amused, would often weave into her rug some figures or symbols especially for the child. Possibly some of the irregularities in antique rugs are due to interruptions of the weaver, although the story is that no faithful Mohammedan would wish to make a rug perfect in symmetry of design and weaving because he might offend Allah, who alone is the symbol of perfection. Furthermore, the representation of human figures, birds, or beasts was forbidden in strict observance of Mohammedan laws. Consequently the original geometric designs were perpetuated.

Floral patterns are now identified with Persian rugs, but the oldest floral patterns were not developed in Persia. Greece and neighboring countries borrowed simple geometric designs from Egypt and Assyria and developed beautiful, complicated floral designs. Persia received this art centuries later.

The present designs in our modern oriental rugs are copies of old pieces. The symbolism attached to designs in antique rugs no longer exists. Swastikas for happiness, latch-hooks for good luck, a geometric figure supposed to represent a dog who preceded Mohammed when he first entered Mecca are all symbols of the early rugmakers, who also wove their life histories into their rugs. The same designs are present today, but no symbolic meaning is intended by the weaver.

ANTIQUE VERSUS MODERN ORIENTALS

A rug, to be considered antique, should be at least 100 years old.[10] Sometimes rugs about 25 years old are called semi-antiques. The colors of antique orientals have been softened and subdued by constant wear and by dirt, and the pile is worn down in places, with the result that there is an effect of light and shadow on the surface. These mellow colors are quite different from the garish brillance of recently loomed orientals.

The yarns used in the antiques were dyed with natural coloring matter; for example, ox blood or madder for red, the safron crocus for yellow, the indigo plant for blue, and walnut shells for brown and black. These have great depth, natural sheen, and softness; they are also color fast.

While the first aniline dyes were developed over 100 years ago, they were of poor quality and did not come into general use until after World War I, when they were greatly improved. In early days, the Persian government outlawed the use of aniline dyes in order to protect the country's reputation for quality rugs. It is reported that the government threatened to cut off the hand of any rug maker who attempted to use the new synthetic dyes.

Today, excellent synthetic dyes from benzine, obtained in turn from coal tar, have replaced the natural dyes. They are colorfast to light and to shampooing but tend to lack the softness of the antiques. To emulate the old coloring, the new orientals are frequently subjected to chemical washes of chlorine or an acetic acid to mute the vivid colors. Glycerine may also be applied to give sheen. Coloring matter in the desired hues is often applied to the washed rugs by a hand-operated dye pencil. The pencil may also be used to cover worn spots on used rugs.

A chemical wash can be detected by comparing the wrong side with the top side. If the former is brighter, the rug has probably been washed.

---

[10] At the British Dealers' Antique Fair, the term "antique" is limited to rugs made not later than 1830.

Sniffing the rug may detect the chemical odor. Repainted rugs often have shiny areas that give off color when rubbed with a wet finger or tissue.

VALUES IN ORIENTAL RUGS

The value of an oriental is measured by the quality and nature of the yarn (silk generally more expensive than wool), the design, the color, the rarity, and the age. The number of knots to the square inch is also a factor with some famous antiques having over 800 knots to the square inch.[11] It is said that some of the ancient weavers went blind on the job. But some closely knotted rugs are too tight and too brittle.

Fine antiques command very high prices, with some palace rugs costing many thousands of dollars. But some excellent scatter rugs are available for much less than one thousand dollars, especially if not in excellent condition.

The modern orientals, sold both at rug auctions and in the stores, are usually less expensive on a square foot basis than the antiques. While generally more expensive than woven rugs and carpeting, there are exceptions.

FACTORS TO CONSIDER IN THE SELECTION
OF AN ORIENTAL RUG

In buying an oriental rug, first consider the interior in which it is to be used. For example, oriental rugs fit into nearly every type of living room except possibly one with Colonial, French Provincial, or Directoire furniture. Bedrooms look best with hooked or rag rugs, or solid-color carpets. Floors in dining rooms, halls, and libraries are usually appropriately covered with machine-made or real orientals. In decorating a room, remember that the rug usually covers the largest or second largest area. Accordingly, if one already has chairs upholstered in vivid, patterned fabrics, and draperies in patterned materials, it would be wise and in good taste to select a plain-color rug, possibly a domestic.

If a consumer decides to buy an oriental rug, he should consider these points as well:

1. *Detection of worn areas.* Careful inspection is necessary by running the hand over the surface of the entire rug to detect low or worn spots. If the rug is small enough, hold it up to the light. If you can see light through the rug, it is badly worn.

2. *The size best suited to the space.* If the room is large, a rug at least 9 × 12 feet in size would be advisable, because too many small scatter rugs seem to cut up the floor space. One large rug with smaller ones in front of doors, the fireplace, or stairs is a better arrangement, because the large rug forms a center for the room. Some people prefer a room-size carpet in a neutral shade over which they throw small scatter-size orientals. With this plan, the small rugs do not slip on hardwood floors, whereas small rugs alone require a felt or rubber mat under them.

---

[11] A skilled craftsman can tie 8,000 to 12,000 knots in a day. Thus, a 9′ × 12′ rug with 150 knots to the square inch will take one person about nine months of steady work, with some allowance for loom set-ups and adjustments.

However, small orientals may slip when placed on a long-piled acrylic broadloom.

3. *The design.* If one has no furniture or draperies as yet, any appealing designs or colors may be used. But if there are other furnishings, their color and type must be considered to make a harmonious ensemble. The outline of the design should be distinct, and whites should be clear.

4. *The closeness of construction and evenness of weave.* Turn the rug over on the back and notice the closeness of the weave. The more knots to the inch, the stronger the rug. An evenly woven rug will be flat on the floor and will not pucker at the ends. The thickness of the rug and the depth of the pile have no definite bearing on durability; some of the thinnest orientals with short pile wear longest, because they are very closely woven of Grade A wool. A new rug should have even pile, and the color should be the same on the surface as it is at the knot.

5. *Place of purchase.* To acquire a thorough knowledge of orientals would take a lifetime. It is therefore advisable for a customer to go to a reliable department store or importer who will stand behind his merchandise. A guarantee by an unethical merchant is meaningless. Some so-called antiques are really modern; they may have been treated with chemicals and filled with dust to make them appear old. Good buys can be obtained at auctions, but considerable expertise is needed in selection. If the customer can spot the dealers present and is careful to bid only slightly higher than a dealer, he may do better than in the stores, but a good deal of time has to be spent consummating the purchase.

CARE OF RUGS

If they are to give long service, all rugs should have proper care. A rug cushion should always be placed under a rug and it should be turned around occasionally. When a domestic rug is new, a certain amount of woolly fluff may brush out of it. This is to be expected, for in the process of shearing, particles of wool often fall back into the pile. The regular vacuuming will, in time, remove all fluff.

If the surface of the pile is not even, however, any long ends, tufts, or knots projecting above the surface should be cut off. Pulling out long ends may injure the construction.

Sometimes a solid-color rug seems to have dark and light spots in it. These marks are called *shading*, which is due to a crushing of the pile in spots—often caused by someone walking or moving furniture on the rug. The crushing of the pile may be somewhat reduced if the rug is turned around occasionally; the wear is thus distributed evenly. Running the sweeper or vacuum cleaner in the direction of the pile will decrease shading. Professional cleaning may prove a cure.

By going over soft floor coverings with a carpet sweeper once a day or every two days or with a vacuum cleaner once or twice a week, one can keep a rug comparatively clean. In vacuuming orientals, avoid going over the fringes. A stiff broom may injure the pile of the rug and so should be used lightly. The sweeping should be in the direction of the pile, not against it. New rugs should be vacuumed as often as old rugs. Hand-hooked rugs should not be shaken or cleaned with a vacuum, as the pile may be loosened by the suction; the old-fashioned carpet sweeper or broom is the best cleaner. If ends of pile or warp of any rug appear above the surface, they should be clipped off level and not pulled out.

In the case of indoor-outdoor carpeting used outdoors, hosing down is a good cleaning method. If used indoors, the carpeting may be sponged with a detergent solution.

Rugs are best kept free of moths by hard use. Rugs used for hangings should be examined frequently to see that moths are not in them. A weekly spraying with an insecticide will generally keep rugs free of moths during the summer months, and vacuum cleaning is also helpful. In the South, where the woodworm sometimes eats the jute backs of rugs, naphthalene can be used as a preventative.

For storage, rugs should be rolled up, not folded, preferably around a pole, and sprinkled with moth crystals that should be removed every few months.

SHAMPOOING AND SPOT REMOVAL

Soap, water, or chemicals may injure domestic wool rugs unless one knows how to use them. Soil embedded in carpets and rugs can best be thoroughly cleaned by commercial cleaning services. Domestic and oriental rugs and carpets that can be removed from the floor may be sent to a rug-cleaning plant for most thorough and efficient cleaning. Wall-to-wall coverings can be done professionally in the home. Care in selection of a commercial rug cleaning establishment is important.[12] Cleaning a carpet or oriental rug on the floor by hand is hard work, but a shampooing device that holds and distributes a special cleaning fluid as it is run over the rug does a satisfactory job. Unless a rug is made of fibers that soil easily, shampooing is not required very often. Prompt and careful treatment of stains is important for good serviceability in any carpet or rug.

For removing spots from acrylic and nylon pile carpets, use a dull-edged spoon to dislodge as much of the soil as possible. With tissues or white cloth, blot up all you can of the soil. Apply a detergent or cleaner sparingly. To avoid spreading the stain, work from the edge to the center. Rinse with water and blot with tissues after each application of cleaner. Then put a half-inch stack of tissues, weighted down with a heavy object, on the cleaned area and leave it overnight. Remove the tissues, which have absorbed moisture from the carpet. Brush up the carpet pile lightly. The spot should have disappeared.

CLEANING SOLUTIONS TO USE AT HOME[13]

1. Detergent solution, a dry powder household detergent (Tide, Cheer, Fab). Mix a teaspoon of detergent, one teaspoon of vinegar to one quart of water.
2. Dry-cleaning solvent. Any approved consumer brand. Read the label carefully. Take notice of safety precautions.
3. Alcohol—denatured or isopropyl.

[12]National Institute of Rug Cleaning, 7355 Wisconsin Ave., Bethesda, Maryland, 20014, will supply names of member cleaning plants in a given area.

[13] "How To Care for Your Carpet of Acrilan, Acrylic Pile" and "How To Care for Your Carpet of Cumuloft Nylon Pile," pamphlets by Monsanto Textiles Division, Monsanto Company, New York.

Type of Stain	Removal Procedure
Dry, Soiling Materials Clay Plaster	1. Crumble and remove with vacuum 2. Apply foam of neutral detergent 3. Blot with tissue 4. Dry thoroughly 5. Gently brush pile
Oily Materials Butter Grease Ball Point Pen Ink Furniture Polish Hand Cream Oil Carbon Black (soot)	1. Remove excess materials 2. Apply a dry cleaning fluid 3. Dry the carpet 4. Repeat application of solvent if necessary 5. Dry the carpet 6. Gently brush pile
Oily Foodstuffs, Animal Matter Coffee Blood Tea Salad Dressing Milk Ice Cream Gravy Sauces Chocolate Egg Vomit Animal Glue Catsup Mustard	1. Remove excess material (blot liquid or scrape semisolids) 2. Apply detergent-vinegar water solution* 3. Dry the carpet 4. Apply dry cleaning solvent 5. Dry the carpet 6. Gently brush pile
Foodstuffs, Starches and Sugars Candy Soft Drinks Alcoholic Beverages Fruit Juice **Stains** Fruit Stain Urine Washable Ink Excrement	1. Blot up liquids or scrape off semisolids 2. Apply detergent-vinegar water solution* 3. Dry the carpet 4. Reapply the detergent-vinegar water solution (if necessary) 5. Dry the carpet 6. Gently brush pile
Heavy Grease, Gum Gum Paint Tar Heavy Grease Lipstick Crayon Rubber Cement Shoe Polish	1. Remove excess material 2. Apply dry cleaning fluid 3. Apply detergent-vinegar water solution* 4. Reapply dry cleaning fluid 5. Dry the carpet 6. Gently brush pile

FIGURE 20.21. Removal of spots and stains from rugs. (Courtesy Eastman Chemical Products, Inc.)

4. Amyl acetate—a common drugstore brand, or nail polish remover without lanolin, or lacquer thinner.
5. Bleach solution, nine parts water, one part of chlorine bleach.
6. Sour solution, one part white vinegar, one part water.

A word of caution: Rings on the surface of a carpet may be caused by excessive soaking. Follow the instructions of the solvent maker, because water alone can cause a brown or yellow stain. Therefore, don't overwet the carpet. Use a towel or tissue to soak up excess water.

551

SUMMARY The decoration of an interior should grow out of the use to which the rooms are put and the personal preferences of the occupants; but a knowledge of period styles in furniture and furnishings is useful and necessary.

Since the rug takes up a large area in a room, it is a very important consideration in decoration. A rug usually proves to be a good buy if it is carefully selected and properly cared for. In modern domestic rugs, colors and patterns can be found that fit with any decorative scheme. If one can afford to possess an oriental, there are innumerable designs from which to choose. Again, care in selection repays the buyer many times over.

PROJECTS 1. Draw the layout of a department that sells soft floor coverings in a large retail store.
   (*a*) Classify carpets and rugs sold in each section; give their names, sizes, colors, approximate prices.
   (*b*) Constructively criticize the layout and stock assortment.
2. Clip advertisements for rugs in your local newspaper.
   (*a*) Classify carpets and rugs offered by various stores.
   (*b*) Tabulate fiber contents, sizes, colors, and prices of each article.
   (*c*) Analyze your data to determine which floor covering is the best value for the price. Which is the poorest value? Rate articles in order from best to poorest.
   (*d*) Support your conclusions.

Alternate: If advertisements of soft floor coverings cannot be obtained, visit a large department or specialty store that carries carpets and rugs. Follow steps *a*, *b*, *c*, *d* above.

GLOSSARY Antique oriental rug—A hand-tied oriental rug at least 100 years old.

Aubusson carpet—A term used for carpets made with a round wire, uncut looped pile, to distinguish them from cut pile carpets.

Axminster machine-made rugs with oriental designs or velvet construction, and are frequently referred to as sheen-type rugs.

Baluchistan rug—A hand-tied oriental rug from Baluchistan, commonly called *Baluchi.*

Bath mat—A floor covering often made of tufted chenille. See Chapter 19.

Broadloom—A seamless woven carpet six to eighteen feet or more in width.

Carpet rayon—A specially constructed fiber and yarn for carpets that has greater tensile strength and is coarser than rayon for clothing.

Carpeting—A soft floor covering that can be made of a variety of different fibers. It is sold by the yard and can be cut to any size.

Carved rug—See *Sculptured rug.*

Caucasian rug—Hand-tied oriental from Caucasia and Transcaucasia on the Black and Caspian seas. Names include Kabistan, Shirvan, Kazak, and Karaja.

Chain warp—A warp that joins or binds together the upper and lower surfaces of a rug.

Chenille blanket—A loosely woven fabric (often cotton warps and large woolen fillings) cut into narrow strips that are pressed V-shaped.

Chenille rug—A floor covering made with chenille (caterpillar) yarn used as a filling. It may be carved. See *Chenille blanket.*

Chinese rug—A hand-tied oriental rug made in China, often characterized by dragons and flowers in circles.

Contemporary style—A present style in home furnishings that emphasizes the mobile and functional in furniture.

Contract carpeting—Floor covering in considerable yardage contracted for by motels, bowling alleys, schools, and institutions.

Domestic rugs—Floor coverings manufactured in the United States.

Drugget—A rug of all wool or wool and cow's hair mixed pile with a ground of jute. It is used for sun porches and summer cottages.

Embossed type rug—See *Sculptured rug.*

Fiber rug—A floor covering made of tightly twisted strips of paper, finished to repel friction and moisture.

Flocked carpet—See *Nonwoven floor coverings.*

Frame—Denotes the number of colors possible in a Wilton rug; for example, five frames means five colors are possible, one frame for each color yarn. Frame holds spools of colored pile yarn in Axminster construction.

Ghiordes—Type of knot used to make pile in Turkish hand-tied rugs.

Grass rug—Made of cured prairie grass.

Hearth rug—A hand-tied oriental rug characterized by designs in the form of arches, one at either end.

Hit-or-miss rug—A floor covering made of many colored twisted rags bound together.

Hooked rug—Handmade by using a large hooked needle to pull yarn or bias-cut strips of fabric through a coarse burlap fabric. Some types are made on the Jacquard loom in round wire construction to imitate the hand-hooked type.

India rug—Hand-tied rugs made in India in the province of Lahore, numdahs, and druggets.

Indoor-outdoor carpeting—Floor coverings suitable for both inside the house and outdoors.

Kilim (ghileem)—Near Eastern oriental woven with a shuttle or needle, with no pile. Kilims are used by the orientals as portiéres, couch covers, and table covers.

Luster rugs—Rugs that are chemically washed to give them sheen. They may be Wilton, Axminster machine-made rugs with oriental designs or velvet construction, and are frequently referred to as sheen-type rugs.

Modern style—A style in home furnishings that emphasized simplicity, angularity, and straight lines in furniture.

Mohair rug—Floor covering with mohair pile and jute back.

Needle-punched carpeting (needle loom)—A nonwoven nonpile carpeting with a felt-like surface. A lap, web, or batt of loose fibers is applied to a base of cotton fabric, burlap, plastic, rubber, etc. Needles having downward-facing barbs are forced into the base, thus causing the tufts of fiber to adhere to the base.

Nonwoven floor coverings—Carpets having tufts that are usually punched through a burlap backing. Flocked carpets are made of precut electronically charged fibers that are stuck to a backing coated with adhesive.

Numdah rug—A rug from India, made of felted goat's hair. Designs are embroidered on the rug by hand.

Oriental rug—Hand-tied rug made in the Near East, India, or China.

Patent back—Carpeting that has its tufts locked in place by a mixture of latex or pyroxylin.

Persian (Iranian) rug—A hand-tied oriental rug made in Iran. Names of Persian rugs include Kirman, Kashan, Shiraz, Teheran, Saraband, Isfahan, Sarouk, Hamadan, Meched, Tabriz, Nain, and Qum.

Pile warp—The warp yarn in a carpet that forms the looped pile.

Pitch—The number of pile yarns to the 27-inch width.

Plush carpet—Floor covering with one level of cut pile made of soft twisted yarns that do not show any yarn texture.

Prayer rug—A hand-tied Near Eastern oriental rug characterized by a design in the form of an arch.

Rag rug—Floor covering made of strips of twisted rags braided, crocheted, or bound together by cotton thread or cord.

Random-tip shears—Carpets and rugs with a high pile sheared at random.

Round-wire carpet—A Wilton construction in which a round wire is used instead of a flat wire to make the pile. Pile is therefore uncut.

Rows to the inch—Rows of yarn tufts to the inch lengthwise.

Rug—A thick, heavy fabric that can be made of a variety of different fibers and textures. Term is often used synonymously with carpet. Rugs are made with ends finished with binding or fringe.

Rug cushion—A fabric of sponge rubber or hair felt placed under the rug to prevent the rug from slipping and to make the rug more soft and cushiony.

Savonnerie—A French rug made in imitation of oriental knotted rugs with rococo patterns.

Sculptured rug—A floor covering with a Jacquard design made with different heights of pile.

Senna knot—Type of knot used to make pile in Persian hand-tied rugs.

Shading—Crushing of the pile of a rug so that it seems to have light and dark spots in it.

Shag—A floor covering with relatively long, loose wool or man-made fibered pile.

Stuffer warp—A warp that passes straight through the carpet to form a stuffing.

Toile de Jouy—Used for draperies. See Glossary, Chapter 21.

Tufted carpet—Made by needling pile yarns into a previously woven backing of jute or cotton.

Turkish rug—A hand-tied oriental rug made in Turkey. Names of Turkish rugs include Bergama, Ladik, Ghiordes, Kulah, and Oushak.

Turkoman rug—A hand-tied oriental rug from Turkestan. Names include Bokhara, Beshir, Tekke Turkoman, and Samarkand.

Tweed—Heavy wool, cotton, or man-made fibered fabric in handwoven effects, used for draperies and upholstery.

Twist—A carpet made with uncut pile. Yarns of different colors may be twisted together to form pile loops.

Underlay—See *Rug cushion.*

Velvet rug—A floor covering woven on a plain harness loom with cut pile. It has solid-color or printed pile.

Wall-to-wall carpeting—A carpet of any fiber or fibers and in any construction that covers the entire floor.

Wilton—A floor covering (usually woolen or worsted) with buried pile, cut or uncut. It is often made with carved designs in plain color or multicolored.

Wire—Each row of pile or tufts on the surface of a rug. See *Rows to the inch.*

Draperies, Curtains, and Upholstery

21

No harmonious decorative scheme comes into being without thought. A carefully considered plan must be worked out before a satisfactory living area or an efficient working space can be created. Each individual reacts in a different way to the design of a space where he or she will live or work. Consequently each person involved in using these areas should be considered by the decorator.

WHAT IS DESIGN? Design, to most people, means the choice and arrangement of certain shapes or forms to produce a decorative effect. Design must include both color and form, for without color, there is no form.

Structure is the composition and foundation of creative decoration. Everything depends upon the structural idea—the relationships between the construction of the room and the shapes or forms of the furnishings in the room. In designing a room, it is important to see the whole rather than only the parts—the furniture, colors, and decorations. For instance, if one has only a floor plan without wall elevations, one cannot determine the height of the ceiling, door opening, windows, and the like. Design is a functional factor of every single object in the decorating and furnishing scheme.

THE CREATION OF STRUCTURAL DESIGNS IN FABRICS

Home furnishing fabrics, like apparel fabrics, are made with structural or printed designs. A structural design is a woven-in pattern as opposed to a printed one. (See *types of printed designs*, Chapter 8.) An intricate structural design, made in Jacquard or dobby weave, is first worked out on point paper. Then cards or narrow wooden strips are made to govern the loom operation. (See Chapter 5.) Structural designs may also be called *visual designs*, when the design shows up in the effect done in the weave. For instance, if one pure color is used in the warp and another pure color is used in the filling, the effect is an iridescent one or even a brand-new shade. This combination of colors in a weave may create a sheen; or a black warp and a gold filling may give a metallic gold appearance. Visual designs are popular in contemporary styles because of their textural interest.

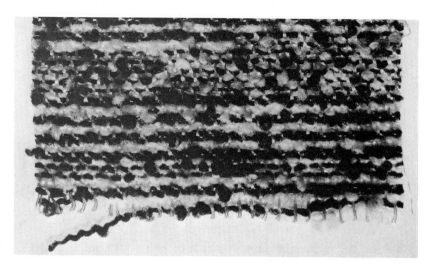

FIGURE 21.1. Construction of a visual design.

Any natural or man-made fibered yarn or blend may be used for a visual design. The designer tries, on her handloom, the fiber and the color in the warp that will give the effect she desires. This trial-and-error method is called *direct designing:* no point-paper patterns are drawn because the weave is usually a basic one. There are unexpected hazards, however, in such an approach to designing. For example, a designer working with spun saran found that its static electricity caused it to pick up pieces of varicolored lint around the plant. As a result, the woven cloth appeared multicolored instead of the two colors she had planned.

Some visual designers who are novices in weaving may sacrifice certain basic qualities in a cloth just for the visual effect. A company lost $50,000 on an upholstery fabric with a cotton warp and jute filling because there were too few ends to the inch to withstand abrasion in use.

When a designer for a fabric house is satisfied with the design she has created on the handloom, she has the design approved by the chief designer. Then the design is checked by the testing laboratory to see if it is

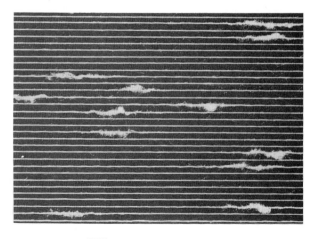

FIGURE 21.2. Curtain and drapery fabric of acetate random slub yarns. (Courtesy Eastman Chemical Corp.)

adequate for its intended uses. If it qualifies it is sent to a mill to be power-woven on a commercial basis.

In addition to designs created by its own staff, a fabric house may buy designs from free-lance designers. There seems to be no sure way of patenting or trademarking a structural or visual design. For by merely changing the count of the cloth, the fiber content, or the color of the yarn, the design can be proved not to be a copy. It is disheartening to a fabric house to find another manufacturer adding one insignificant metallic yarn to a borrowed design so that it is different from the original.

FIGURE 21.3. A South-of-the-Border drapery design. (Courtesy Celanese Fibers Marketing Co.)

**A HAR-
MONIOUS
ENSEMBLE**

To create a harmonious decorative scheme, there are four essential points to be kept in mind: (1) style of the furniture, (2) size of the room, (3) use of the room, and (4) size and shape of the windows.

Two interior decorating terms, drapery and curtain, require clarification. A drapery is any pinch-pleated window covering except a pinch-pleated sheer, which is considered a curtain.[1]

Style of drapery treatment is a first consideration. Draperies and curtains should be used to emphasize and beautify the structural opening with which they are associated. Is the room to become dignified, dramatic, cottagelike, theatrical, or masculine? These factors naturally have more bearing on the choice of hangings than on the grade of the fabric. Draperies, an intrinsic part of home furnishings, help to build up the character and mood of each room, whether it is a room in a home, office, theater, hotel, or restaurant. Depending on the choice of fabric for draperies, one can make a room formal or informal. A formal room would require a fine fabric: velvet, damask, taffeta, satin, or antique satin. Choice

[1] Definition evolved from research of leading retailers and prime producers by Du Pont.

of color can depend on exposure of the room or personal likes or dislikes of the homemaker. A scheme may be built up around a fine oriental rug or an antique Aubusson rug that the homemaker owns or wishes to purchase.

Curtains and draperies are usually not the first decision. Rather, they are a background for the style of furniture, the rug or carpet, and the upholstery to be used. The exception would be a room where a fine French or English blocked chintz or linen is proper. The colors in the drapery would be a guide for the carpet, wall color, and upholstery.

STYLE OF THE FURNITURE

In Chapter 20 the different period styles in furniture were discussed. To select suitable draperies, one needs to know the fabric with the exact design and texture that best typifies the spirit of the period represented by one's furniture. (The table in Appendix E, pp. 598-600 gives the fabrics appropriate to different periods.)

SIZE OF THE ROOM

The size of the room is an important consideration in the selection of appropriate furniture and also in the selection of a drapery design. Ordinarily small designs are best for a small room and large designs for a large room. A striped pattern hung horizontally normally makes a room appear lower and broader. Mirrors on one side of the room with draperies on the opposite side tend to make the room seem larger and more luxuriously draped.

USE OF THE ROOM

Some rooms are used much more than others. Much-used rooms include living rooms, nurseries, and bedrooms; those used less frequently include foyers, dining rooms, and guest rooms. Appropriate color schemes are based on the use for which the room is intended. In general, rooms lived in most of the time should be decorated in muted tones.

The color scheme for a house or an apartment should be thought of as a whole, not room by room. A feeling of shock is experienced by the visitor who walks from a red hall into a lavender living room or into a rose or blue dining room. It is like looking at a display of model rooms in a department store.

Style trends of the moment might influence the young bride or homemaker to choose stark black and white décor, bubble plastic inflated furniture, parsons tables, and chrome frames for chairs, all of which may be fleeting fads. A designer or decorator should offer suggestions on items of major expense, such as carpeting, chandeliers and draw curtains. The fad items will eventually have lost their glamour, and then the articles of better taste suggested by the decorator will create a good background. When the young homemaker's taste has matured, she will be ready to purchase the traditional articles for more permanent family living.

It is important for the skilled and trained decorator as well as for the homemaker to exercise great control in combining colors. There are very real personal psychological reactions to color, and one cannot presume to dictate taste in color to another person. It is too subtle and too personal a matter for mathematical formulas.

SIZE AND SHAPE OF THE WINDOWS

There are various sizes and shapes of windows that have to be draped, curtained, or both. Some windows are tall and narrow, some are short and wide, and some are arranged in groups. Each shape is a problem in decoration.

In general, a high, narrow window looks wider if the drapery extends beyond the window on the wall at either side. The amount of widening would depend on the architectural features of the wall space; for example, the draperies might be brought out six to ten inches on either side of the window frame for balance. However, there is no set rule. One might want to cover as much as three or more feet of wall to balance the room. In fact, it is fashionable to drape a whole wall, whether it contains one or more windows. This treatment usually consists of one pair of curtains with French pleating and heading installed on a traverse rod. The curtains

STRAIGHT FABRIC
COVERED CORNICE

DOUBLE HUNG OR
CAFE CURTAINS

SWAG AND JABOTS

COVERED CORNICE IN
FRENCH PROVINCIAL DESIGN

TREATMENT FOR
A DORMER WINDOW

FIGURE 21.4. Optical effect of drapery lines. (Drawings suggested by Mrs. J. Orton Buck.)

have 150 percent fullness allowed for heavy fabrics such as damasks, brocades, and organzas, and 300 percent for tissues (lightweight fabrics) such as gauze, voile, and net.

A valance—a decorative fabric or board installed across the top of a window—is usually made of buckram or wall board, padded slightly and covered in the same fabric as the draperies. The bottom of the valance is often shaped to carry out the period style of the room. A shirred valance is used most often when the fabric is sheer and unlined.

Curtains for French doors or inswinging casements are held firmly down at the top and bottom of the door or window by small brass rods. If the doors open into another room, the upper panes may be left bare, but if they open to the outdoors, the curtain should cover the entire door.

French doors may be treated with draperies to insure privacy and add color to the room. They may be made so that they can be drawn and treated as a window.

Another window treatment is the use of two long panel draperies that hang at either side of a window or at either end of a group treatment for side decoration.

If there are sufficiently wide strips of woodwork between windows, drapery panels may be hung between the windows. In another treatment, mirrors are used to cover or even to black out an unsightly window.

Sometimes a wide valance is hung across the top of several windows in a group to make them seem like one.

**DRA-
PERIES
AND
CURTAINS**

The types of draperies and curtains are classified on the following pages.

DRAPERIES OR OVERHANGINGS

These are decorative fabrics that are hung at the sides of the windows or doors for artistic effects. They may soften the line of the doors and windows or screen a doorway. They also add a note of color and interest. Draperies may be made of cotton, linen, rayon, silk, wool, man-made fibers, or mixtures of these fibers. (See the Glossary for the names of fabrics commonly used for draperies.) In the choice of draperies, as in that of upholsteries, the fabric should correspond with furnishings in the room. Textures in a formal room should be woven in silklike surfaces in acetates and polyesters. Cotton blended with polyester or rayon or acrylic textures may be used in informal rooms. Linens are more formal, durable, serviceable, and vigorous. Silks are formal, suggesting regalness and luxury. Rayons, acetates, polyesters, acrylics, and glass fibers are used in the same weaves and textures as silks.

Most newer man-made fibers can be laundered or dry-cleaned. Wools are especially appropriate for masculine decoration, such as in hunting lodges, libraries, and dens. Wools and nylons are also adaptable for fabrics used as curtains and seat covers in vehicles of transportation and hotel lobbies and rooms, and in clubs. Wool, a heavy fabric, drapes beautifully but requires care insofar as it attracts moths unless treated. Wools are informal, suggesting warmth, orderliness, and masculinity.

Because of the trend to casual living and informal decoration, satins and Jacquards are declining, whereas open weaves, knits, and sheer panels in natural colors are increasing in demand.

FIGURE 21.5. Swiss tambour muslin curtain. (Photograph courtesy of E.C. Carter & Son, Inc.)

INNER CURTAINS

Since these are hung next to the window frame or glass, they may also be called glass curtains. They may be divided into four groups: sheer, tambour, draw, and sash.

Sheer Curtains. Made of very thin materials and hung on a rod by hooks or casings, they average 1½ to 3 yards in length and usually hang loosely to the sill. A casement curtain is a type of glass curtain hung from an inside rod, the outside rod holding the overdraperies. Casement curtains are usually made of casement cloth of polyester, acetate, rayon, or silk gauze. Fiber glass, heavy lace, filet net, lawn, and voile are particularly well suited to windows of the outswinging leaded type where neighbors are close.

Tambour Curtains. Made in imported Swiss, heavily embroidered batistes, lawns, or net in elaborate and exquisite designs (white on white), these curtains can take the place of glass curtains or draperies, and they may be formal or informal. The net style is often used for ecclesiastical purposes.

Draw Curtains. Used as window shades, they insure privacy or shut out bright light. Equipped with a draw cord or traverse rod, they usually hang from an outside rod to the sill, to the bottom of the apron, or to the floor. They are made of opaque fabrics and are often lined or foam backed.

Sash or Café Curtains. These are hung on a rod attached to the lower window sash or to the lower half of the window casing. Bathroom or kitchen windows can be curtained in this way so that curtains do not hinder the raising or lowering of the windows. Windows that are opened frequently are best treated in this manner so that curtains do not soil or tear by blowing out of the window. French doors may be curtained with a sheer fabric, such as marquisette, ninon, voile, or batiste, held taut at top and bottom by small brass rods.

561

Café curtains (originally styled in France) consist of one, two, or three tiers of fabric that can be installed with (1) plain heading with brass rings sewn on, (2) clips, (3) shirred headings, or (4) fabric loops. The length of the tiers depends on the number of tiers desired; usually tiers overlap each other three inches. Headings and hems of the café curtains may be cut in scallops or squares or left straight. These curtains can be made of any informal fabric.

HOMEMADE CURTAINS

Although curtains and draperies can be purchased ready-made, home-makers may prefer to make their own to achieve greater individuality.

The first thing to do is to estimate correctly the amount of material needed. This estimate requires careful measuring of the window with a ruler or yardstick. (A string or tape stretches and is therefore likely to be inaccurate.) In estimating, add 9 inches to each curtain length: 5 inches for a bottom hem and 4 inches for a top hem. Sheer materials look best when the hem is turned over three times.

Sheer inner curtains usually just clear the sill or hang to the bottom of the apron. A graceful drapery reaches to the bottom of the apron or to the floor. Very formal draperies spread out on the floor.

When sheer materials are shirred on rods, a fullness of three times the width of the window should be allowed. Curtains or draperies may also be

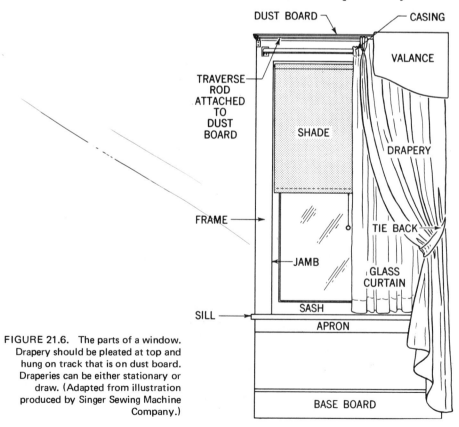

FIGURE 21.6. The parts of a window. Drapery should be pleated at top and hung on track that is on dust board. Draperies can be either stationary or draw. (Adapted from illustration produced by Singer Sewing Machine Company.)

pleated at the top. A Flemish or a French pleat is a box pleat with three loops caught together about 4 inches from the top and hung by a hook or ring. Seven pleats are generally made in 50-inch materials, which leaves a panel 25 inches wide. Five pleats in a 36-inch fabric leave an 18-inch panel. When using a 36-inch width, allow one third again as much fabric as you need for a 50-inch material, whether for draperies, upholstery, or slip covers. If you are using a patterned fabric, allow for repeat of the pattern.

The valance or decoration of ornamental material hung at the top of the window may be of these types:

1. Shirred on an outside rod (not on same rod as the side draperies).
2. Flat (pulled straight, no fullness).
3. French-pleated (three small pleats pinched together at intervals).
4. Box pleated (pleats spread flat and pressed, sewed at even intervals).
5. Side pleated (pleats basted at even intervals and pressed in one direction).
6. Dutch (valance shirred on same rod and placed between the side draperies).
7. Cornice board (a piece of wood carved or cut to serve as a valance and painted in the color scheme of the room).
8. Swag and jabots (top, or swag, hangs in draped curves between two or more points). Side panels are jabots. See Figure 21.7.

READY-MADE CURTAINS

Nearly every type of curtain or casement curtain is available ready-made. Ready-made draperies can also be purchased. The most common types of ready-made curtains are:

1. Ruffled (with tie-backs, with or without valance; well suited to informal rooms, bedrooms, nurseries, and so forth).
2. Crisscross (two panels cross each other at the top and are tied back; appropriate for colonial rooms).
3. Sash curtains (cover the bottom sash of the window; appropriate for kitchens and bathrooms).

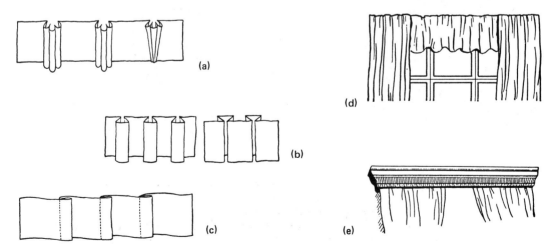

FIGURE 21.7. Types of valences. (a) French-pleated; (b) box-pleated; (c) side-pleated; (d) kitchen; (e) cornice board with wood mouldings.

4. Plain pairs of curtains (sold in pairs; narrow hems down the sides and wider hems across the bottom; may or may not have fringes).
5. Panels (single curtains; one panel is made to cover the entire window).
6. Café (consist of one, two, or three tiers of fabric that usually overlap about three inches).

SELECTION OF MATERIALS FOR DRAPERIES

There are so many types of drapery fabrics that at first it may seem difficult to make an appropriate selection. But if three important factors are considered, *color*, *texture*, and *design*, the task should be easier. Color having been determined, texture can next be settled. Texture means the roughness or smoothness of the surface of a fabric. The one rule that governs texture combination is that textures should be neither too much alike nor too dissimilar. For example, silk velvet should not be combined with rough linen-like textures, or taffeta with monk's cloth. On the other hand, there should be enough textural contrast to create interest. In a room in which the draperies are of damask and the curtains are of gauze, the upholstery may be of brocade, striped taffeta, plain taffeta, or velvet. For an informal room a pleasant combination might be achieved by combining a toile de Jouy for draperies and bedspread with a solid-color antique satin for a wing chair and a small bench. (See Glossary at the end of this chapter for names and identifying features of drapery fabrics.)

FIGURE 21.8. Toile de Jouy: a pictorial design fabric. (Photo by Jack Pitkin.)

In selecting appropriate designs, remember that too much pattern in a room is tiresome and should be avoided. The same principle that applies to color applies to one's selection of design.

In choosing drapery materials, a practical consideration is the effect of sunlight on the different fibers. Nearly all fabrics are weakened somewhat by sunlight. Rayon is about as resistant to sunlight as cotton, and bright acetate is more resistant than cotton. Sunlight decreases the strength of

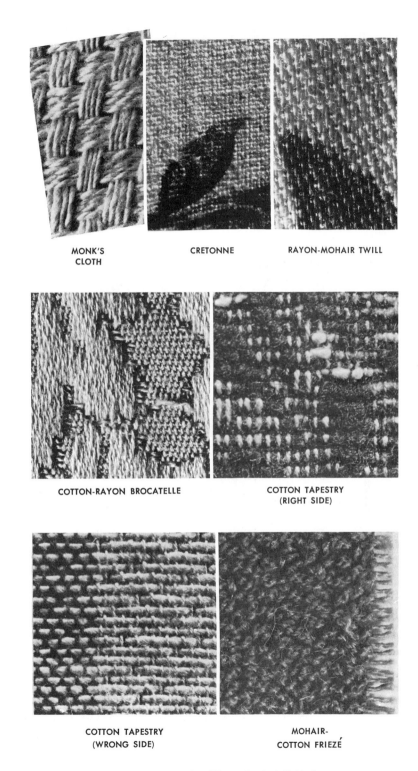

MONK'S
CLOTH

CRETONNE

RAYON-MOHAIR TWILL

COTTON-RAYON BROCATELLE

COTTON TAPESTRY
(RIGHT SIDE)

COTTON TAPESTRY
(WRONG SIDE)

MOHAIR-
COTTON FRIEZÉ

FIGURE 21.9. Selection of fabrics used for draperies. (Photos by Jack Pitkin.)

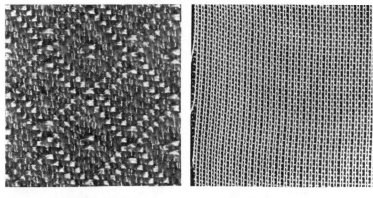

CASEMENT CLOTH   RAYON NINON

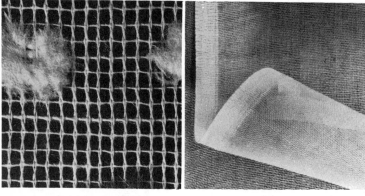

FIGURED MARQUISETTE   ORGANDY

FIGURE 21.10. Selection of fabrics for inner curtains. (Photos by Jack Pitkin.)

pure silk. Strong sunlight also injures nylon. Since both polyester and acrylic fibers are highly resistant to sunlight, they are seldom lined.

About 60 percent of the curtains and draperies produced in 1970 were of man-made fibers, about 28 percent of cotton, and 12 percent of glass. But the percentage of cotton is declining and the glass proportion is up somewhat.[2]

In a survey by Owens-Corning, women were found to look for the following traits (in order of preference) in buying curtains and draperies: (1) ease of care; (2) holding shape; (3) resistance to fading; (4) fire resistance; (5) protection of furniture from sunlight; (6) assurance of privacy.[3]

CARE OF DRAPERIES AND CURTAINS

If instructions for care of draperies and curtains appear on a label attached to the merchandise when purchased, that label should be saved for reference when the curtains must be cleaned.

Most cottons, particularly those blended with polyesters, can be washed in an automatic washer. Many curtains today have durable press

[2] *New York Times*, September 22, 1974, sec. 3, p. 12.
[3] *Ibid.*

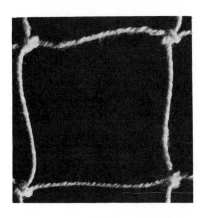

FIGURE 21.11. Informal linen fish net for draperies and curtains.

performance and are tumble dried. No ironing is required. Some all-cotton curtains require starching to give them a crisp finish. If the label indicates that they are permanent starchless finish, then starching is unnecessary. Curtains that require minimum care usually should be thrown over a line or hung at the window (with paper underneath to catch the water) to drip dry. Little if any ironing is generally needed. All-cotton velveteen, velour, and tapestry should be dry-cleaned.

Should the label indicate that the article is hand washable, a neutral soap solution of lukewarm water should be used. The soap solution should be squeezed through the fabric many times until the fabric is clean. Water should be extracted gently. The water for rinsing should be lukewarm to cool. Cotton fabrics containing rayon should be dried flat or hung over a line with the edges straight, away from heat or sun. The strain of drying should come on the cotton (the warp), not on the rayon. Since clothespins may cause threads to bulge or break, they should not be used on delicate fabrics. There is no problem with polyesters or acrylics. Fabrics containing man-made fibers should be pressed with a warm, not a hot, iron.

Linen draperies are usually washable, provided the dyes are fast. They are usually fairly heavy, sturdy cloths and so do not require special treatment in laundering. If ironing is required to remove wrinkles, it is advisable to do so while the fabric is still damp.

The average silk fabric should be dry-cleaned.

Sheer fabrics made of polyester and acrylic fibers are usually machine washable and machine dryable. Glass-fibered curtains are hand washable and do not wrinkle. When washed by hand, such sheer curtains should be dipped in a soap solution, rinsed, and hung to dry. Since glass fibers do not absorb moisture, fabrics should be cleaned and dried quickly, without wrinkling, shrinking, or losing their shape. When used in sheer curtains, glass fibers are smooth and may slip in laundering unless care is taken. Hems may need hand smoothing after washing to prevent puckering.

Wool fabrics and blends should be dry-cleaned. They are generally too heavy to be managed in laundering. To keep moths from attacking the wool in upholsteries and draperies, vacuum-clean and treat for moth prevention. A thorough cleaning of wool fabrics at regular intervals will rid them of odors, dirt, and moths.

Before curtains or draperies of any fabric are stored for a season they should be laundered or cleaned. Dirt and grit tend to rot cotton fabrics.

Soiled silks and rayons look much better when they have been dry-cleaned, for then their natural luster returns.

THE CURTAIN AND DRAPERY MARKET

In 1974 about 1.2 billion square yards of fabric went into the curtain and drapery market, a figure which may rise to 1.8 billion by 1980. Most of the buying is done by young married couples. It is expected that over the next several years, there will be more wives working, fewer children, and more families with incomes above $15,000. A good proportion of this money will be diverted to home furnishings, including draperies and curtains.

UPHOL-
STERY

Fabrics used for covering upholstered furniture and cushions and for slipcovers are classed as upholstery fabrics. Upholstery fabrics may be classified as follows:

1. Textured: a surface that is woven with a nubby yarn in the construction; may be made in any fiber.
2. Velvets: cut loops; thick, dense pile.
3. Damasks (reversible) and brocades (nonreversible): woven in elaborate Jacquard designs including brocades, brocatelles, and damasks.
4. Rib weaves: including tapestries (having large pictorial designs) and reps (having solid colors with crosswise ribs).

Any textile fiber can be used for upholstery, provided the cloth is sturdy enough to resist friction, sunlight, dry cleaning, and, in some cases, laundering. Wool, cotton, nylon, and polypropylene are probably the most satisfactory for upholstery. Silks, being luxury fabrics, should be used with discretion. Rayon and acetate are less expensive and are easier to care for. Plastic-coated fabrics are suggested where durability is paramount. Rayons and acetates are decorative and are best used in homes where there are no young children who may soil or tear fine fabrics. Nylon is strong, resists abrasion, and is easily cleaned.

If upholstery is to have hard usage, inconspicuous patterns and colors that will not show soil should be chosen. A few silk, rayon, or metal threads shot through a cotton or wool upholstery fabric give it luster and

FIGURE 21.12. A chair covered in cotton corduroy.

additional beauty. For durability, yarns should be tightly twisted and the weave close.

Upholstery fabric retains its freshness longer if it is covered during the summer months. Linen and cotton fibers are excellent for summer use as slipcovers; they make a chair or divan upholstered in wool seem cooler. Bright, cheerful designs in chintz or cretonne can change a formal room into an informal one. If upholstery is somewhat shabby, new slipcovers will freshen it. Some of the fabrics commonly used for slipcovers are chintz, cretonne, linen crash, cotton rep, nylon and cotton blends with rayon or polyester, cotton broadcloth, denim, and knitted stretch fabrics.

Some of the most commonly used fabrics for covering upholstered furniture and cushions are textures (in wool or cotton), brocade, damask, plush, velvet, velour, mohair, leather and its substitutes, tapestry, needlepoint, and laminated fabrics. (A description of the fabrics listed here appears in the Glossary.)

The relation between the style, size, and use of the piece of furniture to be covered and the selection of fabrics is the same as that between the room and the draperies and curtains.

CARE OF UPHOLSTERY

Upholstery should be brushed and vacuum-cleaned frequently, not only to remove dirt but to prevent attacks by moths on wool.

To guard against moths, when a new piece of furniture is bought, make sure the upholstery fabric is treated chemically to make it mothproof. A muslin covering inside the upholstery fabric will keep moths from the inside of the furniture.

If moths do get into an upholstered chair, spread paradichlorobenzene crystals (two to three pounds) over it. Then carefully wrap the chair in paper to confine the odor.

Spots should be removed when they first appear, with either soap and water (if the fabric is washable) or a dry-cleaning fluid. A white fabric often can be cleaned at home. Sprinkle dry powdered magnesia on it, rub the magnesia in, and then brush it off. If upholstery is badly soiled, take it to a reliable upholsterer for cleaning.

TAPESTRY Tapestry is an ornamental textile with a long service record. It is basically a handwoven fabric made with a bobbin worked from the wrong side on a warp stretched vertically or horizontally. The bobbin is carried only to the edge of the pattern and not from selvage to selvage. The surface consists entirely of filling threads. If the warp is stretched vertically, the loom is called *high warp;* if horizontally, *low warp.* In the high-warp loom the outline is designed in ink on the warp; in the low-warp loom the weaver places a cartoon (sketch of the design) under and close up to the warp, making inking unnecessary.

The warp yarns may be of wool, linen, or cotton. The warp of wool is elastic and is likely to produce a cloth with a crooked shape; warp of linen or cotton is stiffer. The filling yarn is generally wool, except in Chinese tapestry. Although silk is attractive in satin and brocade, it is flat and uninteresting in the interpretation of large pictures. The texture and vibrant character of tapestry is caused by three factors: the ribs formed by

FIGURE 21.13. An Aubusson tapestry.

the covered warps, which form the highlights; the hatchings, the fine filling threads in vertical series, which form the middle lights; and last, the slits (holes grouped in diagonal series), which form the shadows.

Handmade tapestries are still produced, and machine-made reproductions are woven on Jacquard looms. Two sets of warp and filling yarns are used. The wrong side is smoother than that of a handmade tapestry.

Tapestries are distinguished according to period and origin as follows:

1. Primitive—from Egypt; woven as early as 1500 B.C.
2. Gothic—from France; about the fourteenth century.
3. Renaissance—from France; wide borders; composition clear and picturesque; texture inferior to Gothic.
4. Gobelin (early)—from France; seventeenth century; Gobelins originally a family of dyers who added a tapestry factory; Louis XIV in 1662 made the factory a state institution; early Gobelin tapestries characterized by solemnity, conformity, and dignity; inspired by paintings of Rubens and LeBrun.
5. Gobelin (later)—brightness, individuality, and grace replaced earlier characteristics; inspired by Watteau and Boucher.
6. Beauvais—from a famous factory north of Paris; private but backed by Louis XIV; coarser and less expensive than Gobelin tapestries; mostly landscapes.
7. Aubusson—from the city of Aubusson, 207 miles south of Paris; less expensive than Beauvais; depict especially groups of personages; coarse, loose texture. (See Figure 21.13.)
8. Tapestries produced outside France—German, Swiss, English, Spanish, Russian, Turkish, and Chinese.

Tapestries were used in the Middle Ages as a protection against drafts and as wall decorations. Although in modern homes we do not need them as protection against drafts, we still use tapestries for hangings, either as a background or as pictures. Modern tapestries woven on the Jacquard loom are suitable for fire-screen covers, covers for benches or stools, reupholstering of furniture, knitting or shopping bags, and handbags.

SUMMARY   One who prefers individuality in home furnishing may follow that preference by using his or her own taste in choosing fabrics for draperies and curtains. Those who favor period styles may follow that inclination in decoration, provided appropriate fabrics are coordinated with the furniture and rugs. The most important thought to bear in mind is that harmony of design, color, and the texture of the fabrics must be maintained. In addition, the style of furniture, the size of the room, the use of the room, and the size and shape of the windows are important considerations.

PROJECTS   1. Plan the fabric decorations for a master bedroom (18 X 13 feet) of a suburban home. Two windows face north, and walls are painted in a grayish, pale, warm beige. Furniture is Early American. If possible, include swatches of actual fabric together with prices for ready-made articles or for fabric by the yard.
2. Plan the décor for a living room (20 X 18) of a city apartment. Casement windows open onto an unsightly, dark court. Walls are painted a light gray. Furniture is contemporary with an oriental influence. Wherever possible, the prices of fabric by the yard or the ready-made article should be included.
3. Plan the fabric decorations for a teen-age boy's or a teen-age girl's sunny bedroom in a small ranch-type home of five rooms. The wallpaper in the boy's room is patterned with large motifs of sailing vessels. The wallpaper in the girl's room has a spaced design of varicolored nosegays. The rooms each have a square, medium-sized window with louvers of clear glass. Furniture is contemporary.

GLOSSARY   Antique satin—A fabric made to resemble a silk satin of an earlier century. Has a slub face and a satin back.

Antique taffeta—Originally pure silk fabric with a nubby texture. Now usually polyester warps and silk fillings.

Bouclé.—A fabric made of novelty yarn that is characterized by tight loops projecting from the body of the yarn at fairly regular intervals.

Brocade—A drapery or upholstery fabric in Jacquard weave with raised designs. It has contrasting surfaces or colors that emphasize the pattern. Metallic threads may be shot through the fabric.

Brocaded satin—A satin fabric with raised designs in Jacquard weave.

Brocatelle—A drapery and upholstery fabric made in double-cloth construction with a silk- or rayon-fibered face. Best grades have linen back. The design stands in relief from the ground, giving a padded effect.

Burlap—A coarse, stiff fabric in plain weave. It is made of jute, hemp, or cotton and is used for draperies.

Café curtains—Consist of one, two, or three tiers of fabric that usually overlap about three inches.

Casement cloth—Any medium-sheer drapery fabric suitable for casement windows and draperies.

Chenille—Fabric of silk, wool, cotton, or man-made fibers, made with chenille yarns or tufts, used for draperies and bedspreads. See Chapter 19.

Chintz—Glazed cotton and blends of polyester/cotton fabric, often printed in gay colors, used for draperies, slipcovers, bedspreads, and upholstery.

Contemporary style—See Glossary, Chapter 20.

Corduroy—In cotton blended with polyester for draperies. See Glossary, Chapter 17.

Cretonne—A plain-weave carded cotton fabric, usually printed with large designs. Cretonne is unglazed and is used for draperies and slipcovers.

Damask—A drapery or upholstery fabric of silk, rayon, and cotton, or other combinations of fibers, woven in Jacquard weave with reversible flat designs.

Denim—Twilled cotton fabric made of single hard-twisted yarns. Staple type has colored warp and white filling. Woven-in stripes and plaids are popular for draperies, upholstery, and bedspreads.

Design—The choice and arrangement of shapes or forms and color to produce a decorative effect.

Direct designing—A trial-and-error method in the use of yarns of different fibers and blends to create a visual design. It is done directly on a hand-loom with no point-paper pattern.

Faille—Used for draperies. See Glossary, Chapter 15.

Fiber glass—See Glossaries, Chapters 2 and 15.

Fishnet—Large novelty mesh fabric of cotton or linen, acrylic or polyester, made to resemble fishing nets in white or colors. It is used for curtains.

Frieze—Heavy pile fabric with rows of uncut loops. It is made of mohair, wool, cotton, or man-made fibers and is used for draperies and upholsteries.

Fringes—Thread or cords of any fibers grouped or bound together and loose at one end, used for trimming draperies and upholstery.

Gauze—Sheer, loosely woven plain-weave fabric suitable for curtains. It is made in wool, silk, or man-made fibers.

Gingham—Used for curtains. See Glossary, Chapter 17.

Homespun—A very coarse, rough linen, wool, cotton, or man-made fiber or blend in varied colors; generally in plain weave resembling wool homespun. It is used for draperies and upholstery.

Hopsacking—A coarse, loosely woven fabric in basket or novelty weave. The original hopsacking was used for sacking hops. Now made to resemble the original of linen, spun rayon, or cotton, and used in blends. Also used for dresses and coats.

Lace—See *laces*, Chapter 19.

Louver—A fitted window frame with slatted panels.

Marquisette—A sheer curtaining material of silk, rayon, nylon, polyester, or acrylic fibers woven in leno weave.

Matelassé—A heavy Jacquard double cloth with quilted appearance that is used for draperies and upholstery. See *matelassé* for dresses, Glossary, Chapter 17.

Moiré—A design having a watered appearance, usually on a ribbed textile fabric. When the fabric is sufficiently heavy, it may be used for draperies.

Monk's cloth—A heavy cotton fabric in basket weave (4 × 4 or 8 × 8). It comes in natural color, solid, or stripes, and is used for draperies and couch covers.

Monochromatic scheme—The use of a combination of different shades of one color.

Needlepoint—An upholstery fabric. Designs are usually floral, embroidered with yarn on coarse canvas.

Net—See Glossary, Chapter 19.

Ninon—A sheer plain-weave glass curtaining made in polyester or other man-made fibers. The warp yarns are arranged in pairs.

Organdy—Sheer, crisp, cotton or polyester in plain weave. See Glossary, Chapter 17.

Percale—Plain weave, closely woven fabric in cotton or man-made blends in dull finish that may be dyed or printed. It is used for curtains and bedspreads.

Plastics—Fabrics made of plastic-impregnated or plastic-coated yarns (core of yarn made of cotton, rayon, linen, silk, glass, nylon), plastic-finished fabrics, and all-plastic extruded fibers and yarns suitable for webbing and woven fabrics for porch and beach furniture. (See *saran*, Chapter 15.)

Plush—A heavy-pile fabric with deeper pile than velvet or velour. It may be mohair, silk, rayon, acrylic, or polyester, and is used for upholstery.

Pongee—Used for draperies and casement curtains. See Glossary, Chapter 17.

Poplin—See Glossary, Chapter 17.

Rep or repp—Heavy fillingwise corded fabric, heavier than poplin. It may be silk, rayon, or other man-made fibers, wool, or cotton. It is used for draperies and upholstery.

Sailcloth—A generic name for fabrics used for sails. May be made of cotton, linen, jute, nylon, or polyester. Sailcloth is also used for draperies, upholstery, and sportswear.

Sateen—A mercerized fabric of cotton or cotton blended with polyester in sateen weave used for lining draperies. It may be printed for draperies.

Satin—Silk and cotton, acetate and cotton, or other man-made fiber combinations woven in satin weave. It is used for draperies, upholsteries, bedspreads, and sheets.

Satin antique—See *Antique satin.*

Seersucker—See Glossary, Chapter 17.

Shantung—Used for draperies. See Glossary, Chapter 17.

Sheer curtains—Thin fabrics of polyester, cotton, and blends that hang text to the window glass.

Shiki (shiki rep)—Heavy rayon, acetate, and cotton, or other mixtures identified by wavy fillingwise cords. It is used for draperies.

Structural design—A woven-in pattern as opposed to a printed one.

Swiss (dotted or figured)—Used for curtains. See *Dotted Swiss*, Glossary, Chapter 17.

Synthetic fibers—Man-made fibers. See Chapter 2.

Taffeta—A plain-weave, stiff-finished fabric in silk or the man-made fibers. Used for draperies and bedspreads. See *Antique taffeta.*

Tambour curtains—Imported Swiss, heavily embroidered batiste, lawn, or polyester curtains.

Tapestry—A Jacquard woven fabric in cotton, wool, or man-made fibers. The design is woven in by means of colored filling yarns. On the back, shaded stripes identify this fabric. It is used for draperies and upholstery.

Textured—A surface that is woven with a nubby yarn construction. May be made in any fiber.

Toile de Jouy—Cotton fabric printed in pictorial designs. The original toile was printed by Oberkampf in 1759 at Jouy, France. It is used for draperies and bedspreads.

Tweed-textured—An exaggerated chevron or tweedlike structural design with accentuated nubs.

Valance—A decorative fabric or board that is installed across the top of a window.

Velour—A smooth, closely woven pile fabric usually of cotton, wool, or man-made fibers. The fabric is heavier than velvet and is used for draperies, upholstery, and bedspreads.

Velvet—Silk, rayon, nylon, acrylic cut-pile fabrics. When used for draperies and upholstery it is somewhat heavier than dress velvet.

Velveteen—An all-cotton pile fabric for draperies and upholstery that is heavier than dress velveteen. See Glossary, Chapter 17.

Visual design—When the design shows up in the effect done in the weave.

Voile—A sheer plain-weave curtain fabric of cotton, rayon, or polyester fibers made of hard-twisted yarns.

Whipcord—Hard-woven worsted fabric with fine diagonal cords on the face that is used for draperies and upholstery.

Appendices

Photomicrographs
of
Textile Fibers

A

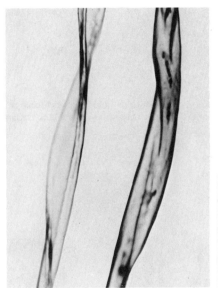

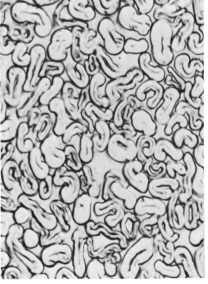

FIGURE A.1. Unmercerized native cotton: longitudinal and cross-sectional views. (Photomicrographs courtesy of the Southern Regional Research Laboratory of the U.S. Department of Agriculture.)

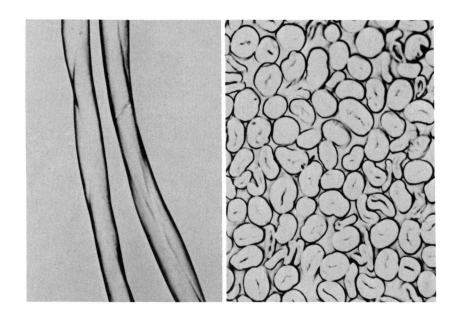

FIGURE A.2. Mercerized cotton: longitudinal and cross-sectional views. (Photomicrographs courtesy of the Southern Regional Research Laboratory of the U.S. Department of Agriculture.)

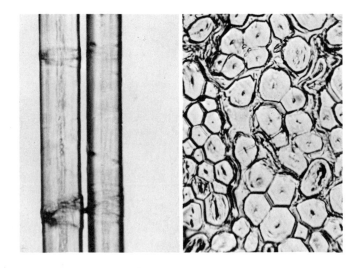

FIGURE A.3. Flax fibers: longitudinal and cross-sectional views magnified 500 times. (Photomicrographs courtesy of the Southern Regional Research Laboratories of the U.S. Department of Agriculture.)

FIGURE A.4. Ramie fibers: longitudinal and cross-sectional views magnified 500 times. (Photomicrographs courtesy of the Southern Regional Research Laboratory of the U.S. Department of Agriculture.)

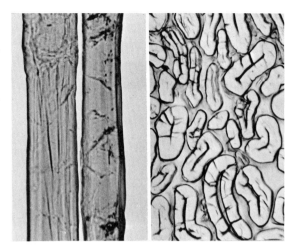

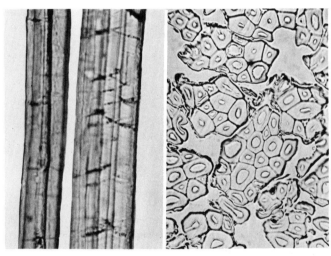

FIGURE A.5. Jute fibers: longitudinal and cross-sectional views magnified 500 times. (Photomicrographs courtesy of the Southern Regional Research Laboratory of the U.S. Department of Agriculture.)

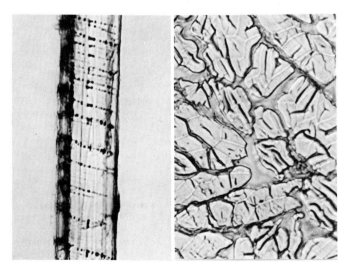

FIGURE A.6. Hemp fibers: longitudinal and cross-sectional views magnified 500 times. (Photomicrographs courtesy of the Southern Regional Research Laboratory of the U.S. Department of Agriculture.)

579

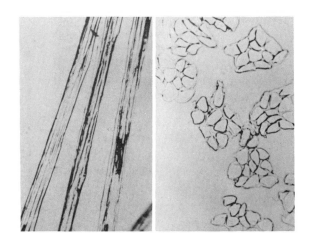

FIGURE A.7. Cultivated raw silk. Left: Longitudinal view of silk fibers, showing the sericin, which forms an outer layer around the fibroin, or main core, of the fiber. Right: Cross sections of raw silk threads reeled from six cocoons. Since each thread is doubled, there are actually twelve filaments bound together by the natural gum, or sericin.

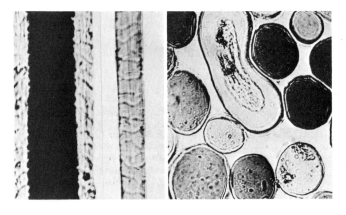

FIGURE A.8. Mohair: longitudinal and cross-sectional views. (Photomicrographs courtesy of the Forstmann Woolen Company.)

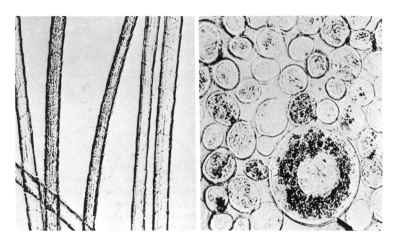

FIGURE A.9. Cashmere: longitudinal and cross-sectional views. (Photomicrographs courtesy of the Forstmann Woolen Company.)

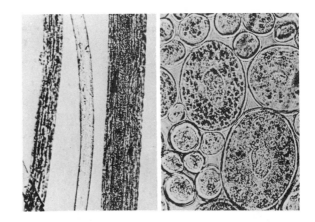

FIGURE A.10. Camel's hair: longitudinal and cross-sectional views. (Photomicrographs courtesy of the Forstmann Woolen Company.)

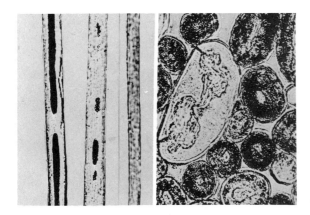

FIGURE A.11. Alpaca: longitudinal and cross-sectional views. (Photomicrographs courtesy of the Forstmann Woolen Company.)

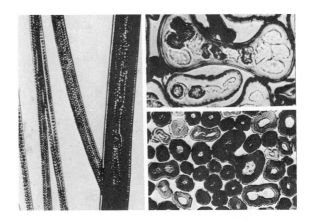

FIGURE A.12. Rabbit's hair: longitudinal and cross-sectional views. (Photomicrographs courtesy of the Forstmann Woolen Company.)

581

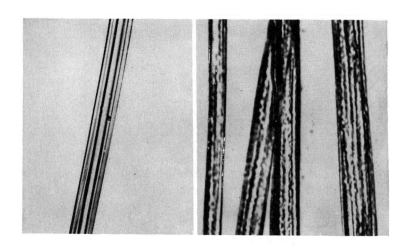

FIGURE A.13.   Vicose rayon. Left: Bright. Right: Delustered. (Photomicrographs courtesy of the United States Testing Company, Inc.)

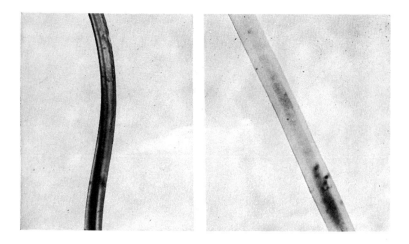

FIGURE A.14.   Left: Cuprammonium rayon (bright). Right: Acetate (bright). (Photomicrographs courtesy of the United States Testing Company, Inc.)

FIGURE A.15. Nylon. Left: Longitudinal view of a semi-dull nylon filament (3-3 denier) magnified 400 times. (Photomicrograph courtesy of Allied Chemical.) Right: Cross-sectional view magnified 660 times. The seventeen filaments are almost perfectly round and very smooth. This is a thread used in sheer stockings and fine knit goods. (Photomicrograph courtesy of E.I. Du Pont de Nemours & Company, Inc.)

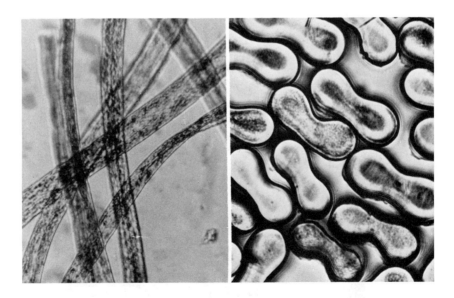

FIGURE A.16. Orlon acrylic. Left: Longitudinal view of continuous filament yarn shows the striated surface of the fiber. Right: Cross-sectional view of staple yarn magnified 500 times. (Photomicrographs courtesy of E.I. DuPont de Nemours & Company, Inc.)

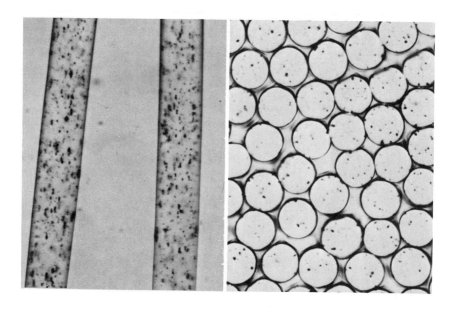

FIGURE A.17. Dacron polyester: longitudinal and cross-sectional views magnified 1000 times. (Photomicrograph courtesy of E.I. DuPont de Nemours & Company, Inc.)

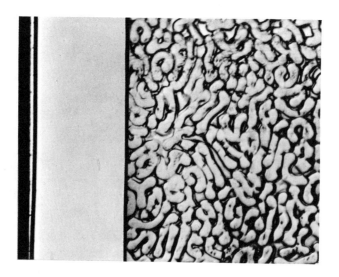

FIGURE A.18. Dynel modacrylic: longitudinal and cross-sectional views. (Photomicrographs courtesy of Carbide and Carbon Chemicals Company.)

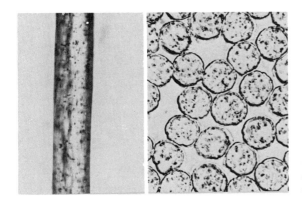

FIGURE A.19. Acrilan acrylic: longitudinal and cross-sectional views. (Photomicrographs courtesy of The Chemstrand Corporation.)

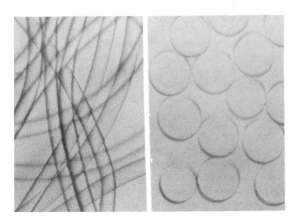

FIGURE A.20. Saran: longitudinal and cross-sectional views. (Photomicrographs courtesy of the National Plastic Products Company.)

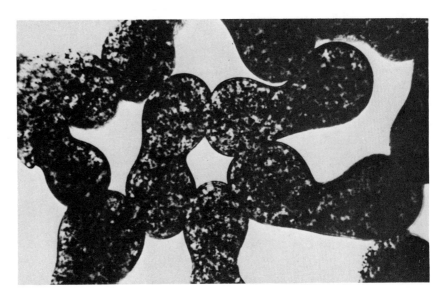

FIGURE A.21. Lycra spandex: cross-sectional view magnified 500 times. (Photomicrograph courtesy of E.I. DuPont de Nemours & Company, Inc.)

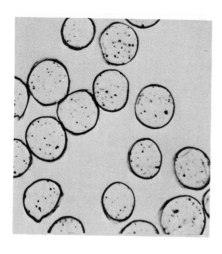

FIGURE A.22. Polypropylene olefin: cross-sectional view magnified 500 times. (Photomicrograph courtesy of E.I. DuPont de Nemours & Company, Inc.)

Generic Groups
of Man-Made Fibers
with Producers' Trademarks

B

Generic Groups of Man-Made Fibers with Producers' Trade Marks*

Generic Name	Characteristics	Some Typical Uses	Representative Trade Names	Features	Producers
Acetate	Excellent hand, good draping ability, moth and mildew resistant, cross-dyed effects with rayon, desirable hand, doesn't pill; fair wrinkle resistance, poor crease retention; must be ironed at low temperature; dimensional stability, low cost, limited strength	Apparel, home furnishings fabrics; also in blends with other man-made fibers	Acele	filament yarn	E. I. Du Pont de Nemours & Co., Inc.
			Ariloft	filament yarn	Eastman Kodak Co., Tennessee Eastman Co. Div.
			Avicolor	solution-dyed filament	FMC Corp., Fiber Division
			Celacloud	crimped staple fiberfill	Celanese Fibers Marketing Co., Celanese Corp.
			Celanese	stable filament, cigarette filter tow, and fiberfill	Celanese Fibers Marketing Co., Celanese Corp.
			Celaperm	solution-dyed filament	Celanese Fibers Marketing Co., Celanese Corp.
			Chromspun	solution-dyed filament yarn	Eastman Kodak Co., Tennessee Eastman Co. Div.
			Estron	filament yarn and cigarette filter tow	Eastman Kodak Co., Tennessee Eastman Co. Div.
			Estron SLR FMC	filament yarn	Eastman Kodak Co., Tennessee Eastman Co. Div. FMC Corp., Fiber Division
			Loftura	slub voluminized filament yarn	Eastman Kodak Co., Tennessee Eastman Co. Div.
			SayFR	fire resistant filament acetate	FMC Corp., Fiber Division
Acrylic	High bulk, warmth, and dimensional stability, woollike hand, pressed crease retention; minimum care, may pill, fair strength	Furlike pile fabrics, blankets, carpets, sweaters, infants' sleepwear; also used for stuffing of pillows, comforters, etc.	A-Acrilan	staple and tow	Monsanto Textiles Co.
			Acrilan	staple and tow	Monsanto Textiles Co.
			Bi-Loft	fibers, filaments	Monsanto Textiles Co.
			Creslan	staple and tow	American Cyanamid Co.
			Nandel	acrylic rotofil yarns	E. I. Du Pont de Nemours & Co., Inc.
			Orlon	staple and tow	E. I. du Pont de Nemours & Co., Inc.
			Zefran	acrylic, dyeable and producer colored	Dow Badische Co.
Anidex	Elastomeric fiber. Stretches and recovers. An elastomer of an acrylic closely allied to acrylic fibers and acrylic plastics	Foundation garments, woven and knitted clothing fabrics	Anim/8		Rohm & Haas Co.
Aramid	Highly aromatic polyamide fiber	Protective clothing for fire fighters, industrial workers, race drivers, military, pilots and tires	Kevlar	filament	E. I. Du Pont de Nemours & Co., Inc.
			Nomex	filament and staple	E. I. Du Pont de Nemours & Co., Inc.

*Compiled from material in 6th edition of Textile Fabrics 1970 and from Man-Made Fiber Fact Book of the Man-Made Fiber Producer's Association, Inc., 1974.

Generic Groups of Man-Made Fibers with Producers' Trade Marks (Continued)

Generic Name	Characteristics	Some Typical Uses	Representative Trade Names	Features	Producers
Azlon	Fibers produced from proteins found in casein, peanuts, soya beans, corn kernels				No domestic producers
Biconstituent Fiber			Source Monvelle	biconstituent nylon-polyester biconstituent nylon-spandex	Allied Chemical Corp., Fibers Division Monsanto Textiles Co.
Glass	Nonflammable; wrinkle, soil, and chemical resistant; very strong; quick drying, no ironing required; poor abrasion resistance	Draperies, curtains, electrical insulators	Beta Fiberglas 401 PPG Vitron	textile glass for decorative purposes filament and staple air bulked yarn glass fibers or yarns	Owens-Corning Fiberglas Corp. Owens-Corning Fiberglas Corp. Owens-Corning Fiberglas Corp. PPG Industries Inc. Johns-Manville Fiberglass Inc
Metallic	Metallic. glitter and sheen. Stainless steel used for functional purposes Metallic	Decorative addition to fabrics, static elimination, heat resistance and conductivity	Lurex Mylar	yarn of slit film polyester fibers for production of metallic yarns	Dow Badische Co. Du Pont E.I. De Nemours & Co., Inc.
Modacrylic	Chemical, fire, mildew resistant; fairly difficult to dye; resilient; strength poor; fair resistance to pilling; fair abrasion resistance; low melting point	Knitted pile fleece and fur like fabrics, carpeting, fire-resistant draperies, wigs	A-Acrilan Acrilan Elura Orlon Sef Verel Dynel	staple and tow staple and tow modacrylic staple and tow modacrylic modacrylic synthetic fur, wigs	Monsanto Textiles Co. Monsanto Textiles Co. Monsanto Textiles Co. E. I. Du Pont de Nemours & Co., Inc. Monsanto Textiles Co. Eastman Kodak Co., Tennessee Eastman Co. Div. Union Carbide Corp.
Novoloid	Lightweight, resilient, highly flame-resistant	Flame-resistant clothing	Kynol	derived from chemical compound "phenol"	Carborundum Corp.
Nylon	Strength and elasticity; abrasion resistance; quick drying, stability in repeated launderings, good color-fastness; fair hand (unless textured); safe ironing at 300° F.—350° F. depending upon type	Hosiery, lingerie, outer garments, carpets, upholstery; in blends for duffle bags, tents, glider ropes, thread, parachutes, tarpaulins, nets	Actionwear Anso Antron Astroturf Ayrlyn Beaunit Nylon	nylon nylon filament and staple soil-resistant carpet yarn nylon nylon continuous filament nylon filament, staple and tow, plied and heat set 2500 denier and white and space dyed	Monsanto Textiles Co. Allied Chemical Corp., Fibers Division E. I. Du Pont de Nemours & Co., Inc. Monsanto Textiles Co. Rohm and Haas Co., Fibers Division Beaunit Corp.

Generic Groups of Man-Made Fibers with Producers' Trade Marks (Continued)

Generic Name	Characteristics	Some Typical Uses	Representative Trade Names	Features	Producers
Nylon (cont.)			Blue "C"	nylon	Monsanto Textiles Co.
			Bodyfree	static-resistant filament apparel yarn	Allied Chemical Corp., Fibers Division
			Cadon	filament yarn and multilobal monofilament	Monsanto Textiles Co.
			Cantrece	nylon	E. I. Du Pont de Nemours & Co., Inc.
			Caprolan	yarns, monofilaments and textured yarns	Allied Chemical Corp., Fibers Division
			Captiva	textured filament hosiery yarn	Allied Chemical Corp., Fibers Division
			Cedilla	textured nylon filament yarn	Fiber Industries, Inc., Marketed by Celanese Fibers Marketing Co., Celanese Corp.
			Celanese	nylon	Fiber Industries, Inc., Marketed by Celanese Fibers Marketing Co., Celanese Corp.
			Cordura	nylon	E. I. Du Pont de Nemours & Co., Inc.
			Courtaulds Nylon	nylon producer crimped filament yarn	Courtaulds North America Inc.
			Crepeset	patented continuous monofilament that develops a regular crimp, also available in anticling yarn	American Enka Co.
			Cumuloft	textured filament carpet yarn	Monsanto Textiles Co.
			Enka	nylon filament, staple	American Enka Co.
			Enkaloft	textured multilobal continuous filament carpet yarn and staple	American Enka Co.
			Enkalure	multilobal continuous filament apparel yarn and textured delayed soiling carpet yarn	American Enka Co.
			Enkalure II	textured multilobal soil hiding continuous filament carpet yarn and staple	American Enka Co.
			Enkalure III	anticling fine denier nylon continuous monofilament	American Enka Co.
			Enkasheer	torque yarn for ladies' stretch hosiery (patented process)	American Enka Co.
			Guaranteeth	apparel and home furnishings nylon and polyester yarn	Allied Chemical Corp., Fibers Division
			Monvelle	biconstituent nylon-spandex	Monsanto Textiles Co.

590

Generic Groups of Man-Made Fibers with Producers' Trade Marks   (Continued)

Generic Name	Characteristics	Some Typical Uses	Representative Trade Names	Features	Producers
Nylon (cont.)			Multisheer	multifilament producer-textured stretch yarn for panty hose	American Enka Co.
			Phillips 66 Nylon	multifilament nylon yarn	Phillips Fibers Corp.
			Phillips 66 Nylon BCF	bulk continuous filament yarn	Phillips Fibers Corp.
			Qiana	nylon	E. I. Du Pont de Nemours & Co., Inc.
			Random-Set	heat-set BCF nylon	Rohm and Haas Co.
			Random-Tone	fashion and styling yarns of BCF nylon fiber	Rohm and Haas Co.
			Shareen	nylon monofilament textured yarn	Courtaulds North America, Inc.
			Source	biconstituent nylon polyester	Allied Chemical Corp., Fibers Division
			Stria	bulked nylon carpet yarn, modified twist	American Enka Co.
			Stryton	variable denier continuous filament nylon yarn	Phillips Fibers Corp.
			Super Bulk	heat-set, high-bulk continuous filament nylon carpet yarn; luxurious thick look of spun nylon	American Enka Co.
			Tango	fine denier nylon	Allied Chemical Corp., Fibers Division
			Twix	bulk nylon carpet yarn, modified twist	American Enka Co.
			Ultron	nylon	Monsanto Textiles Co.
			Variline	variable denier continuous filament yarn (patented process)	American Enka Co.
			Zefran	nylon	Dow Badische Co.
Nytril	Soft, resilient, nonpilling	Furlike rugs			No domestic producers
Olefin	Lightweight, excellent chemical resistance, and good resistance to abrasion, low melting point; fair hand; polypropylene has good strength and low cost	Seat covers, outdoor furniture, marine ropes, shoe and handbag fabrics, indoor and outdoor carpeting, carpet backing, and commercial bagging	Herculon	continuous multifilament, bulked continuous multifilament, staple and tow	Hercules Inc., Fibers Division
			Marvess	staple, tow and filament yarn	Phillips Fibers Corp.
			Marvess III BCF	bulk continuous filament yarn	Phillips Fibers Corp.
		Polypropylene for carpets	Herculon	staple, tow, filament	Hercules Inc.
			Vectra		Vectra Corp.

Generic Groups of Man-Made Fibers with Producers' Trade Marks   (Continued)

Generic Name	Characteristics	Some Typical Uses	Representative Trade Names	Features	Producers
Polyester	Great resiliency, wrinkle resistance, and pressed crease retention; quick drying; some kinds may pill; strength good; abrasion resistance good; hand fair to good depending on type; stable to repeated launderings when heat-set automatic wash-and-wear, safe ironing at 325° F.	Minimum-care fabrics, curtains, knits; in blends for suits, slacks, and dresses; suitable for durable press garments	Avlin	filament yarn and staple polyester	FMC Corp., Fiber Division
			Blue "C"	filament yarn, staple, tow and fiberfill	Monsanto Textiles Co.
			Dacron		E. I. Du Pont de Nemours & Co., Inc.
			Encron	continuous filament yarn, staple, fiberfill	American Enka Co.
			Encron MCS	staple with modified cross sections	American Enka Co.
			Encron 8	octalobal polyester that reduces glitter	American Enka Co.
			Enka	filament and staple polyester	American Enka Co.
			Esterweld	polyester	American Cyanamid Co.
			Fiber 200	polyester	FMC Corp., Fiber Division
			Fortrel	filament yarn, staple, tow and fiberfill	Fiber Industries, Inc., Marketed by Celanese Fibers Marketing Co., Celanese Corp.
			Fortrel 7	continuous filament fiberfill	Fiber Industries, Inc. Marketed by Celanese Fibers Marketing Co., Celanese Corp.
			Golden Touch	high denier per filament Encron polyester for luxurious hand	American Enka Co.
			Guaranteeth	apparel and home furnishings nylon and polyester yarn	Allied Chemical Corp., Fibers Division
			Kodel	filament yarn, staple, tow and fiberfill	Eastman Kodak Co., Tennessee Eastman Co. Div.
			Quintess	polyester multifilament yarns	Phillips Fibers Corp.
			Source	biconstituent nylon polyester	Allied Chemical Corp.
			Spectran	polyester	Monsanto Textiles Co.
			Strialine	slub-effect, variable dyeing Encron polyester	American Enka Co.
			Textura	producer textured polyester yarn	Rohm and Haas Co., Fibers Division
			Trevira	polyester	Hoechst Fibers Inc.
			Vycron	filament, staple, tow and fiberfill	Beaunit Corp.
			Zefran	polyester	Dow Badische Co.
Rayon	Versatile, very absorbent, easily dyed, good creping qualities, doesn't pill; low cost; some kinds stronger than others; fair abrasion resistance; stable to laundering if resin-treated; can be given special wash-and-wear finishes; blends well; excellent colorfastness	Women's men's and children's wear; carpets, upholstery, draperies, and curtains	Avicolor	solution-dyed filament and staple	FMC Corp., Fiber Division
			Aviloc	adhesive treated high strength rayon yarn	FMC Corp., Fiber Division
			Avril	high wet modulus staple	FMC Corp., Fiber Division
			Avril FR	fire resistant, high wet modulus rayon	FMC Corp., Fiber Division
			Beau-Grip	specially treated viscose high tenacity yarn	Beaunit Corp.

Generic Groups of Man-Made Fibers with Producers' Trade Marks   (Continued)

Generic Name	Characteristics	Some Typical Uses	Representative Trade Names	Features	Producers
Rayon (cont.)			Briglo	bright luster continuous filament yarn	American Enka Co.
			Coloray	solution-dyed staple	Courtaulds North America Inc.
			Encel	high wet modulus staple	American Enka Co.
			Englo	dull luster continuous filament yarn	American Enka Co.
			Enka	rayon	American Enka Co.
			Enkrome	patented acid-dyeable staple and continuous filament yarn	American Enka Co.
			Fiber 40	high wet modulus staple	FMC Corp., Fiber Division
			Fiber 700	high wet modulus staple	American Enka Co.
			Fibro	staple	Courtaulds North America Inc.
			Fibro DD	deep-dyed rayon staple	Courtaulds North America Inc.
			Fibro FR	flame retardant rayon staple fiber	Courtaulds North America Inc.
			FMC	rayon	FMC Corp., Fiber Division
			I.T.	improved tenacity staple	American Enka Co.
			Jetspun	solution-dyed continuous filament yarn	American Enka Co.
			Kolorbon	solution-dyed staple	American Enka Co.
			SayFR	fire resistant filament rayon.	FMC Corp., Fiber Division
			Skyloft	bulked continuous filament yarn	American Enka Co.
			Softglo	semi-dull luster continuous filament yarn	American Enka Co.
			Super White	optically brightened rayon	American Enka Co.
			Suprenka	extra high tenacity continuous filament industrial yarn	American Enka Co.
			Suprenka Hi Mod	extra high tenacity high modulus continuous filament	American Enka Co.
Saran	Resistant to water, stains, chemicals, and weather; tough and flexible, stiff; nonflammable, resistant to sunlight; poor strength; safe ironing temperature 150° F.	Auto seat covers, insect screening, awnings, luggage, draperies, doll's hair	Xena	high wet modulus staple	Beaunit Corp.
			Zantrel	high wet modulus staple	American Enka Co.
			Zantrel 700	high wet modulus staple	American Enka Co.
			Lus-Trus	Monofilament yarns	Southern Lus-Trus Corp.
			Vectra		Vectra Corp.
Spandex	Good elasticity, good heat and abrasion resistance, impervious to body acids, lightweight. Long exposure	Foundation garments, swim wear, tops of	Lycra	spandex	E. I. Du Pont de Nemours & Co., Inc.
			Monvelle	biconstituent nylon/spandex	Monsanto Textiles Co.

Generic Groups of Man-Made Fibers with Producers' Trade Marks (Continued)

Generic Name	Characteristics	Some Typical Uses	Representative Trade Names	Features	Producers
Spandex (cont.)	posure to vegetable and mineral oils may cause slight yellowing	men's socks, support hosiery, stretch yarns for apparel			
Triacetate	Less sensitive to heat than acetate, resists pilling, pleat retention, fading, shrinkage, and wrinkle resistant	Apparel and home furnishings	Arnel	filament yarn and staple	Celanese Fiber Manufacturing Corp.
Vinal	Strong, abrasion resistant. Dry wrinkle resistance poor	Industrial	No domestic producers (developed by Japan)		no domestic producers
Vinyon	Nonabsorptive; thermoplastic; water repellent; high strength wet and dry; excellent abrasion and fire resistance	Bonding agent for nonwoven fabrics, batting, heat-sealed paper goods, industrial purposes	Avisco	high-strength and potentiality; inexpensive trademark also applied to rayon and acetate	American Viscose
			Voplex	trademark also applied to olefin	Voplex Corp.

Schools Prominent in Advancing Textile Education

C

Auburn University (formerly Alabama Polytechnic Institute, School of Textile Technology), Auburn, Ala. (B.S. degree)

Clemson University, The School of Industrial Management and Textile Science, Clemson, S.C.

Fashion Institute of Technology, New York, N.Y. (junior college)

Georgia Institute of Technology. The A. French Textile School, Atlanta, Ga. (B.S. degree, evening, extension, and graduate courses)

Institute of Textile Technology, Charlottesville, Va. (education and training in the physical sciences and textile technology leading to the M.S. degree)

Iowa State University, Ames, Ia. (Textile and Clothing Department grants B.S. and M.S. Degrees)

Massachusetts Institute of Technology, Cambridge, Mass. (textile technological courses leading to the B.S., M.S., D.Sc., and Ph.D.)

North Carolina State College, Raleigh, N.C. (B.S. and M.S. degrees)

Philadelphia College of Textiles and Science, Philadelphia, Pa. (B.S. and M.S. degrees)

Purdue University, School of Home Economics, Lafayette, Ind. (B.S. degree in Home Economics).

Rhode Island School of Design, Providence, R.I. (B.S. or B.F.A. degrees)

Southeastern Massachusetts Technological Institute, New Bedford, Mass., and Fall River, Mass. Formerly Bradford Durfee Institute of Technology and New Bedford Institute of Technology. Now combined. (B.S. degree)

Textile Education Foundation, Atlanta, Ga.

Texas Technological College, Lubbock, Tex. (Bachelor of Textile Engineering [B.T.E.] and Bachelor of Textile Chemistry [B.T.C.] degrees)

Art schools with majors in textile design; textile majors in colleges in home economics departments; special textile courses in retailing departments in colleges; specialized adult courses in extension divisions of colleges

Organizations
Engaged
in Textile Research

D

Research is being advanced in such places as the following:[1]
American Association for Textile Technology Inc., New York, N.Y.
American Association of Textile Chemists and Colorists, Research Triangle Park, N.C.
Callaway Institute, La Grange, Ga.
Clemson University, The School of Industrial Management and Textile Science, Clemson, S.C.
Fabric Research Laboratories, Dedham, Mass.
Institute of Textile Technology, Charlottesville, Va.
Lowell Technological Institute Foundation, Lowell, Mass.
National Bureau of Standards, Textile Division, Washington, D.C.
National Cotton Council of America, Memphis, Tenn.
New Bedford Institute of Technology, New Bedford, Mass.
North Carolina State College, School of Textiles, Raleigh, N.C.
Textile Research Institute, Princeton, N.J. (Ph.D. degree)

Research institutes or foundations that experiment with textiles:
Industrial Research Institute, University of Chattanooga, Chattanooga, Tenn.
Mellon Institute, Pittsburgh, Pa.
Research Foundation, Georgia School of Technology, Atlanta, Ga.
Southern Research Institute, Birmingham, Ala.

U.S. Department of Agriculture stations that work with textiles:
Four Regional Laboratories: New Orleans, La.; Peoria, Ill.; Philadelphia, Pa.; and Albany, Cal.
Mississippi Agricultural Experiment Station, Stoneville, Miss.
North Carolina Agricultural Experiment Station, Raleigh, N.C.
Research Station, Beltsville, Md.
U.S. Army Quartermaster Corps., Natick, Mass.

[1] Courtesy of *American Dyestuff Reporter,* with updating.

Period Styles
with Appropriate Woods,
Rugs, and
Upholstery and Drapery Fabrics

E

Period Styles with Appropriate Woods, Rugs, and Upholstery and Drapery Fabrics

Period	Lines	Proportions	Woods	Rugs	Upholstery and Drapery Fabrics
Italian					
Renaissance 1400–1643	curved and straight	massive	chestnut ebony lime, oak sycamore walnut	oriental designs rich in coloring, with ruby red dominant	brocade, damask, satin, tapestry, velour, velvet; large expanse of background in fairly rich colors
Venetian	curved and flowing	large	painted finish; gilt trim; mirrored furniture		same as above; decorative fringes
Spanish					
1451–1504	similar to Italian	similar to Italian		similar to Italian	brocade, cottons (coarse), damask, linen (printed), velvet, plastic-coated fabrics to resemble leather
French 1643–1825					
1. Louis XIV 1643–1715	straight, also rounded	massive	chestnut ebony oak walnut	plain carpeting and designs of the period; also Chinese and some Near-East oriental designs	brocade, damask, satin, tapestry, velvet
2. Louis XV 1723–1774	curves	small and graceful	mahogany oak rosewood walnut	plain carpeting and designs of the period; some oriental designs	brocade, damask, cretonnes, moiré, needlepoint, prints, satin, taffeta, tapestry, toile de Jouy, velvet; pastel grounds, ribbons and flowers, swags, bouquets, medallions, vases; naturalistic flower designs important
3. Louis XVI 1774–1793	straight, a few curves	small, dainty, and light	mahogany rosewood satinwood walnut	same as Louis XV	similar to above; classic influence beginning to be felt; stripes
4. Directoire 1795–1799	transition from straight to straight with ovals, classic influence	small and graceful	ebony mahogany satinwood	plain carpeting and designs of the period; fairly strong colors; Near Eastern oriental and Chinese designs not suitable	materials same as Louis XIV; fabric designs classic; also stripes and small floral motifs
5. Empire 1804–1825	straight with ovals	heavy and massive	ebony mahogany satinwood	plain carpeting or Empire designs in strong, full colors	damask, brocade, moiré, satin, taffeta; medallions, swags, tassels, vase motifs, wreaths, arrow motifs, vertical stripes, scenic chintz, Indian printed cottons
6. French Provincial	straight, some curves	simple and sturdy	beech fruit woods maple walnut	hooked, fiber, and rag rugs	crash (linen), cretonnes, homespuns; small wild flowers, gay plaids

598

Period Styles with Appropriate Woods, Rugs, and Upholstery and Drapery Fabrics (Continued)

Period	Type of Furniture		Woods	Rugs	Upholstery and Drapery Fabrics
	Lines	Proportions			
English					
1. Jacobean 1603-1688	straight	strong and sturdy	oak, walnut	oriental patterns with distinct, vigorously drawn motifs, reds predominating	brocade, chenille, corded fabrics, leather upholstery, needlepoint, velour, velvet
2. William and Mary 1689-1702	straight, changing to curves	lighter	walnut	Chinese designs with blue and old-gold grounds; oriental designs in softened colors and small motifs	chintz, cretonne, damask, leather upholstery, needlepoint
3. Queen Anne 1702-1714	curved, little carving	light and graceful	walnut, some mahogany	similar to William and Mary	brocade, Chinese embroidery, chintz, gros point, needlepoint, petit point, India prints
4. Georgian 1710-1806 (a) Chippendale 1750-1775	straight with flowing lines, more carving	light and graceful	mahogany	oriental designs, small patterns; with Chinese Chippendale, Chinese designs with blue grounds	brocade, damask, leather upholstery, needlepoint, satin, tapestry, velour, velvet
(b) Hepplewhite 1765-1795	curved, except chair legs	small, slender, and sturdy	mahogany, rosewood inlay, satinwood	plain carpeting or contemporary French designs; oriental designs light in coloring with fine patterns and texture	damask, haircloth, striped and figured moiré and satin, trimmings of ribbons and tassel; classic designs
(c) Sheraton 1757-1806	straight, a few curves	delicate, slender, narrow, and refined	mahogany, rosewood inlay, satinwood	similar to Hepplewhite	brocade, damask, haircloth, linens (printed), silks (lightweight); floral motifs on small scale
(d) Adam Brothers 1760-1792	straight, rectangular	graceful	mahogany, maple, pine, satinwood	carpeting matching walls in darker tones;	brocade, moiré, silks (lightweight)
5. Regency 1793-1820	curved	flamboyant	bamboo, black lacquer, mother-of-pearl decorations	Oriental and Indian rug designs	contrasting textures
6. Victorian 1837-1901	curved	fairly large with much ornamentation	black walnut, mahogany, oak	Brussels carpeting, tapestry rugs, Wiltons; in floral designs	brocade, damask, horsehair upholstery, plush, velour, velvet

Period Styles with Appropriate Woods, Rugs, and Upholstery and Drapery Fabrics (Continued)

Period	Lines	Type of Furniture Proportions	Woods	Rugs	Upholstery and Drapery Fabrics
American					
1. Early American 1607-1725	straight	simple and sturdy	ash, cherry, maple, oak, pine	hooked rug designs, rag rugs, plaid carpeting	chintz, crash, cretonne, denim, dotted swiss, homespun, marquisette (dotted), monk's cloth, novelty cottons, organdy, rep
2. Colonial 1725-1790	curved and straight	solid and substantial	black walnut, mahogany	as above; also oriental rugs in close, quiet patterns	same as Early American; also brocades and velvets being introduced
3. Federal 1795-1847	curved and straight	graceful and slender	mahogany, walnut	plain carpeting or designs of the period; oriental patterns with well-colored designs	similar to Georgian
4. American Victorian 1850s	curved	intricate carving	bent and shaped wood, dark, black-finished	Brussels and Axminster carpets and rugs	plush, velvet, velour, damask, tapestry, horsehair
5. Art Nouveau 1875-1900	ship-lash curve	natural growing forms	sculped, combining dark, light, and painted finishes	Brussels, Wilton, Axminster carpets	frieze, plush, velvet, damask
Modern					
Early Modern 1911-1920 Moderne 1930-1940s	straight, angular, and sharp pointed	solid, substantial, and simple	metal, metallic-painted woods, inlaid woods	plain carpeting in light and soft colors; modern designs	armure, casement cloth, chenille, corded fabrics, gauze, modern tapestry, mohair, monk's cloth, rough linens and cottons; large sweeping and block designs, exaggerated in size but simplified in line
Contemporary 1948-	sophisticated simplicity	sturdy, mobile, functional	grained plywoods, glass brick, unbreakable sheet glass plastics	carved and textured; geometric designs; cotton, wood, and synthetic blends	antique satin, bouclé, hand-woven effects, textured cottons, linens, gauze for curtains
Oriental	classical serenity	structural beauty	lattice-work lacquered finished wood	Chinese orientals; Near East orientals; tufted rugs and carpets	gauze, ninon, bouclé, textured cottons, linens, polyesters, glass fibers.

Metric Conversions

F

	When you know the	You can find the	If you multiply by
Length	inches	millimeters	25
	feet	centimeters	30
	yards	meters	0.9
	millimeters	inches	0.04
	centimeters	inches	0.4
	meters	yards	1.1
Area	square inches	square centimeters	6.5
	square feet	square meters	0.09
	square yards	square meters	0.8
	square centimeters	square inches	0.16
	square meters	square inches	1.2
	square kilometers	square miles	0.4
	square hectometers (hectares)	acres	2.5
Mass	ounces	grams	28
	pounds	kilograms	0.45
	short tons	megagrams (metric tons)	0.9
	grams	ounces	0.035
	kilograms	pounds	2.2
	megagrams (metric tons)	short tons	1.1
Liquid Volume	ounces	milliliters	30
	pints	liters	0.47
	quarts	liters	0.95
	gallons	liters	3.8
	milliliters	ounces	0.034
	liters	pints	2.1
	liters	quarts	1.06
	liters	gallons	0.26
Temperature	degrees Fahrenheit	degrees Celsius	5/9 (after subtracting 32)
	degrees Celsius	degrees Fahrenheit	9/5 (then add 32)

References

REFERENCE WORKS AND GENERAL TEXTS

American Fabrics, *A.F. Encyclopedia of Textiles*, 2nd ed. (Englewood Cliffs, N.J.: Prentice-Hall, Inc., 1973).

American Home Economics Association, *Textile Handbook*, 4th ed. (Washington, D.C., 1970).

Booth, J.E., *Principles of Textile Testing* (New York: Chemical Publishing Co., 1969).

Calloway's *Textile Dictionary* (La Grange, Ga.: Callaway Mills, N.C.)

Chambers, Helen G., and Verna Moulton, *Clothing Selection* (Philadelphia, Pa.: J.B. Lippincott Company, 1969).

Computer Technology for Textiles (Atlanta, Ga.: W.R.E. Smith Publishing Co., 1970).

Dictionary of Textile Terms, 8th ed., George E. Linton, ed. (Danville, Va.: Dan River Mills, 1967).

Fairchild's Dictionary of Textiles, 5th ed. (New York: Fairchild Publications, Inc., 1967).

Garrett, Pauline C., *You Are a Consumer of Clothing* (Waltham, Mass.: Ginn & Co., 1967).

Hall, A.J., *The Standard Handbook of Textiles*, 7th ed. (New York: Chemical Publishing Co., Inc., 1969).

Joseph, Marjory L., *Introductory Textile Science*, 2nd ed. (New York: Holt, Rinehart & Winston, Inc., 1972).

Klapper, Marvin, *Fabric Glossary* (New York: Fairchild Publications, Inc., 1973).

Linton, George E., *Applied Basic Textiles*, 2nd ed., revised (Plainfield, N.J.: Textile Book Service, n.d.).

The Modern Textile Dictionary, 4th ed. (Plainfield, N.J.: Textile Book Service, 1973).

Ontiveros, J.R., *Panamerican Textile Dictionary*, Spanish-English, English-Spanish, 2nd ed. (Plainfield, N.J.: Textile Book Service, 1971).

Pizzuto, Joseph J., *Fabric Science*, revised by Arthur Price, Allen C. Cohen (New York: Fairchild Publications, Inc., 1974).

Potter, Maurice D., *Textiles: Fiber to Fabric*, 4th ed. (New York: McGraw-Hill, 1967).

Stout, Evelyn, *Introduction to Textiles*, 3rd ed. (New York: John Wiley & Sons, Inc., 1970).

Tate, Mildred T., and Otis Gibson, *Family Clothing* (New York: John Wiley & Sons, Inc., 1961).

Textile Institute, *Textile Terms and Definitions*, 6th ed. (Plainfield, N.J.: Textile Book Service, 1970).

Wingate, Isabel B., ed., *Fairchild's Dictionary of Textiles* (New York: Fairchild Publications, Inc., 1967).

**REFER-
ENCES TO
SPECIFIC
SUBJECTS**

I. FIBERS AND YARNS

Textile Fibers and Their Properties (Greensboro, N.C.: Burlington Industries, Inc.)

Cook, J. Gordon, *Handbook of Textile Fibers*, 4th ed. 2v. (Plainfield, N.J.: Textile Book Service, 1968).

Dow Badische Co., Textile Fibers Department, Williamsburg, Va., *Zefkrome Type 200 Acrylic Fibers.*

Moncrief, R.W., *Man-Made Fibers* (New York: John Wiley & Sons, Inc., 1966).

Man-Made Fiber Fact Book, Man-Made Fiber Producers Association, 1150 17th St., N.W., Washington, D.C. 20036.

Man-Made Fiber and Textile Dictionary, Celanese Fibers Marketing Co., 1211 Avenue of the Americas, New York, N.Y. 10036.

II. CONSTRUCTION OF CLOTH

Hathorne, Berkely L., *Woven Stretch and Textured Fabrics* (New York: John Wiley & Sons, Inc., 1964).

Knitting Dictionary (New York: National Knitted Outerwear Association, 1966).

Reichman, Charles, et al, *Knitted Fabric Primer* (New York: National Knitted Outerwear Association, 1967).

The Knitter, 106 East Stone Avenue, P.O. Box 88, Greenville, S.C. 29602.

Wheatley, B., *Raschel Lace Production* (New York: National Knitted Outerwear Association, 1968).

III. FINISHING

Textile Finishing Glossary, 4th ed. (Greensboro, N.C.: Cone Mills Corp., Research and Development Division, 1967).

Hall, A. J., *Textile Finishing*, 3rd ed. (New York: American Elsevier Press, Inc., 1966).

Marsh, J. T., *An Introduction to Textile Finishing* (Plainfield, N.J.: Textile Book Service, 1966).

IV. DYEING AND PRINTING

Proud, Nora, *Textile Printing and Dyeing* (New York: Rheinhold Books, 1965).

A.A.T.C.C. Glossary of Printing Terms (Research Triangle Park, N.C.: American Association of Textile Chemists and Colorists,).

V. TEXTILE CLOTHING

The Art of Sewing (series) (New York: TIME-LIFE Books).

The Boys' Outfitter, 71 West 35th St., New York, N.Y.

Newburgh, L. H., ed., *Physiology of Heat Regulation and the Science of Clothing* (New York: Hefner Book Co., 1971).

Sewing and Threads (New York: Coats & Clark, Inc., Educational Bureau).

Deranian Helen, *Finishing Techniques for the Textile Maintenance Industry* (New York: Barclay, 1968).

Lyle, Dorothy S., *Focus on Fabrics* (Silver Spring, Md.: International Fabricare Institute, 1964).

Moss, A. J. Ernest, *Textiles and Fabrics, Their Care and Preservation* (New York: Tudor Publishing Co., 1961).

Fourt, Lyman and Norman Hollies, *Clothing: Comfort and Function* (New York: Dekker Publishing Co., 1970).

Jaffe, Hilde, *Children's Wear Design*, (New York: Fairchild Publications, 1972).

Westerman, Maxine, *Elementary Fashion Design and Trade Sketching* (New York: Fairchild Publications, 1974).

603

VI. TEXTILES FOR HOME DECORATION

Schlosser, Ignace, *The Book of Rugs: Oriental and European* (New York: Crown Publishers, Inc., 1963).

Fairchild's Dictionary of Home Furnishings, Emanuel Hoffman, ed, Verna Small, Bab Foster Buck (New York: Fairchild Publications, 1972).

How To Care for Your Rugs and Carpets (Dalton, Ga.: Carpet and Rug Institute).

Easy Guide to Carpets and Rugs (cu-54), Celanese Fibers Marketing Co., Customers Information Services Department, 1211 Avenue of the Americas, New York, N.Y. 10036.

Easy Guide to Curtains and Draperies, Upholstery and Bedspreads (cu-93), Celanese Fibers Marketing Co., Customers' Information Services Department, 1211 Avenue of the Americas, New York, N.Y. 10036.

Caring for Upholstery Fabrics of 100% Trevira Polyester, Hoechst Fibers, Inc., 1515 Broadway, New York, N.Y. 10036.

Upholstery Fabrics, Fibers Division, Hercules Inc., 910 Market Street, Wilmington, Delaware, 19879.

Herculon for Upholstery (FH-706), Director of Merchandising, Home Furnishings Division, Hercules, Inc., 910 Market Street, Wilmington, Delaware 19879.

Instant Table Decoration with 60 Ideas for Table Setting (pamphlet for distribution in U.S. only), Belgian Linen Association, 280 Madison Avenue, New York, N.Y. 10016 (KYM).

Household Textiles (pamphlets), Good Housekeeping Institute, 939 8th Avenue, New York, N.Y. 10019.

Guides to Sheets, Pillow Cases, Pillows and Mattress Pads, Celanese Fibers Marketing Co., 1211 Avenue of the Americas, New York, N.Y. 10036.

Looking at Creslan from Behind the Blanket Counter, American Cyanamid Co., Berdan Ave., Wayne, N.J. 07410.

Consumer Reports, "Electric Blankets," *1975 Buying Issue Guide* (Mount Vernon, N.Y.: Consumer Union of U.S. Inc.)

AUDIO-VISUALS

I. CLOTHING

A. Ready-To-Wear

How to Give a Fashion Show. 35 mm colored slides. 31-35 minutes; printed commentary; teacher training aids. Fairchild Publications, Visuals Department, 7 East 12th St., New York, N.Y. 10003.

Great Developments in Fashion Series, Professor Rosalie Kolodny. 64 slides (35 mm) in three programs: 1) The Dome Skirt; 2) The Peg Skirt; 3) The Dolman Sleeve. Fairchild Publications Visuals Department, 7 East 12th Street, New York, N.Y. 10003.

Wardrobe (14 minutes, color) IFB, 1961 - 20031 (for renting). The Pennsylvania State University, Audio-Visual services, 7 Willard Building, University Park, Pa. 16802.

B. Hosiery

Association Films, Inc., 600 Madison Ave., New York, N.Y. 10017.

Modern Talking Pictures Service, Inc., 1212 Avenue of the Americas, New York, N.Y. 10022.

II. HOME FURNISHINGS

A. Home Decoration

Home Decorating Slides (35 mm, color). Product information FMC Corp. Fiber Division, 1185 Avenue of the Americas, New York, N.Y. 10036.

Textile Art from Tapestries to Jeans (film strips). American Textile Manufacturers Institute, 1501 Johnson Bldg., Charlotte, N.C. 28281.

B. Draperies

Modern Talking Pictures Service, Inc., 1212 Avenue of the Americas, New York, N.Y. 10022.

III. FIBERS AND YARNS

A. Fibers/Yarns—General

Association Films, Inc., 866 3rd Ave., New York, N.Y. 10022.

Audio-Visual Series. Penn State University, University Park, Pa. 16802.

Yarn and Cloth Construction, 10 minutes (rental). American Viscose, Division of FMC Corp., 1185 Avenue of the Americas, New York, N.Y. 10036.

E.I. Du Pont de Nemours & Co., Motion Pictures Advertising Department, Wilmington, Delaware 19898.

Wingate, Isabel B., *Series: Textiles from Source to Consumer*, Set I (classification and uses of textile fibers; 35 mm colored slides, commentary, glossary, swatches). Set II (yarns). Fairchild Books and Visuals, 7 East 12th Street, New York, N.Y. 10003.

Modern Talking Pictures Service, Inc., 1212 Avenue of the Americas, New York, N.Y. 10022.

B. Fibers—Man-Made

The Way It Is with Man-Made Fibers, 16 mm Sound Motion Picture Section, Advertising Dept., E.I. Du Pont de Nemours & Co., Inc., Wilmington, Delaware 19898.

FMC Fibers and Films, 16 mm Motion Picture, FMC Corp. Fiber Division, Product Information, 1185 Avenue of the Americas, New York, N.Y. 10036. Also, *Rayon Today*, sound filmstrip in color.

Man-Made Fibers, filmstrip in color. Man-Made Fiber Producers Association, 1150 Seventeenth St., N.W., Washington, D.C. 20036.

Textiles Today, filmstrip and book packet (cu-48), Celanese Fibers Marketing Co., 1211 Avenue of the Americas, New York, N.Y. 10036.

C. Fibers—Natural

Cotton—from Fiber to Fabric, 16 mm sound, McGraw-Hill Book Co., Inc.

IV. CONSTRUCTION OF CLOTH

Weaving, 15 minutes, color, Audio-Visual Series, Penn State University, University Park, Pa. (rental).

Wingate, Isabel B., *Textiles from Source to Customer*, (series of manuals with 35 mm colored slides, fabrics). Set III (weaving, knitting, needle punched, etc.), Fairchild Visuals, Fairchild Publications, Inc., 7 East 12th St., New York, N.Y. 10003.

V. FINISHING OF CLOTH

Wingate, Isabel B., *Textiles from Source to Consumer*, Set IV (finishing of cloth), Fairchild Books and Visuals, Fairchild Publications, Inc., 7 East 12th Street, New York, N.Y. 10003.

VI. DYEING AND PRINTING OF CLOTH

Wingate, Isabel B., *Textiles from Source to Consumer*, Set V (coloring), Fairchild Books and Visuals, 7 East 12th St., New York, N.Y. 10003.

International Fabricare Institute, P.O. Box 940, Joliet, Ill. 60434.

The Soap and Detergent Association, 475 Park Ave. South, New York, N.Y. 10016.

Wingate, Isabel B., *Textiles from Source to Consumer*. Set VI (care of textile fabrics), Fairchild Books and Visuals, Fairchild Publications, Inc., 7 East 12th Street, New York, N.Y. 10003.

GOVERN-MENT BULLETINS

Federal Trade Commission, Washington, D.C. 20250.

U.S. Department of Agriculture, Office of Information, Washington, D.C.

Catalogue of government bulletins on textiles (fibers, fabrics, and sewing aids). Also *Consumers Guide*, Washington, D.C. 20250.

U.S. Government Printing Office, Superintendent of Documents, Washington, D.C.

Rules and regulations under the Textile Fiber Products Identification Act.

Compilation of laws administered by the U.S. Consumer Product Safety Commission (includes Flammable Fabrics Act), Washington, D.C. 20207.

TEXTILE TESTING

AATCC Technical Manual (Research Triangle Park, N.C.: American Association of Textile Chemists and Colorists).

ASTM, *Book of ASTM Standards* (Philadelphia: American Society for Testing and Materials), parts 24, 25, 30.

Booth, John E., *Principles of Textile Testing*, 3rd ed. (New York: Chemical Publishing Co., 1969).

"Federal Test Method Standard No. 191," *Textile Test Methods* (Washington, D.C.: General Service Administration, 1968).

Pizzuto, Joseph J., *Fabric Science*, revised by A. Price and A.C. Cohen (New York: Fairchild Publications, Inc., 1974), Chapter 10.

United States of America Standards Institute, *U.S.A. Standard Performance Requirements for Textile Fabrics* (U.S.A.S. L22, 1968), New York, 1968.

Wingate, Isabel B., and Ralph Burkholder, *Laboratory Swatch Book for Textile Fabrics,* 7th ed. (Dubuque, Iowa: W.C. Brown Publishers, 1970).

MAGA-ZINES AND TRADE PAPERS

GENERAL

AATT (American Association of Textile Technologists), 11 West 42nd St., New York, N.Y. 10036. "Proceedings" published in *Modern Textiles.*

ASTM Magazine (American Society for Testing and Materials), 1916 Race Street, Philadelphia, Pa. (monthly).

American Fabrics Magazine, Doric Publishing Co., Inc., 24 East 38th St., New York, N.Y. 10016 (quarterly).

American Textiles Reporter Bulletin (monthly), 106 Stone Ave., P.O. Box 88, Greenville, S.C. 29602. Also publisher of 1975 Clark's *Directory of Southern Textile Mills.*

Journal of Home Economics, American Home Economics Association, 2010 Massachusetts Ave., N.W., Washington, D.C.

Modern Textiles, Rayon Publishing Corporation, 303 Fifth Ave., New York, N.Y. 10016.

Retail Directions, 270 Madison Ave., New York, N.Y. 10017.

Textile Chemist and Colorist, Journal of the AATCC, P.O. Box 12215, Research Triangle Park, N.C. 27709 (monthly).

Textile Organon, Textile Economics Bureau, Inc., 489 Fifth Ave., New York, N.Y. 10017.

Women's Wear Daily, Fairchild Publications, Inc., 7 East 12th St., New York, N.Y. 10003.

Home Furnishings Daily, Fairchild Publications, Inc., 7 East 12th St., New York, N.Y. 10003.

SPECIFIC

A. Outer Clothing

Knitting Times, 51 Madison Ave., New York, N.Y. 10016.

Infants' and Children's Review, Earnshaw Publications, 393 7th Ave., New York, N.Y. 10001.

Parents' Magazine, 52 Valderbilt Ave., New York, N.Y. 10017.

Sportswear on Parade, 60 East 42nd St., New York, N.Y. 10017.

B. Underwear

Corset and Underwear Review, 111 Fourth Ave., New York, N.Y. 10003.

C. Men's and Boys' Wear

The Boys' Outfitter, 71 West 35th St., New York, N.Y. 10010.

Men's Wear, Fairchild Publications, 7 East 12th St., New York, N.Y. 10003 (monthly).

D. Home Furnishings

Curtain and Drapery Magazine, 370 Lexington Ave., New York, N.Y. 10017.

Linens, Domestics, and Bath Products, Target Communications Inc., 909 3rd Ave., New York, N.Y. 10022.

News from West Point-Pepperell Inc., 111 West 40th St., New York, N.Y. 10018.

SOURCES OF INFORMATION FOR CONSUMERS

American Apparel Manufacturers Association, 1611 North Kent St., Arlington, Va. 12209.

American Home Magazine, 641 Lexington Ave., New York, N.Y. 10022.

American Wool Council, 1460 Broadway, New York, N.Y. 10001.

Better Homes and Gardens, 750 Third Ave., New York, N.Y. 10017.

Esquire Magazine, 488 Madison Ave., New York, N.Y. 10022.

Fabrics Containing Verel Modacrylic Fiber, Education Department, Eastman Chemical Products, Inc., 1133 Avenue of the Americas, New York, N.Y. 10026.

Family Circle Magazine, 488 Madison Ave., New York, N.Y. 10022.

Glamour Magazine, 420 Lexington Ave., New York, N.Y. 10017.

Good Housekeeping Magazine, Eighth Avenue at 57th St., New York, N.Y. 10019.

Harper's Bazaar, 717 Fifth Ave., New York, N.Y. 10022.

House Beautiful, 717 Fifth Ave., New York, N.Y. 10022.

International Nonwoven and Disposable Association, 10 East 40th St., New York, N.Y. 10027.

Ladies' Home Journal, 641 Lexington Ave., New York, N.Y. 10017.

McCall's Magazine, 230 Park Ave., New York, N.Y. 10017.

Mademoiselle Magazine, 420 Lexington Ave., New York, N.Y. 10017.

Men's Fashion Association of America, 1290 Avenue of the Americas, New York, N.Y. 10019.

Neighborhood Cleaners Association, 116 East 27th St., New York, N.Y. 10016.

National Institute of Rug Cleaning, 7355 Wisconsin Ave., Bethesda, Md. 20014.

Sears Roebuck and Company, Consumer Information Services, Dept. 703, Public Relations, 7401 Skokie Boulevard, Skokie, Ill. 60076.

Seventeen, 320 Park Ave., New York, N.Y. 10022.

United Piece Dye Works, 111 West 40th St., New York, N.Y. 10018.

608
References

Vogue, 420 Lexington Ave., New York, N.Y. 10017.

Woman's Day Magazine, 1515 Broadway, New York, N.Y. 10036.

Women's Wear Daily, 7 East 12th St., New York, N.Y. 10003.

Consumer Bulletin, Consumer Research, Washington, N.J. 07882.

Consumer's Guide, U.S. Department of Agriculture, Washington, D.C. 20250.

Consumer Reports, Consumer Union of the U.S. Inc., 56 Washington St., Mount Vernon, N.Y. 10553.

Index

Mrs. David J. Kachik
648 North Inverway, Inverness
Palatine, Illinois 60067